The Narrators of Barbarian History

Publications in Medieval Studies

THE NARRATORS
OF BARBARIAN HISTORY

(A.D. 550-800)

Jordanes, Gregory of Tours, Bede,
and Paul the Deacon

Walter Goffart

UNIVERSITY OF NOTRE DAME PRESS

NOTRE DAME, INDIANA

First published in 1988 by Princeton University Press

First paperback edition published in 2005 by the University of Notre Dame Press
Notre Dame, Indiana 46556
www.undpress.nd.edu

Reprinted in 2009

Manufactured in the United States of America

Library of Congress Cataloging-in-Publication Data

Goffart, Walter A.
    The narrators of barbarian history (A.D. 550–800) : Jordanes, Gregory of Tours,
Bede, and Paul the Deacon / Walter Goffart.
        p.   cm. — (Publications in medieval studies)
    Originally published: Princeton, N.J. : Princeton University Press, 1988.
    Includes bibliographical references and index.
    ISBN 13: 978-0-268-02967-8 (pbk. : alk. paper)
    ISBN 10: 0-268-02967-9 (pbk. : alk. paper)
    1. Europe—History—392–814—Historiography.   2. Migrations of nations—
Historiography.   3. Germanic peoples—Historiography.   4. Jordanes, 6th cent.
5. Gregory, Saint, Bishop of Tours, 538–594.   6. Bede, the Venerable, Saint,
673–735.   7. Paul, the Deacon, ca. 720–799?   8. Middle Ages—Historiography.
I. Title.   II. Publications in medieval studies (Unnumbered)
    D56.G64   2005
    940.1'2072022—dc22

                                                    2005026717

For Giles Constable

Contents

Contents

Preface to the Paperback Edition

Almost two decades have passed since the original publication of *The Narrators of Barbarian History*. The book has attracted much notice and been widely cited; and many new studies of Jordanes, Gregory of Tours, Bede, and Paul the Deacon have appeared. This preface briefly presents the disputed questions that have arisen from my book, and also lists additional bibliography, with occasional comments.

Abbreviations

HE   Bede, *Historia ecclesiastica gentis Anglorum*
HL   Paul the Deacon, *Historia Langobardorum*
HR   Paul the Deacon, *Historia Romana*

Reviews of *The Narrators of Barbarian History*

Bachrach, Bernard, in *Francia* 17 (1990) 250–56
Brasington, Bruce, in *Comitatus* 19 (1988) 105–8
Cameron, Averil, in *American Historical Review* 95 (1990) 1172–73
Collins, Roger, in *English Historical Review* 106 (1991) 969
Fouracre, Paul, in *History* 74 (1989) 497–98
Gerberding, R. A., in *Speculum* 80 (1990) 674–76
Heather, Peter, in *Journal of Roman Studies* 83 (1993) 261–63
John, Eric, in *Catholic Historical Review* 75 (1989) 130–31
Lotter, Friedrich, in *Göttingische gelehrte Anzeigen* 241 (1989) 243–57
Pelteret, David, in *Old English Newsletter* 23/1 (1989) 81 (Bede section only)
Pfaff, Richard W., in *Church History* 58 (1989) 372–73
Pohl, Walter, in *Historische Zeitschrift* 249 (1989) 149–50
Sot, Michel, in *Annales. Économies - Sociétés - Civilisations* 44 (1989) 888–90
Straw, Carole, in *Envoi* 2 (1990) 327–31
Tabacco, Giovanni, in *Rivista storica italiana* 101 (1989) 266–69
Wood, I. N., in *Canadian Journal of History* 24 (1989) 92–94

Ch. I, "The First Major Historians of Medieval Europe"

This chapter is my general introduction to *Narrators*. Two aspects of it attracted critical notice. I maintain that a) the four authors were conscious narrators, going about their work deliberately. My accent is on what they did to the information they had, rather than on what their sources did to them. I emphasize the creative side of their historical writing, rather than the passive function of their works as transmitters of "tradition"; b) the four histories in question do not belong to a special and newly minted historical genre of "national history" or *origo gentis*. Both Jordanes and Paul the Deacon wrote Roman histories; their Gothic and Lombard histories did for the Goths and Lombards the same thing as the other narratives did for the Romans, without its mattering that the former were "barbarians" and the Romans were not. The enterprise of writing history was carried forward from classical and early Christian antecedents and did not need the creation of a new genre to incorporate non-Romans.

Most reviewers of *Narrators* did not regard these positions as heretical and abhorrent; several of them commented with approval on precisely these aspects of my work. Three quotes serve as examples: "The insistence that these Dark Age historians were literary figures, who had specific goals in mind, and moulded their narratives to suit their ends, is crucial. So too is the notion that the works of these historians, and not the information they contain, are our real incontrovertible 'facts' " (Wood, as cited above, p. 94). In a particularly warm review, Averil Cameron said: "One of the concerns for which Goffart deserves most respect is his insistence on taking early medieval history on its own rather than on our terms, which up to now have been all too often arrogantly ethnocentric or classicizing" (Cameron, as cited above, p. 1172).[1] Heather expressly supports my claim that "there was no such thing as a self-conscious late antique/early medieval genre of 'barbarian history' " (review cited above, p. 261).

My views have been vehemently contested, however, in one corner of the learned world, namely the Institut für österreichische Geschichtsforschung at the University of Vienna, directed by Herwig Wolfram until his recent retirement. He and his students, most notably Walter Pohl, realized that *Narrators* sharply contradicts the ideas about "ethnogenesis" and related matters that they have been propagating since at least 1979.[2] In defense of their teachings, they have claimed, forcefully and repeatedly, that *Narrators* is tainted by literary-critical theories (notably of Hayden White and Northrop Frye), that it treats the four histories as "mere literature," and that it denies the authors their identity as historians. The more technical

---

[1] See also Brian Croke, "Latin Historiography and the Barbarian Kingdoms," in *Greek and Roman Historiography in Late Antiquity, Fourth to Sixth Century A.D.*, ed. Gabriele Marasco (Leiden 2003), pp. 349–52, 387–88.

[2] For a clear account of what is involved, see the review of Wolfram, *History of the Goths* (Berkeley 1988), by A. C. Murray in *International History Review* 11 (1989) 529–31.

question of an *origo gentis* genre, central to the Viennese enterprise, may be postponed for the moment.

Narrators is about the four historians of its title, each of whom is the subject of a monograph-length chapter; it is not about "ethnogenesis theory," which did not come to my attention until after the book was published.[3] If the present remarks about Chapter I dwell solely on the implications of *Narrators* for ethnic traditions, it is because my two positions, summarized above, impede the Viennese theory. The connection of *Narrators* to an "ethnogenesis theory" completely absent from its pages has been a focus of attention out of proportion to the total contents of the book.

Here is the criticism of Wolfram and Pohl in their own words:

[Goffart] disputes the understanding of the early medieval writer of history as a naïve portrayer of his age and the use of him purely as a "mine of material." [G.] sets about rehabilitating him as a narrator and maintains that he formed his portrayal deliberately and with circumspection. In this way [G.] attaches himself to an anti-exegetical current that lately has won many adherents in English-speaking scholarship through the works of Hayden White, and that judges the factual content of narrative sources very pessimistically. . . . [According to G.] The "narrator of barbarian history" did not mean to write either "national history (*Volksgeschichte*)" or even history itself . . .

Much that contradicts the leanings of the book, however, appears to be rather too casually disposed of. . . . One mainly has the impression that, as a result of [G.'s] concentration on "narration," on the author as creator, the nature and function of the early medieval "historia" falls out of the field of vision . . . Were the investigated works only instructive or polemical collections of examples, arbitrarily put together and altered? Or did it nevertheless matter to have history?[4]

The assertions that should be underscored are that I am "anti-exegetical" and that my authors, after I am done with them, cease to be writers of history. Pohl developed these premises in an article published a little later:

traditional source criticism has understood Paul, like many [other] early medieval authors, as a naïve compiler. . . . It is Walter Goffart's merit to rescue Paul from such source criticism—but he does so at the cost of sacrificing [Paul] as a historian. That history was only the medium, not the goal, of "narrators of barbarian history" is connected with the criticism of Hayden White concerning historical narrative and its "fiction of fact."[5]

---

[3] The accent here is on "theory." "Ethnogenesis" itself is duly mentioned in connection with Wolfram's *Geschichte der Goten* in my review cited n. 14, below.

[4] Walter Pohl, review (1990) cited above among the reviews of *Narrators*; my translation.

[5] Walter Pohl, "Paulus Diaconus und die 'Historia Langobardorum': Text und Tradition," in *Historiographie im frühen Mittelalter*, ed. A. Scharer and G. Scheibelreiter, Veröffentlichungen

It seems that, by my doing, Paul has fallen from the ranks of historians. This is phrased more directly by Herwig Wolfram in the allegation that I reduce my authors to writers of "mere literature." The article quoted here is probably Wolfram's main statement of opposition to my *Narrators* and vindication of his own handling of evidence:

> ethnic traditions in early medieval texts cannot be studied as mere literature belonging only to the time they came to be written down. The methods, skills and techniques of exegesis are also required. . . . [The index to Northrop Frye's *The Great Code*] does not contain the entry "genealogy." This one-sided approach toward an *origo gentis* such as the bible is followed by Walter Goffart with the result that his *Narrators* . . . misses the point because it commits the methodological sin of treating every text polemically as mere literature, that is, as its author's creation *ex nihilo*. Consequently, Goffart dislikes continuity as a whole and neglects any archaic texture, that is, all the prefabricated elements of tradition, which past authors (re)used to construct their texts. As to Goffart's argument that his "Narrators" are authors of politically situated and programmatic literature, this is no different from every other text that was ever written.[6]

Wolfram's and Pohl's indictment of *Narrators* might be summarized as follows: 1) Goffart's fault is to treat each text as mere literature—a creation *ex nihilo* belonging only to the time when it was written down; 2) Goffart should be aware that, in dealing with early medieval historians, one must make allowance for "prefabricated elements of tradition . . . used to construct their texts" which can be distilled by applying "the methods, skills and techniques of exegesis"; 3) because all texts are politically situated and programmatic, that aspect of theirs should be taken for granted without further comment.

The Viennese claims that I deny that Paul the Deacon or the other three wrote history, or that I treat their works as "mere literature" and regard them as creators *ex nihilo*, seem more like smears than serious criticism. As for "exegesis" and "history," the words are deployed by Pohl and Wolfram in senses far removed from common usage. Dictionaries state that "exegesis" comes from Greek "interpretation, explanation," and currently means "critical explanation or analysis of a text" or "critical explanation or interpretation."[7]

---

des Instituts für österreichische Geschichtsforschung, 32 (Vienna 1994), p. 381; my translation.

[6] Herwig Wolfram, "*Origo et religio*: Ethnic Traditions and Literature in Early Medieval Texts," *Early Medieval Europe* 3/1 (1994) 36.

[7] *American Heritage Dictionary; Random House Dictionary of the English Language*, College Edition. For a reasoned rebuttal of the Viennese smears, see Andrew Gillett, "Introduction: Ethnicity, History, and Methodology," in *On Barbarian Identity: Critical Approaches to Ethnicity in the Early Middle Ages*, ed. Andrew Gillet (Turnhout 2002), pp. 14–15.

By that token, *Narrators* is, if anything, overexegetical. But, clearly, Wolf-ram and Pohl have something else in mind. I think that "exegesis" in this special sense is equivalent to what Wolfram does to texts, such as clarifying sixth-century Latin works by reference to thirteenth-century Scandinavian ones, and deploying other practices usually associated with modern com-parative religion and expounded by Karl Hauck.[8] Exegesis of this sort is able to take a single Gothic word out of Jordanes and infer from it elaborate re-ligious crises among the Goths in the dim recesses of their Ukrainian past.[9] It seems more accurate in this context to speak of "post-fabricated" elements of tradition rather than of prefabricated ones. "History," as evoked by Pohl, also looks like something special, much more restricted than the normal (and comprehensive) use of the term. I shall not try to puzzle out what this special sense might be, except to venture that it is probably more recognized in Vienna than in the rest of the learned world.

Origo gentis is another instance of a Viennese adaptation of a common idea. For a long time, scholars who classify medieval sources for purposes of discussion have spoken of "national histories." Sections under this rubric or a variant may be found in the respected works of Herbert Grundmann, Beryl Smalley, and R. C. van Caeneghem (among others). They availed themselves of this category as a convenient pigeonhole for a particular set of histories. None of them argued for the existence of *origo gentis* as a type dis-tinct from other historical genres or gave it a methodological grounding; that was not their goal.[10] With Wolfram, however, *origo gentis* acquired con-crete existence, first as a general category of classical literature, then as a distinct early medieval offshoot: "For the genesis of the *origines gentium* the work of Cassiodorus was . . . revolutionary . . . Cassiodorus's [lost Gothic his-tory] is the first *Origo* of a post-classical people . . . Thus Cassiodorus set the example of medieval *origines gentium*, a series which the Danish Saxo Gram-maticus closed around 1200."[11] What matters to Wolfram at least as much as this genetic argument is the idea, crucial to "ethnogenesis theory," that these new, distinctive *origines gentium* were privileged repositories of ethnic memories, the medium for the continuity of polity-creating "gentile" tradi-tions from the prehistoric past into the medieval future.

---

[8] Karl Hauck, "Lebensnormen und Kultmythen in germanischen Stammes- und Herrscher-genealogien," *Saeculum* 6 (1955) 186–223; "Carmina antiqua: Abstammungsglaube und Stammesbewußtsein," *Zeitschrift für bayerische Landesgeschichte* 27 (1964) 1–33.

[9] For Wolfram and the word *haliurunna*, see my "Two Notes on Germanic Antiquity Today," *Traditio* 50 (1995) 27–29. For his practices as an "exegetic historian," see my "Does the Distant Past Impinge on the Invasion Ages Germans?" in *On Barbarian Identity*, ed. Gillett, pp. 34–35.

[10] For these authors, as well as B. Guenée, see *Narrators*, pp. 3–4.

[11] Herwig Wolfram, "Gothic History and Historical Ethnography," *Journal of Medieval His-tory* 7 (1981) 310–11.

Either the genre defined by Wolfram exists or, as I argue in *Narrators*, it does not. There is no middle ground. The result has been that each side has simply affirmed its positions against the other. Among the many places where Wolfram has expressed his views, I cite: "Einleitung oder Überlegungen zur Origo gentis," in *Typen der Ethnogenese unter besonderer Berücksichtigung der Bayern*, part 1 (Vienna 1990), pp. 19–31; and "Le genre de l'*Origo gentis*," *Revue belge de philologie et d'histoire* 68 (1990) 789–801. The same teaching is repeated in Wolfram's *Das Reich und die Germanen* (Berlin 1990), pp. 58–59, and its English translation, *The Roman Empire and Its Germanic Peoples* (Berkeley 1997), pp. 31–34. I am not sure where Walter Pohl stands about *origines gentium*, but at least one scholar besides Wolfram has spoken in defense of the new definition, namely, Hans Hubert Anton, "Origo gentis – Volksgeschichte. Zur Auseinandersetzung mit Walter Goffarts Werk 'The Narrators of Barbarian History,' " in *Historiographie im frühen Mittelalter*, as n. 5 above, pp. 262–307. This massive article, in which Anton, professor of medieval history at Trier, intermittently credits me with notions that I do not have, is less than compelling.[12] My own opposition to Wolfram's style of *origo gentis* is stated again in "Two Notes on Germanic Antiquity Today," *Traditio* 50 (1995) 22–24.

Narrators was written out of interest in early medieval historiography; its index lists neither "ethnogenesis" nor its country cousin, *Stammesbildung*. Nevertheless, the book has become a stumbling block for the teaching propagated from Vienna. The significance of *Narrators* for "ethnogenesis" should be emphasized in the light of a disingenuous comment by Pohl: "This debate in the US and Canada was rather slow to emerge: Wolfram's book on the Goths came out in 1979, and has been available in an English translation since 1988. The time lost has in recent years been compensated for with polemical fervour worthy of a Gothic onslaught. [n. 4:] The debate was opened by Goffart, 'Germanic Antiquity Today' [1995]."[13] Contrary to Pohl's allegation of silence until 1995, my review of Wolfram's *Geschichte der Goten* appeared in 1982, expressing serious reservations about its methods

---

[12] It is cited with approval by, e.g., Veronica Epp, "Von Spurensuchern und Zeichendeuten. Zum Selbstverständnis mittelalterlicher Geschichtsschreiber," in Johannes Laudage, ed., *Von Fakten und Fiktionen. Mittelalterliche Geschichtsdarstellungen und ihre kritische Aufarbeitung* (Cologne 2003), pp. 43–62, at 45–46, n. 13. I believe that Epp has no first-hand acquaintance with my book and knows it only through the prism of Anton's article. Hans-Werner Goetz, "'Konstruction der Vergangenheit'. Geschichtsbewusstsein und 'Fiktionalität' in der hochmittelalterlichen Chronistik, dargestellt am Beispiel der Annales Palidenses," in the same collection, p. 230 n. 13, argues that the "Kontroverse" between Anton and me would be toned down "wenn man den Konstruktionscharakter auch der Geschichtsschreibung anerkennt."

[13] Walter Pohl, "Ethnicity, Theory, and Tradition: A Response," in *On Barbarian Identity*, ed. Gillett, p. 222.

and arguments;[14] and *Narrators* appeared in 1988. These were the timely beginning of transatlantic opposition to "ethnogenesis theory."

Ch. II, Jordanes

New Publications of Texts

Iordanis De origine actibusque Getarum, ed. Francesco Giunta and Antonino Grillone, Fonti per la storia d'Italia, 117 (Rome 1991). A beautifully printed edition
that is far from superseding Mommsen's. My severe review is in *Gnomon*, 67/3
(1995) 227–29. See further below under "Jordanes in Italy."
Jordanes. *Histoire des Goths*, tr. Olivier Devillers (Paris 1995). An able and learned
translation whose extensive notes, unfortunately, never acknowledge sources.
The introduction is influenced by *Narrators*.

Jordanes wrote both a history of the Romans and one of the Goths, and he
took pains to make readers understand that the two were a connected enterprise, a single work in two parts. It is characteristic of Jordanes studies
that they continue to focus almost entirely on the Gothic part at the expense of the Roman.[15]

The *Getica* and "Ethnogenesis"

As pointed out by Patrick Amory, "Overreliance on the *Getica* is the main
weakness of the ethnogenesis school" (book cited below, p. xix). The *Getica*
of that school is understood to be the work of a patriotic Goth whose expressed views faithfully summarize the contents of Cassiodorus's lost history
of the Goths, itself based on oral Gothic tradition. So conceived, the *Getica*
is a treasure-trove of pure Amal beliefs about the early Gothic past by an
author wholly in sympathy with Cassiodorus's ideas. This ethnogenetic
Jordanes, the backbone of Wolfram's *Geschichte der Goten*, is wholly incompatible with the Jordanes of my chapter—a Latin-speaking Byzantine
(whatever his ethnic origins) who wrote in Constantinople at the moment
when the forces of Justinian were grinding the last Goths of Italy into the
dust. I expressed further thoughts on this question in "Two Notes on Germanic Antiquity Today, 2. Around Jordanes's *Getica*: Tribal Memory vs.
Source Criticism," *Traditio* 50 (1995) 19–29.

---

[14] *Speculum* 57 (1982) 444–47.
[15] Perhaps typically of earlier scholarship, Carlton Huntley Hayes, *An Introduction to the
Sources Relating to the Germanic Invasions* (New York 1909), p. 159 n. 3 (on p. 160), barely acknowledges the existence of the *Romana*. It never occurs to him that it might be relevant to
the *Getica*.

Herwig Wolfram and his disciples have focused their attack on my Jordanes chapter, as one would expect from Amory's comment. The main assault was meant to be carried out by Johann Weißensteiner in a book expanding a preliminary article (cited below); but the book has not appeared. Weißensteiner's article is hard going and unconvincing to the unconverted. Meanwhile, both Peter Heather and Arne Søby Christensen (cited below) have independently expressed views of Jordanes that thoroughly undermine the "ethnogenesis" positions. I have set out my own final thoughts on these and other matters in "Jordanes's *Getica* and the Disputed Origin of the Goths from Scandinavia," *Speculum* 80 (2005) 379–98. As for "ethnogenesis theory," there is an at least even chance that it has enough adherents, notably in the Anglophone world, that it may linger even after its main prop—the *Getica*—has been knocked over.

Jordanes in Italy

A great deal keeps being written in Italy about Jordanes and his more prominent work, but the authors seem unable to shake loose from the positions affirmed fifty years ago by Francesco Giunta and Bruno Luiselli (and also, independently, by Arnaldo Momigliano). These involve moving Jordanes westward to Italy and associating his works with Vivarium and Cassiodorus, who is alleged to have given his personal blessing to Jordanes's abridgment of his Gothic history. The old, long discredited identification of Jordanes with a bishop of Crotone in southern Italy is freshly dusted off. The central idea guiding the Giunta and Grillone edition of the *Getica* (cited above) is that Jordanes was deformed by copyists and that his text should be liberally emended to proper classical standards. Giunta and Luiselli (not to say Momigliano) are names to reckon with in Italian scholarship, and it is apparent that Italian writers on Jordanes are unable to outgrow their fragile opinions and contentions. The result is a Jordanes who remains almost wholly unaffected by what is said of him in *Narrators*. The uniformly negative comments made below about Italian writings on Jordanes should be understood in this context.

The Use of "Native" Sources in the *Getica*

One of the long disputed and still undecided questions about the *Getica* is the use within it of information supplied by oral informants. The survival of distinctively "Gothic" traditions is subsidiary to the main question whether either Cassiodorus's history or Jordanes's incorporates knowledge obtained from unwritten sources. Wolfram and his adherents have magnified this component, but so has Heather, who has bent over backwards to credit both historians with having exploited the oral informants that may be assumed to have been available either in Gothic Italy or from Jordanes's non-Roman acquaintances.[16] My own skepticism on this issue is notorious. The evidence is so thin that the argument can never be concluded either way. It is interesting, nevertheless, to be able to cite a spokesman from a century ago who (far removed recent disputes) shrewdly commented on whether native sources were present in both works:

> We should like to think that Cassiodorus, being in a position of great influence and with every possible opportunity to know the barbarians, had . . . mastered the tribal traditions and legends, [and] had diligently investigated every Germanic source . . . But all we know about the work tends to prove the opposite. . . . Cassiodorus [as he states in *Variae* 9.25] seems to have done more than a scientific historian could do, for he remembered what had been forgotten, and constructed for the reigning family a fine genealogy of seventeen kings, . . . The Gothic history of Cassiodorus was apparently a panegyric . . .[17]

Hayes emphasizes the plain sense of Cassiodorus's own testimony: however available oral information may seem to have been to someone in his position, he gives no hint of having exploited this resource. The same, as Hayes points out, is true of the *Getica*: "Jordanes alleges that the Goths had ancient traditions and poetry, but whether he knew them himself or used them he does not say."[18] Modern commentators have the option of amplifying any trace or presumption that native sources were utilized, but they invariably do so against the grain: neither Cassiodorus nor Jordanes offers any explicit help to the argument.

Second Thoughts on the Jordanes Chapter of *Narrators*

Jordanes is a controversial author for more reasons than "ethnogenesis." His writings have many aspects that remain unstudied (as Andrew Gillett reminds me) while attention has long focused on disputed terrain such as the author's identity, the relations of the *Getica* to Cassiodorus, and the supposed Scandinavian origin of the Goths. I have set out my final thoughts on these subjects in the *Speculum* article cited above, in which I make a number of changes in my previous positions. Where the chapter in

---

[16] Peter Heather, *The Goths* (Oxford 1996), p. 9 (emphasizing oral material exclusively); also Croke, "Latin Historiography and the Barbarian Kingdoms," in *Greek and Roman Historiography*, pp. 361, 362 (on the basis of two strained interpretations of the *Variae*), 366, 369.

[17] Hayes, *An Introduction to the Sources Relating to the Germanic Invasions*, p. 157.

[18] Hayes, p. 159. He also attests (in reference to nineteenth-century scholarship) that the sections "treating of the early wandering of the Goths . . . are generally rejected."

Narrators is concerned, there are aspects that I would modify if I were to retrace my steps.

My main chapter title mentions Jordanes and his "Three Histories," and I argue that the HR has two autonomous parts. In other words, I claim that the two parts of the HR are separate accounts of the world (or universal history) and of Rome. Some critics of *Narrators* disagreed with this subdivision and argued that the HR was a single work. I think they were at least partly right. If I could, I would adjust my language accordingly.

Near the close, I engage in a number of speculations about proper names and express a belief that Jordanes's work was at least blessed by (members of) Justinian's court—that there was something official about it. Speculations usually have foundations of some sort. However that may be, my main arguments are probably weakened by these conjectures. Also, as regards the goals of the *Getica*, the views set out in *Narrators* are superseded by my account in *Speculum*.

The *Getica* has a happy ending. Even if the princely marriage and the birth of a son of noble lineage at the close are disregarded, the work ends with Justinian's triumphing over the Gothic kingdom in Italy in 540. Jordanes makes it crystal clear that he viewed the defeat of the Goths as a happy outcome, and he avoids any reference (in the *Getica*) to the more than ten grim years of Italian war after 540. These are important facts, which have been ignored by a large proportion of students of the *Getica*, past and present. In my efforts to convey this aspect of the book, I gave voice to two dangerous ideas: I pointed out that "comedy" is the term used in literature for writings with a happy ending, and further that the typical comedic plot is the "love story." There is nothing inherently wrong with these ideas; they have practical utility in analyzing the *Getica*. Yet I am sorry I used them; they gave critics, notably Heather, a lever for their own efforts to ignore the happy ending and otherwise undermine my findings. Dr. Johnson advised authors that, if they found a "particularly fine" passage in their compositions, they should strike it out.[19] I wish I had taken this advice in regard to "comedy" and "love story."

In a recent, commendable account of Jordanes, Brian Croke states, "The emerging consensus is that Jordanes is best taken at his word. This means that the *Getica* is a conscientious [history] . . ." (Croke, as cited below, p. 373). Simply put, Croke agrees with Heather's compulsion "to take Jordanes at face value" (*Goths and Romans*, cited below, p. 49). I emphatically dissent from this "consensus." Anyone who ponders the mendacious dating of the *Getica* and *Romana*, and the *suppressio veri* involved in the closing paragraphs of the *Getica*, should think twice about taking Jordanes at his

---

[19] *Concise Oxford Dictionary of Quotations*, 2d ed. (Oxford 2001), p. 132, no.18.

word about anything, including his identity. In another misstep, Croke draws on common knowledge of 551 and, in this way, twists the finality of Jordanes's close into an "anticipation" of things not even hinted at (pp. 363, 367 with n. 43). He should have kept his eye on the happy ending.

Supplementary Bibliography

Amici, Angela. *Iordanes e la storia gotica*, Quaderni della Rivista di Byzantinistica, ed. Antonio Carile, 6 (Spoleto 2002). Much affected by the empty speculations embedded in the Giunta-Grillone edition.

Amory, Patrick. *People and Identity in Ostrogothic Italy, 489–554* (Cambridge 1997), pp. 291–307. An energetic and clear-sighted discussion of the *Getica*.

Bradley, Dennis R. "*In altum laxare vela compulsus*: The 'Getica' of Jordanes," *Hermes* 121 (1993) 211–36.

Buonomo, Luigi Maria. "Introduzione alla lettura delle opere di Giordane," in *Mutatio rerum: letteratura, filosofia, scienza tra tardo antico e altomedioevo, Atti del convegno di studi (Napoli, 25–26 novembre 1996)*, ed. Maria Louisa Silvestre and Marisa Squillante (Naples 1997), pp. 115–46. Nothing of value.

Christensen, Arne Søby. *Cassiodorus, Jordanes, and the* History of the Goths: *Studies in a Migration Myth* (Copenhagen 2002). An important and exhaustive study in which, unfortunately, the woods tend to be obscured by superabundant trees.

Croke, Brian. "Latin Historiography and the Barbarian Kingdoms," in *Greek and Roman Historiography in Late Antiquity, Fourth to Sixth Century A.D.*, ed. Gabriele Marasco (Leiden 2003), pp. 358–75.

Devillers, Olivier. "Le conflit entre Romains et Wisigoths en 436–439, d'après les *Getica* de Jordanès. Fortune et infortune de l'abréviateur," *Revue de philologie* 69 (1995) 111–26.

Gillett, Andrew. "Jordanes and Ablabius," *Latomus* 254 (2000) 479–500.

Heather, Peter. *The Goths*, The Peoples of Europe (Oxford 1996). Differs somewhat from its predecessor.

———. *Goths and Romans, 332–489* (Oxford 1991), esp. pp. 38–52. An important book whose criticism of my *Narrators* is gratuitously vehement.

Jacobs, Edward H. *Accidental Migrations: An Archaeology of Gothic Discourse* (Lewisburg, Pa. 2000), pp. 33–57 ("Jordanes's *Getica* and the Rhapsody of Migration; or, How the Goths Came to Kent"). Jordanes meets Michel Foucault.

Kortüm, H.-H. "Geschichtsschreibung," in *Hoops Reallexikon der germanischen Altertumskunde* 11 (Berlin 1998), p. 485. Espouses outdated ideas about the *Getica*.

Löwe, Heinz. "Vermeintliche gotische Überlieferungsreste bei Cassiodorus und Jordanes," in K. Herbers et al., eds., Ex ipsis rerum documentis. *Beiträge zur Mediävistik. Festschrift für Harald Zimmermann* (Sigmarigen 1991), pp. 26–30. In my view, mistaken.

Mortensen, Lars Boje. "Stylistic Choice in a Reborn Genre: The National Histories of Widukind of Corvey and Dudo of St. Quentin," in *Dudone di San Quintino*, ed. Paolo Gatti and Antonella Degl'Innocenti (Trento 1995), pp. 77–102.

Murray, Alexander C. "Reinhard Wenskus on 'Ethnogenesis,' Ethnicity and the Origin of the Franks," in Andrew Gillett, ed., *On Barbarian Identity: Critical Approaches to Ethnicity in the Early Middle Ages* (Turnhout 2002), pp. 39–68.

Pohl, Walter. "The Politics of Change: Reflections on the Transformation of the Roman World," in *Integration und Herrschaft*, ed. W. Pohl and M. Diesenberger, Forschungen zur Geschichte des Mittelalters 3 (Vienna 2002), p. 278. Very briefly sets out a bizarre, and wholly undocumented, theory of the origin of Jordanes's *Getica*.

Ratti, S. "Les *Romana* de Jordanès et le *Bréviaire* d'Eutrope," *Antiquité classique* 65 (1996) 175–87.

Vermeulen, C. E. P. *Op zoek naar de Gotische Tradition. Een onderzoek in Casssiodorus' Variae en Jordanes' Getica* (Rotterdam 1999).

Weißensteiner, Johann. "Cassiodor/Jordanes als Geschichtsschreiber" in A. Scharer and G. Scheibelreiter, eds., *Historiographie im frühen Mittelalter*. Veröffentlichungen des Instituts für österreichische Geschichtsforshung, 32 (Vienna-Munich 1994), pp. 308–25.

Wolfram, Herwig. *Die Goten, Von den Anfängen bis zur Mitte des sechsten Jahrhunderts. Entwurf einer historischen Ethnographie*, 3rd ed. (Munich 1990). Earlier editions are called "Geschichte der Goten."

———. *History of the Goths*, rev. ed., tr. T. J. Dunlap (Berkeley 1988).

Zecchini, Giuseppe. "Cassiodoro e le fonti dei *Getica* di Giordane," in Zecchini, *Ricerche di storiografia Latina tardoantica* (Rome 1993), pp. 193–209.

Ch. III, Gregory of Tours

Heinzelmann's *Gregor von Tours*

The decisive event in studies of Gregory since my chapter has been the publication of Martin Heinzelmann's *Gregor von Tours (538–594), "Zehn Bücher Geschichte": Historiographie und Gesellschaftskonzept im 6. Jahrhundert* (Darmstadt 1994). There is a less than exemplary translation by Christopher Carroll, under the title *Gregory of Tours: History and Society in the Sixth Century* (Cambridge 2001); the German title evokes Gregory's "concept of society," an idea masked by the loose "society" of the English version. A compact foretaste of the book is given in Heinzelmann, "Histoire, rois et prophète" (cited below).

Heinzelmann, long a pillar of the German Historical Institute in Paris, editor of its journal *Francia*, and a prolific author, is an unequaled expert on Gregory's works. As at least eleven articles on Gregory preceded his book, so this book is not his last word on Gregory, on whom he continues to reflect and refine his ideas.

What is newest and most ambitious about Heinzelmann's book is that he envisions the *Histories* as a unified work with a collective theme and the practical purpose of guiding Merovingian kings along well defined tracks. In place of the more familiar Gregory who narrates variegated particular circumstances and is steeped in the ambivalence of real life, he substitutes a theologian with a plan and enamored of abstractions. The case is strongly argued, with much evidence and deep conviction. Interpretive theories are inevitably contestable, however. Though Heinzelmann and I agree on much, it cannot be overlooked that there is genuine incompatibility between his Gregory and the one found in *Narrators*.

Whether these differences will eventually be resolved remains to be seen; this is certainly not the place even to begin the process of harmonization. What needs to be underscored is that Heinzelmann's book is indispensable for more reasons than its main argument. No one can fail now to ponder his other contributions: an account of the manuscript tradition and critique of earlier scholarship; a prosopography of Gregory's extended family; a searching examination of Gregory's life; a detailed reading of the *Histories*; a demonstration of the value of the chapter headings for understanding chapter contents; and major discussions of Gregory's language and, not least, of his deployment of typology. Future students of Gregory must have Heinzelmann's book by their side and absorb his methods before venturing into the lists of creative scholarship.

Useful but Neglected Research Tools

Two not particularly recent works of fundamental importance for study of Gregory continue still to be less utilized than they should be (I am among the sinners). Denise St.-Michel's *Concordance de l'Historia Francorum de Grégoire de Tours*, Collectum. Collection de textes et concordances de textes de l'Université de Montréal, 2 vols. (Montreal 1979), records all words (except stop-words) in context by book, chapter, page, and line. Pages and lines are less accessible than one might hope; St.-Michel used the first Monumenta Germaniae edition (by Arndt and Krusch, 1884) rather than the second (by Krusch and Levison, 1951), and the Arndt edition may not be widely available. The concordance is not impeccable in details; nevertheless, even an imperfect one is a precious asset for the study of Gregory's language and much else. Hardly less valuable is Margarete Weidemann, *Kulturgeschichte der Merowingerzeit nach den Werken Gregors von Tours*, 2 vols. (Mainz 1982). Although the work includes synthetic chapters, it is mainly a meticulous autopsy and classification of the contents of *all* Gregory's writings under a multitude of topic headings—a virtual card file of Gregorian details.

Was Gregory a "Satirist"?

If I were to rewrite my chapter, I would remove references to "satire," and in particular blot out the idea that Gregory was a satirist. Without ceasing to believe that satire as a literary category is relevant to an appreciation of Gregory's work, I have become keenly aware that the idea of "Gregory the satirist" is not essential to my argument and too easily latched onto by critics as a way to disregard much else that I say.

Chronology of Composition

Alexander Callander Murray points out the persistence to this day of an old temptation in the study of Gregory's *Histories*, namely, that of wresting from it an internal chronology of composition and applying a progression through time to the decoding of Gregory's thoughts.[20] Ostensible differences between one point in the *Histories* and another may, in this way, be ascribed to Gregory's changes of mind or circumstances. Many students of the *Histories* since the nineteenth century have engaged in this exercise, and various schemes—some very recently devised, notably by Ian Wood— pretend to lay bare Gregory's chronological order of composition.[21] These schemes do not work; they fall apart when subjected to severe scrutiny. It is not accidental that Heinzelmann, Murray, and I turn our backs resolutely on such endeavors: Gregory does not allow himself to be pinned down in this way. For all practical purposes (as Murray suggests) the perspective of the *Histories* is that of about the year 590.

Additional Bibliography

A great deal has been and continues to be written about Gregory of Tours, though many such works deal with material mined from his pages, or with his age, rather than with his writings. An attempt at a complete Gregory bibliography has been made and is posted on the world wide web under the title "Gregory of Tours and His World"; the URLs are: http://spectrum. troy.edu/ ~ajones/gotbibl.htm or http:// spectrum.troy.edu/%7Eajones/ gotbibl.html. Though long and comprehensive, it (inevitably) has gaps. A

---

[20] Alexander C. Murray, trans., *Gregory of Tours: The Merovingians*, introduction. I am very grateful to Murray for allowing me to consult parts of this important book in typescript.

[21] Wood advocates this practice in his review of *Narrators* (cited above in the list of reviews), and faults me for not resorting to it. Sympathy for such efforts is voiced by Croke, "Latin Historiography and the Barbarian Kingdoms," p. 383.

shorter list of recent works in English, on which I have drawn, is in Murray, *Gregory of Tours: The Merovingians* (cited below). My selection has three criteria for inclusion, though I have occasionally violated them: studies specifically concerned with Gregory's writings; worthy works of whatever date not cited in *Narrators*; relevant works published since *Narrators*.

Bachrach, Bernard S. *Armies and Politics in the Early Medieval West* (Aldershot 1993) (Collected studies).

———. "Gregory of Tours as a Military Historian," in Mitchell/Wood (2002), pp. 351–63.

Bergmann, Werner, and Wolfhard Schlosser. "Gregor von Tours und der 'rote Sirius'. Untersuchungen zu den astronomischen Angaben in *De cursu stellarum ratio*," *Francia* 15 (1987) 43–74.

Bourgain, Pascale. "Grégoire de Tours en 1994," *Revue Mabillon* 67, n.s. 6 (1995) 295–98.

Bourgain, Pascale, and Martin Heinzelmann. "L'oeuvre de Grégoire de Tours: la diffusion des manuscrits," in Gauthier/Galinié, 1997, pp. 273–317.

Brennan, Brian. "The Image of the Merovingian Bishop in the Poetry of Venantius Fortunatus," *Journal of Medieval History* 18 (1992) 115–39.

Breukelaar, Adriaan H. B. *Historiography and Episcopal Authority in Sixth-Century Gaul: The Histories of Gregory of Tours Interpreted in Their Historical Context* (Göttingen 1994).

Brown, Peter. "Gregory of Tours: Introduction," in Mitchell/Wood (2002), pp. 1–28.

Cameron, Averil. "The Byzantine Sources of Gregory of Tours," *Journal of Theological Studies*, n.s. 26 (1975) 421–26.

Ciccarese, M. P. "Alle origini della letteratura delle visioni. Il contributo di Gregorio di Tours," *Studi storici religiosi (Rome)*, v. 5, fasc. 2 (Rome 1981) 251–66.

The Construction of Communities in the Early Middle Ages: Texts, Resources and Artefacts, ed. Richard Corradini, Max Diesenberger, and Helmut Reimitz (Leiden 2003) (Collection of studies).

Contreni, John J. "Reading Gregory of Tours in the Middle Ages," in Mitchell/Wood (2002), pp. 419–34.

Croke, Brian. "Latin Historiography and the Barbarian Kingdoms," in *Greek and Roman Historiography in Late Antiquity, Fourth to Sixth Centuries A.D.*, ed. G. Marasco (Oxford 2003), pp. 361–87.

de Nie, Giselle. *Views from a Many-Windowed Tower: Studies of Imagination in the Works of Gregory of Tours*. Studies in Classical Antiquity 7 (Amsterdam 1987).

———. *Word, Image and Experience: Dynamics of Miracle and Self-Perception in Sixth-Century Gaul* (Aldershot and Burlington, Vt. 2003) (Collected studies).

DuPlessis, M. "Les aveux d'ignorance de Grégoire de Tours sont-ils contradictoires du caractère de sa langue?" *Revue des langues romanes* 78 (1968) 53–69.

Gauthier/Galinié, 1997 = *Grégoire de Tours et l'espace gaulois*, ed. Nancy Gauthier and Henri Galinié. *Actes du congrès international, Tours, 3–5 nov. 1994*, Revue archéologique du Centre de la France, Suppl. 13 (Tours 1997) (Collection of studies).

Gautier Dalché, Patrick. "La représentation de l'espace dans les *libri miraculorum* de Grégoire de Tours," *Le Moyen Âge* 88 (1982) 397–420.

George, Judith. "Poet as Politician: Venantius Fortunatus' Panegyric to King Chilperic," *Journal of Medieval History* 15 (1989) 5–18.

———. *Venantius Fortunatus: A Poet in Merovingian Gaul* (Oxford 1992).

Godding, R. "Il *Liber Vitae Patrum* di Gregorio di Tours e l'origine dei *Dialogi* di Gregorio Magno," in *Scrivere di santi, Atti del II Convegno di studio dell' Associazione italiana per lo studio della santità, dei culti e dell' agiographia Napoli, 22–25 ott. 1997*, ed. G. Luongo (Rome 1998), pp. 107–28.

Goffart Festschrift = Murray, Alexander C., ed. *After Rome's Fall: Narrators and Sources of Early Medieval History. Essays Presented to Walter Goffart* (Toronto 1998) (Collection of studies).

Goffart, Walter. "Conspicuously Absent: Martial Heroism in the *Histories* of Gregory of Tours and Its Likes," in Mitchell/Wood (2002), pp. 365–94.

———. *Rome's Fall and After* (London and Ronceverte 1989) (Collected studies).

Grégoire de Tours (538–594), Père de l'histoire de France, ed. Patrick Perrin et al. (Rouen 1998).

Gregorio di Tours, 10–13 ottobre 1971. Convegni del Centro di studi sulla spiritualità medievale, 12 (Todi 1977) (Collection of studies).

Halsall, Guy. "Nero and Herod? The Death of Chilperic and Gregory's Writings of History," in Mitchell/Wood (2002), pp. 337–50.

Heinzelmann, Martin. "Grégoire de Tours 'Père de l'histoire de France'?" in *Histoires de France, historiens de la France: Actes du colloque international, Reims, 14–15 mai 1993*, ed. Y.-M. Bercé and P. Contamine (Paris 1994), pp. 19–45.

———. "Hagiographischer und historischer Diskurs bei Gregor von Tours?" in Aevum inter utrumque. *Mélanges offerts à Gabriel Sanders, professeur émérite à l'Université de Gand*, ed. M. Van Uytfanghe and R. Demeulenaere (Steenbrugge and The Hague 1991), pp. 237–58.

———. "Heresy in Books I and II of Gregory of Tours' *Historiae*," in *Goffart Festschrift*, pp. 67–82.

———. "Histoire, rois et prophètes. Le rôle des éléments autobiographiques dans les *Histoires* de Grégoire de Tours: Un guide épiscopal à l'usage du roi chrétien," in *De Tertullien aux Mozarabes: antiquité tardive et Christianisme ancien. Mélanges offerts à Jacques Fontaine*, ed. Louis Holtz and Jean-Claude Fredouille (Paris 1992), pp. 537–59.

Helttula, Anne. "The Accusative Absolute in Jordanes and Gregory of Tours," in *Studies on the Latin Accusative Absolute, Commentationes Humanarum Litterarum*, 81 (Helsinki 1987), pp. 56–77.

Hen, Yitzak. "Clovis, Gregory of Tours, and Pro-Merovingian Propaganda," *Revue belge de philologie et d'histoire* 71 (1993) 271–76.

———. *Culture and Religion in Merovingian Gaul, AD 481–751* (Leiden 1994).

———. "Paganism and Superstitions in the Time of Gregory of Tours: *une question mal posée!*" in Mitchell/Wood (2002), pp. 229–40.

———. "The Uses of the Bible and the Perception of Kingship in Merovingian Gaul," *Early Medieval Europe* 7 (1998) 277–90.

Historiographie im frühen Mittelalter, ed. Anton Scharer and George Scheibelreiter, Veröffentlichungen des Instituts für österreichische Geschichtsforschung, 32 (Vienna and Munich 1994).

James, Edward, tr. *Gregory of Tours: Life of the Fathers*, Translated Texts for Historians (Liverpool 1985, 2d ed. 1991).

———. "Gregory of Tours and the Franks," in *Goffart Festschrift*, pp. 51–66.

———. "A Sense of Wonder: Gregory of Tours, Medicine and Science," in *The Culture of Christendom: Essays in Medieval History in Memory of Denis L. T. Bethel*, ed. E. A. Meyer (London 1993), pp. 45–60.

Jungblut, Jean-Baptiste. "Recherches sur le 'rythme oratoire' dans les 'Historiarum libri,' " in *Gregorio di Tours, 10–13 ottobre 1971*, pp. 325–58.

Loseby, S. T. "Marseilles and the Pirenne Thesis, I: Gregory of Tours, the Merovingian Kings and 'un grand port,' " in *The Sixth Century: Production, Distribution and Demand*, ed. R. Hodges and W. Bowden (Leiden 1998), pp. 203–29.

Löwe, H. "Besprechung: Gregorii Episcopi Turonensis libri Historiarum X. Ed. alteram curaverunt B. Krusch und W. Levison," *Historische Zeitschrift* 177 (1951) 340–43.

Maaz, W. "Gregor von Tours," in *Enzyklopädie des Märchens*, ed. K. Ranke et al. (Berlin and New York 1988) IV, pp. 117–25.

Mitchell, Kathleen. "Saints and Public Christianity in the *Historiae* of Gregory of Tours," in *Religion, Culture, and Society in the Early Middle Ages: Studies in Honor of Richard E. Sullivan*, ed. T. F. X. Noble and J. J. Contreni (Kalamazoo 1987), pp. 77–94.

Mitchell, Kathleen, and Ian Wood, ed. *The World of Gregory of Tours* (Leiden 2002) (Collection of studies).

Moreira, Isabel. *Dreams, Visions, and Spiritual Authority in Merovingian Gaul* (Ithaca 2000).

Murray, Alexander Callander. *From Roman to Merovingian Gaul: A Reader* (Peterborough, Ontario 1999). Contains an extensive selection from the *Histories*, newly translated, along with many other translated sources and excellent introductory commentaries.

———, tr. *Gregory of Tours: The Merovingians* (Peterborough, Ontario). Forthcoming.

———. "*Post vocantur Merohingii*: Fredegar, Merovech, and 'Sacral Kingship,' " in *Goffart Festschrift*, pp. 121–52.

———. See also *Goffart Festschrift*

Noble, Thomas F. X. "Gregory of Tours and the Roman Church," in Mitchell/Wood (2002), pp. 145–61.

Oury, Guy-Marie. "Le miracle dans Grégoire de Tours," in *Histoire des miracles, sixième rencontre d'histoire religieuse, Fontevraud, 1982* (Angers 1983), pp. 11–28.

Pietri, Luce. *La ville de Tours du IVᵉ au VIᵉ siècle: naissance d'une cité chrétienne*, Collection de l'École française de Rome, 69 (Rome 1983).

Pohl, Walter. "Gregory of Tours and Contemporary Perceptions of Lombard Italy," in Mitchell/Wood (2002), pp. 131–43.

Reydellet, Marc. "Pensée et pratique politiques chez Grégoire de Tours," in *Gregorio di Tours, 10–13 ottobre 1971*, pp. 173–205.

———. "Tours et Poitiers: les relations entre Grégoire de Tours et Fortunat," in Gauthier/Galinié, 1997, pp. 159–67.

Reymitz, Helmut. "Social Networks and Identities in Frankish Historiography: New Aspects of the Textual History of Gregory of Tours' *Historiae*," in *Construction of Communities*, pp. 229–68. An important study of the afterlife of Gregory's *Histories*.

Roberts, Michael. "Venantius Fortunatus' Elegy on the Death of Galswintha (*Carm.* 6.5)," in Ralph W. Mathisen and Danuta Shanzer, eds., *Society and Culture in Late Antique Gaul: Revisiting the Sources* (Aldershot and Burlington, Vt. 2001), pp. 298–312.

Rose, Emily M. "Gregory of Tours and the Conversion of the Jews of Clermont," in Mitchell/Wood (2002), pp. 307–20.

Schlick, J. "Composition et chronologie des *De virtutibus s. Martini* de Grégoire de Tours," *Texte und Untersuchungen zur Geschichte der altchristlichen Literatur, 92, Studia Patristica* 7 (1966) 278–86.

Shanzer, Danuta. "Dating the Baptism of Clovis: The Bishop of Vienne vs the Bishop of Tours," *Early Medieval Europe* 7 (1998) 29–57.

Tarriño Ruiz, Eusebia. "Observaciones sobre el acusativo absoluto en Gregorio de Tours," in *Mnemosynum C. Codoñer a discipulis oblatum*, ed. Augustín Ramos Guerreira, Acta Salmanticensia, 247 (Salamanca 1991), pp. 321–32.

Van Dam, Raymond. "Images of Saint Martin in Late Roman and Early Merovingian Gaul," *Viator* 19 (1988) 1–27.

———. *Saints and Their Miracles in Late Antique Gaul* (Princeton 1993) (Collection of translated Gregorian hagiographies).

Winstead, Karen. "The Transformation of the Miracle Story in the *Libri historiarum* of Gregory of Tours," *Medium Aevum* 59 (1990) 1–15.

Wood, Ian. *Gregory of Tours*, Headstart History Papers (Oxford 1994).

———. "Gregory of Tours and Clovis," *Revue belge de philologie et d'histoire* 63 (1985) 249–72; reprinted in *Debating the Middle Ages: Issues and Readings*, ed. L. K. Little and B. H. Rosenwein (Oxford and Malden 1998), pp. 73–91.

———. "The Individuality of Gregory of Tours," in Mitchell/Wood (2002), pp. 29–46.

———."The Secret Histories of Gregory of Tours," *Revue belge de philologie et d'histoire* 71 (1993) 253–70.

Ch. IV, Bede

My Later Writings about Bede's HE

"The *Historia ecclesiastica*: Bede's Agenda and Ours," *Haskins Society Journal: Studies in Medieval History* 2 (1990) 29–45. Rephrases and gives a more concise version of some of the arguments made in *Narrators*.

"L'*Histoire ecclésiastique* et l'engagement politique de Bède," in *Bède le Vénérable entre tradition et postérité. Actes du colloque international Bède le Vénérable: bilan et perspectives (juillet 2002)*, ed. Martine Aubry, Stéphane Lebecq, Michel Perrin and Olivier Szerwiniack (Lille 2005), pp. 149–58.

"Bede's History in a Harsher Climate," to appear in *Tradition and Innovation in the Writings of the Venerable Bede*, ed. Scott DeGregorio (Univ. of West Virginia Press). This article clarifies some of my positions and responds to criticism of *Narrators*. There is overlap between it and the article in French.

"Bede's *vera lex historiae* Explained," *Anglo-Saxon England* 34 (2005) 111–16. Offers a solution for a difficult passage of the Preface to the *History*.

Reactions to the Bede Chapter of *Narrators*

Writers on Bede have shown little inclination to engage with the arguments set out in *Narrators*. The exception is David Kirby, whose Jarrow Lecture for 1992, while limiting its overt rejection of my work to one note, is in its entirety an attempt to portray the contemporary setting of Bede's HE differently from my account. Kirby's rebuttal alleges, in effect, that nothing of any note was taking place in Northumbria that would have affected Bede's composition of the HE; the Kirby of 1992 deserts the insights of the Kirby of 1983, by whom I was inspired (article cited below). I have responded in my contributions to the Lille/Amiens Bede conference and to the collection edited by DeGregorio (both cited above).

The appreciative remarks of Paul Remley (*Old English Newsletter* 25/2 [1992] 62–63) are rare and welcome. In England my Bede chapter seems to have been largely passed over in silence. Besides Kirby's piece just noted, I have come across only occasional comments, such as Roger Collins, "[Goffart's] thesis, that Bede was reacting to the posthumous influence of Wilfrid, may seem a little narrow" (World's Classics *Bede*, cited below, p. xx n. 19), and Alan Thacker, "he depicts Bede as a calculating partisan" (*Beda Venerabilis*, cited below, p. 32). Both single out details and distort what they see. Henry Mayr-Harting, deploring the demise of a reverential atmosphere, considers *Narrators* as part of a "harsher climate" afflicting studies of Bede's *History* (article cited below). A typical sign of the ultra-traditional English approach is that James Campbell and Thacker, both very well informed, follow the correct name for Bishop Wilfrid's biographer, Stephen of Ripon, with the gloss "(Eddius Stephanus)," suggesting that Eddius is a synonym for Stephen rather than a wholly different person (articles "Bede" and "Wilfrid," cited below); and Eddius is retained as the biographer in the commentary by Wallace-Hadrill (cited below). I would prefer a more open and detached dialogue.

Preface to the Paperback Edition

Bede's Attention to Churches Outside Northumbria

My account of the HE emphasizes that at least half its contents are concerned with Northumbrians and Northumbrian affairs. This appraisal is not
wrong. It is strongly confirmed by studies of the afterlife of the HE (lately,
R. H. C. Davis, cited below), which show that its Northumbrian slant
proved a source of embarrassment and of excisions in the Wessex-centered
Anglo-Saxon England of the future. I am inclined to think, however, after
often rereading the HE, that Bede was more seriously concerned with the
rest of England than I allow him to be in *Narrators*. The HE still seems to
me to be very selective in its coverage of the all-English church; but I now
believe that Bede was diligent in dealing with this aspect of his subject and
did as well as he could within the limits of what he set out to do.

Additional Bibliography

Bibliographical guidance
Eckenrode, T. "The Venerable Bede: A Bibliographical Essay, 1970–81," *American
Benedictine Review* 36 (1985) 172–91.
Fry, Donald. "Two Bede Bibliographies: a Progress Report," in *Old English Newsletter*
25/1 (1991) 34–36.
Keynes, Simon. *Anglo-Saxon History: A Select Bibliography* (Binghamton, N.Y.
1987).

There is a lengthy bibliography in the Wallace-Hadrill commentary (cited below).

New texts and tools
(A convenient translation) *Bede, The Ecclesiastical History of the English People, the
Greater Chronicle, the Letter to Egbert*, ed. Judith McClure and Roger Collins, Oxford
World's Classics (Oxford 1994, 1999). The translation of Bede's history is that of
Bertram Colgrave, carried over from the Colgrave-Mynors, Oxford Medieval Texts
edition. It is far from perfect. Colgrave's idiosyncratic annotation has not been re-
tained; its replacement is skimpy and haphazard.

(Bede in French) Olivier Szerwiniack et al., trs. *Bède le Vénérable, Histoire ecclésiastique du peuple anglais*, 2 vols. (Paris 1999). Judicious and well-informed introduction
and notes.

(Major commentary) Wallace-Hadrill, J. M. *Bede's* Ecclesiastical History of the English People: A *Historical Commentary* (Oxford 1988), ed. T. Charles-Edwards, with
Addendum by Charles-Edwards, P. Wormald, et al. (coordinated with the Colgrave-
Mynors edition). A resource that cannot be overlooked, but suffers from having
been a posthumous work brought to completion by pious helpers. The main commentary is very conservative, and only slightly offset by the addenda.

Foley, W. Trent, and Arthur G. Holder, trs. *Bede: A Biblical Miscellany.* Translated
Texts for Historians, 28 (Liverpool 1999).

Wallis, Faith, tr. *Bede: The Reckoning of Time.* Translated Texts for Historians, 29
(Liverpool 1999). This excellent work includes a valuable introduction and a
full translation of Bede's Major Chronicle.

Studies

Bassett, Steven, ed. *The Origins of Anglo-Saxon Kingdoms* (Oxford 1989).

Beda Venerabilis: Historian, Monk and Northumbrian, ed. J. R. Houwen et al.
(Groningen 1996).

Berschin, Walter. "*Opus deliberatum ac perfectum*: Why Did the Venerable Bede
Write a Second Prose Life of St Cuthbert?" in *St Cuthbert* (as below), pp. 95–102.

Brooks, Nicholas. *Bede and the English,* Jarrow Lecture 1999 (Jarrow n.d.).

Brown, George H. *Bede the Venerable* (Boston 1987). On Bede's biblical exegesis and
biblical aids, see the useful comments on pp. 42–61.

Bullough, Donald. "Anglo-Saxon Institutions and Early English Society" (1965);
reprinted in David A. F. Pelteret, ed. *Anglo-Saxon History: Basic Readings* (New
York–London 2000).

Campbell, James. "Bede (673/4–735)," *Oxford Dictionary of National Biography* (Oxford 2004) [http://www.oxforddnb.com/view/article/1922].

———, ed. "Elements in the Background of the Life of St Cuthbert and His Early
Cult," in *St Cuthbert* (as below), pp. 3–19.

Davis, R. H. C. "Bede after Bede," in *Studies in Medieval History Presented to R. Allen
Brown,* ed. Christopher Harper-Bill et al. (Woodbridge, Suffolk 1989), pp.
103–16.

Grocock, Christopher. "Bede and the Golden Age of Latin Prose in Northumbria,"
in *Northumbria's Golden Age,* pp. 371–82. A profound study of Bede's language.

Higham, Nicholas J. *The Kingdom of Northumbria: AD 350–1100* (Dover, N.H.
1993). There are many other titles by this controversial author.

Kirby, D. P. "Bede, Eddius Stephanus and the 'Life of Wilfrid,'" *English Historical Review* 98 (1983) 101–14.

———. *Bede's Historia ecclesiastica gentis Anglorum: Its Contemporary Setting,* Jarrow Lecture 1992 (Jarrow 1993).

———. *The Earliest English Kings,* rev. ed. (London–N.Y. 2000).

Lapidge, Michael. "The Anglo-Latin Background," in S. B. Greenfield and D. G.
Calder, eds., *A New Critical History of Old English Literature* (New York 1986), pp.
5–37.

———. "Anglo-Latin Literature," in *Anglo-Latin Literature 600–899* (London
1996), pp. 1–35. Places Bede in the context of early English learning.

———, ed. *Archbishop Theodore: Commemorative Studies on His Life and Influence*
(Cambridge 1996).

———. "Bede's Metrical *Vita S. Cuthberti,*" in *St Cuthbert,* pp. 77–93 (also in *Anglo-
Latin Literature* 1996).

———. "Hagiography in the British Isles, 500–1550, Retrospect (1968–98) and
Prospect," *Hagiographica* 6 (1999) 69–89.

Mayr-Harting, Henry. "Bede's Patristic Thinking as an Historian," in *Historiographie im frühen Mittelalter* (as cited in Ch. III Additional Bibliography), pp. 367–74.

McCready, William. "Bede and the Isidorian Legacy," *Mediaeval Studies* 57 (1995) 43–73.

Nelson, Janet. "Anglo-Saxon England," in *Oxford Illustrated History of Medieval England*, ed. Nigel Saul (Oxford 1997), pp. 25–60.

Northumbria's Golden Age, ed. Jane Hawkes and Susan Mills (Stroud, U.K. 1999).

Orchard, Andrew. *The Poetic Art of Aldhelm* (Cambridge 1994).

Pelteret, David. "Bede's Women," in *Women, Marriage, and Family in Medieval Christendom: Essays in Memory of Michael M. Sheehan*, ed. C. M. Rousseau and J. T. Rosenthal, Studies in Medieval Culture, 37 (Kalamazoo 1998), pp. 19–46.

Rollason, David. *Bede and Germany*, Jarrow Lecture 2001 (Durham, n.d.).

———. "Bede's *Historia Ecclesiastica*," *The Historian. Magazine of the Historical Association* 73 (2003) 6–10.

———. *Saints and Relics in Anglo-Saxon England* (Oxford 1989).

St Cuthbert, His Cult and His Community to AD 1200, ed. Gerald Bonner et al. (Woodbridge 1989).

Thacker, Alan. "Bede and the Irish," in *Beda Venerabilis: Historian, Monk and Northumbrian*, ed. J. R. Houwen et al. (Groningen 1996), pp. 31–60.

———. "Wilfrid [St Wilfrid] (*c*.634–709/10)," *Oxford Dictionary of National Biography* (Oxford 2004) [http://www.oxforddnb.com/view/article/29409].

Tugène, Georges. *L'idée de nation chez Bède le Vénérable* (Paris 2001).

———. *L'image de la nation anglaise dans l'Histoire ecclésiastique de Bède le Vénérable* (Strasbourg 2001).

Yorke, Barbara. "Anglo-Saxon *gentes* and *regna*," in *Regna and Gentes: The Relationship between Late Antique and Early Medieval Peoples and Kingdoms*, ed. H. W. Goetz et al. (Leiden 2003), pp. 381–407.

———. *Kings and Kingdoms of Early Anglo-Saxon England* (London 1990).

Ch. V, Paul the Deacon

Three Important Articles

Bullough, Donald A. "Ethnic History and the Carolingians: An Alternative Reading of Paul the Deacon's *Historia Langobardorum*," in C. Holdsworth and T. P. Wiseman, eds., *The Inheritance of Historiography, 350–900*, Exeter Studies in History, 12 (Exeter 1986), pp. 85–105; reprinted in Bullough, *Carolingian Renewal* (Manchester 1991), pp. 97–122.

McKitterick, Rosamond. "Paul the Deacon and the Franks," *Early Medieval Europe* 8 (1999) 319–39.

Pohl, Walter. "Paulus Diaconus und die 'Historia Langobardorum': Text und Tradition," in *Historiographie im frühen Mittelalter* (cited in Ch. III Additional Bibliography), pp. 375–405.

Pohl and McKitterick directly take issue with me. Bullough does not; we missed each other's work on this subject owing to overlaps in publication dates. The main thesis of Bullough's article (concerning Paul's "legendary" passages) is based on the improbable premise that thirteenth-century Iceland is relevant to eighth-century Italy. Much more noteworthy are Bullough's brief reconstruction of Paul's career and his excellent summary of the "unbalances, omissions and apparent anomalies" of the HL. His account of Paul's life closely agrees with mine; I am glad to have his support in countering McKitterick's iconoclasm. I deal with Pohl and McKitterick at greater length under topic headings.

Did Paul Have a Central Purpose?

Pohl and McKitterick are both concerned with the motivation of the HL. McKitterick, while loudly dissenting from me, fails to remark that her theory and Pohl's are wholly incompatible. Pohl insists that Paul, amidst the contradictions of life in Lombard Italy, cannot be pinned down to any definite central purpose. McKitterick, on the other hand, provides Paul with the most central of purposes; she claims that he was the officially commissioned advocate for Frankish rule of the Lombard kingdom—a pillar of the post-781 Carolingian regime in Pavia. The views I set out in *Narrators* occupy middle ground between these extremes. My Paul not only has a central focus, namely the Lombard principality of Benevento and its new prince Grimoald III, but also advocates a Benevento friendly to and supportive of the Franks and aligned with the new Pavian regime. The evidence McKitterick musters for a pro-Frankish Paul—she leans exclusively on HL6—is as useful to my theory as to hers. As for Pohl, he is the solitary champion (except, perhaps, unintentionally for Bullough) of his vision of a Paul who weaves and squirms, turning where his sources turn, but without firm sympathies. These premises allow Pohl to mold and shape Paul's history in accord with his own purposes.

There are two associated problems: Paul's biography, and the question whether the HL is finished or incomplete.

Paul's Biography

McKitterick proposes that Paul joined Charlemagne's court as early as the 770s and became a monk at Monte Cassino only after returning from the Frankish kingdom in the 780s. Both views are extreme and unsustainable, no matter how vociferously McKitterick affirms them. Bullough's account and mine of Paul's biography are on more solid ground. Even she backs off later in her article, accepting normal doctrine. Pohl enters this discussion only as regards Paul's date of death, usually given as ca. 799, that is, pre-800. He observes that Paul is unaware of Charlemagne's destruction of the Avar kingdom in 796 and infers a terminus ante quem from that silence. The argument has merit, but changes little even if accepted. The HL continues to fit into the last (Monte Cassino) part of Paul's life, probably in the 790s.

Is the HL Complete or Unfinished?

Here, too, McKitterick is emphatic and categorical: Paul very definitely meant to finish the HL where it ends, with the obituary chapter on King Liutprand. She has an ally in the lengthy but weak work of Helmut Rogan, *Paulus Diaconus 'Laudator temporis acti'. Königsdarstellung und Aufbauprinzip der Buchschlüsse als Antwort auf die Frage nach dem von Paulus intendierten Ende der* Historia Langobardorum (Graz 1993). Pohl, too, leans in this direction. Many earlier scholars besides myself have believed that the HL is incomplete; a recent endorsement of the idea is given by Lars Boje Mortensen, "Impero Romano, *Historia Romana* e *Historia Langobardorum*," in *Paolo Diacono. Uno scrittore* (as cited below), pp. 355–66. The argument for incompleteness hinges on the absence of an introduction and a conclusion, features found in Paul's finished writings. Incompleteness is also suggested by the care with which Paul fills in the background of Ratchis and Aistulf, the successors of Liutprand as Lombard kings, and by Paul's evocation of prophetic holy men. These are solid reasons, which the partisans of completeness should not disregard. I go further by conjecturing that Paul had a plan for a completed HL extending to two additional books, including an account of the Frankish conquest of 774. There is no way to "prove" this conjecture; the one course for making it plausible is the necessarily fallible literary analysis I conduct, which I urge others to improve and strengthen. Neither side is able to provide conclusive proof one way or the other.

The Future of the HL, Its Publication History

Both Pohl's and McKitterick's articles pay sustained attention to the HL after Paul, as reflected by the dispersal of its manuscripts and its use by later medieval authors. This is valuable and much needed work. Both approach this task, however, with the idea that the future of the HL sheds light on its circumstances of composition. For example, McKitterick feels sure the early distribution of HL manuscripts lends weight to her "Frankish" theory of its origins. Mutatis mutandis, Pohl also argues in this sense. It is fair to say, I believe, that the evidence that Pohl and McKitterick collect has no discernible bearing on theories of composition.

The Connection of the HR to the HL

In the article cited above, Mortensen denies that, in ending the *Historia Romana*, Paul already foresaw the HL; instead (he claims), Paul refers only to the prospective addition of a seventeenth book reaching to the end of Justinian's reign. This argument is weak. Paul is firm in offering an HR in sixteen books only and promises a separate continuation. The evident connection between the end of the HR16 and HL1–2 suffices to show that Paul's promised continuation is the HL.

An Edition with Commentary

Lidia Capo, ed. *Paolo Diacono. Storia dei Longobardi* (Vicenza 1992): Latin text with facing Italian translation and an extensive commentary. (Capo worked too early to take account of *Narrators*.) The commentary accompanying this convenient edition is learned and ample, but unfocused. Capo does not envisage her task as primarily shedding light on what Paul was doing and how he molded the past.

Second Thoughts on the Paul Chapter of *Narrators*

I remain convinced that serious readers of the HL need to familiarize themselves with the methods of writing history exemplified by Paul in his earlier works, notably the HR, the *Gesta* of the bishops of Metz, and the Life of Gregory the Great. I give an account of these methods in *Narrators* (and my article in *Traditio* listed below) but do not claim that my results could not be improved upon. Paul, an assiduous user of sources, was not concerned to be a faithful transmitter of the information he received; he used sources to fashion histories of his own, which he no doubt believed conveyed the past more fully and faithfully than the sources on which they were based. Not for a moment do I accept Walter Pohl's allegation that my Paul is denied the role of a historian (quotation cited above, p. xi); in Collingwood's definition of that role, Paul was an imaginative re-creator of the past.

Where the interpretation of the HL is concerned, I have not ceased to believe that the work was crafted with great deliberation and care and is wrongly envisaged as a slavish, haphazard, and fault-ridden combination of Paul's sources. To take a simple example, the placement at the head of HL3 of incidents involving the recluse Hospitius required Paul to lift information from the very end of Gregory of Tours's account of Lombard incursions into Gaul; in other words, Paul carefully adapted Gregory to purposes of his own. In this and dozens of other instances, a serious reader of the HL needs to puzzle out what these purposes and Paul's ordering scenarios were.

I implemented these premises in *Narrators* and am not unhappy with the results; but I am sure that my account is far from being a final reading of the HL and should be refined and improved. I regard my approach to the HL as more enduring than my particular interpretations of Paul's narrative. The hypothesis that Paul wrote the work as a mirror for young Grimoald III of Benevento still seems to me preferable by far to the divergent courses offered by McKitterick and Pohl, and I regard my idea of a planned eight-book HL as a possibility that should not be lightly discarded.

Additional Bibliography

Capitani, Ovidio. "Paolo Diacono e la storiografia altomedievale," in *Paolo Diacono e il Friuli*, pp. 25–44. Takes extended notice of Pohl and me.

Capo, Lidia. "Paolo Diacono e il problema della cultura dell'Italia longobarda," in *Langobardia*, pp. 169–235. The same title in *Il regno dei Longobardi in Italia. Archeologica, società e istituzioni*, ed Stefano Gasparri (Spoleto 2004), pp. 215–25. By the editor of Paul named above on p. xxxiii. Little attention is paid to Paul.

Cingolani, Stefano Maria. *Le storie dei Longobardi. Dall'origine a Paolo Diacono* (Rome 1995). Reviewed negatively by me in *Speculum* 73 (1998) 823.

Costambeys, M. "The Monastic Environment of Paul the Deacon," in *Paolo Diacono. Uno scrittore*, pp. 127–138.

Goffart, Walter. "Paul the Deacon's *Gesta episcoporum Mettensium* and the Early Design of Charlemagne's Succession," *Traditio* 42 (1986) 59–93. Expands the few pages of *Narrators* on this subject; illustrates Paul's method of composition.

Herren, Michael W. "Theological Aspects of the Writings of Paul the Deacon," in *Paolo Diacono. Uno scrittore*, pp. 223–35. A talented philologist and literary scholar, Herren is less qualifed in ecclesiastical history.

Kempf, Dietmar. "Paul the Deacon's *Liber de episcopis Mettensibus* and the Role of Metz in the Carolingian Realm," *Journal of Medieval History* 30 (1994) 279–99. Liberally helps himself to my *Traditio* article in a crude attempt to rectify it.

Langobardia, ed. S. Gasparri and P. Cammarosano (Udine 1990).

Mortensen, Lars Boje. *Civiliserede barbaren* [Paul the Deacon and his predecessors] (Copenhagen 1991). In Danish. Mortensen likes to find fault with me.

Paolo Diacono e il Friuli altomedievale (saec. VI–X), Atti del XIV congresso internazionale di studi sull'alto medioevo, *24–29 settembre 1999* (Spoleto 2001). At least two contributions are *Narrators* conscious. Most contributions have nothing to do with Paul, or simply mine him for largely archaeological reason.

Paolo Diacono. Uno scrittore fra tradizione longobarda e rinovamento carolingio, Atti del Convegno internazionale di studi, *6–9 maggio 1999*, ed. Paolo Chiera (Udine 2000).

Pohl, Walter. His major study is cited on p. xxx, above. Pohl has written assiduously about Paul. His widely dispersed articles are not difficult to find via the Internet; they embody much recycling and self-citation.

Zanella, Gabriele. "La legittimazione del potere regale nelle 'Storie' di Gregorio di Tours e Paolo Diacono," *Studi medievali*, ser. 3, 31 (1990) 55–84.

Preface

Soon after my first term at college began, the introductory course in Western civilization in which I had enrolled prescribed mimeographed readings labeled "The Dark Ages"; their only contents were lurid passages from the *Histories* of Gregory of Tours. At this distance, I cannot explain my negative reaction to the package placed in my hands, but I do recall being convinced that the selection was a caricature, no more representative of "The Dark Ages" than of any other epoch. It has taken me a long time to translate this hunch into a sustained argument.

A more positive impulse helped in its elaboration. Commenting on my *Le Mans Forgeries*, Professor Horst Fuhrmann wrote, "It remains to test whether Goffart . . . does not introduce too much intention (*Absicht*) and circumspection (*Umsicht*) into the forgeries."* Of course my findings should be verified, as scholarship must always be. But the aspect that Fuhrmann believed to need special probing seems rather odd. Why should one be suspected of exaggeration for treating medieval authors (forgers or not) as thoroughly conscious of their actions and wily in carrying them out? The tendency of historical research has been to judge otherwise; inadvertence and artlessness are thought to be the normal condition of writers long dead, a critical equivalent, perhaps, to the presumption of innocence in criminal law. The four narrators whom I shall be discussing do not have to be presumed innocent, because they run no danger of being found guilty; they are neither under indictment nor on trial. If a single theme runs through this book, it is that, like us, Jordanes, Gregory, and the others meant to write what they did and were well aware of what they said and why.

In 1974 I began to hold a seminar on late Roman and early medieval historians and, after a few years, limited its scope to the authors featured here. The possibility this gave me of closely reading the same texts year after year has proved invaluable. My students during these years had to endure my obsessions, and I am more grateful for their forbearance than I can say: the greater part of the learning experience tended to be mine rather than theirs.

My preoccupation with these historians was also indulged outside Toronto. On a snowy February afternoon of 1979 in New York City, when the condition of the streets forced the cancellation of classes, some stalwarts

---

* Horst Fuhrmann, *Einfluss und Verbreitung der pseudoisidorischen Fälschungen*, Schriften der MGH, 24, part 1 (Stuttgart 1972), p. 193 n. 123.

turned up at Barnard College to hear me discourse on "Jordanes and Procopius: The Context of the Gothic Migration Legend." This was the first of
a string of lectures on one or another of the four authors: at the University
of California, Berkeley (1981), the Medieval Academy of America Annual
Meeting (1983), the Conference on Medieval Studies at Western Michigan University, Kalamazoo (1983), the Universities of Toronto and of Ot-
tawa (1983), Dumbarton Oaks in Washington, D.C. (1984), the International Society of Anglo-Saxonists, Cambridge, England (1985), a
workshop convened by the Institut für österreichische Geschichtsforschung at the Abbey of Zwettl (1986), the Accademia Peloritana dei Peri-
colanti, University of Messina (1986), and the University of Catania
(1986). All these audiences have earned my thanks by their kind recep-
tiveness and stimulating questions.

Two studies of Gregory of Tours that I published while this book was in
preparation are not directly within its scope. On the other hand, a topic
directly relevant to Chapter V § 5, but too intricate for inclusion in it, is to
appear as "Paul the Deacon's *Gesta Episcoporum Mettensium* and the Early
Plans for Charlemagne's Succession," in *Traditio* 42 (1986). A much longer
version of Chapter III § 2 appears as "From *Historiae* to *Historia Francorum*
and Back Again," in *Religion, Culture, and Society in the Early Middle Ages:
Studies in Honor of Richard E. Sullivan*, ed. T.F.X. Noble and J. Contreni
(Kalamazoo, Mich. 1987).

Begun during my tenure of a Guggenheim Fellowship in 1979-80, the
text of this book was completed in draft in 1983-84, thanks to the award by
the University of Toronto of a Connaught Senior Fellowship in the Humanities—a nonsabbatical year, free of classes and other responsibilities.
The manuscript gained its full complement of notes and other finishing
touches while I enjoyed sabbatical leave from my university and a fellowship from the Social Sciences and Humanities Research Council of Canada. Of the smaller research grants that came my way in this period from
the Research Board of the University of Toronto, the most noteworthy allowed me to talk at the I.S.A.S. conference in Cambridge. Not least, the
Senior Common Room of St. Peter's College welcomed me as a member
during a four-month Oxford stay in 1986. I am very happy to be able to
acknowledge the generosity and help of these institutions and bodies.

I have incurred a host of debts to libraries and individuals. Some helpers
are singled out in the notes. Many others, left unnamed, have earned my
gratitude; their anonymity spares them any share in the flaws of the end
product. My wife has been the most certain source of counsel and support
since the inception of this project and has even had to endure my neo-
phyte's absorption in word processing. For good measure, she also had to

read the manuscript several times. If imperfections remain, it was not for lack of her efforts to get them out.

The dedication page allows me to acknowledge my indebtedness to a friend with whom I took my first steps into scholarship and whose wisdom and generosity over the years have sustained me and countless others.

Toronto
August 1986

Abbreviations

| VW | *Vita Wilfridi, episcopi Eboracensis*, ed. Wilhelm Levison, MGH SRM VI, 193-263—Ed. and tr. Bertram Colgrave, *The Life of Bishop Wilfrid by Eddius Stephanus*. Cambridge 1972—Tr. J. F. Webb, *Lives of the Saints*. Harmondsworth, Middlesex 1965. Pp. 133-206 |
| Whitby Gregory | *De vita atque virtutibus beati Gregorii papae urbis Romae*, ed. and tr. Bertram Colgrave, *The Earliest Life of Gregory the Great*. Lawrence, Kans. 1968; reprinted Cambridge 1985 |

GREGORY OF TOURS

Bordier	Henri Bordier, *Les livres de miracles de Grégoire de Tours*, 4 vols. Société de l'histoire de France, Paris 1857-64
Buchner	Gregor von Tours, *Zehn Bücher Geschichten*, ed. and tr. Rudolf Buchner, 2 vols. Ausgewählte Quellen zur deutschen Geschichte des Mittelalters 2-3, Berlin 1955-56
Buchner, Einleitung	Introduction to Buchner
CS	*De cursu stellarum ratio*, ed. Bruno Krusch, MGH SRM I part 2, pp. 857-72
Dalton	O. M. Dalton, *The History of the Franks. By Gregory of Tours*, 2 vols. Oxford 1927
GC	*Liber in gloria confessorum*, ed. Bruno Krusch, MGH SRM I part 2, pp. 744-820
GM	*Liber in gloria martyrum, ibid.*, pp. 484-561
K-L	*Historiarum libri X*, ed. Bruno Krusch and Wilhelm Levison, MGH SRM I part 1, 2d ed.
Thorpe	Gregory of Tours, *History of the Franks*, tr. Lewis Thorpe. Penguin Classics, Harmondsworth, Middlesex 1974
Todi Convegno 12	Centro di studi sulla spiritualità medievale, Convegni XII: *Gregorio di Tours* (10-13 ottobre 1971). Todi 1977
VP	*Liber vitae patrum*, as GC, pp. 661-744
VSJ	*De virtutibus s. Iuliani, ibid.*, pp. 562-84
VSM	*De virtutibus s. Martini libri IV, ibid.*, pp. 584-661

JORDANES

Get.	Jordanes, *Getica*, ed. Theodor Mommsen, MGH AA. V. Cited by paragraph number only (¶)
Mierow	Charles Christopher Mierow, *The Gothic History of Jordanes in English Version*, 2d ed. Princeton 1915; reprinted New York 1960
Mommsen, Preface	Theodor Mommsen, Preface to Jordanes, *Romana et Getica*, MGH AA. V, v-lxxiii
Rom.	Jordanes, *Romana*. Same as *Get.*

PAUL THE DEACON

Bethmann-Waitz See *H.L.*

Foulke William Dudley Foulke, tr., *Paul the Deacon, History of the Langobards*. Philadelphia 1907; reprinted as *History of the Lombards*, Philadelphia 1974

H.L. Paul the Deacon, *Historia Langobardorum*, ed. Ludwig Bethmann and Georg Waitz, MGH *Script. rer. Lang.*

H.R. Paul the Deacon, *Historia Romana*, ed. Amadeo Crivellucci. Fonti per la Storia d'Italia 51, Rome 1913—Ed. H. Droysen, MGH AA. II (as an expansion of Eutropius)

Neff Karl Neff, *Die Gedichte des Paulus Diaconus. Kritische und erklärende Ausgabe*. Quellen und Untersuchungen zur lateinische Philologie des Mittelalters, ed. Ludwig Traube, 3, fasc. 4, Munich 1908. Numbers cited in Roman numerals

The Narrators of Barbarian History

The First Major Historians of Medieval Europe

The narrators of this book's title have an established place in the study of the early Middle Ages. In the *Guide to the Sources of Medieval History* by R. C. van Caeneghem, they enter into a class of "National Histories of the Germanic Peoples," with the comment, "Once the Germanic tribes reached a sufficient degree of civilization, they found authors to record their histories and thus provide invaluable information."[1] Herbert Grundmann's influential account of medieval historiography suggests that the same four were nourished by the historical poetry of the nonliterate Germanic peoples, and it places their works in a category of "Volksgeschichte (Origo gentis)."[2] Beryl Smalley's more popular *Historians in the Middle Ages* invokes "The Roman Legacy" and "The Jewish-Christian Legacy" before arriving at "The Barbarian Legacy and the Early Middle Ages":

The ancient world [she says] had no precedent for the history of a barbarian people. Tacitus' *Germania* is descriptive rather than historical. The Chosen People of the Pentateuch hardly counted as barbarian. But the barbarian invaders of the Roman empire moved triumphantly into historiography just as they founded their successor-states on former imperial territory. They produced four great historians: Jordanes (d. 554?) for the Goths; Gregory, bishop of Tours (d. 593/4), for the Franks; Bede (d. 735) for the English; and Paul the Deacon (d. 799?) for the Lombards.[3]

The four major historians normally associated with the barbarian successor-states are the subject of this book.

Caeneghem, Grundmann, and Smalley use slightly different terms, as called for by their varying themes, but all agree in regarding the "barbarians" as forming a very special group of peoples and their narrators as distinctive because associated with them. The premise they share illustrates a pervasive feature in the study of historiography. The histories we have long written give prominence to the Germanic invasions and settlement of the Roman Empire; the periodizations Europeans have used since the seven-

---

[1] Caeneghem, *Guide to the Sources of Medieval History*, pp. 26-27.

[2] Grundmann, *Geschichtsschreibung*, pp. 12-15. Curiously, Grundmann's point of departure is not the historians of late antiquity, but the "oral history," as it were, of the Germanic tribes.

[3] Smalley, *Historians in the Middles Ages*, p. 50. Although one understands what Smalley means about Tacitus, her distinction is somewhat misleading, because ethnography more legitimately belongs to the genre of history than, e.g., biography; see Fornara, *Nature of History*, pp. 12-16, 34-36, 184-89.

teenth century accord the barbarians an assured place.[4] These periods are expected not only to guide us, but also to commit early historians, who are tacitly assumed to speak to our concerns as though they were parties to our ordering of events. The result for Jordanes and the others tends to be that, because they were the first to pay sustained attention to Goths, Franks, and other barbarians, they are said to be not just our informants about these peoples, but also the authors of a new kind of history. The advent of the Germanic barbarians, a weighty event in our estimation, is deemed to be directly mirrored in the history of historiography and to result in the emergence of "national" history, a type of writing about the past not practiced until then.

Another perspective guided medieval collectors of histories. "National" histories were well known to the Middle Ages, but no one cared, when gathering them between two covers, whether one work was about the (Germanic) Goths, the next about the Romans, and a third about the Jews. A twelfth-century library catalogue from a monastery near Bourges lists a "History of the English, the Trojans, the Romans, the Lombards, the Goths in one codex." The manuscript in question, of eleventh-century date, survives at the Ambrosian Library in Milan and contains Bede, Dictys (on the Trojans), Paul the Deacon (on the Romans as well as the Lombards), and Jordanes.[5] Another manuscript—also French, of the same century, and now in Florence—joins Jordanes and Paul the Deacon to many other historians, including Josephus on the Jews, the "Deeds of the Franks" (a condensation of Gregory of Tours), Einhard's *Life of Charlemagne*, and the *History of Apollonius of Tyre* (which, to us, is simply an ancient romance).[6] Peoples or nations were the defining feature, whereas their relative age and respectability were irrelevant. In the Christian perspective of the classifiers, God ruled the world, whose denizens, after Noah's sons and the Tower of Babel, were scattered over the globe in national groups.[7] Only in the Renaissance and afterward were some of these peoples segregated as distinctively "barbarian" or "Germanic," whereas others were assigned to

[4] Dopsch, *Wirtschaftliche und soziale Grundlagen* I, 1-5. Messmer, *Hispania-Idee und Gotenmythos*, pp. 9-51.

[5] Ambrosianus C 72; Mommsen, Preface, pp. l-li; Mynors, OMT, p. lxiii. On Dictys, a pseudo-history believed to date from the first century A.D., Eisenhut, "Spätantike Troja-Erzählungen." The text of Dictys is ed. W. Eisenhut (Leipzig 1978); also see R. M. Frazer, tr., *The Trojan War: The Chronicles of Dictys of Crete and Dares the Phrygian* (Bloomington, Ind. 1966).

[6] Florence Laurentianus LXV, 34. From France, according to Waitz, "Über d. handschriftliche Überlieferung u. d. Sprache," pp. 546-47; Mommsen, Preface, p. xlix. The condensation of Gregory of Tours is cited below, n. 29.

[7] Their dispersion was tracked in the biblical table of nations (Gen. 10) and its descendants, such as that of Hippolytus of Rome. See Borst, *Der Turmbau von Babel* I, 234-35; II part 1, pp. 370-73.

the privileged antiquity of Greece and Rome. It is a point of view dependent on the course of modern historical thinking.[8]

Beryl Smalley believed that classical antiquity lacked a precedent for the
history of a barbarian nation.[9] One might argue the point, but regardless of
whether it did or not, no special talents and methods were needed for learning to write one: there were models. In the cosmopolitan Roman Empire of
the Flavians (A.D. 69-96), the resident Jews were deemed to be aliens, that
is, "barbarians" in the neutral sense of the word. Josephus wrote on the recent *Jewish Wars* and, at greater length, on *Jewish Antiquities* with a view to
making his fellow Jews better known and more acceptable to the Greco-
Roman public. Unintentionally, he provided the Christians of the third
and later centuries with some of their most cherished reading.[10] However
closely Christians after Constantine associated their earthly destiny with
the Roman Empire, the past that their religion and holy book invited them
to identify with could hardly be exclusively Roman.[11] While the emperors
still ruled, the multiplicity of peoples and the particularity of their histories
were clearly illustrated by the Christian *Chronicle* of Eusebius and its Latin
translation by Jerome. To record events in the current unity of the Empire,
only one column of chronicle was needed, but earlier ages demanded a dou-
ble-page spread to accommodate the multiple columns commemorating as
many as nine coexisting kingdoms for as long as they lasted.[12] Roman history itself had always tended to parochialism rather than to an outlook
commensurate with a far-flung empire.[13] Toward 369, a government official
named Eutropius wrote a compact history of the Romans since the foun-

[8] The course of their thinking was hardly simple and has not yet, to my knowledge, been
traced. One aspect of it was the creation of a "German" history, on which, for orientation,
see Borchardt, *German Antiquity in Renaissance Myth*. Another aspect is the privileged status
that Rome (ultimately classical antiquity) enjoyed from Petrarch onward: Lefebvre, *Naissance
de l'historiographie moderne*, pp. 82, 85; Breisach, *Historiography*, pp. 161-62, 164-65.

[9] As above, n. 3.

[10] Rajak, *Josephus*, pp. 223-29. The first third of the *Jewish Wars* is concerned with historical
background, and an eminently sensible outline of a "national" history appears in *Jewish Antiquities* 1.2.5-6 (below, II n. 322). Josephus is very prominent among the sources of Eusebius's
H.E. (for which see below, n. 21), and two translations of his *Jewish Wars* into Latin were
made in the fourth century; it was available to Latin Christians as a "Church" history well
before Eusebius was translated (the statue of Josephus in Rome was probably erected by Christians: Rajak, p. 229). Josephus meant his massive *Antiquities* "to be a counterpart to . . . [the
monumental] *Roman Antiquities* [of] Dionysius of Helicarnassus": Blatt, *Latin Josephus* I, 12.
Eusebius himself conceived of his *H.E.* as the history of a nation: Markus (as below, n. 16),
p. 7.

[11] On the association between Empire and Church, see, among many, Meslin, "Nationalisme, état et religions." By accrediting Oriental chronological data, Christian authors overthrew the whole system of Greek prehistory: Bickerman, "*Origines gentium*," p. 73.

[12] Jerome *Chronicon*, ed. Rudolf Helm (Berlin 1956): nine columns, p. 83; one, p. 188 to
the end. Other configurations: five columns, p. 27; seven, p. 66; six, p. 102; four, p. 131; two,
p. 163.

[13] Fornara, *Nature of History*, pp. 23-28, 52-54. See also Wiseman, "Practice and Theory."

dation of their city. It was as tidy a model as one might hope to find for the history of a people.[14] Two centuries later, Jordanes, the first of our quartet, saw no incongruity in preceding his account of the Goths with one of the Romans; and Paul the Deacon, years before writing about the Lombards, developed the ten small books of Eutropius into a sixteen-book history of the Romans from Janus to Justinian.[15] Like the eleventh-century collectors who casually aligned the Trojans side by side with the English, Jordanes and Paul did not question that Romans, Goths, and Lombards were equivalent entities, however differentiated their histories might be.

The title *Narrators of Barbarian History* speaks to a modern audience in the terms with which it is familiar, but it should not be understood to mean that the authors in question wrote a type of history sharply contrasting in subject to that practiced in earlier centuries. That Jordanes and his peers were concerned with Goths and other "barbarians," though not an incidental detail, is not the main reason for studying them. The Constantinopolitan perspective of Jordanes overshadows his Gothic theme. Gregory of Tours was primarily concerned with current events rather than with the Franks, and he was intent on portraying the depravity of all men rather than of a subgroup among them. Bede was Northumbrian rather than English and cared more about the Christian face of his compatriots than about their ethnic peculiarities. Paul waited so long to write about his fellow Lombards, applying his pen to other subjects, that he left their history unfinished. Our four authors are less compelling for occasionally addressing themselves to the peoples whom we call Germanic barbarians than they are for being the leading practitioners of narrative history in Latin within the two hundred fifty years that separate Justinian, for whom Jordanes may have worked, from Charlemagne, at whose court Paul the Deacon briefly sojourned.

Jordanes and Gregory lived close enough to the conventional "end of Rome" that they force us to ask when we may stop calling historians "ancient" and start using the term "medieval." The acclimatization of Christianity in the Roman Empire of the fourth century muddies the issue and invites caution in the drawing of boundaries. In the later Roman Empire, Christian and nonsectarian (rather than "pagan") historians coexisted and overlapped, so much so that the start of a new era in historiography has to be situated considerably later than the triumph of the new religion.[16] Chris-

---

[14] Eutropius *Breviarium ab urbe condita*, ed. Franz Rühl (Leipzig 1919); ed. H. Droysen, MGH AA. II (with two Greek translations and later Western adaptations, including Paul the Deacon's). We shall hear much of Eutropius.

[15] Below, ch. II § 5 and ch. V § 3.

[16] Momigliano, "Pagan and Christian Historiography"; Momigliano, "L'età del trapasso"; Markus, "Church History and Early Church Historians"; Laistner, "Some Reflections" (concerned mostly with the fourth century); Demandt, "Geschichte in der spätantike Gesells-

tian history, such as the pioneering *History of the Church* by Eusebius of Caesarea, was written many decades before the pagan Ammianus Marcellinus revived the old-fashioned manner of Tacitus in writing a multivolume account of the recent past.[17] Between Eusebius and Ammianus, the works of other non-Christian historians, such as Aurelius Victor and Eutropius, saw the light.[18] In the East Roman Empire, where Greek was the dominant tongue, the duality of Christian and classical modes in the writing of history was perpetuated into the sixth century and even made a comeback at later times.[19] Latin literature, however, displays a sharper line of demarcation. Traditional nonsectarian history seems to have expired with an enigmatic collection of imperial biographies known as the *Augustan History*, whose date continues to elude scholarship; the only apparent certainty is that the work belongs no earlier than the last decade of the fourth century.[20] From then on, the outlook of Latin historiography was uniformly Christian even in works whose subject matter had no direct relation to the Church or the

---

chaft." Novel and important observations on the relations of traditional and Christian historical writing are made by Press, "Development of the Idea of History," and Sordi, "Dalla storiografia classica alla storiografia cristiana."

[17] Eusebius first wrote the *H.E.*, before the end of the third century: Barnes, *Constantine and Eusebius*, p. 128. Ammianus's first installment was published in 392, the rest before 397: Blockley, *Ammianus Marcellinus*, pp. 12-16. Matthews, "Ammianus' Historical Evolution," pp. 37-38, develops the challenging argument that the "the closest affinities to Ammianus' historical manner are in the Greek tradition," in other words that he is more a successor of Dexippus than of Tacitus.

Another early Christian work with a claim to being called a history, dated 315, is Lactantius *De mortibus persecutionum*, ed. J. Moreau, Sources chrétiennes 39 (Paris 1954); its form resembles the traditional one of a catalogue of emperors.

[18] Sextus Aurelius Victor *Liber de Caesaribus*, ed. Franz Pichlmayr (Leipzig 1911), pp. 75-129; ed. and tr. Pierre Dufraigne, Collection des universités de France (Paris 1975). For Eutropius, n. 14 above. Very close to him in time is Festus *Breviarium*, ed. J. W. Eadie (London 1967). I call them nonsectarian because unable to find notable traces of any sort of religion in their pages; for comparison, see the third-century work of Herodian *Ab excessu divi Marci*, ed. C. R. Whittaker, Loeb, 2 vols. (London 1969-70), whose many casual references to pagan cults have no parallel in fourth-century historians. See also Syme, "Fiction in the Epitomators."

[19] The pagan histories of Eunapius and Olympiodorus belong to the early fifth century; the three (surviving) continuators of Eusebius *H.E.*—Socrates, Sozomen, and Theodoret—belong to the mid fifth. Classicizing works resume in the 470s, with Priscus of Panium, then Malchus and Candidus. Theodore Anagnostes wrote Church history in the early sixth, and Evagrius toward its close; in between, classicizing history was exemplified by Procopius, Agathias, and Theophylact Simocatta. On the Church historians, see in brief Altaner, *Patrology*, pp. 273-75. On classicizing historians down to 500, R. C. Blockley, *The Fragmentary Classicising Historians of the Later Roman Empire*, 2 vols., Arca: Classical and Medieval Texts, Papers and Monographs 6, 10 (Liverpool 1981-83). Procopius and Agathias will concern us in connection with Jordanes.

[20] *Scriptores historiae Augustae*, ed. E. Hohl, 2 vols., rev. ed. (Leipzig 1971). For a brief account, Birley, "The *Augustan History*," esp. pp. 123-24 (on the date). On the current state of discussion, see Syme, "Controversy Abating and Credulity Curbed." For continuing dissent from the currently accepted date, see below ch. IV n. 1. The first known borrowing from the *H.A.* (and thus its firm *terminus ante quem*) is in Jordanes; see below, ch. II n. 295.

saints. Gregory, Bede, and Paul were ordained clergymen, and Jordanes, perhaps a layman, was no less conspicuously Christian than they.

Although simplicity recommends that our historians should be called medieval, the Latin historiography of the sixth, seventh, and eighth centuries prolonged the Christian strain in the historical writing of late antiquity. When Gregory of Tours and the others evoked historical classics, they mentioned the Bible as well as Eusebius's *Church History*, the universal *Chronicle* of Eusebius and Jerome, Orosius's *Seven Books of History against the Pagans*, and other works of the patristic age.[21] Regardless of whether they directly modeled their own writings on them or not, such was the tradition they appealed to and within which they wished to rank. All of them recognized, to be sure, that peoples once alien to Roman history had a major place in their narratives; to this extent, they supplied fuel to modern notions of "national" histories and *Volksgeschichte*. But they did not imagine that the Franks, Lombards, and others marked an interruption in the course of Christian literature, such as to turn historiography toward uncharted paths. None of them had a subjective sense of doing something that had not been done before. As the Christian Church had lived in the Roman Empire, so it lived on in the successor-kingdoms of the West; and it was with that universal entity (in its Latin manifestation) rather than with alien newcomers that they primarily identified their literary endeavors. The commitment of Gregory, Bede, and Paul to their religion, expressed in a variety of ways, is the dominant feature of their works.[22]

Our four narrators were not the only Latin historians of the centuries they span. At the risk of unfolding a catalogue, some attempt must be made to survey the comparable writings within the same two hundred fifty years. The period in question is famous for being culturally impoverished, and so, to some extent, it was. Nevertheless, our authors, though eminent, cannot be said to rise up out of a desert.

Their peers included a considerable number of chroniclers, taking up

[21] The version of Eusebius accessible to Westerners was the translation of Rufinus, available to us only in the major edition of Theodor Mommsen, *Eusebius Werke*, II part 2, Die griechiche christlicher Schriftsteller der ersten drei Jahrhundert (Leipzig 1903-09); a handier edition, without facing Greek, would be valuable. The translation dates from the very early fifth century. For an appreciation of Rufinus's work, see Christensen, "Rufinus of Aquileia." For the Eusebius-Jerome *Chron.*, n. 12 above. Paulus Orosius *Historiarum adversum paganos libri VII*, ed. Karl Zangenmeister, Corpus scriptorum ecclesiasticorum Latinorum 5 (Vienna 1882); tr. Roy J. Deferrari, *The Fathers of the Church: A New Translation* (Washington, D.C. 1964). Among our authors, only Gregory was acquainted with Sulpicius Severus *Chronicon* (ca. 400), which is not really a chronicle; below, ch. III nn. 198-99. As pointed out by Laistner, "Some Reflections," p. 242, Cassiodorus (*Institutiones divinarum et humanarum lectionum* 1.17) also restricts his list of historians to Christian authors, and Josephus.

[22] Jordanes is less straightforward, as will be seen; in the Gothic history (*Getica*) his commitment is to the East Roman Empire.

where those of the fifth century had left off. Original continuations, some very ambitious, were given to the Eusebius-Jerome *Chronicle*, by Count Marcellinus (in the East Roman Empire), Victor of Tunnuna (an African, but writing in the East), Marius of Avenches (in Frankish Gaul), John of Biclar (in Visigothic Spain), and the anonymous "Copenhagen Continuator of Prosper" (in Italy).[23] Not least, Isidore of Seville and Bede himself compiled entirely new chronicles, using Eusebius-Jerome as a source rather than as a trunk to be developed.[24]

Chronicles aside, Italy after Justinian's conquest witnessed several contributions to historical literature. The great Cassiodorus, after retirement from public life to the monastery he had established at Vivarium, made a point of encouraging needed translations from Greek. One of these was of Josephus's *Jewish Antiquities*, complementing the *Jewish Wars* which had been twice rendered into Latin in the fourth century. Another translation, carried out by Epiphanius, was a history of the Church from Constantine to the First Council of Ephesus (430), continuing the Latin version of Eusebius's *Church History* by Rufinus (ca. 402). Epiphanius's long work, composed of extracts from the fifth-century histories of Socrates, Sozomen, and Theodoret, is called *Historia tripartita*.[25] Elsewhere in the peninsula and in a more original vein, an author whose name and circumstances are wholly unknown produced an interesting essay in parallel biography, setting the emperor Constantine alongside the Ostrogothic king Theodoric.[26] In Rome, a sequence of papal biographies—a papal chronicle—went through its first redaction in the sixth century and was recast in the seventh into the collection known as the *Liber pontificalis*. This work of unnamed authors, regularly continued pope by pope until interrupted in the 880s, was the first official history undertaken in the West, and the only one until the Carolingian royal annals in the very late 700s.[27]

Other regions of the West also contributed more than chronicles. In the

---

[23] These are all among the *Chronica minora*, ed. Th. Mommsen: Count Marcellinus, Victor, Marius of Avenches, and John of Biclar in MGH AA. XI, 60-108, 184-206, 232-39, 211-20, respectively; the *Continuatio Havniensis Prosperi*, in MGH AA. IX, 298-399 (alongside other texts).

[24] Isidore of Seville *Chronica*, ed. Mommsen, MGH AA. XI, 424-81; Bede *Chronica maiora*, ed. Mommsen, MGH AA. XIII, 247-327.

[25] On the Epiphanius translation, see now Cameron, "Cassiodorus Deflated," p. 185. On the *Antiquities*, Blatt, *Latin Josephus* I, 9-20, 25; Schreckenberg, *Die Flavius-Josephus-Tradition*, pp. 56-60.

[26] *Excerpta Valesiana*, ed. Jean Moreau, new ed. (Leipzig 1968). The work is called after its original editor, Henri de Valois (brother of Adrien, a notable early student of Gregory of Tours). See Barnish, "The Anonymous Valesianus II."

[27] *Liber pontificalis*, ed. Louis Duchesne, 2 vols. (Paris 1886). The difficult history of its origins is masterfully presented by Duchesne I, xxxiii-lxxvii, ccxxx-xlv. In the case of so important a text, it would be rewarding to retrace and verify his reasoning in detail. Also see Bertolini, "Il *Liber pontificalis*."

first half the sixth century, the Briton Gildas composed a hortatory tract, *On the Ruin and Conquest of Britain*, of which more will be heard. Gildas did not intend to be a historian, but the first twenty-six paragraphs of his treatise form a historical introduction: the unique narrative of Britain after the end of Roman rule.[28] Near the other limit of our period, an anonymous Frankish contemporary of Bede, residing in Paris or nearby, wrote a brisk and colorful account of the Frankish kings, drastically abridging Gregory of Tours but also adding personal touches, some highly legendary, and continuing down to his own times. The work is known as *Gesta regum Francorum* or *Liber historiae Francorum* and was well liked in the Middle Ages.[29]

In most lands, accounts of the lives and posthumous miracles of saints were very numerous. For us to segregate them from history on the grounds that hagiography is a different genre would be as inappropriate as to exclude biography in other epochs. In the early Christian context, the deeds of the saints were considered to be no less factual and eventful than those of ordinary men.[30] Two types of hagiography merit special notice even in a brief survey. Christians revered and celebrated the heroes of their bloodstained beginnings. We have long been aware that many, perhaps most, passion narratives are anything but authentic reports of events; they were a form of popular fiction widely, but anonymously, practiced in the last centuries of antiquity (probably later as well). The ecclesiastical authorities, even of the time, occasionally thought authorial imaginations went too far, as in narrating the passion of St. George.[31] The level of indulgence was high,

[28] Gildas *De excidio Britonum*, ed. and tr. Michael Winterbottom (London 1978). On the date, see below, ch. III n. 252.

[29] *Liber historiae Francorum*, ed. Bruno Krusch, MGH SRM II, 238-328; tr. Bernard S. Bachrach (Lawrence, Kans. 1973); abridged ed. and tr. Herbert Haupt, *Quellen zur Geschichte des 7. und 8. Jahrhunderts*, Ausgewählte Quellen zur deutschen Geschichte des Mittelalters 4a (Darmstadt 1982), pp. 338-79. A monograph on this work, by Richard Gerberding, is in press.

[30] The relations of history and hagiography will concern us again, particularly in connection with Gregory and Bede, the two of our authors with a notable hagiographic output. Whether history and biography belong together is the more fundamental question, but, for better or worse, late antiquity had answered it in the affirmative before hagiography influenced the discussion: Fornara, *Nature of History*, pp. 184-89.

Hagiography has recently gained more than its share of attention among historians; e.g. Friedrich Lotter, "Legenden als Geschichtsquellen"; Fuhrmann, "Die Mönchsgeschichten des Hieronymus"; Uytfanghe, "Avatars contemporains"; Lotter, "Methodisches zur Gewinnung"; Leonardi, "L'agiografia latina"; Doignon, "Tradition classique et tradition chrétienne."

[31] The basic work is still Delehaye, *Passions et genres*. Also, Dufourcq, *Étude sur les gesta martyrum romains*; Delehaye, *Étude sur le légendier romain*; Giuseppe Lazzati, *Gli sviluppi della letteratura sui martiri nei primi quattro secole* (Turin 1956); Sozio Pezzella, *Gli atti dei martiri. Introduzione a una storia dell'antica agiografia* (Rome 1965). If I underscore the fictional character of most of these narratives, it is only to suggest that they are better suited to telling us about the authors and their audiences than to documenting the Roman persecutions. Banning of two martyr narratives by ecclesiastical authorities: Dobschütz, *Das Decretum Gelasianum*, pp. 41, 57, 473-75.

however, and tales of spectacular torture and heroism in the face of death were, for many centuries, the most cherished of hagiographic reading in the Church. Bede, as we shall see, gathered the substance of over four dozen such narratives within the covers of a modest-sized martyrology.[32] The other end of the hagiographic spectrum was occupied by a rich series of signed lives of bishop-saints, inaugurated in the third century by Pontian's *Life of St. Cyprian*, given renewed vigor in the late fourth century by the *Life of St. Martin* of Sulpicius Severus, and continued without interruption into the Carolingian era and beyond. Though several of these accounts (for example, the *Life of St. Augustine* by Possidius) steer clear of miracles, all of them remain well within the hagiographic genre. They stand out for being, most often, acknowledged by their authors and for setting out credible models of Christian leadership.[33] Together with chronicles, they best allow us to see that, contrary to what "the Fall of Rome" is sometimes taken to mean, historical writing was carried on uninterruptedly from late antiquity into the Middle Ages. If hagiography were given notice proportional to its volume and prominence, many more works would enter the present list.

Two seventh-century authors are almost distinguished enough as historians to be joined to our quartet. Isidore of Seville, the most accomplished post-patristic intellectual until Bede, wrote voluminously on many subjects. Besides compiling a major chronicle, as noted above, he composed a *History of the Goths, Vandals, and Sueves*; and there is much of interest to historical thought in his celebrated encyclopedia, the *Etymologies*.[34] Yet Isidore's *History of the Goths* (which is independent of Jordanes's) consists for the most part of an assemblage of extracts from chronicles and is almost the least assuming of his works. A good assessment of it within the wider setting of Visigothic historiography already exists.[35] The other omission needing

---

[32] Philippart, *Légendiers latins*, p. 40. Hardly any medieval legendaries devote less than two-thirds of their contents to martyrs; the proportion was of the order of 95 percent in the ninth century and 75 percent in the thirteenth. For Bede's martyrology, see below, ch. IV nn. 63-66.

[33] On these *vitae* down to the seventh century, see Heinzelmann, "Neue Aspekte"; Lotter, "Methodisches zur Gewinnung," pp. 309-11 (stresses the irreconcilable difference between aretological-hagiographic *vitae* and rhetorical-idealizing ones). On the avoidance of miracles in the latter type, Uytfanghe, "Controverse biblique," pp. 216-17. We shall be looking more closely at several episcopal hagiographies; notably, the Northumbrian *Vitae* of St. Cuthbert and Wilfrid of York (ch. IV) and Paul the Deacon's *Vita s. Gregorii papae* (ch. V). The interesting discussion among Beaudouin de Gaiffier, Jocelyn Hillgarth, and Jacques Fontaine, in *Spoleto Settimane* 17 (1970) 186-87, shows how hard it is to discern change and development within so long-established a hagiographic genre.

[34] On Isidore, see the brief, well-chosen remarks of Hillgarth, "Ireland and Spain," pp. 3-5. Isidore *Historia Gothorum Vandalorum Sueborum*, ed. Th. Mommsen, MGH AA. XI, 267-303; tr. G. Donini and G. B. Ford, Jr., 2d ed. (Leiden 1970). About history in the *Etymologiae*, Borst, "Das Bild der Geschichte."

[35] Hillgarth, "Historiography in Visigothic Spain," pp. 287-99.

apology is that of an anonymous Frank conventionally known as Fredegar (more ponderously, as pseudo-Fredegar). Fredegar often ranks as a chronicler, because his point of departure was an expanded version of the Eusebius-Jerome *Chronicle*; but he extensively modified the Eusebian core, went on with a personal condensation of Gregory of Tours, and concluded with an original continuation from the 580s to the 640s. The chaotic quality of his Latin is famous.[36] Despite the shortcomings of his education, Fredegar was a genuine historian, worthy of sustained study.[37] The serious obstacles to doing so are his anonymity, uncertain date and provenance, and other technical problems. He is still better suited to erudite research than to a sustained effort at interpretation.[38]

Although this survey is not exhaustive, the works and authors mentioned constitute a large fraction of the total for the period in question. The volume seems small by later medieval and modern standards. By those of earlier epochs in Latin historiography, however, it is not contemptible.[39] Even when, as here, the hagiographic component is mentioned only in passing, enough is left to suggest that the writing of history, whatever its quality, was practiced by many hands, in many places. These, then, were the minor works by comparison with which Jordanes, Gregory, Bede, and Paul are considered major.

Besides claiming attention for their association with barbarians, our narrators are the outstanding witnesses to the long epoch that their works span. If for no other reason, their epoch merits a moment's pause. Bede, the most celebrated of the four, is credited with composing "the masterpiece of Dark Age historiography"; the others are the "Dark Age" historians whom he outstrips.[40] Many medievalists of today use the term "Dark Age(s)" as a compendious and, in their intention, neutral way to refer to the earliest medieval centuries.[41] The obscurity that was once thought real

[36] Fredegar *Chronicon*, ed. Bruno Krusch, MGH SRM II, 18-168; tr. (omitting bks. I-III) J. M. Wallace-Hadrill, *The Fourth Book of the Chronicle of Fredegar and Its Continuations*, Nelson's Medieval Classics (London 1960); ed. and tr. (omitting bks. I through II, ch. 52) Andreas Kusternig, *Quellen zur Gesch. des 7. u. 8. Jhrdt.* (above, n. 29), pp. 44-270. Krusch's edition is essential, not least because it systematically distinguishes copied sources from Fredegar's alterations and additions. On the date, Goffart, "Fredegar Problem Reconsidered," and Erikson, "Problem of Authorship" (Erikson and I independently arrived at the same result by complementary routes). On Fredegar's Latin, Wallace-Hadrill, as above, pp. xxviii-xliii; Kusternig, pp. 18-33.

[37] A pioneering effort to do justice to Fredegar is Wallace-Hadrill, "Fredegar and the History of France."

[38] Buchner, "Kulturelle und politische Zusammengehörigkeitsgefühle," p. 570, also intentionally by-passes Fredegar, who is pertinent to his theme.

[39] It is much richer than, e.g. during the more than two centuries between Suetonius and Aurelius Victor.

[40] The phrase about Bede is by Campbell, "Bede," p. 160.

[41] For the pejorative origins of the term, see Mommsen, "Petrarch's Conception of the

has been attenuated by the advance of scholarship (and tolerance), but the earliest centuries of the Middle Ages still run no risk of rivaling Periclean Athens or Medici Florence. In a consecrated metaphor whose credit has yet to be seriously shaken, Rome fell and Christian Europe arose out of its ruins. The trough of this curve is occupied by our historians.

A general introduction to their works might be expected to elaborate on the dismal nature of the times in which they were fated to live. The epoch has recently been dubbed a "civilization of insecurity," one in which a lively belief in miracles was indispensable to ensure the psychological survival of the individual and collectivity.[42] If the exercise of pinning names on periods and encapsulating their character is unavoidable, at least the temptation of making real people fit within these simplifications should be resisted. Where our "Dark Age" quartet is concerned, it is hard to see in what way the conditions they endured were self-evidently more perilous and less fortunate than those of other times, including our own. As far as we know, their personal safety and comfort were rarely threatened. Jordanes in Justinian's Constantinople shared in one of the high points of late antiquity. Gregory, bishop of Tours, was able to criss-cross Gaul with greater freedom and security than Sidonius Apollinaris had experienced a century earlier.[43] Though Gregory once fell afoul of a Frankish king, he extricated himself within a few weeks and was apparently unscarred by the experience. Bede, a monk of Jarrow (near today's Newcastle-on-Tyne), lived at what then seemed to be the ends of the earth, but the institution he belonged to had been furnished with books, pictures, and other refinements from the more developed world to the south and was an outpost of material as well as ideological modernity. And not only modernity vis-à-vis the "barbaric" Anglo-Saxons: Roman Britain, despite its imposing physical remains, had never managed to generate an intellectual of any sort, let alone one of Bede's stature.[44] Paul the Deacon, a monk of Monte Cassino, had personal experience of Charlemagne's court as well as of several parts of Italy. Though directly affected for a while by the Frankish conquest of

'Dark Ages.' " About current usage, cf. below, ch. III n. 506. Also see Voss, "Problème du moyen âge dans la pensée historique en France."

[42] Uytfanghe, "Controverse biblique," p. 205, endorsing the views of an unidentified recent authority. Against the temptation to make "security" a criterion for defining an epoch, see Burckhardt, "On Fortune and Misfortune in History," pp. 356-57.

[43] In Sidonius's time, Gaul was divided among at least three governments less able to safeguard the free movement of persons than the occasionally quarreling Frankish kings of Gregory's day.

[44] There are no pagan British writers and so few Christian ones that, down to the age of Gregory the Great, no group of British authors exists in Dekkers, *Clavis patrum Latinorum*. Pelagius (ca. 352-427) appears among "heretical" writers, St. Patrick among Irish ones, and Faustus of Riez with the Gauls among whom he worked; even Gildas, though properly dated, is displaced (for efficiency) to the seventh century.

the Lombard kingdom (774), he overcame these troubles and ended his literary career, as he began it, in the service of the very resplendent ducal
house of Benevento. The times these men experienced were no more
tragic, perilous, or gloomy than other epochs, and by comparison with
some were notably benign. To anyone reared in the twentieth century, the
plagues, bloodshed, and assorted disasters that all four intermittently record
seem almost nondescript. To suggest that they document the "Dark Ages"
would validate a historical metaphor that was not in their heads and would
impair their ability to drive it from ours.

Our narrators form a family of historians only from a modern point of
view. Time and place separated them from each other to such an extent
that references from one to the other are rarely applicable except in minor
and incidental ways. Paul the Deacon, the last in date, read and excerpted
all three of his predecessors and was noticeably influenced by at least two of
them. Bede consulted Gregory of Tours but discloses no self-evident traces
of dependence on him. Jordanes and Gregory were aware only of earlier historians, such as Orosius.[45] In modern times, the four have normally been
studied one at a time, in a perspective of national history, or as successive
entries in histories of medieval Latin literature. To judge from bibliography, Jordanes and Paul belong mainly to Germany and Italy; Bede is little
read outside England; Gregory alone can boast a genuinely international
following, one does not quite know why.[46] They have posed different problems to researchers and have not all been examined with equal skill and
intensity. Bede has been best favored in the volume and quality of study he

[45] Paul used Jordanes only as a source of information; he both drew upon Gregory and Bede
and entered into the spirit of their writings. The direct evidence for Bede's acquaintance with
Gregory *Hist.* lies outside the *H.E.* (see below, ch. IV n. 290). Jordanes appeals to Orosius in
the opening sentence of the *Get.* ("Maiores nostri, ut refert Orosius"); on his frequent use, see
Mommsen, Preface, pp. xxvii, xliv. Gregory rarely mentions Orosius and owes comparatively
little information to him, but is imbued with his vision of earthly events as a series of calamities. According to Banniard, "Aménagement de l'histoire chez Grégoire de Tours," pp. 23-26,
Gregory drew his information about Attila's campaign from Jordanes or Cassiodorus's Gothic
history, perhaps at second hand, via the poet Fortunatus. Banniard has no proof of this, only
a need to provide Gregory with a source about the events of 451; yet Gregory quotes from the
lost history of Frigeridus, who, because well informed about Aëtius, ought to have been able
to tell him about 451 as well.

[46] These are generalizations, of course. A great study of Bede is owed to a German, Wilhelm
Levison, and there has been recent, noteworthy work on him in Italian, German, and Dutch.
Jordanes, owing to his account of Gothic migration, has long attracted attention in Scandinavia; there is a growing list of work on him in English, a Hungarian translation (1904), and
even a major recent edition, translation, and commentary of the *Getica* in Russian: Elena
Cheslavovna Skrzhinskaia, ed., *[Jordanes] O proiskhozhdnii i deianiiakh getov* (Moscow 1960).
For illustration of the wide following of Gregory of Tours (including a Danish translation), see
the bibliography in Gregorio di Tours, *La storia dei Franchi*, ed. and tr. Massimo Oldoni, 2 vols.
(n.p. 1981) I, lxx-lxxix.

has inspired. Jordanes, on the other hand, is a hornet's nest of unresolved controversy. Even his standing as an original author raises problems that must be dealt with before his works are examined. Both Gregory and Paul are particularly challenging as narrators, the one for his sprawling discursiveness and unique concentration on the years of his lifetime, the other for an unparalleled level of fragmentation. Besides, the textual tradition of Gregory's *Histories* needs attention, whereas the simple facts of Paul's biography are more elusive than one would like them to be. Each of the four, in sum, is a distinct case and will be treated accordingly.

The question that will be mainly asked of them is, What was each one doing and for whom? Together with other early historians, they have rarely been written about except in a context of source analysis and appraisal of their testimony. They have been mined for information and have had their ore sifted through a fine mesh of criticism, so that their evidence, suitably refined, might take its due place in modern narratives. The quality of our reconstructions of the past depends on source criticism—an indispensable occupation. But the outlook of source criticism as commonly practiced tends to be narrower than that of historiography.[47] An author approached as though he were a body of ore is prized mainly for pure metal content. One taken seriously in his own right stands a chance of having his opinions and literary talent valued as an integral part of the information he conveys; he may just possibly be seen not only as a reporter of the past, but as a component of the past that he transmits. This is the standpoint from which our quartet will be examined.

Jordanes, Gregory, Bede, and Paul are best known to us for a single narrative apiece—their "barbarian" histories. All of them wrote more than that. Bede's bibliography is daunting; the others were less accomplished but nevertheless have several titles to their names. These complementary works will not be neglected. They include in the case of Jordanes the *Roman History*; in that of Gregory of Tours the *Eight Books of Wonders*; in Bede's at least the *Life of St. Cuthbert* in verse and prose and his *History of the Abbots of Wearmouth-Jarrow*, as well as the contemporary writings of the same sort by other Northumbrians; and in Paul the Deacon's the *Roman History*, the *Life of Gregory the Great*, and the *Deeds of the Bishops of Metz*. Many of these compositions lack source value. Paul's *Life of Gregory the*

---

[47] A pioneer in the effort to read early historians otherwise than as providers of certifiably accurate facts was Spörl, *Grundformen hochmittelalterlichen Geschichtsanschauungen*. Also see, along the same lines, Beumann, "Methodenfragen der mittelalterlichen Geschichtsschreibung," pp. 1-8. These two and others, such as Siegmund Hellmann and Heinz Löwe, are credited with working out the "documentary character of historiography": Schmale, "Mentalität und Berichtshorizont, Absicht und Situation hochmittelalterlichen Geschichtsschreiber," p. 14. Also see Ernst, "Zeitgeschehen und Geschichtsschreibung," pp. 143-45.

Great, the extreme case, adds nothing at all to our knowledge of the pope. From a perspective of historiography, the question whether an author supplies firsthand or original information is a subsidiary and even irrelevant consideration. How Jordanes and Paul handled Roman history is important even if all their material comes from works known to us. The same holds true for Bede's rewriting of the *Life of St. Cuthbert*. The pigeonholing of our authors in a category of "national" history or *Volksgeschichte* has had the disadvantage of isolating a single work from the sum of their writings. Breaking this isolation is a step toward recovering the identity of each one.

It will be assumed that they, like us, did not write for posterity but had nearer preoccupations and aims. Manuals on the critical handling of source material sometimes attribute to narrative histories the reprehensible trait of being "intentional."[48] In the sense of this distinction, old coins "*unintentionally*" land before the numismatists of today; they were normally minted or counterfeited for immediate circulation. Charters, notarial registers, and the like are also understood to have had practical and local purposes, not including that of becoming objects of learned research. In contrast to them, a written history is assumed to have been deliberately addressed to posterity as well as to a living audience, and to merit suspicion on this account unless the author's innocence is established. Owing to this taint, narratives tend to get highest marks for credibility if least motivated or ostensibly deliberate, and vice versa. It is presumably a compliment that, at some time or other, all four of our narrators have been called naïve. Such reasoning needs qualification. Histories are intentional only insofar as they—exactly like coins, account books, charters, or whatever—had a practical context. They may not be critically utilized unless attention is paid to the local circumstances of their composition and issuance. The future, however, is another matter. Narrators can try to impose their views on posterity, but they are virtually powerless to resist the views that posterity imposes on them. This disparity of force guarantees that histories, at any considerable distance from when they were written, are just as unintentional as the rest of the haphazard débris that we call sources.

The four authors with whom we are concerned undertook, for a variety of reasons, to record and interpret the past. Though more often honest and high-minded than not, their endeavors were never innocent; nor should

---

[48] Bloch, *The Historian's Craft*, p. 60, "the innumerable varieties of documents at the disposal of the historian are divided [into two chief categories:] The evidence of the first group is intentional; that of the second is not"; the latter, Bloch adds, has no desire at all to influence the opinions of contemporaries or future historians (p. 61). This distinction goes back to the nineteenth-century German classification of sources as *Überreste* ("leavings") and *Tradition* ("handings on"); see Bernheim, *Lehrbuch der historischen Methode und der Geschichtsphilosophie*, pp. 255-59, 465-506.

anyone wish them to be. Their portrayals were conscious and deliberate, and worthy of sustained attention for precisely this reason. The relationship between their words and the meaning they were intended to bear when set down is a problem we shall be continually facing. We may rest assured, however, that our authors no more intended to deceive modern scholars than to become the "fathers" of one or another branch of the European saga. Just like us, they were time-bound and fully absorbed by responsibilities and preoccupations more immediate than the hypothetical impact they might have on unborn generations. Gregory wrote primarily about the very recent past; Jordanes gives the impression of descending to the time of writing; Bede and Paul drew a veil over their own generation. Conceivably, the importance of current events to them was in inverse ratio to the space those events occupy in their writings. However that may be, we need, at least temporarily, to forget what we want of them (such as "national" history) and to take sustained interest instead in the local circumstances of their lives.

If context is important, it is rivaled by the need to grasp each author's work as an artistic whole, often illuminated by his other writings. History is a type of literature; the task of our narrators was, in Sallust's phrase, to turn deeds into words. Their works begin and end; the contents are more or less cohesive; they argue and entertain. Gregory of Tours is famed for realism; Jordanes ends on a conspicuously joyful note; Paul interweaves dry reports with flowing legends; Bede is known to have a plot. Their information has often been detached from their modes of presentation, whereas the two are necessarily of a piece.

Erich Auerbach on Gregory and Robert Hanning on Bede are almost alone in having examined members of our quartet as artists. Although no one denies that histories are literature, it has hardly been supererogatory for Hayden White to spell out what this commonplace implies: historians tell stories about the past and can do so only with "the aid of some enabling and generally fictional matrix"; the appeal of a narrative presentation of real events—its capacity to explain and render the past assimilable—"arises out of a desire to have real events display the coherence, integrity, fullness, and closure of an image of life that is and can only be imaginary"; the muddle of events and data is translated into "an image of continuity, coherence, and meaning" by the imaginative magic of storytelling.[49] As a result, the information that a historian conveys may hardly be distinguished from the

[49] The quotations are from, respectively, White, "Fictions of Factual Representation," p. 30, and "The Value of Narrativity in the Representation of Reality," pp. 27 and 15. For additional accounts of White's ideas, see his "Historicism, History"; "The Historical Text as Literary Artifact"; and, most fully, *Metahistory*.

manner in which he presents it; an "enabling and generally fictional matrix" shapes the facts at least as much as it is shaped by them. White's teaching makes short work of the long-cherished belief that evidence or "source value" has priority in the assessment of histories.[50] In a more positive vein, he draws attention to the stories historians devise in their efforts to evoke a past endowed with coherence, fullness, and meaning. Stories are infinitely varied, but they fall into limited categories that literary critics have taken pains to describe (in White's words, "types of figuration are finite"). What kinds of stories our narrators were telling will often concern us; the answers are a help in determining how they wished to be understood and what should be read in their lines, as well as between them. Literary criticism is not usually taught in historical seminars, and no claim to special expertise is made here. Nevertheless an effort will be made to show three of our authors (Bede excepted) in the role of literary creator.[51]

In an engaging recent essay subtitled "Against Exegesis," Marcia Colish argued that, "many medieval historians . . . are just as easy to read as their modern counterparts. They can be understood without the need for an elaborate critical superstructure."[52] She developed her point by setting three medieval authors side by side with three modern ones (writing on different subjects) and showing—not without playfulness—the identity of historical approach each pair took. Although, in her examples, the ease of reading referred to comes near to being ease of dismissal, her guiding idea seems entirely sound. With or without exegesis, the goal worth striving for is to bridge the time gap, eliminate obscurities, and render early historians as immediately understandable and eloquent as modern ones.

Within the period 550-800, the composition and issuance of each of the histories for which our quartet is famous was an event of comparable magnitude to the major happenings they record. As events, literary compositions leave more direct and stable traces than do incidents that must be observed and set down. They are more knowable even than carefully reported occurrences and have the advantage of disclosing states of mind rather than fleeting actions. Nevertheless, the histories that have come down to us are

---

[50] For a defense of this tradition against White, see Momigliano, "Biblical Studies and Classical Studies," "Rhetoric of History and History of Rhetoric," "Considerations on History in an Age of Ideology." Momigliano, whose skill in exposition and argument is of a very high order, deprecates the place of rhetoric in written history: "rhetoric has long been for the historian an effective (never essential) device to be used with caution" (*Settimo contributo*, p. 59). His statement makes sense only if rhetoric is defined restrictively as a "device," such as "purple prose," rather than as the skill indispensable to any writer.

[51] Figurations finite: White, "Historicism, History," p. 66. I have followed White in relying on Frye, *Anatomy of Criticism*, an introduction to literary analysis that is within even a historian's reach. See also in this connection, Fontaine, "Unité et diversité"; Olten, "Rapport du texte."

[52] Colish, "Historical Writing Then and Now," p. 270.

not self-explanatory, and their eventfulness may be grasped only in the context that gave them birth. Major narratives were rarities, each one a distinct case, isolated in place and time. What it took to bring these four into existence is the common problem that will be grappled with in the next chapters.

Jordanes and His Three Histories

1. The Inauguration of "National" History

The Latin historians of late antiquity address their narratives to the affairs of Rome, of the Christian Church, and even, if translations are included, of the Jews.[1] In the middle of the sixth century, however, one history departs from the Mediterranean focus of noteworthy events and seems correspondingly novel. This is a work bearing the title *On the Descent and Exploits of the Getae (De origine actibusque Getarum)*, by an author who calls himself Jordanes.[2] The Getae of his title were no strangers to classical antiquity; they had feature roles in the histories of Herodotus, Trogus Pompeius, and others. But the Getae of Jordanes are, in fact, Goths, and they are shown originating from remote, northerly Scandza and eventually migrating into the Roman world.[3] An even greater novelty of this work is that Jordanes, by his affirmation, was himself a Goth, the native chronicler of his own people.[4] His Gothic history—usually called the *Getica*—looks like a milestone in the passage from antiquity via the barbarian invasions into the Middle Ages. The moment appears to have come when one of the invading tribes, now settled, generated a literate member able to convey the experience of his people in the language of civilized historiography. It looks as though, from this start, the road points ahead to Gregory of Tours writing about the Franks, Bede about the Anglo-Saxons, and Paul the Deacon about the Lombards, as well as to the other "national" histories that dot the landscape of early medieval literature.

[1] As examples of Roman history, Aurelius Victor *Caesares* (ch. I n. 18); Eutropius (ch. I n. 14); Ammianus Marcellinus *Res gestae*, ed. and tr. J. C. Rolfe, Loeb, 3 vols. (London 1935-39); *Epitome de Caesaribus*, ed. Franz Pichlmayer, Teubner (Leipzig 1911); *Historia Augusta* (ch. I n. 20). Concerning the Church, Rufinus translated Eusebius's *History* (ch. I n. 21) within two or three years of the time when Sulpicius Severus composed his *Chronicle*, which is more a history of the Church than anything else: Sulp. Severus *Chronicon*, ed. C. Halm, Corpus scriptorum ecclesiasticarum Latinarum 1 (Vienna 1866) 3-105. St. Jerome declared the intention of tracing the history of the Church: *Vita Malchi, praef.*, PL XXIII, 55. On Josephus's histories of the Jews and their wide influence, see above, ch. I nn. 10, 25.

[2] See under Jordanes in the List of Abbreviations.

[3] On the Getae, *Oxford Classical Dictionary*, 2d ed. (Oxford 1970), ss.vv. "Getae" and "Thrace," pp. 466, 1065. Their identification with Goths, as, e.g. by Orosius *Hist.* 1.18, dates back to Jerome: Wolfram, *Gesch. d. Goten*, pp. 21-23. The migration from Scandza has no attestation outside Jordanes.

[4] *Get.* ¶ 316. See below, § 4.

Although Jordanes and his *Getica* can be presented in the way just out-lined or one similar to it, neither the author nor his work is as straightfor-ward as appears at first sight. For one thing, the *Getica* does not exist in iso-lation; it follows a history known as the *Romana*, itself in two distinct parts. Jordanes is responsible for a three-part historical compilation. Part I is a brief account of universal chronology on the Christian pattern, closing with Augustus inaugurating the fifth and final world empire; part II is a Ro-man history from the birth of Romulus to the twenty-fourth year of Justin-ian (A.D. 550-51). Parts I and II form the *Romana*.[5] The Gothic history, also ending in 551, is simply part III. It does have a preface and a named sponsor of its own, but Jordanes provides a general preface dedicated to someone else, clearly stating that he meant all three sections to go to-gether. His affirmation is borne out by the manuscript tradition.[6] Jordanes, otherwise unknown, needs to be assessed as the creator of a little historical library, centered in Justinian's reign, and not solely as the author of a "na-tional" Gothic history.

Another complication concerns the relative originality of Jordanes's *Ge-tica*. When the great Cassiodorus served the Ostrogothic kings of Italy, he wrote a history of the Goths in twelve books.[7] Priority among the "na-tional" histories clearly belongs to this work rather than to Jordanes, who was active some twenty years later. The Gothic history of Cassiodorus is completely lost; only one authentic fragment of it survives, quoted by its author in a letter.[8] On the other hand, Jordanes used Cassiodorus's twelve books. His own work was occasioned, he tells us, by a friend's request that

[5] Jordanes announces his plan for the *Rom.*: "to collect in the form of a little story both the series of years and also the deeds of those men who strove mightily in the state (*res pub-lica*)" (¶ 6). The *annorum seriae* ends with the Incarnation (¶ 85). Jordanes then addresses his patron again, saying he must now go back to the beginnings of Rome (¶ 86), which he had mentioned but set aside temporarily so as to survey *externa regna* (¶ 52). The same device of going back to earlier times in order to fill out a story occurs in *Get.* ¶ 246.

[6] For the general preface, *Rom.* ¶¶ 1-5. For the link between the two *libelli*, ¶ 4: to the one on Rome he has joined "aliud volumen de origine actusque Getice gentis, quam iam dudum . . . ededissem." The message of his work is conveyed by both works together: "legens ergo utrosque libellos, scito quod" (¶ 5). More details in the preface to the *Get.* ¶ 1: at a friend's request, he interrupted his *adbreviatio chronicorum* (= the *Rom.*) so as to abridge Cassiodorus on the Goths.

On the text tradition, Mommsen, Preface, p. xlvi. A new ms of the *Getica* came to light in the 1920s, when given to the Archivio di Stato of Palermo by the art historian Nino Basile; it is of the later eighth century, in an Irish hand, probably from Bobbio; see *CLA* 1741. It be-longs to class 3: Sthamer, "Eine neue Jordanes-Handschrift in Palermo," p. 45.

[7] The *testimonia* are conveniently assembled in Manitius, *Gesch. d. lat. Lit.* I, 42.

[8] Cassiodorus *Variae* 12.20.4 (536), ed. Å. J. Fridh, Corpus Christianorum, ser. Lat. 96 (Turnhout 1973) 487: "exemplum quod in historia nostra magna intentione retulimus." The incident is not in Jordanes *Get.*

he should abbreviate the history of his illustrious predecessor.[9] As a result, the *Getica* is rarely regarded as being exclusively the work of its designated author. Cassiodorus intrudes, forcing us to determine the extent of his participation. In theory at least, the *Getica* may be Cassiodoran in all essentials, an adequate substitute for the longer history; and so it is affirmed to be in a major recent survey of medieval Latin literature, in which Jordanes is passed over as an incidental adjunct to his supposed principal.[10] Alternatively, Jordanes may have merely used his predecessor's narrative as a source and subordinated it to his own different designs. Intermediary positions are also available.[11] Because Cassiodorus's history has vanished, the problem of assigning responsibility is the more delicate and arduous for having to be pursued on the basis of little else than internal study of the *Getica*.

Jordanes may hardly be called a neglected historian, but almost all commentators have focused on the *Getica* to the exclusion of his other works and have believed, more out of faith than of fact, that the authentic voice of Cassiodorus rings through the Constantinopolitan abridgment. Several approaches have not been tried. In view of the integrity of the three parts, it is hardly satisfactory to devise a reason for the Gothic history without simultaneously explaining why the audience for the *Getica* needed the *Romana* as well. Twenty years separate Jordanes from his ostensible Cassiodoran model; greater attention needs to be paid to the possibility that these eventful decades stood in the way of the epitomator's sharing the outlook of his source. Some of the Cassiodoran history may be reconstructed independently of the *Getica*, and it seems, by this test, to have been reproduced in a highly selective way. Jordanes, although a self-confessed Goth, was a thoroughgoing Byzantine in outlook; his summary of universal history gains its distinctive traits from Greek sources, and his Roman history embodies a characteristically Eastern point of view. In the *Getica*, he did not stress dependence on Cassiodorus; instead, he wished readers to understand that he had limited access to his predecessor's history and drew upon other sources as well. The most direct indication that the *Getica* is original with Jordanes resides in that its narrative culminates in a blessed event—the birth of a child of mixed Roman and Gothic blood, symbolizing the assimilation or fusion that would take place once the emperor Justinian had suppressed Gothic independence. The whole of the *Getica* is organized to bring about this happy outcome, an outcome that, for reasons of date as well as political tendency, could have had no place in Cassiodorus's history. When these

---

[9] As above, n. 6.
[10] Brunhölzl, *Gesch. d. lat. Lit.* I, 29-31.
[11] Giunta, *Jordanes e la cultura.* More, presently, about this division of opinion.

and other ideas are developed, Jordanes and his historical collection gain a different appearance from the one currently prevailing.

2. Cassiodorus and Jordanes: A Strained Collaboration

The *Getica* is rarely mistaken for impartial history; its tone is transparently tendentious. Commentators have rightly inferred that Jordanes, who wrote in the 550s, was promoting a cause. Even greater emphasis has been given, however, to Jordanes's total dependence on Cassiodorus, whose Gothic history, composed in the 520s or early 530s, also promoted a cause.[12] If the tendentious *Getica* embodies the faithful abridgment of this single source, the objectives of Cassiodorus needed to be wholly compatible with those of Jordanes. It must have been possible for the lost tract for the 530s to be turned without deformation into the surviving tract for the 550s. Regardless of whether Jordanes and Cassiodorus knew each other or not, they had to have formed a harmonious partnership in ideology. This is a strange and improbable assumption.

The relationship of the *Getica* to the Gothic history of Cassiodorus has been central to modern assessments of Jordanes, overshadowing the question why the *Getica* is in a three-part collection. Critics tend to fall into a "German school," which considers Jordanes to be a pale, servile shadow lurking behind a basically Cassiodoran epitome, and an "Italian school," which decries the virtual elimination of Jordanes and maintains that he had an identity of his own.[13] The German approach, generally preferred, rests on the research of Schirren (1858), Köpke (1859), and Mommsen (1882).

Schirren detected the florid language of Cassiodorus, well known from surviving writings, in many paragraphs of the *Getica*. He also showed that most of the authors referred to by Jordanes were familiar to Cassiodorus and need not have been cited in the *Getica* otherwise than at second hand.[14] Köpke drew an appealing conclusion: precisely because the abilities and learning of Jordanes were much less than believed, the value of his book

[12] For a fair interpretation of the "cause" promoted by each one, see the quotations below at nn. 29-30.

[13] The two schools are characterized by Wagner, *Getica*, pp. 57-59. A vigorous early statement of the "German" argument is by Köpke, *Anfänge*, pp. 50-93. To the contrary, Giunta (as above, n. 11), p. 147. Whereas the "German" inclination is to eliminate Jordanes and take the *Get.* to be substantially Cassiodoran, the opposite tendency is to have the *Get.* reflect the individuality of both authors at once. The divergence between the opposing points of view is not wide.
Representative spokesmen for the "Italian school" include Cipolla, "Considerazioni"; Giunta, "Considerazioni sulla vita e sulle opere di Jordanes," and as above; Arcari, *Idee e sentimenti politici*, p. 196; Giordano, *Jordanes*. Possibly, the "school" has tacitly yielded to the other side; see Luiselli, "Sul *De summa temporum*," and "Cassiodoro e la storia dei Goti."

[14] Schirren, *De ratione*. See, also, the important review of Schirren's book by Gutschmid.

was much greater; for the less competent he was, the more Cassiodoran his book must necessarily be.[15] Mommsen, besides editing Jordanes, lent the weight of his incomparable prestige to Schirren's conclusions.[16]

However great the contribution these scholars made to internal analysis of the *Getica*, they dealt only incidentally with many aspects of the book, such as its contents and bias. Schirren's research demonstrated no more than that Jordanes depended heavily on Cassiodorus.[17] Mommsen, well aware that mere dependence was no guarantee of fidelity, drew attention to subjects on which Jordanes differed markedly from his precursor.[18] Later commentators played down the contrasts. They were content that Cassiodorus's dominant voice should have been substantiated by Mommsen, Köpke, and Schirren. The work of the pioneers has never been fundamentally reconsidered or elaborated.[19] Because no compelling alternative has been offered by the "Italian school," the common inference has been that, although Jordanes is the nominal author of the *Getica*, the history chiefly embodies Cassiodorus's narrative and ideas, and is to be "valued less as a monument of historiography than as an expression of Cassiodorus's political objectives."[20]

There have been two major efforts in recent times to place Jordanes's incidental role and Cassiodorus's preponderant responsibility beyond all possible doubt. In 1948, Wilhelm Ensslin sought to show that behind Jor-

---

[15] As above, n. 13. Köpke's argumentation is firm and eloquent, but uses little evidence. As a principle of interpretation, he proposed, "Die groben Irrthümer, die öfter hervorgehoben worden sind, kommen auf Rechnung des Jordanis, der bessere Theil gehört dem Cassiodor" (p. 84); yet, he was aware that the share of each could not be objectively delimited (p. 68). He consistently treated the *Rom.* and the *Get.* as separate books (p. 60).

[16] Mommsen, Preface, p. xlii. Mommsen's critical edition of Jordanes's entire output is still unrivaled. Two of the earliest manuscripts were destroyed by fire while in his temporary custody.

[17] Schirren, *De ratione*, pp. 9-28, detected traces of Cassiodorus's style throughout the *Get.*; pp. 29-43, he showed that Cassiodorus was acquainted with almost all the authors Jordanes mentions; pp. 44-64, he developed arguments for attributing various passages of the *Get.* to Cassiodorus. A rich body of evidence is assembled, and the case is argued as well as possible, with little account taken of contrary possibilities.

[18] Mommsen, Preface, pp. viii-xiii, at once contested by Schirren, review in *Deutsche Literaturzeitung*.

[19] The teaching of Schirren and Köpke seems to have been canonized in Wattenbach, *Deutschlands Geschichtsquellen*, 5th ed., I, 66-75, reproduced almost verbatim in Wattenbach-Levison, *Geschichtsquellen*, p. 75-81; also, Manitius, *Gesch. d. lat. Lit.* I, 213. Other examples: J. B. Bury in Gibbon, *Decline and Fall* I, 458; O'Donnell, *Cassiodorus*, p. 53.

Maintaining the tradition, Krautschick, *Cassiodor u. die Politik*, p. 25, asserted: "Schon Carl Schirren hatte nachweisen können" that Jordanes almost exclusively transcribed Cassiodorus. Schirren's excellent work was merely a beginning and in fact "proved" very little. The most sustained attempt to go beyond him and define more precisely the Cassiodoran and other components of the *Getica* is by Hachmann, *Goten u. Skandinavien*, pp. 35-81, 475-98. Hachmann's recognition that more along these lines needed to be done merits applause; his results, based on shaky criteria, are disappointing.

[20] Löwe, "Cassiodor," p. 14.

danes's first two parts—the *Romana*—lay the Roman history of Q. Aurelius Memmius Symmachus, another lost work from the age of Theodoric. Ensslin contended, on the basis of many parallel passages, that Jordanes was a mere abridger of Symmachus in the *Romana* as he was of Cassiodorus in the *Getica*.[21] Arnaldo Momigliano, in 1955, built in part on Ensslin's results when he addressed himself to the few paragraphs of the *Getica* that seem to be necessarily composed by Jordanes because concerned with the period after Cassiodorus's history ended. For reasons of content—chiefly a passage celebrating the union of the famous Roman family of the Anicii with the Ostrogothic royal line of the Amali—Momigliano maintained that the text Jordanes had abridged was an augmented version of Cassiodorus's history, updated to the 550s by the original author with a view to being summarized by Jordanes for propagandistic use.[22] Cassiodorus, on this hypothesis, was not just a written source but was personally involved in Jordanes's enterprise. The theses of Ensslin and Momigliano, in their combined force, promised to clinch the positions of the "German school."

Neither argument gained lasting acceptance.[23] The idea that Cassiodorus continued his history of the Goths to the 550s hinged on the belief that no one but he could possibly be responsible for the reference to the Anicii found near the end of the *Getica*.[24] Critics insisted, however, that Jordanes's reference to the Anicii was open to other, equally plausible expla-

[21] Ensslin, "Des Symmachus Historia Romana als Quelle für Jordanes."

[22] Momigliano, "Cassiodorus and Ital. Culture," reprinted in his *Studies in Historiography* and his *Secondo contributo*; my references hereafter are to the first reprinting. Momigliano reaffirmed his thesis in his 1971 article "Cassiodoro," reprinted in *Sesto contributo* (after which it is cited here).

Momigliano was anticipated, but weakly, by Cappuyns, "Cassiodore," coll. 1366, 1403, 1404. Convinced that all the *Get.* was fundamentally Cassiodoran, Cappuyns inferred his Constantinopolitan continuation from the reference of Jordanes (*Get.* ¶ 1) to Cassiodorus's history of the Goths "from long ago until now (*usque nunc*)," which, on a literal reading, means that the Cassiodoran history known to Jordanes extended to 551. Momigliano avoided this argument, whereas Krautschick, *Cassiodor u. die Politik*, p. 19, revived it. An able refutation is given by Barnish, "Genesis and Completion," p. 348.

[23] On the reception of Ensslin's argument, see Croke, "A.D. 476," pp. 92-93. For favorable reception of Momigliano's, see, e.g. Courcelle's review in *Latomus*; Fuchs's review in *Museum Helveticum*; Wes, *Ende des Kaisertums*, pp. 187-92 (with refinements); Wolfram, *Gesch. d. Goten*, pp. 6 n. 8 (endorsing Wes), 441-42. The theory retains eloquent defenders: Barnish, "Anonymous Valesianus II," p. 577, and "Genesis and Completion"; Krautschick, *Cassiodor u. die Politik*, pp. 4-40 (cf. my review in *Speculum*). Cameron, "Cassiodorus Deflated," p. 185, expresses approval for Momigliano's thesis as well as its critics.

[24] "Nobody except Cassiodorus could represent the union between Matasuntha and Justinian's cousin as a union not of the royal family of Ravenna with the imperial family of Constantinople, but between the Amali and the Anicii. Here, it seems to me, Cassiodorus has put his seal" ("Cassiodorus and Ital. Culture," pp. 194-95). Momigliano also stressed that the *Getica*'s reference to the Anicii was solitary, abrupt, and most of all unexplained: "It seems to me clear that this passage is a shortened version of something more circumstantial about the same subject"; Jordanes was summarizing "here as elsewhere," and the subject points directly, once more, to Cassiodorus as source (p. 194). For more on this argument, see below, nn. 249-50.

nations.[25] Ensslin's elaborate demonstration that Jordanes's *Romana* abridged the lost history of Symmachus called for comparably elaborate disproof and eventually received it in an excellent study by Brian Croke.[26]

The lack of a decisive argument did not alter the prevailing direction of Jordanes criticism. One could still believe that the *Getica* belonged at least as much to Cassiodorus as to Jordanes. Ranke, too, had been of this opinion: "Jordanes provided only a name behind which the actual origin [of the book] was hidden; he was a redactor rather than an author."[27] So conceived, the *Getica* embodies both the history personally commissioned by Theodoric the Ostrogoth and its abbreviation carried out two decades later in Justinian's Constantinople; it is a product of hyphenated authorship, Cassiodorus-Jordanes, virtual collaborators in a common enterprise.[28]

Yet the agreement of the two authors could not be total. Once their political orientation is taken into account, at least some difference becomes unmistakable. The old exposition of Adolf Ebert adequately states the case:

Cassiodorus's object . . . was to elevate the Gothic conquerors to parity with the Roman population that had become their subjects: by the identification of the Goths with the Getae . . . the former were established as already a world-historical people in earliest times . . . ; and since not only the great bravery but also the high scientific culture of these dim ancestors of the Goths was celebrated in Cassiodorus's history, [the Goths] were attributed a nobility that made them at least equal to the Romans. In Cassiodorus, the praise of the Gothic people forms only a pedestal for the splendor of the Amal house, in which all praise attains its peak, a house that is proved to have a noble family tree reaching back into distant antiquity. To be ruled by such a lineage together with such a people as the Goths could no longer seem to the Romans to be a disgrace.[29]

Several of the views ascribed here to Cassiodorus are substantiated only by the *Getica*, rather than by writings certifiably his own. Nevertheless, the thrust of his thought is correctly characterized. Ebert went on to specify the views of Jordanes:

The [Cassiodoran] idea of the world-historical parity of birth of the Goths and Romans . . . is by no means effaced in Jordanes; his abridgement is still a panegyric

[25] Bradley, "Composition of the *Getica*"; Wagner, *Getica*, pp. 39-57; Baldwin, "Purpose of the *Getica*"; O'Donnell, *Cassiodorus*, pp. 270-71; Reydellet, *Royauté*, pp. 261-62.

[26] Croke, "A.D. 476," pp. 90-115. Ensslin's study is forbiddingly unreadable; Croke earns our gratitude for having taken the pains to dominate it. Ensslin's thesis continues to circulate; see Callu, "Première diffusion," p. 99 (the thesis is assumed to be proved).

[27] Ranke, *Weltgeschichte*, p. 327.

[28] Hellmann, "Gregor von Tours," p. 8; Andersson, "Cassiodorus and the Gothic Legend of Ermanaric," p. 129; Dagron, "Discours utopique"; Lönnroth, "Goten in der mod. Geschichtsauffassung," p. 59; Wolfram, "Gothic History," p. 311; see, also, Bollnow, as below, n. 81.

[29] Ebert, *Allgemeine Gesch. d. Lit. des MAs* I, 560.

of the Gothic people. With a pride worthy of a Roman's, he commemorates the deeds of their bravery: he has the same object of equalization [as Cassiodorus—to bring about] an enduring reconciliation with the Roman Empire of the Germanic peoples (*Volkselemente*) incorporated within it. But since, at the time that [Jordanes] wrote, the Ostrogothic power had been completely broken by Byzantium, he had to orient his idea of reconciliation toward Roman emperorship; and since he flatters Justinian as the thriumpher over the highly praised Goths, he places the hopes of the latter's restoration on the son of Matasuinth, granddaughter of Theodoric, and of Germanus, a [cousin] of Justinian—a son also called Germanus, who unites in himself the Anician lineage with that of the Amals. This hope, which, to be sure, presupposes the dependence of the Goths on the Roman emperorship, clearly corresponded to the personal wishes and views of Jordanes, who cared more for the interests of the Amals than for those of the Goths, and who, in his Roman-clerical culture, held the world-rule of Rome to the end of time to be a dogma.[30]

These lines are a fair statement of the case for the two authors' harmony of political outlook. Both of them praise the nobility of the Goths and their kings, the Amals, and strive for reconciliation between them and the Romans: this is their common ground. But Cassiodorus presupposed the enduring rule of the Goths over the Italo-Romans, whereas Jordanes envisaged their subjection to the emperor. Each had a very different view of how his story ended.

In Ebert, and in Jordanes criticism as a whole, these differing assumptions about political régimes are treated as incidentals, irrelevant to the compatibility of Cassiodorus's narrative with Jordanes's. But is the contrast minor? Does not the ending of a story tend to color its entire course?[31] One need look no further than the uncontested facts of composition to realize that Jordanes may not have taken so readily to hyphenation with Cassiodorus, or Cassiodorus with him, as is generally assumed.

Cassiodorus, an Italo-Roman and a senator, worked in Ravenna at a Gothic court that was Arian in religion. Himself a Catholic, he took pains not to offend the religious susceptibilities of his patrons.[32] Potentially, he had access to excellent sources of information about the Gothic past, in-

---

[30] *Ibid.*, pp. 560-61. Along the same lines, Manitius, *Gesch. d. lat. Lit.* I, 214, "es ist aber kaum anzunehmen, dass Cassiodors Standpunkt ein wesentlich anderer war, obwohl sich die Zeiten geändert hatten" (in the direction opposite to the normal flow of time); Wolfram, "Überlegungen," pp. 489-90. Wolfram's habitual reference to a Gothic *Origo gentis* or *Origo Gotica*, meaning Cassiodorus's *History* or Jordanes's *Getica* or both, seems to be without precedent in the literature on this subject. Cf. below, n. 52.

[31] Momigliano, "Cassiodoro," p. 491, stresses the identity of outlook of Cassiodorus and the *Getica*; differences are disregarded.

[32] Vyver, "Cassiodore et son œuvre"; Cappuyns, "Cassiodore," coll. 1350-57; Momigliano, "Cassiodorus and Ital. Culture," pp. 188-99. For an important point concerning Cassiodorus's restraint in religious matters, see Mommsen, Preface, p. xliii n. 82.

cluding oral traditions. His desire to reconcile his fellow Italo-Romans to Theodoric's Goths, and vice versa, can be clearly inferred from his surviving letter collection, the *Variae*, published in 538.[33] That the same tendency should have been imprinted upon his Gothic narrative is only to be expected. Theodoric himself (d. 526) sponsored the history. Cassiodorus had certainly finished it by 533 if not earlier.[34] Besides extolling the Goths and their Amal dynasty, his account must have taken for granted that they had a future as the ruling force in Italy. A history designed to reconcile the Amals and their Roman subjects would hardly have been needed if the days of Gothic government had been thought to be numbered.

Jordanes exists for us only in his three-part collection, and notably in the brief autobiographical remarks written into the *Getica*.[35] The context he lived in bore no resemblance to that in which Cassiodorus had composed his history. Jordanes claimed to be descended from Goths long resident in the East Roman Empire and to have been, for a time, secretary to a barbarian general serving the Empire.[36] Catholic and possibly a clergyman, he was hostile to the Arian Christianity that the independent Goths professed, and he shows himself to be a loyal and admiring subject of the emperor Justinian, whose wars for the suppression of the Goths in Italy and Spain he reports with unqualified approval.[37] Most probably, Jordanes worked in Constantinople, which he casually calls "the city" (*urbs*).[38] The date of completion that he features is 551. As he affirms, Amal kingship was now a thing of the past, and he does not regret its termination.[39] The *Romana* informs us that 550 was when Justinian organized an army to deliver the final blow to Ostrogothic resistance.[40] What attraction Jordanes might have had at that date to Cassiodorus's old theme of Romano-Gothic parity and reconciliation, and what need there was for him to voice it once again, are perplexing questions. No obvious answers come to mind. Whereas Jordanes and barbarian descendants like him were simply imperial subjects,

[33] Krautschick, *Cassiodor u. die Politik*, pp. 41-49, 107-17, is the latest authority on this subject; cf. above n. 26. Cassiodorus's *Chronicle* also points in a direction of conciliation.

[34] Below, § 3.

[35] Below, § 4.

[36] *Get.* ¶¶ 265-66.

[37] Hostility to Arianism, *Get.* ¶¶ 132-33, 138 (cf. Orosius, *Hist.* 7.33.16-19); approval of Justinian's conquests, *Rom.* ¶¶ 363, 366, 375, 386-87; *Get.* ¶¶ 171-72, 303, 313, 315.

[38] Perhaps the most impressive example is *Get.* ¶ 168, in which the context cries out for *urbs* to be Rome, but the sense is Constantinople. For other examples, see n. 119 below.

[39] Whether Amal kingship ended with Theodahad in 538 or with (the non-Amal) Vitiges in 540 is left unclear. The eventual end of Amal kingship is announced early in the book (*Get.* ¶ 81); the end of Gothic kingship is asserted after the surrender of Vitiges (*Get.* ¶ 313).

[40] *Rom.* ¶ 383. The event is placed after the death of Theodora (548) and Totila's ravaging of Sicily (550).

the Goths of Italy in 551 were forced to choose between total submission to the Empire or desperate struggle.[41] Constantinople in the 550s was a favorable setting for writing Gothic history because Cassiodorus's twelve books had accompanied the great statesman on his temporary exile from Italy and were potentially available.[42] Beyond this, the impulse behind the *Getica* is obscure. The time and place seem, at first sight, to have been better suited to burying the Goths than to commemorating their valor. Jordanes was undoubtedly promoting a cause, one that must have overlapped at least to some extent with Cassiodorus's.[43] But what this cause may have been is hardly self-evident.

Even if Jordanes and Cassiodorus had agreed in politics, the *Getica* would closely reflect its main source only if Jordanes were a deliberately faithful summarizer, or (as sometimes believed) too simple-minded to be anything else. Either assumption is fragile.[44] Epitomes, abridgments, and adaptations obscure and misrepresent their models at least as often as they accurately mirror them. Little would be known, for example, of the real Gregory of Tours if his *Histories* had to be reconstructed from the summaries in Fredegar and the *Liber historiae Francorum*.[45] The bad Latin of Gregory's summarizers—far exceeding what Mommsen called the *tenuitas* of Jordanes—proves to be no guarantee of servility in abbreviating the model.[46] Ensslin's effort to attach the *Romana* to a single Italian source had great potential importance for confirming Jordanes's inability to be original, but the single source for the *Romana* proved to be a frail reed. Croke's demolition of Ensslin's argument also undermines the accepted reading of the *Getica*.[47] Jordanes cannot be assumed to be a faceless, unintrusive copyist. One has to reckon in both works with an author who, for all his literary shortcomings,

[41] On the condition of the Goths in Italy in 551, Stein, *Bas-Empire* II, 593-99 (Justinian would not negotiate); Wolfram, *Gesch. d. Goten*, pp. 438-42.

[42] The best account of Cassiodorus in Constantinople is now Cameron, "Cassiodorus Deflated," pp. 183-86; Jordanes bears witness to the presence of his history in Constantinople (*Get.* ¶¶ 1-2).

[43] Otherwise, Jordanes would not have claimed Cassiodorus's history as his model. Giunta, *Jordanes e la cultura*, pp. 170-73, very clearly perceived the difference of Jordanes's politics from Cassiodorus's.

[44] Reydellet, *Royauté*, p. 256: "Et même, en admettant qu'il y ait imitation, on peut se demander si elle est fidèle à son modèle." On this problem, see also Guenée, *Histoire et culture historique*, pp. 211-14, 51.

[45] See below, ch. III § 2. The summarizers leave out Gregory's four last books, orient his narrative toward the past, and prefer political history to other subjects. Without wanting to, they wholly misrepresent the original.

[46] On the Latinity of Fredegar, ch. I n. 36 above. On the *Liber historiae Francorum*, Bruno Krusch in MGH SRM II, 218. On Jordanes's Latin, a useful point of departure is Kappelmacher, "Iordanis."

[47] As above, n. 26.

had a mind and a pen of his own and presumably used them because he had better things to do than reproduce a single model.

Scholarship alone does not explain the strength and persistence of the idea that Jordanes was a slavish abridger. Schirren's effort to make the *Getica* Cassiodoran remains just about where he left it; his pioneering analysis has never been developed into a precise and compelling argument.[48] The role of Cassiodorus has been magnified for other reasons. Over the centuries, the tale of Gothic emigration from Scandinavia in the first pages of the *Getica* has generated a profound commitment among those who regard the Goths as their distant ancestors. The barbarian songs and legends of the *Getica* have met with comparable reverence.[49] The *Getica* holds a hallowed place, perhaps second only to Tacitus's *Germania*, as a repository of the antiquities that furnish modern Germany with its earliest history. It has become a kind of sacred scripture, and its migration story is the linchpin of the principle, cherished since the early romantics, that Scandinavian and German antiquity are one and the same.[50]

Nothing is more important for the historical authenticity of this primordial Gothic past than that it should spring from the riches of ethnic oral memories that Cassiodorus might have tapped in Ostrogothic Ravenna.[51]

[48] As above, n. 19: the efforts of Hachmann in this direction are commendable but isolated.

[49] For an instructive account of this commitment, uncritically espoused by the author, see Moisl, "Anglo-Saxon Royal Genealogies," pp. 217-31. Moisl shows that these tales have acquired special emphasis within the past fifty years as a result of the writings of O. Höfler, K. Hauck, and R. Wenskus. Such an early student of Jordanes as Sybel, *De fontibus Jordanis*, p. 38, denied any historical value to the origin myth; that had also been the view of Mascov, *Geschichte der Teutschen* I, 2-3 (the standard German history of the eighteenth century). Cf. Goffart, *Barbarians and Romans*, pp. 12-31, and Bollnow, as below, n. 81. Jordanes refers to ancient songs four times (*Get.* ¶¶ 28, 43, 72, 79); brief commentary in Opland, *Anglo-Saxon Oral Poetry*, pp. 57-59. Contrary to Mierow's translation, his various references to the utterances of the *maiores* should not be given a personal and ethnic cast, as though he were invoking his Gothic "elders." None of these passages involves a personal pronoun. Some clearly refer to classical *maiores*, and the term itself is almost equivalent to our expression, "the sources." On the classical ethnographic commonplace that songs either precede history or are its primitive form, see the fascinating accounts of Momigliano, "Perizonius, Niebuhr and the Character of Early Roman Tradition" and "Place of Ancient Historiography." Roman history has also experienced a debate over the historicity of its "ancient songs."

[50] For the genesis of this principle, See, *Germanen-Ideologie*, pp. 34-37, esp. 36: in nineteenth-century German scholarship, the Scandinavian Middle Ages became *Germania germanicissima*, the "preparation chamber" (*Rüstkammer*) of the Germanic spirit, the pure, unfalsified antiquity of Germanic culture. On the other hand, Scandinavians persisted in regarding the same material as documenting their Middle Ages (pp. 80-82).

[51] As a result, scholars insist, against all odds, on making Jordanes a Ravennan: Dagron, "Discours utopique," p. 293; Wattenbach-Levison, *Geschichtsquellen*, p. 75 (Jordanes as one of the representatives of classical education whom Theodoric assembled at his court!); Ermini, *Storia della letteratura Latina medievale*, p. 471; Barnish, "Anonymous Valesianus II," p. 577. The opinion gains a semblance of legitimacy from the class-3 mss (containing the *Get.* only), which call the author *episcopus ravenatis civitatis*. Cf. Momigliano, "Cassiodorus and Ital. Culture," p. 196 with n. 80. But see below, nn. 110-17.

Jordanes, despite his Gothic blood, is too Constantinopolitan to be a reliable mouthpiece for Gothic folk memories. Only the Cassiodoran source, reverently copied by an abridger lacking a mind of his own, offers solid guarantees of conveying those precious postulated vestiges lately called the "tradition," "tribal saga," or "heroic memory" of the Goths.[52]

Similar results are attained from a complementary direction. An observed tendency of research into Germanic antiquities has been to minimize the directly accessible texts, which are usually late in date, and to subordinate them to "the better antecedents"—the vanished tales or writings of earlier date whose vestiges are deemed to be incorporated, in debased form, in the materials that survive.[53] Jordanes fits perfectly into this pattern of deprecating the time-bound text we have and preferring the lost precursor of which much may be imagined. If Jordanes's *Getica* is the "ruin" of the preferable Gothic history of Cassiodorus, every trait indicating conscious composition in Justinian's Constantinople may be disregarded, and whatever fragments seem attractive in a Germanistic perspective may be attributed to the Ravennan prototype. Imagination is best served by treating the *Getica* as a collection of extracts, and not as a planned literary design.

The existing consensus about Jordanes and his works is based on a narrow capital of research and a large fund of pious hope. Abandonment of the assumption of a harmoniously Cassiodoran *Getica* is the condition for finding out what Jordanes's historical collection might be about.

3. The Gothic History of Cassiodorus

The twelve books of Gothic history by Cassiodorus are lost to us but well attested among his works, and Jordanes leaves us in no doubt that he used them. What we do not know is how much was used, how faithfully the source was reproduced, and how closely Jordanes shared its outlook. After the preface to the *Getica*, Jordanes never mentions Cassiodorus again; quotations and borrowings are unacknowledged. Several modern attempts have been made to detect the passages bearing a demonstrably Cassiodoran stamp; those seriously concerned with utilizing information from the *Getica*

---

[52] E.g. Wolfram, *Gesch. d. Goten*, pp. 39 (*heroische Memoria, Stammessage*), 62 (*Überlieferung der Goten*), 309 (*Hausgeschichte*), 333 and 393 (*amalische Hausüberlieferung*); most often used is "*Origo Gothica*," as though there had been a book bearing that name: 60, 61, 313, 314, and *passim* (cf. above n. 30). In Wolfram, "Überlegungen," p. 487, the phrase "der von Jordanes überlieferten Stammesgeschichte der Goten," makes the author secondary, or even incidental, to the work circulating under his name (Wenskus, *Stammesbildung*, p. 462, has a very similar phrase).

[53] See, "Altnordische Literaturgeschichte als Textgeschichte," esp. 527-29 (the texts supposed to be "blosse Trümmer ihre besseren Vorstufen," p. 536). See, also, his *Kontinuitätstheorie*, p. 9: "Da die altertumskundliche Sichtweise die überlieferten Objekte häufig nur als Mittel zur Rekonstruktion nicht überlieferter Objekte benutzt, neigt sie natürlich von vornherein in besonderen Masse zu Spekulationen und Hypothesen."

are virtually forced to engage in this risky exercise.[54] A simpler procedure is to find out what may be known about Cassiodorus's lost history apart from the *Getica*, solely on the basis of Cassiodorus's surviving writings. Such an inquiry reveals little about the Gothic past, but it is a first step toward finding out what sort of source was available to Jordanes and how much of it he altered and omitted in abridgment.[55]

There are two clues to the date of Cassiodorus's history. It was written "at the command of King Theodoric" (who died in 526), and it was completed by 533, when, in a letter Cassiodorus composed, the young king Athalaric describes the history as one of his minister's achievements.[56] Little precision may be extracted from Theodoric's "command." It need not mean that the history was finished or even started in his reign. The one apparent certainty is that Cassiodorus wished to place his work under the great king's patronage. Athalaric's statement, for its part, simply establishes the date by which the Gothic history was considered finished. These sparse facts enter into the two hypotheses about the date of the lost Gothic history that have recently been advanced. After outlining them and indicating their flaws, a third possibility will be presented. The lack of evidence permits little more than informed guesses.

In 519, Cassiodorus wrote a little *Chronicle* celebrating the consulate of Theodoric's son-in-law, Eutharic. Jordanes's *Getica* stresses that Eutharic was an Amal, descended from a collateral branch, and that his marriage to Amalasuntha therefore joined Amal to Amal. Very probably, Cassiodorus was Jordanes's source. Several commentators have taken this interest in Eutharic to mean that 519 was the year of Cassiodorus's twelve books as well as of the *Chronicle*.[57] The argument is superficial. Eutharic and his bloodline are prominent in the *Getica*, but not very. Besides, it would have been

---

[54] Schirren, *De ratione*, pp. 9-19, 44-64; Köpke, *Anfänge*, pp. 74-77; Cipolla, "Considerazioni," pp. 116-34; Hachmann, as above, n. 19. The exercise is deprecated by O'Donnell, *Cassiodorus*, p. 49. Nevertheless, serious efforts to place Cassiodorus's contribution on an objective footing are preferable to eclectic selections of grain from chaff.

[55] The same thing is done by Croke, "Cassiodorus and the *Getica*." Working independently, he and I attain convergent results by different steps. I am very grateful to Dr. Croke, of Macquarie University (Sidney, Australia), for letting me see this important study in typescript.

[56] *Anecdoton Holderi*, ed. Å. J. Fridh, Corpus Christianorum, ser. Lat. 96, pp. v-vi lines 28-29; Cassiodorus *Var.* 9.25.4-6. The *Anecdoton* is understood to be by Cassiodorus himself, an extract from a longer (lost) work: Momigliano, "Cassiodorus and Ital. Culture," pp. 189-90; it lists his *cursus honorum* and writings alongside those of two other Italian contemporaries, Boëthius and Symmachus. We learn comparatively little from the assertion that Cassiodorus wrote the history at Theodoric's command. The spectrum of possibilities entirely compatible with the truth ranges from a formal commission at once executed to a casual suggestion piously carried out after the king's death.

[57] O'Donnell, *Cassiodorus*, pp. 44-46; Krautschick, *Cassiodor u. die Politik*, pp. 31-34. To the contrary, Barnish, "Genesis and Completion," pp. 336-37.

superfluous, in the year of his consulate, to emphasize his legitimacy: Theodoric had gained the assent of Constantinople to Eutharic's succession to the Ostrogothic throne; the year of the son-in-law's consulate was a moment of unparalleled power and security for the dynasty.[58] A much more suitable occasion for making the same point occurred after both Eutharic and Theodoric were dead. It mattered very much to the child king-Athalaric that he should be able to claim Amal blood on the father's as well as the mother's side, for there was a grown-up Amal cousin to dispute his throne.[59] Nothing recommends 519 for the Cassiodoran Gothic history, except perhaps as a *terminus post quem*.

The argument for pinpointing the history to 533, long after its royal sponsor had died, is more elaborate. In that year, Cassiodorus wrote two letters containing information of great value for assessing his history. The earlier one is a panegyric of Amalasuntha, the queen regent and Theodoric's daughter, addressed to the Roman Senate. In its course, Cassiodorus points out that the queen incarnates the special excellences of nine Ostrogothic kings, from the *felicitas* of Amal to the *sapientia* of her father.[60] The later letter of 533, already outlined and soon to be quoted, indicates that the Gothic history was finished and specifies that it showed the reigning king, Athalaric, to be the seventeenth Amal to rule over the Goths. Athalaric duly appears as seventeenth in the *Getica*'s full genealogy of the Amals.[61]

The attempt to date the composition of Cassiodorus's history to the year of these letters centers on the proposition that the "genealogy" of Amalasuntha, as set out in the letter eulogizing her, differs in vital details from the genealogy of the *Getica*. This discrepancy is taken to mean that Cassiodorus

---

[58] *Get.* ¶¶ 80, 251 (both stress the reunion of the *stirps*), 298 (a few words of personal praise), 304 (Athalaric orphaned). Though not mentioned, Eutharic is the raison d'être of *Get.* ¶¶ 174-75 (how his forebears moved to the Visigothic kingdom). On the condition of the Ostrogothic monarchy in 519: Stein, *Bas-Empire*, II, 225-26, 247 (triumph of the conciliatory policy of the reign); Ensslin, *Theodorich der Grosse*, pp. 309-10; Wolfram, *Gesch. d. Goten*, pp. 404-405; Barnish, "Anonymous Valesianus II," p. 595 (excellent relations with the then pope). Krautschick, *Cassiodor u. die Politik*, p. 22, acknowledges the favorable situation of 519 but maintains that the senators had before then to be reconciled to Eutharic. Are histories really useful for such purposes?

[59] Krautschick, *Cassiodor u. die Politik*, pp. 61-94, stresses this period and cites earlier studies (notably Sundwall's). Wolfram, *Gesch. d. Goten*, pp. 409-10, is very eloquent on the claims of Theodahad to preference over Athalaric. I am not suggesting that Cassiodorus's Gothic history was a lawyer's brief designed to convince anyone of a single point.

[60] Cassiodorus *Var.* 11.1.19. The context deserves to be summarized: But how can feminine examples (for which, see below, n. 64) suffice for her who outdoes men in praiseworthiness? If that royal cohort of relatives looks down upon her, one sees at once her heralds as though in the purest mirror; for she outshines A in such-and-such, B in thus-and-so, etc.

[61] Cassiodorus *Var.* 9.25.4; *Get.* ¶¶ 79-81.

had only just begun to compose his narrative: his "genealogy" of Amalasuntha embodies a first draft, whereas the table of Amal kings copied by Jordanes into the *Getica* is Cassiodorus's final and significantly modified version. On these premises, Cassiodorus mainly wrote the history during 533, between the early letter and the later one.[62]

The condition for this conclusion is that the nine kings in the letter about Amalasuntha should form a genealogy of the queen's ascendants in direct line. There is no reason, however, why such should be the case.[63] Cassiodorus was not tracing a family tree, but citing a string of precedents for the queen's merits. For his panegyrical purposes, it did not matter whether the kings referred to were ascendants of the queen or members of a collateral branch. Roman emperors were routinely praised for embodying the qualities of predecessors with whom they had no blood relationship at all.[64] In much the same way, Cassiodorus's selection of Amal kings was guided by the imperatives of eulogy, not genealogy. His letter cannot document an authorial change of mind.

Much as we might prefer a firm date, we have only the termini 519 and 533. Because Cassiodorus was thoroughly conversant with the early kings of the Ostrogoths when he eulogized Amalasuntha in January 533, his history was presumably finished by at least the previous year. Political considerations favor composition in the days of Athalaric and Amalasuntha rather than earlier. Cassiodorus left royal service very soon after their accession (526) and returned as praetorian prefect in 532, after Amalasuntha had disposed of the Gothic faction that had dominated the government since the beginning of the reign. His interval of repose was a suitable time for the composition of a work that celebrated the cooperation of Goths and Romans, extolled the example of Theodoric, and buttressed the legitimacy of Athalaric by detailing the Amal ancestry of his father, Eutharic. In this

[62] Wolfram, "Überlegungen," pp. 493-94; also Wolfram, "Theogonie," pp. 80-82, in which the dating is taken for granted. Wolfram assumes, but makes no effort to demonstrate, that the kings in Cassiodorus's letter form a genealogy rather than a collection of relatives.

[63] Cf. above, n. 60, for Cassiodorus's words; the kings are mentioned as relatives (*parentes*) whose virtues are reflected in the queen. A reference to relatives does not imply an order of descent (genealogy). Various Gothic songs or lays are conjectured to lie behind this passage, or are circularly inferred from it. Wagner, "Germanische Namengebung," says that the songs existed "in my opinion (*m. E.*)." No qualifications in Wolfram, "Überlegungen," pp. 493-94. To the contrary, See, *Kontinuitätstheorie*, pp. 39-40.

[64] Cassiodorus begins with the intention of comparing Amalasuntha to empresses ("Ordo flagitat dictionis Augustarum veterum pompam moderna comparatione discutere"), then shifts sex and introduces the royal relatives. A series of good emperors are invoked by Pacatus *Panegyricus Theodosio dictus* 11.6, ed. Édouard Galletier, *Panégyriques latins*, 3 vols. (Paris, 1949-55), III, 78-79; also see *ibid.* I, 27 (comparison with heroes of the republican period). Eutropius *Brev.* 8.5.3: down to the present (i.e. 369) the Senate acclaims the emperors with the words "Felicior Augusto, melior Traiano."

case, a political context more plausible than any other seems to be the best attainable substitute for an authoritative date.[65]

Cassiodorus wrote a history of the Goths, "setting out in twelve books their descent, dwelling places, and way of life (*originem eorum et loca moresque XII libris enuntians*)."[66] As is only to be expected, it was not a piece of disinterested research so much as a celebration. Cassiodorus fashioned it by culling successes from the flower-flecked meadow of Gothic events (*Gothorum historiam defloratis prosperitatis condidisti*). Since he spoke of Alaric and the Sack of Rome, some space was apparently allotted to the Visigoths. As dependents of Theodoric, living since 507 under the protection of his armies and the supervision of his agents, they could hardly have been alien to a history written in Ravenna.[67] The longest description Cassiodorus provides of the contents of his history assigns pride of place within it to the Ostrogothic dynasty. The audience for this description is the Roman Senate, the speaker is King Athalaric, with Cassiodorus furnishing the words in which his own accomplishments are praised:

[Cassiodorus] extended his labors even to our remote ancestry, discovering in books that which scarcely the hoar memories of our forefathers preserved. He drew forth from their hiding place the kings of the Goths, concealed by long forgetfulness. He restored the Amals to their proper place in all the luster of their lineage, proving indubitably that for seventeen generations we have had kings for our ancestors.

He turned Gothic descent into Roman history, collecting as into a single wreath the varied flowers that were formerly strewn here and there in the fields of books.

Consider how much he loves you when he praises us: he showed that the nation of your sovereign is admirable from of old, [allowing it to be seen] that, just as your nobility descends from your forefathers, so you are [now] ruled by an ancient line of kings.[68]

With the disarming naïveté for which he is famous, Cassiodorus gave the Roman senators to understand that their pride had been bolstered by his research into Gothic antiquities. They might be ruled by fur-clad monarchs, but his diligent study had shown that furs were compatible with an ancestry no less venerable than that of the great families of Rome.

The sentence of Athalaric's discourse that promises to illuminate Cassiodorus's work begins the second paragraph: *originem Gothicam historiam fecit*

---

[65] Concerning this period of Ostrogothic history, see Krautschick, *Cassiodor u. die Politik*, pp. 161-84, and my review in *Speculum*.

[66] *Anecdoton Holderi*, ed. Fridh, p. vi line 29-30. The translated extract benefits from emendations by Hermann Usener and Mommsen; the unemended text reads, "originem eorum et loca mores in libris enuntians."

[67] Cassiodorus *Var.* 12.20.4. On Theodoric's protectorate, Wolfram, *Gesch. d. Goten*, pp. 303-305, 384-85.

[68] Cassiodorus *Var.* 9.25.4-6. I have adapted the tr. in Hodgkin, *Italy and Her Invaders* I, 26-27.

esse Romanam. These few words are open to a variety of interpretations and have been often glossed. Schirren understood them to refer only to the long historical interconnection now shown by Cassiodorus to have existed between the Goths and Romans.[69] A more widely favored interpretation is expressed by Hodgkin's translation, "he made 'the Origin of the Goths' a part of Roman history."[70] So understood, the phrase is somewhat patronizing toward the Goths but also suggestive of an idea of reconciliation, as though to say that the Goths had been incorporated into Roman history—both accepted and dignified by admission into the historiographic club. Though attractive, Hodgkin's translation and those like it may go further than the words and context allow.

A third theory, currently favored, holds that Cassiodorus meant his history to make the Goths seem civilized and reputable: he "sets the Goths on the horizons of the Roman Empire as being in the canon of thoroughly respectable non-barbarian peoples whose origins are on a par with those of the Romans."[71] In Cassiodorus's usage, it is claimed, *origo* stands for "tribal history," whereas *historia Romana* means "universal (or world) history." So interpreted, the phrase about turning *origo* into *historia* not only elevates a one-time tribe to universal standing, but also shows that Cassiodorus wished to extend to the Goths the providential character of the Romans.[72]

The main flaw of this reading is the belief that there was something "universal" about Roman history. A people did not have to be barbarous to be

---

[69] Schirren, *De ratione*, p. 71. Along the same lines, Cappuyns, "Cassiodore," col. 1365: "l'*Histoire* prétendait rattacher la dynastie elle-même et ses fastes au passé de Rome" (also, to give the Gothic tribes a Roman genealogy, col. 1352). Nothing tends to substantiate this reading.

[70] *Italy and Her Invaders* I, 27. Cf. Reydellet, *Royauté*, p. 263: "Des origines gothiques il a fait une histoire romaine."

[71] Krautschick, *Cassiodorus u. die Politik*, p. 30 n. 4.

[72] Wolfram, *Gesch. d. Goten*, pp. 454-55, interprets *origo* as "particulare Stammesgeschichte," contrasted to *historia Romana* as "allgemeine Weltgeschichte"; cf. Wolfram, "Gothic History," p. 311, "Roman history as world history became the goal of every *origo gentis*." Can this generalization (even if true) refer to anything but the single example of Cassiodorus? In the *Anecdoton Holderi*, Cassiodorus states that his Gothic *historia* contains, among other things, the *origo* of the Goths (above nn. 56, 66). One would ordinarily read this to mean that *origo* was a dimension of the history of any people, not something peculiarly barbarian. Besides, Roman history was not, by definition, world history; it had long tended to consist of a series of narrow imperial biographies (below, n. 78).

According to Wolfram, "Überlegungen," p. 489, Cassiodorus is the first author of the *origo* of a "nichtantike" people. Yet the Goths of the *Getica* are identified with the thoroughly ancient Scythians and Getae. No inclination may be found in Cassiodorus (or Jordanes, for that matter) to claim modernity for the Goths. Note, however, that the three *testimonia* about Cassiodorus's history outside the *Get.* mention only Goths. Contrary to Krautschick, *Cassiodor u. die Politik*, pp. 30-31, and others, who believe that Cassiodorus sought respectability for the Goths by making them as old as possible, there can be no certainty that his history paraded the Goths in Getic dress. One cannot assume that a travesty of this kind would have won over skeptics unfriendly toward the Goths.

the subject of an *origo gentis* (at least one *origo* of the Romans had been written), and the genre of universal history, illustrated by Justin's epitome of Trogus Pompeius, was distinct from the history of Rome and by no means coincided with it.[73] In fact, Roman history was notably parochial in character.[74] As for the providential character of Rome, it was proper to Christian chronicles, with which the twelve-book history of the Goths had nothing in common. Cassiodorus was not about to suggest to the staunch Catholics of Italy that the Arian Goths had become privileged sharers in God's long-range plans for the governance of the world. The entire argument about parity and providentiality presupposes that certain non-Romans were classed as "barbarian/disreputable" whereas others were deemed "nonbarbarian/respectable." Reasoning of this sort belongs to our times rather than to late antiquity.[75] One may speculate that "Cassiodorus intended, with his Gothic history, to prove the antiquity and parity of the Gothic people with the Roman,"[76] but this is not a meaning that may be extracted from the words placed in Athalaric's mouth.

A more straightforward and prosaic interpretation is available. Momigliano suggested that *origo* in this passage is best translated as "history," a rendering of the word also found in Jordanes's *Getica*.[77] Literally, then, the passage would read "he made Gothic history to be Roman history." These words make sense only if a specific meaning is given to *historia Romana*. The context helps. To hear Athalaric, the main feature of Cassiodorus's history consisted of the succession of Amal kings ("He restored the Amals to their proper place"). The difficult phrase comes next, possibly to epitomize this main feature—the catalogue of Gothic kings. "Roman history" can, of course, have many meanings; but, for a long time before Cassiodorus, its written versions had almost always assumed the form of serial biography,

---

[73] The argument of Wolfram, "Überlegungen," pp. 488-89, relies heavily on Bickerman, "*Origines gentium,*" pp. 65-81, and Grundmann, *Geschichtsschreibung*, pp. 12-17—excellent studies, but not primary sources for the literary context of Cassiodorus's history. Something more directly within Cassiodorus's reach than Bickerman's article has to be found if one aspires to identify the model of *origo* he followed. For one that may have influenced Jordanes, see n. 322, below. See Momigliano, "Origins of Universal History"; Wiseman, "Practice and Theory," p. 378. Orosius *Hist.* owed much of its "universal" dimension to Justin's epitome of Trogus Pompeius: *Epitoma historiarum Philippicarum*, ed. and tr. E. Chambry and L. Thély-Chambry, 2 vols. (Paris n.d.).

[74] Fornara, *Nature of History*, pp. 23-28.

[75] On the contrasting modern and ancient perspectives of "barbarians," see Goffart, "Theme of Barbarian Invasions." Wolfram, "Gothic History," pp. 314-15, assembled every pejorative notion about barbarians in ancient literature and presented the collection as though representative of "the ancients' perspective"; this may be rhetorically effective, but it can have little point other than to discredit the testimony of antiquity.

[76] Krautschick, *Cassiodor u. die Politik*, p. 160.

[77] Momigliano, "Some Observations on the *Origo gentis Romanae*," p. 149. E.g. *Get.* ¶ 315, calls for "history" rather than "beginnings."

37

the succession of imperial reigns. One need only recall Suetonius, Herodian, Lactantius, Aurelius Victor, books VII-X of Eutropius, the *Epitome*, book VII of Orosius, and the *Historia Augusta*.[78] In a context featuring a long line of Gothic kings, Cassiodorus is likely to have evoked this literary tradition when referring to *historia Romana*: by resurrecting the forgotten Amals, he had made possible a Gothic history cast as serial biography; that is, in the form long customary for histories of the Roman Empire. Cassiodorus might not have repudiated the resonance of his studied brevity—the note of reconciliation and acceptance—but at a literal level his words merely summed up the description just given. He had done for the Goths what Aurelius Victor and others had done for the Romans.

Another important aspect of Athalaric's discourse concerns the research Cassiodorus engaged in: *lectione discens quod vix maiorum notitia cana retinebat*.[79] He had assembled an account of the Gothic past from books, as a bouquet culled from far-flung wildflowers.[80] What is more, he learned from these books that which the Goths themselves had forgotten, including the identity of their ancient kings. Bollnow has suggested how deep a shadow this passage casts on the widespread belief that Cassiodorus relied on Gothic oral traditions.[81] To be sure, a passing comment such as this offers only a hint; it is not an author's precise and exhaustive description of his sources of information. The line nevertheless implies that Cassiodorus's Ravenna did not prize an oral "heroic memory" as a fountain of Gothic history. On the contrary, memory was fallible; time eroded it; the written word was needed to remedy its lapses into forgetfulness. It is in the *Getica*, rather than in certifiably Cassiodoran writings, that appreciative references

[78] Suetonius *XII Caesares*, ed. and tr. H. Ailloud, Collection des universités de France, 3 vols. (Paris 1964-67); Herodian, above, ch. I n. 18; Lactantius *De mortibus persecutorum*, above ch. I, n. 17; Aurelius Victor, above ch. I, n. 18; Eutropius, above ch. I, n. 14; *Epitome*, above, n. 1; Orosius *Hist.* 7, above, ch. I n. 21; *Historia Augusta*, above ch. I, n. 20. See Johne, "Zur Problemen der Historia-Augusta Forschung": such histories did double duty as histories of the Empire as well as of the emperors in question. Serial biography is, of course, not proper to Rome; cf. modern histories of England as a succession of kings, then prime ministers, of the U.S. as a succession of presidents. The scheme combines the advantages of a chronology attached to a magistrate with a personalization of the course of events.

[79] For the translation, see the extract above at n. 68.

[80] Contrary to the opinion of O'Donnell, *Cassiodorus*, pp. 52-53, metaphors of this sort are not a "Cassiodoran literary motif," but common literary coin. Greek "anthology" is Latin "florilegium"; also see *Oxford Latin Dictionary* (Oxford 1982), s.v. "flos. 11."

[81] Bollnow, "Herkunftssagen." Köpke, *Anfänge*, p. 92, affirmed that the kings whom Cassiodorus called "hidden" had to be those of the Getae, "denn die Volkskönige, welche die Heldensage feierte, lebten ja in Aller Munde, unmöglich konnten sie *oblivione celati* sein." Because there is no evidence at all for heroic songs on everyone's lips, sturdy affirmations of faith like Köpke's are rare today. But the faith endures. From a different standpoint, Baldwin, "Sources for the *Getica*," pp. 144, 146, emphasizes the ability of both Cassiodorus and Jordanes to acquire oral information. Whether or not they availed themselves of their opportunities is a different matter.

to Gothic songs and legends occur. If Cassiodorus did not spurn the oral or traditional information that may have been available to him, he also did not set a high value on its contribution. To conceive of his history as largely embodying the "tradition of the Goths" seems to contradict the plain sense of his words. Briefed by his chief minister, the Amal Athalaric did not blush to point out how defective the "Amal dynastic tradition"—if there were one—had turned out to be.

The scope of the first Gothic history may be only sketchily ascertained from Cassiodorus's surviving writings. That the work was in twelve books suggests great length, but, as Cappuyns pointed out, the inference is not mandatory.[82] The length of a papyrus scroll, or *volumen*, set the standard for ancient books, as, for example, in Livy, Augustine's *City of God*, or even Gregory of Tours.[83] Twelve such books form a stately collection. Jordanes's preface refers explicitly to twelve *volumina* of Cassiodorus and contrasts them to the one small *libellus* into which they were to be compressed. But Jordanes's word *volumina* is plagiarized from Rufinus; Cassiodorus himself speaks only of *libri*.[84] The very popular *Breviarium* of Roman history published by Eutropius in 369 is divided into ten *libri*, yet it amounts in all to fewer than a hundred pages of modern print.[85] In late antiquity, histories on Eutropius's modest scale were more common than the substantial seven *volumina* of Orosius. Unless Cassiodorus engaged in a great deal of padding (a task not beyond his powers), the information he could gather about the Goths would have favored book divisions on the Eutropian pattern rather than on Livy's. Twelve books of this length would, roughly speaking, have exceeded Jordanes's *Getica* by little more than a quarter. There are obvious attractions to supposing that the twelve books were of modest size. Their appeal would presumably have varied in inverse proportion to their length. But no certainty is possible.

Cassiodorus's history set out the *origo*, *loca*, and *mores* of the Goths, and, from Athalaric's standpoint, it was chiefly notable for displaying a long lineage of Gothic kings, perhaps as a set of biographies in the manner of Roman histories. One-word characteristics of nine of these kings are given in Cassiodorus's letter about Amalasuntha: Amal's *felicitas*, Ostrogotha's *patientia*, Athala's *mansuetudo*, Winitharius's *aequitas*, Vuinimund's *forma*, Thorismuth's *castitas*, Walamer's *fides*, Thiudimir's *pietas*, and Theodoric's *sapientia*. In a letter of 536, Cassiodorus quotes his history for an act of spe-

---

[82] Cappuyns, "Cassiodore," coll. 1365-66; Wagner, *Getica*, p. 59.

[83] *Oxford Classical Dictionary*, 2d ed., s.v. "Books, Greek and Latin," pp. 172-75.

[84] For Jordanes's borrowing from Rufinus, see nn. 190-95 below. For Cassiodorus's usage, the three *testimonia*, n. 7 above.

[85] In the Teubner edition of Rühl (37 lines per page), the books of Eutropius range from 144 lines (bk. V) to 322 lines (bks. VII, X); the average is 275 lines, which makes fewer than 7.5 pages per book.

cial magnanimity by Alaric when sacking Rome; the anecdote is visibly developed from material in Orosius. A final clue to the contents is furnished by Cassiodorus's *Chronicle* of 519, which embodies more than twenty entries about Gothic affairs down to the consulship of Eutharic. Presumably, all or almost all these incidents were mentioned and developed in the history.[86]

These are the few traces of the long Gothic history uncontaminated by Jordanes. They shed light on the relationship of Cassiodorus to the *Getica* by showing Jordanes in the act of altering Cassiodoran information or leaving it out. In his *Getica*:

—A pair of very early Ostrogothic kings are mere names on a genealogical list.[87]

—Because Amal and Athala are mere names, nothing is heard of their respective *felicitas* and *mansuetudo*; Winitharius receives attention, but nothing approximating his *aequitas* is mentioned; the same silence attends the *castitas* of Thorismuth; *fides* is attributed not to Walamer, but to his Gepid counterpart Ardaric; the virtue of *sapientia* is never associated with Theodoric.[88]

—The incident illustrating Alaric's magnanimity is omitted.[89]

—The Goth Radagaisus, a very well attested invader of Italy, is omitted.[90]

—The capture of Rome follows directly after the Battle of Pollentia instead of being separated, as in reality, by eight years.[91]

—The attack of Litorius on the Visigoths ends in a return to amity rather than in Litorius's historical capture and death.[92]

—Theodoric's campaign against Odoacer is drastically abridged.[93]

—Further incidents of Theodoric's reign are left out.[94]

---

[86] Cassiodorus *Chronicon*, ed. Mommsen, MGH AA. XI, 120-61. I refer to entries by year A.D. Barnish, "Genesis and Completion," pp. 332-33, 338, presupposes that differences between the *Chronicle* and Jordanes's *Getica* document Cassiodorus's changes of mind between writing the first and writing the Gothic history. The argument is circular unless the Cassiodoran substance of the *Getica* is an ascertained fact. Like Croke (n. 95 below), I assume that the *Chronicle* is a fair foreshadowing of what Cassiodorus said in the long history.

[87] *Get.* ¶ 79: Amal and Athala.

[88] Winitharius, *Getica* ¶¶ 121-22; Thorismuth, ¶ 250; Ardaric and Walamer, ¶¶ 199-200. Ostrogotha's conduct (¶¶ 98-99) might be interpreted as *patientia*; Hunimund has *pulchritudo* (¶ 250); Thiudimir's *pietas* might be illustrated, without reference to the word, in ¶ 253 or ¶¶ 278-79 (avenging Walamer). Two-thirds of Cassiodorus's characterizations are missing.

[89] In *Get.* ¶ 156, Alaric expresses his magnanimity by sacking Rome rather than burning it. Cf. above, n. 67 and n. 8.

[90] Cassiodorus *Chron.* under A.D. 400: Alaric and Radagaisus lead the Goths into Italy.

[91] *Get.* ¶¶ 154-56, but cf. Cassiodorus *Chron.* 402, 410.

[92] *Get.* ¶ 177; cf. Cassiodorus *Chron.* 439.

[93] *Get.* ¶¶ 292-95 jump a year and end the war with Zeno apparently still alive; cf. Cassiodorus *Chron.* 489-93, a careful list of incidents, showing that the campaign ended after Zeno's death.

[94] Notably Cassiodorus *Chron.* 500, 502.

Although based on very limited material, the comparison of the *Getica* with authentic Cassiodoran utterances is unusually revealing.[95] If Cassiodorus's skeletal *Chronicle* manages to say much more than the *Getica* about Theodoric, then surely there is something very odd in the way Jordanes treated the greatest Goth of all. (Just how odd his treatment is will eventually be seen.)[96] According to Athalaric's letter, Cassiodorus composed a celebration of Ostrogothic kings. The *Getica* matches these specifications only partially. Even the little we have directly from Cassiodorus shows that he did better. To be sure, Jordanes abridged; but that observation cannot serve as an explanation or excuse, since abridgment is a conscious process. An abbreviator appropriates the text he is shortening and makes it serve his own purposes—provided, of course, that his purposes differ from those of his model. Even the minor comparisons that are in our power to make between pure Cassiodorus and the *Getica* are a warning against assuming that Jordanes felt duty-bound to convey the history of his predecessor as faithfully as he could.

The general orientation of Cassiodorus's history may be easily inferred from his surviving writings, but the specific terms in which he couched those views depended on the course of politics. There are more than ten years within which the history might have been composed. If Cassiodorus wrote it under Theodoric and before 523, he would have been bound to stand aloof from Constantinopolitan ideas and to be cordial toward the Vandals. Many paragraphs of the *Getica* are irreconcilable with the view that Cassiodorus wrote them in or before the early 520s.[97] The advent of the child Athalaric with his mother as regent marked a notable decline in Ostrogothic power; hostility toward the Vandals and subservience toward the Eastern Empire became the order of the day.[98] Although some parts of the *Getica* sound too Byzantine to be considered Cassiodoran under any circumstance, the possibility of a late date for the long Gothic history muddies the problem of attribution.[99]

These vicissitudes imply a more general lesson. Cassiodorus must be as-

[95] The excellent analysis by Croke, "Cassiodorus and the *Getica*," which also takes Jordanes's *Rom.* into account, lengthens the list of contrasts between the two authors.

[96] Below at nn. 232-41.

[97] As noted before, the orientation of the *Get.* is Constantinopolitan. Except when Gaiserich is specifically in question, the Vandals are spoken of with contempt (see below, nn. 309-12). The treatment of the Vandals in the *Get.* was Mommsen's basis for assigning Cassiodorus's history to the period after Theodoric's death, or at least after 523: Mommsen, Preface, pp. vii-viii.

[98] Krautschick, as above, n. 59.

[99] For example, it is hard to imagine Cassiodorus calling Constantinople "the" city, or noting that the plague had raged in the capital nine years earlier (when, possibly, he was still in Italy), or expressing anxiety about the raids of Bulgars and Slavs into the Balkans. No casual references of the same kind suggest an Italian provenance.

sumed to have tailored his history in different ways depending on whether he wrote it under Theodoric or under Athalaric. If this is so, it surely follows that even more allowance needs to be made, in analyzing the *Getica*, for the intrusions of a Constantinopolitan abridger working twenty years later than his main source. Whenever Cassiodorus wrote, he envisaged a future for the Amals. For his summarizer, however, the Amals had been toppled from royalty, and their last survivor, the son of a Roman father, remained Gothic only on the distaff side. So glaring a change in circumstances left its mark on more than just the ending of the *Getica*.

4. Jordanes's Ambiguous Origins

Jordanes is so famous as the first historian of Gothic blood that one easily forgets how faint a trace he gives of his nationality. The point arises only in the last lines of the *Getica*. Readers are not to believe, he says, that he has shown partiality toward the Goths as a result of personally descending from them: *quasi ex ipsa [gente] trahenti originem*.[100] Offsetting the hesitancy of *quasi*, an earlier clue to exotic nationality comes from the parents cited in Jordanes's unexpected lapse into autobiography—the main source of information about him. In narrating the installation of barbarian splinter groups in East Roman territory after Attila's realm fell apart (454), Jordanes mentions that, among those settled in Scythia Minor and Lower Moesia, there was a body of Alans led by Candac: "To this Candac, as long as he lived, my grandfather Paria—the father of my father Alanoviiamuth—was notary. To [Candac's] sister's son Gunthigis, also known as Baza, Master of the Soldiery, son of Andagis, son of Andela, descended from the Amal lineage (*prosapia*), I, Jordanes, though unlearned, was notary before my conversion."[101] If one were to judge from the profession of notary, Jordanes and his grandfather might have been Scytho-Moesian provincials among whom Candac's Alans settled; but the names Paria and Alanoviiamuth tend to confirm the claim Jordanes eventually makes to Gothic origin.

A few more details about him are available. His Catholicism is implied by the portrayal (drawn from Orosius) of the emperor Valens "infecting" the Goths with Arianism and suffering divine punishment on this account.[102] Two men whom Jordanes addresses as "brother" are associated with his historical labors. The "very noble and magnificent" Vigilius com-

---

[100] *Get.* ¶ 316. Cf. ¶ 43: they [i.e. the Goths] used to sing of various men "quorum in *hac* gente magna opinio est." Should we not expect *nostra*?

[101] *Get.* ¶ 266. Jordanes treats *Get.* ¶¶ 265-67 as a digression, spun off from the story of the Ostrogoths in ¶ 264.

[102] Above, n. 37. Arianism briefly appears in the *Get.*, then vanishes; Valens is more wicked for infecting the Goths with heresy than they for cultivating it. Jordanes is not militantly anti-Arian; for a test passage, see n. 310 below.

missioned the short *summa temporum* and the Roman history, the entire three-part collection is dedicated to him. As for the *Getica*, it was sponsored by a certain Castalius, addressed without honorifics, whom Jordanes affirms to be a friend of both Vigilius and himself. [103]

Little may be done with the lines of concentrated autobiography except to spell out what they seem to say. Just because Jordanes's grandfather served an Alan and his father had "Alan" compounded in his name, there is no reason to believe that Jordanes was partially or wholly Alan. (The occasional claim that he was pro-Alan is also forced.) [104] Neither does the affirmation of Gothic descent necessarily signify that all his immediate ancestors were Goths. If 454 is taken as the starting point of his sketch and 551 as the year of the histories, the indicated period is disturbingly long. Close to a century seems to be spanned by the three short generations from grown-up Paria to less-than-senile Jordanes, and by the two generations from Candac to Gunthigis-Baza. This chronology strains credulity, but not to the breaking point. [105] The rest is also somewhat improbable, without exceeding the bounds of possibility at least to us. The careers of Jordanes and his grandfather as Gothic *notarii* to generals are no less unique than Jordanes being a Goth writing history. Jordanes's confession of being *agramatus*, not illiterate but lacking a liberal education, tends to be substantiated by the linguistic shortcomings of the *Getica*. On the other hand, Jordanes associates this deficiency only with the period when he was *notarius*. Unlike Gregory of Tours, he does not deprecate his ability to write history. [106]

A final peculiarity involves Jordanes's religion. Even in the Eastern Empire, most Goths appear to have stayed Arian. [107] The Catholicism of Jordanes is illustrated without being explained. His service to Gunthigis-Baza ended, he says, when he underwent a *conversio*, but this word need not refer to a change of creed unless glossed in this sense. *Conversio* may also indicate

---

[103] *Rom.* ¶¶ 1-5 (*novilissime et magnifice frater*, ¶ 5; Castalius as *communi amico*, ¶ 4); Castalius as *frater*, *Get.* ¶ 1, also *ut vicinus genti*, ¶ 3, whatever that might mean (*vicinus* and *gens* are a frequent pair throughout the *Get.*).

[104] Jordanes's partly Alan origin was first argued by Grimm, "Über Jornandes," p. 177. The idea was endorsed by Mommsen, Preface, p. x, whose object was only to separate the identities of Jordanes and Cassiodorus. Forthright affirmation, Giunta, "Considerazioni," p. 246; Jordanes as an offspring of Alan nobility who reckoned himself a Goth, Brincken, *Weltchronistik*, p. 88 (she also has him be notary to a king of the Alans). These notions persist though having no basis: Callu, "Première diffusion," p. 90. For a systematic refutation, see Friedrich, "Kontroversen Fragen," pp. 380-88.

[105] Croke, "Cassiodorus and the *Getica*," estimates that Jordanes must have been in his seventies. He is more content to live with this possibility than I.

[106] Friedrich, "Kontroversen Fragen," pp. 388-89.

[107] Le Bachelet, "Arianisme." As late as the 570s, Goths fighting for Byzantium petitioned the emperor for a church in which they and their dependents might practice Arian Christianity: John of Ephesus *Historia ecclesiastica* 3.13, 26, tr. E. W. Brooks, Corpus scriptorum Christianorum orientalium no. 106, Scriptores Syri 55 (Louvain 1936), pp. 102-103, 113-14.

the assumption of the monastic or clerical state, or, as a minimum, that Jordanes withdrew from worldly employment and lived as a layman in religious retirement.[108] The "very noble" Vigilius called him from this retreat to write history, a task that Jordanes claimed was unsuited to his current way of life (*conversatio*). None the less, he carried out the commission and responded to Castalius's suggestion besides. One would dearly like to know whether Jordanes's name, an obvious evocation of baptism, was given him by his parents or assumed when he entered religious retirement. The same name was borne by a second-generation barbarian general in East Roman service: Jordanes, son of John the Vandal, a convert to Catholicism in 465 and consul in 470.[109] This Jordanes seems to have been so called since birth.

Many commentators have tried to turn the historian Jordanes into a dignitary of the Latin Church. The fact inspiring these efforts is that his sponsor Vigilius bears the same name as the reigning pope from 537 to 555. Pope Vigilius was in Constantinople with a large entourage from 547 to 554, being pressured by Justinian into endorsing the condemnation of the Three Chapters and eventually succumbing.[110] Among those attending him in these difficult years was Jordanes, bishop of Crotone in Bruttium (modern Calabria).[111] Jean-Pierre Callu (1985) is the latest of many scholars to identify this bishop with the author of the *Getica*, deeming him to be a Goth turned Catholic and elevated to the episcopate in Italy.[112]

For this identification to be accepted, it is essential that the Vigilius addressed as "very noble and magnificent brother (*nobilissimus et magnificus frater*)" should be the pope. Jordanes's authority would, of course, be greatly enhanced if he had been the holder of a Western bishopric, not far from

---

[108] Friedrich, "Kontroversen Fragen," pp. 393-402, exhaustively examines the matter, with negative results: Jordanes's *Stand* cannot be determined with certainty; the spectrum of possibilities extends from a layman to an ordained clergyman. Grimm, "Über Jornandes," pp. 171-79, believed that the conversion involved a change of name from Gothic Jornandes to Christian Jordanes. (The form Jornandes was frequent in scholarship before the editorial work of the nineteenth century, and Grimm believed it should be retained.)

[109] Martindale, *Prosop. Later Rom. Emp.* II, 620-21.

[110] Grimm, "Über Jornandes," pp. 182-83, first made this identification, whose only basis is homonymy, as shown by Friedrich, "Kontroversen Fragen," pp. 429-30. (Momigliano, "Cassiodorus and Ital. Culture," p. 208 n. 81, indicates that the identification was anticipated in 1690.) On Pope Vigilius, Caspar, *Geschichte des Pappstums* II, 234-86; Fliche and Martin, *Histoire de l'Église* IV, 457-79; Richards, *Popes and the Papacy*, pp. 125 (his background), 139-57.

[111] The identification was first made by Selig Cassel in 1848: Mommsen, Preface, p. xiii n. 22.

[112] As a representative sample, Köpke, *Anfänge*, pp. 57-59, specified that Jordanes must have first studied Cassiodorus's history in Bruttium; Momigliano, "Cassiodorus and Ital. Culture," p. 196; Luiselli, "Sul *De summa temporum*," pp. 108-23, based his argument on the circumstantial consideration that Jordanes being a bishop in Bruttium would fit admirably with the idea that the *Get.* is Western; Callu, "Première diffusion," pp. 92-95.

Cassiodorus's monastery at Vivarium, and associated with the head of the Latin Church. Many perplexities surrounding the *Getica* would be solved as a result. Nevertheless, the hypothesis is untenable. Though persistently revived, it was proved impossible long ago by Mommsen and Johann Friedrich.[113] The form of address to Vigilius is wholly improper for anyone, let alone a bishop, to use in writing to the pope, and it cannot be redeemed by the excuse of mere clumsiness, for even a bad writer minds decorum more reverently than he minds syntax.[114] An additional and decisive obstacle comes at the close of Jordanes's dedication. He invites the very noble Vigilius "to be converted to God, Who is the true freedom"; to avoid being "attached to the world"; to heed the gospel injunction not to love the world, whose glamor passes, but to do God's will; and to love God and his neighbor.[115] These are admirable sentiments, but hardly the sort of thing to say to the pope in question. Vigilius had endured hard years in Constantinople, defending ecclesiastical principles as best he could. It would have been a crowning irony, amid these trials, for him to be treated to a homily on *contemptus mundi* by one of his Italian familiars.[116] Jordanes, in preaching as he does and in adopting a nonclerical formula of address, shows that he had not been commissioned by the pope. The honorifics he attaches to Vigilius's name suit a layman; his edifying remarks are entirely fitting for a *conversus* to address to someone still enfolded in worldly cares. Besides, if

[113] Mommsen, Preface, pp. xiii-xiv; Friedrich, "Kontroversen Fragen," pp. 429-34. Friedrich underscored how improbable it is that Vigilius, a native Roman and the son of a consul, would have commissioned an uneducated Goth to write a short Roman history for his instruction (p. 431). Kappelmacher, "Zur Lebensgeschichte des Iordanis," showed that the notations in medieval mss indicating that Jordanes was a bishop lacked any authority.

[114] Momigliano, "Cassiodorus and Ital. Culture," p. 196, dismisses this objection: "I am inclined to suspect that Jordanes was a clumsy man . . . a boorish provincial bishop of Gothic extraction who did not know how to talk to his fellow exile, the Bishop of Rome." But cf. Lotter, "Zu den Anredeformen," p. 516: there was a fundamental distinction between clerical and lay titles of address. Mommsen, Preface, p. xiii, spoke sharply against those who built castles "sola similitudine nominis non admodum rari." Krautschick, *Cassiodor u. die Politik*, p. 19, departed from Momigliano on this point.

[115] *Rom.* ¶¶ 4-5: "diversarum gentium calamitate conperta ab omni erumna liberum te fieri cupias et ad deum convertas, qui est vera libertas. Legens ergo utrosque libellos, scito quod diligenti mundo semper necessitas imminet. Tu vero ausculta Iohannem apostolum, qui ait: 'Carissimi, nolite diligere mundum neque ea que in mundo sunt. Quia mundus transit et concupiscentia eius: qui autem fecerit voluntatem dei, manet in aeternum.' Estoque toto corde diligens deum et proximum, ut adimpleas legem et ores pro me, novilissime et magnifice frater."

O'Donnell, "Aims of Jordanes," bases on this passage the unusual theory that Jordanes's histories are permeated by religious otherworldliness closely reminiscent of Augustine and Salvian. No attentive reader of the *Rom.* and *Get.* could come to this conclusion; these lines to Vigilius are almost its sole basis.

[116] This objection was initially made by Ebert, *Allgemeine Gesch. d. Lit. des MAs* I, 561 n. 3; Mommsen, Preface, p. xiv; Friedrich, "Kontroversen Fragen," p. 432. Also see Barnish, "Genesis and Completion," p. 354.

Jordanes had been bishop of Crotone, or otherwise a dignitary, the concealment of this fact in his lines of autobiography would need to be explained.[117] The rapprochement between Jordanes's Vigilius and the homonymous pope is, admittedly, intriguing, but there may be a better use for this coincidence (as we shall see) than to turn Jordanes into someone whom he never claims to be.[118]

The efforts applied to tracing the intricacies of Jordanes's life story tend to obscure its salient feature; namely, that all we know about him is what he chooses to tell us. To complement and, in part, to offset the information that he intentionally conveys there is the discreetly eloquent evidence furnished by his writings.

The impact made by Jordanes's three-part collection of histories is not Gothic at all, but overwhelmingly Byzantine. *Urbs* stands for Constantinople; the East is qualified as "our regions" (*nostrae partes*); the fourth-century Visigothic king Athanaric is shown contemplating Constantinople as though it were heaven on earth, and Theodoric the Amal stands at the pinnacle of his glory when the emperor Zeno honors him with the ordinary consulate; the Western emperors of the fifth century are incidental to those of the East; the *Getica* was written "to the praise of him who conquered [the Goths]," namely, Justinian.[119] Jordanes, whose language contains occasional Grecisms, speaks often and feelingly of raids into the Balkans by Bulgarians and Slavs, and he cannot mention a third-century plague without recalling the one that afflicted Justinian's capital in 542.[120] His brief universal chronicle, ostensibly based on that of Eusebius and Jerome, embodies a sequence of four empires before Rome's and a world era in which the Incarnation falls in A.M. 5500—features characteristic of Byzantine rather than Latin chronography.[121] Little else interests him in early Roman history than the record of world conquest, a suitable background to Justinian's enterprises. In his account of later events, Jordanes reacts to ideas launched by recent Greek historians: the *Romana* has the special value of reinterpreting the *New History* of Zosimus, while the *Getica* echoes the ethnographic opinions of Procopius in order to dismiss them.

These and other traits, which will be examined at greater length, warn

[117] Partisans of these identifications disregard Jordanes's silence, as though it were perfectly all right for him to be at once candid about his family and reticent about his identity (and his conjectured Alan blood, n. 104 above).

[118] Below, § 10.

[119] *Urbs*: Get. ¶¶ 38, 168, 289-90; *regia urbs*, ¶¶ 107, 143. The East: Get. ¶ 132; cf. Friedrich, "Kontroversen Fragen," pp. 403-404. Athanaric and Theodoric: Get. ¶¶ 142-44, 289. Western emperors: Get. ¶¶ 236, 239-41; clearer evidence in the *Rom.*: Croke, "A.D. 476," p. 101. Justinian: Get. ¶ 316.

[120] Jordanes's Greek: Mommsen, Preface, p. xxvii; Croke, "A.D. 476," p. 99. Raids, *Rom.* ¶ 388; Get. ¶¶ 37, 119; plague, Get. ¶ 104.

[121] Brincken, *Weltchronistik*, pp. 89-90.

us against dwelling on Jordanes as a "national" historian of the Goths. He was only too right to disclaim partiality toward tribal ancestors. If it were not for the few lines of autobiography, everyone would agree that Jordanes was simply a Byzantine. As a writer of history in the 550s, he was in good company. Procopius, John Malalas, John the Lydian, and others were all working at much the same time.[122] Jordanes, by long being overshadowed by Cassiodorus and by writing Latin rather than Greek, has been kept from the attention he deserves as one of the remarkable gathering of historians who flourished in the reign of Justinian.

5. Parts I and II of Jordanes's Historical Collection

The idea that the *Getica* was composed with a view to propaganda found an eloquent early exponent in Ranke and was forcefully revived by Momigliano.[123] The work looks as though it had a message and, owing to its date, it can hardly have been alien to Justinian's efforts to complete the conquest of Italy. Ranke and Momigliano were surely right to exclude the possibility that Jordanes meant simply to address posterity. But whatever designs he had were traced on a broad canvas. His Gothic history comes last in a larger collection designed to circulate as a whole. Whatever propagandistic purpose Jordanes or his sponsors had needs to be related to the total package, not just to the narrative about the Goths.

The three parts of Jordanes's work have already been introduced. Two of them are encompassed in the single title "Summary of the Ages and the Descent and Exploits of the Roman People" (*De summa temporum vel [= et] origine actibusque gentis Romanorum*). The title of the third part applies to the Getae-Goths the same formula as to the Romans minus one noun: "The Descent and Exploits of the Getae" (*De origine actibusque Getarum*). Jordanes takes pains in the preface to Vigilius to outline the contents of these various tracts. He regards the Roman state as the final empire of Daniel's prophecy and twice qualifies it as "holding" in the Pauline sense of averting the dreaded advent of Antichrist and the end of the world.[124] The apparent function of part I is to set the chronological scene for this final empire by

[122] Vasiliev, *History of the Byzantine Empire*, pp. 179-84; Stein, *Bas-Empire* II, 702-34. Cf. Croke, "A.D. 476," p. 118, stressing that the Latin chronicler Count Marcellinus falls within the Byzantine chronicle tradition. Wattenbach-Levison, *Geschichtsquellen*, p. 81, acknowledged the contemporaneity and comparability of Jordanes to Procopius. Jeffreys, "Attitudes of Byzantine Chroniclers," 203, 205, forthrightly treats Jordanes's *Romana* as a Byzantine chronicle.

[123] Schirren, *De ratione*, pp. 85-93; Ranke, *Weltgeschichte* IV part 2, pp. 326-27; Momigliano, "Cassiodorus and Ital. Culture," pp. 194-96.

[124] The Pauline passage, 2 Thess. 2.7-8. For this interpretation, Suerbaum, *Vom antiken zum frühmittelalterlichen Staatsbegriff*, pp. 270-71. Cf. Löwe, "Von Theoderich dem Grossen zu Karl dem Grossen," p. 356. For commentary, see Reydellet, as below, n. 163.

summarily unfolding the ages from the Creation down to the advent of Augustus and the birth of Jesus Christ. From this point, Jordanes deliberately backtracks to Romulus, more amply recording "the exploits of men who strove mightily for the [Roman] state."[125] This is part II. Unlike parts I and III, it has no proper conclusion, only a reference to current hardships and a parting recommendation that the interested reader should pursue the subject in the consular annals.[126] The *Getica* then begins, with its separate preface to Castalius. This third and last part is noteworthy for having a happy ending: a child is born embodying the hopes of its Roman and Gothic parents; applause is invited for the glorious Justinian as author of this fortunate outcome. The Goths are the subject of a cheerfully finished story, whereas the final empire of Daniel's prophecy labors on in pain and suffering.[127]

As already observed, Jordanes's "Summary of the Ages" has characteristically Byzantine traits.[128] The advertised (and, in part, real) source is the *Chronicle* of Eusebius-Jerome, the common ancestor of Latin chronicles. But Mommsen maintained, for good reasons, that "some Alexandrine chronicle (*chronicon quoddam Alexandrinum*)" had also been used.[129] Alexandria was a center of chronicle production in late antiquity and decisively affected Eastern chronography.[130] This source presumably supplied Jordanes with the long series of Hebrew patriarchs whose "generations" fill the space between the Creation and Ninus, the first king in the Eusebian series of reigns. The same work may also explain the choice of the Ptolemaic dynasty to embody the "Greek empire" from Alexander on.[131] Empires appear to have a privileged relation to eponymous cities; as Ninus's city of Nineveh

---

[125] See above, n. 5.

[126] *Rom.* ¶¶ 384-85, African affairs, ending with the murder of seventeen Moorish chieftains and resulting in peace "iubante domino" for all Africa; ¶¶ 386-87, a great victory by the Lombards, allies of the emperor, over the Gepids; then the final ¶ 388: "Hi sunt casus Romanae rei publicae preter instantia cottidiana Bulgarum, Antium et Sclavinorum. Que si quis scire cupit, annales consulumque seriem revolvat sine fastidio repperietque dignam nostri temporis rem publicam tragydiae. Scietque unde orta, quomoda aucta, qualiterve sibi cunctas terras subdiderit et quomodo iterum eas ab ignaris rectoribus amiserit. Quod et nos pro captu ingenii breviter tetigimus, quatenus diligens lector latius ista legendo cognoscat." There is a noteworthy switch from the African and Lombard victories, favorable to the Roman state, to the doleful sounds of the final paragraph introduced by a reference to current Bulgarian and Slavic raids. Any sense of a climax or conclusion is avoided.

[127] About the cheerfully finished story, § 8 below. Daniel's prophecy, *Rom.* ¶ 84: "[Romanorum imperium] ubi et usque actenus, et usque in finem mundi secundum Danielis prophetia regni debetur successio."

[128] Above, n. 121.

[129] Mommsen, Preface, pp. xxvii-viii.

[130] Adolf Bauer and Josef Strzygowski, "Eine alexandrinische Weltchronik," *Denkschriften der kaiserlichen Akademie der Wissenschaft* (Vienna), philol.- hist. Klasse, 51, no. 2 (1906), 87-92; Croke, "Origins of the Christian World Chronicle."

[131] *Rom.* ¶¶ 8-11 (*capita familiarum* in lieu of kings), 72-84 (Macedonian kings).

had been to the Assyrians, so Alexandria was to the Greeks, and Rome or New Rome is to the final empire.[132]

Alongside the succession of rulers and empires, the conspicuous feature of part I, perhaps also from the Alexandrine chronicle, is the attention paid to the Jews even after the chronological series switches from patriarchs to Assyrian and other imperial reigns. Three long entries are concerned with the prehistory of Rome, two short ones with nondescript Persian affairs.[133] All other narrative, unless detailing the circumstances in which world rule passed from one people to the next (*translatio imperii*), forms a continuous trail of Jewish history.[134] The cumulative logic of these entries suggests that, as the Roman Empire was about to begin, Jewish independence came to an end: "when [Cleopatra, the last Greek 'emperor'] ruled, the Jews associated themselves in friendship to the Romans and now live by their laws, because Pompey took away the sovereignty (*regnum*) from Aristobulos and instituted (*praefecerit*) his brother Hircanus."[135] Although the message of Jordanes is not entirely clear, it seems as though a "national" history of the Jews is blended into the chronological summary of his first part. Its outcome for them is rather similar to that endured by the Goths in part III: the Jews (without changing religion) are absorbed into the Empire.

The Roman history that forms part II is about half as long as the *Getica* and is largely pasted together from well-known histories and chronicles. There is an almost sixty-year gap in the transmitted text, from the onset of Diocletian's persecution through the reign of Constantius II, as a result of which we cannot tell how Jordanes portrayed Constantine and the foundation of Constantinople.[136] The seven kings of Rome have individual entries, but the five centuries of consular rule are compressed into a narrative of unrelieved conquest.[137] After the defeat of Hannibal, chronological order even yields to geographic coverage.[138] Of the politics of the republican period—the Gracchi, Marius and Sulla, Pompey and Caesar, and all the other incidents of internal turmoil—nothing whatsoever is mentioned ex-

[132] *Rom.* ¶¶ 12, (14?), 52, 71; exception, ¶¶ 49, 57.

[133] Prehistory of Rome, *Rom.* ¶¶ 38, 51, 52; Persian affairs, ¶¶ 62, 69.

[134] Passage of world rule: *Rom.* ¶¶ 11-12, 49, 57, 71, 84. Almost every paragraph until ¶ 59 is concerned with Jewish affairs; entries concerning the Jews diminish only in the post-exilic period.

[135] *Rom.* ¶ 84: "qua [i.e. Cleopatra] regnante Iudaei in amicitias Romanorum se sociantes eorum iam legibus vivent, quia Pompeius regnum ab Aristobolo sublato Hircanum fratrem eius praefecerat."

[136] *Rom.* ¶ 302; the gap opens with the announcement of Diocletian's Christian persecution (A.D. 303) and ends with the death of Constantius II in Cappadocia (when on his way to contest Julian's usurpation, 361). There is a much smaller lacuna at ¶ 137.

[137] Kings, *Rom.* ¶¶ 87-110; consuls, ¶¶ 111-254.

[138] Geographic coverage, *Rom.* ¶¶ 210-34. The reason is a change of source (indicated below, n. 150), but Jordanes selected deliberately; he had already used this source in ¶ 111.

cept the Actium campaign that sealed Augustus's triumph.[139] Once the imperial régime begins, the usual pattern of serial biography is adopted (the kings are treated in the same way). The entries gain breadth with Diocletian and become genuinely interesting as political commentary from Marcian (450-57) onward.

Jordanes is notably negative about the earliest emperors. Nero and Domitian, predictably, "did not profit the state," but that the same condemnation should be attached to Nerva, Hadrian, and Antoninus Pius, whose worst sin was to avoid war, prepares us for the idea that the martial Trajan was "preferable to almost all the emperors."[140] It also prepares us for the less predictable judgment that Julian the Apostate, explicitly so called, was "a man of distinction and necessary to the state."[141] His fighting the Persians, as Trajan had, evidently made up even for apostasy.

In carrying out what is called an "abridgment of chronicles," Jordanes gave short shrift to chronology.[142] His Roman history is articulated in a 253-year period of kings and a 458-year period of consuls before debouching upon the age of the emperors. From Augustus onward, each emperor is introduced in a formulaic sentence that includes the years and months of his reign.[143] Owing to the use for the consular period of a source that surveys conquests in geographic order, such emperors as Claudius, Trajan, and Aurelian briefly intrude into the republican age.[144] The imperial reigns, comparatively short as they are, make the period after Augustus seem much more time-bound than that of the kings and consuls, whose atemporality is enhanced by the lines of geographic coverage. Even so, the age of the emperors is not free of chronological muddles. The simultaneity of Eastern and Western events between 395 and 476 is straightened into a narrative that makes only thematic sense.[145] Jordanes extracted facts from the chronicles he used and dispensed with their scruples in keeping to the order of time. Nevertheless, in the *Romana*, sketchy chronology does not result in glaring historical errors.

---

[139] *Rom.* ¶¶ 251-54.

[140] Criticized emperors, *Rom.* ¶¶ 261, 265, 266, 269, 271; Trajan ¶ 267.

[141] *Rom.* ¶ 304.

[142] *Get.* ¶ 1: he was engaged in an *abbreviatio chronicorum* when Castalius interrupted him.

[143] E.g. *Rom.* ¶ 279, "Marcus Aurelius Antonini Caracallae filius templique Heliogabali sacerdos imperator factus regnavit ann. IIII"; ¶ 293, "Probus regnavit an. VI m. IIII." Shorter period, ¶ 289: "Post cuius [Claudii] mortem Quintilius frater eius a senatu Augustus appellatus octavo decimo imperii sui diae Aquilaeia occisus est." A similar formula opens each papal biography in the Roman *Liber pontificalis*.

[144] *Rom.* ¶ 217, Trajan, Aurelian, also Gallienus; ¶ 225, Claudius. The source is Festus, above, ch. I n. 18.

[145] E.g. Arcadius, Eastern events, *Rom.* ¶¶ 319-21; Western ¶¶ 321-22 (beginning at "Hesperica vero plaga"). Theodosius II, Western, ¶¶ 323-30; Eastern, ¶ 331. Marcian, Eastern, ¶¶ 332-33; Western, ¶ 334.

Despite the patchwork of sources, the *Romana* is less derivative than it might potentially have been. The remarkable thing is that Jordanes pieced together a new history of Rome instead of merely continuing an existing work of the same compass. When Paul the Deacon undertook a similar task two centuries later, he acquitted it by using the *Breviarium* of Eutropius as his core and augmenting it with a beginning and a continuation.[146] Eutropius was as well known in Jordanes's day as in Paul's; the *Breviarium* had recently been honored with a second translation into Greek. Jordanes drew upon Eutropius but only for ten brief extracts, none of them concerning the republican period. Moreover, he went out of his way, in a passage of the *Getica*, to speak well of two third-century emperors whom Eutropius had disparaged.[147] Jordanes was under no obligation, of course, to behave like Paul the Deacon. Yet his avoidance of the very obvious Eutropius, in preference for other guides, bears witness to the originality of his concept and draws attention to the choices he made.

Jordanes's authorities for the kings and the Republic are Florus primarily and Rufius Festus as a poor second.[148] Whereas the neglected Eutropius specializes in numerical data, the authors whom Jordanes favored are extraordinarily chauvinistic. Augustine, in *The City of God*, classed Florus among "the historians who set out to sing the praises of the Roman Empire, rather than to recount Rome's wars."[149] Florus was somber at least about civil strife, but Jordanes skipped these parts.[150] Festus, though drier than Florus, is even less moderate in tendency. He surveys the Empire region by region—uniquely anticipating the form of Mommsen's *Provinces of the Roman Empire*[151]—with the sole purpose of explaining how each one came under Roman domination. In a notorious passage, Rome's wars with Carthage are packed into the phrase "Ter Africa rebellavit."[152] Rome's right to world conquest is never doubted, and neither Florus nor Festus betrays any com-

[146] See below, ch. V § 3.

[147] Greek translation: Eutropius *Brev.*, ed. Droysen, p. xxv; ed. Rühl, p. vii. Eutropius in Jordanes: *Rom.* ¶¶ 235, 257, 259, 264, 267, 282, 290, 294, 304. Rehabilitations: *Get.* ¶ 106 (on the grounds that they made a treaty with the Goths). Cf. Eutropius *Brev.* 9.5.1. Mommsen, in MGH AA. V, 85 n. 2, reproduced Orosius at this point for comparison with Jordanes, but Eutropius was the common source.

[148] Florus *Epitoma de Tito Livio*, ed. Paul Jal, Collection des universités de France, 2 vols. (Paris 1967); on its use by Jordanes, I, cxviii-ix. For Festus and his date, see ch. I n. 18 above.

[149] Florus *Epit.* 1.22.1. Augustine *De civitate Dei* 3.19, ed. B. Dombart and A. Kalb, Corpus Christianorum, ser. Lat. 47 (Turnhout 1955), p. 87; tr. Henry Bettensen (Harmondsworth, Middlesex 1972), p. 118. Hagendahl, *Augustine and the Latin Classics*, p. 663, points out that modern commentators agree with Augustine's assessment of Florus.

[150] Florus *Epit.* 2.1-9, 11-13, 15-18, 21. Jordanes drew very little from Florus's second book.

[151] Mommsen, *Die Provinzen von Caesar bis Diocletian*, on which see, in brief, Gooch, *History and Historians*, pp. 465-67.

[152] Festus *Brev.* 4, ed. Eadie, p. 47. The translation "Africa rebelled three times" would somewhat distort the original (*rebellare* means more than "to rebel"), but not very much.

passion toward the defeated and conquered. Augustine's friend Orosius, author of the one history of Rome along Christian lines, continually adverts to the slaughter and destruction attendant upon empire-building.[153] Jordanes relied on Orosius in the *Getica* as well as the *Romana* and could hardly have missed these passages, but he had no use for them. He valued the Empire-centeredness of his authorities at least as much as the (hardly unique) information they provide. Where the victims of conquest are concerned, Jordanes condescends only to copy Florus's line (which had once caught Augustine's eye) that the Second Punic War had been as damaging to the victors as to the vanquished.[154]

Though disregarding Orosius's compassion, Jordanes comes nowhere near emulating the wary nonsectarianism of Eutropius's *Breviarium*. Details of Christian history, not many but enough to count, are effortlessly integrated into his narrative. The birth and passion of Jesus Christ come at the start of the imperial period.[155] We hear of persecutions, or harm to the Church, by nine emperors, one usurper, and a would-be usurper, in the course of which special mention is made of the martyrdom of Peter and Paul and the travails of John the Evangelist.[156] Philip the Arab has his usual role as first Christian emperor, and the trio of Theodosius I, Marcian, and Justinian are singled out as rulers specially favored by the Almighty.[157] The only novelty among these Christian entries is a set of references to translations of the Bible into Greek, from that of Aquila under the emperor Hadrian to the sixth under Alexander Severus. No other Latin chronicler records this information until Isidore of Seville.[158] Of course, vast tracts of Church history are left out of the *Romana*: no evangelization, no councils, no heresies (except that Valens was Arian and Basiliscus Nestorian), no Church fathers, no hint of a miracle.[159] Even so, Jordanes's religion leaves a conspicuous mark. Paul the Deacon, monk of Monte Cassino, composed his *Historia Romana* in response to a complaint that Eutropius omitted Christian information.[160] Yet Jordanes, for all his attention to military exploits and good words for Julian the Apostate, is more lavish than Paul in portraying a Roman Empire that was recognizably Christian.

Jordanes's lack of Christian compassion toward the victims of imperial-

---

[153] E.g. Orosius *Hist.* 5.1. For a synopsis, Lacroix, *Orose et ses idées*, pp. 112-17. See also Mommsen, "Orosius and Augustine," p. 334.

[154] *Rom.* ¶ 181; the source is Florus as above, n. 149.

[155] *Rom.* ¶¶ 256, 258.

[156] *Rom.* ¶¶ 262 (Peter and Paul), 265 (John the Apostle), 281, 284, 287, 302, 304, 308 and 312, 322, 342, 359.

[157] *Rom.* ¶¶ 283; 315, 317; 332-33; 363, 366, 381.

[158] *Rom.* ¶¶ 270, 276, 277, 280. Isidore of Seville *Chron.* 270, 279, 284, 292 (MGH AA. XI, 458-61). See Mommsen, Preface, p. xxviii.

[159] *Rom.* ¶¶ 308, 342.

[160] Below, ch. V § 3.

ism is perhaps better ascribed to anxiety for the contemporary Empire than to blind patriotism. He records Justinian's conquests with pleasure and satisfaction and has only harsh words for Totila's revival of the Gothic cause in Italy.[161] In a curious change of a line from Florus, he even manages to portray Augustus as a Justinian before the fact: "The Germans, Gauls, Britons, Iberians, Asturians, and Cantabrians lived beneath the western sky and, after long subjection, had fallen away. Augustus went personally against them, forcing them to serve again and to live by Roman laws."[162] We are to understand that there had been earlier defections from imperial control than those of the recent past, and they had been mastered. Yet the *Romana*, like other histories of Justinian's day, is far from striking notes of generalized triumph and confident supremacy. If the "Roman state" (*Romana res publica*) continues to embody Daniel's final empire, Jordanes adds the qualification that it does so "at least ostensibly" (*vel imaginarie*).[163] He tells in closing of having related the Empire's "calamities (*casus*), except for the daily incursions of Bulgarians, Antes, and Sclavini"; the reader is asked to observe "that the *res publica* of our time is worthy of [portrayal in] tragedy"; it had originated, grown, subjected all lands to itself, and lost them again owing to unskilled rulers (*ignari rectores*)."[164] The Empire, in Jordanes's conception, has experienced the fate of a hero in the grip of Fortune. Once borne to an almost paradisal condition, it reached its acme long ago and fell, like Adam, to a merely mortal state. Justinian's successes brought the Empire no closer to regaining its primitive timelessness.

Jordanes is so often cited as attesting to a belief in the continuity of the Empire that the details of his outlook merit close scrutiny.[165] On a superficial level, a Constantinopolitan like him could scarcely fail to acknowledge the endurance of the *res publica* to which he belonged or to illustrate in his work the direct links of that state to the Rome of Romulus. But these views do not prevent Jordanes from also being one of the most explicit early witnesses to an *Untergangsstimmung*, a developed sense that the Empire had

---

[161] *Rom.* ¶¶ 366, 375, 385-87 (more of the same in the *Get.*); ¶¶ 379, 382 (hostility to Totila).

[162] *Rom.* ¶ 249: "Germanos Gallos Brittones Spanos Hiberes Astures Cantabros occiduali axe iacentes et post longum servitium desciscentes per se ipse Augustus accedens rursus servire coegit Romanisque legibus vivere."

[163] *Rom.* ¶ 2: "ut tibi, quomodo Romana res publica coepit et tenuit totumque pene mundum subegit et hactenus vel imaginariae teneat, . . . referam." Reydellet, *Royauté*, pp. 291-93, after an important discussion of the (rare) word *imaginariae*, interprets it as "d'une manière symbolique" or, with Ferdinand Lot, "théoriquement, idéalement."

[164] Above, n. 126.

[165] Brincken, *Weltchronistik*, p. 89, insisted on the absence of any trace of an *Untergangsstimmung*; Reitter, *Der Glaube an die Fortdauer*, p. 11. Along the same lines, Wattenbach-Levison, *Geschichtsquellen*, p. 77. What needs to be understood is that when "fall" is taken in the sense of "expulsion from paradise," it does not exclude continuity.

fallen from a once-high estate. A striking passage evokes Belisarius entering Rome in 536 to be received "by that formerly Roman people and by a Senate whose very name had almost gone to the grave along with its vigor."[166] But Jordanes was not referring only to the West. There is no trace in him of our facile contrast between luckless West and fortunate or triumphant East.[167] With the advent of Justin in 518, he says, "the worn-out state was able to breathe a little." The *res publica* also gained from the accession of Justinian nine years later.[168] Yet the only change that these rulers embodied was one from inept to skillful government. As much as ever, the Empire itself was a fit subject for tragedy. The exiles from the paradise of world power had to earn whatever security they enjoyed by the sweat of their brows.

Jordanes is all too clear as to when Fortune smiled on the Roman people. Florus and Festus told the story, and their accounts were so edited that scarcely a hint of civil war detracts from Rome's total freedom to dominate the world. The fall, however, is implied rather than stated and needs to be more precisely circumscribed. Jordanes's vision of the contemporary Empire was hardly peculiar to himself. It expressed an almost official point of view, set out, for example, in Justinian's own laws: world dominion had been lost by the negligence of earlier rulers.[169] The first clearly identifiable spokesman for this outlook belongs somewhat earlier, to the generation of the emperor Anastasius (491-518). He is the historian Zosimus, whose unfinished *New History*—a title meant in the pejorative sense of a "history of deplorable innovations"—was written near 504.[170] Zosimus by-passes early Rome, barely pausing at Augustus, and becomes more detailed from the third century onward, for which he uses important sources. Although his narrative ends, unintentionally, in 410, Zosimus often expresses the sense that the Empire he lived in (that of Anastasius) was a shadow of former

[166] *Rom.* ¶ 373, "consul Belesarius Romanam urbem ingressus est exceptusque ab illo populo quondam Romano et senatu iam pene ipso nomine cum virtute sepulto."

[167] E.g. Paschoud, "Influences et échos," pp. 317-18. For details, Goffart, "Zosimus," pp. 429-30.

[168] *Rom.* ¶ 359; Justin made Justinian emperor "consulens et rei publicae utilitatibus" (¶ 362).

[169] The point is developed in my "Zosimus," pp. 421-26, 430-32.

[170] On the interpretation of Zosimus's title, I accept the argument of Cracco-Ruggini, "Publicistica et storiografia bizantine," pp. 166, 181-83. Scholars currently divide over the issue whether Zosimus blindly reproduces his sources (mainly the late-fourth-century pagan historian Eunapius) or, instead, deploys them to express views belonging to his own times; for a summary of the controversy, see Blockley, *Classicising Historians* I, 2, 97-98. Blockley regrets that no clear method has been developed for distinguishing non-Eunapian (i.e. Zosimean) matter in the *New History*. This observation cuts both ways, however. There is no method either by which passages deemed to be from a source, such as Eunapius, can be "purified"; that is, cleared of the epitomator's editing and other intrusions. Cf. Jordanes: his *Rom.* is certainly derivative, yet it speaks with the accents of its age, not of Florus's or Eusebius's.

greatness, an island of survivors in a sea of barbarism. Zosimus was or at least wrote as a pagan, and he portrayed Christian emperors, notably Constantine and Theodosius, as bearing a heavy responsibility for the fall of the Empire. The *New History* seems to have been, when written, a piece of ambitiously radical revisionism. [171] That the Catholic *conversus* Jordanes, fifty years later, should fully agree with Zosimus in celebrating the apostate emperor Julian (execrated by the prominent historians of a century before) is perhaps the most conspicuous sign of how respectable a characteristically "pagan" interpretation of Roman history had become. [172] An arresting feature of Justinian's zealously Christian reign is its endorsement of Zosimus's vision of fallen empire. [173] Of course, in circles close to the régime, Christianity could not be deemed to be the main cause of decline; the outcome was the same, but a less repugnant explanation was needed than Zosimus had supplied.

In Jordanes, as we have seen, the course of imperial history is reminiscent of Adam's, or mankind's, tragedy—the expulsion from paradise. The Christian scheme of universal history, assigning to Rome the privilege of being the final empire, receives its due in the *Summa temporum* of part I; but the mundane Roman history of part II reduces the ostensibly privileged *res publica* to the common condition of humanity. For the rest, Jordanes develops two ideas taken directly or indirectly from the *New History* of Zosimus. The first, in Zosimus's formulation, was that Rome, which had waxed great by laudable rivalry among aristocratic consuls, set upon its downward course when the Romans heedlessly "entrust[ed] the burden of such a great empire to one man's whim and power." [174] Jordanes, as a Christian, could not follow Zosimus in condemning the principate of Augustus. Doing so undermined the happy coincidence of the Incarnation with the Augustan peace, a dogma of Christian chronography. [175] But if Augustus was beyond criticism, his successors were not. No reader of Jordanes can suppose that

[171] The fact of reviving the pagan Eunapius a century later is a sufficiently clear indication of Zosimus's radical revisionism. More generally, see Zosime, *Histoire nouvelle*, ed. François Paschoud, Collection des universités de France, I (Paris 1971) xxiii-vii (scope and ending), xii (paganism), lxiii-vi (repertory of passages illustrating his religious and political inclinations).

[172] The church historians who, near 445, continued Eusebius, rivaled with each other in defaming Julian: Socrates *H.E.* 3, *PG* LXXXII, 1085-1122; Sozomen *H.E.* 5-6.1-2, ed. J. Bidez and G. C. Hansen (Berlin 1960) pp. 188-239; Theodoret *H.E.* 3, ed. L. Parmentier (Leipzig 1911), pp. 177-206. Cf. earlier and more moderate Christian commentators: Jerome *Chron.*, ed. Helm, pp. 242-43 (abstains from praise); Augustine *Civ. Dei* 5.21, ed. Dombart and Kalb, p. 157 (Julians's worthy character was blinded by sacrilegious curiosity).

[173] As above, n. 169.

[174] Zosimus *Historia nova* 1.5.2, tr. Ronald T. Ridley, Byzantina Australensia 2 (Canberra 1982), p. 2.

[175] Mommsen, "Augustine and the Christian Idea of Progress" and "Orosius and Augustine"; Lacroix, *Orose et ses idées*, pp. 145-49; Keen, "Medieval Ideas of History," p. 299.

the Roman Empire was at its height in the first and second centuries A.D. Of the emperors down to Marcus Aurelius, only three—Claudius (the conqueror of Britain), Titus, and Trajan—rate a favorable word.[176] Till then and thereafter, the criterion for approval is not peace but military enterprise, especially against Persia, and there is too little of it to record. Our vision of the imperial period, or Orosius's for that matter, has little in common with that of Jordanes. Eutropius had judged that, until Trajan, the Empire was only defended rather than "nobly increased."[177] Even this attenuated notion of a defensive *pax Romana* has no place in Jordanes's perspective. As he saw it, the Empire started to be merely managed once past Augustus's consolidations; it eroded right from the start under many inept rulers and was intermittently shored up by a few able ones. So it continued, much diminished, under Justinian and would run on, episodic emperor upon emperor, like an interminable soap opera. The details differed from Zosimus's; the negative point of departure is the same.

Very early in the account of the imperial régime, Jordanes makes it apparent that Rome had fallen from its paradisal condition, but a serious additional disturbance of its equilibrium had taken place in the relatively recent past. Zosimus is particularly famous for promising to supply a negative counterpart to Polybius's account of the making of Rome's empire. As Polybius had documented the rise of Rome to world power in the brief span of fifty-three years, so Zosimus undertook to show how its empire was unmade in just about the same span of time. This promise, however, is left hanging. Not only does Zosimus never revert to the fifty-three years after once mentioning them, but every modern attempt to carve out five suitable decades in his narrative has proved unsatisfactory.[178] There is nothing mysterious about Zosimus's silence; he would have kept his promise if the *New History* had not been cut short in 410, probably by the author's death. In the *Romana*, Jordanes makes up for that silence by spelling out the age of disaster: Marcian became emperor in 450 and saved "the realm that his dainty predecessors, ruling turn by turn for almost sixty years, had made small."[179] The fifty-three Polybian years of growth were undone by the fifty-five years from Arcadius and Honorius through Theodosius II, or the sixty years from the same beginning to the death of Valentinian III (455). To Jordanes, just as to his contemporary Procopius, the emperors Honorius and Valentinian III

[176] *Rom.* ¶¶ 260, 264, 268-69.
[177] Eutropius *Brev.* 8.2.2.
[178] Paschoud, *Cinq études sur Zosime*, pp. 184-206; Paschoud, "Influences et échos," pp. 305-37.
[179] *Rom.* ¶ 332: "Regnum quod delicati decessores prodecessoresque eius per annos fere sexaginta vicissim imperantes minuerant . . . reparavit."

epitomized the background of negligent loss whose result was the lamentably "ostensible" empire in which they lived.[180]

The Roman history of Jordanes is a document of extraordinary interest for penetrating the mentality of Justinian's reign. Its perspective, once understood, readily explains why Eutropius or Orosius could not serve Jordanes as a model. An original selection of extracts needed to be made in order to convey a novel synthesis: a grim vision of the Roman past consistent with the harsh military exigencies of an age striving to repair the ruins piled up by all too many "dainty" emperors. Jordanes held out no prospect of amelioration. The lesson he proposed to the very noble Vigilius was *contemptus mundi*. By reading these histories, he would "know that anxiety always grips him who is attached to the world"; the downfall of diverse nations taught one "to desire to be detached from all tribulation and to be converted to God, Who is the true freedom."[181] Hope resided in the pursuit of religious perfection. None was to be found in the course of an empire that, even though Christianized, promised only unending toil and calamity.

The pessimism of the *Romana* brings to mind Peter Brown's fine assessment of Justinian: "The true measure of the man . . . was not the belle époque of 533 to 540; it was the quality revealed in the harsh years that followed . . . [the quality of] the slightly uncanny old man, who worked until dawn every night in the seclusion of the Great Palace."[182] As a narrator of this reign, Jordanes was not among "the alienated and the embittered" through whose eyes, as Brown points out, Justinian is mainly seen. Yet the *Romana* is a not a panegyric. Jordanes's most genuine kindness to Justinian—an analogy designed to save him from being blamed for the recent plague—occurs in the *Getica*, which also closes with explicit praise for the emperor.[183] In the *Romana*, no praise is intended when Justinian is portrayed triumphing from the spoils of domestic opponents "as though a great alien host had been laid low," in contrast to Belisarius who, a few lines later, triumphs "from the Vandal spoils."[184] Both ceremonies occurred some twenty years before the time of writing. Justinian is also shown committing an error of judgment in 549: "But, as often happens, the turn of events clashed with the emperor's decision (*voluntas*)"; Belisarius was recalled to

---

[180] I first made this point in "Rome, Constantinople, and the Barbarians," pp. 298-99.

[181] The text is cited above, n. 115.

[182] Brown, *World of Late Antiquity*, p. 155.

[183] *Get.* ¶¶ 104-106. This is the passage in which Jordanes clearly departs from Eutropius (above, n. 147).

[184] *Rom.* ¶ 364, "sociosque eorum, qui evaserant a caede, proscriptos, veluti grande hoste prostrato de manubiis triumphavit"; ¶ 366, "cuius notu remuneratus consulque ordinarius mox designatus, de manubiis Vandalicis Belesarius triumphavit."

Constantinople with disastrous results for Italy.[185] Isolated in a basically appreciative context, these sentences cannot turn Jordanes into a critic of the régime. At most, they provide him with a small claim to the historian's virtue of uttering distasteful truth. Thanks to the dignified authors on which it relies, the *Romana* is serious and sober in details as well as in its interpretation of where the Roman Empire had come from and was going. Jordanes engaged in compilation in order to achieve an original result: a Christianized adaptation of Zosimean history, in which the "pagan" theme of the ruin of the Empire was sublimated into ascetic contempt for the world. If there had ever been a recent moment for euphoria, it passed with the resumption of war with Persia in 540 and its train of accompanying calamities.[186] What remained by the 550s was the limited expectation that incessant bailing would outpace the leaks and keep the *res publica* afloat. It was an effective synopsis of the Byzantine future.

Our consideration of parts I and II of Jordanes's historical collection is drawing to a close. They are not trivial works. Jordanes's outlook is so metropolitan that the place where he wrote is hardly arguable. His narrative and opinions align him more closely with Justinian's court than with a circle having a discernibly alternative identity. The other historians of Justinian's reign wrote in Greek, the language of their public. Jordanes's audience read Latin. The case is not unique, for Constantinople was a bilingual capital, and its emperors had never yet ceased to originate from Latin-speaking provinces. Earlier in the sixth century, the Eastern Empire had given birth to an important continuation by Count Marcellinus (who was apparently assured of a receptive public) of Jerome's Latin-language *Chronicle*. Whether Marcellinus's public was also meant to be Jordanes's is better considered after all three parts of the latter's collection have been studied. By common consent, the *Getica* is Jordanes's most important and absorbing composition.

6. How Closely Did Jordanes Reproduce the Gothic History of Cassiodorus?

The first question to consider in turning to the *Getica* is, again, its relationship to Cassiodorus's Gothic history; Jordanes himself started part III by indicating the scale of his indebtedness. Modern views on this subject have already been discussed.[187] A precise and objective answer would be possible had the twelve-book Gothic history survived. Since it is lost, all that may be done is to attempt, by conjecture, to detect Cassiodoran style,

---

[185] *Rom.* ¶ 381.
[186] *Rom.* ¶¶ 376-83 (378, "cladem . . . in Esperia plaga"), 388; ¶¶ 384-87, recent successes.
[187] Above, § 2.

phraseology, ideas, and sources in the body of Jordanes's work. These efforts are not vain, but they easily go astray unless carried out with caution and restraint.[188] One needs, for a start, to exhaust those resources of the text that can be exploited without recourse to guesswork. The obvious point of departure is to find out precisely how Jordanes describes his dependence on Cassiodorus. Almost all commentators affirm that he claims to summarize the long Gothic history.[189] His own account is more qualified.

The *Getica* opens with a short preface addressed to Castalius. Unlike the general preface to Vigilius, that to the *Getica* is not wholly Jordanes's composition. About half the words and the whole course of the argument are plagiarized from the preface of Rufinus to his translation of Origen's *Commentary on the Epistle to the Romans*.[190] Jordanes did not casually pick this model in order to make up for defective powers of invention. He singled it out because its message was much the same as the one he wished to convey.[191] Like Jordanes, Rufinus responded to a request to abridge (as well as, in his case, to translate), and he apologized that his version was rather distant from Origen's original.[192] In part, Rufinus set out the conventional idea that he was unequal to his patron's request, but his regrets also had factual dimensions.[193] He was afraid, he said, of being drowned in the ocean depths of Origen's interpretation (*sensus*), and, what was worse, he had been unable to find the whole of Origen's fifteen-book *Commentary* at the booksellers.[194] All three of these points return, with suitable alterations, in Jordanes's adaptation. He seized upon Rufinus's factual excuses and built them into an explanation of his less-than-literal relations to Cassiodorus. The choice of this Rufinian preface as a model clarifies Jordanes's

---

[188] Cf. above, n. 54. Momigliano, "Cassiodorus and Ital. Culture," pp. 283, 197: "These researches, however acute, never produced conclusive results." As with every effort to detect traces of lost sources, there is no method for determining how they were altered or adapted by the borrower.

[189] E.g. Mierow, p. 13; Hodgkin, *Italy and Her Invaders* I, 26; Brunhölzl, *Gesch. d. lat. Lit.* I, 30.

[190] This source was discovered by Heinrich von Sybel. For the text, MGH AA. V, 53-54 (footnote).

[191] Köpke, *Anfänge*, pp. 66-67, recognized that Jordanes's predicament fundamentally resembled Rufinus's and that this resemblance determined Jordanes's choice of literary model. The implications escaped him.

[192] *Loc. cit.* (n. 190): "suades, ut nostra voce quindecim eius volumina . . . explicemus . . . atque in Latino opere integram consequentiam dare. . . . Addis autem, ne quid laboribus meis desit, ut omne hoc quindecim voluminum corpus . . . adbreviem et ad media . . . coartem."

[193] On the "modesty topos," Curtius, *European Lit. and Latin Middle Ages*, pp. 83-85.

[194] *Loc. cit.* (n. 190): "in quibus ille dum sectatur apostoli sensum, in tam profundum pelagus aufertur, ut metus ingens sit illuc eum sequenti, ne magnitudine sensuum velut immanitate opprimatur undarum. Tum deinde nec illud aspicis, quod tenuis mihi est spiritus ad inplendam eius tam magnificam dicendi tubam. Super omnes autem difficultates est, quod interpolati sunt ipsi libri. Desunt enim fere apud omnium bybliothecas, incertum sane quo casu, aliquanti ex ipso corpore volumina."

intentions. If he had wished to affirm a close dependence on the long Gothic history, he would have selected a different model to imitate or, as in the preface to Vigilius, used his own words.

Except for one controversial sentence, Jordanes's adaptation of Rufinus is straightforward. Castalius had asked him to interrupt his "abridgment of chronicles" (that is, the *Romana*) so that he might, using his own words, compress into one small *libellus* the twelve *volumina* of Cassiodorus "On the Descent and Exploits of the Getae." *Volumina* is Rufinus's word, referring to the fifteen full-size books of Origen's *Commentary*.[195] As the preface unfolds, Jordanes states that he has made additions to Cassiodorus from several Greek and Latin historians, "mixing matter of my dictation into the beginning, the end, and quite a lot in the middle."[196] Like Rufinus about Origen, he admits that his eloquence cannot match Cassiodorus's.[197] He also regrets that, because the long Gothic history was not beside him as he composed, he has been unable to adhere slavishly to Cassiodorus's meaning (*sensus*). The parallel intended is with Rufinus on the deep waters of Origen's interpretation.[198] These statements, added together, suggest that the *Getica* contains a free abridgment of Cassiodorus, deliberately interpolated with extracts from other authors. It could not possibly embody an exact image of the Cassiodoran model. Although Jordanes may have exaggerated the extent of his personal activity, what he wished readers to believe about it seems plain.

Precisely how much access did Jordanes have to his main source? The story he tells is that, some time before he wrote the *Getica*, he was allowed by Cassiodorus's steward to have the twelve books for three days.[199] In describing what he did during this period, Jordanes does not say *legere*, "to read," but *relegere*. In modern discussions, his use of the latter verb has often been understood to mean that he had two periods of access to the Gothic history, one long and leisurely, the other the three days of "re-reading" referred to. Harald Fuchs even devised an elegant emendation, four words without textual basis, spelling out this chronology of a careful and a

[195] Texts in nn. 192 and 194. Rufinus uses *libri* once, but *volumina* three times. Of course, the fact of plagiarism is not proof of distortion; the possibility that Cassiodorus's books were full-sized cannot be excluded. (Note that Jordanes *ut nostris verbis* copies Rufinus *ut nostra voce*.)

[196] *Get.* ¶ 3: "Ad quos et ex nonnullis historiis Grecis ac Latinis addedi convenientia, initium finemque et plura in medio mea dictione permiscens."

[197] *Get.* ¶ 2: precisely matching Rufinus (n. 194), "nec illud" to "tubam"—Jordanes's most direct plagiarism.

[198] *Ibid.*: "super omne autem pondus, quod nec facultas eorundem librorum nobis datur, quatenus eius sensui inserviamus." The parallel with the passage quoted in n. 194 is obvious; note, also, the resemblance involved in the use of *sensus*.

[199] *Ibid.*: "sed, ut non mentiar, ad triduanam lectionem dispensatoris eius beneficio libros ipsos antehac relegi."

cursory reading.[200] When more closely examined, Jordanes's preface does not lend itself to such an interpretation. The literary underpinnings—the regrets of Rufinus at being unable to acquire the whole of Origen's *Commentary*—are there to buttress the plain import of Jordanes's sentence. He meant to indicate a grave handicap, not to report two periods of reading. There is no force to the corollary objection that three days are absurdly few for mastering twelve books.[201] As mentioned earlier, the length of Cassiodorus's narrative is unknown and unknowable.[202] If its book divisions were on the same modest scale as those of Eutropius's *Breviarium*, the total would have come to not much more than the *Getica* itself. The idea that Jordanes refers to only one reading is best confirmed by the authority of Thomas Hodgkin, whose testimony comes from outside the modern controversy. In translating the passage, Hodgkin rightly saw that the context calls for *relegere* to be synonymous with *legere* (the same equivalence often occurs in none other than Rufinus): "I did some time ago, by the kindness of his steward, receive those books for a three days' perusal."[203] Here, as before, one may doubt Jordanes's truthfulness;[204] the three days' reading is his counterpart to Rufinus's lack of success at the booksellers. But there can be no arguing with the import of his remarks. Regardless of whether his statement was candid or not, he wished readers to understand that his access to the twelve books had been too brief to do them precise justice.

Neither Rufinus nor Jordanes was discouraged by the inadequacy of his contact with the work central to his enterprise. Jordanes cheerfully sums up what the three days had made possible; in Mierow's translation: "The words I recall not, but the sense and the deeds related I think I retain entire."[205]

---

[200] Grimm, "Über Jornandes," p. 187; Schirren, *De ratione*, pp. 92-93; Köpke, *Anfänge*, p. 67; Hachmann, *Goten u. Skandinavien*, pp. 37-38; Luiselli, "Sul *De summa temporum*," p. 114; O'Donnell, *Cassiodorus*, p. 47; Momigliano, "Cassiodorus and Ital. Culture," p. 193 (takes the word as Jordanes's "admission" that he had read the work before); Fuchs, review in *Museum Helveticum*, p. 251.

[201] Croke, "Cassiodorus and the *Getica*," argues that three days *is* adequate time—a possibility that deserves to be at least voiced in order to prevent the too easy canonization of the alternative.

[202] Above, nn. 82-84.

[203] Hodgkin, *Italy and Her Invaders* I, 26. Luiselli, "Sul *De summa temporum*," p. 114 n. 48, showed that *relegere* does not have to mean "re-read," but persuaded himself that Jordanes meant it in this sense because, five times, he uses *legere* for "read." But *relegere* is not a simple synonym; it can denote a way of reading (see C. T. Lewis and C. Short, *Latin Dictionary*, Oxford 1879, s.v.). Croke, "Cassiodorus and the *Getica*," suggests "skim read." This is in keeping with the context; Jordanes says he has had no access to the twelve books or, to be strictly accurate, merely three days to sail over them. Gutschmid, review of Schirren, pp. 149-50, recognized the "reproachful tone." Some restraint in Manitius, *Gesch. d. lat. Lit.* I, 213 n. 1.

[204] Hodgkin, *Italy and Her Invaders* I, 28-29 with n. 1 (p. 29), endorsed the view of Hermann Usener that the three days' use "is of course humbug." This avoids having to interpret *relegere* as two readings, but raises the problem of Jordanes's veracity.

[205] Mierow tr., p. 51; *Get.* ¶ 2, "quorum quamvis verba non recolo, sensus tamen et res actas

He had been faithful to Cassiodorus in his fashion. This statement comes just before the equally positive reference to the inclusion of extracts from other historians.[206] Despite apologies, Jordanes was content with the *Getica*. Readers should not expect a close copy of Cassiodorus, but they would find the whole of Cassiodorus's interpretation and events, mixed in with material from other historians. No promises are made that sources will be identified, though some are, and no later references to Cassiodorus in fact occur. All in all, Jordanes seems to tell us that he blended one main source and a series of minor ones into a basically new work, much as he did in the *Romana*. His description offers no encouragement at all to those wishing to identify the *Getica* directly with Cassiodorus, but it is thoroughly consistent with what is otherwise known about Jordanes's methods.

7. The *Getica*: A Celebration of Goths?

Even if heavily indebted to the Gothic history of Cassiodorus, the *Getica* is a book written in the 550s by a thoroughly Byzantine author who intended it to be the last and longest component of a three-part historical library of his own devising. Jordanes was a compiler, not an independent researcher. As seen above with parts I and II of his writings, the most direct approach involves observing the selection and deployment of his sources. This is the normal way to make the most of a historical compilation.[207] With the *Getica*, something else needs to be tried, since not only Cassiodorus's twelve books, but also other authorities, such as Priscus, are wholly or largely lost.[208] Jordanes, though he copied the books of others, shaped them in an original fashion. For a start, something may be learned about the *Getica* by examining its contents and its shortcomings in matters of historical fact.

---

credo me integre retinere." Rufinus expressed his confidence by trusting that God, through his sponsor's prayers, would make possible what, to Rufinus, seemed impossible (a more obviously rhetorical turn of phrase than Jordanes's).

[206] Above, n. 196.

[207] See Guenée, as above, n. 44.

[208] On Priscus, Blockley, *Classicising Historians* I, 48-70, 113-23, esp. about Jordanes 113-14. Ablavius is cited three times (*Get.* ¶¶ 28, 82, 117) and is very puzzling. For a rundown of opinions about him, Wagner, *Getica*, pp. 62-68. Mommsen, Preface, pp. xxvii-ix, stressed his importance. Ablabius's existence outside the *Getica* used to be based on an ingenious emendation by W. Meyer of Cassiodorus *Var.* 10.22.2, a letter of 535, seeking peace from Justinian: "Considerate etiam, principes docti, et Ablabi vestri historica monimenta. Recolite, quantum decessores vestri studuerint de suo iure relinquere, ut eis parentum nostrorum foedera provenirent" (ed. Fridh, p. 405). But this emendation is uncalled for. I am very grateful to Professor Evangelos Chrysos, of the University of Ioannina, for pointing out to me that the ms reading *abavi* makes excellent sense: Justinian was asked to ponder the *historica monumenta*, i.e. archives, of *abavi vestri*, i.e. his imperial predecessors; he was not being directed to a historical narrative. Jordanes's references to a historian Ablavius are therefore unique and unconfirmed. He is a less certain authority than Priscus.

The *Getica* is more loosely articulated than parts I and II. Jordanes specifies a division into three segments: "the period when both tribes, Ostrogoths and Visigoths, were united," "the Visigoths apart from the Ostrogoths," and "the ancestry and deeds of the Ostrogoths."[209] Comprising 127, 114, and 128 paragraphs, respectively, the segments are almost uniform in length. The first is a notably uneven compound: migration legends; tales of the Scythians, Amazons, Getae, and Dacians disguised as Goths; an acclamation of Gothic chiefs leading into the genealogy of the Amals; and an abstract of Gothic relations with the Roman Empire in the third and fourth centuries. The unity of the Goths in this period is nowhere emphasized.[210] The Visigothic segment is more tightly controlled, but close to half the paragraphs are occupied by a disproportionate narrative of Attila's great campaign of 451.[211] Another obtrusive digression traces the Vandal kingdom of Gaiseric through Justinian's conquest of 533.[212] The Ostrogothic segment is the most straightforward. Attila again occupies much space, with a lengthy account of his death and the breakup of the Hunnic Empire, but the Ostrogoths manage nevertheless to remain at the forefront of the story.[213]

Throughout, very little reference is made to precise chronology. The narrative once leaps from the fourth century B.C. to Sulla (who died in 78 B.C.) and skips lightly from there to Julius Caesar, Tiberius, and Domitian (who died in 44 B.C., A.D. 37 and 96 respectively).[214] Although Gothic kings are prominent, their presentation bears little resemblance to the formulaic order of Roman kings and emperors in the *Romana*.[215] Digressions, often consisting of elaborate geographic descriptions and catalogues of peoples, vie for attention with the unfolding of events. Jordanes avoids this device elsewhere.[216] He did not completely exclude colorful or spicy anec-

[209] *Get.* ¶ 246. The three sections are, respectively, ¶¶ 3-130, 131-245, 246-314. The preface occupies ¶¶ 1-2.

[210] On the contrary, as noted below. A fundamental division is presupposed even in *Get.* ¶ 98: "cuius [i.e. Ostrogothae regis] adhuc imperio tam Ostrogothae quam Vesegothae, id est utrique eiusdem gentis populi, subiacebant" (Mommsen accepts the reading *gentes*).

[211] *Get.* ¶¶ 178-227; i.e. 50/114 of the second segment, 44 percent if paragraphs were of equal length.

[212] *Get.* ¶¶ 67-72.

[213] Huns, *Get.* ¶¶ 254-64, 265-67 (the Ostrogoths turn up briefly at the close of ¶ 264). Wolfram, "Theogonie," p. 81, may be right to say that the Amal genealogy is the backbone of the book. Nevertheless, the Amals are absent from all of section 2. The narrative is less coherent in their absence.

[214] *Get.* ¶¶ 67-68. Philip of Macedon and Alexander are in ¶ 66!

[215] For the formula, n. 143 above. *Get.* ¶¶ 90 (Ostrogotha just turns up), 116 (Ermanaric), 146, 158, 164 (the closest one comes to a formula is the indication, in 121, 164, 170, of position in the Amal line), 176, 218, 229, 234 (rare reference to a regnal year), 244-45 (almost a formula, but at the very end), 246-50, 288, 304.

[216] Listed in the analytical table of contents: Mommsen, Preface, pp. xviii-xx (Mierow, pp. 47-50).

dotes from the Roman history; the downfall of Cleopatra, the two wives of Valentinian I, and the adventures of Illus under Zeno stand out from the relation of *res gestae*.[217] Legendary tales are somewhat more prominent in the *Getica*. For example, Visigothic kings are most memorable for the dramatic circumstances of their deaths.[218]

Despite the legends and unverifiable barbarian exploits, much of the *Getica*, especially in the Visigothic segment, narrates Roman history and may be checked, often from sources consulted by Jordanes and even, in many cases, on the basis of his own part II. Whereas his *Romana* is creditably accurate, the *Getica* harbors conspicuous blunders. The emperor Maximinus was not succeeded by Philip the Arab.[219] Few would agree that Troy in the third century A.D. could have only "lately recovered" from the Trojan War.[220] The emperor Gratian allegedly "retreated from Rome to Gaul because of the Vandals" and was killed by the usurper Eugenius; in reality, the Vandals came nowhere near Gratian, whose main capital was always Trier, as it was that of his slayer, the usurper Maximus.[221] In the fanciful version of the *Getica*, the Battle of Pollentia (402) triggers Alaric's Sack of Rome (410) and is soon followed by a second sacking, this time at the hands of Athaulf.[222] Although the Visigoths are never shown as residents of Pannonia, the Vandals and Alans are said to have fled from there to Gaul for fear that the Goths "should return."[223] Wallia, king of the Visigoths from 415 to 418, is credited with a twelfth year of rule.[224] The Romans break their treaty with the Visigoths in 439, on account of the doings of Gaïnas, dead in 400.[225] Beaten in one Gallic battle, Attila cannot resist returning for a second try; it turns out "in much the same way as before."[226] The author of the *Romana* did not have to look far in order to avoid these enormities. Their occurrence in the *Getica* is a further indication that he treated

[217] *Rom.* ¶¶ 250-54, 310-11 (from Socrates *H.E.* 4.31), 349-53.

[218] One problem is how to define a legend. The account of migration from Scandza in the fifteenth century B.C. is imaginary, rather than documentary, but wholly lacks circumstantial details (*Get.* ¶ 25-26); the death and burial of Attila are colorful (¶¶ 254-58), but may be from a historical source (Priscus). What follows is a conservative list: the broken bridge (¶ 27), the foundation of Marcianople (¶ 89), the origin of the Huns (¶¶ 121-24), Ermanaric and Sunilda (¶¶ 129-30), the burial of Alaric (¶ 156), the death of Athaulf (¶ 163), the death of Thorismund (¶ 228). See, for comparison, *Get.* ¶¶ 49-57, 58-60, 84-86, 103, 183, 208, 214-15, 276-79.

[219] *Get.* ¶ 88; cf. *Rom* ¶¶ 281-83.

[220] *Get.* ¶ 108. A blunder or humorous hyperbole?

[221] *Get.* ¶¶ 141, 145; cf. *Rom.* ¶¶ 309, 312, 316.

[222] *Get.* ¶¶ 154, 156, 159.

[223] *Get.* ¶ 161; cf. *Rom.* ¶ 322.

[224] *Get.* ¶ 166. Cf. Bury, *Later Roman Empire from Death of Theodosius I*, 205; Stein, *Bas-Empire* I, 267.

[225] *Get.* ¶ 176; cf. *Rom.* ¶ 320.

[226] *Get.* ¶¶ 225-27. Jordanes is not alone. Procopius *Wars* 3.4.24, 29, ed. H. B. Dewing, Loeb, 7 vols. (London 1914-40), implies two Western campaigns.

the Goths to history of a very different sort from that written in parts I and II.

When, some pages ago, the *Getica* was compared to what may be independently known of the substance of Cassiodorus's Gothic history, it was found that Jordanes omitted or, more rarely, garbled astonishing quantities of pertinent information.[227] Internal evidence leads to the same conclusion, particularly in the cases of the Visigothic kingdom of Toulouse and of the great Ostrogoth, Theodoric.

Jordanes's narrative of the Visigoths in Gaul involves an almost systematic substitution of alien history for Gothic. Concerning Wallia, we hear first of the elimination of Roman usurpers, then of Gaiserich and the Vandals in Africa down to their suppression; Theodorid I and Thorismund are almost entirely overshadowed by Attila; the reign of Theodorid II is fully occupied by the affairs of the Sueves in Spain; Euric, greatest of the kings of Toulouse, is almost incidental to an account of the last decades of the Western Empire; and Alaric II occasions only an anticipation of his downfall and that of his kingdom.[228] The topics Jordanes features are not irrelevant to the rulers in question; in the most conspicuous instance, the Visigoths were no doubt the key to victory over Attila. Yet a sincere historian of the Goths might have found other things to say as well. He is unlikely to have reduced the great Athanaric (whom Isidore of Seville would consider to be the first Gothic king) to the role of a goggle-eyed visitor to Constantinople, or to have tucked away the emperor Avitus, friend and protégé of Visigothic kings, as an afterthought to an account of his son, the *dux et nobilissimus senator* Ecdicius, last leader of Roman resistance in southern Gaul.[229] One keenly misses the version of Cassiodorus. The evasive approach Jordanes adopted seems poorly designed for a genuine celebration of Goths.

Nowhere is the ambiguous relation of Jordanes to his theme more glaring than in the treatment of Theodoric. Some have imagined, for this reason, that Cassiodorus stopped short of his patron's rule.[230] That view is a high price to pay in order to exculpate Jordanes. To suppose (with Brunhölzl) that Cassiodorus stressed the ancient Goths at the expense of recent ones

[227] Above at nn. 87-91.

[228] By a rough count, *Get.* ¶¶ 164-243 (Wallia to Alaric II) contain 469 lines of which about 244 (52 percent) are irrelevant to Visigothic history. There is next to nothing on the internal organization (let alone internal history) of the kingdom of Toulouse.

[229] Athanaric: *Get.* ¶¶ 142-44; cf. Stein, *Bas-Empire* I, 186, 188, 191, 193; Wolfram, *Gesch. d. Goten*, pp. 68-83. His conflicts with Valens in the 360s are reported by Ammianus, an author known at least indirectly to Jordanes (Mommsen, Preface, pp. xxiii-iv). Avitus: *Get.* ¶ 240; cf. Stein, I, 368-74.

[230] Schirren, *De ratione*, p. 92; Cipolla, "Considerazioni," p. 115 (decides against the possibility).

is only another device for reconciling the *Getica*'s anomalous treatment of Theodoric with the idea of a slavish abridgment of the long Gothic history.[231] The main flaw of the *Getica* in regard to Theodoric resides in what Jordanes chose to omit. The fourteen years during which Theodoric ruled the Ostrogoths in the Balkans (474-88) are to all intents suppressed; the vicissitudes of his campaign against Odoacer are glossed over; the account of his thirty-six-year reign in Italy is limited to foreign affairs.[232] Information could hardly have been lacking in Constantinople. There were extensive sources about the reign of Zeno, during which Theodoric was active in the Eastern Empire, and even Procopius and John Malalas, contemporary fellow-Byzantines of Jordanes, found flattering things to say about Theodoric in Italy.[233] Nothing of the sort graces the *Getica*.

The unlikelihood that Jordanes's silences concerning Theodoric were accidental tends to be confirmed when the little that he does narrate about the great Ostrogoth turns out to fall far short of glorification. By his account, Theodoric, at age seven, becomes a token of peace with the Romans and, as a hostage, wins imperial favor. Sent home eventually, with great gifts, he at once takes off on his own and seizes Singidunum without returning it to the Romans. He joins his father, Thiudimir, in successfully invading imperial territory.[234] Thiudimir, "perceiving his own and his son's good fortune and still not content"—a phrase often applied to usurpers and, by the historian Socrates, to Alaric marching on Rome—pushes on to threaten Thessalonica.[235] By this move, the Goths exact an advantageous

[231] According to Brunhölzl, *Gesch. d. lat. Lit.* I, 30, Jordanes's summary shows that Cassiodorus's center of gravity was "ältere Geschichte," in line with his object of proving Gothic antiquity and thus respectability. "Ancient" is undefined, but the comment seems to leave out of account that only one-third of the *Get.* concerns events before the 370s.

[232] Theodoric in the Balkans: *Get.* ¶ 209 (swallowed up in the account of Zeno's pouring honors upon him); cf. Bury, *Later Roman Empire from Death of Theodosius* I, 411-22; Wolfram, *Gesch. d. Goten*, pp. 335-46 (I have followed Wolfram's 474 rather than Bury's 471, but retain an open mind); Demougeot, "Bedeutet das Jahre 476 das Ende des römischen Reiches im Okzident?" pp. 376-78; Šašel, "Antiqui barbari." Italian campaign: *Get.* ¶¶ 292-94; omits an early setback and Visigothic assistance, about which Bury, I, 423-24; Wolfram, p. 350. Theodoric's rule in Italy, *Get.* ¶¶ 295-302; modern accounts, of course, have more to say, much of it based on Cassiodorus's *Variae*.

[233] Malchus Fragm. 18, 21, ed. Blockley, *Classicising Historians* II, 421, 427-29; Procopius *Wars* 5.1. 9-39, esp. 26-31; Johannes Malalas *Chronographia* 15, ed. Ludwig Dindorff, Corpus scriptorum historiae Byzantinae (Bonn 1831), pp. 383-84. Malalas incorporates Theodoric's career in the reign of Zeno and gives no indication that he was a Goth or a barbarian. On Procopius's account of Theodoric (and much else), see now Cameron, *Procopius*, pp. 192-93, 198-99. Reydellet, *Royauté*, pp. 287-88, recognizes that Jordanes's Theodoric is an ambiguous figure.

[234] *Get.* ¶¶ 269 (born *bona spei*), 271 (hostage), 281 (return), 282 (acts *inscio patre*, keeps Singidunum), 283, 285.

[235] Socrates *H.E.* 2.34 (Gallus), 5.25 (Eugenius), 6.6 (Gaïnas), 7.10 (Alaric), cf. 7.33 (John). I doubt that the phrase is peculiar to Socrates. Cf. *Get.* ¶ 222, Attila is talked out of

peace, but Thiudimir shortly dies (like Alaric after sacking Rome), naming Theodoric as his heir. The emperor Zeno then summons Theodoric to Constantinople and loads him with honors: adoption as son in arms, a triumph, the eponymous consulate, and an equestrian statue. That he was made a patrician is omitted. Even so, the Constantinopolitan phase looks, to a reader of the *Getica*, like the high point of Theodoric's life.[236] But Theodoric "chose rather to seek a livelihood by exertion after the usual manner of his people."[237]

In proposing to Zeno that he should conquer Italy in the emperor's name, Theodoric remembers enough of his Constantinopolitan upbringing to utter traditional Roman sentiments about the utility of barbarians: "If I prevail, I shall hold [Italy] by your grant and gift; if I am overcome, Your Piety loses nothing, indeed . . . you will save the cost I now entail."[238] He marches to Italy with the Goths, wins one battle, besieges Ravenna for three years, and ends the campaign by first promising Odoacer his life and then killing him. With Zeno's consent (though Zeno had in fact died and been replaced), he becomes the ruler of Goths and Romans alike.[239] His Italian reign, as portrayed, boils down to a few initiatives in foreign affairs. He arranges a long series of marriages between his family and neighboring barbarian kings. The general he sends to seize Sirmium also helps Mundo, a chief of outlaws, ruffians, and vagabonds, to destroy the Roman army of Illyricum; Mundo becomes Theodoric's grateful subject. Another general of his wins a battle over the Franks, and a third serves creditably as guardian over the Visigoths.[240] Dying, Theodoric names his grandson king and urges his assembled companions and chieftains to love the Senate and people of Rome and to retain the goodwill of the emperor, as next after God.

The total impression is of an authentically untrustworthy barbarian who

---

marching on Rome by the example of Alaric, who did not long survive its capture; Attila's followers feared for his *fortuna*.

[236] *Get.* ¶ 289. The omission of the patriciate is striking; Malchus Fragm. 20 (18), ed. Blockley, *Classicising Historians* II, 445; Procopius *Wars* 5.1.9; Ensslin, *Theoderich der Grosse*, p. 44.

[237] *Get.* ¶ 290 (quotation from Mierow tr., p. 135): "elegit potius solito more gentis suae labore querere victum." This sounds more complimentary to our ears than it did, one imagines, in the sixth century.

[238] *Get.* ¶ 291. For the idea that no sight is more pleasing to Romans than that of barbarians fighting each other, *Panegyrici latini* 3.16-17; cf. Burian, "Der Gegensatz zwischen Rom und den Barbaren," pp. 95-96. Orosius 7.43: barbarians spontaneously offer to kill one another for the greater delectation of the Roman emperor. Later than Jordanes, Menander Protector fragm. 5.2: "This . . . was a very wise move, since whether the Avars prevailed or were defeated, both eventualities would be to the Romans' advantage" (R. C. Blockley, ed. and tr., *The History of Menander the Guardsman*, Arca 17 [Liverpool 1985], p. 51).

[239] *Get.* ¶ 295 (cf. Malalas above, n. 233). Zeno died April 491; Theodoric became supreme in March 493: Stein, *Bas-Empire* II, 57-58, 76.

[240] The striking passage concerns Mundo, *Get.* ¶¶ 300-301. About him, Wosniak, "Lombard-Gepidic Wars," pp. 142-47, and Croke, "Mundo the Gepid."

is occasionally softened by the generosity and kindness of the Empire. The facts related are quite inadequate to document Theodoric's fame. Jordanes, rightly expecting that readers of the *Getica* would be aware of the king's reputation, bridges the gap between common knowledge and his narrative by sustaining a semblance of praise.[241] His own highly ambivalent version of Theodoric's career loses none of its force from such dilution.

These comments on the oddities of the *Getica*—its loose construction, historical howlers, and conspicuous avoidance of the ostensible subject— are not meant to disparage Jordanes but to portray him as a more complicated and difficult author than he is generally taken to be. Parts I and II of his little historical library reveal the hand of a Byzantine fully in tune with the circumstances of the 550s; Jordanes relates many vicissitudes of Belisarius's first campaign against the Goths that are not carried into part III, and he is grimly conversant with the Gothic revival under Totila.[242] The author of the *Getica* familiar to modern scholarship is a naïve Goth who eagerly reports the past of his people, mechanically copies Cassiodorus, and fears that he might be thought to exaggerate Gothic glory. A better candidate for the role of author is the sober and able complier of the *Romana* whom we have learned to know. The *Getica*, with its colorful legends, glaring blunders, and vast omissions, is a carefully structured piece of literature. The problem we face, once its obvious shortcomings are catalogued, is to determine another reason for its composition than admiring commemoration of the Goths and their Amal kings. In the latter perspective, the *Getica* is too contemptuous of its subject to make any sense. The ambiguous contents of the book are predictable anyway from its time of composition: the early 550s cannot have been a propitious moment for a Constantinopolitan to set about sincerely celebrating the Goths.[243] A different orientation is suggested if the *Getica* is examined in the light of its climax. The most startling and subversive feature of Jordanes's narrative is its happy ending.

8. The *Getica*: History with a Happy Ending

The dramatic close of the *Getica* has won prominence from Momigliano's interest in its reference, unique in Jordanes's works, to the great Roman family of the Anicii, and to the union of that family with the

---

[241] A child of good hope (¶ 269), a goodly child (¶ 271), eschews comfort when his people are in want (¶ 290), expresses proper Roman sentiments (¶ 291), Zeno sorry to see him go (¶ 292), while he lives the Goths resist the Franks (¶ 296), cares for and protects Amalaric (¶ 298), wins victories through generals (¶¶ 300, 302), has hegemony over Western peoples (¶ 303).

[242] *Rom.* ¶¶ 370, 374, 375; 378-83.

[243] Above, at nn. 39-43.

Gothic Amals.[244] An even better reason for closely studying this passage is its relation to the book as a whole. Jordanes writes that, with the surrender of Vitiges, the Gothic sovereignty and people were vanquished by Justinian through his very faithful consul Belisarius; Vitiges was taken to Constantinople, made a patrician, and died after two years of enjoying the emperor's favor; Justinian then united Vitiges's widow, Matasuntha (Theodoric's granddaughter), to his cousin, the patrician Germanus; and to this couple, after Germanus's premature death, a son was born, also named Germanus: "In him the union of the Anician family with the Amal stock continues, with the Lord's favor, to promise hope to both lineages [or peoples]."[245] The *Getica* goes on for two more paragraphs, but only to bring the author to the front of the stage, inviting applause for himself and Justinian. The action effectively terminates with the birth of Germanus and the hopeful promise that his mixed blood holds for the two *genera* of Anicii/Romans and Amali/ Ostrogoths.

Readers of the *Getica* have been well prepared for this ending, though not for its Anician twist. Three-fifths of the way through the opening segment (¶81), the full Amal genealogy is laid out, with careful attention to the last links in the chain:

Vitiges united with Matasuntha, from whom no child issued. Both were brought to Constantinople by Belisarius, and, when Vitiges died, the patrician Germanus, son of the brother of the emperor Justinian's father, took [Matasuntha] in marriage and made her a patrician ordinary; and he had by her a son also called Germanus. When [the elder] Germanus died, she resolved to remain a widow. However, we shall tell in its proper place, if the Lord lends assistance, how and in what way the sovereignty (*regnum*) of the Amals was destroyed.[246]

---

[244] Momigliano, "Cassiodorus and Ital. Culture," pp. 189-95; see above, n. 25. Also on the ending (without reference to the Anicii), Schirren, *De ratione*, pp. 90-92; Wattenbach-Levison, *Geschichtsquellen*, p. 78, which anticipates the exaggerations of Wes, *Ende des Kaisertums*, pp. 191-92.

[245] *Get.* ¶¶ 313-314: "nec mora ultro se ad partes dedit victoris cum Mathesuentha iugale regiasque opes. Et sic famosum regnum fortissimamque gentem diuque regnantem tandem pene duomillensimo et tricesimo anno victor gentium diversarum Iustinianus imperator per fidelissimum consulem vicit Belesarium, et perductum Vitiges Constantinopolim patricii honore donavit. Ubi plus biennio demoratus imperatorisque in affectu coniunctus rebus excessit humanis. Mathesuentham vero iugalem eius fratr[uel]i suo Germano patricio coniunxit imperator. De quibus post humatum patris Germani natus est filius idem Germanus. In quo coniuncta Aniciorum genus cum Amala stirpe spem adhuc utriusque generi domino praestante promittit." Note that the only memorable date mentioned is 540, the surrender of Vitiges. Unless one remembers the date Jordanes advertises for the *Romana* (year 24 of Justinian), one might imagine that Matasuntha's widowhood, remarriage, and bearing of Germanus Postumus took place nearer to 545 than to 550. The period after Vitiges's death (542) has a timeless quality, which affects *adhuc*. Barnish, "Genesis and Completion," p. 353, rightly regards *spem adhuc utriusque generi* as being meant in a broad sense, not familial but racial (his word) and political; see below.

[246] *Get.* ¶81: "Mathesuenthae Vitigis est copulatus, de quo non suscepit liberum; adduc-

The cast of characters is listed; young Germanus is identified with the destruction of Amal kingship; and a vital detail, never again mentioned, is spelled out: because Matasuntha had vowed not to remarry, she or her son was the end of the line.

In case this genealogy might not be retained by forgetful readers, its relevant parts occur again very near the start of the third, or Ostrogothic, segment. The context is an account of the detached branch of the Amals from which issued Eutharic, the husband of Theodoric's daughter, Amalasuntha, and, by her, the father of Matasuntha. Jordanes supplies little more at this point than a reminder of essential names and relationships. With the marriage of Eutharic and Amalasuntha, the two branches of the Amals were joined. Of the two children of this union, the son died while still a boy; the daughter, Matasuntha, was brought to Constantinople and, by her second husband, Germanus, cousin of the emperor, she bore a posthumous son, whom she called Germanus.[247] The double anticipation of this ending assures us that little Germanus marks the point at which Jordanes concludes his story. The weight given to Germanus's birth is deliberate.[248]

Its importance cannot have resided in the Anicii, even though their abrupt appearance is more than an incidental detail. There probably was a factual basis for the reference, as Momigliano conceded; various suggestions have been made as to what this basis might be.[249] Yet Momigliano was right

tique simul a Belesario Constantinopolim: et Vitigis rebus excedente humanis Germanus patricius fratruelis Iustiniani imp. eam in conubio sumens patriciam ordinariam fecit; de qua et genuit filium item Germanum nomine. Germano vero defuncto ipsa vidua perseverare disponit. Quomodo autem aut qualiter regnum Amalorum distructum est, loco suo, si dominus iubaverit, edicimus." To underline the completed character of the history to be narrated, ¶ 82, "Nunc autem ad id, unde digressum fecimus, redeamus doceamusque, quomodo ordo gentis, unde agimus, cursus sui metam explevit."

[247] *Get.* ¶ 251: "Eutharicus, qui, iunctus Amalasuenthae filiae Theodorici, item Amalorum stirpe iam divisa coniunxit et genuit Athalaricum et Mathesuentham. Sed quia Athalaricus in annis puerilibus defunctus est, Mathesuentha Constantinopolim allata de secundo viro, id est Germano fratruele Iustiniani imperatoris, genuit postumum filium, quem nominavit Germanum."

[248] The conceivable alternative ending is the surrender of Vitiges, the one event of genuine historical importance narrated at the close of the *Getica*. But Jordanes gives us little reason to infer that this is his proper terminal point. He dwells only for a moment on the surrender, noting the passing of Gothic sovereignty after 2,030 years. His comment is too brief and incidental to qualify as the end of the narrative. He moves into the sequel in the same sentence and without change of tone. The surrender of 540 is never anticipated, whereas the birth of Germanus is associated with the end of Gothic kingship and twice drawn to our attention. After it occurs, narrative stops (as it does not after Vitiges's surrender); Jordanes turns directly to the audience and invites applause. Cf. the interpretation of Sybel, n. 252 below.

[249] Wes, *Ende des Kaisertums*, pp. 189-90, casts doubt on the Anician link. It is defended by Wagner, *Getica*, pp. 54-59. Krautschick, *Cassiodor u. d. Politik*, pp. 17-18, disputes the latter's view that there was nothing remarkable about Jordanes's comment.

Alan Cameron, in a communication ("Cassiodorus, Jordanes and the Anicii") to the 11th Byzantine Studies Conference, showed that Germanus Senior could not possibly have Anician blood and that, in any case, the Eastern Anicii prized their imperial ancestry over their

to insist that this kinship, whatever it amounted to, hardly suffices to explain why the obvious tie of Germanus Postumus to the imperial family is subordinated to his merely noble relatives. There is a problem, but Cassiodorus is not its solution. Although as a Westerner he was certainly conscious of the Anicii and admired them, it does not follow that (as Momigliano intimated) all authors except him would have silenced the Anician link and, instead, taken the occasion to celebrate the union of "the royal family of Ravenna with the imperial family of Constantinople."[250] For there was no "royal family of Ravenna" in the 550s.

The exaltation of Amal royalty by association with imperial purple would have been out of character with Jordanes's handling of Gothic kings. As early as paragraph 81, he stresses the end of Amal kingship. Moreover, he insists that King Vitiges surrendered the sovereignty of the Ostrogoths to Belisarius and Justinian.[251] At the time of Matasuntha's marriage ten years later, the royal Amals belonged to history. What was left to them was a genealogy extending sixteen generations into the past and forming a resplendent lineage. No harm would come from allowing this line to join with families of comparable antiquity. Jordanes's pairing of the Amals with the Anicii situated the ex-kings of the Goths in the social slot appropriate to so ancient a line—not the emperorship of Constantinople, but the blood nobility of the city of Rome.

The function of the passage in which the Anicii figure acquires its proper value when recognized to be the carefully prepared climax of the entire *Getica*. Long ago, Heinrich von Sybel interpreted it with admirable clarity. Throughout the book, he said, Jordanes prepared the opinion that he openly declared at the end: "The Romans and Goths, who had long been friends and allies, were now to be completely joined together; Germanus

---

Anician forebears. He maintained, however, that in order to account for Jordanes's sentence, there had to be some sort of link between Germanus and the Anicii (perhaps by marriage). So long as this is conceded to be the case, Cassiodorus's hand might be discerned behind this name, but only (to depart now from Cameron) on condition that none but Cassiodorus had a motive for evoking Germanus's tenuous Anician connection.

[250] Momigliano, "Cassiodorus and Ital. Culture," pp. 194-95; cf. n. 24 above. The crux of his argument is that an account which neglects the imperial and royal connections and portrays the marriage "as a union of the Roman family of the Anicii with the Amali" is intelligible only as Jordanes's abridgment of something longer by Cassiodorus: the latter would have made sense of the hardly self-evident connection between Germanus and the Anicii, and he alone, owing to reverence for the Anicii, had a compelling reason to subordinate royalty to nobility. Momigliano leaves out of account Jordanes's other announcements of the marriage (above, nn. 245-47): Germanus's kinship to Justinian is mentioned each of the three times; but that to the Anicii only once, in a very special context. I gather from Cameron (as n. 249), that Cassiodorus is no longer taken to be related to the Anicii.

[251] As just seen above, n. 245. A reader of the *Get.* is notified as early as ¶ 81 that the goal of the book is the end of Amal royalty, an event compatible with the continuation of the Amal family.

Junior is displayed as the outstanding example of this affinity, and both peoples are to consider [this example] with the utmost respect."²⁵² To portray the fall of the Ostrogothic kingdom in 540 as a happy event in itself would surely have struck a false note in a history of the Goths. Even the death of the elder Germanus is distractingly realistic, though unavoidable. Jordanes made the most of the assets available to him. He provided a marriage, however brief, between (in effect) a prince and a princess, each symbolic of his people; a child was born to them, uniting noble *genera* and promising hope to both. The author then materialized to praise the valiant general and triumphant emperor whose conquest he had recorded.²⁵³ Lines like these, far from straightforwardly aligning facts, are what Henry James ironically described as "a distribution at the last of prizes, pensions, husbands, wives, babies, millions, appended paragraphs, and cheerful remarks."²⁵⁴

There is no mistaking the dramatic import of Jordanes's closing words: he is supplying a happy ending to his story. He concludes, characteristically, with a family festival, not the ideal one—a wedding—but at least a blessed event, in the wake of which "a new society crystallizes" and benefits from a "a general assumption of post-dated innocence in which everyone lives happily ever after."²⁵⁵ The vision that Jordanes projects is of a new society, symbolized by the infant Germanus, in which Romans and Goths intermarry and, in their progeny and in submission to Justinian's empire, become one. This new society does not belong to an uncertain future; the child is born, the society he symbolizes exists.

Jordanes's happy ending bears a paradoxical relationship to external events: the news was terrible in 551, yet a baby was supposed to fill the audience with joy and hope. Momigliano and others have suggested that the birth of Germanus Postumus was a good time for someone to write a Gothic history with an optimistic ending. This is quite wrong; the time could not have been worse chosen, for "the surprising death of Germanus Senior in 550 put an end to all expectations."²⁵⁶ Jordanes himself, in the *Romana*, shows clear awareness that baby Germanus was politically irrelevant and that the situation in early 551, when the *Getica*'s blessed event is situated, was not at all joyous.²⁵⁷

---

²⁵² Sybel, *De fontibus Jordanis*, pp. 44-45.

²⁵³ *Get.* ¶¶ 313 (fall of the kingdom), 314 (marriage, death, birth), 315-16 (cheers for the Goths, Justinian, Belisarius, and the author).

²⁵⁴ Quoted in Kermode, *Sense of an Ending*, p. 22.

²⁵⁵ Frye, *Anatomy of Criticism*, pp. 44, 162.

²⁵⁶ Demandt, "Spätrömische Militäradel," p. 627. Germanus died a few months after marrying Matasuntha. For the view that early 551 was a good moment for Jordanes's enterprise, Momigliano, "Cassiodoro," p. 496; Barnish, "Genesis and Completion," p. 359; also see below, § 10.

²⁵⁷ See below, at nn. 360-62, about *Rom.* ¶ 383.

Elaborate celebrations greeted the birth of children to the emperor, but no evidence suggests that an imperial relative as distant as little Germanus occasioned public festivity.[258] Even in the remote eventuality that he did, Jordanes at the critical moment deliberately diverts us from this interpretation: he omits Germanus's imperial kinship and features the Anicii instead. The infant was not memorable because marginally imperial; much more than ceremonial formality made his birth a happy event. He gave hope to the Anicii/Romans and the Amali/Ostrogoths by being the innocent babe exemplifying their total union because the blood of both flowed in him.

Jordanes writes as though this union were an accomplished fact; newborn children are not contingencies. Yet, in the season of Germanus's birth, the Ostrogoths were farther than ever from union with the Romans, and the birth changed nothing. Neither as fact nor as symbol does the ending of the *Getica* reflect real life in 551. Jordanes's words certainly imply public jubilation; they have been read in this way by everyone, Momigliano included. Yet Constantinople had no reason whatever for festivity concerning Ostrogothic affairs. The Byzantine position in Italy had been miserable since the advent of Totila in 541 and would not improve until the total defeat of the Italian Goths in 552.

The "happy ending" of the *Getica* is a deliberate literary contrivance. Why Jordanes wished to conclude on this optimistic note has much to do with the purpose, the intended destination, and, most of all, the date of both his books—issues that will be considered in due course. The more urgent question is what the ending implies for an understanding of the *Getica* as a whole.

"Happy endings" are not incidental features of the narratives that contain them; they are signposts of a type of plot whose general outline is familiar to everyone: "take two or more persons who belong together (for instance, a pair of lovers), . . . separate them violently, subject them to all sorts of hair raising adventures by land and sea, reunite them at the end, cause them to recognize one another, and so let all end happily."[259] That a historical narrative should be cast in the form of a traditional, happily ending love story is neither implausible nor strange. Works whose overt or underlying theme is deliverance, rather than mere survival, tend to end on a hopeful note; "[At their close] . . . we normally have the vision of a group

---

[258] Constantine Porphyrogenitus *De caeremoniis aulae Byzantinae* 2.21-22, ed. J. J. Rieske, 2 vols., Corpus scriptorum historiae Byzantinae (Bonn 1829-30) I, 615-20; Otto Treitinger, *Die oströmische Kaiser- und Reichsidee nach ihrer Gestaltung im höfischen Zeremoniell*, 2nd ed. (Darmstadt 1956), pp. 108-10. I am very grateful to Professor Evangelos Chrysos for bibliography on this aspect of the subject.

[259] J. H. Delargy, quoted in Scobie, "Storytellers, Storytelling, and the Novel," p. 252.

of people going off the stage or page to begin a new kind of life."[260] Jordanes, in his Roman history, gave survival its painful due. But he also had
news of a deliverance and, presumably, an audience to which that message
could appropriately be conveyed.

As just noted, a plot of this sort normally involves two lovers, male and
female. They "belong together" but are blocked by restrictions that the
course of the action tends to remove. Their union is usually impeded by
obstructive characters, such as a father or other parental figures; some structural obstacle, such as an absurd law, often intrudes as well. To even the
scales, there are helpful characters who assist the lovers' romantic quest.
One of them is normally instrumental in effecting the twist in story that
dissolves the impediments and allows all to end happily. The wedding or
other family festival marking the desired union of the lovers presupposes a
general reconciliation; because the "bad" characters are merely deluded
rather than villainous, it is understood that their obstructions end, and that
they like everyone else share in the joy of the outcome.[261]

Does the happy ending of the *Getica* refer only to the Anicians and the
Amals, or do the two families simultaneously symbolize the Romans and
the Ostrogoths as a whole? The book as a love story must signify that at least
the Amals were predestined for union with a Roman family. Its unmistakable message is one of fusion and assimilation. This idea seems to have been
translated into social terms and extended to all the Romans and Ostrogoths. Constantine and Theodosius I, the great Christian emperors, are
among the few genuinely "helpful" Romans in the *Getica*. Jordanes records
the recruitment under the first of 40,000 Goths "whose corps and service is
renowned to the present day in the state, namely, the *foederati*." This military corps founded by Constantine was revived, we learn, when Theodosius welcomed the Gothic troops of the deceased Athanaric, and "they were
called *foederati*."[262] The corps Jordanes referred to was not, in fact, a fourth-
century institution but a comparatively recent one, a major element of the
sixth-century army list; its renown "to the present day" was a more certain
and useful fact than its Constantinian creation. Procopius specifies in the
Wars that, though once restricted to barbarians "who had come into the
Roman political system . . . on the basis of complete equality," the *foederati*
of Justinian's day were open to enlistment by native Romans and barbarians
alike.[263] If union with the very noble Anicii supplied the very noble Amals

[260] Frye, *Myth of Deliverance*, p. 14.

[261] Frye, *Anatomy of Criticism*, pp. 44, 163, 172-77.

[262] *Get.* ¶¶ 112, 145.

[263] Procopius *Wars* 3.11.3-4; Jones, *Later Roman Empire*, pp. 663-64. These *foederati* should
not be confused with "federates" of the sort associated with the fifth-century barbarian kingdoms in Gaul. Recognition of the anachronistic character of Jordanes's *foederati*: Teall, "Barbarians in Justinian's Armies," pp. 296-97; Chrysos, "Gothia Romana," pp. 53-54.

with their due place in society, the mixed corps of the imperial *foederati*—perhaps standing for the whole Roman army—was a no less worthy and suitable destination for the Amals' erstwhile subjects. In other words, the plot of the *Getica* centers on the love between two peoples, Romans and Goths, not just between two families.

If these considerations help to clarify the close of Jordanes's tale, at least as much may be learned from determining its starting point. To look for this beginning in the migration of the Goths from Scandinavia would be a mistake.[264] Despite all the modern attention this legend has received, even a superficial reading of the *Getica* reveals that the move from Scandza and its Scythian sequel have very limited bearing on any later part of the book. The early legends are saved from isolation mainly by serving to tag the Gepids as detached Goths and the Huns as demonic Goths.[265] For the genuine Goths, whether Visi- or Ostro-, the tale of their origin in the distant North and most of their Scytho-Getic adventures are colorful but inconsequential. The tagging of the Amazons as Goths is, as we shall see, the exception that proves the rule.[266] Down to paragraph 76 the narrative is a prologue or hors d'oeuvre.

The *Getica* properly speaking starts *in medias res*: "A long time [after the forty years of Coryllus's rule], during the reign of the emperor Domitian, the Goths feared his avarice [and as a result] broke the treaty that they had long observed with other emperors."[267] Before this, Jordanes had mentioned Sulla, Julius Caesar, and Tiberius, but neither they nor other Romans had had any contact with the Goths.[268] That contact, however made, took place off-stage. The Goths suddenly materialize in a guise not very distant from the one they have at the end, as treaty partners of the Romans enjoying imperial bounty, and the action moves at once into the first of its most characteristically recurring incidents: fearing interruption or denial of their consecrated Roman subsidies, the Goths attack the Empire.[269]

---

[264] *Get.* ¶¶ 4-25. For discussion, below § 9.

[265] *Get.* ¶¶ 94-95, 121-22: these are the only later allusions to the migration story; for the reason why Jordanes linked the origin legends, § 9 below.

[266] Below at nn. 290-91.

[267] *Get.* ¶ 76: "Longum namque post intervallum Domitiano imperatore regnante eiusque avaritiam metuentes foedus, quod dudum cum aliis principibus pepigerant, Gothi solventes." For Coryllus, ¶ 73. In between, Jordanes sets a geographic digression on "Gothia, which the ancients used to call Dacia and which the Gepids now inhabit" (¶¶ 74-75). Dacia became Gothia after being evacuated by the Romans in the third century: Wolfram, *Gesch. d. Goten*, p. 10.

[268] *Get.* ¶¶ 67-68. Adapting a passage of Orosius about the Getae, Jordanes eloquently asserts that even Caesar avoided tangling with the Goths. When Rome was already at its third emperor (Tiberius), "Gothi tamen suo regno incolume perseverant." I would read this to mean that they "retained their own sovereignty" rather than that they "existed under their own kings."

[269] *Get.* ¶¶ 76-77: they begin by devastating the banks of the Danube long held by the Em-

In this opening, the notoriously "bad" emperor Domitian leads off the series of Roman characters whose wickedness obstructs the union of the Goths and Romans. He is soon followed by Philip the Arab and several others, all traditionally "bad," down to Arcadius and Honorius. The recurring badness of Roman emperors in the love story consists in neglect of the Goths or an interruption of gifts to them.[270] A special role of this sort is played by the heretic emperor Valens, whose divine punishment of death by fire hardly makes up for the propagation of Arianism among all the Gothic peoples (this impediment is no sooner mentioned by Jordanes than buried in silence).[271] Other obstructors include the generals who drove the Visigoths to rebel and thus prepared the disaster at Adrianople, as well as the treacherous Stilicho, (wrongly) held responsible for Alaric's rampage.[272] In all these cases, Roman history came to Jordanes's assistance. It was comparatively simple to deploy a cast of villains whom tradition already painted black.

Impediments associated with both the aspiring lovers were necessary if the story was to attain its conclusion through appropriate vicissitudes. With no tradition of written history to lean upon, the author had to show greater resourcefulness when dealing with the Gothic side. Here, too, the reign of Domitian is the scene for Jordanes's initial move. The war that the emperor's avarice occasioned resulted in a great Gothic victory over the Romans. When it was won, the Goths "acclaimed their leading men, by whose ostensible good fortune they were victorious, not as plain men but as demigods, that is, Ansis."[273] Jordanes then steps self-consciously forward

---

pire, killing the soldiers and their generals, then defeat the provincial governor, and ultimately win a great victory over the Roman general Fuscus, sent against them with a great army. In proper history, these events of A.D. 86-87 involve the Dacians: *Cambridge Ancient History* XI, 168-71; Iliescu, "Bemerkungen zur Gotenfreundlichen Einstellung," pp. 426-27. There were no Goths within reach of the Roman frontier until the end of the second century.

[270] Domitian: Eutropius *Brev.* 7.23.1. Philip (*Get.* ¶89) is not bad in fourth-century accounts, but becomes so in *H.A. Aurel.* 34.1 and Zosimus *Hist. nova* 1.23.1 and 1.19-22. Diocletian and Maximian (¶110); in the case of the first only, qualities balance faults (Aurelius Victor *Caesares* 39; Eutropius *Brev.* 9.21). Arcadius and Honorius (¶146) were highly esteemed by the fifth-century Church historians, but opinions shifted by Jordanes's time: Zosimus *Hist. nova* 5.1 (emperors only in name, cf. Orosius *Hist.* 7.32); Procopius *Wars* 1.2.6 (Arcadius), 3.2.8-10, 25-26, 3.4 (Honorius only).

[271] *Get.* ¶¶ 131-32, 138; about his reputation, see above, § 4 with n. 102 (the Church historians also spoke badly of him).

[272] *Get.* ¶¶ 134-37 (Ammianus *Rer. gest.* 31. 4-5); ¶¶ 154-55 (Orosius's main chapter about Stilicho comes just before the capture of Rome: *Hist.* 7.38). The idea of Stilicho's treachery long antedated Jordanes. Moderns generally agree that Stilicho's execution (408) and Alaric's inability afterward to reach a satisfactory arrangement with Honorius's court led to the long siege of Rome: Hodgkin, *Italy and Her Invaders* I, 766. Behind Jordanes's idea that an act of treachery incited Alaric to take Rome, there may lie the historical ambush of Alaric by Sarus, which infuriated Alaric and triggered the seizure of the city: Stein, *Bas-Empire* I, 259.

[273] *Get.* ¶ 78, "tum Gothi . . . magnaque potiti per loca victoria iam proceres suos, quorum quasi fortuna vincebant, non puros homines, sed semideos id est Ansis vocaverunt."

and proceeds, with protestations of truthfulness, to list the genealogy of "those heroes," who turn out to be only the Amals.[274] As we have seen, he carries the recitation right down to the infant Germanus and the end of Ostrogothic kingship.

Whatever the documentary value of the genealogy may be, the historical context for its recitation is contrived.[275] It was really the Dacians rather than the Goths who defeated Domitian's army, but because this flaw derives from the identification of Goths with Getae and of Dacia with Gothia, it lacks specific relevance to the Gothic acclamation.[276] The two inconsistencies that undermine the terms of Jordanes's own story are more noteworthy. When the victory over the Romans took place, the *principatus* over the Goths was apparently exercised by Dorpaneus; yet, no such name appears among the men by whose *fortuna* the Goths were victorious.[277] Even more oddly, the Ostrogoths themselves lacked a logical relationship to the war. They are said, right afterward, to have then been settled at the Black Sea, with the Visigoths to the west of them.[278] If so, their Amal chiefs had no business being in Dacia to be hailed as demigods in connection with a victory on the middle Danube. Although the acclamation is crucial to the design of Jordanes's plot, inconsistencies isolate it within the course of his narrative.

The scene loses none of its force for being a dramatic contrivance. Just before unfolding the genealogy that links the beginning and end of the action, Jordanes narrated the event central to his plot. By his account, normality for the Goths involved living under the patriarchal leadership of the

---

[274] *Ibid.*: "quorum genealogia ut paucis percurram vel quis quo parente genitus est aut unde origo coepta, ubi finem effecit, absque invidia, qui legis, vera dicentem ausculta." The term "heroes" occurs in ¶ 79.

[275] For the agreement of the genealogy in number of generations with the seventeen mentioned in Cassiodorus *Var.* 9.25.4, see above, n. 61. Cassiodorus must have drawn up such a list. It is hardly certain, however, that he rather than Jordanes attributed it to native tradition: "ut ipsi [i.e. Gothi] suis in fabulis referunt" (*Get.* ¶ 79). On the contrary, Cassiodorus states that several kings on his list were "hidden" from the Goths and only uncovered by his research among books (above, n. 81).

[276] Above, n. 269. Wolfram, "Methodische Frage zur Kritik," claims that these incidents (notably the Gothic acclamation after the victory) take place "in grauer Vorzeit," a half-millennium before the time of writing. Yet we do not, in relation to ourselves, regard the fifteenth century as "hoary," let alone as *Vorzeit*, and late Romans cannot have imagined that any of the Christian centuries belonged to the distant past.

[277] Compare *Get.* ¶ 76 ("Gothis autem Dorpaneus principatum agebat") with the list in ¶ 79. Jordanes does not specify which Amal coincided with the victory over the Romans.

[278] *Get.* ¶ 82: "Nunc autem ad id, unde digressum fecimus, redeamus doceamusque, quomodo ordo gentis, unde agimus, cursus sui metam explevit. Ablabius enim storicus refert, quia ibi super limbum Ponti, ubi eos diximus in Scythia commanere, ibi pars eorum, qui orientali plaga tenebat, eisque praeerat Ostrogotha, utrum ab ipsius nomine, an a loco, id est orientales, dicti sunt Ostrogothae, residui vero Vesegothae, id est a parte occidua." One could hardly be given a more relentless reply to the question how the Ostrogoths got their name. About Ablabius, see above, n. 208. Jordanes's cross-reference is to ¶¶ 38, 42.

Amals as subsidized friends of the Romans.[279] Domitian disturbed this calm by his avarice; and, in reaction, the Goths further disturbed it by being victorious. The enthusiasm generated among them by this victory only made matters worse. The Amals, though heroic, were mere men. The Goths who acclaimed them as demigods—that is to say, who elevated them from patriarchal chieftaincy to kingship—made the mistake of according divine honors to human beings.[280] The Goths' acclamation created a structural barrier, additional to the human obstructors: it brought into being "the absurd or irrational law" fundamental to the social order that would keep the hero and heroine apart.[281] The perpetuation of this absurdity in the guise of the successive Gothic kings formed the obstacle that Belisarius eventually broke down, allowing the new, long-desired society to materialize in rediscovered innocence.

Because the institution of Gothic kingship was itself a mistake, Jordanes did not, in principle, have to go out of his way to create Gothic counterparts to his cast of Roman obstructors. He would have found it hard, in any case, to fashion "bad Goths" without doing obvious violence to his main source, the panegyrical history of Cassiodorus. No harm would come from naïve endorsement of Cassiodoran praise and tales of valor, provided it was established that kings of the Goths obstructed the action by the simple fact of reigning. Once elevated to more than patriarchal rank—mere men masquerading as demigods—they were clearly impostors.[282] On this understanding, Kings Ostrogotha, Cniva, Geberich, and so forth could go through their paces, damaging the Empire as well as fighting fellow barbarians, without incurring the author's censure. Cassiodorus was mainly edited by omission. Nevertheless, as already observed, Jordanes took pains to cut

---

[279] *Get.* ¶ 42: "Tertia vero sede super mare Ponticum iam humaniores et, ut superius diximus [i.e. ¶ 38], prudentiores effecti, divisi per familias populi, Vesegothae familiae Balthorum, Ostrogothae praeclaris Amalis serviebant." Cf. the *capita familiarum* in the patriarchal age of the Hebrews, n. 31 above. Jordanes is the sole authority for Baltha as the family name of the Visigothic kings of Toulouse: Wolfram, *Gesch. d. Goten*, p. 24.

[280] The mistake resembles the error at the root of paganism, as told by Johannes Malalas *Chron.* 2, ed. Dindorff, pp. 53-56: the gods were real but merely men who had accomplished great things; thankful contemporaries accorded them divine honors, and ignorant posterity wrongly imagined that they were gods. These ideas antedate Malalas, but regardless of their ultimate source, they were expressed by a coeval of Jordanes. *Semideus* = kings, heroes: Statius *Thebaid* 3.518, 5.373. Jordanes specified "heroes." See also Cerfaux and J. Tondriau, *Culte des souverains*, pp. 105-106, 143, 187, 263, 276, 413. See, *Kontinuitätstheorie*, p. 47, stresses that *semidei* originates from "der antiken und nicht der germanischer Vorstellungswelt." It would not be surprising to learn that Jordanes designed the scene in such a way as to evoke the act of a Roman army acclaiming its general as *imperator*.

[281] Frye, *Anatomy of Criticism*, p. 169. The account of the victory over Fuscus might also have been meant as a prefiguration of the Battle of Adrianople.

[282] Their role might be likened to that of the stock *miles gloriosus* in New Comedy, though (in Jordanes's tendency not to have them speak) lacking the *miles*'s eloquence: Frye, *Anatomy of Criticism*, pp. 39-40, 165, 172.

down a few demigods to less-than-heroic scale: Ermanaric monstrously punishes Sunilda for her husband's treason, suffering suitable retribution himself; the Almighty thwarts Alaric's designs and occasions his untimely death; the kings of Toulouse, about whom much could be known, dwindle to shadows; and Theodoric, highly praised by Greek historians, falls short here of any admirable achievement.[283] Some Goths, the better documented ones, had been more obstructive than the others.

Goths who proved helpful to the lovers are as few as helpful Romans. Athaulf may fall within this category once he had married the Roman princess, Galla Placidia; so does his successor, Wallia, who made peace with Rome, harried the Vandals out of Spain, and returned provinces to the Empire.[284] The outstanding member of the class is Jordanes's travesty of Athanaric, stripped of all his well-attested earlier career as an enemy of the Empire; he visited Constantinople in order to gaze in wonder at the city and its emperor and, thus edified, died a happy man.[285] A more straightforward cluster of helpers appears toward the close, as the Gothic counterparts to Belisarius in clearing away the obstacles between Romans and Goths. Sinderith surrendered Sicily, Evermud turned his back on his royal father-in-law and willingly submitted, and Vitiges himself had the wisdom to capitulate voluntarily and without delay.[286] The ease of conquest resided not just in Belisarius's skill, but in the futility of defending what was, after all, only the absurdity of Amal kingship.

Jordanes's irony, once detected, calls back to mind the disillusioned narrator of the *Romana*. But a tale that ends happily should remain light-hearted and needs playful touches. One of them is the obsessive behavior that possesses the Goths until the action of the tale cures them.[287] From the moment of their first involvement with the Roman Empire, they are portrayed in the part of dependents anxious for their subsidies and unbalanced when the expected Roman remittance fails to arrive. This undignified conduct is seen again and again, amusing us with the spectacle of men who go frantic whenever their alimony is withheld or endangered.[288]

---

[283] Ermanaric: *Get.* ¶¶ 129-30; for his medieval reputation, Caroline Brady, *The Legends of Ermanaric* (Berkeley 1943), p. 3 and *passim*. Alaric: ¶ 157. For the Visigoths and Theodoric, see above, nn. 228-29, 232-41. Concerning Ermanaric's killing of Sunilda and the fate of those preparing Alaric's tomb, cf. Chastagnol, "Supplice de l'écartèlement": a way to blacken rulers is to attribute unusually brutal killings to them.

[284] By association with Galla Placidia, Athaulf visibly changes from a despoiler of Rome into an auxiliary of the Empire: *Get.* ¶¶ 159-63; Wallia seems to serve spontaneously: ¶¶ 164-66, 174.

[285] On Athanaric, n. 229 above. Persecutor of Christians, Orosius *Hist.* 7.32.9. Isidore of Seville regarded him as the first Gothic king: *Hist. Goth.* 6, MGH AA. XI, 269.

[286] *Get.* ¶¶ 308, 313.

[287] On this feature, Frye, *Anatomy of Criticism*, pp. 168-69.

[288] *Get.* ¶¶ 76, 89, 146, 270-71 (most eloquent), 272.

Yet the running joke bears thinking about. Are we supposed to laugh because the Goths are anxious dependents or because they go on armed rampages? If merely worried about their material well-being, the Goths would
collectively assume the part of a character who entertains by being single-
mindedly intent on filling his belly.²⁸⁹ But that does not quite fit the case.
Other stimuli than the withdrawal of support also provoke the Goths to
desperate deeds. A violent response is unleashed whenever Roman emperors are "negligent" or less than virile toward them.

At an early point, Jordanes dwells at surprising length on the Amazons'
being Gothic. Except for two paragraphs and the inevitable geographic
digressions, the entire Scythian section is devoted to the Goth-Ama-
zons.²⁹⁰ Jordanes even calls attention to the disproportion of his treatment:
"Why does a discourse that began with Gothic men dwell so long on their
women?"²⁹¹ Why indeed? Amazons are women who, because their menfolk
have departed, spurn their femininity and assume unnatural roles.²⁹² There
is nothing incongruous, later on, in the Goths' being dependent; we are
meant to take their expectations of Roman support and firm handling as
thoroughly dignified. The occasions for amusement occur when Roman
negligence awakens in the Goths the ancient—and humorous—Amazon
strain. The Visigoths, along with despising the cowardly new emperors of
395, "fear their [own] valor would be destroyed by a long peace," and Alaric
persuades them "to seek a kingdom by their own exertions rather than to
serve others in idleness"; the Ostrogoths, resenting the paltry scale of Roman gifts, are "eager to display their wonted valor"; "peace became distasteful to men for whom war had long furnished the necessaries of life";
and Theodoric decides "to seek a living by his own exertions, after the
manner customary to his race."²⁹³ In Jordanes's ironic perspective, Gothic
deeds of valor are manifestations of Amazon behavior, triggering laughter,
in the same way that Gothic kingship emanates from an absurd law. The
two themes are, in fact, closely linked. The logic of the plot calls for the

²⁸⁹ Such as the stock parasite, Frye, *Anatomy of Criticism*, p. 175.

²⁹⁰ The period of Scythian residence embraces *Get.* ¶¶ 44-58, in the last of which Jordanes
moves to the next, Moeso-Dacian phase of Getic/Gothic history. Geographic digressions occupy ¶¶ 45-46, 53-55. Of the balance, only ¶¶ 47-48 are concerned with Gothic men. Even
¶ 44 mainly establishes that the male Goths (Scythians) were the husbands of the Amazons.

²⁹¹ *Get.* ¶ 58: "Sed ne dicas: de viris Gothorum sermo adsumptus cur in feminas tamdiu per-
severat? Audi et virorum insignem et laudabilem fortitudinem." But, for their exploits, the
men are transposed to Moeso-Dacia. For a similar use of a rhetorical question to draw attention, see ¶ 171. H.A. *Aurel.* 34.1, reports that, at Aurelian's triumph, there appeared ten
women survivors of the many who had fought in men's clothes among the Goths; the placard
borne before them said they were *de Amazonum genere*.

²⁹² *Get.* ¶¶ 49, 56-57 (expose male children, hate childbearing).

²⁹³ Respectively, *Get.* ¶¶ 146-47, 272, 283, 290.

80

Goths' aspirations to masculine enterprise to be reversions to the freakishness of their primitive ancestors. Their proper condition is feminine. In the marriage that, at the close, symbolizes the joining of Goth and Roman, the Amal who is united to an Anician is a female. Jordanes's romantic intrigue casts the Goths, predictably, in the part of the heroine, glimpsed, wooed, and betrothed by the manly, bountiful Empire before the action even begins.

Jordanes's plot has room for two characters who simply entertain. The first appears right after the Gothic victory over Domitian and the listing of the Amals.[294] He is the Roman emperor Maximinus Thrax (234-38), son of "a Goth named Micca and . . . an Alan woman named Ababa," who "after rustic life came from the pastures into military service." Jordanes appeals to the lost Roman history of Quintus Aurelius Symmachus—Boëthius's father-in-law and fellow victim—as the source of information about Maximinus. Even if mediated by this lost work, the amusing details, including Maximinus's barbarian parentage, stem from the controversial *Historia Augusta*, here documented for the first time.[295]

Jordanes carefully frames his account of Maximinus. In the opening and closing paragraphs, the sober facts of his career are set out: distant ancestry and parents, *cursus honorum*, accession to the emperorship "by vote of the army, without a decree of the Senate," three-year reign culminating in a persecution of Christians (mentioned twice), and violent death.[296] The slapstick comes in between. Fresh from his pastures, the eight-foot boor stumbles upon the emperor Septimius Severus holding military games and asks in his native tongue to join in; he wrestles sixteen camp servants to the ground without pausing for breath, runs tirelessly beside the emperor's trotting horse, converses with Severus, and wrestles with seven very strong recruits as continuously and victoriously as before.

[294] *Get.* ¶¶ 76-82. In ¶ 82, he speaks as though moving out of a digression back to a straight track, but Maximinus proves to be another digression.

[295] *Get.* ¶¶ 83-88. On Symmachus, Momigliano, "Cassiodorus and Ital. Culture," pp. 185-86; *Anecdoton Holderi*, ed. Fridh, p. v lines 11-12, "parentesque suos imitatus historiam quoque Romanam septem libris edidit." This and Jordanes's one extract, specified to be from bk. V, are all that is known of the history. The source, *H.A. Maximini duo* 1-4, ed. Hohl, II, 3-6 (visibly developed from material in Herodian 6.8); cf. Hohl, "Die 'gotische Abkunft' des Kaisers Maximinus Thrax"; Schwartz, "Jordanès et l'Histoire Auguste." For the first attestation of the *H.A.*, Callu, "Première diffusion," pp. 100-15.
This passage on Maximinus is so interesting for reasons alien to the *Getica* that one tends not to notice that it relates to nothing else in the narrative and is therefore puzzling. But Maximinus's irrelevance to the plot is consistent with his role as a bringer of comic relief.

[296] *Get.* ¶¶ 83, 88. The references to Christian persecution are not in the *H.A.* Mommsen, Preface, p. xxxix, concluded from this that the passage came, as Jordanes claimed, from Symmachus's history. Except for this addition, the resemblances suggest a direct copy of the *H.A.* with superficial inversions and word changes.

The humor is obvious; but, besides entertaining, the scene serves to remind us that certain traits make a Goth-Alan funny whereas others most certainly do not.[297] However jolly Maximinus was on the military playground, he was totally out of place as emperor. Charged with usurpation, long deplored as the first emperor of purely military origin, and a persecutor of Christians in the bargain, Maximinus incarnated the reason why barbarians were excluded from the imperial throne.[298] With naïve irony, Jordanes personally points to the moral: "We have borrowed this for our little work from Symmachus's history in order to show that the tribe which we are discussing came as far as the summit of Roman rule."[299] Maximinus was an object lesson of what happened when it did.

We are told by Jordanes (and not by the *Historia Augusta*) that Maximinus descended from those Goths who had settled in Moesia and Thrace many centuries before (the Getae-Goths in Moesia dated back, allegedly, to a son of Hercules);[300] yet Maximinus's parents seem to have still been recognizable as Goth and Alan, respectively. This ethnic combination has a familiar ring. It occurs more loosely in the passage, earlier examined, in which Jordanes discloses details about his parentage. The geo- and ethnographic settings are the same; Jordanes's presumably Gothic grandfather, Paria, worked for an Alan; his father had "Alan" compounded in his name, and he himself, though *agramatus*, served an Alan as notary before his *conversio*. Perhaps this moment of authorial self-revelation should be taken both more lightly and more seriously than critical tradition demands. Its echo of Maximinus's homeland and parentage is one of several reasons for probing whether the passage might, like the lines on Maximinus, be designed to furnish comic relief. The author who takes pains to establish his "low" character by admitting to barbarian parents and inadequate education is well designed to take a humorous part, perhaps as master of ceremonies, in his own book.[301]

Jordanes often intrudes into the Gothic history, though he is virtually absent from the *Romana*. We have observed him drawing attention to the Goth-Amazons, reciting the Amal genealogy (with a call for audience attention), pointing out the moral of Maximinus's reign, and filling in his

[297] Cf. Frye, *Anatomy of Criticism*, pp. 175-76.

[298] Herodian 6.8–8.5; Aurelius Victor *Caesares* 25 ("primus e militibus"); Eutropius *Brev.* 9.1.1 ("cum nulla senatus . . . auctoritate"); *Epitome* 25; Orosius *Hist.* 7.19.1-2 (author of the sixth persecution). Jordanes *Rom.* ¶ 281, records the facts from Orosius, without editorial comment. An author from within the Roman world who stressed that Maximinus was Gothic was unlikely to be Gothophile.

[299] *Get.* ¶ 88: "Quod nos idcirco huic nostro opusculo de Symmachi hystoria mutuavimus, quatenus gentem, unde agimus, ostenderemus ad regni Romani fastigium usque venisse."

[300] *Get.* ¶ 59; cf. ¶ 38.

[301] For a suggestive stock character, see Frye, *Anatomy of Criticism*, p. 175.

own background.[302] First-person commentary is not limited to these occasions. An additional instance comes at the very end. As the Anicii and the Amali retire to live happily ever after, the author steps forward to celebrate the Goths, Belisarius, and Justinian as well as his own handiwork. No one is to think that he has unduly glorified his Gothic ancestors, for he has "spoken [not] so much to their praise as to the glory of him who conquered them."[303] Duly appealed to, the audience is bound to respond with loud applause.

Jordanes does not strike a joyful note only at the end of his Gothic narrative; the whole book, once past the prologue, is integrated by a comprehensive plot. It traces the adventures of two lovers, Roman male and Gothic female, who have met and plighted their troth off-stage just before we first glimpse them as an engaged couple. Their union is impeded by the absurd institution of Gothic kingship, by the resultant impostors, by bad Roman emperors, and by Gothic lapses into atavistic behavior; and it is fostered by such kindly helpers as Constantine, Theodosius, Athanaric, Wallia, Justinian, and Belisarius. A Moesian rustic entertains and defines the social level that Goths are not to exceed, and a Moesian master of ceremonies keeps the action moving without excessive concern for historical accuracy. The happy outcome is an infant in whose veins the noblest Roman and Gothic blood combines to animate a single innocent body.

The *Getica* is a complex and subtle book. It is a very serious work, by the same author who, in the *Romana*, faces up to the reality of an empire fallen from paradisal bliss. He is well aware that the end of the Ostrogothic kingdom is as desirable an outcome as the end of the Huns and Vandals. He has little use for Gothic heroes and takes greater pains to keep the story running than to get the facts straight. But these attitudes, not really difficult to discern for anyone with modern resources, are concealed by a mask of sincerity and naïve wonder made possible by the literary convention of a tale ending

---

[302] *Get.* ¶¶ 58, 78, 88, 266. Other paragraphs with first-person intrusions: (section 1, thirty-eight times) ¶¶ 1-3, 9-10, 12, 16, 19, 29, 31, 37, 38, 39, 42, 45, 48, 52, 54, 61, 70, 71, 73-75, 81-83, 93-96, 104, 114, 119, 121, 127-29; (section 2, eight times) 172, 174, 176, 194, 197, 243-45; (section 3, eight times) 246, 251, 252, 256, 261, 268, 315, 316.

Kappelmacher, "Iordanis," col. 1927, points to Jordanes's intensive use of the first person as a special characteristic of his, departing from historical style. Yet Polybius *Hist.* 36.12 not only uses the first person, but comments on his doing so.

[303] *Get.* ¶¶ 315-16: "Haec hucusque Getarum origo ac Amalorum nobilitas et virorum fortium facta. Haec laudanda progenies laudabiliori principi cessit et fortiori duci manus dedit, cuius fama nullis saeculis nullisque silebitur aetatibus, sed victor ac triumphator Iustinianus imperator et consul Belesarius Vandalici Africani Geticique dicentur. Haec qui legis, scito me maiorum secutum scriptis ex eorum latisima prata paucos flores legisse, unde inquirenti pro captu ingenii mei coronam contexam. Nec me quis in favorem gentis praedictae, quasi ex ipsa trahenti originem, aliqua addidisse credat, quam quae legi et comperi. Nec si tamen cuncta, quae de ipsis scribuntur aut referuntur, complexus sum, nec tantum ad eorum laudem quantum ad laudem eius qui vicit exponens."

happily. There could not have been anything Cassiodoran about this device. On the contrary, Jordanes's plot can only have twisted Cassiodorus's message out of the shape it had, in order to suit the conditions of the 550s.

More was involved than a change of political orientation. Jordanes assumed that universal and Roman history could be presented with candor and forthrightness, whereas the truth about the Goths needed to be conveyed so gently as to be visible only between the lines. This contrast was basic to his historical collection. Where the Goths were concerned, a lighthearted plot had to be devised because the intended audience was unsuitable for, and unprepared to accept, the one-sided tale of Roman triumph, in the mode of Florus, that might have been fashioned (perhaps more easily) out of the same facts.[304] The problem of Jordanes's audience—that is, of the destination of his little library—will be fully considered after complementary aspects of the *Getica* are attended to.

9. The *Getica*: Roman Victories and Scandinavian Origins

The *Getica*, though not a candid history of the Goths, offers more to readers than the ironic tale of Goths and Romans that has just been examined. A sincere dimension of its design is the commemoration of Roman success over the barbarians and even the promise of further successes to come. Jordanes went to the trouble, as noted earlier, of portraying the Gepids as blood relatives of the Goths, latecomers in the emigration from Scandza and companions in Arianism; and, in an adaptation of the biblical legend of the fallen angels, he turned the Huns into demonic Goths by tracing their origin to banished Gothic witches coupling with unclean spirits.[305] The probable reason for contriving such unifying connections was to give the Goths a generic or symbolic character. They stood for all northern barbarians as well as for the Goths of the sixth-century kingdoms in Italy and Spain.[306] Late Roman convention called for acclaiming the emperor as "conqueror of all barbarians" (*victor omnium barbarorum*).[307] The *Getica* served in part to substantiate this acclamation.

One detail of Byzantine ethnography that Jordanes did not endorse was the classification, found in Procopius and Cyril of Scythopolis, of the Van-

[304] For Florus, n. 149 above.

[305] Above, n. 265.

[306] Not, of course, the Bulgarians and Slavs, or Westerners, such as the Franks and Sueves. But "Goth" in sixth-century Byzantium had something generic about it. Hence, e.g., the assimilation of Odoacer to a Goth in Jordanes's statement that Italy was ruled by "Gothic" kings after the overthrow of Romulus Augustulus (*Get.* ¶ 243, *Rom.* ¶ 345). The same notion occurs in Count Marcellinus *Chron.* Also the concept of "Gothic" peoples including Vandals and Gepids, as below, n. 308.

[307] E.g. Vegetius *Epitoma rei militaris* 2. *praef.*, ed. C. Lang (Leipzig 1885) p. 33: "domitori omnium gentium barbarorum." See Christ, "Römer und Barbaren," p. 281.

dals as a Gothic people, the fourth after the Ostrogoths, Visigoths, and Gepids.[308] The Vandal passages of the *Getica* embody contradictory emotions. Most often, the Vandals are treated with contempt, knocked about by the Goths or in flight before them.[309] The exception occurs when Gaiserich is mentioned. Here, genuine admiration intrudes, even for the craftiness of his dealings with the Roman emperors. Without the slightest allusion to his resolute Arianism and persecutions of African Catholics, he is shown as a God-sanctioned king, whose admirable succession ordinance guaranteed prosperity to the Vandals until its violation brought about their collapse.[310] The note of Byzantine propaganda is unmistakable, for Justinian's attack in 533 had been justified by Gelimer's breach of Gaiserich's succession law (in fact, Gelimer was only the last of several violators).[311] The contradiction in Jordanes's treatment of the Vandals possibly results from a juxtaposition of borrowed Cassiodoran matter and his own contributions.[312] Either way, Belisarius duly suppressed the Vandal kingdom. It is interesting, nevertheless, that Jordanes clung closely enough to his sources to avoid any suggestion of kinship between Vandals and Goths. Procopius's audience was ready to accept the Vandals as a breed of Goths; Jordanes's public, presumably, was not.

The other tribes that are laid low, or destined soon to be by the end of the *Getica*, are either generically Gothic or alleged to be. Ethnic kinship, however demonic, seems to have been Jordanes's excuse for introducing an interminable romance of the Huns, starting from a double origin legend, moving through the great battle in Gaul, and on to Attila's "base death" and the dissolution of his empire. With space in all three segments, the Hunnish story almost forms a book within a book, partly based on Priscus's *History*. From Jordanes's standpoint, it was a useful device for omitting properly Gothic history.[313]

As for the two other branches of the Gothic diaspora, Jordanes antici-

[308] See Goffart, "Table of Nations," pp. 120-21, 124 n. 112.

[309] *Get.* ¶¶ 26, 89, 113-15, 161-63, 166, 173. Cf. Mommsen, Preface, pp. vii-viii; Barnish, "Genesis and Completion," p. 340. Contempt ceases as soon as Gaiserich makes his appearance as Vandal king.

[310] *Get.* ¶¶ 167-69 (Vandal succession and Byzantine reconquest, 170-72), 184-85, 244. On Gaiserich's religious policies, Courtois, *Vandales*, pp. 289-93.

[311] Bury, *Later Roman Empire from Death of Theodosius* II, 124-26; Stein, *Bas-Empire* II, 311-12. On Vandal succession, explicitly contradicting Jordanes, Courtois, *Vandales*, pp. 238-42.

[312] Stein, *Bas-Empire* II, 143, 252-53; Wolfram, *Gesch. d. Goten*, p. 383. The relations of the Ostrogoths and Vandals abruptly changed to hostility at the advent of the pro-Catholic and pro-Byzantine Hilderic (523). The passages listed above, n. 309 (with exceptions, notably ¶ 28), reflect what might be expected of the Cassiodoran history. Cassiodorus would surely not have extolled and championed Gaiserich's succession ordinance.

[313] *Get.* ¶¶ 121-28, 178-228, 253-63. Blockley, *Classicising Historians* I, 113-14 (finds non-Priscan influences as well). On the avoidance of proper Gothic history, see above, nn. 228, 232.

pated their imminent end. The Visigoths seemed to be taking their time dying. Their sovereignty should have been swept away with the violent death of Alaric II or that of his son, Amalaric, but Theodoric's viceroy, Theudis, had kept them united as long as he lived.[314] Near the close of the *Getica*, we hear that a general with an army had been appointed by Justinian to go to Spain, presumably to administer the coup de grâce. (The outcome was considerably less decisive.)[315] For the fate of the Gepids, the last paragraphs of the *Romana* must be consulted. In a battle of record proportions, they had been crushed by the Lombards, "allies of the Roman emperor." An added detail explains why it was preferable to record this promising success outside the *Getica*. None other than the niece of the Ostrogothic king, Theodahad, had been given as wife to the Lombard king by Justinian; she was an Amal who did not fit in with Jordanes's happy ending.[316] However that may be, his Gepid prediction was better founded than the Visigothic one. Though not in the battle of 551 or 552, the Lombards did eventually destroy the Gepids. (It was the prelude to their invasion of Italy, undoing Justinian's conquest.)[317]

Jordanes's celebration of the Goths is ironic, that of the victorious Empire sincere; the author of the *Romana* may hardly be thought to have been otherwise disposed. The cultivation or preservation of venerable Gothic traditions was not among his designs.[318] The only chance that such traditions might have had of landing in the *Getica* is if they were in the Cassiodoran history and if Jordanes saw no harm in appropriating them. There surely is Cassiodoran matter in the *Getica*, although its identification is hardly facilitated by the detection of the story structure Jordanes adopted.[319] Yet even if the Cassiodoran hand could somehow be certified in a given passage, there is no guarantee that it would record ancient Gothic

[314] *Get.* ¶¶ 245 (clearly indicates, but wrongly, that the Visigothic kingdom ended with Alaric II), 298, 302. Possibly, Jordanes's point of view was that the legitimate Visigothic line ended with Alaric II and that Visigothic independence after his death was "artificial." But this is not spelled out.

[315] *Get.* ¶ 303; Thompson, *Goths in Spain*, pp. 16-18. See also below, n. 363.

[316] *Rom.* ¶ 386; Stein, *Bas-Empire* II, 528, 534; Wozniak, "Lombard-Gepidic Wars," pp. 148-52. The bride, a refugee to Byzantium from Thuringia, was the grandniece of Theodoric.

[317] In alliance with the Avars: Hodgkin, *Italy and Her Invaders* V, 137-39, esp. 138 n. 1. See also below, ch. V §§ 7-8.

[318] He claims acquaintance with Gothic songs, but does nothing to authenticate this source. Even assuming his autobiographical statements are true, he never specifies when and from whom he would have acquired Gothic information. See above, n. 49 (and the articles by Momigliano cited there); ancient ethnographers had given enough currency to the idea that nonliterate peoples remembered their past in songs (e.g. Tacitus *Germania* 2) that a Constantinopolitan author did not need direct exposure to such songs in order to assert their existence.

[319] In part at least, the findings of Schirren are persuasive. The point that cannot be verified is how faithfully Jordanes reproduced his main source.

memories. Cassiodorus himself made much of books and deprecated the forgetfulness of the *maiores*;[320] not he, but the less-than-sincere Jordanes, is responsible for invoking ancient songs and tales.

These reflections need to be kept in mind as one approaches the famous origin legend that opens the *Getica*. The migration from Scandza has occasioned a flood of modern commentary, but no consensus has been attained.[321] It was pointed out a few pages ago that the first seventy-five paragraphs of the *Getica* are, at best, a prologue. Their contents are marginally relevant to the plot of Jordanes's book. The Goths' talent for archery, war with Vesosis the Egyptian, incarnation as Parthians, Scytho-Getic exploits, and philosophic education in the care of Decineus, together with tedious descriptions of the Don, Dnieper, Caucasus, Dacia, and Danube, are no sooner set down than forgotten.[322] The origin legend itself is picked up again only in connection with the Gepids and Huns.

Concerning the Goths, the prologue launches two enduring themes. The first, discussed earlier, is that the Amazons were Goths; their strain of unfeminine behavior, materializing in their distant descendants, proves to be a recurrent impediment to the romance with Rome.[323] Also important is Jordanes's determination to project the political geography of the sixth century onto the distant past. Although the whole first segment of the *Getica* is alleged by Jordanes to be about the united Goths, he never allows us

---

[320] Above, n. 81.

[321] For orientation, Wagner, *Getica*, pp. 103-22; Svennung, *Jordanes u. Scandia*; Svennung, "Jordanes und die gotische Stammsage"; Schwarz, "Herkunftsfrage der Goten"; Wolfram, *Gesch. d. Goten*, p. 6 n. 8. In a revisionist sense, Weibull, *Auswanderung*, against which strict orthodoxy was reaffirmed in the review by Schwarz in *Historische Zeitschrift*; also revisionist, Hachmann, *Goten u. Skandinavien*, pp. 15-143.

[322] Even if these paragraphs contribute hardly anything to the plot, they may nevertheless have a structural function. Josephus had set out a program for writing the history of his people: "I had . . . already contemplated describing the origin of the Jews, the fortunes that befell them, the great lawgiver under whom they were trained in piety and the exercises of the other virtues, and all those wars waged by them through long ages before this last in which they were involuntarily engaged against the Romans" (*Antiquitates Iudaica* 1.2.6, tr. H. St. J. Thackeray, Loeb, IV [1930], 5). Jordanes refers to the *Antiquitates* (*Get.* ¶ 29), and his *Getica* is a suitable approximation of this pattern. (A possible parallel between the Jews and the Goths was observed in connection with the opening segment of the *Romana*, nn. 134-35 above.)
The Josephan plan is particularly useful in motivating the presence in the *Get.* of various Gothic educators and lawgivers, most of all, Decineus (*Get.* ¶¶ 67-73); also Zalmoxes (¶¶ 39-40, without details). The role ascribed by Herodotus to Zalmoxes among the Scythians is reenacted in Strabo by Dekaineos alongside the Dacian king Burebista. The latter is Jordanes's Decineus, complete with his king. For a careful discussion of the sources for these educators, see Krautschick, *Cassiodor u. die Politik*, pp. 142-46. Jordanes has good reason to prefer a Dacian Moses to a Scythian one (Scythia was reserved for Amazons). Contrary to Krautschick, p. 160, I am not attracted to the idea that Decineus is Cassiodorus in disguise. Roman readers of the long Gothic history, who could hardly fail to penetrate the disguise if it had been presented to them, probably would have derided Cassiodorus's pretenses.

[323] Above, nn. 290-93.

to contemplate their existence as a united people; nor is their division into western and eastern branches brought into relation with the attack of the Huns in the 370s. When the Huns arrived, Jordanes maintains, the Ostrogoths and Visigoths already lived apart as a result of an unexplained quarrel.[324] Their separation was, it seems, a matter of very long standing. Jordanes begins the Scythian paragraphs by specifying that, as soon as the Goths had become more refined and wiser, they lived "divided among the [first] families of the people (*per familias populi*), the Visigoths serving the family of the Balthae, the Ostrogoths the renowned Amali." These two Gothic branches and their patriarchal lineages—not royal dynasties—were an established fact when the Goths first entered into contact with the Romans.[325] The prologue was meant to draw together present and past, not to trace historical developments.

The Gothic origin legend, though virtually isolated, is firmly argumentative. Jordanes does not begin with a geographic survey, similar to the sketches that Orosius and Bede provide of the wider setting of their narratives. The places to which the *Getica* draws our attention in the opening paragraphs never concern us again; Jordanes's interest is intense, but not geographic.[326] He casts the paragraphs in question—thirty-four of them— in the form of a tight argument and takes pains to intrude personally at strategic moments. He is the master of ceremonies even in the prologue, and his task is to clear up the confusion that appears to surround Gothic origins.

A few simple propositions suffice for him to set the record straight. The nearest fringes of the trackless ocean, he says, contain known islands, running from Ceylon in the east to the Orkneys, Thule, and Scandza in the northwest; Scandza is where the Goths come from.[327] Britain is another island; it has its geo- and ethnography. The geo- and ethnography of Scandza

---

[324] *Get.* ¶ 130.

[325] Even *Get.* ¶ 98, in which reference is made to the unity of the Ostrogoths and Visigoths, treats the two branches as pre-existing entities rather than as offshoots of a common trunk. In the logic of the argument, Gepids and Huns have as much claim to springing from the trunk as the two branches with "Goth" in their names.

[326] That the *Get.* opens with a geographic survey is repeated everywhere: e.g. Dagron, "Discours utopique," pp. 296-99; Giordano, *Jordanes*, p. 30, "La prima [parte] è una grande e particolareggiata esposizione della geografia del mondo antico." But the claim does not bear examination. Orosius surveyed the world (*Hist.* 1.1.14-2.106), Bede the British Isles (*H.E.* 1.1), and Paul the Deacon Italy (*H.L.* 2.14-24), and intended to do so. But Jordanes follows a road map (only islands interest him); he is going somewhere, not conveying generalized geographic information.

[327] In greater detail: the innumerable writers who have described the earth have also located islands large and small (*Get.* ¶ 4), not in the impassable ocean (¶ 5), but in the clearly known nearer borders, along which islands are inhabited, such as Taprobane in the East (¶ 6). The ocean in the West also has islands, such as (¶ 7) the Orkneys (¶ 8) and, at its farthest bounds, Thule. The same ocean contains Scandza (¶ 9).

is distinct.[328] Long ago, the Goths migrated from the latter island to Europe and, after about five generations, moved on to Scythia.[329] The silly legends current in "our *urbs*"—Constantinople—that have the Goths coming from Britain are false because contradicted by authoritative books.[330]

Jordanes's narrative of Gothic origins has no existence apart from this comprehensively argumentative structure; its individual parts cannot properly be dealt with as though autonomous. The possibility of a casual borrowing from Cassiodorus is virtually nil. Moreover, the whole discussion is expressed in the conceptual framework and nomenclature of Greco-Roman geography. When the Goths give the name "Gothiscandza" to their landing place on the European coast, they precisely conform to the concept embodied in Livy's story that Evander and Aeneas, on attaining Italy, each gave the name of Troy to his landing place.[331] As for Scandza itself, the idea that an authentic Gothic tradition should have referred to an island of that name is no more plausible than that hoary legends among native peoples of North America should refer to the State of Alaska or the Yukon Territory, let alone to Hudson's Bay.[332] Jordanes had a use for Scandza. The narrative momentarily pauses so that he might assure Castalius, the patron just addressed in the preface, that this island was the starting point of the history he wished to learn.[333] Scandza mattered because it excluded the British alternative.

This argument could hardly have been made in a vacuum. As it proceeds, Jordanes takes pains to invoke authors and books: Orosius, innumerable geographers, Livy, Greek and Latin authors, Strabo, Cornelius (Tacitus), Dio, Ptolemy the geographer, Pomponius Mela, old Gothic

---

[328] *Get.* ¶¶ 10-15 (Britain), 16-24 (Scandza).

[329] The two migrations are cursorily described, more briefly than the description of Scythia that comes next (the three ships are mentioned only in connection with the Gepids, *Get.* ¶ 94): King Berig leads the Goths forth; they call their landing place Gothiscandza, a name said to be still used today (¶ 25). They fight the Ulmerugi, drive them from their homes, and subdue the Vandals. Their numbers increase so that a new migration takes place under Filimer, about the fifth king from Berig (¶ 26). They reach the delightful land of Scythia. On their trek a bridge breaks irreparably, forever cutting off the leading group from the rear echelons (¶ 27). The Goths in Scythia under Filimer defeat the Spali and go to farthest Scythia. So the story is told in ancient songs, and Ablabius agrees (¶ 28). Other authorities concur (¶ 29). Description of the land and people of Scythia (¶¶ 30-37).

[330] *Get.* ¶ 38. As was kindly pointed out to me by Professor Chrysos, the text reads *nostro urbe* (several mss correct to *orbe*, which makes no sense at all, and one to *nostra*). It is hard to see how anything but *nostra* can be meant.

[331] Livy *Ab urbe condita* 1.1.3-4. The Greco-Roman conceptual framework is not a modern discovery; Jordanes himself went out of his way to affirm the learned and bookish basis of his discourse.

[332] Alaska is an Aleutian word for "mainland": George R. Stewart, *American Place Names* (New York 1970), p. 6. Yukon is derived from an Amerindian word for "great river": William B. Hamilton, *Macmillan Book of Canadian Place Names* (Toronto 1978), p. 309.

[333] *Get.* ¶ 9.

songs, Ablavius, several ancients, and Josephus.[334] All these readings outweighed the silly legends (*fabulae aniles*) about Britain that lacked any written basis. There had to be a target for this arsenal, or at the least a wider
Constantinopolitan setting for Jordanes's debate. What the target or setting might be will concern us after additional aspects of the origin legend
are reviewed.

Jordanes's chronology in these paragraphs compresses past and present to
the latter's advantage. To be sure, the Goths leave Scandza *quondam*, as
though to say "Once upon a time"; these were the Gothic *principia*. But
roughly dated incidents of Gothic migration and settlement are few by
comparison with the attention Jordanes pays to places. The timelessness of
geography favors the present, and ethnography is datable. Although the
description of Britain and its inhabitants is chronologically fuzzy, that of
Scandza is not.[335] Any doubt about the near contemporaneity of its ethnography is dissolved by the reference to a certain Roduulf, king of the
Ranii (or of seven tribes), who spurned his own kingdom in order to flee to
the more desirable bosom of Theodoric the Ostrogoth. The report that the
Danes had driven the Herules from their home also sounds like recent
news.[336] Scythia, as described, is even more clearly contemporary to the
writing of the *Getica*. The first listed of its inhabitants are the Gepids, occupying their sixth-century territory. After them come the Sclaveni, the
Antes, and eventually the Bulgarians "notorious for the calamities that our
negligence brings about"—a vivid echo of Justinian's reign as portrayed at
the close of the *Romana*.[337] On a smaller scale, the *quondam* of the Gothic
migration is offset by the immediate report that the place to which, on
landing, they gave a name is said to be called Gothiscandza "even today";
"today" returns soon after in the account of the trek to Scythia.[338] Jordanes
was more careful to evoke the sixth-century setting of his argument over

[334] *Get.* ¶ 4, Orosius, innumerable geographers; ¶ 9, Virgil; ¶ 10, Livy; ¶ 12, Strabo; ¶ 13,
Tacitus; ¶ 14, Dio; ¶ 16, Ptolemy (also ¶ 19), Pomponius Mela; ¶ 28, ancient songs, Ablavius;
¶ 29, ancient writers, Josephus. On Ablabius, above, n. 208.

[335] *Get.* ¶¶ 13-15 seem to describe pre-Roman peoples (who fight with scythed chariots).
No recognizable allusion is made to current times and conditions.

[336] *Get.* ¶ 24: seven tribes are listed with the Ranii last, *quibus* Roduulf was king. Does the
relative pronoun refer to the whole series or to the last tribe only? Mommsen believed that
Roduulf was identical with a memorable king of the Herules in Procopius *Wars* 6.14.11-21:
MGH AA. V, 154, s.v. "Roduulf"; for a different view, Wagner, *Getica*, p. 193. See also Svennung, *Jordanes u. Scandia*, pp. 182-83. On the Danes dislodging the Herules, *Get.* ¶ 23. The
incident is undated, but would hardly be noted unless understood to be comparatively recent
(like Roduulf's emigration).

[337] *Get.* ¶ 37; cf. *Rom.* ¶ 388.

[338] MGH *AA*. V, 60 lines 8, 19. Reindel, "Bajuwaren," p. 452, recognizes, in connection
with *Get.* ¶¶ 280-81 (perhaps the earliest reference to Bavarians), that Jordanes's geography
is contemporary to himself rather than to the period discussed.

origins than to impress upon readers the very distant antiquity of King Berig's leading the Goths "like a swarm of bees" to the Continent.[339]

The lands associated with the most ancient Goths are not presented in an impartial fashion. Britain, the island that they did not come from, seems distinctly unattractive. Surrounded by a sluggish sea equally resistant to oar and sail, its land is better suited to the support of beasts than of men. Frequent ocean inroads soak its soil, making it exhale such mists that even on days called fair the sun is hidden from sight. Many of the inhabitants live in woods, sharing their wattle huts with their animals; they paint their bodies iron-red and often wage war; all of them, kings included, are wild.[340] The dismal characteristics of Britain occasion the error that Jordanes's argument seeks to correct, for Scandza, when its various features are added up, also lacks appeal. Although it invites confusion with Britain because both are repulsive islands of the northern ocean, Jordanes carefully points out the emphatic differences between them.[341] Scandza is inhospitable to men and cruel even to beasts. Deprived of honey and the sun's light, its inhabitants live like beasts in caves, feeding on flesh and eggs without grain, in dire poverty but dressed in rich furs. Taller and more spirited than even the Germans, they continually fight with the ferocity of animals (in fact, exactly like the Huns).[342] There was no need for Jordanes to explain why the Goths decided to leave "the workshop of peoples or surely the womb of nations." As the case of Roduulf showed, even a Scandzan kingdom was worth abandoning for the warmth of Italy. The Goths were well to be out of there.

The mainland region where they landed is less than clear to Jordanes, whose geographic muse is, for once, silent. He has the Goths multiply there for "about" five generations and implies that their great numbers forced further migration. "While [their leader, Filimer] sought a most suitable and appropriate settling place, he reached the land of Scythia, which they call *Oium* in their language; he delighted in the great bountifulness of its districts."[343] The Goths had reached "the soil they had longed for." Although

[339] The 2,030 years of the Goths are mentioned only at the very end (*Get.* ¶ 313); the first datable person one meets is the Egyptian king Vesosis in the fourteenth century B.C. (¶ 47): Orosius *Hist.* 1.14.

[340] The line about people and king being equally *inculti* is straight out of Pomponius Mela.

[341] Jordanes's unexplained intrusion of Britain is the puzzle of this section, from which many have inferred that he was writing disinterested geography. But there is a logical connection, apparent once *Get.* ¶ 38 is reached. The goal of the geographic hunt through the islands is to show that Britain and Scandza can be confused.

By detaching ¶ 38 from its context, theories have been devised about the Goths in Britain, the assumption being that Jordanes reports an authentic Germanic legend in the course of dismissing it; see Wagner, *Getica*, pp. 60-102.

[342] *Get.* ¶ 24, "pugnabant beluina saevitia"; ¶ 128 (Huns) "vivunt beluina saevitia."

[343] *Get.* ¶ 27.

the elaborate description of Scythia that comes soon after does not revert to the delights of the land, other than to list rich coastal cities, its attractiveness is beyond doubt. The Huns would also find Scythia very appealing. Whereas Scandza merited flight, Scythia was a desirable destination—so desirable, in fact, that it was, at the time of writing, fully occupied by dauntingly warlike peoples.[344]

One mysterious incident punctuates the Gothic migration. As Filimer led the army and its *familiae* into Scythia, a bridge that they were crossing collapsed "irreparably," cutting off half the Goths from the other half, "nor was it possible ever again for anyone to go forward or back."[345] Although Jordanes refers to travelers hearing mysterious noises out of the nearby bogs even "today," the more arresting fact is that the legend of the fallen bridge stands totally by itself in the *Getica*. The cut-off Goths, half the progeny of those brought out of Scandza, vanish without trace. Jordanes has no further use for them.[346] His interest appears to reside not in them, but in the finality of the break and the impossibility of going back. An impenetrable barrier separated the Scythian Goths from their Scandzan background; even if the northern island were worth going back to, which it surely was not, the road to it was broken beyond repair.

A final component of these paragraphs consists in Jordanes's appeals to authorities. Those writers attesting merely to geography add little more than the weight of their sonorous names. The passage that has rightly drawn most modern attention occurs after the Goths are ensconced in Scythia:

So also [the tale] is generally remembered in almost historical fashion in their ancient songs. And Ablavius, outstanding ethnographer of the Gothic people, attests

---

[344] The description begins with the Gepids, living where they settled after the collapse of Attila's empire (*Get.* ¶ 264); then Venethi, Sclaveni, Antes, and (skipping over less-known tribes) Bulgars; finally, two groups of Huns also active in the sixth century. All these were recognizable as contemporaries to Jordanes's audience.

The delightfulness of Scythia was not a traditional motif; cf. Solinus *Collectanea rerum mirabilium* 15.1-19, ed. Mommsen (Berlin 1895), pp. 82-86: everything nasty, including the use of hollowed skulls as drinking vessels (cf. below, ch. V n. 198).

[345] *Get.* ¶ 27: "et exercitus mediaetate transposita pons dicitur, unde amnem traiecerat, inreparabiliter corruisse, nec ulterius iam cuidam licuit ire aut redire. Nam is locus, ut fertur, tremulis paludibus voragine circumiecta concluditur quem utraque confusione natura reddidit inpervium. Verumtamen hodieque illic et voces armentorum audiri et indicia hominum depraehendi commeantium attestationem, quamvis a longe audientium, credere licet."

[346] A device of this sort might be deployed to explain the existence of two branches, but only if the lost or cut-off branch turned up again to be recognized as long lost. Nothing of the kind occurs in the *Get.* The Goths unable to proceed to Scythia simply evaporate. Wagner, *Getica*, pp. 223-34, discusses the relations of the passage to folk memories of travel through the Pripet Marshes, which he denies.

this in his very true history. And several ancients agree in this opinion, including Josephus, a very truthful annalist, who everywhere cultivates the rule of truth and unwinds histories from their beginnings. But we do not know why [Josephus] omits what we have said about the beginnings of the Gothic people; only commemorating that they are of the stock of Magog, he states that they are called Scythian in nation and in name.[347]

The vague demonstratives (*quemadmodum, quod, haec*) that Jordanes employs make it difficult to determine how much of what he has narrated is confirmed by the ancient songs and by Ablavius. No assurance at all is given that they refer to Scandza as well as Scythia. They and the other *maiores* and Josephus are all said to agree with each other; but since, as Jordanes specifies, Josephus omits the *principia*, one might reasonably infer that everyone else, less scrupulous than Josephus about "unwinding histories from their beginnings," omits them too. The Goths pose no problem as inhabitants of Scythia; Isidore of Seville, their later historian, would have them come only from there.[348] The detail badly needing confirmation is the migration to Scythia from Scandza. Jordanes's lines of authentication are phrased in a sufficiently ambiguous and evasive way as to suggest that the journey from Scandza might be hard to verify outside the *Getica*. The broken bridge, symbolizing collective amnesia, helped to explain why no Goth or anyone else had ever heard of the Scandzan homeland before.

The opening of the *Getica* is argumentative on several levels. Most broadly, it was meant to replace a British hypothesis with a Scandzan one. Concurrently, Jordanes stressed the repulsiveness and unattainability of Scandza; and he showed that Scythia was so fully peopled with Sclaveni, Bulgarians, and others that it could hardly accommodate the Goths again. Besides, Britain was closed to them, since it had no part in their past. The reason to commemorate the land that one originates from is that, in theory, it is a place to which one may return if need be; Aeneas, fleeing the ruin of Troy, sought out the ancient home of the Trojans and began by finding the wrong one.[349] Jordanes's apparent design was to seal off or foreclose whatever possibilities of relocation the Goths might have thought themselves to have. Like Roduulf, and Aeneas for that matter, they were best off in Italy.

---

[347] *Get.* ¶¶ 28-29: "Quemadmodum et in priscis eorum carminibus pene storicu ritu in commune recolitur: quod et Ablavius descriptor Gothorum gentis egregius verissima adtestatur historia. In quam sententiam et nonnulli consensere maiorum: Ioseppus quoque annalium relator verissimus dum ubique veritatis conservet regulam et origines causarum a principio revolvat. Haec vero quae diximus de gente Gothorum principia cur omiserit, ignoramus: sed tantu Magog eorum stirpe comemorans, Scythas eos et natione et vocabulo asserit appellatos."

[348] *Hist. Goth.* 1, MGH AA., XI, 268. Scythia is not mentioned in Isidore's second edition of this work.

[349] Virgil *Aeneid* 3.94-95, 105, 129, 163-67, 180.

But why Britain and the laborious invention of a Scandzan alternative? No trace survives outside the *Getica* of "silly legends" ascribing British origins to the Goths, but there is contemporary evidence that the Ostrogoths were once offered a home in Britain. Procopius's narrative of the Italian conquest, which was published in the same year 551 that Jordanes appeals to for both his works, relates a negotiation between Belisarius and the Goths during the siege of Rome in 538. On this occasion, the Gothic proposal to have only Sicily as their home was countered by an offer of Britain, "which is far greater than Sicily, and was formerly subject to the Romans."[350] The talks broke down, and the idea of the Goths going to Britain never surfaces again. Yet there is more than this isolated tangency between Procopius and the origin legend of the *Getica*. A few chapters after the negotiation, Procopius launches into his famous digression about the sixth-century Herules, including an account of how some of them trekked northward from the Danube to Thule. The opening of the *Getica* is full of parallels to Procopius's digression, not simple correspondences but those that result when one story turns another upside down. (The chronological relation between Procopius's work and Jordanes's presents no difficulties; the *Romana* and *Getica* were composed later than 551, as will presently be shown.[351])

Procopius's Herules had ancestral homes just north of the Danube. They forced their king, Rodolph, into a war in whose disastrous outcome he perished. Some of the shattered Herules wandered to the former lands of the Rugi and then farther south to ultimate settlement in Roman territory, "not that they became allies of Rome, however, or did them any good." The balance of the Herules—the preferable ones—stayed on the barbarian side of the Danube and found a home "on the very edge of the inhabited world." Trekking northward across various lands, they eventually "passed the peoples called Dani without encountering opposition from the barbarians thereabouts." At the ocean, they "took to the sea [and] reached the island of Thule . . . [which is] ten times the size of Britain." There they stayed. Thule has thirteen populous tribes, each with its king. It is a land of midnight sun in summer and continuous darkness in winter; but only one of its tribes, the Scritiphini, has "an uncivilized way of life." The other tribes live like other men except for worshipping many gods, of whom they

[350] Procopius *Wars* 6.6.27-36, tr. Averil Cameron, *Procopius*, The Great Histories, ed. H. Trevor-Roper (New York 1967), p. 212. On spring 551 as the time when Procopius published *Wars* 1-7, Rubin, "Prokopios von Kaisareia," p. 354. The last book of the wars, narrating Narses's campaign and seeing the Gothic war through to late 552, was published in spring 553.

[351] See § 10. It is generally taken for granted that Jordanes could not have consulted Procopius; e.g. Grimm, "Über Jornandes," p. 187.

regard Ares as the greatest. "The most populous tribe among them is that of the Gauti," near whom the Herules settled. Procopius cites no authorities; on the contrary, he declares that he, in properly Polybian fashion, was "very anxious" to go to Thule to see it for himself.[352]

Jordanes acknowledges that Thule is among the islands on the northern edge of the known world, but his contrast to Britain is another such island, called Scandza. It has twenty-seven peoples, not seven as Ptolemy claims, and is thoroughly distasteful, for more reasons than its extremes of light and darkness and the wretched Screrefennae (Scritiphini). There, the Dani drove the Herules from their homes, and a tribal king, Roduulf (Rodolph), preferred to emigrate to Gothic Italy and lived happily as a result. The Goths (Gauti) made their southward move long before him. After landing on the Continent, they defeated the Ulmerugi (Rugi) and seized their lands. At their Scythian destination, they practiced the cruel cult of Mars (Ares), whom they had always worshipped. As basis for all this, Jordanes cites his assiduous reading.[353]

It is hard to conceive that these coincidences between Procopius and Jordanes could have come about by chance or as slightly divergent interpretations of the same core of information. The very fact that Jordanes casts the opening of the *Getica* as an argument acquires its point when Procopius is found to feature almost the same names and incidents while stringing them together in a diametrically opposite direction. Possibly, the offer of Britain in 538 gave rise in Constantinople to unattributable *fabulae aniles*; one may hardly affirm that it did not. For the rest, however, the specific relationship of the *Getica* to Procopius seems plain. The latter's beguiling evocation of barbarians who set off for the distant north, relieving the Roman Empire of their obnoxious proximity, called for a careful rebuttal. Jordanes, as a prelude to his story of Roman-Gothic fusion, stood the Procopian narrative on its head, turning the facts around in both time and space. Regardless of the silly tales in circulation—such as the Herules migrating from the Danube to Thule—the Goths were in the Roman orbit to stay. There was nowhere else in the world for them to go.

Someone had thought there was. In relating the Gothic surrender to

---

[352] Procopius *Wars* 6.14-15, tr. Cameron, pp. 214-19. The Gauti of Procopius are the well-attested Scandinavian Gautar (the Geats of the Old English *Beowulf*), who continuously resided in medieval southern Sweden. The relevance of this passage of Procopius to Jordanes has been noted before, e.g. Svennung, *Jordanes u. Scandia*, pp. 194-97, who holds that Procopius complements Jordanes without contradicting him.

[353] Thule and Scandza, *Get.* ¶ 9; Ptolemy, ¶ 19; extremes of light and dark, ¶ 20; Screrefennae, ¶ 21; Dani and Herules, ¶ 23; Roduulf, ¶ 24; the Gothi depart, ¶ 25; Ulmerugi, ¶ 26; Mars, ¶¶ 40-41. Schnetz, "Jordanes beim Geograph von Ravenna," p. 95, plausibly argues that the text of Jordanes should be emended to read "Scretefennae."

Narses late in 552, Procopius claimed that the survivors were permitted to "leave Italy at once" with their money in order "to live independently with the other barbarians" beyond the emperor's reach.[354] His version, which made allowance for a minority of 1,000 Goths to withdraw north of the Po, did not remain unchallenged. Agathias's account of the same events affirms that all the Goths submitted and were allowed to return to their Italian homes, free to enjoy their property in security. The good Herules were not alone, therefore, in being portrayed by Procopius as departing for remote, extra-imperial destinations, and neither was Jordanes the only sixth-century historian who took pains to contradict him.[355]

In an unwitting marriage of opposing tendencies, Felix Dahn ended his famous novel *Ein Kampf um Rom* by having the Goths who had survived the defeat of 552 take to the sea to make their way back to the Scandinavian homeland.[356] The fate of origin legends is to be believed, and Dahn's consciously fictional concord of ends with beginnings is one of many interpretive roles that Berig's three ships crossing the Baltic have assumed in modern times. Jordanes had different ambitions. His account of the migration from Scandza to Scythia was so marginal to the course of later Gothic history that he never mentioned it again as relevant to any but secondary actors. The origin story was not designed to elicit belief in its details, still less to immortalize the substance of ancient ethnic songs. Its purpose came from a contemporary Constantinopolitan debate of which the *Getica* itself formed a part. Jordanes set out an alternative to existing tales of recent barbarian wanderings and sought, by contradiction, to prevent them from being credited. The Gothic love story, beginning *in medias res*, had little need for reinforcement out of the distant past; what mattered was that no other outcome than the Italian fusion that it proposed should win a hearing. There were contrary possibilities. The one advocated by the eloquent Procopius has come down to us in the form of a digression suggesting, if taken literally, that the Empire could look forward to such a thing as a barbarian final solution: they would leave for the ends of the earth. The salvation that the *Getica* promised in its happy ending had a simpler and more attainable form.

[354] Procopius *Wars* 8.35.33-38, tr. Cameron, pp. 282-83.

[355] Cameron, *Agathias*, p. 43. Procopius's idea that barbarians could be made to turn tail was anticipated, more than a century earlier, by Synesius of Cyrene *Discours sur la royauté*, tr. Ch. Lacombrade (Paris 1951), p. 68.

[356] A Viking fleet happened by and took aboard the Gothic remnants: "Nach Norden! gen Thuleland! Heim bringen wir die letzten Goten." I rely on the summary of Simon, "Concept of Germanic Heroism," p. 103. Dahn's novel, completed in 1876, is regarded as the greatest of the *Professorenromane* and his own masterpiece.

10. The Date, Destination, and Authorship of Jordanes's Historical Library

The *Getica* closes with the birth of the half-Amal Germanus in 551; the plague of 542 is specified to have occurred nine years earlier. The last reign narrated in the *Romana* is that of Justinian, said to be in his twenty-fourth year of rule at the time of writing; this regnal year ended on 31 March 551. Neither work refers to the expedition of Narses to Italy in 552 and its successes. As a result, scholars normally cite 551 as the year in which Jordanes's works were completed.[357]

The same year seemed to Momigliano, as it had to Schirren and Ranke, to provide the *Getica* with a political motive. Justinian's aim in marrying Matasuntha to his cousin Germanus in 550 was to undermine Ostrogothic resistance in Italy, and this policy met with some success; it was part of the preparations being made for a decisive campaign, commanded by the patrician Germanus, to put down Totila and his followers and to reaffirm the conquest achieved in 540. Even though Germanus unexpectedly died, he left a posthumous son, "a promise of reconciliation and peace between the two races." In view of these circumstances, Momigliano concluded, "[Jordanes] did not summarize the Gothic history [of Cassiodorus] simply because it flattered his patriotic sentiments. His work had a clear political message. It invited the Goths to cease resistance, but also gave encouragement to those who worked in Constantinople for a *modus vivendi* between Goths and Romans."[358]

So conceived, and further explained by Momigliano along the same lines, the composition of the *Getica* falls within the fleeting instant between the stillbirth of the elder Germanus's politically promising expedition and the grim realities of Narses's campaign. The hopes attached by the *Getica* to the infant Germanus are, on this hypothesis, carried over to the child from his parents' aborted campaign. Jordanes's book conveys a mo-

---

[357] The datable elements of the *Rom.* and the *Get.* are in perfect accord with each other: Germanus Senior died in late summer 550 (Procopius *Wars* 7.40.9); his posthumous child could not have been born much earlier than Feb. 551; the plague, *Get.* ¶ 104; Jordanes offers year 24 of Justinian as the terminal date for the entire, two-part work: *Rom.* ¶ 4. Scholarly consensus, e.g. Grimm, "Über Jornandes," p. 184; Hodgkin, *Italy and Her Invaders* I, 23, 25; Kappelmacher, "Iordanis," coll. 1915-16; Momigliano, "Cassiodorus and Ital. Culture," p. 192 with n. 65; Wagner, *Getica*, pp. 18-30 (very full survey of opinions); O'Donnell, "Aims of Jordanes," pp. 239-40 (somewhat eccentric). On the plague, which affected Constantinople for four months, see Allen, "The 'Justinianic' Plague" (none in antiquity was deadlier or more widespread). Jordanes's advertised completion date coincides almost precisely with the date of Procopius's *Wars* 7, the endpoint of his first installment (n. 350).

[358] Momigliano, "Cassiodorus and Ital. Culture," pp. 192-93.

mentary illusion of reconciliation and peace that, unknown to the author, Narses would prove vain.[359]

The idea of a narrative based on evanescent hopes is not inherently improbable; but Jordanes himself reveals that no false expectations were nursed in the winter of 550-51. The *Romana* is outspoken about the effect of Germanus's death:

[the patrician] breathed his last in the city of Sardica, leaving a pregnant wife, who after his death gave birth to his posthumous son and called him Germanus. Totila, learning how luck had favored him (*felicitas sibi*), taunted the Romans and devastated almost the whole of Italy.[360]

Germanus's death in the early autumn of 550 nullified the threat of his Amal marriage and, at once, produced deplorable consequences; the posthumous child was irrelevant. Jordanes ends the *Romana* on a different note from the *felicitas* of Totila in 550-51, but Totila's relief at the widowing of Matasuntha is the *Romana*'s factually ironic counterpart to the happy ending of the *Getica*.[361] We have no reason to imagine that Jordanes or anyone else in Constantinople harbored illusions about the political potential of baby Germanus for an imperial effort to suppress the Italian Goths.[362] Besides, his birth in the *Getica* signifies an accomplished union, not a contingent future to be hoped and worked for.

By supplying many clear indications, Jordanes makes it easy for his readers to establish the date before which his works had to be written. But it is as risky to believe him in this respect as it is to imagine that the Gothic master of ceremonies whom he sketches in self-revelation is a true picture of himself. Unquestionably, readers of the *Romana* and the *Getica* are invited to dwell on the year ending in March 551. But Jordanes, without saying so, reports later events: in the *Romana*, a Lombard victory over the Gepids; in the *Getica*, the organization of a Byzantine expedition to Visigothic Spain. Although these incidents are hard to date with precision, they probably occurred no earlier than the summer or autumn of 551. They

---

[359] Along the same lines, see now Krautschick, *Cassiodor u. die Politik*, pp. 21-25; Barnish, "Genesis and Completion," p. 359.

[360] *Rom.* ¶ 383: "[Germanus Patricius] in Sardicense civitate extremum halitum fudit, relinquens uxorem gravidam, quae post eius obitum postumum ei edidit filium vocavitque Germanum: qua felicitate sibi Totila conperta totam pene insultans Romanis devastat Italiam."

[361] The passage about Totila is followed by accounts of events more favorable to the Romans in Africa and the Balkans (*Rom.* ¶¶ 384-87); then the *Rom.* ends. For the discord between external events when Germanus Postumus was born and Jordanes's interpretation of the birth, see also above at n. 256.

[362] Cf. Gutschmid's review of Schirren, p. 149: "ein neugeborenes Kind einem Mann wie Totila gegenüber als König aufzustellen, daran konnten doch selbst Fanatiker der Legitimität nicht in Ernste denken." The various speculations on this subject are gathered by Wagner, *Getica*, p. 56 n. 209.

cannot have fallen within the twenty-fourth year of Justinian, as Jordanes implies.[363]

Some commentators have supposed that Jordanes added these events after having finished the rest; another adjusted the advertised year of composition only to the extent needed to incorporate the two discrepancies.[364] Such temptations should be resisted. If Jordanes knew about the Gepid defeat and the Spanish intervention, he could not avoid being also aware of the next stage of the campaign against Totila. Narses was appointed to replace the deceased Germanus in winter 550-51 (possibly before Matasuntha gave birth), and he set out from Constantinople in April 551 to take command.[365] Jordanes's failure to refer to the new commander was not accidental. He wanted it understood that he knew nothing whatsoever about the concluding phase of the Italian war; he was as innocent as baby Germanus. An author who pretended, in the *Getica*, that the surrender of the Ostro-

[363] These anomalies, partly observed by Köpke, *Anfänge*, pp. 54-56, were most clearly shown by Stein, *Bas-Empire* II, 820-21 (his concern was to establish the date of the Byzantine expedition to Spain); see now the sensible treatment of Barnish, "Genesis and Completion," p. 352, who believes that both events may belong to 552.

Jordanes reports that, in Spain, Athanagild revolted against King Agila and called for Byzantine help, and that Liberius with an army had been appointed (*destinatur*) to support him (*Get.* ¶ 303). Athanagild rebelled between Jan. and Dec. 551 (Stein, II, 562 n. 2); Liberius returned to Constantinople from Sicily only in 551 (Procopius *Wars* 8.24.1). Even if it is conceded that Jordanes reports no more than an "appointment," rather than the departure of Liberius's expedition, it is inconceivable that the report—an integral part of the *Get.*, not an afterthought—could have been written before 31 March 551. Stein's date, 552, is not excluded.

The victory of the Lombards over the Gepids seems to appear under 551 in Procopius (*Wars* 8.25.7-15). When in the year is hard to determine because the narrative is ordered topically within each year segment. Procopius specifies that many Lombards had already joined Narses for the march to Italy. These events cannot be situated before 31 March. Stein may be right in believing that the battle occurred as late as 552 (II, 533-34, 821); Wozniak, "Lombard-Gepidic Wars," p. 151, dates the battle to May/June 552.

Liberius's return from Sicily (*before* the Spanish expedition) and the Lombard-Gepid battle are both noted in Procopius's bk. VIII (published 553), not in the installment published in 551. These events happened well after the death of Germanus Senior. On the other hand, there is little merit to the allegation of O'Donnell, "Liberius the Patrician," p. 67, that Liberius's Spanish expedition is mere confusion on Jordanes's part and never took place. All that seems clear is that Liberius was back in Constantinople by April 553.

[364] Wagner, *Getica*, pp. 22-26, was determined to defend the advertised year of composition, but accepted Stein's corrections and therefore assumed additions (O'Donnell, as above, n. 357, seems to agree with him). Stein, *Bas-Empire* II, 821, rather lightheartedly adjusted Jordanes's date to 552, disregarding the advertised date; but he did maintain that Jordanes would not have failed to report Totila's defeat if he had known of it. Wagner, pp. 28-29, has Jordanes die before Totila's defeat so as to excuse him for having failed to record it. Barnish, "Genesis and Completion," p. 353, is content with completion a year after Germanus's birth. The question why then, rather than years later, is never posed.

[365] Procopius notes Narses's appointment at the very opening of 551, i.e. within year 24 of Justinian (*Wars* 8.21.6); he may well have been named to succeed Germanus before Germanus Postumus was born. Narses set out some time after being appointed (8.21.20). For the date, Stein, *Bas-Empire* II, 597.

gothic kingdom occurred once and for all in 540, and who therefore silenced the many Ostrogothic activities in the ten years afterward, could not
afford to report its second suppression even in the *Romana*. Jordanes at least
did us the favor of not being rigorous in the deployment of his dramatic
date. His inconsistency assures us that 551 was not when he wrote. That
year is nothing more definite than a *terminus post quem*.

A more certain, if approximate, date of composition may be inferred
from the firm premise of the *Getica* that Ostrogothic sovereignty had ended
and now belonged to history. The certainty and confidence Jordanes manifests in portraying the Goths as no longer independent outweighs his ostensible ignorance of any other Gothic submission than that of Vitiges.
The first surrender had been reaffirmed when Narses, in a second conquest,
stamped out the last embers of Ostrogothic royalty. Jordanes was in a safe
position to turn the clock back to such moments of innocence as Vitiges's
surrender and the birth of the infant Germanus, because, at the time of
writing, innocence of a sort had been regained and could be relied on to
endure at least for a while.

Narses's Italian campaign dragged on for almost a decade, but the
suppression of the Ostrogothic *regnum* was achieved in its initial months.
Totila was defeated and killed in late June 552, and his successor Teia in
October of the same year. Cumae, with the Ostrogothic treasure and royal
insignia, surrendered voluntarily in the winter of 553-54.[366] A formidable
army of Franks and Alamans remained at large needing to be dealt with,
and many Ostrogothic strongholds continued to resist, especially north of
the Po. Although Narses's task went on, the war seemed in Constantinople
to be won as of 554.[367] The thoughts of the capital turned to reorganization
and reconstruction. Justinian drew up a long ordinance setting out the legal
order of the new Italy; it survives under the name of *Sanctio pragmatica ad
petitionem Vigilii* and bears the date 13 August 554. Pope Vigilius was on the
point of returning to Rome. He was acccompanied by the fundamental law
under which, with the great legal corpus of Justinian, the Italians were now
to live and manage their affairs.[368]

The possibility that Jordanes's historical collection was related to the circumstances of 554 seems more likely on internal grounds than the alternative that the *Getica* was designed as propaganda for the opening of the war.
Jordanes does not incite his audience to side with any faction or to take a
political stand. His presupposition, rather, is that conflict is a thing of the
past. Italy had been delivered; the helpful acts of a Roman and several

---

[366] Stein, *Bas-Empire* II, 597-607.

[367] *Ibid.*, 607-11; Wolfram, *Gesch. d. Goten*, pp. 444-45.

[368] Stein, *Bas-Empire* II, 613-14, 669. Vigilius died in Sicily (Jan. 555) before reaching
Rome.

Goths had saved it from the encumbrance of Gothic sovereignty. Its inhabitants, second-generation as well as ancient, had a new life before them under the direct governance—never before experienced by Italy, at least not since 395—of the emperor of Constantinople.[369] As this new society began, the Italians would profit from a little enlightenment about the empire under whose sway they had come and about the course and sense of their recent past. The *Romana* and the *Getica* look as though, together, they were meant to serve this purpose: they are a historical and ideological complement to the imperial statute issued "in answer to Vigilius's petition."

Everything that has been learned about Jordanes's little library favors this conclusion. Although written in Constantinople by someone familiar with Greek who engaged in quiet polemic with a contemporary Greek historian, the corpus was destined for speakers of Latin, presumably including Romans as well as Goths.[370] An Italy that had lived under "Gothic" kings since 476 could do with being reminded of the place of the Roman Empire in God's providential design and with adjusting whatever conception it still had of the Roman past to the grimly realistic form prevalent in Justinian's capital. The travails of the Empire went on, with a hostile Persia to the east and Slavic and Bulgarian raids into the emperor's backyard. All subjects whom these hardships might even indirectly affect would benefit from knowing about them. Yet there was also hopeful history, which the *Getica* served to impart. Its audience was expected to take pleasure in being addressed by an eastern Goth who had once worked for a remote Amal. It would respond positively to a summary of Cassiodorus's twelve books about the Goths, as well as to the tale of a half-Gothic emperor extracted from Symmachus's Roman history. In order to spare feelings, the sad but unavoidable fact of Arianism was no sooner touched on than forgotten. By no means all Italians had been anti-Gothic; Cassiodorus epitomized the many

[369] The possibility of speaking of Western and Eastern empires began only in 395, and though emperors mainly resident in the East ruled the West in the fourth century (Constantine, Constantius II, Julian, Theodosius I) the prefectoral organization of the government left little scope for anyone to imagine even then that the West was being controlled by the East.

[370] Jordanes speaks very favorably of Belisarius and sets him almost on a par with Justinian: *Rom.* ¶¶ 366, 368, 370, 375 (*fidelissimus consul*, repeated in *Get.* ¶¶ 307, 313), 377, 381; *Get.* ¶¶ 171 (*vir gloriosissimus*, full listing of titles), 172 (*sollers dominus* [= Justinian] *et fidelis ductor*), 307, 308 (*dux providentissimus*), 313, 315 (Justinian and Belisarius jointly called *Vandalici Africani Getici*). From a political standpoint, such praise might almost be said to be predictable. Belisarius, recalled to Constantinople in 549, remained at court in great honor, treated as the loftiest of dignitaries (Procopius *Wars* 8.21.1-3); his name heads lists of notables sent to wait on Pope Vigilius in 552-53, taking precedence over one man much senior to him in date of ordinary consulship (Stein, *Bas-Empire* II, 592, 650, 665-66, 823). Belisarius's transitory fall from grace occurred only in 562-63 (*ibid.*, p. 779).

Jordanes's emphatic praise of Belisarius, coupled with his total exclusion of Narses (and avoidance of praise for Germanus Senior), gives him something of a Procopian sound. However else they might differ, they were at one in extolling Belisarius.

willing collaborators.[371] For this part of the audience, as well as for those Goths who could read Latin, the tale of Roman-Gothic relations needed to be treated in a gentle, sympathetic, and positive fashion. Jordanes did so. The key resided in focusing on the Amals and wiping out by silence all Gotho-Italian history after their surrender. Justinian's Pragmatic Sanction embodied the same *damnatio memoriae* of Totila and his works.[372] (The message was not weakened by Totila's appearing in the *Romana* as a usurper who perpetrated nothing but harm.[373]) The condition for peace and reconciliation after Totila was that Gothic relations with Romans should be approved and applauded down to 540 and forgotten thereafter. On this basis of mutual respect and even affection, the Romans and Goths of Italy might joyfully unite and be blessed by their own editions of the infant Germanus.

The three-part collection was designed to do more than inform its audience and inculcate a lesson of amity and fusion. It also taught, by the example of its author, the Gothic *conversus* to Catholicism with a name redolent of the waters of baptism. Religious conversion was too inappropriate to this medium to be dealt with more directly than by delicate hints.[374] Another conversion received sustained attention: namely, that of the Gothic past. No promise was made to reproduce the narrative of Cassiodorus pure and unalloyed; the program was, in fact, quite the reverse—to fashion an emasculated history of the Goths that, beneath an outer shell of guileless wonder, portrayed their kingship as an error, their supposed Roman emperor as a disaster, and their greatest leaders as variously flawed. Simultaneously, the very un-Cassiodoran message of relentless imperial victory over barbarians was openly conveyed. God's original chosen people, the Jews, had submitted to Roman laws; all the peoples of the world had fallen before Roman arms; the same power that had dispersed the Huns and terminated the Vandal and Ostrogothic *regna* would soon master the Gepids and Visigoths. The moral to be drawn by everyone from this spectacle of irresistible might was spelled out to the very noble Vigilius: "having per-

[371] Stein, *Bas-Empire* II, 124-30; Courcelle, *Histoire littéraire*, pp. 203-10, 225-31.

[372] *Sanctio pragmatica* 1-2, in *Corpus iuris civilis* III: *Novellae*, ed. R. Schoell and G. Kroll (Berlin 1895), 799. Totila is called *tyrannus*, and all his acts are declared invalid. All acts by Gothic kings through Theodahad are confirmed. The two years of Vitiges appear to occupy a no-man's-land between *approbatio* and *damnatio*; only married into the Amal family and preoccupied by war, he had not been able to govern very much.

[373] *Rom.* ¶¶ 378-83. Totila is never called king, but "in regno . . . asciscitur" (adjusting the faulty punctuation of Mommsen's edition). He is consistently portrayed as damaging, cruel, destructive, hostile, fierce, etc. Many of these terms come from Count Marcellinus *Chron.*, Jordanes's main source.

[374] See above, n. 108: Jordanes's reference to "before my conversion" leaves it to the reader to determine what conversion he had in mind.

ceived the downfall of various nations, you should desire detachment from all tribulation and conversion to God, Who is the true freedom."

Instruction, pacification, and admonition were all part of the lesson, but a final consideration may help most to explain why Constantinople saw profit in Jordanes's "edition" of the Cassiodoran history, even if it meant praising a dynasty that, besides being Arian, had put to death the great Roman senators, Boëthius and Symmachus.[375] The *Getica* affirmed that the Goths, though now suppressed, had once been true sovereigns of the lands they ruled, abrogating whatever *regnum* had preceded theirs. Gothic kingship might have emanated from an absurd law, now fortunately repealed, but the law had been in force for as long as it lasted; namely, until the surrender of Vitiges in 540. So, indeed, had Gaiserich ruled Africa by divine authority. The Western *regnum* of the Roman people had ended with the overthrow of Romulus Augustulus in 476. That fact is spelled out without qualification in the *Romana* as well as the *Getica*, and the Senate and people of Rome who greeted Belisarius in 536 are pointedly called "formerly Roman."[376] Justinian's acquisition of Africa and Italy was not to be understood to have rekindled a flame of Roman *regnum* in these lands, joining separated brethren to the dominant stock of the Empire. On the contrary, the Vandals and Goths had ruled lawfully, by God's ordinance or imperial assent, and Justinian's domination succeeded theirs, rather than that of the Western emperors.[377] The Pragmatic Sanction set 538, not 476, as the term of Italian legality. In short, the *Getica*'s celebration of the ancient nobility of the Goths and their kings had the Italo-Romans as its ultimate target, and among them especially, one supposes, the Roman senators.[378] The reality of Gothic history, formerly narrated by Cassiodorus, deserved to be reaffirmed, however ironically, by New Rome, so as to forestall any Westerners imagining that their imperial identity had been recovered. Agathias, the historian who, a generation later, wrote a continuation of Procopius, gives "a curious impression that Italy was populated entirely by Goths."[379] The idea embedded in Jordanes's *Getica* had had its effect at least on him.

Once the Pragmatic Sanction of 554 is evoked, the name Vigilius returns to prominence. Might there now be reason to react more favorably than before to the opinion that Pope Vigilius set Jordanes to work, just as he petitioned for Justinian's statute? Vigilius is a common name, and the sponsor addressed by Jordanes is conspicuously tagged as a layman. Rather than

[375] Stein, *Bas-Empire* II, 254-58.
[376] On 476 as embodying "the view from Constantinople," see Croke, "A.D. 476," pp. 115-19.
[377] *Get.* ¶ 169 (Gaiserich), ¶ 295 (Theodoric).
[378] Along the same lines, see Reydellet, *Royauté*, pp. 289-90.
[379] Cameron, *Agathias*, p. 118.

struggle against these obstacles, one might observe that all three names connected with the composition of the *Romana* and *Getica* are unusually eloquent. Their associations are more numerous and richer than tends to be the case with most authors and patrons.

Vigilius is homonymous with the pope, but also reminds one of Justinian, the sleepless emperor, son and brother to Vigilantias. In the context of reconquered Italy and the purpose of the *Getica*, he fulfilled a biblical prophecy of affliction followed by new life: "And as I watched (*vigilavi*) over them . . . to demolish and destroy and harm, so now will I watch over them to build and to plant."[380] Although Justinian could not openly advertise sponsorship of histories meant to reconcile Italy to his rule, no one was better suited than he to be their patron. The lay Vigilius might be his disguise.

Together with Vigilius, Jordanes and Castalius are "speaking names" (*redende Namen*). The former evokes baptism, religious conversion, and the waters that inspire Christian writers. Besides, a Jordanes had been famous in the 460s as a half-barbarian general and convert from Arianism.[381] Aquatic meaning also attaches to Castalius, the "mutual friend" of Vigilius and Jordanes, who bears no honorific titles but who allegedly prompted the writing of the *Getica*. Paulinus of Perigueux, a fifth-century poet, graced his longest composition with the lines, "Let frantic hearts demand Castalian dews; Other drink is fit for men reborn in Jordan."[382] He meant that pagan and Christian authors were moved by different stimulants. Castalius, rare as a personal name, designates "a fountain of Parnassus, sacred to the Muses."[383] By interrupting Jordanes, as the preface says, and diverting him from Roman to Gothic history, Castalius personified the very Muse-like function of literary inspiration.

There may have been a *conversus* of Gothic descent named Jordanes whom a lay patron, Vigilius, commissioned to write history and whom a mutual friend Castalius invited to summarize Cassiodorus. The factuality of

---

[380] On the two Vigilantias, see Stein, *Bas-Empire* II, 743-44; Corippus *In laudem Iustini Augusti*, ed. Averil Cameron (London 1976), pp. 121, 127, 168. Jordanes's preface begins "Vigilantiae tuae." The biblical passage: Jer. 31:28. It complements Jer. 1:10, "I have set thee over the nations . . . to root out and pull down, to destroy and to overthrow." For less appropriate texts involving vigilance, see H. Lesêtre, "Vigilance," in *Dictionnaire de la Bible* 5 (Paris 1922) 2422.

[381] *Prosop. Later Rom. Emp.* II, 620-21: Fl. Iordanes, cos. 470. Above, n. 109.

[382] Paulinus Petrocorensis *De vita Martini* 4.252-53, ed. M. Petschenig, Corpus scriptorum ecclesiasticarum Latinorum 16 (Vienna 1888), p. 91; tr. in Curtius, *European Lit. and Latin Middle Ages*, p. 236.

[383] *Lemprière's Classical Dictionary of Proper Names in Ancient Authors*, 3d ed., ed. F. A. Wright (London 1984), p. 130; cf. Lewis and Short, *Latin Dictionary*, s.v. "Castalia." The name occurs once as a *praenomen* in the *Prosop. Later Rom. Emp.* II, 184 (Castalius Innocentius Audax, prefect of the city of Rome 474-75). Two instances of Castalius are in the index to the *Inscriptiones Latinae urbis Romae: Corpus Inscriptionum Latinarum* VI, part 7, fasc. 1 (Berlin 1974), p. 983.

these persons, and of what is deliberately said about them, cannot be disproved. Yet the names they bear are exceptionally well suited to the roles they perform, almost too well. One might do worse than to retain an open mind about their historicity and to weigh other possibilities.

11. Conclusion

The disappearance of the "first national history," composed by Cassiodorus, is as integral to the fate of Ostrogothic Italy as the campaigns of Justinian's armies. What it looked like will never be known. Besides being overtaken by political events, the twelve-book Gothic history, by having had to be resolutely nonsectarian, may in time have displeased even its author.[384] Its necessary reticence on religious matters had honorable precedents in the histories of such post-Constantinian pagans as Aurelius Victor and Eutropius; but ancestry of this sort was no recommendation in the sixth century. A Latin narrative that extolled defeated Goths and paid scant attention to Providence could have had little future. Cassiodorus's enduring, though indirect, legacy to historical literature was the *Historia ecclesiastica tripartita* composed at Vivarium.[385]

Before vanishing, the twelve books on the Goths contributed to Jordanes's *Getica*, but Cassiodorus would be poorly served if we imagined that his celebration of the Amals and their people could be reconstructed on the basis of its Byzantine travesty. In what age did Cassiodorus's narrative begin? How far into antiquity were his Getae traced? Answers can be only speculative. We know he made much of an Amal line reaching back fourteen generations from Theodoric, perhaps to the first century A.D. In order for the equivalence of Goths to Getae to have a concrete basis, his Goths—those of Theodoric's Italian kingdom—had to originate earlier than the dynasty, but they had no practical use for the mythical past antedating even the Trojan War that the *Getica* fancifully supplies. Jordanes's extravagance is a humorous touch among many others militating against faithful repro-

---

[384] Cappuyns, "Cassiodore," col. 1369, considered irrelevant the absence of the Gothic history (as well as other writings of his public life) from the list of Cassiodorus's writings heading his *De orthografia* (the list might embrace only those writings relevant to the Bible). What mattered for the fate of that history, Cappuyns held (col. 1366), was the condition of Italy: after 554, Cassiodorus's opinions were outdated, and he may have left the history behind in Constantinople. This reasoning seems sound except in its dating: the likelihood is that Cassiodorus's history was an anachronism, and had been for quite a few years, when Jordanes used it.

[385] Of course, Cassiodorus only commissioned this work. Cappuyns, "Cassiodore," coll. 1376-77, proposed that the *Historia tripartita* was carried out while Cassiodorus was in Constantinople; Cameron, "Cassiodorus Deflated," p. 185, adopts this view and suggests that the work was written in connection with the defense of the Three Chapters. For him to side with Justinian on this issue would have been more consistent with his record. Either way, the orientation of the *Hist. trip.* needs more thorough elaboration. See, also, Laistner, "Value and Influence."

duction of his main source. Cassiodorus, for all his panegyrical intent, had reason to be serious about the Goths whenever he could. Should his schoolmaster's hand be detected behind the *Getica*'s evocation of Decineus initiating the Scythian Goths into philosophy? Jordanes's irony offers a more probable explanation.[386] Provided distant nobility was secured for the Amals, together with a plausible antecedent for their people, nothing forced Cassiodorus to intrude fictions from the distant past that might dim the historical exploits of the Goths from the third century onward. There were skeptical Romans to be impressed; sobriety was a defense against raised eyebrows and derision. Even if formed of short books rather than *volumina*, the Cassiodoran history probably was far more distinguished than an improved *Getica*. Its loss leaves a large and irreplaceable gap. In many known instances, our documentation of late antiquity has been harshly curtailed. The case of the Gothic history invites particular regret because of Cassiodorus's literary talent, the novelty of his theme, and his unique opportunities for securing authentic information.

Nevertheless, the idea that Cassiodorus inaugurated a new form of history can have only a narrow, technical, and postulated basis. The work he composed marked as abortive a beginning as Theodoric's Italy itself. If the conjectures made here about its contents are correct, its nonsectarian reserve and its accommodation of the Amals to the imperial scheme of serial biography would have resulted in a very different end-product from all later accounts featuring barbarian peoples. Because less Christian, it may have been markedly more "Roman" than they. In any case, the long Gothic history came into the hands of no other author than Jordanes, whose assignment was to transform his model rather than to copy it. No properly Cassiodoran influence passed through the *Getica* to distant posterity. Except for incorporating odd scraps of borrowed information and verbiage, the pages that applaud the suppression of Amal kingship guaranteed that Gothic history of the Cassiodoran kind would be swept from sight.

The anonymous Constantinopolitan whom we know of as Jordanes worked hard and skillfully enough that he deserves to be assessed in his own right, not just in relation to his main source. Despite writing two lines critical of the reigning emperor, he is likely to have been in the employ of Justinian's court or otherwise near it, carrying out a task designed to forward the interests of the Byzantine state in its conquest of Italy. That some personal initiative entered into the elaboration of his materials seems beyond doubt. Though less trustworthy as an informant than he has long been taken to be, he can no longer be denied the status of a conscious and sometimes original author. His works date from no earlier than 552 and are well

[386] See above, n. 322.

suited to 554, the year of the *Sanctio pragmatica*; but an exact year of composition after 552 cannot be established. In placing history at the service of public policy, he more faithfully reflected the *sensus* of the Cassiodoran model than if, in drastically altered circumstances, he had slavishly abridged it.

To attribute a Gothic history to Jordanes is to mistake a fraction for the whole. Jordanes produced a single work formed of three parts and distributed in two "little books" (*libelli*). The preface to Castalius mentions Jordanes having to interrupt his *Romana* in order to abridge Cassiodorus on the Goths, and the preface to Vigilius announces that the book for Castalius is now joined to the completed account of Roman history.[387] An author who parades in "low" disguise should not be expected to be candidly informative when he volunteers details about his processes of composition. The two prefaces emphasize to readers the integral relationship of the *Getica* to the *Romana*, and that is all they were probably meant to do. Not that we need reminding: the textual tradition joining the two *libelli* is eloquent enough.[388]

The three-part collection was meant to furnish reconquered Italy with a comprehensive, up-to-date initiation into universal, Roman, and contemporary history—first the providential ordinance of earthly rule since the Creation; then the tragedy of the final empire fallen from the paradise of effortless might to the common condition of humanity; and finally the comforting spectacle of recent victory over many, if not all, barbarians. Within the limits of his commission, Jordanes did not lack the seriousness of a historian. Nowhere perhaps is this more apparent than when, in the *Romana*, he Christianizes Zosimus's theme of fallen empire into a metaphor of the expulsion from paradise. If God took flesh in the reign of Augustus, it was not incongruous for the Roman Empire to have then begun to earn its survival by the sweat of its brow. The idea was strikingly original and admirably suited to Byzantine conditions. Only a little less seriousness was called for to contest Procopius's insidious suggestion that present-day barbarians, if properly handled, would turn their backs on the Mediterranean and go far away to live among their kind. Jordanes's response—the origin legend of the *Getica*—lacks historicity but was meant no less earnestly for that. The barbarians were here to stay and had to be dealt with on that basis. Jordanes shared in the intellectual life of a great capital then witnessing an outpouring of memorable historiography. He was neither isolated nor a court hack.

Although basically factual, the *Romana* was, in intent, as much a work

[387] *Get.* ¶ 1, *Rom.* ¶ 4.
[388] Above, n. 6.

of propaganda as the *Getica*. The Roman past that Jordanes conveyed to Italian readers was shaped by a Constantinopolitan perspective in which the straight line of imperial succession had passed from Gratian to Theodosius I (379) and never again detoured toward the West.[389] No dubious adjustments of past events were needed, only the presentation of the point of view espoused by the conquering power. Roman history had, by the doing of others, been withdrawn from its native land and acclimatized to the Bosphorus. The time had now come for the Italians to learn the authorized version. Perhaps Jordanes engaged in special rectifications with a view to his Western audience; the passing reference to the "formerly Roman people" is a case in point.[390] We would be in a better position to judge if his paragraphs on Constantine had not been deleted early in transmission and, especially, if Symmachus's Roman history (or an equivalent) had survived as a basis of comparison. Jordanes stressed that Bosphoran Romanity had superseded the Italian variety, but he saw no need to mislead Justinian's new subjects about the parlous condition of the Empire. If the edifying lesson drawn for Vigilius was also meant for them, then they were to keep clear of politics and cultivate their souls.

In the *Getica*, historical sincerity is a function of purpose rather than of contents. Of course, not every line is fanciful. Where do the tribal names of the early paragraphs come from? Even if they do not, as often argued, authenticate the legend of Scandinavian migration, Jordanes must have drawn them from sources rather than invented them from nothing.[391] Other items occurring only in the *Getica*, such as Gothic exploits in the third and fourth centuries, Ostrogothic ones in the later fifth, Ermanaric and Sunilda, and the colorful deaths of the Visigothic kings, may sometimes deserve to be stamped as originating from respectable antecedents. The effort to extract historical data from the *Getica* and to certify them for incorporation into our narratives cannot stop, but it will necessarily be arduous. For the transmission of trustworthy information had no part in what Jordanes set out to do in his second *libellus*. Unless directly applicable to his purposes, as in the interminable account of Attila's doings, truthful history survived its passage through his hands only by accident. Jordanes wanted the Goths to be remembered; the reality of their existence was the condi-

---

[389] Gratian (*Rom.* ¶ 310) is treated as direct successor of Valentinian I (¶ 309); Valens, though Gratian's senior, goes to his death against the Goths as part of Gratian's entry (¶ 314). Both Valentinian I and Gratian ruled in the West. But Jordanes then has the succession pass from Theodosius I (¶ 315) to Arcadius (¶ 319) to Theodosius II (¶ 323)—all Eastern.

[390] Above, n. 166.

[391] Partisans of the historicity of Jordanes's migration legend regard his lists of Scandzan tribal names as crucial proof: Svennung, *Jordanes u. Scandia*, pp. 32-110; Wagner, *Getica*, pp. 103-222. To the contrary, e.g., Lönnroth, "Goten in der mod. Geschichtsauffassung," p. 62.

tion for effacing the Romanness of Italy and for painting Justinian's conquest evenly Gothic, as it would look to Agathias. But any Goths vaguely resembling the sixth-century variety were adequate for his purposes. Their authentic past was superfluous and often unwelcome baggage.

Jordanes wished to be thought of as having abridged Cassiodorus and having conveyed the spirit of his history, though he also went out of his way to circumscribe the limits of his dependence. The congruence between the *Getica* and its source resided in the assumption that Goths and Romans were friends whose fates had long been linked. How Cassiodorus had elaborated this theme in the perspective of an enduringly bicultural Italy inevitably eludes us. For Jordanes, the endpoint was radically different, and the vicissitudes of Roman-Gothic relations had to be reinterpreted with a view to this outcome. The mutually desired goal of the long, checkered friendship was the fusion of the Goths into the population of Justinian's empire. To sustain this theme, Jordanes devised the plot whose structural components and detailed elaboration we have examined—a love story ending happily in whose terms historical incidents could, without total distortion, be both commemorated and traced to the required conclusion. Despite many lighthearted touches—the Goths as Amazons, the boor-emperor Maximinus, the "stammering, confused, and barely literate" master of ceremonies[392]—the *Getica* with its happy ending not only complements the reference to tragedy at the close of the *Romana*, but also shares in some of the latter's seriousness. The origin legend gave the lie to Procopian fantasies about return migrations; the space devoted to vanquished Huns and Vandals underscored the fate of the Ostrogoths; and expectations were raised that the days of the Gepids and Visigoths were numbered. In the guise of a Gothic history, the *Getica* celebrates Justinian's energy, persistence, and annexations. There is nothing ironic about the round of applause bringing the story to an end.

Jordanes seems to have envisaged both an untutored audience and a more sophisticated one. As a tract meant to have practical impact in conquered Italy, the collection was addressed to readers who had little choice but to accept Jordanes as the naïve narrator he claimed to be. For their sake, Cassiodorus and Symmachus were featured as sources, Arianism vanished as soon as mentioned, Vandals were cast as defeated foes rather than as a species of Goths, the Amals were united to the Anicii, and the narrator posed as an uneducated blood relative, from among the Gothic stragglers in

[392] The quotation, referring to Jordanes as author, is from Maenchen-Helfen, *World of the Huns*, p. 17.

Moesia.[393] How readily the *Getica* lends itself to being understood in a simple, literal fashion is shown by its reception in modern times. But if receptive passivity were expected of all sixth-century readers, there would have been little point in Jordanes leaving a trail of suggestive clues inviting discovery of the deeper level of his narrative. Narrower circles in the capital, and even in Italy, were given incentives for reading between the lines. Less inclined, perhaps, than moderns to believe that naïve bumblers were able to marshal authorities in two languages and to write extensive histories, they might have been spurred to attentiveness by the *Getica*'s very style.

However far Jordanes was from wishing to portray the Goths as an emerging people, the *Getica* has better claims than Cassiodorus's lost work to being regarded as the "first national history"; but they are only a little less shaky. Gregory of Tours, Isidore, and Bede went about their labors wholly unaware of Jordanes's writings. Not surprisingly, the *Getica* surfaced in Italy. Its first probable effect was to supply Scandinavia as point of departure for the Lombard migration legend composed toward 650. This *Origo gentis Langobardorum* also betrays the influence of the *Getica* by casting the Vandals as the Lombards' first opponents.[394] The Ravenna Geographer, whose date is uncertain, was another early user, profuse in expressions of respect.[395] By the latter half of the eighth century, the Jordanes collection was well known, but as a source rather than a prototype. Paul the Deacon used Jordanes's works among many others, toward 770, in compiling a *Historia Romana*. His original narrative of the period 364-552 markedly departs from Jordanes's Byzantine orientation.[396] Jordanes's influence from 800 onward deserves to be carefully studied; the sequel to his often ironic narrative was that, in the historical records of the Middle Ages, the Goths won the enduring place that, in life, Justinian denied them.[397] But this began to

[393] Cf. the overstatement of Maenchen-Helfen, *World of the Huns*, p. 17 n. 101: "It is inconceivable that anyone in Constantinople would have read more than a page of a book written in such atrocious Latin as the *Getica*."

[394] *Origo gentis Langobardorum* 1, ed. Waitz, MGH *Script. rer. Lang.*, pp. 2-3: the proto-Lombards fight the Vandals on the home island of Scadanan, then move; there is no reference to a sea crossing or landing. An early variant version of the Lombard tale, in Fredegar *Chron.* 3.65, mentions Scathanavia as being located between Ocean and the Danube. See also Hachmann, *Goten u. Skandinavien*, pp. 17-32, esp. 23-27 (the best account of the early influence of Jordanes). Cf. below, ch. V nn. 168, 170.

[395] Hachmann, *Goten u. Skandinavien*, pp. 18-19, proposes "soon after 800"; so also Staab, "Ostrogothic Geographers," p. 31. *Ravennatis anonymi geographus*, ed. Joseph Schnetz, *Itineraria Romana* II (Leipzig 1940). Interestingly, the anonymous interpreted *relegere* as "read" (1.1; see above, n. 203), and he identified Scandza with *Antiqua Scithia* (1.12), a return to the normality of the Goths being Scythians.

[396] Below, ch. V.

[397] Jordanes is well preserved in ms collections; the three classes of the text tradition existed in the ninth century; see Kappelmacher, "Iordanis," coll. 128-29. The modern influence of Jordanes is even more impressive; see Weibull, *Auswanderung*, pp. 22-28; J. Svennung, *Zur Geschichte des Goticismus* (Stockholm 1967); See, *Germanen-Ideologie*, pp. 19-30. Most re-

happen only two centuries or more after the *Romana* and the *Getica* were composed. In the interval, Western historians coped on their own with the problem of incorporating non-Romans as leading actors in the course of events. Jordanes's collection had little to do with shaping the earliest tradition.

cently, Wolfram, *Gesch. d. Goten*, seems to have been conceived in the form of an updated *Getica*.

Gregory of Tours and "The Triumph of Superstition"

1. The Historian and His Context

Georgius Florentius Gregorius, a native of Clermont in the Auvergne, was chosen bishop of Tours in 573, at the age of thirty-four. In the ecclesiastical geography of the Frankish kingdom, Tours was one of eleven metropolitan sees. It was greater still by virtue of its fourth-century bishop, St. Martin, the leading confessor of Gaul, whose tomb witnessed frequent miracles.[1] The life of Bishop Gregory bears little resemblance to that of his cherished predecessor, the Pannonian soldier-turned-monk.[2] Born to privilege and wealth, he was the great-grandson, grandnephew, and nephew of bishops of Langres, Lyon, and Clermont, and resolved as an adolescent to enter the clergy. He was elevated to the episcopate by the favor of the royal court, in succession to a maternal cousin.

Authors were rare among Gregory's more than 110 fellow bishops in the kingdom, and neither then nor in any earlier age, as far as we may tell, had anyone at Tours engaged in literary composition. Yet, when Gregory died, after two decades in office, he left a considerable body of writings, few of which appear to have been published in his lifetime.[3] He probably regarded its major components as being historical: eight books of *miracula* (distributed among five separate titles), which we class as hagiography, and ten books of *historiae*. The latter work, known since Carolingian times and still

---

[1] There are many accounts of Gregory's life: e.g. K-L, Preface, pp. ix-xix; Pietri, *Ville de Tours*, pp. 247-334 and *passim*. Pietri also gives a full account of Tours. The totals of metropolitan sees and, in the next paragraph, of bishoprics are from the *Notitia Galliarum*: ed. Otto Seeck, *Notitia dignitatum* (1876, reprinted Frankfurt 1962), pp. 261-74. Both figures, probably too high, are offered only as approximations.

A recent, not widely circulated asset to studies of Gregory is St.-Michel, *Concordance*. It is based on Arndt's edition and includes all words in context (not excepting *et*, relative and demonstrative pronouns, etc.). A more select concordance to Bede's *H.E.* appeared fifty years earlier; see below, ch. IV n. 8.

[2] Sulpicius Severus *Vita s. Martini*, ed. and tr. Jacques Fontaine, Sources chrétiennes 133 (Paris 1967); see, also, F. R. Hoare, *The Western Fathers* (London-New York 1954, reprinted New York 1965), pp. 3-144. Sulpicius's life is a great classic of early Christian literature (above, ch. I n. 33). If the real Martin resembled the figure portrayed by his biographer, he was a notably eccentric miracle worker. See now Stancliffe, *St. Martin and His Hagiographer*.

[3] The only writings of his known to have appeared in his lifetime are the first books of the VSM; see Bonnet, *Latin de Grégoire de Tours*, p. 13.

commonly today as *The History of the Franks,* has ensured his fame. He is a celebrated historian, and deservedly so.

Gregory does not pose the arduous critical problems of a Jordanes or a Fredegar. He would exist for us, as a leading patron and friend of the poet Fortunatus, even if he had never written a line.[4] Although most of our ample information about him comes from his own testimony, the tenor of his works encourages us to believe that he is sincere. Bishop Gregory pleads, but as a Christian teacher, celebrating sanctity and reproving wickedness in two complementary accounts of his age. One is a tour d'horizon of the marvels accomplished by the Almighty, largely through His saints; the other, a history conceived as a chronological narrative of wondrous *grandeurs* coexisting with all-too-human *misères.* Obviously different in design, both works are profoundly similar in quality and sound.

It is easier to affirm Gregory's high repute as a historian than to discover its basis. He passes among Frenchmen as the first of "our" historians, among medievalists as an indispensable informant about Frankish times and preserver of documents otherwise lost, among philologists as a prime witness to a Latinity in headlong change. Some of these ideas are captured in the admiring words of Rudolf Buchner:

Gregory of Tours' "Books of Histories" rank among the most indispensable sources of our European development. Through their fresh, vivid, plastic tales, as through no other source, we learn [to know] a whole century—from the time when, toward 498, the raw Clovis "humbly bowed his neck" in order to "adore what he had burned," down to the end of that wild, stormy, barbaric sixth century, in which, by the fusion of Romans and Germans, by the interpenetration of their natures and cultures, a part of the foundation was laid for the proud edifice of European history.[5]

In this fragment from a much longer assessment, Buchner accents what contemporary Europeans may extract from Gregory. The bishop's own presence in the *Histories,* though not unnoticed, seems limited to the charm of his storytelling. Everyone agrees in recognizing Gregory's outstanding talent for anecdote. It says much for his gifts that many incidents having little claim to being commemorated at all have, by his doing, gained

---

[4] Fortunatus *Opera poetica,* ed. F. Leo, MGH AA. IV, 2, attests that Gregory occasioned his longest poem (the verse *Vita s. Martini*) as well as the total collection of his poems; within the latter, Gregory is prominent in 5.3-5, 8-17; 8.11-21; 9.6-7; 10.5-6, 10-12, 14 (Gregory's archdeacon made bishop of Poitiers), 15 (Gregory's mother, compared to the mother of the Maccabees: the latter had seven sons, but her one outshone them all). Cf. Dalton I, 83-84; he shrewdly comments, "On the whole, we gather from the various poems that the relations of the two men were more intimate than we should infer from terse allusions [to Fortunatus in Gregory's works]." But Gregory implies more than he says; see below, n. 149.

[5] Buchner, Einleitung, p. vii.

a secure place in our vision of the Merovingian age.[6] But neither an ability to narrate anecdotes, however realistically, nor the merit of being useful to a posterity curious about its past, takes us very far toward determining Gregory's identity as a historian.

Most commentators since the nineteenth century have, in effect, evaded this question by asserting that Gregory was naïve—a blunt, sincere, and artless recorder of the world around him. The literary historian J.-J. Ampère, who dubbed Gregory the Herodotus of his age, set out the basic thesis: "Gregory presents [everyday life] naïvely, just as he sees it."[7] To Augustin Thierry, he was an "intelligent and saddened witness to the confusion of men and the chaos reflected in the disorder of his narrative," for, as Ampère had said, "The style of Gregory of Tours is itself a faithful image of the situation that he describes."[8] Emil Walter, in the 1960s, struck the same note: "The inadequacy of Gregory's historical writing reflects typical defects of the Merovingian age."[9] This had been stated the other way around by Thierry: the Frankish period encountered "a historian marvelously appropriate to its nature."[10] Thierry evoked Gregory's "naïve talent," Dannenbauer his "naïve enjoyment of a variegated world," Latouche his "naïve and disarming clumsiness."[11] The same view could be expressed without reference to naïveté, as in an authoritative guide to medieval sources: "What he heard, what he saw, he narrated without further goal than to preserve the memory of events."[12] Even Siegmund Hellmann, whose study of Gregory is a milestone in the critical literature, preceded his analysis of the *Histories* with an account of the Merovingian age that seems to be directly apprehended but comes from little else than Gregory's narrative.[13] "There must be an element of truth," Walter concluded, "in the unanimous conviction of all modern interpreters that Gregory conveyed undistortedly and simply

---

[6] Notably, the story of Sicharius and Chramnesindus, brought to prominence by the exposition of Auerbach, *Mimesis*, ch. 4; the reprint (Garden City, N. Y. 1957) is used here. The same minor and local feud also won prominence somewhat earlier: Monod, "Aventures de Sichaire," *Revue historique* 31 (1886) 259-90. It occasioned a public quarrel between Monod and Fustel de Coulanges, who assailed the former's critical method: Fustel, "De l'analyze des textes historiques," *Revue des questions historiques* 41 (1887) 5-35; replies by both, *ibid.*, pp. 540-48, 549-53.

[7] Ampère, *Hist. lit.* II, 294. This paragraph owes much to Thürlemann, *Gregor von Tours*.

[8] Thiérry, *Récits*; Ampère, *Hist. lit.* II, 309.

[9] Walter, "Hagiographisches," p. 306.

[10] Thiérry, *Récits*, p. 4.

[11] *Ibid.*, p. 3; Dannenbauer, *Entstehung Europas* II, 68; Latouche, "Grégoire de Tours," p. 82.

[12] Wattenbach-Levison, *Geschichtsquellen*, p. 105. This statement is already in Wattenbach, *Deutschlands Geschichtsquellen*, 5th ed., I, 96, together with at least nine-tenths of what is said about Gregory in the 1950s edition.

[13] Hellmann, "Gregor von Tours," reprinted in his *Ausgewählte Abhandlungen* (the reprint is cited here).

what he saw and heard."[14] The point at issue here is not whether Gregory was truthful. Rather, it is whether the age speaks through an ingenuous Gregory or whether, instead, he deliberately shaped the age he depicted. Ampère's premise of naïveté effaces the historian's mediatory presence. To open Gregory's pages is, so it appears, to plunge immediately among the bloody Merovingians. No meddlesome interpreter distracts us from grasping the raw events by intruding his editorial and artistic intelligence.

The naïve Gregory, mirror of his barbarous epoch, was a creature of romantic literary criticism. Long in decline, he was suitably exposed a few years ago by Felix Thürlemann and mainly survives in the guise of a candid reporter.[15] But he merits a brief pause. The writings that featured him include memorable aperçus, such as that of Adolf Ebert:

An interest in the personal, the individual, as being that which may be directly apprehended, is proper not only to a historiography in decay (as Loebell says) but also to one that is beginning, and constitutes, besides, the true nature of the memoir genre; it is precisely this [interest] that imparts a peculiarly gripping attractiveness to Gregory's works, one that triumphs over all its weaknesses and inadequacies. However shapeless and awkward the narrative is, however much it dissolves history into starkly isolated stories that do not manage to connect internally with one another, yet by virtue of the all-individual indwelling life that he reproduces with naïve fidelity, the work retains an unconquerable freshness that attracts ever anew.[16]

Although Ebert's terms are sometimes questionable, he effectively defines the lasting appeal of Gregory's works. He foreshadows not only Buchner's reference to "vivid tales," but also the much admired dissection of Gregory's language and style by Erich Auerbach.[17] The underlying contention, rarely denied, is that Gregory has the virtues of his defects. The conventional skills that he lacks, sometimes to an embarrassing degree, are outweighed by an irresistibly attractive originality.

Once the naïve Gregory is outgrown, however, it can no longer be

---

[14] Walter, "Hagiographisches," p. 299. For another, unavowed, edition of the naïve Gregory, see Charles M. Radding, *A World Made by Men: Cognition and Society, 400-1200* (Chapel Hill, N.C. 1985) pp. 58-64, according to whom Gregory "had few ideas greatly different from the general mass of his society."

[15] Thürlemann, *Gregor von Tours*, pp. 50-58. Noting that naïveté is a genuine topos in scholarly writing about Gregory, he draws attention (pp. 54-55) to the observation of Albet Pauphilet, *Le legs du moyen âge. Études de littérature médiévale* (Melun 1950), p. 41, that naïveté, in the sense of unmannered sincerity, was the "grande vertu nouvelle" that the eighteenth century attributed to the Middle Ages and delighted in repeating. For Gregory the reporter, e.g. Reydellet, *Royauté*, p. 349: "le parti qu'il adopte de raconter simplement, sinon toujour objectivement, les faits et les gestes de la monarchie mérovingienne."

[16] Ebert, *Allgem. Gesch. d. Lit. des MAs* I, 571. Ebert was also perceptive in recognizing the unity of Gregory's hagiographic and historical writings.

[17] Buchner, as above, n. 5; Auerbach, as above, n. 6. Approval is not unanimous; see C(hatillon), "Illusoire *Mimésis.*"

enough to understand what there is about his works that delights us. More subtle approaches began to be developed early in this century, notably by Hellmann and Godefroid Kurth. [18] That Gregory was a conscious artist who employed literary effects and interpreted the events he reported is no longer doubted. It is even ventured that his flawed Latin may conceal "thinking that is more powerful, clear and sophisticated—on its own ground—than he has generally been given credit for."[19] In other words, he was a thoughtful historian. The task of coming to terms with him as one of that tribe needs to be taken in hand.

An established course tending in this direction has been to compare Gregory to his peers, the Christian historians of barbarian peoples, especially Bede, his junior by a century and a quarter. By this test, Gregory's *Histories* comes out as a confused adumbration of better things to come. R. A. Markus concluded that his work

is a medley of historiographical forms rather than a real synthesis . . . a medley, in which first a stretch of ecclesiastical, then a predominantly national history with ecclesiastical episodes included in it, are grafted onto what began as a chronicle. . . . [Gregory's] achievement . . . does not obliterate the impression of a writer who is more at the mercy of his sources and his models and less able to dominate his materials than Bede.[20]

Unlike Bede, then, Gregory lacked direction. Robert Hanning observed that Gregory's work does not leave an impression of "uniformity of purpose and execution. The attempts at interpretation in the tradition of the Christian theology of history remain in contrast to Gregory's keen awareness of harsh barbarian reality; the miracles of Frankish saints and the feuds of Frankish warriors compete for our attention at every turn." Hanning considered this competition disturbing: "Gregory's hagiographical interludes create friction with the realistic and concrete sections of his narrative"; whereas in Bede, hagiography "harmonize[s] perfectly with the flow of British history."[21]

The comparison with Bede, though helpful and enlightening in some respects, is foreordained in its outcome. If the principals had both sought to confect a stylish dessert, it might be granted that Bede's was delicately smooth perfection whereas Gregory's was a lumpy and hesitant compound of ill-assorted ingredients. But histories, at least in this epoch, have no common recipe. Unless allowance is made for goals, the balance of ap-

[18] Hellmann, as above, n. 13; Kurth, "De l'autorité."
[19] Nie, "Roses in January," p. 266; cf. Dill, *Society in the Merovingian Age* p. 348, "The present writer is inclined to think that Gregory is much more of a literary and historical artist than modern critics will allow."
[20] Markus, *Bede*, pp. 5-6.
[21] Hanning, *Vision of History*, pp. 69-70.

proval is bound to tip toward the author whom the comparer regards as normative—in this case, Bede. Reversing the terms of discussion, Robert Latouche found Gregory to be far preferable to his Welsh predecessor Gildas, whose "grandiloquent pedantry has condemned Great Britain to knowing virtually nothing of its past."[22] In these staunchly Gallic terms, Gregory triumphs even over the latecoming Bede.

"When Fortunatus . . . saluted [Gregory] as *lumen generale*," M.L.W. Laistner wrote, "he spoke the unvarnished truth; for no one acquainted with the bishop's works, and with his *History* first and foremost, can fail to realize that Gregory is a figure unique in the Merovingian Age."[23] This is handsome praise, concluding a wise and discerning appreciation. There have been many comparably positive assessments of Gregory in recent decades, which will be encountered in due course. Gregory, it is agreed, is not only invaluable as a source but is also a far more talented and accomplished author than his age allows us to expect. But is such praise handsome enough?

In striving for a wider basis of judgment, the commentators who aligned Gregory with Bede have, regardless of outcome, set an example worthy of emulation. For Gregory is a landmark in the Latin branch of Christian historiography. In the general preface to the *Histories*, he evokes a public avid for nourishment: all sorts of things are going on, and no one has the training to record them; "Woe to our days," people say, in which current events lack a man of letters to write them down.[24] Gregory's prefatory lines should not be mistaken for literary history. "Our days"—which moderns sometimes gloss as days of Merovingian barbarity—had, in reality, nothing to do with the public's complaint. The lean years for historical writing extended far beyond any time that Gregory's contemporaries could remember, and the hiatus could not have been occasioned by educational decline. Sidonius Apollinaris, the most accomplished man of letters in fifth-century Gaul, proved deaf to two requests that he should turn his hand to history. In this refusal, he differed from other skilled authors only in that his decision is known to us. He considered historical writing to be most inappropriate for members of the clergy.[25] Bishop Gregory broke a silence that had

---

[22] Latouche tr. (as below, n. 37), I, 17.

[23] Laistner, *Thought and Letters*, pp. 129-35, here 134-35.

[24] *Hist.* 1.*praef.*, K-L p. 1: "nonnullae res gererentur . . . nec repperire possit quisquam . . . qui haec aut stilo prosaico aut metrico depingeret versu: ingemescebant saepius plerique, dicentes: 'Vae diebus nostris, quia . . . [non] reperitur rethor.' " More fully, n. 190 below. The lines about "Woe to our days etc." are taken as literary history by Manitius, *Gesch. d. lat. Lit.* I, 217. The practice reaches back at least to the eighteenth century; see the famous work of the abbé Du Bos, *Histoire critique* I, 13-14

[25] Sidonius *Epistolae* 4.22, 8.15, ed. André Loyen, 3 vols., Collection des universités de France (Paris 1960-70), II, 160-61; III, 126. The first letter is interesting for the history of historiography. In counseling that his correspondent, Leo (a high official), rather than he,

lasted more than one hundred fifty years. Since the time when Orosius had issued his *Seven Books against the Pagans* (417), the West Roman provinces had witnessed varyingly severe disruptions of civil tranquillity but no generalized cultural blackout. Such barbarian troubles as there were did not prevent Christian letters from pouring forth abundantly in Gaul and elsewhere in the Latin sphere. Among them were polemics with historical overtones, as well as chronicles, biographies, and hagiographies, some of them of enduring merit.[26] But they included nothing known to Gregory (or, for all practical purposes, to us) that might be called history. The historiographic "tradition" Gregory looked back to was as far removed from him as if a fiction writer today were to undertake to be the first novelist since Jane Austen.

Not content to be the first historian since Orosius, Gregory also revived an all-but-abandoned dimension of the historical genre. He had no classical education to speak of. His two tags from Sallust's *Catiline* required no familiarity with the work itself and, though he occasionally cited Virgil and consistently observed the rules of prose rhythm in the ancient manner, he informs us, candidly or not, that his grounding had been in Christian letters alone.[27] So far as we may tell, no profane histories were familiar to him except two fifth-century compositions—quite substantial ones—that are known to us only by grace of his few quotations; Buchner has rightly emphasized how profoundly they differ from Gregory in the manner and preoccupations of their accounts. Yet there is something obtrusively classical, or old-fashioned, about Gregory's *Histories* that sets it apart from Eusebius, Orosius, Bede, and others like them.[28] As though he were another Thucydides or Ammianus, he narrated primarily as a contemporary and eyewitness. Out of the ten *Libri historiarum*, six concern his own times. The first four books serve as an introduction, and the next six are annals in the classical sense of the term.[29] Gregory's choice of ten books reminds one of the Livian decades.[30] Not long after, Isidore of Seville would set down that

should take up history, Sidonius implies that a lofty politician writing history has the stature to silence his critics, whereas a clergyman is fair game, no matter what or how he writes.

[26] Chadwick, *Poetry and Letters*. For the period after Chadwick's book ends, see the list of writings in Dekkers, *Clavis patrum Latinorum*, 2d ed., nos. 957-1022a.

[27] Kurth, "Grégoire de Tours et les études classiques" I, 1-29; M. Manitius, "Zur Frankengeschichte Gregors von Tours." However limited Gregory's knowledge of authors might be, he composed metrical prose in the classical manner; see the important study by Jungblut, "Recherches."

[28] Gregory and the fifth-century historians, Buchner, Einleitung, pp. xv-xvi. Reydellet, *Royauté*, p. 435, recognizes Gregory's affinity to the major Roman historians.

[29] This division of the *Hist.* is commonplace, if not universally endorsed; see, e.g., Laistner, *Thought and Letters*, p. 131. For another view, see below, n. 54.

[30] Only to the extent that Livy is the author whom one immediately associates with books grouped in tens. Another ten-book collection is that of apostle legends ascribed to Abdias, which is believed to have been assembled toward Gregory's time and probably in Gaul; ed.

"history means, in Greek, *apo tou istorein*; that is, to see or know. For among the ancients no one used to write history except someone who had been present and had seen what was to be written down."[31] Much of this famous teaching, to which Isidore added that the eyes are more reliable than the ears, derives, presumably, from Josephus.[32] Whether Gregory had been exposed to this source or not, or found the same teaching in Aulus Gellius, he was well aware that what one saw was inherently more credible than what was merely heard: once doubting Thomas had seen, he believed.[33] Gregory never explains why he considered the decades and centuries prior to his episcopate less worthy of detailed portrayal than the few years after 573, but this is the order of importance embodied in his work.

We may be certain merely from literary context that Gregory could not have thought he was embarking on just another Christian history. Like the active bishops of his day, he built churches at Tours and its environs, promoted cults, and engaged in politics at the royal courts. Even his (largely lost) commentary on the Psalms, and the little tract on computing the hour for night offices on the basis of the stars, set him apart only in a minor way from his peers.[34] If he had composed a chronicle, he would have had a contemporary and not too geographically distant counterpart in Marius, bishop of Avenches.[35] Eyewitness history was another matter. Gregory the Christian historian stands out as an original intellect within a far wider frame of reference than the Merovingian age. The alternative to the Gregory of romanticism, naïvely recording the world around him, is one who, if not so fully aware as we can be of his place in the history of historiography, could not avoid being an even more deliberate and conscious artificer than yet imagined. It is that very unusual intellect, only a little senior to Pope Gregory the Great, which one may hope to discover in his writings.

2. The History of the Franks, or Histories?[36]

As with most classics, Gregory is generally read in the modern languages and long has been. Two full translations into English have appeared

Johannes Albert Fabricius, *Codex apocryphus Novi Testamenti*, 2 vols., 2d ed. (Hamburg 1719).

[31] Isidore *Etymologiae* 1.41.1.

[32] Josephus *Bellum Judaicum praef.* 5.14-15. For Aulus Gellius as another possible source, see below, n. 42. Cf. Momigliano, "Historiography on Written and Oral Tradition."

[33] *VP* 17.*praef.* Gregory seems to say that the minimum condition of faith is that we should, like Thomas, at least believe the evidence of our eyes.

[34] Pietri, *Ville de Tours*, pp. 313-26. About the tract on computing the night office, see below, nn. 87-88. Commentaries on the Psalms are legion.

[35] Marius of Avenches *Chronica*, ed. Mommsen, MGH AA. XI, 232-39 (not an extensive chronicle; it ends in 581); Monod, *Études critiques*, pp. 147-63.

[36] I discuss this subject more fully in "From *Historiae* to *Historia Francorum* and Back Again," pp. 55-76.

within the past fifty years. Readers of these versions almost always encounter Gregory's main work as *The History of the Franks*, the title that also pre-
dominates in the critical literature. Moreover, modern versions, in English
and other languages, often specify that Gregory's work went through two
redactions or drafts. The first, it is said, consists of books I-VI minus sixty-
eight chapters; the second consists of this version plus books VII-X and the
formerly missing chapters of books I-VI. Several printed texts of Gregory,
including an influential edition of the Latin original, take pains to indicate
the two posited stages of composition.[37]

When Gregory ended the *Histories* with a résumé of his episcopate, he
gave a list of his writings, headed by *decem libros historiarum*, "ten books of
histories."[38] He called his work *Historiae*, "Histories," and presumably
wished it to bear this name. He was not responsible for the familiar title
Historia Francorum, "History of the Franks," whose earliest occurrence is in
manuscripts of late Carolingian date.[39] Gregory's choice of title has long
been noted by modern scholars as an interesting fact, but it was Bruno
Krusch who took the novel step, in the Monumenta Germaniae edition of
1937, of deliberately setting *Historiae* in place of the traditional and common name. It is the most conspicuous change attributable to him.[40]

Although the revised title is accepted in many recent studies of Gregory,
its bearing on the contents has attracted less attention than it deserves.[41]

[37] For the English translations, see List of Abbreviations, under Dalton and Thorpe.
French: Grégoire de Tours, *Histoire des Francs*, tr. Robert Latouche, Classiques de l'histoire de
France au Moyen Âge, 2 vols. (Paris 1963); its predecessor was Henri Bordier, tr., *Histoire
ecclésiastique des Francs par saint Grégoire, évêque de Tours, suivie d'un sommaire de ses autres
ouvrages et précédée de sa vie écrite au Xe siècle par Odon, abbé de Cluni*, 2 vols. (Paris 1859-62).
Bordier was influenced by the translation of Wilhelm Giesebrecht, which still underlies all
German versions: Gregor von Tours, *Zehn Bücher fränkischer Geschichte*, Die Geschichtsschrei-
ber der deutschen Vorzeit, 2 vols. (Leipzig 1851) (not available to me); 2d ed. (Leipzig 1878);
see now the Buchner version noted in the List of Abbreviations (its title lacks the Franks).
Oldoni's Italian version (above, ch. I n. 46) bears the title *Storia dei Franchi*; but Krusch's title
is also used: Oldoni, "Gregorio di Tours e i *Libri Historiarum*."
The two redactions are featured in the translations by Giesebrecht, Dalton, Latouche, and
Thorpe. The latter three found this doctrine in *Grégoire de Tours, Histoire des Francs*, ed.
Henri Omont and Gustave Collon, Collection de textes pour servir à l'étude et à l'enseignement de l'histoire, fasc. 2, 16 (Paris 1886-93); or *ibid.*, ed. René Poupardin, Collection de
textes, fasc. 47 (Paris 1913).
[38] *Hist.* 10.31, K-L pp. 535-36.
[39] K-L p. ix: the ms classed as C2, in which this title appears, is of the tenth century and is
an important early witness to Bede's *History*; the standard title became *Historia Francorum*
(sometimes qualified as *ecclesiastica* like Bede's) in the D-class mss.
[40] The title was observed by Monod, *Études critiques*, p. 41; more explicitly by G. Waitz in
Gregory of Tours *Opera*, ed. Wilhelm Arndt and Bruno Krusch, MGH SRM I, part 1 (Han-
nover 1885) p. vii (referred to hereafter as Arndt ed.). Krusch's announcement of his change
has a personal ring: "titulum genuinum ab auctore ipso in ultimo capite . . . traditum nunc
tandem restitui, suppressis titulis falsis editorum anteriorum, qui auctoritate nulla confirman-
tur" (K-L p. ix). Buchner, p. 406.
[41] A practice has lately arisen of referring to Gregory's *Histories* as *libri historiarum*, as for

Whatever the subject of Gregory's narrative may be, he had no intention of featuring the Franks in his title. His unqualified word *Historiae* points in the special direction he took in recording mainly contemporary history— the times that he had seen, rather than just heard of or read about.[42] The label *History of the Franks*, though consecrated by millennial usage, departs from the author's intentions. Whenever it is retained, the advertised substance is not what Gregory offered so much as what medieval and modern readers have wished to find in him.

The claim that Gregory's *Histories* had two redactions was first voiced in the seventeenth century, but its concrete basis belongs to an epoch surprisingly near Gregory's lifetime. The earliest manuscripts of the *Histories*, precious codices of Merovingian date copied within a few generations of Gregory's death, contain a shortened six-book text. The same abridged version of the *Histories* was in the hands of the first known users of Gregory, toward 660 and 727. Yet the full *Histories*, preserved in less venerable manuscripts (notably a twelfth-century codex from Monte Cassino), extends to ten books and began to circulate in this longer form no later than the eighth century.[43]

Attempts have been made to use this textual history as a springboard toward fuller comprehension of Gregory's work. Charles Le Cointe, who objected to what the *Histories* showed of the underside of the Merovingian Church, inaugurated the theory of two versions in 1666 by arguing that only the short recension found in the oldest manuscripts was authentic; all other writings claiming to form part of Gregory's narrative were forgeries or alien interpolations.[44] Nineteenth-century scholars were less skeptical about the contents and more concerned with Gregory's working methods and chronology of composition. They agreed with Le Cointe only in taking

---

example by Brown, *Relics and Social Status*, p. 3, and Oldoni (as above, n. 37). Yet, one rarely refers to Augustine's *Books about the City of God*, or to Orosius's *Books of History against the Pagans*. In Gregory's case, the extension, especially when filled out to "Ten Books of Histories," seems cumbersome and superfluous except for occasional use. Ganshof, *Gregorius van Tours*, p. 31, rightly points out that the simple rendering of *Decem libri historiarum* is *Historiae*.

[42] Isidore of Seville *Etymologiae* 1.41.1 (above, nn. 31-32). A possible source for this idea is Aulus Gellius *Noctes Atticae* 5.18, tr. J. C. Rolfe, Loeb, 3 vols. (London 1927-28), I, 433-437. Cf. Gregory of Tours VP, *praef.*, ed. Krusch, p. 662. Manitius, "Zur Frankengeschichte Gregors von Tours," p. 555, defended the idea that Gregory directly consulted Gellius's work. On the predominance of contemporary events in Gregory's *Histories*, see n. 54 below.

[43] On the textual tradition, Krusch, "Handschriftlichen Grundlagen"; on the earliest mss, pp. 679-89 (they comprise CLA 670, 671, 742a-b, 1122, 1544, and 1584). For the first users, see below, nn. 59-60.

[44] Le Cointe, *Annales ecclesiastici Francorum*. His attack on Gregory is in vol. II. For a summary of his views, see Bordier IV, 297-98. The heirs of his outlook in the nineteenth century were Kries, *De Gregorii Turonensis vita et scriptis*, and Lecoy de la Marche, *De l'autorité de Grégoire de Tours*.

it for granted that the six-book version was prior to that in ten books; Gregory had developed the short recension into the long.[45]

How this assumption succeeded in living on into the second half of the twentieth century is a mystery of Gregory studies, or an object lesson in scholarly carelessness. The issue was definitively settled in 1699 by Thierry Ruinart, the first critical editor of Gregory's works, whose preface contained a lengthy refutation of Le Cointe's charges that the text of the *Histories* had been deformed. Ruinart's positions were endorsed by Arndt in 1885, in the first Monumenta edition of the *Histories*, and restated in Krusch's edition of 1937. Ruinart showed that the sixty-eight chapters lacking in the earlier (six-book) manuscripts could not possibly have been "added" by Gregory to a draft that did not contain them, for the short recension is full of references to material present only in the ten-book text. Ruinart made the crucial point that the ten-book recension was primary; this was the work that had left the bishop's hands, which in closing he asked to be kept intact and unchanged.[46] The short recension, though very old, does not convey Gregory's *Histories*; it derives from Gregory's unique draft and embodies the deliberate abridgment of a later editor.[47] Ruinart explained:

Unless I am much mistaken, these scribes [of the six-book manuscripts] wished to have a history of the kings of the Franks, divorced from alien tales and facts of limited interest; as a result, they took pains to copy those things that Gregory wrote on this subject [i.e. the Frankish kings] and omitted other matters that did not pertain to their theme. [This is why the excised chapters largely concern churchmen, including Gregory himself.] Indeed Fredegar did exactly the same thing: compiling an epitome of Frankish history from Gregory's writings, he omitted much that was not pertinent to Frankish affairs.[48]

[45] The complicated story is traced in my "From *Historiae* to *Historia Francorum*," pp. 59-62.

[46] Ruinart, Preface (unpaged) ¶¶ 86-120; Arndt ed., pp. 18-19. For the decisive part of Ruinart's demonstration, Preface ¶¶ 93-96. Another important argument involves the presence in six-book mss of a fragment from bk. VII: see Arndt ed., p. 19; Krusch, "Handschriftlichen Grundlagen," p. 681; also Ruinart, Preface ¶¶ 89-90.

[47] As a result, the six-book mss should not be mistaken as witnesses to Gregory's work or as "Gregory mss." The work they primarily contain is that of the anonymous editor; they are secondary and indirect witnesses to Gregory's text. These implications, somehow unnoticed by the Monumenta editors and by all those who insisted on believing that the six-book mss accurately mirrored Gregory's Latin, are only just beginning to be applied to the text of the *Histories*. See Zelzer, "Zur Frage des Autors." I am extremely grateful to Dr. Martin Heinzelmann, of the Deutsches historisches Institut Paris, for having drawn this study to my attention and having sent me a copy.

The common ancestor of the text tradition of the *Histories* is removed by several steps from Gregory's final text: Bonnet, review of Arndt ed., p. 166; Buchner, Einleitung, p. xxxv; Löfstedt, "Zu Gregorius Turonensis *Hist. Franc.* 2.31."

[48] Ruinart, Preface ¶ 90.

A "History of the Franks" had not been Gregory's goal, but that is what his seventh-century public wished to read, and what the editor of the six-book abridgment supplied.

The unambiguous teachings of Ruinart and Arndt on this subject were persistently ignored. It took until 1911 for Max Manitius to acclimatize their views in the German-speaking world.[49] France and England turned a blind eye; the doctrine of two drafts continues to be well entrenched in their most widely accessible versions of Gregory (1963, 1974), along with the corollary that the six-book draft preceded that in ten.[50] One reason why this obsolete and false doctrine so long endured is that, once Le Cointe was laid to rest, the two-draft hypothesis proved harmless and roused no passions. Nothing startling, intriguing, or valuable about Gregory and the *Histories* ever came to light as a result. The doctrine imparted a semblance of learned profundity while leaving the common wisdom about Gregory alone.

There is one exception to this rule of innocuousness; and, predictably, its premises differ from the norm. Gustavo Vinay was aware of the teachings of Arndt and Krusch and did not mistake the six-book version for an early stage in Gregory's labors. On the contrary, he sought to establish that the shortened version was Gregory's own work, an abridgment of the ten books that he had personally mapped out but was unable to turn into a final, fully revised edition. Vinay's argument hinges on a comprehensive interpretation of the *Histories*, one of the most sustained attempts ever made to define Gregory's identity as a historian. He argued that Gregory himself discarded a long series of hagiographic and autobiographical passages from the early books of the *Histories*, doing so "in his last years out of the natural exigency to give full effect to his new, clearer, limpid, harmonic perception (*modo di vedere*)."[51]

However deserving of respect, Vinay's argument can persuade only if one first accepts his vision of Gregory as an author who came to understand late

---

[49] Manitius, *Gesch. d. lat. Lit.* I, 220. In the same year, Giesebrecht's teaching was modified: as above, n. 37, 4th ed., by Siegmund Hellmann, Die Geschichtsschreiber der deutschen Vorzeit, 2. Gesamtausgabe, VIII (Leipzig 1911) xxxiii n. 3 (on xxxiv); nevertheless, Hellmann reproduced all of Giesebrecht's original introduction.

[50] Latouche tr., I, 11-13 with n. 8. Though familiar with Buchner's edition, he was particularly attached to the reasoning of Monod, *Études critiques*. Thorpe tr., pp. 21 with n. 97, 26 with n. 120, 32 with n. 185, 316 with n. 101.

Wallace-Hadrill, review of K-L, p. 403, endorsed the teaching of the Monumenta edition: "there never were two distinct redactions of the History; Gregory did not publish his work piecemeal"; but he seems to take a different view of the matter in "Work of Gregory of Tours," p. 51.

[51] Vinay, *San Gregorio*, pp. 75-79, 173-92 (= app. 1, "Sul testo dei primi sei libri dell'*Historia*"); the quotation, p. 78.

in life that the proper subject of his *Histories* was the constructive ferocity of the barbaric Franks. Every technical consideration weighs against the belief that Gregory heavily blue-penciled his writings. Vinay inadequately explained the survival of the ten-book version (closing with Gregory's strong plea that his works should be left intact[52]); and he offered no compelling reason why Gregory, rather than a later editor, should be responsible for the abridgment. Vinay's two-draft hypothesis matters in a way that the more common one does not; but his explanation of the textual tradition makes much less sense than Ruinart's.[53]

In the twenty years of his episcopate, Gregory wrote ten books of "histories." The first book hastens from the Creation to about A.D. 400; the next three proceed briskly to 575; and the last six, at a completely different, leisurely pace, span a mere fifteen years.[54] The work was neither composed all in one piece nor systematically set down *pari passu* with the events even in the most contemporary books. Enough traces of inconsistency and anticipation exist to indicate authorial second thoughts, too few to define a datable process of revision. Although books I-IV form an introductory unit and may have been written as one, early in Gregory's episcopate, neither they nor other parts were issued by Gregory as separate publications.[55] There is little to gain from trying to get behind the *Histories* as we have it. Gregory did not cover all his tracks, but the work is homogeneous enough to discourage a sustained concern with his chronology of composition.[56]

---

[52] "I conjure you all . . . that you never permit these books [all his works are meant, not just the *Histories*] to be destroyed, or to be written over (*rescribi*), or to be reproduced in part only with sections omitted": *Hist.* 10.31, Thorpe, p. 603 (slightly revised). Wallace-Hadrill, "Work of Gregory of Tours," pp. 50, 70, endorses Krusch's use of this passage as a guide to editing the text ("Handschriftlichen Grundlagen," p. 678) and memorably enlarges it into a principle for interpreting the *Histories*. Imprecations similar to Gregory's close the Apocalypse, the last book of the Bible, as well as various early Christian writings: Monod, *Études critiques*, p. 66.

[53] For details, see my "From *Historiae* to *Historia Francorum*," pp. 63-64. The account of Vinay's theory by Wallace-Hadrill, "Gregory of Tours and Bede," pp. 99-100, is unfortunately detached from the wider context of two-draft hypotheses.

[54] The assignment of six whole books to a few years deserves more notice than it sometimes gets (cf. n. 29 above). Brunhölzl, *Gesch. d. lat. Lit.* I, 137, regards only books I-III as introductory, presumably because Gregory's ability to be an eyewitness begins in book IV. This choice gives the *Histories* the appearance of focusing on fifty years rather than a mere fifteen or sixteen. An identical position was taken by Bordier (above, n. 37) I, vi. Köpke, "Gregor von Tours," p. 317, already recognized perfectly well that Gregory's six books for sixteen years compared with four books for five millennia.

[55] For Gregory's few known publications in his lifetime, see above, n. 3. Bonnet, *Latin de Grégoire de Tours*, p. 11 n. 3, believed that a cross-reference by Gregory to a book of his (as, in the *Histories*, to the *Vita patrum*) was proof that the work in question had been published. This is possible but cannot be confirmed.

[56] On this subject the point of departure is Krusch, in K-L pp. xxi-xxii, according to whom Gregory worked hard at expanding and correcting the work and left it incomplete, without its final polish, at his death; but the genesis of the *Histories* cannot be educed from the manu-

We are well advised to concentrate on the finished ten books, alongside the finished *Miracula*, just as their author left them at the close of his life.

The *Histories* proved irksome to seventh-century readers. Though the work was unique and invaluable as a source about the early Merovingian kings, Gregory seemed to have diluted this subject with capsule biographies of the bishops of Clermont and Tours and with many other incidental matters. The farther he went, the slower his pace. The unflattering portrayal he gave in books VII-X of certain royal personages could not have been altogether pleasing after 613, when the son of Chilperic and Fredegonde, Chlothar II, became the sole and apparently well-loved ruler of the Frankish kingdom.[57] The public hungering for history that Gregory evokes in his general preface may have been a poetic fiction.[58] The first real public he won could thank a considerate editor for supplying a brisker narrative than Gregory had written: a six-book abridgment so designed as to be, in effect, the first "History of the Franks." This is the text preserved by the earliest manuscripts.

The tendency toward Frankish royal history embodied in this edition became even firmer in the Fredegar chronicle (ca. 660). Fredegar worked with only an abridged Gregory. He left out book I altogether, substituting other material and enriching it with an account of Frankish origins from Troy, along with much else. Out of what was left of Gregory, he formed as his own third book a *Historia epitomata* composed of seventy-three chapters drawn from books II-IV and only nineteen from books V-VI.[59] Gregory's testi-

---

scripts. Oldoni tr. (above, ch. I n. 46) I, xxxvi-vii, spells out the chronology very firmly, without indicating on whose authority; cf. Vogüé, "Grégoire le Grand," p. 226 n. 1: Gregory's chronology of composition poses almost insoluble problems.

Buchner, Einleitung, p. xxii, argues that Gregory cannot have known the full course of the famous Sicharius and Chramnesindus feud when he wrote his first account of it; therefore, its beginning (*Hist.* 7.47) is separated from its termination (9.19). Buchner's reasoning would work if no other variables were involved than the acquisition of information; but why should one think so? Similarly, Thompson, *Goths in Spain*, p. 72 n. 7, tries to date events in the Hermenegild rebellion (580-85) by assuming that Gregory's reports are in strict order of time. The argument is frail. These many reports have only one chronological boundary: *Hist.* 5.38, 6.18, and 6.43 all presuppose Hermenegild's defeat and capture, whereas 8.28 announces his execution; yet, the rebel's capture was separated from his death by a scant year. One might plausibly infer, without certainty of course, that Gregory was aware of Hermenegild's death when he started writing about him and had artistic reasons for setting out the chapters as he did. Users of Gregory have been understandably tempted to believe that he wrote as the facts came to his ears (the phrase "hot off the fire" has been used in connection with him). In the view of Buchner (*loc. cit.*), Gregory wrote *laufend*; Latouche tr., I, 8-11, is even more committed to this idea. No compelling evidence that such was the case has yet been supplied.

[57] Fredegar *Chron.* 4.42, ed. Krusch, p. 142. A warm eulogy of Chlothar follows the grisly account of Brunichild's execution. Nevertheless, Fredegar was not a contemporary of Chlothar II and may have looked back through rose-colored glasses.

[58] K-L p. 1 (partly quoted above, n. 24). Of course, Gregory's statement does not *have* to be poetic fiction.

[59] Ed. Krusch, pp. 88-118. The title *Historia epitomata* is not Fredegar's, but conventional.

mony was valued in inverse ratio to its contemporaneity, and he turned into a political historian. The tilt toward the past was further accentuated in the *Liber historiae Francorum* (727), whose nameless author was unacquainted with Fredegar. Again, book I of Gregory was disregarded, and out of sixty-seven chapters excerpted from books II-VI, fifty-five came from books II-IV.[60]

The severe selectivity of the *Liber historiae Francorum* proved to be the nadir in the fortunes of Gregory's *Histories*. From then on, the work began to regain its losses and to circulate in a form more closely approximating the original.[61] The new interest in those portions of Gregory formerly considered superfluous went hand in hand with the idea that his work was *historia Francorum*, as Paul the Deacon showed when he noted, in reference to Gregory, that the facts of some defeat "of the Franks" could be read in "their history."[62] Paul's copy belonged to the Carolingian edition of Gregory, still abridged but at least reunited with its last four books.[63] As time passed, successive copyists were interested enough to seek out and fill in missing chapters. An almost complete text of Gregory was attained by the beginning of the tenth century.[64] The nameless editor responsible for it took the most constructive step in the reconstitution of the *Histories* until the work, almost a millennium later, of Ruinart and the Monumentists. In 1937, Krusch capped the long, collective effort to recover those parts of Gregory's narrative that early readers, and perhaps not only they, had deemed distracting and superfluous: he struck out *Historia Francorum* and reinstated Gregory's own title, *Historiae*.

The two-draft hypothesis is obtrusive in writings about the *Histories*, yet it is far more easily dispensed with than retained. Greater effort is needed to do justice to the title *Historiae* now heading Gregory's major work in the authoritative edition. It is difficult to clear the mind of a descriptive label that one encounters everywhere, that one probably becomes familiar with before reading Gregory, and that one finds emblazoned in the versions that come most readily to hand. That Gregory should be anything but the historian of the Franks is a new and almost subconsciously resisted teaching.

---

[60] MGH SRM II, 245-304. An alternative and often-used title for the *Liber historiae Francorum* is *Gesta regum Francorum* (see CLA 98), another indication of what the public wished to read about.

[61] Krusch, "Handschriftlichen Grundlagen," p. 699; the *Liber historiae Francorum* itself attests to this in that the author's six-book version of Gregory had been augmented out of a ten-book text; see Krusch, "Zu M. Bonnets Untersuchungen," p. 433.

[62] Paul the Deacon *H.L.* 3.29, ed. Bethmann-Waitz, p. 108.

[63] On the Carolingian edition, an amalgam of Gregory, Fredegar, and the *Liber historiae Francorum*, see Krusch, "Handschriftlichen Grundlagen," pp. 707-708, 690-704. The last books of Gregory are abridged along the same lines as the first six in the Merovingian edition: *ibid.*, p. 690. The fact is very damaging to Vinay's theory.

[64] See my "From *Historiae* to *Historia Francorum*," p. 66.

Krusch's innovation caused at least one critic to affirm that the traditional title was basically correct.[65] Vinay sought to enhance Gregory's Frankish-mindedness by having him personally blot out his supposed excess of hagiography and autobiography.[66] Even east of the Rhine, a recent account of medieval Latin literature still affirms that "the Franks are for Gregory a chosen people. . . . Faith in the mission of the Franks stamps the great work of history."[67] Perhaps the Merovingian abridger knew best. The subject he highlighted was conceivably the one Gregory really wished to stress. The greater likelihood, however, is that the full text, with its ecclesiastical by-ways and eyewitness *longueurs*, goes hand in hand with Gregory's ethnically undefined title. Here, at least, is an issue more likely than the two-draft hypothesis to advance understanding of Gregory. His fame was earned by an often shortened *History of the Franks*. It remains to be seen what he amounts to as an author of *Histories*.

3. *Miracula*: A Christian Historian's Answer to Philosophy

B efore entreating posterity to keep his works intact, Gregory specified what they were: "I have written ten books of *Histories*, seven of *Wonders* (*Miracula*), and one about the *Life* of the fathers (*Vita patrum*); I commented in one book on the Book of Psalms; and I also composed one book about the *Offices of the Church*."[68] He was not always of the same mind about the extent of the *Wonders*. In introducing *The Glory of the Confessors*, last of the collection, he listed the *Vita patrum* as the next-to-last in an eight-book whole, not a separate tract; and in the many references to it in the *Histories*, the reader is directed to an individual "book of his life" (that is, of the saint just mentioned) rather than to the collective work into which, sooner or later, Gregory gathered the various *vitae*. The seven or eight books of *Miracula* are distributed among five titles: I. *The Glory of the Martyrs*; II. *The Passion and Miracles of St. Julian Martyr*; III-VI. *The Miracles*

---

[65] Ganshof, *Gregorius van Tours*, p. 7: "that, nevertheless, the work is in the very first place a history of the Franks or rather of the Frankish kingdom may scarcely be seriously doubted." Wallace-Hadrill, review of K-L, p. 404, expressed momentary reservations about the wisdom of Krusch's choice.

[66] As above, n. 51.

[67] Brunhölzl, *Gesch. d. lat. Lit.* I, 138. In the more reserved accents of Manitius, *Gesch. d. lat. Lit.* I, 221, Gregory narrated the history of the Merovingians without sparing them or exaggerating.

[68] *Hist.* 10.31, K-L pp. 535-36: "Decem libros Historiarum, septem Miraculorum, unum de Vita Patrum scripsi; in Psalterii tractatu librum unum commentatus sum; de Cursibus etiam ecclesiasticis unum librum condidi." This forms part of a listing of his achievements as bishop of Tours. Gregory explains why he writes "life" rather than "lives" of the Fathers: *VP, praef.*, ed. Krusch, pp. 662-63. All page references to the *Miracula* or its parts are to the Krusch ed.

A noteworthy recent enterprise embracing all of Gregory's writings is Weidemann, *Kultur-geschichte der Merowingerzeit*, a massive and encyclopedic collection, undertaken with great care, of the factual information that may be extracted from Gregory's works.

of St. Martin; (VII. *The Life of the Fathers*); and VII. (or VIII.) *The Glory of the Confessors.*[69] The *Wonders*, then, unlike the *Histories*, may have been envisaged as distinct parts before being formed into a comprehensive collection.

Gregory's catalogue accords the *Histories* the same preference within his entire corpus that is assigned to the *Martyrs* in the collection of *Wonders*. St. Julian (of Brioude in the Auvergne) takes precedence, as a martyr, over the confessor Martin of Tours; in turn, the four books about St. Martin are so situated as to place him at the head of the confessors. Since the "fathers" of the *Vita patrum* were comparatively recent saints, Gregory's decision, recorded in the *Histories*, to treat this tract as separate from a seven-book *Wonders* may be a later and more final idea than the eight-book order described in the *Confessors* and maintained in the text tradition.[70] Gregory regarded the *Histories* as not only his longest but his principal work; next in weight were the *Wonders* and *Fathers*, followed by the minor *Psalter Commentary* and *Ecclesiastical Offices*.

Gregory had more minor writings to his credit than he chose to list. No trace survives of the collection he once says he made of the Masses of Sidonius Apollinaris and introduced with a special preface.[71] Modern editions of his works include two additional items. One is an account of the Seven Sleepers of Ephesus, "interpreted" from the Greek by a resident Syrian named John and rendered by Gregory into Latin; he refers to it in the *Martyrs*, after a summary of the story.[72] The other is an expurgated selection from a narrative, deemed apocryphal, of the miracles and passion of St. Andrew; it ends with Gregory's disclosure that the apostle's feast, 30 November, was his own birthday.[73] Whether he was also responsible for a version of the *Acta Thomae*, as Bonnet believed, is less certain.[74] The lost

---

[69] Eight-book collection: GC, *praef.*, ed. Krusch, p. 748. References to *liber vitae eius: Hist.* 1.45, 2.21, 2.37, 5.8-10, etc. Gregory refers to GC and GM as *libri miraculorum*, to VSJ and VSM as *virtutes* or *miracula* of Julian or Martin. For a full listing of these cross-references, see K-L, Index, p. 551, s.v. "Gregorius, ep. Turon.," *in fine.*

[70] Of the twenty saints, one is of uncertain date and four died before 500. The rest belong to the sixth century, and ten died after 550.

[71] *Hist.* 2.22.

[72] Ed. Krusch, pp. 848-53; p. 853, "explicit passio sanctorum martyrum septem dormientium apud Ephysum, translata in Latinum per Gregorium episcopum, interpretante Iohanne Syro, quae observatur 6. Kal. Augusti." The facts are also given in GM 94.

[73] Ed. Max Bonnet, MGH SRM I, 826-46; the reference to Gregory's birthday, p. 846, together with a profession of stylistic inadequacy (*sermone rusticus*); expurgation, p. 827. Zelzer, "Zur Frage des Autors," is specially concerned with confirming Gregory's authorship.

[74] Bonnet, *Latin de Grégoire de Tours*, p. 9. Not accepted by Manitius, *Gesch. d. lat. Lit.* I, 219. Laistner, *Thought and Letters*, p. 132, set the account of Thomas on a par with that of Andrew. The skepticism of Arndt, MGH SRM I, 11, concerning the *Miracula s. Andreae* seems to have been eventually overruled. On both apostle texts, see Lipsius, *Die apokryphen*

collection of Masses was in the nature of an edition; the accounts of the Seven Sleepers and St. Andrew were adaptations, lacking the originality of Gregory's other compositions. They would, among other things, have introduced an element of thematic dispersal and confusion in the order of the writings that he lists. He chose to omit them. Although the *Histories* is famous for being a jumble, Gregory had, in some respects, a tidy mind.

The individual books of *Wonders* have the orderliness that comes from deliberate planning. The *Martyrs* and *Confessors*, which frame the collection, closely resemble each other in design; Gregory underlines the parallelism in a preface.[75] At the start, a combination of hierarchy, history, and geography determines the succession of items, until the narrative settles down to Gaul, passing from city to city. There are signs, in both, of some muddle in the latter half, as though additions were made somewhat haphazardly to an unfinished draft; but the parallel endings featuring the Italian town of Nola (St. Felix in the *Martyrs*, Paulinus in the *Confessors*), as well as a concluding tale of avarice, evidently formed part of the original outline.[76] In *The Miracles of St. Martin*, the first book concerns events that took place before Gregory became bishop, in precisely the same way that the four introductory books of the *Histories* precede his accession to the episcopate.[77] The next three books about Martin parallel Gregory's years at Tours, and a precise chronological track may be traced, if one cares to do so, from references to the saint's annual feasts.[78] The *Vita patrum*, unlike

---

Apostelgeschichten und Apostellegenden I, 137-70. Against the attribution, conclusively, Klaus Zelzer, "Zu den lateinischen Fassungen der Thomasakten," *Wiener Studien* 84 (1971) 161-79; 85 (1972) 185-212; and "Zu Datierung und Verfasserfrage der lateinischen Thomasakten," *Studia Patristica* 12 (1975) 190-94.

[75] GC, *praef.*, ed. Krusch, p. 748: "Et quoniam primum libellum de Domini miraculis inchoavi, velim et huic libello de sanctorum angelorum virtutibus adhibere principium."

[76] GM: the Lord (1-7), Our Lady (8-10), John the Baptist (11-15), the apostles (26-32), martyrs of Italy (33-46), of Gaul (47-88), of Spain (89-92), of the East (94-102), Felix of Nola (103), punishment of avarice (105), the sign of the cross (106).

GC: Angels (1), Hilary of Poitiers (2), Eusebius of Vercelli (3), Martin of Tours (4-14), regions, beginning with Touraine (15-25), Limoges (27-28), Clermont (29-36), Auxerre (40), Dijon (41-43) etc., Paulinus of Nola (108), examples of punished avarice (109-10).

The most apparent confusion involves the dispersion of entries in GC: Bourges, 79-81, 90, 100; Paris, 87-89, 103; Limoges, 27-28, 101-102. In both tracts, the succession of localities often suggests a systematic pattern of distribution, but not one that is consistently carried out. The settings of Gregory's stories jump around. The table of contents to GC lists chs. 105-107, but they were never written.

[77] VSM 2.*praef.* VSM 2.1 is the only place where Gregory records his accession (the event is also alluded to in VSM 3.10). *Hist.* 4 ends with the murder of King Sigibert, rather than Gregory's accession two years before; Gregory chose the resounding public event nearest to it in time.

[78] Schlick, "Composition et chronologie," p. 286 (a major study of the *De Virtutibus sancti Martini*). See, also, on the chronological order of miracles, Heinzelmann, "Source de base de la littérature hagiographique latine," pp. 237-40.

any of the other eight books, is formed of twenty independent *libelli*, each with its own preface. The underlying sameness of subject matter does not prevent studied adaptations of structure to particular needs.

In the view of one modern commentator, the *Wonders* is a "usually wearisome array of impossibilities," and though such outright dismissals are rare, the eight books have more often been deemed an embarrassment, to be disregarded, than a precious clue to Gregory's outlook and identity as a historian.[79] Vinay, who strove as hard as anyone to understand Gregory, conceived of him as being, in part, a grandiose failure: his intense sensitivity remained incoherent; it could not "be translated into an organic vision of history and life," because the age into which Gregory was fated to be born denied him the needed intellectual resources.[80] Vinay came to this view via a resolute disparagement of Gregory's writings on the saints; "the *libri miraculorum* are the work of the pious and good bishop who feels and reasons like any other of his good and pious confreres," and his miracle-centered faith was, throughout his life, that of the little boy who learned in the family circle to regard holy dust and other relics as the sovereign defense against all ills.[81] So conceived, Vinay's Gregory gains stature only in the *Histories*, as the admirer of barbaric vigor and energy "who saw what was firm, positive, and constructive" in the turbulent passions of the invaders.[82]

Vinay's conclusion tempts one to ask, maliciously, whether admiration for barbaric vigor is necessarily less infantile than belief in miracles. The pertinent issue, however, is whether Gregory may rightly be said to have fallen short of "an organic vision of history and life." Vinay was not alone in expressing this view; the scholars whom we earlier saw comparing the *Histories* with Bede's narrative also came away with a sense of incoherence.[83] In their case as in Vinay's, the conclusion gains force from one-sided emphasis of Gregory's *Histories*.

Gregory was the first Latin Christian to write history on an ambitious scale in well over a century, and he was even more unusual for addressing himself predominantly to current events. These characteristics belong just as much to the author of the *Wonders* as to that of the *Histories*. The miracles that Gregory collects are not, either in fact or intent, a succession of

[79] Quotation from Brehaut tr., Preface, p. xvi. Foakes-Jackson, *History of Church History*, p. 108, intimates that Gregory was not really a Christian. Lof, "De san Agustín a san Gregorio de Tours," pp. 36-37, points out the low esteem of the major nineteenth-century historians of dogma for the cult of martyrs, which they deemed to be a second-class Christianity. That opinion has markedly improved since then seems doubtful.

[80] Vinay, *San Gregorio*, p. 169.

[81] *Ibid.*, pp. 98, 16-17.

[82] *Ibid.*, p. 169; cf. his contrast between the "mediocre" Gregory of the *Miracula* and the "imaginative and original author" of the *Histories* (p. 58).

[83] Above, nn. 20-21.

happenings vying with each other in prodigiousness and incredibility; some are no more remarkable than the cure of a headache or sore tooth.[84] Minor or major, the miracles are narrated with verisimilitude, as historical events involving real people in their relationship to the saints; and they occur in exactly the same geographic compass and time period as the *Histories*. The *Wonders* has traditionally been mined for autobiographical details; it tell us much about Gregory's life that we would not otherwise know.[85] But its importance for an understanding of the *Histories* does not end there. The same author—a Christian who (unlike Sidonius Apollinaris) believed that contemporary events narrated historically had didactic value—greets us in the *Wonders*, just as, conversely, many tales of miracles greet us in the *Histories*. There is reason to look more closely at what he might have been doing in his second major project.

One of the least items in his catalogue sheds light on Gregory's concept of the miraculous and sets it off from ours. That book, which he called *The Offices of the Church* (*De cursibus ecclesiasticis*), was first published in 1853 from a unique manuscript lacking an attribution to him; its title in the sole manuscript is *The Course of the Stars* (*De cursu stellarum*).[86] It is mainly "a brief account of simple astronomy so that the clergy could perform certain ceremonies at the proper time of the night."[87] The work is illustrated with images of star locations, and its information has proved, on modern verification, to be impressively accurate.[88] Whereas the didactic quality of the *Histories* and *Wonders* is of the kind associated with pulpits, that of the *Offices* is of a practical, schoolmasterly sort that Gregory does not elsewhere display. The book reminds one, on a small scale, of Bede on the reckoning of time.

However that may be, its wider interest stems from Gregory's disproportionately long introductory paragraphs about the Seven Wonders of the World, commentaries that enjoyed a small medieval circulation apart from the treatise they head.[89] Here, as in the title of the eight-book collection, Gregory is concerned with *miracula*, "wonders," as distinct from more individualized *virtutes*, "miracles," worked by God through saints and their

[84] VSM 2.60 (headache), 3.1 (fish bone in throat), 3.60 (toothache). See below, n. 100.

[85] Accounts of Gregory's early life and family background seldom indicate how essential the *Miracula* are as source of this information; e.g. Monod, *Études critiques*, pp. 25-32. On this subject, see below, nn. 341-43.

[86] See Krusch ed., pp. 854, 857.

[87] Tr. William C. McDermott, *Gregory of Tours: Selections from the Minor Works*, in Edward Peters, ed., *Monks, Bishops, and Pagans* (Philadelphia 1975), p. 207.

[88] *Ibid.*, p. 208. Cf. Manitius, *Gesch. d. lat. Lit.* I, 221, who noted the parallel with Bede on time reckoning.

[89] Krusch ed., pp. 856-57.

relics.[90] Gregory sets out a straightforward argument: philosophers, in their learned leisure, have singled out seven *miracula* "as more marvelous than others"; they include Noah's Ark and Solomon's Temple as well as classical splendors, such as the Colossus of Rhodes, the Theater at Heraclea, and the Pharos of Alexandria; these wonders, even if some were built pursuant to God's command, "were none the less established by men" and therefore have perished or are subject to destruction; there are other wonders, however, that come directly from God, "which in no age grow old, by no accident fall, by no loss are diminished, except when the Master shall have ordained that the universe be destroyed"; these are the tides, the annual fruitfulness, the phoenix, Mt. Etna, the springs of Grenoble, the sun, and the moon and stars.[91] Although Gregory does not explain why this contrast of human to divine wonders is appropriate as an introduction to the *Offices*, his rationale is easily inferred from the contents. Before detailing the reckoning of time from the stars, he wished to remind readers emphatically that stellar motion, like the tides and course of the sun, proceeds from God and is not an inevitable operation of nature.

The significance of Gregory's reasoning was observed and spelled out by Godefroid Kurth:

> Wonders (*le miracle*), to Gregory's way of thinking, are not extraordinary and exceptional acts of Providence momentarily suspending the course of natural laws. . . . [T]hey are, on the contrary, regular and daily manifestations of divine power. . . . One may say that Gregory knows nothing more natural than the supernatural; he is so imbued [with this belief] that he would be unable to conceive of the world otherwise than as a machine whose maker (*auteur*) comes at every moment to correct, suspend, or change its workings.[92]

Kurth's "machine," implying a *tertium quid*, is not quite right. Gregory is as far removed as we may imagine from any acceptance of objectivity in nature. That is why he classes the heavenly bodies, tides, and seasons as divine "wonders," in relation to which prodigious human accomplishments occupy a lowly and perishable place. There was no call for a self-propelled mechanism to stand between the Almighty and the manifestation of His power on earth.

However starkly expressed, Gregory's view of natural phenomena was not peculiar to him or to his age, but derived from the common Judeo-Christian doctrines of divine creation and omnipotence. Philo, in the first century, had already affirmed that the miracles of the Hebrew Scriptures

---

[90] Gregory uses the two terms as synonyms (see above, n. 69, for his references to VSJ and VSM), but though *virtutes* "miracles of saints" were *miracula*, many "wonders" were not *virtutes*.

[91] CS, ed. Krusch, pp. 857-63; tr. McDermott, pp. 209-18.

[92] Kurth, "De l'autorité," p. 122.

were far less amazing than the created world, whose wonders men overlook because of their frequency.[93] According to Augustine, " 'all natural events are filled with the miraculous.' 'The events of every day, the birth of men, the growth of plants, rainfall,' are all 'daily miracles,' signs of the mysterious power of God at work in the universe."[94] Men take for granted, Augustine said, the slow miracle that, in a vineyard, turns irrigation water into wine and are amazed only at Christ's making wine out of water " 'in quick motion,' as it were"; yet the slow, habitual processes happen just as much by God's will as the rapid ones.[95] Gregory the Great, also fastening upon a miracle of increase, stressed how much less astonishing it was for a multitude to be fed from one loaf than that the Almighty Lord who accomplished this should produce great harvests from a few seeds and create everything from nothing.[96]

The "natural science" of the Church fathers centered on Creation, miracle, and resurrection, all three linked by the common theme of an omnipotent God unconstrained by any natural necessity. In respect to these doctrines, Christianity "was in no way whatever the heir of Greek philosophy."[97] The nature of the philosophers operated inevitably, necessarily, predictably; and the assurance it gave, grounded in common sense, that spring would follow winter also implied that death would unavoidably follow birth. God's freedom from natural limitations, in the Christian scheme of things, promised freedom to men from the condition to which they seemed fated—the tyranny of natural law; and the visible, "quick motion" miracles that God "does not disdain to work . . . in heaven and earth [were meant to arouse] the soul, hitherto occupied with visible things, to the worship of himself, the invisible God."[98]

Skeptical (as Augustine would be) toward the inadequately established verities of the philosophers, the Latin fathers Tertullian and Hilary of Poitiers had stoutly advocated the literal acceptance of miracles.[99] So did Gregory of Tours. In the introduction to the *Offices*, his contrast of human

[93] Grant, *Miracle and Natural Law*, p. 186.

[94] Ward, *Miracles and the Medieval Mind*, p. 3.

[95] Brown, *Augustine of Hippo*, p. 416. For a fuller exposition, see Uytfanghe, "Controverse biblique," pp. 211-12. Uytfanghe sees Augustine's emphasis on *miracula cottidiana* as part of his effort to "relativize" and spiritualize the concept of miracle. But, in Gregory, such belief is by no means incompatible with the conviction of daily divine intervention in human affairs.

[96] Gregory the Great *Dialogi*, 3.37.8, ed. Adalbert de Vogüé, 3 vols., Sources chrétiennes 251, 260, 265 (Paris 1978-80) II, 416. Cf. the passages of Augustine cited by Uytfanghe, "Controverse biblique," p. 226 n. 46.

[97] Grant, *Miracle and Natural Law*, p. 263. Cf. Uytfanghe, "Controverse biblique," p. 206: the idea of an autonomous nature was foreign to Hebrew thought.

[98] Augustine *Civ. Dei* 10.12, ed. Dombart and Kalb, p. 287; tr. Bettenson, p. 390.

[99] Grant, *Miracle and Natural Law*, pp. 193, 212, (on Augustine) 218. Augustine's early views had been reserved: Uytfanghe, "Controverse biblique," p. 211; Saxer, "Reliques, miracles et récits de miracles," p. 261.

to divine wonders implicitly challenged the "philosophers" who had drawn up the initial list. Regardless of the distinctions pre-Christian sages might make, ostensibly ordinary and regular operations of nature did not differ from sudden, arbitrary acts of divine power; a continuum existed between expected and unexpected aspects of God's providential rule; and these facts dissolved human pretensions to wisdom and proved them vain. Openness to wonders was the true and only science offering men liberation from the death-bringing life they endured.

In this perspective, one should not expect the eight books of *Miracula* to be a record of amazing happenings. Nor, in many cases, are they. As Kurth observed, "[Gregory] often takes the most ordinary events of daily life as interventions from on high." Dalton noted the same trait: "he attributes to supernatural power a persistence of intervention in trivial no less than in great affairs which the most ardent advocates of miracle in our own times would find superfluous."[100] To grade wonders by degree of supernaturalness hardly concerned Gregory: his object, rather, was to multiply them; "no [ecclesiastical author] has related more miracles than Gregory of Tours."[101] One basis for disbelief had always been that miracles were a thing of the past, richly documented in the Gospels but vanished from the world of everyday experience.[102] The whole thrust of Gregory's *Wonders* is to illustrate the ordinariness of the miraculous, available today, near at hand, in the most commonplace objects. Far from wishing to stake out a monopoly for his own St. Martin of Tours, his narratives celebrate a host of saints, great and small, ancient and modern, and portray the dissemination through every part of Gaul of their holy graves and powerful, wonder-working relics.[103] Gregory himself, who laid no claims to special merit, details personal experiences of the miraculous at every stage of his life and thrusts himself forward as a leading witness to divine generosity.[104] Unlike the mi-

[100] Kurth, "De l'autorité," p. 184; Dalton I, 18.

[101] Delehaye, "Receuils antiques des miracles des saints," p. 305. According to Uytfanghe, "Controverse biblique," p. 218, Gregory departs sharply from tradition at least "par le nombre de miracles qu'il relate." Uytfanghe's judgment that Gregory overdoes the part of miracle in sanctity falls in the order of ideas indicated above, n. 79.

[102] E.g. Sulpicius Severus *Dialogi* 1.26; Augustine *Civ. Dei* 22.8. Uytfanghe, "Controverse biblique," pp. 210-11, lists respectable Church fathers, such as the historian Eusebius, who believed that miracles were now superfluous and a thing of the past.

[103] Brehaut tr., p. xvi (about the four books of VSM), "Gregory is here a promoter and advertiser"; Wallace-Hadrill, "Work of Gregory of Tours," p. 53, "Pilgrims . . . needed instruction and entertainment. . . . It is just possible, also, that . . . St. Martin's reputation no longer went unchallenged. . . . [In] any case the cult of St. Martin was a fire that needed regular stoking." What really needs explanation, however, is the attention Gregory lavished upon dozens of saints other than his special patrons Julian and Martin. There was no room for games of rivalry and prestige in Gregory's outlook; the saints sustained each other.

[104] An incomplete list: GM 10, 50, 83, 86; VSJ 25; VSM 1.32, 34, 2.1, 32, 60, 3.*praef.* (apologies for relating miracles from which he benefited), 60, 4.1, 2; VP 2.2-3; GC 43, 45,

ser's hoarded treasure, the riches of heaven were profusely poured out upon humanity, only to be reached for in order to be grasped. Both the *Martyrs* and the *Confessors* close with tales of avarice, the message of each book underscored by its contrary.[105]

Gregory's determination to multiply the holy is nowhere more apparent than in his positive and uncritical approach to authentication. In the famous fourth-century *Life of St. Martin* by Sulpicius Severus, the first miracle that the saint performs after becoming bishop of Tours involves the discrediting of a false cult; the people venerated a tomb, thinking its occupant to be a martyr, but Martin summoned up the dead man's spirit and made him confess that he was only an executed robber.[106] Much as Gregory loved the patron of his see, this example went unheeded in his *Wonders*. On the contrary, supernatural interventions always operate in the other direction: ancient tombs are certified to contain saints; the long-lost burial places of bishops are found; holy men and women lacking a cult finally obtain one. St. Martin himself, in his only personal appearances in Gregory's *Confessors*, calls forth a bishop and a religious lady from their graves, lending his prestige to the certification of their holiness and animating their cult.[107] The episcopal authority Gregory wielded, far from being exercised to restrain popular devotion, stoked the delicate flames of belief by increasing the objects of reverence.

The same impulse lay behind Gregory's approach to relics. Though Tours gloried in the corporeal remains of St. Martin, gained (as the *Histories* relates) at the expense of rivals from Poitiers, Gregory never intimates that a saint's body, or a fragment of it, should be more highly prized than relics of a humbler kind.[108] He may have known that popular piety discriminated among holy objects, just as it preferred martyrs with passion narratives to those without;[109] but Gregory gave no encouragement to such fastidiousness. Where relics were concerned, anything would do: a little dust, a shred of bark, oil from a lamp, wax from a candle, a bit of rope. Gregory the Great

---

65; *Hist.* 8.14. For a delicately humorous portrayal of his unworthiness, GM 83. There are, besides, many miracles experienced by members of his immediate family, and others that he has personally seen; for a repertory, see Kurth, "De l'autorité," p. 123 nn. 4-5.

[105] GM 105, GC 109-11.

[106] V. *Martini* 11.

[107] Authentication: GM 5 *in fine*, 11, 48, 55, 62; GC 4, 5, 8, 17, 18, 21, 27, 30, 35, 79, 83, 100, 103. St. Martin intervening to authenticate: GC 4-5 (the second story is particularly gripping).

[108] Tours gets the relics, *Hist.* 1.48.

[109] Preference for martyrs with narratives: GM 63. Nothing known to me directly attests that whole bodies were preferred to humbler relics; but Gregory the Great and the Gelasian Sacramentary took pains to explain that objects placed in contact with holy tombs were just as effective as whole bodies, and various miracles (e.g. a cloth running blood) were reported tending to prove this point. See Hermann-Mascard, *Reliques des saints*, pp. 45, 49; McCulloh, "Cult of Relics."

was of the same mind. What mattered was simply association with the saint, in life or after death.[110] Early chapters of the *Confessors* successively celebrate miracles by a stone on which St. Martin sat, a tree that he moved, a chapel at which he prayed, oil from a lamp at his tomb, a grape from a vine that he planted, and a modern apparition of his close to Langres.[111] In these circumstances, the possibilities for fragments of the holy to proliferate were, in effect, unlimited. To focus devotion on bodily relics, as in the major Carolingian transfers of Roman martyrs to the north, imposed scarcity and fostered "quality control" by ecclesiastical authority.[112] If quality ever was on Gregory's mind, he kept the thought out of the *Miracula*. His implied message is, rather: Accept relics of any kind and the Almighty will authenticate them.

Gregory's lack of discrimination *vis-à-vis* miracles and relics is consistent with his view that the tides and heavenly bodies were directly and continually actuated by God, not just set in motion at the Creation. Properly, that is, uncritically understood, sudden miraculous events were hardly less frequent or common than the predictable happenings that philosophers called natural phenomena. The ubiquity of the miraculous is not an idea incidentally reflected in the *Wonders*. It is the work's central teaching, an unstated lesson conveyed by sheer repetition.

As noted above, Gregory's hagiographic side has troubled his modern admirers. How can the sharp-eyed observation of human folly attested by the *Histories* be harmonized with the relentless credulity of the *Wonders*? Vinay answered that Gregory never outgrew a child's faith. A more widespread opinion is that Gregory's *Miracula* simply reflects "a time of dense superstition": sixth-century Gaul was "something like the primitive districts of Haiti," "a country devoid of general education . . . with a faith prone to excessive reliance on miracles"; Gregory gained his outlook "from his social environment," in which miracles were "the chief interest."[113] According to a recent commentator, the impetus came not just from the environment, but rather from its emphatically dismal character: "the simplicity of [Greg-

---

[110] Dust, GM 48, GC 52, 73, 95; bark, GM 67, 77; oil, GC 9, 69; wax, *VSJ* 40; rope, GC 85. These references are not exhaustive. On Gregory the Great, see McCulloh, as n. 109.

[111] GC 6-11.

[112] Hermann-Mascard, *Reliques des saints*, pp. 57-60. She speaks of a "pénurie de reliques dans les églises du nord" in the eighth century. Gregory was unaware of any scarcity.

[113] For Vinay, n. 51 above. Dalton I, 257; Brehaut tr., pp. ix, xvi. See also Latouche, "Grégoire de Tours," pp. 90, 92 (distorting Kurth's teaching). A variation on this theme, with special reference to the understanding of nature, is found in Sprandel, "Vorwissentschafliches Naturverstehen." According to him, Gregory's outlook on nature was sometimes sophisticated, more often primitive; the former was attributable to his Romance connection, the latter to "die Mentalität von Germanen" that permeated the Merovingian court in which Gregory moved more often than among Gallo-Romans. Besides being circular, Sprandel's analysis—in its confident fragmentation of Gregory—is astonishingly simplistic.

ory's] belief in miracles was the suitable reaction to characteristic Mero-vingian conditions of primitive violence and crudity," as though to say that Gregory and his contemporaries, sunk in the penumbra of Frankish barba-rism, totally despaired of human resources and set their hopes only in super-natural intervention.[114]

This interpretation by environmental conditioning runs the risk of being less sophisticated than the credulity it is meant to explain. If Gregory had lived in a society overgrown with dense superstition, he is unlikely to have gone to the lengths he did merely to cast back to his audience a faith with which, presumably, it was already richly imbued. As reflected in Gregory's works, his contemporaries in all walks of life were credulous and uncritical, but they were also guided by practical common sense. They knew that, as a rule, nothing untoward occurred when one committed perjury, seized church property, oppressed the poor, worked on Sundays, or otherwise of-fended against divine precepts.[115] To them, as to us, the absence of a thun-derbolt from heaven, smiting the offender, was as predictable as tomorrow's sunrise. That comfortable certainty was precisely what Gregory sought to counteract. In opposition to the view of a predictably indifferent nature, operating as it was bound to do, he did not conjure up a contrary philoso-phy. *Their* basis was philosophy; his was history—the evidence, preferably of an eyewitness, recording the multitudinous factual moments when, in defiance of human wisdom and alleged natural necessity, the unexpected occurred.

It comes as a surprise to anyone reared on the idea that Merovingian Gaul marks a low point in humane letters that Gregory should still have considered it timely to place himself at the service of Christianity in its combat with the allurements of classical culture.[116] Yet the first preface of the *Wonders*—that to the *Martyrs*—invokes the *locus classicus* of Jerome's repudiation of Cicero, amplified in Gregory's rendition into "the clever ar-guments of Cicero and the false tales of Virgil."[117]

Gregory's audience had something to do with the relevance of Jerome's ostensibly outdated dream. In both the *Wonders* and the *Histories*, the in-cidents narrated gravitate between Clermont in the South and Tours in the

[114] Walter, "Hagiographisches," p. 306.

[115] The inference seems to follow from the various stories designed precisely to counteract such transgressions by documenting instances when, by exception, they were miraculously punished. E.g. perjury, GM 19, 38, VSJ 19, 39, GC 91, 92, *Hist.* 7.29; Sunday work, GM 15, VSJ 11; violation of sanctuary, VSJ 10, 13, GC 66; seizure of Church property, GM 71, 78, VSJ 14, 15, 17; GC 70, 78. Skepticism toward saints and miracles is comprehensively docu-mented by Graus, *Volk, Herrscher und Heiliger*, pp. 451-55.

[116] Lot, *Invasions germaniques*, p. 237.

[117] GM, *praef.*, ed. Krusch, pp. 487-88; tr. McDermott, pp. 130-32. The theme does not die out with Gregory; e.g. *Vita s. Eligii*, *praef.*, ed. Bruno Krusch, MGH SRM IV, 663-65 (the alleged, and perhaps real, author is Audoënus, bishop of Rouen in the mid seventh century).

North; they are solidly attached to the most Romanized districts of Gaul.[118]
Vienne, whose bishop would soon be reproved by Gregory the Great for
lecturing on profane authors, lay within the same vast region.[119] The horizon of Gregory of Tours rarely extends north and east of the Loire; it
reaches at the farthest to Trier and Cologne, without ever, except for politics, crossing the Rhine.[120] For all we may tell, no rumor of Christianity in
Ireland came to his ears, and the distinctive Christianity of the Bretons,
just down the Loire from Tours, might just as well have never existed.[121]
The conversion of Arians to orthodoxy interested him; but, regardless of
the attention he pays to Clovis's baptism, he is unconcerned with the evangelization of heathens as a current-day activity. It is not from him that we
learn that many Franks still needed religious instruction, or that the Thuringians and Alamans (both under Frankish sway), let alone the Anglo-
Saxons, had yet to hear the word of God; even the Lombard holy man
whom he met, and whose life story he asked to hear, fails to relate how he
became a Catholic in the first place.[122] In short, Gregory averts his gaze
from terrains of potential conversion. His focus is sharply circumscribed,
and his more distant vision reaches out, not into the northern gloom, but
toward the Mediterranean and the East. Although circumstances may have
limited his information, it need not follow that he knew no more than what
he wrote. In part at least, his geography seems deliberately tailored to the
intended audience. The pastorate he undertook to exercise through his
writings could hardly have been directed elsewhere than among the educated, Roman-descended, and hereditarily Christian elements of the
Frankish kingdom. The palpable events they were invited to contemplate
were mainly those occurring in their own neighborhood. Addressed to such
ears, the tale of Jerome's attachment to classical letters was not wholly
anachronistic. Neither were Gregory's efforts to combat "philosophy."

[118] On the cultural contrast between "Roman" and "barbarian" Gaul, see Riché, *Éducation
et culture*, p. 220. The place of Tours and Clermont in Gregory's writings is most obvious in
Hist. 1-4 and from the starring roles of Sts. Julian and Martin in the *Miracula*.

[119] Laistner, *Thought and Letters*, p. 109.

[120] Trier, GC 91-92, *Hist.* 8.13-17 (Gregory travels there); Cologne, GM 61, 62 (Xanten).
Attention to activity beyond the Rhine: *Hist.* 3.4, 8 (Thuringians), 4.10, 14 (Saxon rebellion), 23, 29, 5.15 (battle between Saxons and Swabians, location not specified).

[121] The British Isles might as well not exist (Kent is mentioned, but not located, *Hist.* 4.25,
9.26). Yet the Irish monk, Columbanus, came to Guntram's kingdom in Gregory's lifetime:
Bullough, "Colombano," pp. 116-17. On Brittany, Pietri, *Ville de Tours*, pp. 294-98. Gregory
says much about Breton politics, but nothing about the Breton Church. Pietri, p. 296, infers
from his silence that contact was lost. This seems unlikely. Gregory, well informed about Breton chieftains, was bound to know about its Church. He even gives prominence to a potential
informant: *Hist.* 5.21, 8.34.

[122] The king of Kent who married a Merovingian princess (n. 121) is not identified as pagan.
The Lombard, *Hist.* 8.15. The only nonroyal conversion of a barbarian that Gregory does report is in *VP* 12.2; it occurs in Auvergne.

In a recent study, Sofia Boesch Gajano has drawn attention to three pervasive traits of the *Wonders*: the "actuality" of the miracles Gregory described; the episodic quality of his narrative; and the absence of any attempt to edify by holding up saints as models of life or conduct. [123] These are useful topics to explore in our continuing examination of the less familiar of Gregory's major works.

The *Wonders* occasionally contains a capsule history, such as the passion of St. Julian at the hands of Roman persecutors, and a number of miracles described either occur in a definably distant past or lack chronological specificity. [124] Passages like these are exceptional. In the large majority of cases, no matter how ancient the saint, Gregory sets down events of his own time or relates miracles to the present, such as by detailing his source of information. His reason for appealing to the span of living memory is set out in the preface to the first book about St. Martin: "The miracles that the Lord our God [performed through] St. Martin in the flesh He now deigns to confirm daily to strengthen the belief of the faithful. . . . Therefore let no one doubt past miracles when he beholds the gift of present signs given forth, since he sees the lame made straight, the blind given sight, etc."[125] Gregory was consistent with this program: relics of the Lord's cross were now at Poitiers; His tunic was active at Galata, outside Constantinople; there were relics of the Virgin at Marsat in the Auvergne, and John the Baptist expelled demons at Tours; Gregory had admired wool brought from the wool-bearing tree in Jericho and learned, from a certain Theodore, of the apostle Thomas's wonder-working church in India; heaven-sent visions had lately allowed the bishop of Langres (Gregory's great-grandfather) to rediscover the martyr Benignus, and the bishop of Cologne to find Mallosus of Xanten; King Guntram's envoy to the martyrs of Agaune was saved by them from shipwreck, and so was a deacon of Gregory's by the relics of the Roman martyrs he was carrying. [126] This selection of incidents from the *Martyrs* typifies Gregory's focus in time and place. The miracles now experienced authenticated those of the past which were known only indirectly from written testimony. The Incarnation was an academic notion if located in the days of Caesar Augustus; it was credible if the miracle of the Word taking

[123] Boesch Gajano, "Il santo," pp. 32-43.

[124] *VSJ* 1; *GC* 44, incident from the life of St. Severinus; 62, miraculous cure of the emperor Leo's daughter (almost certainly apocryphal, since no such emperor fits the specifications); *VP* 2.1, Illidius cures an unnamed emperor's daughter.

[125] *VSM* 1.*praef*, ed. Krusch, p. 585: "Miracula, quae dominus Deus noster per beatum Martinum antistitem suum in corpore positum operari dignatus est, cotidie ad conroborandam fidem credentium confirmare dignatur. . . . Nemo ergo de anteactis virtutibus dubitet, cum praesentium signorum cernit munera dispensari, cum videat clodos eregi, caecos inluminari. . . ."

[126] *GM* 5, 7, 8, 17, 32, 50, 62, 75, 82.

Flesh occurred repeatedly in the present. The impulse that drove Gregory to concentrate predominantly on contemporary Gaul was as proper to the *Wonders* as to the *Histories*; for events immediately experienced "strengthen belief," whereas knowledge of past occurrences gained through the written word goes unheeded.

None of the books of *Miracula* has an explicit theme; no argument is developed and no effort made to explain anything more challenging than a single incident. The books are orderly, as we have seen, but their contents lack any structure of argument or organic theme. They are uniformly episodic: a succession of incidents, each meant to stand in isolation and often drawing the reader inward by dramatic devices.[127] Even when connections are obvious, as in the five chapters of the *Martyrs* featuring Arian heretics, Gregory simply runs on from one episode to the next.[128] He plainly asserts that sheer quantity will have greater impact than any verbal attempt at persuasion, such as a thread of argument woven through a more compact whole; as he puts it, the eloquence he lacks will be compensated for by "the very accumulation of numerous miracles."[129]

Boesch Gajano's third trait—the normal absence of edifying comments about the lives of holy men—complements Gregory's preference for narrating isolated episodes occurring in his lifetime. The lesson of recent miracles was one of deeds, not words. For words in books were futile, incapable of convincing or of occasioning changes in conduct. Gregory claims to have personally experienced their impotence. Tutored by the priest Avitus at Clermont, he had bent over the Scriptures, but "they did not bring me to discernment . . . because I am unable to heed them."[130] If words could move, and not just entertain, men would be living by the Gospels, as they manifestly were not. The theme of imitation is raised on several occasions in the prefaces to the *Vita patrum*; in the narrative, however, the burden falls on miracles rather than on any sustained portrayal of exemplary conduct.[131] As Marc Reydellet has observed, "The idea yields to its material representation. Sanctity is perceived only in as much as it is manifested by concrete acts, miracles, and the very name of *virtutes* given to them, in its passage from the abstract sense [= 'virtues'] to the concrete, perfectly sums

---

[127] E.g. GM 5, 9, 30 (Mummolus), 33 (Bordeaux); GC 49. The general idea is that Gregory often goes far beyond narrating a miracle; he sets the scene, makes the characters interesting, has them speak, includes arresting details, etc.

[128] GM 77-81. One might maintain that GM 77-89 form a thematic unit extending beyond its Arian chapters. But Gregory does not draw attention to the unifying feature.

[129] VSM 2.*praef.*, tr. McDermott, p. 135.

[130] VP 2.*praef.*, ed. Krusch, p. 668-69: "mihi non ad iudicium contingerent, quae ipso praedicante audivi vel cogente relegi, qui ea nequeo observare."

[131] VP, *praef.*, 4.*praef.*, 9.*praef.*, 16.*praef.*, 20.*praef.* Boesch Gajano, "Il santo," pp. 41-43, focuses on VP as the exception that proves the rule: referring to exemplary conduct but, all the same, mainly concerned with miracles.

up the mental evolution (*évolution des esprits*)."[132] The verbal re-creation of forgotten examples of conduct was a pointless exercise among men possessing rich stores of skepticism. A preacher aware that words alone were powerless to move even himself needed better resources to sway his flock. The advantage of history was not that it painted a gallery of worthies and villains, but that it recorded happenings that existed outside books. Events recalled by a narrator to men who half knew them already were beyond argument.

However uncritical Gregory was toward the phenomena he accepted as miraculous, he took pains to define the conditions within which miracles had the capacity to persuade. They were not all alike. Man's defective capacity to perceive the truth required that miracles performed in a saint's lifetime should be distinguished from posthumous ones emanating from the power (*virtus*) of relics. After relating how Bishop Illidius of Clermont cured the emperor's daughter at Trier (implicitly, in the fourth century), he explained:

> Perhaps, as men are often inclined to mutter, someone will prattle, saying, "[Illidius] can't be taken for a saint just on the strength of doing one miracle." For if one considers what the Lord spoke in the gospel, "Many will say to me in that day, Lord, Lord, have we not cast out devils in Thy name and performed many miracles? And I shall reply to them saying, I never knew you" (Matt. 7:22-23), one assuredly realizes that the *virtus* proceeding from the grave tends more to renown than that which any living person manifested in the world; for the latter may be soiled by the constant hindrance of worldly endeavors, whereas the former is clearly devoid of all stain.[133]

Typically, Gregory both disparaged the prattlers and personally endorsed their objection: only posthumous miracles were certain. He returned more briefly to this distinction in the *Confessors*, in connection with the recently deceased Bishop Felix of Bourges. A blind man recovered his sight at Felix's tomb, "and the people recognized him as a friend of God whom they, owing to the impediments of worldly dimsightedness, had not merited to know fully in the flesh. [They now] began to approach his presence with continual prayers."[134] *Obsistentibus mundanis caliginibus*: the world of social involvement was bathed in fog, within which any certainty about important things was impossible. But the effects of saintly *virtus* after death were one truth that men could clearly apprehend, provided, however, that the time frame was suitably circumscribed.

Gregory defined the relevant span in continuing to discourse about Illi-

[132] Reydellet, *Royauté*, p. 389.
[133] VP 2.2, ed. Krusch, pp. 669-70.
[134] GC 100, ed. Krusch, p. 812. Cf. VP, *praef.*: contrast between long-dead saints (miracles at their tombs) and more recent ones.

dius, the fourth-century bishop of Clermont: "Therefore because those things which St. Illidius carried out before this time [= the present] have, we believe, been forgotten and not come to our knowledge, we shall set out those which we have experienced by the witness of our own eyes or have learned were perceived by faithful men."[135] Gregory's time frame was very narrow. The past beyond the observer's memory was as good as lost, and the society of the living was enveloped in mists; but within what was left, there were transcendental truths that the eye could see, affirmations of divine power that were apprehensible to the senses. And such facts were anything but rare.

Gregory was no more superstitious than Augustine had been. Where he parted from patristic tradition was in the centrality he accorded to the *virtutes* of present times in his pastorate. Augustine had been sufficiently gripped by these phenomena to accord them a disproportionately long chapter of *The City of God*.[136] They accounted for an incomparably larger share of Gregory's output. With him, history was the medium, current time the frame, and miscellaneous but unarguable happenings the theme. The special quality of the incidents in the *Wonders* has been well characterized by Boesch Gajano:

these miracles [those of St. Martin] are, one might say, fortuitous: prayer near the tomb generally precedes the cure but is not causally connected to it. Although Gregory, in the preface to book III, underlines the importance of the soul's disposition, [the preface] to book IV again places the accent primarily on the *virtus* of the tomb: its power expresses itself visibly in the cure of physical ailments; only by analogy does that healing efficacy extend to moral [ills]. The narrative does not necessarily concern the rewarding of the good or punishment of the wicked—only cured men, women, and children: the *virtus* will in any case act unexpectedly, one might say irrationally. This holds true for the unending series of miracles related, each one focused on a single case, each turned upon itself. This episodicity, this fortuitousness encapsulates the sense and, one might say, the fascination of Gregory's hagiography.[137]

One might even go beyond fascination. Gregory's handling of miracles is not a casual personal gift, but the expression of an outlook that is too consistently elaborated in his writings to have been subconscious. In effect, he repudiated philosophy in all its systematizing manifestations. To the apparent regularity of nature, going through its predictable paces not perceivably touched by God, he opposed a multiplicity of hard, contrary facts testifying

[135] VP 2.2, ed. Krusch, p. 670 (continuing the quotation at n. 133).

[136] Augustine *Civ. Dei* 22.8.

[137] Boesch Gajano, "Il santo," pp. 39-40. For a largely statistical analysis of the 295 miracles of the *Miracula s. Martini*, see Giordano, "Sociologia e patologia del miracolo." More than 90% are cures; blindness and paralysis head the list of ailments.

to the free and ostensibly haphazard intrusions of divine power right here and now. Only a historian, rooted in particulars, could collect this evidence; and only the incidents, bit by discrete bit, rather than any linking commentary, had the capacity to persuade.

Gregory, it has been said, "is not a man of theory."[138] The fathers of the Church seem to have had little more impact on him than the grammarians. The only theology he shows himself capable of consists in recitation of the Creed and in unwinding strings of biblical quotations, the latter, usually to little effect.[139] The *persona* Gregory projects in his many lapses into self-portrayal is capable of many things, but not abstract thought. Perhaps he would not have welcomed the notion that his works embodied an explicit philosophy, yet an attempt should be made all the same to place them in a philosophical setting.

His younger contemporary, Pope Gregory the Great, devoted the last book of his *Dialogues* to exploring the subject of bodily resurrection. In its course, he retold Plato's allegory of the cave in late sixth-century form. It is as though he were furnishing the bishop of Tours with his intellectual credentials:

Born as bodies in the blindness of this exile [Pope Gregory says], we hear tell about the heavenly home, about its citizens the angels of God, about the spirits of the perfectly just which live with them; but corporeal beings [that we are], because unable to grasp invisible things by experience, [we] doubt the existence of what [we] cannot see with bodily eyes. Our first father could not have had this doubt. Expelled from the joys of paradise, he recollected what he had lost because he had seen it. But [all other men] cannot sense or recollect what they are told because none of them possesses the experience of the past [that Adam had].

Let us suppose a pregnant woman cast into a dungeon in which she gives birth to a son. After being born, the child is nourished and grows up in this dungeon. If his mother happens to speak to him of the sun, the moon, the stars, the mountains and the plains, the birds that fly and the horses that run, he who was born and reared in the dungeon knows only its darkness. He hears that all this exists, but since he has no experience of it, he doubts its reality. Thus, men born in the blindness of this exile, when they hear that there are lofty and invisible things, doubt their reality, for they know only those paltry visible things among which they were born.

This is why the Creator of things invisible and visible, the Son of the Father, came to redeem the human race and to send the Holy Spirit into our hearts, so that animated by it we might believe what we cannot yet know by experience.[140]

---

[138] Reydellet, *Royauté*, p. 424.

[139] Creed, *Hist* 1.*praef*. Disputations with a king, two Arians, a Jew, and a would-be Sadducee: *Hist*. 5.44, 5.43, 6.40, 6.5, 10.13. Only the last of Gregory's interlocutors was moved by Gregory's argument, but he was a priest of Tours. The main lesson of these dialogues is their futility. See also below, n. 361.

[140] *Dial*. 4.1.2-4, ed. Vogüé, III, 19-21.

The obvious difference between the pope's version and Plato's is that the Christian heaven, revealed to men, is set in the place Plato assigns to an "intelligible world" to which the soul ascends in life by abstraction from "the prison" that is "revealed through sight."[141] The common premise that the world apprehensible to sight and the other senses is comparable to a dungeon has diametrically opposite and incompatible complements. Meditation, abstraction, philosophizing—the activities of the human spirit—are alien to Pope Gregory's rendition. The Redeemer and the Holy Spirit are free gifts of the Almighty to humankind, "animating" belief in a transcendental reality that men will partake in only after physical death. Pope Gregory's basic doctrine is clear to the point of banality, and it was, presumably, beyond contestation among Christians.

For both Gregories, however, there remained the grave pastoral problem of how to penetrate the skepticism and doubt of their congregations, of how to overcome the understandable reluctance of men to grasp anything except visible experience. It was very well for divine revelation to be the source of truth, but how else was that revelation to be communicated if not through books? The point of departure for Pope Gregory's allegory is that the Scriptures and Christian letters are unconvincing. Men hear what they say about heaven, but the readings remain mere talk, at best conveying what others, but not the listeners, have experienced.

In this problem of Christian disbelief, Plato exacted a sweet revenge. He, after all, had shown that words, properly organized, could express truth. Language was not just sophistic trickery, but could lead one out of the cave and toward the light. The foundation of humanistic culture had been the faith he pioneered in the potential of language—the inherent power of properly constructed verbal sequences to compel assent.[142] Together with many other Christians, Gregory of Tours celebrated the Lord's "destruction of the vanity of worldly wisdom"; but, where the persuasive force of language was concerned, the destruction cut both ways.[143] Its unavoidable consequence was to discredit the artfully combined words in which the Christian message was also phrased. In a baptized world, discourse no longer persuaded as it once had. For the language in which Christian truth was clothed was indistinguishable from, and no more credible than, the language in which philosophical "vanities" were expressed. By undermining the instrument that it shared with pagan culture, Christianity had, in its triumph, created a population of skeptics. Few witnesses are more forth-

---

[141] Plato *Republic* 7.517B, tr. Paul Storey, Loeb, 2 vols. (London 1935) II, 129-30.

[142] The passage after the dash is paraphrased from Frye, *Great Code*, p. 9.

[143] *VSM* 1.*praef.*: the Lord called fishermen and rustics to this destructive task. The passage is adapted in part from Sulpicius Severus, *V. Martini praef.* 3, on which see the commentary of Jacques Fontaine, Sources chrétiennes 134 (Paris 1968), pp. 384-89.

right than the two Gregories in testifying to the vanished force of properly constructed verbal sequences. Only experience, not words, commanded credence.

Pope Gregory's account of the dungeon outlines this dilemma without explicitly portraying it as a pastoral problem. He concludes on a factual note: for Plato, the process of intellectual abstraction was man's link between the world of the senses and metaphysical truth; in Pope Gregory's teaching, however, the link was "the only Son of the Father," incarnated among men "to redeem the human race and to send the Holy Spirit into our hearts." Precisely how the Incarnation overcame human disbelief in what was merely heard Gregory does not explain, at least here. For our purposes, it is enough to observe that the pope evoked this problem in a narrative concerned with recent saints and miracles in Italy, the one of his works that, in subject and even style, stands closest to Gregory of Tours.[144]

The latter, as we have seen, had a clear sense of how to communicate Christian truth as an appeal to the experience rather than to the intellect of his listeners. He would set before them the wonders of today. God's free, inexplicable, and unexpected intrusions into daily life, served up "hot off the fire," were Bishop Gregory's challenge to the skepticism of his audience;[145] and history, conceived in the *Wonders* as an aggregate of such episodes, was the form he gave to his militant anti-intellectualism. The properly philosophical dimension of Gregory's endeavor was a matter of language. Because words on a page were futile, he would turn his back on style and assign persuasiveness to the facts.

On no fewer than twelve occasions—eight in the *Wonders*—Gregory notified readers of his defective Latin, sometimes contrasting it to that of properly trained writers.[146] Not only did he not conceal his linguistic failings, he seized every reasonable pretext for advertising them. These passages have drawn much modern attention. Although it has been recognized that confessions of inadequacy are conventional in literature, the majority view continues to be that Gregory told the simple truth about his shortcomings as an author and is the best example of his famous statement that the cultivation of liberal letters was declining, indeed perishing, in the cities of Gaul.[147]

---

[144] Gregory the Great *Dial.*, ed. Vogüé, I, 118-20; Auerbach, *Literary Language*, pp. 95-103, qualified by Vogüé, I, 31-42.

[145] The quoted phrase is from Auerbach, *Literary Language*, p. 109 (rendered as "hot from the oven" by the translator of *Mimesis*, p. 79).

[146] The most circumstantial are asterisked: VSJ 4; *VSM 1.*praef.*, 2.*praef.*; VP, praef., 2.*praef.*, 8.*praef.*, 9.*praef.*; *GC, praef.*; *Hist., praef., 1.*praef.*, 5.6, 10.31.

[147] Buchner, Einleitung, p. xxxvi; Bonnet, *Latin de Grégoire de Tours*, pp. 77-79. Dalton I, 20 n. 1, cites a collection of commentators. Better, Beumann, "Gregor u. der *sermo rusticus*": authors used to affect literary inadequacy for the sake of ingratiation, but by the sixth century

The interpretation of these passages as sincere confessions is not self-evidently flawed. Gregory's tone is humble, and his apologies are based on awareness of the genuine faults of his Latin. Proper grounding in letters, he sometimes suggests, would do greater justice to his subject. Irony at the expense of fine writers is sometimes present, but less apparent than admiring respect.[148] Gregory was no more hostile to the masters of eloquence than to the philosophers who compiled the man-made wonders of the world. They were not enemies, like the heretical Arians. Christian letters were, after all, scarcely less studied and refined than pagan writings. The masters of style included friends of Gregory's, such as the poet Fortunatus in Poitiers, and such revered figures from the past as *Sollius noster*—the one-time bishop of Clermont, Sidonius Apollinaris.[149] Gregory, though well disposed toward fine writers, was apparently unable to emulate their standards. Yet he would not, for that reason, keep quiet. His eloquence was of no account; he had weighty matter to convey, stacks of it, and it made up for the insufficiency of his tongue.

Hardly any issue in the interpretation of Gregory seems more important than that of his self-consciousness. In a justly celebrated essay, Erich Auerbach, influenced by the Romantic image of the naïve Gregory, maintained that his "grammatically confused, syntactically impoverished, and almost sophomoric Latin" was a given quantity, the only instrument he was equipped with; that he "half-unconsciously" became a writer; and that—as Ampère had taught—"the pattern of events [Gregory] has to report meets his style halfway."[150] Characteristically, the view Auerbach adopted here (and later discarded) can apply only to the *Histories*, for that work might just conceivably have been affected by an external "pattern of events," such as what Auerbach called "a progressive and terrible brutalization."[151] In the *Wonders*, however, there can be no question of barbarous Latin meeting

---

(e.g. Eugippius), the claim was meant in earnest, as praise of simple language (*laudatio sermonis rustici*).

Concepts of Merovingian Latin have developed considerably in recent times; see Uytfanghe, "Latin mérovingien, latin carolingien," and especially Heinzelmann and Poulin, *Les vies anciennes de sainte Geneviève*, pp. 11-15 (Heinzelmann).

[148] Circumstantial list of his faults, GC, *praef.*; only proper writers can do justice to great miracles, VSM 1.*praef.*; on irony at the expense of fine writers, see Beumann, "Gregor u. der *sermo rusticus*," pp. 84, 85, and Auerbach, *Literary Language*, p. 105.

[149] Fortunatus: cited as hagiographer in GM 41, GC 44, 94, *Hist.* 5.8; indication of friendship, VSM 1.13-16; set on a par as stylist with Sulpicius Severus, VSM 1.*praef.* (see also above, n. 4). *Sollius noster*: VSJ 2, *Hist.* 2.25, 4.12. Sollius was Sidonius's second name, by which he called himself in some of his writings; see *Poems and Letters*, ed. and tr. W. B. Anderson, Loeb, 2 vols. (London 1963-65) I, xxxii.

[150] Auerbach, *Mimesis*, pp. 78, 80, 79.

[151] *Ibid.*, p. 79. Cf. Auerbach, *Literary Language*, p. 103; this view is anticipated in *Mimesis*, p. 81, but contradicted there by the idea of a Gregory conditioned by his barbaric context (n. 150).

barbarously chaotic events halfway. Gregory chose his miracles and their time frame, not they him, and the witness he caused them to bear to divine power, generosity, and beneficence in the here and now was, to Gregory at least, a thing of sublime beauty. Yet, the deliberately narrowed subject made no difference to Gregory's language. The works of God and His saints were conveyed in the same defective Latin as the *Histories*, and were insistently declared to be by the hand of an untrained writer. Gregory fastened upon the miracles of today in order to penetrate walls of skepticism concerning the existence of a loftier existence; and, as he continually protested, these concrete events were conveyed in artless and incorrect words. Gregory's insistence on his rusticity suggests that language played as integral a part as subject matter in his pastoral strategy.

A prose meant primarily to describe concrete events, miraculous or not, should owe as little as possible to art. If, as Auerbach showed, Gregory's language was "imperfectly equipped to organize facts," it may well be that Gregory had a principled objection to the pretension that facts might be organized, as though from above, by language.[152] Gregory's humble and regretful deference to high standards of eloquence, without being feigned, was nevertheless offset by indications that his self-deprecation was a mark of positive virtue. He likened himself to the fishermen and rustics whom "the Lord . . . chose for the destruction of the vanity of worldly wisdom"; he was encouraged and pleasantly surprised to be told that "few understand the philosophizing orator, but many the peasant's speech (*loquens rusticus*)."[153] Auerbach eventually recognized that Gregory showed genuine "self-awareness [of] his distinctive worth" as a stylist; he was the "most intense" representative of a wider "drive [among Christian authors] to write in a colloquial style."[154] One might go a step further and recognize that Gregory's *rusticus loquens* expresses contempt for literary language itself, regardless of whether refined or colloquial. Others, like Augustine, might espouse a *sermo humilis* exemplified by the Latin Bible and claim for it "a new eloquence of its own," but Gregory simply advertised his ineptitude.[155] Casual usage won attention for content. The gross errors Gregory ascribed to himself in the preface to the *Confessors* were evidently indifferent and venial, perhaps even virtuous, for words were only an instrument in men's hands, subordinate to the truly important external facts they described and dramatized. Emphatically distancing himself from the philosophers and

[152] Auerbach, *Mimesis*, p. 78. Cf. Jennifer Tolbert Roberts, "Gregory of Tours and the Monk of St. Gall: The Paratactic Style of Medieval Latin," *Latomus* 39 (1980) 179.

[153] VSM 1.*praef*., ed. Krusch, p. 586 (see also n. 143); *Hist.*, *praef*., K-L p. 1.

[154] Auerbach, *Literary Language*, pp. 107, 103; cf. above, n. 151.

[155] Quotation from Auerbach, *Literary Language*, p. 50.

even from Christian masters of fine language, Gregory transposed eloquence from the manner of discourse to its substance.[156]

Gregory's surprising evocation of Jerome's dream, in the first preface to the *Wonders*, ends like Pope Gregory's version of Plato's allegory with a reference to the Incarnation. The bishop of Tours called on the example of Jerome in order to underline his personal determination to spurn the allurements of classical letters. Pursuant to the Pauline injunction, "If there be good speech let it be for instruction, that it might grant grace to its readers," his subject matter would be only "that which builds the church of God and by sacred teaching enriches needy minds." He would have nothing to do with "lying stories" or "the wisdom of philosophers which is hostile to God." He launched into a lengthy *praeteritio*, listing examples of what he would eschew. There is no mention here of "clever arguments" or philosophic wisdom. Mythology is at the forefront, with Homeric and Virgilian accompaniments—the stock in trade, as it then was, of the elementary teacher of literature (*grammaticus*).[157] Jerome's conversion had been from one sort of literature to another: "Since then, I have read the divine books with more care than I formerly applied to reading mortal ones."[158] Gregory's resolve, on the contrary, was detached from the written word: "Having glanced at all these things built on sand and bound to perish, we return rather to divine and evangelical miracles."[159] As mythology was composed of incidents (however false), so its Christian opposite consisted of miraculous happenings and not of teaching or books. Gregory went on, with reference to the gospel of John, to the greatest miracle of all, the one most relevant to letters, namely, that of the Word made Flesh, born in Bethlehem, acknowledged as savior by Simeon while a child in arms and as son of God by Nathaniel in Galilee.[160] In a world redeemed by God Incarnate, deeds daily worked by the Almighty spoke for themselves without need of enhancement: "He Who produced water in the desert to quench the burn-

[156] VSM 1.*praef.*, ed. Krusch, p. 586: "Confidimus ergo . . . quia, etsi non potest paginam sermo incultus ornare, faciet eam gloriosus antistis praeclaris virtutibus elucere." In other words, certain facts have their own eloquence (and not all such facts need be holy).

[157] GM, *praef.*, tr. McDermott, pp. 130-31. Cf. Riché, *Éducation et culture*, pp. 229-30; Marrou, *Histoire de l'éducation*, p. 377.

[158] Jerome *Epistolae* 22.30, ed. Jérome Labourt, Collection des universités de France, I (Paris 1949), p. 146.

[159] GM, *praef.*, tr. McDermott, p. 131 (somewhat modified); ed. Krusch, p. 488, "Sed ista omnia tamquam super harenam locata et cito ruitura conspiciens, ad divina et evangelica potius miracula revertamur." Gregory alludes to Matt. 7:26: those who hear the Lord's words and do not do as He teaches are like the fool who builds his house on sand. McDermott, p. 131 n. 15, comments, "a peculiarly inept quotation." Gregory seems to express the view that wise men found themselves on God's word, foolish ones on mythology or, more broadly, pagan letters.

[160] GM, *praef.* Gregory stresses historical witnesses to the divinity of Christ.

ing thirst of a people is able, I believe, to reveal [the miracles of St. Martin] through my tonguelessness."[161]

The model for Gregory's kind of eloquence could hardly have come from elsewhere than the Bible. Bonnet, Antin, and others have shown the effect of scriptural studies on his prose, but great as that influence was, the biblical cast of his writings has more than a literary basis.[162] The Latin Bible, Auerbach observed, "remained a foreign body in Latin literature as long as the classical tradition survived and . . . [men] preserved a feeling for classical style."[163] Gregory, asserting his incapacity to be a stylist, espoused the alternative he found on the *sacra pagina*: divinely eloquent matter expressed in a language defying classical dictates. He is more notable for emulating the substantive contents of the Bible than for imitating its *sermo humilis*. The contemporary scene he portrayed—more fully in the *Histories* than in the *Wonders*—is one in which miracles often identical to those of the New Testament exist side by side with the deeds of kings, *viri fortes*, prophets, and a vengeful God characteristic of the Old. The Book of Kings, rather than Jerome or Orosius (both mentioned), supplies the three events that, in the preface to book II of the *Histories*, typify the course of history.[164] There were things to say, Gregory implied, that compelled assent even in a world in which the persuasive force of properly constructed verbal sequences had been discredited. The inspired character of the Scriptures came not from a whisper in the ears of long-dead authors, but from the facts that those books recorded. And these facts continued to occur. The revealed Word, by His deeds in the here and now, gave voice to Gregory's tonguelessness, and contemporary Gaul, portrayed without art, corroborated the letter of revelation.

In the Platonic scheme of things, the words of literary language were "primarily the outward expression of inner thoughts or ideas" and "a verbal imitation of a reality beyond [language]." The Church fathers had shared this form of expression with the pre-Christian philosophers. Its central concept, unifying human thought and imagination, was "a monotheistic 'God,' a transcendent reality or perfect being that all verbal analogy points to."[165] But, as Pope Gregory attested, language of this sort had gone the way of "the vanity of worldly wisdom" and could no longer be relied upon to persuade men even of Christian truths. Gregory of Tours showed philosophical

---

[161] VSM 1.*praef.*, tr. McDermott, p. 134 with n. 25.
[162] Bonnet, *Latin de Grégoire de Tours*, pp. 53-61; Antin, "Notes sur le style de Grégoire de Tours"; Antin, "Emplois de la Bible."
[163] Auerbach, *Literary Language*, p. 46.
[164] *Hist* 2.*praef.*, K-L p. 36; see below, n. 265. For a still useful guide to miracles of saints imitating those of the Scriptures, see Brewer, *A Dictionary of Miracles*, part I.
[165] Frye, *Great Code*, pp. 7, 8, 9 (for Frye's typology of language, modifying Vico's, see p. 5).

sensitivity when he insisted that, to persuade, miracles should be posthumous, attributable to the *virtus* of relics, and either seen personally or learned from trustworthy witnesses; and he most fully disclosed the philosophical implications of his work when he distanced himself from the form of writing hitherto dominant even among zealous Christians. [166] The novel doctrine he exemplified was that, in the expression of a reality beyond language, miracles had assumed the role formerly assigned to ordered words. Ever since God had taken Flesh and shown that He manifested Himself continually in the world, words had been dethroned and relegated to being mere instruments of description, subordinate to the concrete, this-worldly manifestations of the divine that could be haltingly and artlessly rendered on the page in just the same way as deplorable profane events were narrated.

Gregory asked not to be taken seriously as a writer, but he presented himself unblushingly as the authority, at first or second hand, for what he said. His prominent place within the *Wonders* and the *Histories* is paralleled by a host of other men and women, whose personalities, with their warts, passions, and domestic imbroglios, wholly outweigh reflective considerations as a scheme of explanation. Personalization permeates Gregory's writings and constitutes one of its widely recognized features. The saints are individualized human beings; their miracles affect persons, usually named; and the testimony of human observers, including Gregory, provides the record of their deeds. Even the Old Testament is hastily unwound, in the preface to the *Miracles of St. Julian*, as a succession of holy personages, from Abel to Daniel. The biblical summary of the *Histories* takes much the same form. [167] Gregory, besides holding center stage as the witness on whom credibility depends, assumes a social role in the prefaces to *The Miracles of St. Martin* and the *Histories*: pressed by a needful public, he will speak.

The place of personalities in Gregory's writings comes close to being the principled consequence of his affirmation of God's freedom at the expense of an objective natural order. Nature itself is personalized. Its operations, the predictable ones as well as the unexpected, are directly identified with the Creator and His friends, the saints, living through their earthly relics. Gregory rarely assigns specialized functions to individual saints, such as (to note the main exception) the punishment of perjury by Sts. Pancras and Polyeuctus. [168] What we do see, at every turn, is God (through the saints)

---

[166] On the culturally ascendant language, *ibid.*, p. 12. White, "Fictions of Factual Representation," pp. 35-36, associates great historians with linguistic self-consciousness.

[167] As men who sought justice, Gregory lists (*VSJ, praef.*): Abel, Enoch, Noah, Abraham, Isaac, Jacob, Joseph, Moses, David, Solomon, the three boys in the furnace, Daniel in the den. These are directly paralleled in *Hist.* 1.2, 3, 4, 7, 8, 9, 10, 12, 13, 15.

[168] GM 39, 102.

wielding power over nature: curing disease, extinguishing fire, taming animals, controlling rain, calming waves, conquering death. Little is heard about fruitfulness, whether by way of harvests or of children; but chastity, prominently featured among the saints, is the alternative expression of the same force.[169] Even more apparent is the divine power wielded over men in remitting and punishing their sins. The wrongs of men against God and the saints are taken personally and retributed in righteous vengeance. Gregory rarely shocks our sensibilities more than when exemplifying this idea. As a gluttonous Arian priest drops dead and is swept off to burial, "the priest of our religion said, rejoicing, 'God has truly avenged his servants.' "[170] However perturbed Gregory was by the many feuds in his environment, he portrays divine justice as resting squarely on, and sanctioning, the same direct response to personal injury that is shown underpinning contemporary society; "he visualizes [divine vengeance] as nothing less than God's own feud in support of his servants."[171] Earth and heaven are closely joined; the natural and moral order of the world, as Gregory conceived it, seems to be not a debased reflection of remote, metaphysical perfection, but personally animated by God and His saints. The latter, moreover, are present through their terrestrial relics as a living force, participating in society as perfect persons alongside imperfect ones and responding as they see fit when men treat them with prayerful reverence or reckless contempt. One might say that the special role of the saints was to multiply, almost as nerve ends, God's capacity to be a living presence among men.

Bishop Gregory was confident in the God-governed world he inhabited, in the validity of his personal experiences, the power of his nonstyle, the meaningfulness of the wonders taking place about him, and the importance of conveying to his public the multiple ways in which God and the saints lived among them. The Gallo-Romans dwelling south of the Loire, to whom his writings were mainly addressed, need not have been less open to the miraculous than he, but nothing compelled them to translate their credulity into *reverentia*—a specific pattern of Christian conduct.[172] For credulousness was not alone in guiding their behavior. As Gregory suggests, they also trusted in the regularity of nature and the normality of divine nonintervention; they both expected the written word to assume artistic shapes and were indifferent to its precepts by comparison with the certainties of

[169] GC 18, 32, 34 (sixtyfold fruit from virginity), 41 (in the form of strict monogamy), 51, 60, 75, 77.

[170] GC 79. A deliberately humorous story; no names or locality are specified.

[171] Wallace-Hadrill, "Bloodfeud of the Franks," p. 127.

[172] A key text is *VSM, praef.* Brown has made *reverentia* a memorable aspect of Gregory's thought: *Relics and Social Status*, esp. pp. 8-10. I doubt, though, that *rusticitas* should be taken as its opposite. There are too many instances of rusticity in a positive sense, e.g. Gregory's style, Abbot Portian (*VP* 5.*praef.*).

lived experience. Profane philosophy, in however debased a sense, still enjoyed enough credit among them to sustain a stolid skepticism toward the teachings of the Church. Gregory wrote as a pastor to dispel the confusions of this flock.

Himself free of such confusions, Gregory knew "nothing more natural than the supernatural." Sudden cures, premature deaths, unexpected releases from chains, and other prodigies were no less regular or ordinary as phenomena than the tides and the course of the heavenly bodies; for the one rule of the universe was God's eternal and very personal governance. Once men were persuaded by multifarious experiences, seen or heard, of this central fact, they might learn to lead their lives with fitting reverence in daily social intercourse with the Almighty Ruler and His friends, the saints. Gregory's belief in miracles was simple, in the sense of being resolutely uncritical, but there was nothing naïve or unreflective in the place he accorded to the miraculous in the faith he taught. He did not lack "an organic vision of history and life." His religion, it seems fair to say, was one of events rather than "of the Book" (and its patristic elucidations); and if he placed his narrative gifts at the service of religious instruction, it was on the considered premise that an artless historical record of contemporary happenings was the only medium capable of promoting and edifying the Church of God. Perhaps no other Christian thinker has come nearer than he to placing *res gestae*—present events no less than those of the past, at the center of his theology.

It makes little sense, then, to distinguish the *Wonders* as hagiography from the *Histories*.[173] Both multibook works incorporate the same mode of storytelling and affirmations of stylistic rusticity, along with the same premises and pastoral concern. Saints and miracles are no strangers to the *Histories*—irksomely so, as noted above, to early readers avid for information about the Frankish kings.[174] The narrative focuses, as in the *Wonders*, on individual incidents rather than connected themes, and the accent is predominantly on persons and events within living memory. The main difference is that the *Wonders* is an account of unrelieved good news: the bountifulness of divine gifts, the proximity of the holy, and its ready accessibility

[173] In this sense, but more reserved, see Walter, "Hagiographisches," p. 292; at n. 8, he cites several acknowledgments of the unity of Gregory's *œuvre*, notably by Ebert. In an unpublished paper ("Genre and Treatment of the Miracle in *De Gloria Beatorum Confessorum* and the *Historiae* of Gregory of Tours," 20th International Congress on Medieval Studies, Western Michigan University, Kalamazoo, Mich., May 1985), Karen A. Winstad examined three miracles that appear in both GC and the *Hist.* and indicated contrasts tending, in her view, to differentiate hagiography from history. The contrast is not wholly persuasive. E.g. the story of the Two Lovers is much more "historical" in *Hist.* 1.47 than in GC 31; but what was a piece of pure edification doing in the *Hist.* to begin with?

[174] Above, n. 48.

to men. In keeping with its philosophical implications, the work is consistently "abstract": the happenings it records are detached from the wider course of events. In the more comprehensive perspective of the *Histories*, the *virtutes* of the saints lose their isolation and are complemented by a less amiable dimension of life on earth. Gregory's terms for that complement are *strages gentium*, "the slaughter of peoples," and *miserorum excidia*, "the downfall of worthless men." Between profane *strages* and holy *virtutes*, there seems to be no middle ground. But that outlook and the other aspects of Gregory's *Histories* call for extended treatment.

4. *Historiae*: Candid but Chaotic Commemoration?

In the years of his episcopate, Gregory had two major works in course of composition—the *Wonders*, which we have now examined, and the *Histories*. Book I of the *Miracles of St. Martin* and books I-IV of the *Histories*, which are explicitly addressed to the years prior to Gregory's election to Tours, may have been finished before 580, in an early burst of literary productivity; but inferences about internal chronology cannot claim to be firm.[175] It has been maintained, on plausible grounds, that each book of *The Miracles of St. Martin* was immediately given to the public; the poet Fortunatus set the *Miracles* to verse when it was still only three books long.[176] None other of Gregory's works, whenever completed, is known with certainty to have circulated in his lifetime. Side by side, the major projects were worked at intermittently over twenty years and brought to a close in Gregory's declining months. The death of King Guntram in 593, not noted in the *Histories*, is referred to incidentally in the last book of *The Miracles of St. Martin*.[177] Gregory is believed to have died in 594.

Gregory did not undertake a history of the Franks. Well before Krusch restored the unqualified term *Histories* to his title, it was acknowledged, as by Ferdinand Lot, that he composed "a history of his times."[178] Gregory had little interest in the Franks as such. Ethnicity of any sort, his own included, was incidental to his concerns.[179] To be sure, sustained attention was paid to the kings of the Franks. Gregory not only speaks of those contemporary to himself but explores their ancestry in some detail. Clovis's descendants were the government, the basis of legality and source of much turbulence. Whether as Franks or something else, they were an obligatory subject in an exposition of current events. Yet there is much else besides them in the *His-*

[175] Above, n. 56.
[176] Above, n. 3.
[177] VSM 4.38. On the relationship of Guntram's death to the ending of the *Hist.*, n. 309 below.
[178] Lot, *Invasions germaniques*, p. 253.
[179] Goffart, "Foreigners."

tories. The topics range in their diversity from a paternity suit involving the first successor of St. Martin, through a feud that claimed the life of Gregory's brother, to a nun's revolt that almost dissolved St. Radegund's convent at Poitiers. At intervals, obituary notices occur, commemorating unholy as well as holy bishops and abbots. Reports of abnormally bad weather and natural calamities are another intermittent feature. Not least, the *Histories* has a decidedly personal touch. Without actually focusing on Gregory, more of the contents relate to him than to anyone or anything else.[180]

Does the *Histories* contain an inner, privileged core of material that lay closer to Gregory's interests than did digressions about religious figures, or that fulfilled a basic plan relegating holy men and autobiography to the margins? Vinay developed this argument (endorsed by Oldoni) on the basis of the phrases in which Gregory, ending a block of material, says that he will now return *ad coepta, ad propositum*, or *ad historiam*.[181] Such changes of direction clearly mean that Gregory had wandered from his "subject" and now regained his former track. Bearing this out, the context tends to involve a transition from a slow-paced passage (such as a series of obituaries) to the continuation of action previously set in motion.[182] Yet it does not follow that Gregory segregated certain kinds of information, distinguishing them from "my subject par excellence" or "my inner core history." He acknowledged what we can plainly see: namely, that his work contains, along with everything else, one or more threads of continuous action. In relation to these he says, "Let me pick up where I left off," or "Let me return to the running story." The running story was not better than the moments of arrested motion, or preferred to them; digressions were not, in principle, marginal, nor was continuous action privileged. When ending the *Histories*, Gregory emphatically asked that his works should not be changed in any way.[183] Such a plea would make little sense if the *Histories* were compounded of dispensable incidentals attached to an essential political core.

Gregory's own ideas of what he was doing are one route toward a better understanding of the *Histories*. The words opening the preface to book I were, presumably, his point of departure. In a parallel position, Josephus said: "The war of the Jews against the Romans was the greatest of our time."

---

[180] Diverse topics: *Hist.* 2.1, 5.5, 9.39-43, 10.15-17. Obituaries: *Hist.* 4.32-33, 5.7-10, 12, 42, 45-46, 6.6-9, 15, 37-39, etc. On natural events and the autobiographical component, see § 7 below. On the paternity suit (*Hist.* 2.1), see Canart, "Nouveau-né qui dénonce son père," p. 310; Gregory and the near-contemporary *Acts of Simon and Jude* supply the earliest known stories of this type.

[181] Vinay, *San Gregorio*, pp. 79-80; Oldoni tr., I, xlii.

[182] *Hist.* 2.4 *in fine* (closing a digression about Arian persecution, 2-4), 4.28 *in fine* (after the domestic lives of Chlothar I's four sons, 24-28, hardly incidental to a political core), 5.13 (after obituaries 7-12).

[183] Above, n. 52.

Other historians, such as Eusebius, are comparably informative.[184] Gregory began with an unhelpful clause: "As I am about to write of the wars of kings with hostile peoples, of martyrs with pagans, of the Churches with heretics."[185] We learn little more from these words than that royal as well as ecclesiastical affairs will be narrated, and that conflict is the stuff of history. Gregory has other, interesting things to say in this preface; but, as we shall see, their purpose is not to clarify his theme.[186]

There is a fuller account of Gregory's intentions in the general preface, which, again presumably, was a final touch, supplied only as the ten books neared completion. The subjects evoked here improve somewhat on the vague opening of book I: "many things are going on, some virtuous, some vile; the wildness of peoples rages; the anger of kings is stirred up; the Churches are attacked by heretics, protected by Catholics; the faith of Christ glows in many, cools in some; and the churches themselves are either enriched by the devout or stripped bare by the faithless."[187] The martyrs are gone—hardly relevant beyond book I. Otherwise, Gregory has amplified the subjects formerly set out without visibly modifying them. Nevertheless, he has taken the suggestive step of phrasing them in the present tense. His stated motive for writing is, as with many historians, "to commemorate those dead and gone, so that they might be borne to the notice of those to come."[188] Gregory's version of the customary assertion of truthfulness is that, though his diction is crude, he has refused "to conceal either the struggles (*certamena*) of the dissolute or the life of the just."[189] If this were all he said, we would be only a little better informed about his enterprise than by the preface to book I, and would continue to miss a reason for reading on. Gregory does not claim attention on the grounds that angry kings, wild peoples, and enriched or imperiled churches are inherently fascinating. The focus is elsewhere.

The general preface breaks new ground, and beckons us onward, when defining the author's role and chronological scope. In a manner better suited to an epic poet than a historian, Gregory takes it upon himself to be spokesman for his society, simultaneously suggesting that he is rather less than the public really wants. Very many people, he says, lament the passing of literary studies from the cities of Gaul; they bemoan the absence from their midst of an eloquent man of letters who might publish the deeds of the present in written form (Gregory links the sought-for *rethor* with the

---

[184] Josephus *Bell. Jud. praef.* 1.1; Eusebius *H.E.* 1.1.1-2.

[185] *Hist.* 1.*praef.*, K-L p. 3.

[186] Below, n. 359.

[187] K-L p. 1.

[188] *Ibid.* E.g. similar sentiments close Bede's preface, *H.E.* ed. Plummer, I, 8.

[189] K-L p. 1: "etsi incultu effatu, nequivi tamen obtegere vel certamena flagitiosorum vel vitam recte viventium."

pompous phrase *promulgare in paginis*).[190] Hearing these plaints, Gregory volunteers to speak "though in unpolished address." He is a second-best but compensates for this by intelligibility: "Few understand the philosophizing public speaker, but many the *loquens rusticus*."[191] The subjects listed in this preface are in the present tense. Except for tense, they might, as a group, belong to any age after Christ; there is nothing characteristically Merovingian about them. It is Gregory's social context that defines his chronological focus. The public wants *gesta praesentia*, contemporary history, and that, just as in the *Wonders*, is what Gregory supplies.

A writer's audience, Walter Ong observes, is always a fiction.[192] The historical reality of a complaining public assailing Gregory is secondary to the idea he conveyed by placing the *Histories* in a context of social need. For it is hardly true, as we have seen, that Merovingian Gaul was uniquely disadvantaged in not having previously found a historian. More than a century and a half, far beyond living memory, had passed without commemoration, and no one before had seemed to mind.[193] Gregory implies that men are in principle distressed if all sorts of things take place and no one records them. Historians might like to think this is so, but experience suggests that indifference is more normal than concern. No provocative theme—such as the rise and degeneracy of the Frankish kings, or "the story of the barbarian settlement of a Roman province"[194]—is recommended to our attention. There had to have been a more immediate and compelling reason for the public's plaint than a desire to inform posterity about nondescript happenings.

The muted alternative is suggested by the yearning that the public expressed for a skilled man of letters, someone who would commit events to words—*promulgare gesta in paginis*. Their call was for a *philosophans rethor*; the answer, Gregory's rusticity. Either way, more than mere commemoration would take place. For the public, in bewailing the lack of a historian, wished to understand; it hoped that *gesta praesentia*, by being translated into

[190] *Ibid.*: "Decedente atque immo potius pereunte ab urbibus Gallicanis liberalium cultura litterarum, . . . nec repperire possit quisquam peritus dialectica in arte grammaticus, qui haec aut stilo prosaico aut metrico depingeret versu, ingemescebant saepius plerique, dicentes: 'Vae diebus nostris, quia periit studium litterarum a nobis, nec reperitur rethor in populis, qui gesta praesentia promulgare possit in paginis.' " On the epic poet as spokesman of his society, Frye, *Anatomy of Criticism*, pp. 54-56.

[191] *Ibid.*: "Ista . . . intuens dici, . . . praesertim his inlicitus stimulis, quod a nostris fari plerumque miratus sum, quia: 'Philosophantem rethorem intellegunt pauci, loquentem rusticum multi.' " For "unpolished address," see above, n. 189.

[192] Ong, "A Writer's Audience Is Always a Fiction."

[193] Above, nn. 25-26.

[194] Quotation from Wallace-Hadrill, "Work of Gregory of Tours," p. 70. Cf. Foakes-Jackson, *History of Church History*, p. 97: "[Gregory's] theme is the emergence of the pagan and savage nation of the Franks from a collection of heathen hordes into a great Christian nation."

language, would gain a sense that they did not have for those who had lived them. Although Gregory's logic skips a step, the implication of his stylistic contrast seems plain. The audience, instead of the artful words it pined for, would get a narrative anyone might grasp; but regardless of whether the historian used studied or plain language, he would do something to the *gesta* he set down. His hard task, Gregory says elsewhere, quoting Sallust, was to put *facta* into *dicta*, deeds into words.[195] If the goal were only to enlighten "men to come," Gregory's society would endure the lack of a spokesman with equanimity. What it wanted—or, more certainly, what Gregory would compose, wanted or not—was an interpretation of contemporary history. Far from intimating that he would "narrate what he heard and what he saw without wider goal than to preserve the memory of events," he thrust himself forward as author of the plainspoken elucidation badly needed by his times.[196]

No historical model for such a program comes easily to mind. The Eusebius-Jerome *Chronicle*, Eusebius's *Ecclesiastical History* (in the Latin version of Rufinus), and Orosius's *Histories against the Pagans*, all of which Gregory cites and uses to a limited extent, offer little guidance to a historian of his own age.[197] Save for the last eight chapters of Orosius, their concern was the past, and their scale and ambitions had nothing in common with Gregory's.

Another mentioned source is the two-book *Chronicle* of Sulpicius Severus, which Gregory had special reason to study with care because of Sulpicius's personal relations with St. Martin and Martinian writings. Set alongside Gregory's narrative, Sulpicius's *Chronicle* looks like its diametrical opposite: heavy in biblical history, which accounts for three-quarters of the whole, and light on recent events.[198] A small resemblance is nevertheless apparent. Sulpicius set before Gregory a design of ecclesiastical history quite unlike Eusebius's, a design that dwells on biblical time and authorizes an abrupt transition from the Christian macrocosm to the Gallic homeland. Sulpicius starts with the Creation and presents a full range of Old Testament vicissitudes. Though beginning, after Christ, with such major events as the persecutions and the Arian controversy, his account sharply narrows toward the end, without apology or explanation, to the Western,

[195] *Hist.* 4.13. Aulus Gellius *Noctes Atticae* 4.15, provides a discussion of Sallust's remark. On Gregory's acquaintance with Gellius, see above, n. 42.

[196] Quote from Wattenbach-Levison, *Geschichtsquellen*, p. 105. Cf. Reydellet, *Royauté*, p. 349 (anticipated by Giesebrecht tr., I, xxxii): "Il n'écrit pas pour le présent, mais surtout pour la postérité." This is hard to reconcile with Gregory's ostentatious adoption of a social role.

[197] On these and other sources, Kurth, "De l'autorité," pp. 130-36; K-L, Preface, pp. xix-xx.

[198] Sulpicius Severus *Chronica* 1–2.25 (Bible), 2.26-50 (from the Incarnation to present times). See also Stancliffe, *St. Martin and His Hagiographer*, pp. 80, 82-83, 174-82.

and largely Gallic, dispute concerning Priscillian and his supporters. Even before this, the survey of Arianism tends progressively to focus on the Gallic bishop, Hilary of Poitiers.[199] Like Sulpicius, Gregory reached back to the Bible and had no qualms about leaping from there almost directly into the provincial confines he and his public lived in.[200] If allowance is made for the reversal of emphasis from biblical past to Gallic present, Sulpicius's *Chronicle* offers a faint foreshadowing of Gregory's plan. Perhaps the influence is there, although Gregory does not say so. Even if it were, only a minor feature of the ten books would be explained.

Because the scope and ordering of the *Histories* are hard to derive from the Christian historians whom Gregory cites, it is tempting to believe that he simply did his best, on his own, to compose a straightforward account of his era; "times were bad, and were going to get worse. Christians still needed reassurance," that is, reassurance about God's providence, similar to that which Orosius had given after the calamity of 410.[201] The premise here seems to be that Gregory contemplated current politics with anxiety and earnest concern about their course: the Merovingians were very important, and their lack of harmony was a social danger; the Gundovald rebellion (which occupies all of book VII) was a perilous crisis; the Treaty of Andelot, reconciling Kings Guntram and Childebert II, was a welcome development; and so forth. The facts were deadly serious, and that was why they deserved reporting.[202] In his narrative, Gregory sought—so some maintain—to piece together the course of external events in a manner comparable to that of grave historians, ancient and modern. Eusebius and Orosius set him an example of how to do this as a Christian. But he did not quite come up to their standards.

There is straightforward reporting of political facts in the *Histories*. One may even find it, though rarely, in whole chapters. Not everyone would

---

[199] *Chronica* 2.29, 31-32 (persecutions), 35-45 (Arianism, narrowing focus from 39, Gallic bishops always qualified as *nostri*), 46-50 (Priscillianism).

[200] *Hist.* 1.16 (Gaul first mentioned), 17 (Incarnation), 29ff. (Gaul becomes main subject), 44-47 (early bishops of Clermont, with domestic details), 39, 48 (St. Martin).

[201] Quotation from Wallace-Hadrill, "Work of Gregory of Tours," p. 56. Cf. Oldoni tr., I, xxxviii, at Gregory's accession "the kingdom was traversing . . . the most convulsive moment of Merovingian history"; Pietri, *Ville de Tours*, p. 302; Reydellet, *Royauté*, p. 350, the story of a man "à la recherche désespérée d'un ordre au sein du chaos qui apparaît à ses regards."

[202] Pietri, *Ville de Tours*, p. 308, comments about Gregory's inclusion of several strictly local tragedies: "Mais si Grégoire a résolu de faire figurer dans son œuvre, en contrepoint au récit des faits historiques majeurs, ces anecdotes crapuleuses ou scandaleuses, c'est parce que ces événements—il le sent profondément—sont les produits d'une époque déréglée, les symptômes d'une maladie qui envahit le corps social tout entier." She fails to specify the time limits of the *époque déréglée* and seems to take for granted that it was comparatively recent. Why should this be so? If Gregory thought that depraved times reached back to the days of Cain and Abel, he had to be a very different sort of commentator from one who perceived a recent decline from an age of virtue.

agree on the specifications for such passages (their contents are not homogeneous); but on a generous standard, and as a sample, only seven occur out of the fifty-one chapters of book IV, three in book VI, and two in book VIII.[203] The first chapter of book VI, detailing a related set of grave happenings in 581, perhaps best illustrates the type.[204] More consistently, such narrative plays an introductory role as the opening of chapters whose main part focusses on persons or circumstances somehow associated with the initial phrases. For example, Gregory gives a brief, dry account of the wives and children of Chlothar I, then continues with the scurrilous tale of how this king "came to marry the sister of his own wife." A few books later, the statement that Chilperic forced certain Jews of his kingdom to be converted broadens into the grim story of how Priscus, who resisted conversion, was murdered by the convert, Phatir.[205] Dry or neutral chapters and sentences of this kind, conveying dynastic or political information, are numerous enough to be noticeable; they tend to be essential to our understanding of the context of affairs. But they are subordinate elements of Gregory's narrative, designed to outline general circumstances, establish transitions, or set a scene. Though readers would be at a disadvantage without them, the interest and individuality of the *Histories* lie elsewhere. The dispassionate reporting of political facts does not seem to have ranked high among Gregory's priorities.

The main reason for doubting that Gregory was a simple, unreflective narrator of the world around him is his unmistakable and by no means haphazard editing of the historical record. Despite the copiousness of the *Histories*—six books for fifteen years, eight for barely a century—pertinent matters of all kinds are left out. Buchner stated, "It may be assumed that [for books V-X, coinciding with the period of Gregory's episcopate] he fully reports the really essential outward facts."[206] Though this is possible, we may hardly be confident that it is. Gregory omits a great deal, only a fraction of which was beyond his knowledge. Taking stock, however incompletely, of what Gregory passed over helps us to realize how far he was from striving after a full and comprehensive record of events.

[203] *Hist.* 4.1, 8, 10, 29, 38, 41, 45; 6.1; 8.35, 38. Books VI and VIII each have forty-six chapters.

[204] K-L pp. 265-66: "Anno igitur sexto regni sui Childeberthus rex, reiectam pacem Gunthchramni regis, cum Chilperico coniunctus est. Non post multum tempus Gogo moritur; in cuius locum Wandelenus subrogatur. Mommolus a regno Gunthchramni fuga dilabitur et se infra murorum Avennicorum monitione concludit. Apud Lugdunum sinodus episcoporum coniungitur, diversarum causarum altercationis incidens neglegentioresque iudicio damnans. Sinodus ad regem revertitur, multa de fuga Mummoli ducis, nonnulla de discordiis tractans."

[205] *Hist.* 4.31 (Chlothar I), 6.17 (conversions).

[206] Buchner, Einleitung, p. xxx. Cf. Gibbon, *Decline and Fall*, ch. 38 n. 117, ed. Bury, IV, 138: "in a prolix work (the five last books contain ten years) he has omitted almost everything that posterity desires to learn."

The most obvious gaps involve isolated details. Gregory's loathing of the Arian heresy is notorious, yet he seems not to have noticed that Jerome and Orosius plainly ascribe this heresy to the emperors Constantius II and Valens. The first Arians in the *Histories* are the Vandals. Perhaps this is why the Vandals parade before us bereft of Gaiseric, their greatest king and a fine example of unpunished wickedness.[207] Near total silence envelops Justinian, the outstanding ruler of Gregory's own century. He is referred to only at the moment of his death, and his Western campaigns are associated with an unnamed "emperor" and scattered in such a way as to conceal their unity of origin.[208] The Merovingian Childebert I achieved little else in an armed foray into Spain than to bring home the relics of St. Vincent of Saragossa and have them placed in the church that eventually became St. Germain des Prés. In the *Histories*, Childebert's expedition, the relics, and even the king's building of a Paris church to St. Vincent are all mentioned, but not the link between them: that Childebert translated the relics from Saragossa.[209] Some of these lacunae may have been accidental. That all were seems improbable.

Is Gregory at least a comprehensive historian of Merovingian politics and the Gallo-Roman church? Of course he supplies information, sometimes in abundance, but a few examples suggest how far he is from conventional political and ecclesiastical narrative. The generation of Frankish kings central to the *Histories* ascended in 561, at the death of Chlothar I. In less than a decade, and in close conjunction, the oldest of the four kings, Charibert, died of natural causes; another, Chilperic, came under severe pressure from his brothers for having murdered his Visigothic wife. The two events gave rise to major territorial readjustments. Neither is properly dated or sorted out by Gregory in book IV. There is a brief reference to contention over Charibert's territories, but the most we learn comes out of book IX, in which Gregory transcribes, without commentary, the text of a

---

[207] *Hist.* 1.38 (Constantius II and Hilary of Poitiers, with reference only to *heretici*), 41 (Valens punished for drafting monks); cf. Jerome *Chron.*, ed. Helm, pp. 234-35, 240; Orosius *Hist.* 7.29.2-5, 32.6, 33.1-4, 15, 19. According to Gregory (*Hist.* 2.2), a certain Trasamund is the Vandal king responsible for crossing from Spain to Africa, as well as the first specifically Arian persecutor (the real Vandal king Transamund belongs to the last decade of the fifth century). Gaiseric's only appearance is in GM 12, disguised as a certain Gauseric, king of the Huns.

[208] *Hist.* 2.3 (Vandals "overcome by the [Eastern] Empire"; this is completely out of chronological order; we are soon going to hear about Attila); 3.32 (an unnamed emperor recalls Belisarius and appoints Narses in his place); 4.8 (an imperial army invades Spain in the days of Agila); 4.40 (Justinian dies and Justin becomes emperor; the latter is characterized). Justinian is mentioned only to establish the date in GM 30, but in GM 102 he makes his most prominent appearance in Gregory's works, being outwitted by a pious lady whose riches he tries to gain for the treasury. To go by this story, Gregory had a more accurate sense of Justinian than his silence leads us to expect.

[209] *Hist.* 3.29 (Spanish expedition and the relics), 4.20 (the Paris church). Vieillard-Troïekouroff, *Monuments religieux*, pp. 211-12; Reydellet, *Royauté*, pp. 322-27, 409.

recent treaty containing sketchy references to these twenty-year-old arrangements. Many blanks, necessarily, cannot be filled in.[210]

A pervasive obstacle to our understanding the politics Gregory reports is that, except for royalty, the actors come abruptly before us without origins or a social context. A certain Parthenius is well known to modern historians of late Roman Gaul: a grandson of the emperor Avitus, he studied in Ravenna, held office as *patricius* of Provence, undertook an embassy to the Ostrogoths in Italy, was a friend there of the poet Arator (who sent him a copy of his *De actibus apostolorum*), and served the Merovingian Theudebert I.[211] In Gregory's *Histories*, Parthenius turns up only after the latter's death, as a tax official lynched by outraged Franks. No more is said of his past than that he murdered his wife and a friend on baseless suspicion of adultery.[212] It is unusual for Gregory to add, after mentioning that King Guntram appointed Mummolus patrician: "I think a few things should be said about the beginnings of [Mummolus's] career"; less surprisingly, Mummolus's beginnings cast him in a bad light.[213] So do those of the few other persons whose rise Gregory details. Normally, the actors are isolated from their past, and from their families, friends, and neighbors. Duke Ansovald was, from the information we casually gather about him, a leading servant of King Chilperic and the apparent strongman of Chlothar II's minority. Perhaps to his credit, the *Histories* tells us only enough about him to suggest the depth of our ignorance.[214] Even the lengthily described intrigues surrounding Gundovald's rebellion leave us with as many questions as answers. Another contemporary pretender, Sigulf, earns no more than a casual allusion.[215] Gregory was familiar with the works of at least two political historians, but it was no part of his own design to educe the surface coherence of *gesta praesentia*.[216]

The Church—that is, an abstract collegial body, as distinct from a gallery of churchmen—has little more claim to his interest. From the many episcopal elections he describes, no set attitude emerges toward the pres-

[210] *Hist.* 4.21-22 (Chlothar's succession), 26 (Charibert), 29 (Chilperic pressured by his brothers), 45 (contention over the late Charibert's cities), 9.10 (the treaty concluded), 20 (its text read out). Du Bos, *Histoire critique* I, 26, complained of Gregory's inadequacies as a profane historian.

[211] Stroheker, *Senatorische Adel*, no. 383; Riché, *Éducation et culture*, p. 64; *Prosop. Later Rom. Emp.* II, 833-34 (Parthenius 3); Heinzelmann, "Gallische Prosopographie," p. 663 (Parthenius 2).

[212] *Hist.* 3.36. Gregory's reserve can mislead modern writers; Parthenius is just a tax official in, e.g. James, *Origins of France*, p. 44.

[213] *Hist.* 4.42. In book VII, Mummolus fulfills the promise of his beginnings.

[214] *Hist.* 5.3, 47, 6.18, 45, 7.7, 8.11, 31. Among other things, Gregory leaves us wondering how he detached himself from Rigunth's train in the crisis after Chilperic's murder (6.45).

[215] *Hist.* 7.27.

[216] Buchner, Einleitung, pp. xv-xvi. About them, see Stroheker, "*Princeps clausus*. Zu einige Berührungen"; Hansen, "Sulpicius Alexander."

ence or absence of royal intervention. Each case is distinct, sometimes occasioning overt or implied disapproval, sometimes not. In Gregory's telling, no principle is at stake; circumstances and personalities are what matter.[217] A marvelous scene portrays King Charibert, no favorite of Gregory's, exploding the fatuousness of an episcopal council that nullified a decision of Chlothar I in the name of so paltry a thing as canon law. Yet Gregory did not despise canon law, whose rules he succeeded, for a while at least, in having applied to the case of Praetextatus of Rouen.[218] In the same way as prominent laymen, the churchmen we hear about seem to exist in social isolation. Gregory's family circle has been carefully pieced together from scattered references, mostly in the *Wonders*. His fellow bishops could no doubt have boasted of similarly resplendent relatives.[219] But even Gregory, in the *Histories*, is largely detached from any explicitly stated context. By assembling scattered clues, we can gain a little insight into how the Lombard Vulfolaic chanced into a monastery in the Limousin before becoming a stylite ascetic near Trier. Gregory, who could have more than satisfied our curiosity in a few lines, does not.[220] Lacking a clear-cut focus, Church history, even as exemplified by Eusebius, tends to fragmentation; but the unavoidable dispersal of the subject cannot alone account for Gregory's approach.

Much more is left out. O. M. Dalton, who also surveyed Gregory's omissions, was struck by his lack of a pictorial sense—the physical appearance of people, the layout of buildings, costume, and scenery. Despite being very well traveled in Gaul, he was no Arthur Young assessing the cultivation and value of "cornfields, vineyard, and woodlands."[221] Gregory, for all his interest in people and his cast of hundreds, may hardly be called a social historian, and he is only marginally useful to anyone striving to reconstruct Merovingian institutions.[222] His indifference to ethnicity has been remarked on by Fustel de Coulanges, Dalton, and many others. Gregory lived among and names a dozen or more peoples, and only once, because it mattered to the incident he was relating, did he go so far as to note that some of them were distinctive in hair style and dress. Franks frequently occur in the *Histories*, at court and elsewhere, but a close reading of the text is

---

[217] *VP* 5.3, 7.1-2; *Hist.* 3.2, 17, 4.3, 5-7, 11, 15, 18, 26, 35, 5.5, 35, 6.7, 9, 15, 38-39, 46, 7.31, 8.20, 22, 39, 9.23-24, 10.26. Gregory's disapproval of personalities rather than of process is clearest in *Hist.* 3.2, 4.6-7, 11. The principle he does care about is that bishoprics should go to clerics rather than to laymen (6.46, 8.22).

[218] *Hist.* 4.26 (Charibert), 5.18 (Praetextatus).

[219] For Gregory's family, see below, nn. 341-43. On other lineages, Heinzelmann, *Bischofsherrschaft*.

[220] Goffart, "Foreigners," p. 92 with n. 32.

[221] Dalton I, 25-27.

[222] E.g. he contributes little to an account of taxation, and what he incidentally provides tends to be ambiguous; Goffart, "Old and New in Merovingian Taxation."

needed to learn that they had a language of their own. That they actually spoke it is left unsaid. As though linguistic homogeneity prevailed in the North, the one interpreter we encounter turns up near the Mediterranean, helping a group of Lombard marauders to converse with a reclusive holy man. A salutary consequence of this indifference is that no ethnic group in the *Histories* behaves worse or better than any other.[223] Last but not least, one might observe that, among the many references to the weather and natural occurrences, none is made to a mild winter, a fine summer, or a bounteous harvest, surely not because there never were any to report.[224]

Gregory was not bound to include all these matters in the *Histories*. Some he may not have known; the rest, including instances of good weather, he knew perfectly well and chose to omit as having no place in the sort of work he was writing. The possibility of casual forgetfulness and muddle is not unlimited. There was a plan or design for the *Histories*, and it did not allow for the inclusion of proper notice of Justinian, of Franks speaking Frankish, of family connections, and so forth. Gregory was conscious and militant in assuming the accents of the *loquens rusticus*. He seems to have been no less deliberate in selecting what was and was not relevant to his *Histories*.

To leave facts out is not necessarily to suppress them, but there is an unambiguous case of Gregory's doing precisely that—the account of Bishop Avitus's conversion of the Jews of Clermont. Gregory was not predisposed to applaud attempts at Jewish conversion. Two instances involving King Chilperic pass before us with obvious marks of Gregory's scorn. That of Avitus glows with warmth and the aura of miracle. One of the Jews of Clermont threw rancid oil at a convert parading on the day of his baptism; Avitus kept the Christians from stoning the aggressor to death, but at the next major feast they razed the synagogue to the ground. Amidst this tension, Avitus sent the Jews a message affirming that he did not coerce them, but that they might either join his flock or leave the city. A day later, more than five hundred accepted baptism and the rest moved to Marseille.[225]

Gregory goes on at such length about Avitus's pious exhortations and the joy of baptism that we almost overlook the ultimatum in the bishop's message. Even at that, an important fact is passed over. A poem by Fortunatus, based on a report sent to him by Gregory, supplies a parallel account of the incident. It clearly indicates that the Jews accepted Avitus's offer because

[223] For a fuller account, Goffart, "Foreigners," pp. 80-99. The contrary view set out by Michel Rouche, "Francs et Gallo-Romains chez Grégoire de Tours," *Todi Convegno 12*, pp. 141-69, fails to convince.

[224] On weather, see below, nn. 325-27. Gregory does once mention an abundant vintage, *Hist.* 10.30, but in an otherwise deplorable context.

[225] Chilperic's conversions: *Hist.* 6.5, 17; those of Avitus, 5.11. For a fuller discussion, Goffart, "Conversions of Bishop Avitus." Rouche, "Les baptêmes forcés," combines suggestive aperçus with uncritical handling of the evidence.

a mob threatened to put them to the sword.[226] Gregory's *Histories*, contrary to the report sent to Fortunatus, omits the armed siege. The Jews' decision came about only "by the bishop's persuasion, as I believe."[227]

Anxious to defend the historian's truthfulness, Kurth commented: "Evidently, Gregory, who wrote ten years after the event, yielded to the temptation to idealize."[228] Gregory should be spared exculpation. He was not, in this case, departing from his normal standards. If the exploit of Avitus is "idealized," so also are many other passages of hagiography, or all of them. What Gregory gained here by *suppressio veri* was an instance of Jewish conversion such as he—speaking for his society—wished it to be: through prayer, persuasion, and the exploitation of fortuitous circumstances. Avitus's nonviolent, close-to-miraculous success offered a salutary contrast to Chilperic's abhorrent use of force. "Happy endings," a modern authority observes, "do not impress us as true, but as desirable, and they are brought about by manipulation."[229] Gregory saw no harm in sacrificing a fragment of historical truth so that something better might arise from his *dicta* than did from the *facta*. It is likely that he took such liberties more often than in this single detectable instance.[230]

If one wishes to dip into the *Histories* only in order to cull information, or if one believes that the Franks and their kings were crucial to early medieval history, it is comforting to assume that Gregory composed a straightforward narrative, inspired by the seriousness of the events he observed, and meant in all candor to inform posterity. Such a notion, however, is hardly compatible with Gregory's high level of selectivity and still less with the suppression of fact in his account of Avitus's conversions. These observations have little bearing on Gregory's veracity. He was too well trained a Christian to imagine that precise correspondence to outward appearance was the condition of truthfulness. Rather, they suggest that Gregory shaped and controlled the contents of the *Histories*, and that very little may be confidently done with his testimony until one comes to terms with his design. That he had a plan is hardly a novel idea. The *Histories* is too obviously ordered into chapters and books to suggest haphazard composition. But commentators have not gone very far toward puzzling out

[226] Fortunatus *Carmina* 5.5, ed. Leo, pp. 107-12; for a paraphrase, Goffart, "Conversions of Bishop Avitus," pp. 486-87.

[227] K-L p. 206: "ut credo, obtentu pontificis" (I follow the reading of A1 rather than Krusch's *obtentum*).

[228] Kurth, "De l'autorité," pp. 175-76.

[229] Frye, *Anatomy of Criticism*, p. 170.

[230] Cf. Banniard, "Aménagement de l'histoire chez Grégoire de Tours," showing how Gregory breaks with tradition in portraying Attila's campaign; but Banniard's interpretation is questionable.

Gregory's principles of organization. At best, he has seemed to start along a clear road and to have then lost control.

R. A. Markus, in a passage quoted earlier, suggested that Gregory began writing a chronicle and successively grafted onto it "a stretch of ecclesiastical, then a predominantly national history with ecclesiastical episodes." The result, Markus held, was a medley markedly inferior to Bede's harmonious whole.[231] A similar view, set out by Hellmann and lately echoed by Reydellet, is that Gregory's basic idea was to narrate Frankish history in the context of universal history and of the history of the universal Church, but that this plan was overwhelmed by the impact upon him of ongoing events; minute happenings so moved Gregory as to undermine his strong book divisions and to replace order with chaos.[232]

These assessments are thoughtful, but much in them needs to be set right. Gregory did not mean either to write a chronicle or to situate the Franks in a universal context. His attention in book I to the Judeo-Christian macrocosm proceeded only from a need, as he affirms, to "explain clearly" to his public—by way of introduction—"how many years have passed since the world began." Even at that, his choice of subjects is not guided by any desire to trace the rise and fall of nations. Anyone wishing a chronicle might consult Jerome. Gregory's concern was to select paradigmatic events, such as Cain's murder of Abel (the beginning of wickedness among men), the crossing of the Red Sea (a symbol of baptism), and the Babylonian captivity (a symbol of the soul's enslavement to sin).[233] So rapid is his passage through the Bible that, on the verge of the Incarnation, he supplies the first intimation of Gaul—the foundation of Lyon—the goal that he attains a mere ten chapters later.[234] The usual empires of universal history go unnoticed. Even Rome is represented almost exclusively by a string of persecuting emperors, the prototypes, one might say, of the barbarian persecutors who come next.[235] Gregory's rundown of the years of the world supplies a context, but it is not one of "universal history" in any con-

---

[231] As above, n. 20.

[232] Hellmann, "Gregor von Tours," p. 98; Reydellet, *Royauté*, p. 400.

[233] Gregory runs through five of the six world ages in *Hist.* 1.2-15, spelling out what will be briefly recapitulated in 4.51 and 10.31. The fact that the world has persisted so long in its wickedness offers assurance that the end of time had no reason to be near at hand. Paradigmatic events: 1.2, 4, 15; also 1.6, Babylon as symbol of the frailty of human achievements; the conduct of the Israelites, 1.12, 16. Model figures, listed in *VSJ, praef.*, are another feature of the biblical summary (above, n. 167). On the crossing of the Red Sea, see Roberts, "Rhetoric and Poetic Tradition in Avitus's Account."

[234] *Hist.* 1.18, 28.

[235] Cursory reference is made to non-Jewish rulers since the Creation, *Hist.* 1.17; otherwise, the first five ages are purely biblical and Hebraic. Caesar and Augustus are briefly noted (1.18); the Roman Senate disparaged (24); Roman persecutors (21, 27-30, 32, 35, 41); an Alaman persecutor (32-33), more barbarian persecutors of Christianity (2.2-6). Christian emperors are not stressed (1.36-38, 42-43).

ventional sense of the term.[236] As for "national" history, Gregory had no model for it (other than the Old Testament), and he never isolated ecclesiastical affairs from temporal ones in the way Eusebius was able to do. Gregory's subjects may be ill-assorted, but they should not be confused, as Markus confuses them, with a clumsy assemblage of historical genres. Besides, to maintain with Hellmann that particular occurrences subverted a basic plan to write Frankish history disregards Gregory's declared priorities. He never claimed that the Franks were his theme.

If one avoids comparing him with Bede, or paying more attention to his early books than to the later ones, Gregory proves to be more firmly focussed than he might seem. His concern, as the general preface says, was with *gesta praesentia*, and these *gesta*, properly speaking, begin only in book V, after a four-book introduction extending from Adam to the murder of Sigibert I (Gregory's installation as bishop of Tours, which he does not mention, had taken place two years before). His coverage in books V-X of the events of a mere decade and a half may lack coherence. Loebell spoke of its being history reduced to elementary particles.[237] But such a remark concerns inner elaboration rather than the delimitation of a theme. Gregory was the self-appointed spokesman for the slice of Gaul that he regarded as his society. His coherent topic, however he treated it, was the historical experience of his generation, set in the perspective of a summarily filled-in past.

Granting, then, that Gregory held firm to his commitment, he nevertheless puzzles us in as much as the *Histories* combines a tidy and self-explanatory outer structure with a disconcerting looseness of subjects and emphasis within. Hellmann rightly drew attention to the strong book divisions. In Buchner's words, "the work is not without order and planning," but it frequently manifests "freedom from any schema, from restraint."[238] The problem of explaining this inconsistency exists even if one agrees with Buchner that Gregory's freedom from restraint is a part of his "undying attraction." Hellmann called his choice of contents "authentically barbarian," but this and other statements tending to explain Gregory's

---

[236] On the strength of beginning with the Creation, Gregory's work has often been taken to be a "universal chronicle": Morghen, "Introduzione alla lettura di Gregorio di Tours," pp. 15-16; Brincken, *Weltchronistik*, pp. 96-98 (admits that one cannot do justice to Gregory if he is treated as a world chronicler alone); Krüger, *Die Universalchroniken*, pp. 22, 31, 37-42. As Krüger recognizes (though for other reasons), there is something wrong with the definition of a genre that classes Gregory under so unsuitable a rubric. Also representative, Reydellet, *Royauté*, p. 367, Gregory begins as a chronicler, i.e. as something other than the historian of the Franks whom he starts to be at *Hist.* 2.7. This, of course, presupposes that the Franks were his subject. Long ago, Giesebrecht tr., I, xxxiii, correctly concluded that Gregory never intended to write *eigentlich Weltgeschichte*.

[237] Loebell, *Gregor von Tours und seine Zeit*, cited by Hellmann, "Gregor von Tours," p. 69.

[238] Hellmann, "Gregory von Tours," p. 71; Buchner, Einleitung, p. xx.

methods by reference to his supposedly chaotic age are too obviously circular to merit further attention: the chaos is known from little else than his testimony.[239] As Gregory chose the subject matter of the *Wonders* so was he responsible for deciding what entered his principal work. A sustained effort has to be made to account for the curious disparity between the outer orderliness and the inner liberties of the *Histories*.

Gregory's ability to fashion tidily structured books has already been observed in examining the *Wonders*. The basic articulation of the *Histories* is equally satisfactory, even if our curiosity about his choice of ten books remains unsatisfied. Gregory, not wishing to tarry in the distant past, is already in the sixth century by the start of book III and within reach of his own memories by that of book IV, though this span is still treated as introductory. The properly contemporary books are annalistic. Book V opens with year one of Childebert II (it ran from December 575), and Childebert's regnal years are consistently noted thereafter. Gregory's focal cities, Tours and Clermont, pertained to Childebert's (sometimes disputed) share of the Frankish kingdom.[240] Gregory did not feel forced to start all of books V-X with the opening of a regnal year. A Visigothic transition links books VIII and IX. Book VII, concerning the critical events following the murder of King Chilperic, is limited to a few months, by far the shortest span of all. One transition from book to book is less than clearly motivated, others are merely reasonable and sound, and a few embody impressive effects: the adventures of St. Martin's successor as a sequel to Martin's death; the death of the saintly queen Chlothild echoing that of good King Theudebert I; and, most of all, the relationship of the holy bishop Salvius of Albi to the doom of King Chilperic.[241] The bracketing or "framing" of Chilperic by Salvius of Albi is a device that reappears on several occasions. The beginning and end of the tale of how Gregory's brother was killed feature the deacon Lampadius; Chlothar I is associated with St. Martin in his arrogance and, long after, in his death; Ragnachar is by Clovis's side as the latter marches to his first victory, and he is the last of the fellow kings whom Clovis treacherously does to death.[242] There is nothing casual about such writing.

Even within books, Gregory occasionally displays an ability to organize and compose on a larger-than-episodic scale. It only needs to be understood

---

[239] Buchner, p. xx; Hellmann, p. 68. *Hist.* 3 starts in 511; book IV basically in 548, when Gregory was ten, but he was seventeen by 4.9 and twenty-one by 4.20. Book divisions: *Hist.* 8.45 (death of Leuvigild), 9.1 (Reccared seeks peace).

[240] *Hist.* 7 runs from approximately October 584 through June 585.

[241] Unclear transition, *Hist.* 9/10; St. Martin's death and successor, 1.48, 2.1; deaths of Theudebert I and Chlothild, 3.36-37, 4.1 (in fact, Chlothild predeceased Theudebert); Salvius and Chilperic, 5.50, 6.46, 7.11.

[242] Lampadius, *Hist.* 5.5; Chlothar I, 4.2, 21; Ragnachar, 2.27, 42.

that he did so in "stranded" narrative and with hardly any explicit transitions.[243] Book VII contains the outstanding example of such writing. Between chapters 4 and 43 (almost the whole book), Gregory's attention focuses with rare intensity on the political aftermath of Chilperic's death and the course of Gundovald's rebellion. As the focus shifts back and forth among the various participants, the action moves consistently forward, only once delayed, to Guntram's triumph over Gundovald and the flight to sanctuary of the surviving conspirators.[244] Something of the same coherence in the tracing of a complex tale through a connected string of chapters is found in the account of Chramn's rebellion in book IV and in that centering on the ravaging of Auvergne in book III.[245] Gregory's narrative style would not be seriously faulted if these chapters were representative, rather than atypical, of the way he traces tangled events; coherent narration (beyond single chapters) is something he seems occasionally to lapse into. Yet it is hard to accept the idea that these exceptions are flukes of the sort that may occur at random if enough words are written. Our judgment of "chaotic" narrative derives from a sense of what we would accept as a proper history of Frankish or Merovingian affairs. Gregory had something else in mind.

5. *Historiae*: The Moral Sense of Events

The traces of orderliness in the *Histories* do not get us closer to Gregory's guiding design than does the study of his omissions, but they do force us to consider whether the right consequences have been drawn from his promise to provide contemporaries with an interpretation of the *gesta* they had experienced. It seems unlikely, after what we have seen, that he meant to explain recent history in one of the ways in which we expect historical sense to be made, Orosius's among them. His insistence in the *Wonders* on the persuasive force of contemporary events points in a direction far more in keeping with the pastoral functions of his office.

Gregory has long been recognized in scholarship, sometimes with regret, as a Christian moralist. Hellmann referred to him as a *Sittenprediger* and spoke of his "measuring [the figures of his age] judiciously against the inexorable precepts of a Higher Power."[246] It hardly seems far-fetched to suppose that what he believed his public needed from a narrative of *gesta praesentia* was not a worldly-wise exposition of politics and warfare, but moral enlight-

---

[243] On stranded narrative, Clover, *Medieval Saga*, pp. 61-108.
[244] *Hist.* 7.29.
[245] Chramn, *Hist.* 4.10-21; ravaging of Auvergne, 3.4-18.
[246] Hellmann, "Gregor von Tours," pp. 67, 63. Cf. Monod, *Études critiques*, pp. 121-23; Wallace-Hadrill, "Work of Gregory of Tours," pp. 57-58.

enment. So conceived, the *Histories* was meant to be, above all, a vehicle of Christian instruction.

This different point of departure suggests a new background for the *Histories* in Christian literature.[247] The established biblical setting for a concern with current events is that of a prophet who foretells calamity should the people and their leaders persist in their habitual ways, and who summons them to repentance and reform. Two works in Gregory's immediate past adopt this prophetic pattern and, though apparently not known to him, help to give perspective to his enterprise. They are Salvian's *On the Governance of God* and Gildas's *Ruin of Britain*.[248]

Salvian of Marseille, who wrote in the 440s, was deeply moved by the setbacks recently suffered by the Roman West at the hands of barbarians and saw in them manifest proof that God's judgment was exercised here below.[249] The disasters being currently experienced were God's merited punishment for the depravity of Salvian's fellow Romans. Although Salvian's treatise has proved fascinating to modern historians of late antiquity, it almost wholly disregards politics and conventional *res gestae*.[250] Salvian, a moralist and preacher, sought to assign responsiblity for public disasters to the evil lives of the ordinary Roman Christians whom he could expect to reach. The failings he castigates, usually in abstract terms—addiction to amusements, gluttony, drunkenness, sexual laxity, egoism, avarice, manipulation of the tax apparatus, oppression of the poor by the rich—were selected so that his listeners might recognize the contribution of their personal sins to the general calamity.[251] The description of these offenses, as close as Salvian comes to historical details, occupies far less room than his theoretical exploration of God's present judgment.

Gildas is, of course, the famous narrator of the British "dark age," that is, the period between the Roman evacuation and Gregory the Great's mission to the English. He wrote *The Ruin of Britain* toward 540.[252] Like Sal-

[247] Largely anticipated by Hanning, *Vision of History*, pp. 46-49.

[248] Cf. Hanning, *Vision of History*, pp. 45-48.

[249] Salvian *De gubernatione Dei*, ed. and tr. Georges Lagarrigue, Sources chrétiennes 220 (Paris 1975), with a full introduction and bibliography. Concerning the date, Lagarrigue, pp. 11-15, offers the termini 440-50. It seems to me that the Burgundian settlement of 443 (*Chronicle of 452*, ed. Mommsen, MGH AA. IX, 660), which Salvian does not mention, has a good claim to being the *terminus ante quem*.

[250] E.g. Bury, *Later Roman Empire from Death of Theodosius I*, 307-308; Stein, *Bas-Empire I*, 344-47. Because Salvian documents "decline," he has tended to be read as a neutral reporter. Badot, "Utilisation de Salvien," restores the work to its theological context (rich bibliography).

[251] *De gubern. Dei* 4-7 are full of assorted misconduct, with special attention to amusements (6.10-89), taxation (5.17-35), and sexual laxity (7.8-107). No one is named; regions and cities are singled out as being specially addicted to various sins.

[252] Cited above, ch. I n. 28. On the date: O'Sullivan, *The "De excidio" of Gildas*, pp. 77-178; Dumville, "Gildas and Maelgwn" and "Chronology of *De excidio Britanniae*," in Lapidge

vian or an Old Testament prophet, Gildas is a moralist exhorting his contemporaries to penance and reform. His main targets, less diffuse and more socially prominent than Salvian's, are the British kings and clergy, whose sins and vices are denounced, sometimes with personal details: "Britain has kings, but they are tyrants. . . . Britain has priests, but they are fools."[253] Gildas not only denounces but offers salutary advice, consisting mainly of biblical precepts, and his concern for history far exceeds Salvian's. Paragraphs 2 through 26 (about one-eighth of the whole treatise) fill in the background to the present condition of Britain. However meager in dates and concrete details, they have not undeservedly earned Gildas the name of historian. Their inclusion seems attributable to the absence of a crisis as immediate as that in Salvian's Gaul. The victory at Badon Hill had gained the Britons a security from the Saxons that had now lasted nearly a half-century.[254] Gildas, informing his listeners of almost forgotten disasters, strove to shock them with the disclosure that a period of ostensible tranquillity in the not so distant past had been shattered by calamities greater than any before. The cyclical rhythm of history ensured that the current peace was transitory. The time to prepare for the future was now.[255]

Salvian and Gildas allow us to see that, in Christian letters as in the Old Testament, a burning concern with current events did not have to be translated into sustained historiography. Their works also suggest that a moralist's attention to historical circumstances is in inverse relation to the immediacy of critical events. Gregory of Tours was well versed in the biblical prophets but, as far as we may tell, was unacquainted with Salvian or Gildas.[256] Even so, he could be just as preoccupied with moral issues as they. He advertises his identity as a Christian at the very start of the *Histories*. He is even more famed than Salvian and Gildas for vividly commemorating the vices of his contemporaries.[257] His resolution, examined earlier, to apply himself only to such matter as "builds the Church of God" did not refer to the *Wonders* alone: *gesta praesentia* merited attention for the religious instruction and edification they afforded. But if the crumbs of history in Sal-

---

and Dumville, eds., *Gildas: New Approaches*, pp. 51-59, 61-84. O'Sullivan argues for ca. 515-30, and preferably earlier within this span; Dumville, who is very critical of O'Sullivan, tends to confirm the long-accepted approximation. See also Lapidge, "Gildas's Education." More will be heard of Gildas in ch. IV.

[253] Gildas *De excidio* 27.1, 66.1.

[254] *Ibid.* 25.2–26.3. The present generation is that of the grandchildren of the victorious leader (25.3); therefore, men have forgotten (26.3).

[255] *Ibid.* 20.2–23.5.

[256] Cf. Bonnet, *Latin de Grégoire de Tours*, p. 57.

[257] Gregory's creed: *Hist.* 1.*praef.* Dalton I, 86: "The picture [Gregory conveys of his contemporaries] is a dark one; all that can be said to relieve the darkness is that in history the villains are apt to attract the recorder's eye." Dill, *Society in the Merovingian Age*, p. 279: "the moral picture of the Merovingian age is often truly appalling."

vian swell into an estimable share of Gildas's tract, Gregory outdoes Gildas by dwelling so fondly on the *gesta* themselves as almost to banish overt commentary from his pages. Moreover, he has room for saints alongside the sinners.

To judge from the *Histories*, no disaster remotely comparable to the one underlying Augustine's *City of God* and Orosius's *Seven Books*, or those inspiring Salvian and Gildas, pressed Gregory into picking up his pen. He lacked a focal event in the present or even the memory of one in the past. If he was aware of "the Fall of the Roman Empire," he never says so. [258] His repeated refusal to express the subject of the *Histories* in any but the vaguest and most general terms must be taken seriously: all sorts of things were going on, as they always do, and no one, predictably, was bothering to write them down. [259] In an age of scattered rather than concentrated calamity, he had not only to work harder than Salvian and Gildas to detect the vestiges of God's judgment, but also to exercise discretion and restraint in distilling lessons from occurrences that became memorable chiefly as a result of his telling.

Three or four times, including the famous preface to book V, Gregory contrasts the bad conduct either of kings or of their subordinates to the good example of their predecessors. The particular evil in two instances is civil war and, in a third, impotence in war against the Arian Goths. [260] The repetitiveness of Gregory's analysis is striking; even when putting words in the mouths of others, he more or less clearly calls for reform. But one would be hard put to regard these passages as expressions of an urgent crisis. The lines come and go without its being possible to claim that the *Histories* focuses on them. That current events personally moved Gregory goes without saying. The *Wonders* spells out the supreme importance he believed present miracles had for religious knowledge—an idea that might mean, by extension, that chance occurrences were deeply relevant to moral knowledge in general. But he did not expect his point of view to be taken for granted by his public. To go by the general preface, the crisis on the public's mind was the collapse of literary studies in Gaul. Gregory was unperturbed by this, and though he assumes the role of a social spokesman, his voice is far

---

[258] He was no more aware of the rise of Rome. Caesar and Augustus turn up in *Hist.* 1.18 to establish monarchy; the first reference to Gaul involves the foundation of Lyon, but basically as a prelude to the famous martyrs of that city (1.28-29). Gildas, by contrast, has a strong sense of Britain as a province of the Empire.

[259] Above, nn. 185-87.

[260] *Hist.* 4.48, 5.*praef.*, 8.30 (Guntram speaks Gregory's lines), 5.34 (Fredegonde does). Wallace-Hadrill, "Work of Gregory of Tours," pp. 60-61, takes *Hist.* 5.*praef.* to express Gregory's sense of Frankish mission. There is little doubt that these passages express Gregory's indignation at the behavior and rule of Clovis's grandsons, i.e. the Merovingians contemporary to his episcopate.

homelier and more autobiographical than the impassioned admonitions of Salvian and Gildas. Moralist though he is, and never claiming to be dispassionate, he has sometimes charmed modern readers into believing that he had no other concern than to relate the facts as best he could.

This impression of detachment has a certain surface plausibility, but is not encouraged by Gregory himself. He had a clear notion of the moral pattern of history and, after letting readers familiarize themselves with it on their own in the opening book, took care to spell it out explicitly in the preface to book II. Much of the responsibility for the fragmentary and discontinuous appearance of Gregory's narrative rests with his avowed decision to include "miracles of saints" alongside "slaughters of peoples." Vinay drew attention to the troublesome place of *virtutes* in what he wished to be a history of Frankish kings, and he was not wrong to point to the saints as a major cause for Gregory's ostensible lack of inner order.[261] For different reasons, other commentators have also been troubled by the way miracles compete with feuds for the reader's attention.[262] This was not his fault, Gregory asserted: such was the nature of history.

"Startling though it may seem, the concept of history in the objective sense—that is, as the aggregate of past events—was unknown to antiquity."[263] That this sense of the term should have arisen in the setting of Christian time, flowing finitely between Creation and Second Coming, is not surprising. Even at that, Gregory does not invoke the term *historia*, but his meaning is clear, and he does not hesitate to provide this aggregate of events with a simple characterization. He explains, in the preface to book II, that history includes the deeds of the blessed as well as those of the damned; Eusebius, Sulpicius Severus, Jerome, and Orosius "wove together the wars of kings and the miracles of the martyrs," and sacred history does so, too.[264] Five biblical examples are laid out at length, and though two are conventional, the next three illustrate a crucial lesson. The careful reader of Scriptures will find, we are told, that under Samuel the Just the sacrilegeous Phineas was killed, and that under David Stronghand the alien Goliath was cut down; "Let him remember, however," that many disasters, droughts, and famines afflicted the earth in the days when the prophet Elias

[261] Vinay, *San Gregorio*, pp. 78, 104.

[262] Above, nn. 20-21.

[263] Fornara, *Nature of History*, p. 91; also see Press, "Development of the Idea of History," pp. 286-88.

[264] *Hist.* 2. *praef*, K-L pp. 36-37: "Prosequentes ordinem temporum, mixte confusequae tam virtutes sanctorum quam strages gentium memoramus. Non enim inrationabiliter accipi puto, se filicem beatorum vitam inter miserorum memoremus excidia, cum idem non facilitas scripturis, sed temporum series praestitit. Nam sullicitus lector, si inquirat strinue, invenit . . . [biblical examples]. Sic et Eusebius, Severus Hieronimusquae in chronicis atque Horosius et bella regum et virtutes martyrum pariter texuerunt. Ita et nos idcircum sic scripsemus, quod facilius saeculorum ordo vel annorum ratio usque nostra tempora tota repperiatur."

started and stopped rain at will and turned the widow's poverty into riches, that Jerusalem endured many ills in the time of Hezekiah, whose life God increased by fifteen years, and that many massacres and miseries oppressed the people of Israel in the days when the prophet Elisha restored the dead to life and wrought many other miracles.[265] Gregory does not mean that miracles offset miseries. His idea is that, typically, a prophet's holiness and miracles coexisted with the woes of the age he denounced and also deserve attention. "I do not believe it should be regarded as lacking reason if we commemorate the life of the blessed among the disasters of the worthless, for that is the way they are presented, not by the levity of writers, but by the course of events."[266] Nowhere is Gregory more precise than here in disclosing the inner design of the *Histories*.

In commenting on this preface, Vinay took Gregory's phrase *series temporum* to mean "chronological order" and made it central to the argument: "[Gregory] thus denies the irrationality of an exclusively annalistic order, but the very fact of denying it shows that he confusedly realized [its shortcomings]."[267] Vinay's interpretation misses the point. Gregory is not annalistic until book V, and his chronology, never strict, is loosest in the very book he was prefacing.[268] His words *series temporum* mean "course of events," or "history." The combination of blessed and wretched, repeated no fewer than eight times, forces us to realize that Gregory's overriding concern is to justify a distinctive feature of his narrative. Though he invokes Eusebius and the others, and is not wholly wrong in saying that their histories "wove together" martyrs and wars, Gregory is far from being their pupil when he portrays *virtutes sanctorum* alongside *strages gentium*. In a manner proper to himself, he suggests the impossibility of relating the course of events in a unified or homogeneous way. At any given time, the disasters of some coexist with the miracles of others, and both must be successively recorded. Gregory insists on including the light beside the dark; but his main point, perhaps, in multiplying contrasting pairs, is to intimate that he will not try to efface the chasm between them or, as we might say,

---

[265] *Ibid.*: "invenit inter illas regum Israheliticorum historias sub Samuhel iustum Fineen interisse sacrilegum ac sub David, quem Fortem manu dicunt, Golian alophilum conruisse. Meminiat etiam sub Heliae eximii vatis tempore, qui pluvias cum voluit abstulit et cum libuit arentibus terris infudit, qui viduae paupertatem oratione locopletavit, quantae populorum strages fuere, quae famis vel quae siccitas miseram oppraesserit humum; quae sub Ezechie tempore, cui Deus ad vitam quindecim annos auxit, Hierusolima mala pertulerit. Sed et sub Heliseum prophetam, qui mortuos vitae restituit et alia in populis multa miracula fecit, quantae internitiones, quae miseriae ipsum Israheliticum populum oppraesserunt."

[266] As n. 264.

[267] Vinay, *San Gregorio*, p. 69; cf. Nie, "Roses in January," p. 282.

[268] *Hist.* 2.2-3 runs from 406 to the 530s; 2.4, back to the fourth century for Athanaric's persecution of Christians; 2.5-7, the Huns invade Gaul, 451; 2.8, ranges from 425 to 455; 2.9, back to the fourth century; etc.

to justify the ways of God to his readers. He affirms that the coexistence of these opposites in the *series temporum* is the objective character of history. In ordering events *mixte confusequae*, he will narrate the recent past not in the intentionally one-sided manner of the *Wonders*, but "as it really was."

The adjectives *mixte confusequae* refer to the *series temporum*, "history," and not to Gregory, who attributes no confusion to himself. Oldoni concluded that this preface is "a programmatic refusal of any sort of structure," as though Gregory wished us to think him haphazardly moved by the winds of historical accident.[269] Gregory, however, kept the structure of his narrative well in hand. He excluded from the *Histories* nine-tenths of the contemporary *virtutes sanctorum* that he recorded in the *Wonders* and saw to it, in this way, that *strages gentium* should outweigh miracles by a large margin. Far from being an excuse for confusion, the preface to book II sets out Gregory's concept of the inner morality of history and, by the same token, outlines the possibility for meaningfully ordering past and recent events.

6. *Historiae*: Miracles and Slaughters

In keeping with what Gregory maintained was the objective character of events, the interweaving of light and dark guided his choice of subject matter and, less obviously, the narrative mode in which incidents are narrated. For a start, he makes little allowance for the gray middle ground. The course of events is a compound of "slaughters of peoples" or "the disasters of worthless men," on the one hand, and "miracles of the saints," on the other. *Strages* and *excidia* are very strong words, representative perhaps of Orosius's sort of history but not Eusebius's, and no more likely to typify the *gesta praesentia* lived by Gregory's public than they do ours. Albert Hauck observed that "Gregory of Tours' interest . . . was drawn to the spectacular. . . . [T]he everyday, because self-evident, he considered not worth description or not needing it."[270] What Gregory mostly conveys, according to Godefroid Kurth, "are the high exceptions and the low exceptions. Rarely does one encounter a portrayal of everyday existence, the life of average people. We are often obliged to infer it from the two exceptional categories [of miracles and crimes]."[271] Auerbach believed that "what Gregory relates is his own and his only world."[272] This seems not to be the case. An ordinary, normal world, which the author and his audience inhabit, is sketchily evoked, as we shall see. But the animation of the *Histories*, monopolizing Gregory's attention and narrative skill, belongs to a realm of extremes and excesses. Without explaining all the omissions noted earlier,

[269] Oldoni tr., I, xliii.
[270] Hauck, *Kirchengeschichte Deutschlands* I, 172.
[271] Kurth, "De l'autorité," p. 173.
[272] Auerbach, *Mimesis*, p. 79.

the two extremes are the main clue to what Gregory thought relevant or not to his narrative. In the *Wonders*, Gregory's accent was on the fortuitous character of the miraculous; the unexpectedness of divine bounty had much to do with its didactic value. Consistent with this outlook, the fortuitous *virtutes sanctorum* are complemented, in the *Histories*, by equally unpredictable occurrences among the *miseri*. Hauck came close to realizing this when he suggested that Gregory typically narrates "outbreaks of passionate *Kraftgefühl*."[273] The middle ground was almost swept out of the picture, and its small place must be recalled in any attempt to grasp the sort of history Gregory was writing. Not only did he not "conceal the struggles of the dissolute or the life of the just," but he paid attention to little else.[274]

The impact of Gregory's program on the *Histories* is even greater when measured by his deployment of narrative modes; that is, the relative elevation he gave to the leading characters, and their power of action, by comparison with the readers.[275] For most chapters, not all, Gregory availed himself of only two modes. The more prominent one is irony, giving readers the sense of observing irredeemable sinners in a depraved world. The other mode is romance, which portrays persons (mainly saints in the *Histories*) whose power of action is clearly superior to the human norm.[276] Gregory is often taken to be "realistic," which in modern fiction calls for heroes with the capabilities of ordinary men. But his realism is not of this kind. He generally avoids the middle ground in mode as well as subject matter. Some of his most "realistic" touches—a girl fouling a baptismal font with menstrual blood, horses urinating—are in passages of hagiographic romance; and the impressive "realism" of scenes featuring wrongdoers lends conviction to what are, from the first, portrayals of fallen humanity.[277]

Gregory's romantic mode has already been illustrated by the account of Avitus's conversion of the Jews of Clermont.[278] Less elaborate instances occur at irregular intervals. In book IX, we hear of pious Queen Ingoberga (mother-in-law of Ethelbert of Kent), whom Providence warned about her death ("or so I believe") and who prepared for it by abundant charitable legacies. Her death is directly followed by the story of a freeborn girl, unnamed, who like the biblical Judith seized a sword and mortally wounded Duke Amalo when he tried to rape her. The aura of miracle, faintly suggested by Ingoberga's premonition, is the normal though not the obligatory

---

[273] As n. 270.
[274] Above, n. 189.
[275] Frye, *Anatomy of Criticism*, pp. 33-34. Cf. Fowler, *Kinds of Literature*, p. 242. The ultimate source of this classification is Aristotle *Poetics* 2.
[276] Frye, *Anatomy of Criticism*, p. 34, without specific reference to Gregory.
[277] Realistic touches: *Hist.* 2.2, 3.15. About scenes of wrongdoing, nn. 284-98 below.
[278] Above nn. 225-27.

signpost of these passages.[279] Glowing effects are sometimes achieved with great economy of means:

> The wife of Namatius built the church of St. Stephen in the suburb outside the walls of Clermont-Ferrand. She wanted it to be decorated with coloured frescoes. She used to hold a book in her lap . . . and tell the workmen what she wanted painted on the walls. One day as she was sitting in the church . . . there came a poor man to pray. He saw her in her black dress, a woman already far advanced in age. He thought that she was one of the needy, so he produced a quarter loaf of bread, put it in her lap and went on his way. She did not scorn the gift of this poor man, who had not understood who she was. She took it, and thanked him, and put it on one side. She ate it before her other food and each day took a blessing-portion from it until it was all eaten up.[280]

Invariably, Gregory makes his unreserved approval totally clear. A grim tale, like that of the slain abbot Lupentius, is transmuted into beauty by the miraculous recovery of the abbot's mutilated body and the innocence thus proved. The accounts of Hospicius of Nice, Salvius of Albi, and Aredius of Limoges are capsule hagiographies.[281] The long story of the Two Lovers in book I, and the even longer one of Attalus and Leo the Cook in book III, each develops a romantic motif combined in Jerome's famous *Life of Malchus*: in the first, the preservation of chastity by a married couple; in the second, escape from unjust captivity.[282] Gregory's praise of King Guntram reaches its acme in an account of how a poor woman gained a cure for her son by snipping bits off the royal mantle and using them as a medicine.[283] Similar cures occur often in the *Wonders*, whose stories, though generally attached to holy graves, bear a strong family resemblance to the romantic passages of the *Histories*. They all take place close to the border between earth and heaven.

---

[279] *Hist.* 9.26-27.

[280] *Hist.* 2.17, tr. Thorpe, pp. 131-32.

[281] *Hist.* 6.37 (Lupentius), 6.6 (Hospicius), 7.1 (Salvius), 10.29 (Aredius). There cannot be anything casual or accidental about (almost) ending the *Hist.* with an obituary eulogy of Aredius.

[282] *Hist.* 1.47 (a *shorter* version appears in GC 31), 3.15. For the *Vita s. Malchi*, PL XXIII, 55-62; tr. M. I. Ewald, in *Early Christian Biographies*, ed. R. J. Deferrari, *The Fathers of the Church: A New Translation* (Washington 1952), pp. 287-97; a monk and nun captured by desert raiders and enslaved succeed in remaining chaste though forced to marry by their master; they flee, are pursued, and manage to return to their homeland (and monasteries). The preservation of chastity and difficult journeys home are common motifs of Greek romance, which (unlike its Christian offshoots) normally ends with a marriage. Pizarro, "A Brautwerbung Variant," contains interesting observations about brief dramatic scenes in Gregory, but goes astray in finding "realistic Migration-age terms" in the story of Attalus (p. 114), and in imagining that "tales of escape from captivity and return home must have been fairly common among the oral traditions of western European families during and after the invasions" (p. 116). Hellenistic (and later) fiction is rich in captures and escapes that have nothing to do with the *Völkerwanderung*.

[283] *Hist.* 9.21. Cf. Sulp. Severus *Vita s. Martini* 18.4. There is a New Testament prototype.

Gregory's use of the contrasting ironic mode merits special attention because preponderant in the *Histories* and less obvious than the passages of romance. The story of Munderic is a conspicuous example. "A man called Munderic, who claimed to be of royal blood, was so swollen with pride that he said: 'What is King Theuderic to me?' "[284] Munderic's precise identity, his family, home district, past history, are all a blank and remain so. The sense of discontinuity is overpowering. But we are immediately told what was in his head and what to think of him. Full of pride, in rebellion against his overlord, he is a prisoner to his delusions, plainly inferior to our more prudent selves. Munderic, without ever advancing his cause, gathers a crowd of (by definition) "gullible" peasants. The story then moves in a direction that sharply intensifies the irony. King Theuderic responds to Munderic's challenge by behavior every bit as reprehensible as his. He tries one trick that fails, then talks a subordinate, Aregisel, into perjuring himself in order to extract the rebel from his fortified refuge. Aregisel takes on the task, delights in perjury, and succeeds in his mission, but not so fully as to keep Munderic from detecting the betrayal and killing Aregisel before being himself butchered by the assembled troops. Munderic is far from being a tragic hero, yet the vileness of his adversaries imparts a trace of nobility to his last moments. The spectacle presented is of a deluded protagonist destroyed by adversaries no less evil than he—an encounter of bad with worse. It is the formula of many of Gregory's most gripping stories.

Gregory sometimes makes a more sustained effort to engage our sympathies and succeeds in doing so without even seeming to try:

The next night the leading men [of Gundovald's rebellion] secretly took away all the treasure that they could find in the city [of Comminges], together with the church plate. When day dawned, they flung open the gates and allowed in the army [of King Guntram]. All the common people were butchered, and the priests of the Lord God, with those who served them, were cut down at the very altars of the churches. When [the troops] had killed everyone so that there remained not one that pisseth against a wall (1 Kings 25:34), they burned the whole city, with the churches and other buildings, leaving there nothing but the bare earth.[285]

The author seems dispassionate. Since the army is that of a legitimate monarch whom Gregory esteems, he might be recording the carrying out of a just sentence rather than an atrocity. But the reader has no trouble realizing, and sharing, Gregory's profound indignation. Hardly another passage of the *Histories* attains this level of tragic intensity. Here, as often elsewhere, Gregory proves himself a master of understatement.

Even praiseworthy figures star in Gregory's scenes of subhuman action.

[284] *Hist.* 3.14, tr. Thorpe, p. 173 (a little changed).
[285] *Hist.* 7.38.

Clovis, along with his glory as the champion of Catholicism, bears responsibility for episodes of crude treachery.[286] The *rex bonus*, Guntram, is not spared either. On one occasion, after his troops suffer a costly defeat in war against the Visigoths, he is shown going to pieces:

Greatly alarmed, the king ordered the roads through his kingdom to be barred, so that no one from the kingdom of Childebert [II] might have passage over the territory of his realm. [Guntram] explained, "My army was destroyed by his wickedness, for he made a treaty with the king of Spain, and it's by his doing that those [Gothic] cities won't submit to my rule." To this complaint he added another bone of contention, namely, that King Childebert was planning to send his senior son, Theudebert, to Soissons. This made King Guntram suspicious; he said, "My nephew is sending his son to Soissons in order to have him enter Paris, and with the thought of taking away my sovereignty." Never could such an idea have crossed the back of Childebert's mind, if one may presume so to say. [Guntram] also launched many accusations against Queen Brunichild, claiming that [Childebert's actions were] by her advice, and also adding that she wanted to invite the son of the late Gundovald [a slain usurper] to marry her. On this account, he ordered a synod of bishops to gather on the first of November. Many of those who proceeded to this meeting from the most distant parts of Gaul were forced to turn back when on the road. For Brunichild exonerated herself by oaths of the accusation [against her]. And so, with the roads open again, a passage was cleared for those who wished to go to King Childebert.[287]

Nothing serious took place. Guntram was within his rights as king and did nothing more harmful than to inconvenience a few bishops and travelers for a few weeks. His worst action, in Gregory's view, was to summon a synod for insufficient reasons (the sparseness of this sentence—the climax of the chapter—is particularly effective).[288] The bishops obliged to take the road against their will are ironically contrasted to the willing travelers stopped by Guntram's barriers. There is more humor still in the accusation about Brunichild and Gundovald's son. A decade earlier, the newly widowed queen had entered into a subversive marriage with Chilperic's son, Merovech.[289] Guntram, it seems, remembered Brunichild as a nuptial adventuress. As for Childebert II, he was the reigning sovereign over Tours; Gregory intervenes emphatically to exculpate him from reprehensible ambitions. As a prudently loyal subject, the bishop makes himself absolutely

---

[286] *Hist.* 2.40-42. Unless one goes along with the idea of a naïve Gregory writing more or less in his sleep, these stories can have been narrated in the way they are only with a view to filling out aspects of Clovis's personality of which little had been said until then.

[287] *Hist.* 9.32. Guntram's first appearance as a reigning king contains a recital of his sexual irregularities; it begins, "Gunthchramnus autem rex bonus" (4.25, K-L p. 156).

[288] K-L p. 451: "unde etiam synodum episcoporum in Kalendas Novembris congregare praecepit."

[289] *Hist.* 5.2, 14, 18. Merovech was Brunichild's nephew by marriage.

clear, and contemporaries knew whether to laugh or nod assent. Many historians, even without considering Guntram "good," might have portrayed this moment of his reign with indulgence and forbearance. Gregory preferred to hold up the king's behavior to ridicule.

Gregory's resort to the ironic mode is not limited to fully rounded incidents such as the ones just described. The essential element, pervasively present, is that, at the start of chapters or other segments in this mode, the reader is allowed to realize that he, though ordinary, exists on a higher plane than the characters, often of lofty rank, whose activities are brought before him; he is looking downward on a scene with which he would on no account wish to associate himself.

The signposts to scenes of this kind are not always so plain as they are in the story of Munderic. To take an example at random, "Lupus, duke of Champagne, had long been harassed and despoiled by those who were hostile to him, especially Ursio and Berthefried. These two now made a pact to have him killed." In case we were tempted to regard the conspirators as run-of-the-mill Franks behaving in ways that early readers would have accepted as normal, Gregory soon injects the widowed Queen Brunichild to be taunted by them as a figure of pathos.[290] We are not wrong in the first impression that Ursio and Berthefried are scoundrels. Again, "While King Chilperic was still in residence at Nogent-sur-Marne, Egidius, bishop of Reims, arrived on an embassy with the chief notables of Childebert's court. A conference was arranged and they made plans to deprive King Guntram of his kingdom."[291] Gregory's account is only ostensibly detached. More than his sympathy for King Guntram, his principled hatred for civil war tags the plotters as evil men rather than as ordinary politicians.

Sometimes, one needs to read beyond the first sentences. As Gregory begins to narrate the last days of Duke Desiderius—much spoken of before in a possibly negative vein—we see that political circumstances were closing in on the protagonist. He prepared to make war on the Visigoths, having previously, "they report," settled his private affairs. His expedition became known and the Goths were ready. Outside Carcassone, they withdrew before Desiderius and his forces, which gave chase. Few pursuers were left, and with worn-out horses, by the time Desiderius reached the city gate. The Goths sallied out, killing him and so many of his few attendants that hardly anyone survived to tell what happened. Desiderius's second-in-command turned tail, went to the king, and obtained his dukedom.[292] The story

---

[290] *Hist.* 6.4, tr. Thorpe, p. 329.

[291] *Hist.* 6.3, tr. Thorpe, p. 328.

[292] *Hist.* 8.45. Desiderius is, to begin with, only discreditable by association with King Chilperic, whose orders he carries out (5.13, 39; 6.12, 31). He is a leading supporter of Gundovald after Chilperic's murder, and behaves badly (7.9-10), but abandons the pretender long before

has room for gallantry and heroism if one chooses to fill in the available blanks. Gregory was no friend of the Arian Goths, and he occasionally dignifies shady characters with brave ends. No trace of approval is present here. Because overt disapproval is also absent, Gregory might be taken to be merely neutral, yet the circumstances he depicts lend themselves only to a satiric reading. Desiderius's war was a personal initiative, perhaps a last-ditch effort to win royal favor. He allowed it to be noised about. The tactics were rash and the death futile. Altogether an empty *excidium miseri*.

If we try to define the emotion Desiderius's death is supposed to arouse, we find no trace of tragic pity or fear, only a discreet touch of ridicule. Gregory's irony is often comic. In the name of society, for whom he speaks, he celebrates its deliverance from a malefactor who richly deserved his end. Gregory took pains to avert the danger that the scoundrel justly expelled from society should slip into the dignified role of a sacrificial victim.[293] Overweighing the scales against the villain-victims, as he does in the cases of Parthenius, Andarchius, and Rauching, is an effective but unsubtle way to deal with this problem.[294] Gregory proves more skilled when he deploys secondary characters and has them deflect guilt from society by taking it upon themselves. This is the role of Aregisel in the story of Munderic, of Claudius in that of Eberulf, and many others.[295] Another sort of deflection is produced by highlighting the hideous death of the innocents whom the protagonist dooms along with himself, such as Chramn's wife and daughters, the faithful servant of Merovech, the *pueri* of Phatir, and the butchered priests and people of Comminges.[296] In the account of how a certain Waddo is killed when attempting to seize an estate, the tears of his wife and children trying to dissuade him from his course, and the self-sacrifice of the bailiff defending the property, ensure the victim's total isolation from any claim to sympathy.[297] Leudast, who ranks high among Gregory's *bêtes noires*, is shown earning his death by a reckless folly balanced only by the

---

anyone else (7.34). Nevertheless, he has reason to fear Guntram's enmity (7.43) and only half returns to royal favor (8.27).

[293] Frye, *Anatomy of Criticism*, pp. 45, 42.

[294] *Hist.* 3.36, 4.46, (Rauching) 5.3, 9.9.

[295] Aregisel, *Hist.* 3.14 (for a brief account of his role, n. 284 above); Eberulf and Claudius, 7.21, 29.

[296] *Hist.* 4.20 (Chramn is strangled before the hut he is in is burned down with his unstrangled wife and daughters in it), 5.19 (Gailen, who helped Merovech kill himself, is put to death with the utmost cruelty), 6.17 (guiltless of Phatir's crime, his *pueri* are assured of royal punishment after their master makes his escape; the bravest of them kills them all, then rushes from sanctuary and is cut to pieces by the mob outside). For Comminges, see above, n. 285; the killing of the population forestalls sympathy for Mummolus and the other slain supporters of Gundovald.

[297] *Hist.* 9.35.

revolting manner of his execution. Predictably, the royal authors of his death are as worthless as he. [298]

Yet the consignment of assorted men and women to dire fates, or merely their tagging as evil, does not seem to have been the goal of Gregory's ironic passages. Someone like Munderic had been dead for many decades and, when alive, had not, as far as we may tell, been very dangerous or done grave harm. Gregory had no personal animus against him, or for that matter against Aregisel. Duke Desiderius may have been a *miser* deserving of his foolish end, but rather for being deluded than for manifesting exceptional villainy. The high proportion of dismal incidents in the *Histories*, and the involvement in them of figures as respectable (and as acceptable to Gregory) as Clovis and Guntram, assure us that Gregory's irony is directed less at the actors than at the broad range of activities we see them engaging in. Without being solemnly denounced as devil's work and subhuman conduct, such ostensibly respectable exertions as warfare, political maneuverings, the filling of state coffers, and the administration of justice join with unambiguous crimes, such as rebellion, adultery, rape, and murder, in being colored very dark. A wide variety of acts that are entirely legitimate by our own standards, and were no less so among the Romans, fall afoul of Gregory's irony. [299] His basis of condemnation is Christian and not mysterious. The quickest way to define it is to evoke Augustine's contrast between a *civitas terrena* and a *civitas Dei*. The denizens of the "earthly city" strive furiously after the goods of this world. [300] This reprehensible striving after the merely terrestrial, in its many concrete manifestations (some socially sanctioned, some criminal), is what Gregory wishes us to learn to execrate.

The *Histories* is full of scenes of subhuman action. It is not "the facts"—Merovingian reality, as one might say—that drove the author to ironic narrative, any more than other facts drove him to compose hagiographic romance. King Guntram's panic might have been gently portrayed; Duke Desiderius might have been cast as a hero or as unlucky in politics; Bishop Avitus might have yielded credit to a fanatical mob for the Jews' conversion; and so forth. The images we grasp were consistently shaped so as to give one sort of impression or its diametrical opposite; and history, in Greg-

---

[298] *Hist.* 6.32.

[299] E.g. *Hist.* 8.30, 9.3 (warfare), 6.3, 31 (politics), 5.28, 34 (filling state coffers), 6.8 (justice).

[300] David Knowles in Augustine, *Civ. Dei*, tr. Bettenson, pp. xvi-xviii; Brown, *Augustine of Hippo*, pp. 308-10, 314-27. There is no evidence that Gregory was acquainted with any work of Augustine's.

ory's conception, had the objective character of mingling and intertwining such scenes.

A narrative fashioned in this way imposes a great distance between the author and the subnormal events that he reports. If Gregory had wished to convey his absorption in the gravity of Merovingian politics, incident would join with incident in one or more continuous chains, each making more sense than its links. The end of Duke Desiderius would be the culmination, for better or worse, of his earlier appearances; Munderic would not blaze suddenly and at once go out; Guntram's fit of pique would blend into the portrayal of a personality. Gregory may be read, and generally has been, as attempting to constitute meaningful chains of incidents. He has recently been argued to present a developing and somewhat optimistic account of the Merovingian kings.[301] Such readings can be sustained, but only on the assumption that Gregory imperfectly realized his aim and that his desire to write coherent political history was unintentionally thwarted. Once Gregory's scenes are analyzed in the spirit in which they were written, it becomes apparent that he deliberately avoided writing conventional history. Chains are broken by the omission of links; the author focuses attention on isolated, discontinuous scenes; and every effort is bent, as irony demands, on conveying a vivid and unforgettably negative impression without betraying overt disapproval. The details of any action are subordinated to the reader's knowing its moral color. It matters little, typically, what the plans Chilperic hatched with Childebert's envoys exactly were so long as their scheming is seen as heinous.[302]

The seriousness of such history is moral and didactic. Thorough representation of political imperatives, family relationships, or other practical details is a secondary consideration. The stage setting needs only to look convincing; and, for the first readers of the *Histories*, contemporaneity made it very convincing indeed. What matters is that the scene should illustrate the ugliness of merely human gropings. Gregory is in dead earnest when he brings to life what we, after Augustine, would call the *civitas terrena*, the community whose denizens hunger after earthly rewards and often do very well for themselves here below by specializing in such pursuits. Side by side with the saints, whom Gregory also allows us to glimpse, and in contrast with them, the high and low *miseri* scuttle about in their base and empty *certamena*. Current events are placed in correct—that is, moral and Christian—perspective when the strivings men prize most are seen for the vile things they are.

Vile gropings, no matter how numerous, form only a part of the *Histories*.

[301] Reydellet, *Royauté*, pp. 350-435. Cf. Vinay, *San Gregorio*, pp. 101-44.
[302] Above, n. 291.

The saints are also represented, and so are the author and his public. Unlike Salvian, Gregory is not a gloomy, still less a despairing witness. Eight books of *Wonders* attest to his awareness of contemporary good news. The preface to book II, and its profound implications for the texture of the *Histories*, assure us that Gregory had a conscious literary design. It remains to explore how his narrative coheres and what sense it conveyed.

7. *Historiae*: Plot, Prodigies, and "Autobiography"

The subjects vaguely advertised in Gregory's general preface and in that to book I, and the two types of events announced in the preface to book II, militate against the idea that the *Histories* is held together by a developing story or plot. Gregory's procedure does not contrast only with that of Jordanes. Though Bede's device for integrating the *Ecclesiastical History* is more restrained than Jordanes's, he too has a plot. When, in the last book, we learn of the conversion of the Irish monastery of Iona to the Roman reckoning of Easter, we know, and have been prepared to know since the beginning of book III, that the happy climax of his narrative has been reached.[303] In a modest definition easily applicable to historiography, plot is "a series of events which constitutes a change."[304] Paul the Deacon's *Lombard History* easily qualifies for having a plot on these undemanding terms, but it is hard to find one in Gregory's *Histories*.

A narrative that starts with the Creation, takes the Jews to Egypt, back to the Promised Land, and on to Babylonian captivity, records the Incarnation, persecutions, Constantine, and barbarian incursions, then proceeds to the conversion of Clovis to Catholicism and the expulsion of Arian kings from Gaul: such a narrative cannot be said to be devoid of change. But the changes all lie in the summarily remembered past, barely extending beyond book II. They are only a background to *gesta praesentia*. Even if current events were assumed to start in book III or IV, rather than in V, an impression of mere activity prevails. Several times, Gregory states through his own or someone else's mouth that the third generation of Merovingians marked a deterioration by comparison with their forebears.[305] The allegation, though possibly true, is not unequivocally borne out by the facts he reports about either Clovis or his sons, nor is it meant to be. The *Histories* does not exist to make this point. All sorts of crimes and miracles happen; kings and bishops die, naturally or not, and are replaced; but nothing ever changes.

Gregory tends to arrest or efface historical development even on a small

---

[303] For Jordanes's plot, ch. II § 8 above; for Bede's, ch. IV n. 79.
[304] Kernan, "Theory of Satire," p. 271.
[305] Above, n. 260.

scale. The rebellion of the Visigothic prince Hermenegild, also known from independent evidence, extended over five years and ended with the rebel's imprisonment (580-84). A year later, he was put to death. The years of his uprising coincide with the annalistic books of the *Histories*, but Gregory's account takes only two steps. His initial report, coinciding with the outbreak of the rebellion, narrates the full course of events down to the prince's imprisonment. Two later chapters recapitulate the story to this same point, sometimes adding new details. The next step comes only in book VIII with the abrupt announcement of Hermenegild's execution.[306] The case of the domestic usurper, Gundovald, is even more striking. Gregory notes his arrival from Constantinople in 581 and, in other passages, makes clear the conditions of the Merovingians in that year.[307] During the usurpation itself, in 585, Gundovald is shown explaining to a crowd why he had been invited to Gaul some years before. Yet the political circumstances Gregory places in his mouth are not those of 581, known both to us and to him, but the different ones of the moment when he spoke.[308] In these cases, as in all others, Gregory focuses our attention on individual scenes and incidents wherever they fall. We are not encouraged to memorize details and, from their accumulation, to gain an impression of meaningful action.

Gregory's resolve to maintain an appearance of inconclusiveness is best shown by the way in which, in book X, he terminates his detailed account of the intrafamily rivalries of the Merovingian kings that pass for Frankish politics. If he had so wished, the *Histories* might have ended with the death of King Guntram. The fact is recorded in *The Miracles of St. Martin* and might have been commemorated in the *Histories* as well. Gregory's avoidance of Guntram's death is not accidental. His final computation of years in the last lines of book X descends to a date later than this king's demise, showing that the *Histories* was still being written when it occurred.[309] Greg-

---

[306] *Hist.* 5.38; 6.40, 43; 8.28. The independent source is John of Biclar *Chronica*, ed. Mommsen, MGH AA. XI, 215-17. Concerning the rebellion, which was rather different from Gregory's account, see Collins, "Mérida and Toledo," pp. 215-18. Also cf. above, n. 56.

[307] *Hist.* 6.24. The Merovingians in that year: a child on one throne, 5.1; Guntram childless, 5.17; Chilperic rapidly losing all his sons, 5.18, 22, 34, 39, 6.23, 34.

[308] *Hist.* 7.36.

[309] Guntram's death is noted in VSM 4.37. The series of final regnal dates in *Hist.* 10.31 points to 594, but the year cited for Guntram is the last of his life and reign (592), the implication being that he was no less living than Childebert II or Pope Gregory. On this passage, K-L, Preface, p. xviii; Monod, *Études critiques*, pp. 48-49.

The normal assumption is that the *Hist.* had to be finished in Guntram's lifetime because his death goes unmentioned; e.g. Buchner, Einleitung, pp. xxiv-v. But Gregory is not naïve. Whether or not to mention Guntram's demise was a matter of choice. Reydellet, *Royauté*, p. 427, has an excellent sense of Gregory's conscious decision. Oldoni tr., I, lxx, also envisages a deliberate omission of the death, but for the improbable reason that Gregory was disappointed in Guntram. The discussion of the ending of the *Hist.* by Gardiner, "Notes on the

ory portrayed Guntram as a lover of peace, a genuine friend and benefactor of the Church, and the last of his generation.[310] To close with his death would have darkly implied the curtailment of something good or the end of an era. However presented, the event would have been bound to look conclusive. Gregory preferred that we should take leave of the Merovingians with the sense of a secure and unchanging dynasty. As book X advances, Guntram is still alive and ruling; Childebert II reigns and has two sons. And, in the fourth from last chapter—the final scene involving royalty— the young Chlothar II, scion of the third branch of the family, is solemnly baptized and received by King Guntram as his godson.[311]

As an ending, Chlothar's baptism resembles the role of the infant Germanus at the close of Jordanes's *Getica*. An innocent child is born or reborn, symbolizing a society knit together again before leaving the stage to live happily ever after.[312] Gregory's scene, however, is not like that at all. Readers of the *Histories* know that Chlothar II is the son of the royal pair whom Gregory vehemently dislikes (namely, the murdered Chilperic and the still-living Fredegonde) and that his baptism as Guntram's godson, proposed since 585, has been repeatedly arranged and delayed.[313] Even if the offspring of such parents could symbolize a fresh start, much of his innocence has worn off by 591. As for social concord, the previous chapter dramatizes Fredegonde's idea of how to achieve it: she settles a feud by organizing a banquet, inviting the three surviving principals, and having them assassinated.[314] The christening itself is briefly interrupted when envoys of Childebert II approach Guntram to complain (not for the first time) that, by sponsoring Chlothar, he will violate his treaty with their master. The ceremony goes forward clouded by Childebert's objection.[315] In such a context, the sacramental rebirth of Chlothar II can hardly be taken to herald social peace and regeneration. Its implication is rather that the Merovingians, besides enduring, will also persist in the violence and family turmoil that Gregory has accustomed us to. The radically imperfect society

---

Chronology of Fredegar IV," though interesting, suffers from his unawareness that Gregory knew of Guntram's death.

[310] See especially *Hist.* 5.17, 6.19, 33, 7.13-16, 19, 32-33, 40, 8.1-7, 9-10, 37, 45, 9.11, 20. Reydellet, *Royauté*, whose account of Gregory on Guntram is very full, concludes (p. 435): "From a merely literary standpoint, Guntram is, among all the kings Gregory knew, the one who has the most presence and human warmth in the *History of the Franks*."

[311] *Hist.* 10.28. Reydellet, *Royauté*, p. 327, thinks it really is a (happy) ending.

[312] Above, ch. II nn. 253-55.

[313] About Chilperic, in brief, *Hist.* 6.46; assorted crimes of Fredegonde after Chilperic's death, 7.20, 8.31, 44, 9.34, 10.9, 18. The delays in the baptism, 8.9: July 585 was already the fourth time that Guntram was called to the ceremony. The record may have later been made to seem more respectable. According to Fredegar *Chron.* 4.3, Chlothar II was baptized soon after his father's death, not six years later.

[314] *Hist.* 10.27.

[315] *Hist.* 9.20.

that we were introduced to no later than book V leaves the stage as permanent and flawed as ever.

The baptism of Chlothar II portrays the absurd life of the *civitas terrena*. The three chapters that follow, and complete the *Histories*, persist in denying us a climax. They have a strong dash of Gregory and his particular world. First comes a long, hagiographic obituary of Aredius of Limoges, not just another saint but a personal friend of Gregory's, very dear to him.[316] Next is a brief record of abnormalities in nature as of April 591. It is the last of the many entries about prodigies that will soon concern us in greater detail.[317] For a final chapter, Gregory launches into something virtually new, though also, as he remarks, recapitulative: a systematic account of all the bishops of Tours, including himself. This list of bishops with their accomplishments, however local in scope, is a much more proper chronicle than the rundown of biblical and other non-Gallic events in book I. Whereas the latter seems to be a generalized history formed out of paradigmatic incidents (such as Cain killing Abel or persecutions of the Church), the final chapter of the *Histories* systematically sets out sober and creditable facts about Gregory and his predecessors.[318] Far from supplying an ending, the episcopal chronicle, with its implications of apostolic succession and the perennity of the Church, presents us with an orderly, middle-ground continuity, tacitly contrasting with the turbulent biology of Merovingian descent. The parting note is struck by Gregory in person, listing his writings, again deprecating their style, but also asking that they should be scrupulously preserved. He makes himself no less memorable at the close than he does in the general preface, where he began.

The reader of Gregory's *Histories* is given no suggestion of a plot or set of meaningful changes. Instead, in the words of Augustin Thierry, "C'est comme une gallerie mal arrangée de tableaux et de figures en relief."[319] One is promenaded through a panorama of personages and events and shown, frame by frame, how they are to be envisaged and understood. The interpretation Gregory offers consists mainly of sorting events into appropriate, self-explanatory pigeonholes. We have seen the two most important slots.

[316] *Hist.* 8.15, 27, 10.29; GM 36, 41, VSJ 28, 41-45, VSM 2.39, 3.24 (particularly personal), 4.6, VP 17.*praef.*, 3, 5, GC 9 (*vir summae bonitatis*), 102 (his mother). He is the intimate to whom Gregory gives greatest prominence.

[317] *Hist.* 10.30. See below, n. 325.

[318] *Hist.* 10.31. From the eighth century onward, the genre of *gesta episcoporum* would have many representatives. Gregory's chapter may have the distinction of being the first comprehensive episcopal chronicle to survive (it is still uncertain how much of what would become the Roman *Liber pontificalis* already existed in the sixth century; see ch. I n. 27). Michel Sot, *Gesta episcoporum. Gesta abbatum*, Typologie des sources to Moyen Âge occidental fasc. 31 (Turnhout 1981).

[319] Bordier, *Livres de miracles* IV, 276, citing Thierry, *Récits.*

The slots that we are about to consider may or may not serve the same explanatory function, but their conspicuousness is beyond doubt.

When beginning the *Histories*, Gregory announces an interest in the end of the world. Because some persons fear its approach, he will count the years since the Creation. Casual allusions aside, the subject returns only in books IX-X, in the limited context of false prophets and miracle workers.[320] These references, and the chronological summaries going with them, are thematically linked with the prodigious occurrences more frequently mentioned: signs in the heavens, floods, pestilence, unseasonable flowerings, and other abnormalities. Human victims sometimes result, as from famine, landslide, or plague, but as an exception rather than the rule.[321] *Signum* in Gregory may mean either a miracle or a prodigy. In the latter sense, the term refers basically to occasions when nature departs markedly from its ordinary course.

The passages referring to Last Things convey an ambiguous message. Gregory suggests that he shares the fears of those worried about the end of the world, and he endorses conventional ideas about Antichrist, but he also insists, citing Mark 13:32, that the final days are a secret that the Father shares with no one. Though solicitous for the anxious faithful, Gregory is in fact no more inclined than most Christian historians before and after him to search the horizon for signs of the End.[322] In book X, the relationship of false prophets and miracle workers to Antichrist is evoked only to be immediately linked with a peasant who, driven mad by a swarm of flies, turned into a false Christ and proved a merely local nuisance.[323] There is little reason to infer that Gregory, when nearing the close of the *Histories*, became convinced that the Second Coming was at hand. His consistent tendency was to depreciate apocalyptic thinking by vulgarizing it and, in this way, to raise a barrier between human fears and God's well-guarded secret.[324]

The associated passages concerning prodigies extend from the very severe winter after King Theudebert's death (548) to the epidemic, fire from heaven, drought, and other afflictions of 591 in the penultimate chapter.

---

[320] *Hist* 1.*praef.* (K-L p. 3, "eos, qui adpropinquantem finem mundi disperant"), 9.6 *in fine*, 10.25 *in.* Casual allusion in 5.*praef.*, K-L p. 193 lines 3-5.

[321] Famine, *Hist.* 7.45; landslide, 4.31; epidemic, 5.34. For a full and able treatment of this subject, see Nie, "Roses in January."

[322] Disclaimer about the end of the world, K-L p. 5 lines 2-10. Gregory closes with the statement, *Our* end is Christ, Who will bestow eternal life on us if . . . Cf. Isidore of Seville *Chron.* 418, ed. Mommsen, p. 481: "Therefore let each meditate upon his own end . . . for when each individual departs this life, that is the end of time for him."

[323] *Hist.* 10.25; cf. 9.6. Nie, "Roses in January," p. 271, may be right that *Hist.* 6.45-46 have an apocalyptic flavor, but to my mind this is literary color rather than seriously meant.

[324] I disagree with Nie, "Roses in January," pp. 279-88, as with other readings of the *Hist.* that presuppose a development in Gregory's outlook.

The entries are usually brief and to the point, and though they have something of the chronicle about them Gregory makes no apparent attempt to locate them at a precise chronological point within the course of each year. He usually deploys them as transitions in his narrative, occupying moments at which he wishes the reader to pause and clear his mind.[325]

The relationship between abnormalities in nature and perverse human actions is most precisely spelled out in the civil wars of book IV and continues to be strongly emphasized in books V-VI, in connection with royal quarrels and King Chilperic's wickedness.[326] Nevertheless, Gregory persists thereafter in observing prodigies. In 585, a very conspicuous *signum* in the night sky made him fearful: "we suspected that some affliction would be sent us from heaven"; but nothing happened. When it was later learned that God had destroyed certain distant islands by fire, Gregory agreed with the widespread view that the frightening *signum* had been the reflection of this conflagration. In other cases, the abnormality simply takes place, and Gregory records the facts without concern for interpretation.[327]

God was no less in charge of freaks in nature than He was of bringing to an end the world He had created. Gregory agreed with patristic tradition, as we have seen, in regarding nature as suffused with the miraculous. The "wonders" of God included the regular tides, seasons, and moving bodies in the heavens, as well as such irregular and individualized phenomena as miracles of healing, multiplication, or whatever.[328] From "the factual, analytical description [Gregory] sometimes gives," it does not follow that he accepted the autonomous existence of "an accustomed and recognizable order of nature."[329] He certainly recognized normality, by comparison with which earthquakes, famine, and plague were "prodigies." But even normal nature was unpredictably arbitrary. When Gregory says of a fire that "it must have come from God," he means that its cause is not human but "natural," in the same divinely actuated sense that tidal motion is natural. Elsewhere, the grafting of a fruit tree is contrasted to natural growth, in a re-

[325] *Hist.* 3.37, 10.30. Prodigy passages as narrative pauses are particularly noticeable in the last books: *Hist.* 8.8, 17, 23-25, 9.5-6, 17, 44 (last chapter), 10.23, 30 (penultimate chapter).

[326] Nie, "Roses in January," pp. 265-72.

[327] *Hist.* 8.17, 24; Nie, "Roses in January," pp. 273-74. See, also, Meslin, "Merveilleux comme langage politique," pointing out the great place in Roman religion of the study and interpretation of prodigies; it remained untouched by Greek philosophy.

[328] Above, nn. 90-96.

[329] Contradicting Nie, "Roses in January," p. 279. She is perfectly right about Gregory's interest in natural phenomena (pp. 266-67, 276), but may not grasp his reasoning. The "accustomed order" is, in Gregory's view, arbitrary and subject to being effortlessly changed by the Creator. Nevertheless, its regularities can be observed. Gregory's concern with the latter is similar to his interest in the authentication of other events; namely, to establish that a given incident is genuinely miraculous. Cf. Wallace-Hadrill, "Work of Gregory of Tours," pp. 54-55. For an unacceptable approach to Gregory's treatment of natural phenomena, see above, n. 113.

newed opposition of human to divine agency.[330] Gregory gives God a low profile in the passages on prodigies and Last Things; but, though only implied, His role is unmistakable. A forthright explanation is placed in Fredegonde's mouth: "Time and again [God] has sent us warnings through high fevers and other indispositions, but we have never mended our ways."[331] Whether flowing along its customary channels or on a rampage, nature was in God's direct care.

Gregory offers the equivalent of a theory of prodigies early in the *Histories*, when he summarizes the homily of Avitus of Vienne on the Rogations, a three-day period of supplication instituted by Avitus's predecessor, Mamertus (ca. 475). Vienne had suffered several earthquakes; packs of wolves and stags had entered the town and roamed through it unafraid; similar terrors continued for a whole year. On Easter Eve, when the church was thronged amidst hopes of relief from anguish, the royal palace burst into flames, and the people, convinced that the whole city would now be consumed and swallowed up, fled for dear life. Only Bishop Mamertus was left at the altar praying for God's mercy, and the tears he shed quenched the fire. In the next weeks, Mamertus instituted among the people the fasts, processions, and almsgivings of the Rogations and celebrated this festival just before Ascension Day. Thereupon, "All the horrors came to an end."[332] Gregory assumes it is understood that prodigies are warning signs, or direct expressions, of divine anger with mankind, to be responded to by acts of contrition and prayers for mercy. In periods of civil war, misrule, or other manifest evil, observers easily discern the reasons for divine wrath. In humdrum times, the causes are obscure, but the manifestations of God's displeasure are no less eloquent for that. It is never untimely for men to be warned to entreat divine mercy.

In the case of Bishop Mamertus, ominous events are combined with a beneficent miracle; two books later, Gregory builds a prodigy into an exceptionally vehement account of human folly.[333] At a fortress high over the Rhône, not far downstream from Geneva, a bellowing out of the ground was heard for sixty days before half the hill collapsed into the river with everyone and everything on it. The blocked river backed up, sweeping away the villages along its banks as far upstream as Geneva. It was a fearful disaster. In a very full independent account, Marius of Avenches notes the event but makes no reference to sounds out of the earth.[334] Gregory contin-

---

[330] *Hist.* 5.33: a village burned by "incendium divinitus ortum," for it had "nullum paenitus incitamentum . . . ignis alieni" (K-L p. 238). Grafting fruit trees, 4.9.

[331] *Hist.* 5.34.

[332] *Hist.* 2.34.

[333] *Hist.* 4.31. Cf. Nie, "Roses in January," pp. 259-60.

[334] Marius of Avenches *Chron.* 563, ed. Mommsen, p. 237.

ues: afterward, thirty monks could think of nothing better to do than to go to the site and dig for bronze and iron; the earth bellowed again; the monks took no notice, "so strong was their lust for gain"; another landslide occurred, burying them all alive; their bodies were never recovered. Gregory expects us to know that monks should spend their lives praying for divine mercy. So denatured were these thirty that the longest-advertised and most violent expression of divine wrath could not shock them into what should have been their profession. The second landslide lacks realism but drives home the lesson.

In Gregory's narrative, the rather few but noticeable passages in this category all record experiences of the unpredictable hostility of a natural order whose very endurance is a matter of doubt. Through them, Gregory discreetly evokes the Lord of Nature Himself. The scenes differ from those of miracles. Miracles are personalized. Saintly mediators are customary, and the beneficiaries (or victims) tend to be individual men and women. Prodigies, however, are witnessed or endured by large numbers. They are the social manifestations of God and, to this extent, remind us of the God of the Old Testament, Whom they further recall by re-creating the drama of the errant people suffering merited threats or punishments, and collectively pleading (or not, in their folly) for mercy and help. Gregory's Mosaic God is not committed to any one "nation," or to any group otherwise "chosen"; but universality does not silence Him. In conspicuous signs and even painful afflictions, He manifests His power concretely to collectivities of no set size in order to rekindle their cooled faith. If the *miseri* persist in their blindness and crimes, it is not for lack of admonition.

Gregory takes no notice of good harvests or fine weather. His glowing description of Dijon stands out in its uniqueness.[335] Otherwise, bountiful nature is taken for granted. The recognized evidence of God's goodness is limited to the miracles He procures through the holy men and women whose deaths are recorded. The panorama Gregory unfolds includes these saints along with the more numerous *strages* and *excidia*, sporadically punctuated by signs of divine anger. Every now and then, something neutral seems to come before us. There are passages of straightforward political history, as we saw earlier, but these should not be mistaken for accounts of blameless everyday life. When, in the opening chapter of book VI, Gregory dryly reports the outlines of an acute political crisis, his total restraint results not from acceptance of the routine character of the events he has described, but from the confidence that we will recognize their disastrous im-

[335] *Hist.* 3.19. The eulogy of the city is incidental to a commemoration of his much-admired great-grandfather, Gregory of Langres (whose name he took in lieu of George, his name at birth).

plications and supply the emotions he omits.[336] The same tends to hold true for the many straightforward reports of this kind.

For a whiff of normality, readers must look elsewhere, to a discreet but unmistakable element of the *Histories*. The society that wished to learn about *gesta praesentia*, and in whose name Gregory spoke, was not assumed to be composed of perjurers, homicides, and voluptuaries. Gregory closely identifies with his public and maintains continuous rapport with it in the narrative. The audience lacks prominence, but the author is a frequent presence. Together, they appear to occupy the sought-for middle ground.

In the past century, Giesebrecht and other scholars were so impressed by Gregory's role in the *Histories* that they classified his work among historical memoirs. Without going so far as that, Auerbach pointed out that the *Histories* was "much closer to personal memoirs than to the work of any Roman historian"; and Vinay maintained that it embodied an "ibrida concezione politico agiografico autobiografica."[337] Gregory appears in as many as a quarter of the chapters of books V-X. The relationship of the *Histories* to what might be loosely termed "autobiography" needs scrutiny.

It is doubtful that "memoir" or "autobiography" is the right word. Although Gregory injects himself as actor as well as narrator, he neither invites us to share his memories nor claims to tell us the story of his life. The most conspicuous moment of reminiscence features Salvius of Albi's disclosure of his vision presaging the doom of Chilperic's family.[338] The passage, carefully positioned at the close of a book, is an effective narrative device rather than an insider's revelations. Gregory is very visible at the trial of Bishop Praetextatus of Rouen (the closest he comes to heroism) and at King Guntram's visit to Orléans in 585. In both cases, he enters and leaves inconspicuously; the action moves independently of him.[339] The reverse takes place in connection with Chilperic's stay at Nogent-sur-Marne early in book VI. Gregory opens with his summons to court and ends, several chapters later, with his leave taking from the king, but is largely absent from the intervening action. His summons and departure serve as a frame

---

[336] Above, nn. 204-205.

[337] Giesebrecht tr., I, xxxiv; Misch, *Geschichte der Autobiographie*, p. 367 with n. 146; Auerbach, *Mimesis*, p. 74; Vinay, *San Gregorio*, p. 79; Reydellet, *Royauté*, p. 401. Cf. Lefebvre, *Naissance de l'historiographie moderne*, pp. 78-79, pointing out that the special originality of France in Renaissance historiography was the creation of memoirs that claimed to be at the same time historical narratives; he added, "À dire vrai, [ce genre national] ne date pas précisément de la Renaissance. Après tout, Grégoire de Tours a fait quelque chose d'analogue [and so did Commines]."

[338] *Hist.* 5.50.

[339] *Hist.* 5.18 (after an opening scene, Gregory evokes "us," the bishops, deliberating; one speaks; Gregory takes the floor and becomes prominent for several scenes; then he has "us," the bishops, reassemble and withdraws into the group); 8.1-7 (in 2, Guntram comes to visit Gregory, who is most assertive in 6, a brief scene).

for the narrative, which is no more vivid when he is an eyewitness than when he is not.[340] He consistently keeps events at a distance from himself, as though the sphere they belonged to were not his own. The *Histories* records Gregory's experiences without existing for that purpose. It does so at the occasional intervals when *gesta praesentia* happen to intersect his life, such as when distinguished malefactors took sanctuary at the tomb of St. Martin.

The *Histories* records only an ill-assorted scattering of Gregory's relatives. Prosopographies of late Roman Gaul accord him a resplendent lineage. His is one of the best documented of the senatorial families.[341] Most of the information, however, must be culled from the *Wonders*, in which it serves to authenticate miracles.[342] In the *Histories* we meet only his brother, Peter; his great-grandfather, Bishop Gregory of Langres; his distant cousin, Gundulf; and his niece's husband, Nicetius.[343] A certain Justina plays a creditable part in the story of the revolt of the Poitiers nuns; we need Fortunatus to identify her as another of Gregory's nieces.[344] When accused of being an Arvernian interloper (that is, from Clermont) in Tours, Gregory replied that all save five of its bishops were his relatives, but he gave no names.

---

[340] *Hist.* 6.2 (Gregory materializes), 3-4 (scenes without him), 5 (leaves court).

[341] Kurth, "Sénateurs en Gaule," pp. 104-106; Stroheker, *Senatorische Adel*, no. 183 with p. 239 (plus twenty-one other numbers); Heinzelmann, *Bischofsherrschaft*, pp. 213-54; Pietri, *Ville de Tours*, pp. 249-54, 792.

[342] Gregory's entry in Stroheker's prosopography makes this immediately apparent (n. 341). Scholars often attribute family pride to Gregory without properly distinguishing what he says from what they take pains to find out. E.g. Stroheker, *Senatorische Adel*, p. 112, "He is full of pride at being able to ascribe all branches of his family to the highest senatorial aristocracy"; Buchner, *Einleitung*, p. xx, claims that he is the spokesman for the Gallo-Roman noble *Schicht*; Pietri, *Ville de Tours*, p. 251, "Bref, de ces ancêtres paternels Grégoire pouvait déclarer avec une légitime fierté qu'ils étaient *de primoribus senatoribus . . . ut in Galliis nihil inveniatur esse generosius atque nobilius.*" The quoted words are applied to Bishop Gallus of Clermont in *VP* 6.1. Yet Gregory emphasizes Gallus's magnificent descent only to underline his humility: he turned his back on nobility and entered holy orders (the theme is stated in *VP* 6.*praef.*). We have to consult *VSJ* 23 and *VP* 2.2 to learn that Gallus was Gregory's uncle. It need not follow that Gregory despised his family tree, but a little caution is in order before speaking of pride.

The shrewdest comment on the subject comes from Kurth, "Sénateurs en Gaule," p. 104: "Gregory never fails to feature the dignities of his family. If this little weakness [of his] has been overlooked, it is because he resorts to an innocent artifice that, one might say, strikes a compromise between Christian humility and patrician vanity. Every time he says of someone that he is a relative, he refrains from drawing attention to his noble origins. On the other hand, every time he boasts of the nobility of a member of his family, he abstains from noting the bond of kinship." Kurth may have struck the right note, but I am unconvinced. It is easy to be supercilious if one owns Gregory's *opera omnia*, with a good index, and is able, as a result, to unmask the author's "petit faible" and interested in doing so. But what of ordinary readers? It is not entirely convincing to suppose that they were expected to go to the trouble of assembling the fragments and, at the cost of these efforts, be duly impressed.

[343] I.e. relatives who may be identified as such without the help of other information: *Hist.* 5.5 (Peter and Gregory of Langres), 6.11, 5.14.

[344] *Hist.* 10.15; Fortunatus *Carmina*, 8.13, 9.7.81-84.

Although his predecessor, Eufronius, is said by the then king to come from "one of the noblest and most distinguished families in the land," we would not realize that he was Gregory's cousin unless we remembered Eufronius's relationship to Gregory of Langres when, one book later, our Gregory mentions his own descent from the same bishop.[345] It cannot be fairly claimed that the author of the *Histories* expressed ingenuous pride in his senatorial ancestry, or paraded the incidents of his life. Nothing is said of his early years. His accession to Tours, mentioned in the *Wonders*, rates a mere allusion in the *Histories*. Only one friend of his, otherwise unknown, is mentioned. No reference occurs to his visiting his mother when sent on official business to Guntram's capital. A more assertive author, instead of just listing his accomplishments as bishop in the final chapter (alongside those of his predecessors), might have recorded them one by one, at each appropriate chronological point.[346]

Gregory comes before us in the *Histories* in either of two guises. He is the native of Clermont and resident of Tours, who without apology reports incomparably more about these cities than about any others and treats their episcopal successions as a thread of continuity from end to end. He is also the self-conscious author directly addressing his readers in five prefaces, a postface, occasional apostrophes, and a continual flow of brief remarks—reminders of earlier matter, cross-references to other writings (such as the *Wonders*), explanations of what direction the narrative is about to take, and so forth.

Clermont holds an astonishing place in books I-III. For a start, the narrative that opens with the Creation, Exodus, and Babylonian captivity (*inter alia*) descends in the same book to the sexual misconduct of an early bishop of Clermont and the more edifying character of several successors.[347] A special degree of animosity is reserved for certain Clermontans: the descendants of Sidonius Apollinaris, the family of Hortensius, and Bishop Cautinus (in whose case Gregory quotes Sallust to avert a charge of mal-

[345] *Hist.* 5.49; Gregory's point was that he was hardly foreign to Tours; he was not boasting. On who these bishops were, see Kurth, "Sénateurs en Gaule," pp. 105-106. About Eufronius, *Hist.* 4.15, linked to Gregory only through 5.5.

[346] Accession, *VSM* 2.1; allusion to it, *Hist.* 5.48. His friend Galienus, *Hist.* 5.49 (cf. above n. 316: Aredius was clearly a friend of his, but is not so called). His accomplishments, *Hist.* 10.31. Visit to his mother, *VSM* 3.60, GC 84; on Chalon-sur-Saône, not Cavaillon, as her residence in widowhood, see Michel Carrias, review of Vieillard-Troïekouroff, *Monuments religieux*, in *Revue d'histoire de l'Église de France* 73 (1977) 110-12; Pietri, *Ville de Tours*, p. 253 with n. 40.

Gregory's supposed senatorial pride is more often noted than his string of stories and statements disobliging to senators: *Hist.* 1.24, 31, 47, 6.9; *VP* 2.*praef.*, GC 5. In his view, entrance into religion was a renunciation of what senators stood for. The stories about Sidonius Apollinaris (*Hist.* 2.22-23) stress his charity, humility, and helplessness, rather than magnificence.

[347] *Hist.* 1.44-47. All four were deleted from the seventh-century abridgment of the six-book mss (above § 2). *Hist.* 1.32-33 are also about Auvergne.

ice).[348] As for Tours, it is also present as early as book I, with the life and death of St. Martin. Hardly any story personally involving Gregory is detached from his official capacity as bishop. The episcopal chronicle closing book X (but different in form from anything else in the work) gives Tours even more prominence at the end than Clermont has at the beginning.[349] The sense of ecclesiastical purpose and continuity implied by this chronicle terminates the *Histories* on a note of serenity that comes nearest to being paralleled by the account, in book II, of early church constructions in Tours and Clermont.[350]

That Gregory emphasizes his own cities is less surprising than the lack of an apology for doing so. He faults his style but never feels called upon to explain his ostensible chauvinism. Was any excuse necessary? We have observed that the *Wonders* and *Histories* were tailored for a Gallo-Roman public,[351] and, although next-to-nothing is knowable about Gregory's audience, it seems probable that the society in whose name he spoke, or the readers whom he expected his books to reach, lived primarily in Clermont and Tours. Within this context, the feud of Sicharius and Chramnesindus, the quarrel of Ingitrude and Berthegund, the lawsuit of Count Eulalius of Clermont against the wife who had deserted him, and other matters of concern to the two localities had self-explanatory reasons for being commemorated among dismal *gesta praesentia*.[352] Alongside the history of the kingdom itself, they rather than other cities had a claim to priority in the selection of miracles and slaughters. The prominence of Clermont and Tours makes better sense if they were common to Gregory and his readers than if he featured them only because of their association with himself.

As author and narrator, Gregory is neither self-effacing nor consistently intrusive. His most frequent occurrences on the page take the form of asides that are more noticeable in modern translation (owing, for example, to the English "I") than they are in the formulaic phrases of the original, here taken from book VII alone: *sicut superius diximus, cui in libro superiore meminimus, cui supra meminimus, ut diximus, sicut iam supra diximus, sic enim dix-*

---

[348] Relatives of Sidonius: *Hist.* 2.11, 37 (are with the Arian Goths), 3.2, 9-10, 12, 18 (particularly damaging), GM 44 (Gothic connection, cf. *Hist.* 2.20), 64 (bungled church construction), VP 4.1. The family of Hortensius: *Hist.* 4.13, 35, VP 4.3, 6.4. Cautinus, *Hist.* 4.7-11, 13, 31. Further chapters on Clermont: *Hist.* 2.13, 16-17, 20-25, and many more.

[349] *Hist.* 1.39, 48. Gregory's official capacity: in defense of Church and city, 5.4, 6.10, 7.47, 9.30; safeguarding sanctuary, 5.18; Church affairs, 5.18, 9.2, 39-43, 10.12, 15-16; intercedes for endangered notables, 5.39, 8.6, 18; defends his position, 5.49; deals with kings, 6.2, 5, 8.2-3, 5, 14, 9.20.

[350] Early churches of Tours and Clermont, *Hist.* 2.14-17; see the passage quoted at n. 280 above.

[351] Above, nn. 118-22.

[352] *Hist.* 7.47, 9.19 (Sicharius and Chramnesindus); 5.21, 9.33, 10.12 (Ingitrud and Berthegund); 8.27, 45, 10.6, 8 (Eulalius's wife).

imus, quos superius nominavimus.[353] If it were not that Gregory prefers first-person forms, one might think that the effect of such phrases was indistinguishable from the passive *sicut iam superius indicatum est* and *ut supra dictum est.*[354] The same book contains only two interjections that are clearly editorial: "crimes, which I prefer to pass over in silence" and "I believe this was not pleasing to the martyr."[355] Gregory is more obtrusive when calling attention to complementary books, especially his *Miracula* (or their constituent parts), as he often does, and no less so when announcing that a pause (or digression) is over and he is returning to his main thread.[356] There is no doubt, in these cases, that Gregory is sustaining the relationship of a storyteller with his public.

His most emphatic addresses to readers occur, of course, in the prefaces that not only introduce the whole work but also head books I, II, III, and V. Gregory calls attention to his existence even at the opening of books without prefaces. He is summoned to Chilperic's presence (book VI); he feels bound to pause in order to commemorate the holy Salvius of Albi (book VII); he assists at Guntram's visit to Orléans and is visited by the king (book VIII); he is present at Radegund's death and burial (book IX); his deacon returns from Rome with news of Pope Gregory's election and first weeks (book X).[357] Only the start of book IV lacks any intrusion by the author, perhaps as a contrast to book V, the first of the contemporary books, in which Gregory plays a larger part by far than anywhere else.

Nowhere does Gregory draw closer to his public than at his point of departure—the preface to book I. In it, as we saw, his prospective subject matter is reduced to vague conflicts of kings with enemies, martyrs with pagans, Churches with heretics.[358] From these generalities, he shifts at once to an extended *captatio benevolentiae*, his only other concern. So as to set the reader's mind at rest, he will show that he (too) is a good Catholic. He knows that some people worry about the approaching end of the world. Sympathizing with their anxieties, he will clearly lay out all the years of the world, on the assumption that doing so brings comfort and peace of mind.

---

[353] *Hist.* 7.7, 10, 31, 33, 35, 40, K-L pp. 330, 332, 351, 353, 357, 363.

[354] *Hist.* 7.19, 28, K-L pp. 339, 346.

[355] *Hist.* 7.3, 31, K-L pp. 328, 351.

[356] See above, nn. 69, 181-82.

[357] The least memorable of the prefaces heads book III; its simple message, underscoring the principal exploit of Clovis in the previous book, is that Catholics prosper (at least in the next world), whereas heretics come to bad ends, and Catholics gain kingdoms, whereas heretics lose them, and their souls.

Gregory at the opening of books without prefaces: *Hist.* 6.2, 7.1, 8.1-2, 9.2, 10.1. Although these passages are different from the prefaces, they should make us wonder whether the cessation of prefaces after book V is as portentous as Nie, "Roses in January," pp. 287-88, is inclined to think.

[358] Above, n. 185.

By then apologizing for his faulty Latin and defective education, he compliments his betters and appeals to those on the same plane as himself. Only one thing really matters, he insists: to accept without hesitation the teachings of the Church, for even sinners may by pure faith gain God's forgiveness. In other words, being an author or historian, as he is about to be, is a matter of no consequence. God will judge Gregory and readers alike only on their adhesion to Him. To drive home the lesson, Gregory strikes a final note of humility by running through the Creed from end to end. Bishop though he is, he does not disdain to share with his readers the elementary affirmation that he holds in common with them.[359] The preface is a triumph of self-deprecation and identification with the audience.

Kurth, who recognized the prevalence of high and low exceptions in the *Histories*, believed that "the life of average people"—"real" life—had to be inferred from Gregory's exceptional categories.[360] In fact, the *Histories* evokes normality more directly than just by implication. Gregory avoided entering into personal details except when events intersected his life, but he gave himself and his public enough presence on the page as to assure us that the commonplace and unspectacular was no less typical of his world than of our own. On three occasions, he shows himself engaging in theological argument with non-Catholics; the dialogue is tedious and, without fail, neither side sways the other.[361] Few passages of the *Histories* are more realistic.

Like the Old Testament prophets, and like Salvian and Gildas, Gregory was severely critical of the world around him, and vividly portrayed its vices. But with a difference. He does not depict himself as a voice crying in the wilderness or isolated in a jungle of depravity. Clermont and Tours were normal localities, provided with saints as well as sinners, with Churches proceeding securely through time under good and bad bishops, and populated by ordinary residents worthy of protection from tax assessors and collectors of royal fines. There were normal Catholics out there, no worse or better than Gregory himself and capable of being reached by a storyteller's

---

[359] K-L p. 3: "Scripturus bella regum cum gentibus adversis, martyrum cum paganis, eclesiarum cum hereticis, prius fidem meam proferre cupio, ut qui ligirit me non dubitet esse catholicum. Illud etiam placuit propter eos, qui adpropinquantem finem mundi disperant, ut, collectam per chronicas vel historias anteriorum annorum summam explanitur aperte, quanti ab exordio mundi sint anni. Sed prius veniam legentibus praecor, si aut in litteris aut in sillabis grammaticam artem excessero, de qua adplene non sum inbutus; illud tantum studens, ut quod in eclesia credi praedicatur sine aliquo fuco aut cordis hesitatione reteneam, quia scio, peccatis obnoxium per credulitatem puram obtenire posse veniam apud Deum.

"Credo ergo . . ."

[360] Kurth, "De l'autorité," p. 173.

[361] *Hist.* 5.43, 6.5, 40. Momigliano, "Medieval Jewish Autobiography," pp. 333-34, points out that the twelfth-century convert Hermann quondam Judaius considered interfaith debate a barren occupation. Cf. above, n. 139.

parables rather than a prophet's denunciations. Gregory himself showed in his administration of Tours that, with the aid of God and the saints, moderate and upright conduct was adequate for meeting the crises of Merovingian life. This neutral middle ground, shared by author and public rather than narrowly autobiographical, holds a modest place in the *Histories*; but, thanks largely to Gregory's own prominence, it cannot be missed. What is more difficult to determine than its existence is the function it is meant to serve.

The middle ground is not talked about. Its presence in the *series temporum* needs no explanation. The reason for its being there at all seems to be that it is the occasion for talking. Gregory's insistent evocation of himself and his public, and of the cities he and they shared, has a structural function in the *Histories*. It substitutes for the nonexistent plot. People wished to know what had happened; Gregory responded to their need, told them and then stopped. The events themselves, spectacular as they are, form no pattern except the common, repetitive one of good and evil visible in the Bible, Eusebius, and Orosius. Nothing important changes. The action of the work as a whole resides in the process of telling and listening, and ends when author and audience part. The *Histories* is a collection of short stories held together, perhaps by the accidents of time, but especially by the relationship of teller and listener among ordinary persons sharing a common creed. Gregory's final word is for his successor-soon-to-be, that shadowy figure representative of the future who would succeed him as bishop of Tours. He is asked not to alter the delicate web spun between Gregory and the men and women, as blameless as himself, to whom he explained *gesta praesentia*. To recognize that all this is literary artifice diminishes none of its force.

8. *Historiae*: The Union of Satire with History

What sort of man was Gregory? The question is hard to answer because, apart from flattering poems by Fortunatus, Gregory's own testimony must provide the reply. His statements are more illustrative of the face he wished to present to the world, however sincerely, than of the individual we might know if fuller information were available.[362] Many modern commentators, without taking this distinction into account, have

---

[362] Booth, *Rhetoric of Fiction*, pp. 70-72, 75, 76: no matter how sincere an author is, the authorial *persona* is a fictional creature developed to suit the work; the likes and dislikes revealed in a work are those of the implied author. One might argue that Booth's statement does not apply outside fiction; cf. Fowler, *Kinds of Literature*, p. 118, who objects that Northrop Frye tends to blur the line between fiction and nonfiction. What Fowler calls the nonfiction author's contract with the reader may require that the implied author should be identical to the real one. But this condition leaves out of account the necessarily limited or partial self-revelation that any author makes of himself; e.g. a travel book calls for a different persona than a history.

formed an idea of Gregory from his writings. There is a comfortable consensus about Gregory's personality; the summary given here, though drawn (without quotation marks) from only four authorities, is broadly representative. Gregory, it is agreed, was a man of solid good sense and character, a practical bishop seeking to make the best of a bad world, not an idealist hoping for heavenly conditions on earth. He was so honest that he supplies the means for testing his judgments. Though very well born and aware of it, he was, personally, the most modest of men, referring to himself only in passing and in deprecating terms. He manifested unfeigned loyalty toward the Frankish royal family, as to a necessary support of the social order. He avoided altercation whenever possible and, though much inclined to mercy, never questioned prevailing ways, such as the use of torture in judicial proceedings. His religious faith was of the common sort, without sophistication. The reverence he professed for paternal authority is a conspicuous indication of his old-fashioned moral standards. All the same, he was disinclined to severe asceticism, enjoyed food and wine, and had tender feelings for little children. Lewis Thorpe called him "lovable," and he is unanimously thought to have been the best sort of ordinary man. [363]

Gregory, the source of these opinions, looks as he does because he took pains to do so. The prefaces we have already examined add significant traits to his self-image. In lieu of stating a historical theme, he twice advertises his pessimistic view of human affairs: wars, persecutions, heretics; quarreling peoples, furious kings, cooling faith, plundered churches. Pessimism is again affirmed when he deplores the conduct of the current cohort of Merovingians. [364] These conditions force him to write, for everyone longs to understand *gesta praesentia*. He will not hesitate to tell the truth about good and bad men alike. But not in the choice words that the audience seems to want: he rejects pompous writing. Unable to emulate the *philosophans rethor*, he is not ashamed to be a mere *rusticus loquens*. Even if he cannot claim backwoods origins, he is able to express blunt country wisdom.

The Gregory we see is a prudent, modest, ordinary man who happens to write, though incorrectly, and displays no arresting eccentricities. His image has impact because it situates him in a category of humanity quite different from fiery prophets, fathers of the Church, and Gallic bishops. The history of literature contains a tribe of authors who are as conspicuous as Gregory in their writings and as highly conscious of their public, and who, to go by what they tell us of themselves, are all "straightforward, honest, pessimistic, indignant men who dislike ostentatious rhetoric, come from

---

[363] Dalton I, 13-17; Kurth, "De l'autorité," pp. 119-29; Latouche tr., I, 13-15; Thorpe tr., pp. 14-16. See also Monod, *Études critiques*, pp. 122-25; Buchner, Einleitung, pp. xvii-xviii.

[364] See above, nn. 185-91, 260.

the country, and have simple moral codes."[365] This is the profile of the satirist, ancient and modern, and it closely matches Gregory's self-portrait.

Satire, in one definition, is a "literary mode painting a distorted verbal picture of part of the world in order to show its true moral, as opposed to its physical, nature."[366] As a genre, it is closely allied to the root meaning of *satura* as a mishmash, grab bag, or medley, characterized by the same formlessness that most commentators have found in Gregory. The genus satire, even if limited to being "a convenient expression to cover a variety of literary works that have many characteristics in common," helps us to realize that the paradox of inner chaos and outer order in Gregory's *Histories* is only apparent.[367] Although satire tends to change character with every author, it retains certain common traits, notably: an obtrusive author, much concerned with his public; fragmentation and digressive shapelessness; an absence of plot, resulting in the reader's ending more or less where he began; and, not least, a fondness for ideas, especially moral ideas.[368] Another way to think of the genre is as extroverted autobiography, in which the author, instead of focusing confessionally on his own life and thoughts, reaches out toward society and comments on it in a personal way.[369] We have observed almost all these features in the *Histories*. There can hardly be a more precise description of Gregory's procedure than that he painted a distorted verbal picture of the Gaul he lived in so as to show its true moral nature.

The *Histories* illustrates a mad but permanent world whose sway extends homogeneously from biblical antiquity to the Merovingian present. "[T]he current scene is only the latest instance of a process whose dimensions extend through all history"; any expectation of reform or improvement is excluded because the world is portrayed just as it is.[370] Gregory is a solicitous narrator, yet uninhibited in evoking places and incidents close to himself. He and his public give the *Histories* its touch of normality and principle of coherence; "[the satirist] speaks to [the audience] on topics which concern them and him as members of a community or group."[371] It is no news to Gregory that the history he narrates is a scrambled medley. On the contrary, as we have seen, he takes an early opportunity to explain himself.

[365] Kernan, "Theory of Satire," p. 163.

[366] *Oxford Anthol. of Eng. Lit.* I, 2331.

[367] Hodgart, *Satire*, p. 5.

[368] Satire changes with author: *Oxford Classical Dictionary*, 2d ed., p. 953. Solicitous author: below, n. 371. Fragmentation: below, n. 373. Plot: Kernan, "Theory of Satire," p. 171, the most striking characteristic of satire is the absence of plot; at the end, we see the same world, the same fools, and the same satirist as were met at the beginning. Moral ideas: Elliot, *Power of Satire*, pp. 265, 105, 107-109.

[369] Frye, *Anatomy of Criticism*, pp. 308-12; what Frye calls the anatomy genre. Its suitability is questioned by Fowler, *Kinds of Literature*, pp. 118-20.

[370] *Oxford Anthol. of Eng. Lit.* I, 1557; Pinkus, "Satire and St. George," p. 43.

[371] Clark, "Art of Satire," p. 136.

History has the objective character of being *mixta confusaque*; it is altogether fitting that these "varied and intermingled" events should be set out in the disorder inherent to them. [372] Gregory's vision of the past, without doing more violence to history than any other, also matches to perfection the characteristics of a literary genre. Satire "is always a farrago"; it "enjoys the episodic forms"; it involves "a mob of characters whirling about in a great variety of scenes and a succession of seemingly loosely related events with little apparent development" and has "powerful tendencies to fragmentation and meaninglessness."[373] Gregory knew what he was doing. His explicit justification of confusion within the *Histories* points as directly toward satire as does the mask he assumes of "a blunt, honest man with no nonsense about him."[374]

Gregory composed in a sophisticated, characteristically urban literary form that is more readily associated with imperial Rome and the England of Queen Anne than with Frankish Gaul. [375] When the first-century Roman critic Quintilian said "Satire is our very own (*satura tota nostra est*)," he was referring to a type of extended composition that Latin poets, notably Horace, had pioneered. Lucilius, another of its founders, was credited with having made satire-language unliterary, colloquial, even coarse. Satirists occupied an appreciable part of the Latin poetic corpus. [376] Gregory's neighbor, Fortunatus, was conversant with at least Horace and Martial, if not Juvenal. There was much Gregory might have learned from so well trained a man of letters as his Italian protégé, who was himself a literary innovator. [377] Gregory's consistent use of rhythmic prose has long been thought to undercut his professions of being uneducated. [378] After what we have seen, his pretensions to rusticity should be taken even less literally than they have yet been.

Gregory composed prescriptive satire. His portrayals of folly, vice, and crime are contrasted to the explicit norm of the saints, comparable to Horace's ideal of the gentleman and Juvenal's of ancient Roman virtue. [379] Like

[372] See above, nn. 264-65.

[373] The quotations, respectively: Carnohan, *Lemuel Gulliver's Mirror for Man*, p. 22; Paulson, *Fictions of Satire*, p. 5; Kernan, *Plot of Satire*, p. 97; Kernan, "Satire," p. 215.

[374] Kernan, "Theory of Satire," p. 157.

[375] Horace, Juvenal, and Swift tend to be indispensable figures in any general account of satire.

[376] *Oxford Classical Dictionary*, 2d ed., pp. 953-54; Hendrickson, "Satura Tota Nostra Est," pp. 1-15; Anderson, "Roman Satirists and Their Tradition," pp. 33-37.

[377] On Fortunatus's reading, see Manitius's index to his verse, in MGH AA. IV, part 2, pp. 132-37. Fortunatus as a literary innovator: Reydellet, *Royauté*, pp. 297-347 (less of one than Gregory). Also see Navarra, "Venanzio Fortunato."

[378] Above, n. 27.

[379] Payne, *Chaucer and Menippean Satire*, p. 39, contrasts prescriptive satire to the type in which "the concept of the norm itself" is attacked or parodied, e.g. Lucian's or Menippus's.

the poets, Gregory is, or comes close to being, a first-person narrator, much more of one than history usually calls for.[380] In keeping with the Lucilian tradition, he adopted unliterary and colloquial accents, and only half apologized for doing so. The glaring difference, of course, is that Gregory wrote prose rather than verse. He was a historian, committed to consecutive and even annalistic composition. Even though he focused on current events— a more certain spur to indignation than the events of the past—the degree of fragmentation permissible to the poets was unavailable to him. He could not quite emulate "the miscellaneous thoughts extracted from the satirist by the slings of the world."[381] Yet the assemblage of vivid, variegated, and isolated scenes he aligned in the *Histories* comes much closer to approximating this model than the progression of serious events expected in orderly history. That the dominant features of the *Histories* should closely resemble those of satire is beyond coincidence. Gregory lived too close to the classics for the hypothesis of spontaneous or accidental reinvention to be probable. No less a model than Sidonius supplied the assurance that satire and contemporary history (or historical style) necessarily attracted each other.[382]

In the view of one authority, "Satire never fails to assume the coloration of the dominant rationalistic philosophy" of the period in which it is written, such as Cynicism and Stoicism in antiquity and Humanism in the Renaissance.[383] It goes against the grain to associate Gregory with "rationalism" of any sort, but one may wonder whether the term is wholly inappropriate to the outlook we saw expressed in the *Wonders*.[384] As far as Gregory was concerned, the humble "fisherman's wisdom" of Christianity, centered on creation, miracle, and resurrection, was an objective certainty, confirmed by empirical observation rather than reason. It was the more assured for being concrete and detached from mere speculation. Some men and women had, in fact, "taken up the cross of severe observance." Living and dying by Christ's name, they had left earthly remains whose perceptible power, illustrated by continual miracles, bore witness to the truth they had

---

[380] Hellmann, "Gregor von Tours," p. 93.

[381] Kernan, "Theory of Satire," p. 154. A classic explanation of what incites the satirist is Juvenal's line *facit indignatio versum*; i.e. though all else counsels silence, indignation forces him to write.

[382] Sidonius *Epistolae* 4.22.5 (a letter in which he explains why he will not write history), ed. Anderson, II, 148: "sic se illi protinus dictioni color odorque satiricus admiscet." Anderson equates *dictio* with *scriptio historica* in the next sentence; Loyen (Coll. des univ. de France) considers it to be the style of such a work. The moral Sidonius drew from this observation was that, because satire inevitably earns hatred, the writing of history was inappropriate for clergymen. Gregory evidently disagreed with this conclusion. On Sidonius himself as a satirist, see Weston, *Latin Satirical Writing*, pp. 136-38. It was not the form he was most at home with.

[383] Randolph, "Structural Design of Formal Verse Satire," p. 374.

[384] Above, § 3.

exemplified in life and to their conquest over death. The lessons of Holy Writ were mysterious and complex, beyond even a bishop's ability to decipher, but anyone could grasp from a venerable teacher as much of the message of the Church as Gregory had received from Avitus of Clermont: that Jesus Christ was the son of God and savior of the world, and that His friends, the saints, were to be fittingly served.[385] These facts, learned by word of mouth and borne out daily by observation of their continuing effects on earth, were an adequate guide to human conduct.

The heart of Gregory's inverted rationalism appears to have been his derivation of meaning from random, unpredictable events, perceived by his own and his audience's senses. The source of wisdom was neither reason nor revelation but the data of experience. Events were unambiguous. They continually confirmed the concreteness of Christian truth: God's sole governance of the created world. The historian of his times was in the best position to convey these certainties. As the historical record of prodigies documented God's admonitions to humanity, and as that of current miracles documented the eternity assured to the blessed, so did the record of "slaughters" and "downfalls" attest to the folly of alternative ways of life.

In place of Augustine's *civitas terrena* (which he may not have known), Gregory substituted the mad and vicious world of satire, contrasting it to the sense and beauty of the coexisting world of the saints. "In its most serious function," it has been said, "satire is a mediator between two perceptions—the unillusioned perception of man as he actually is, and the ideal perception, or vision, of man as he ought to be."[386] In Gregory's adaptation of this bipartite scheme to Christian history, the saints and their miracles were of the utmost practical importance. "The heroic vision is essential to the satiric; the satirist shows his anti-hero falling as far below the norms of decency and intelligence as the true hero rises above them"[387] Gregory's Gaul was populated with anti-heroes. Even the kings whom he most highly esteems fall astonishingly short of the heroic.[388] But the image the *Histories* projects does not contain only flawed creatures. Gregory's duo of miracles and slaughters is much less pessimistic than the purely ironic and "unillusioned" history epitomized by the familiar modern sayings that the past consists of "the crimes, follies, and misfortunes of mankind" or "the endless repetition of the wrong way of living," and that written history is a set of "lies about crimes."[389] So conceived, history has an oppressive realism con-

---

[385] VP 2.*praef.*, ed. Krusch, p. 669 lines 3-7.

[386] Bullitt, *Jonathan Swift and the Anatomy of Satire*, p. 1.

[387] *Oxford Anthol. of Eng. Lit.* I, 1557.

[388] See § 9; the kings in question are Clovis, Theudebert I, and Guntram, all of whom Gregory took more pains to blacken than he needed to.

[389] Gibbon, *Decline and Fall*, ch. 3, ed. Bury, I, 77, after Voltaire (1767), "En effet, l'histoire n'est que le tableau des crimes et des malheurs," in *Concise Oxford Dictionary of Quotations*

ducive only to despair. For Gregory, however, the saints embodied "man as he ought to be" as a realized actuality, not as an abstract ideal or potential. Because God had become man, one could be certain that some men had fulfilled all that mankind might ever hope to achieve. The saints allowed Gregory to retain a concrete "vision of the world transformed" in the midst of identifying all run-of-the-mill politics and warfare with folly, vice, and crime.[390] Christian salvation perceived as empirical fact allowed a historian to speak in the accents of a satirist and yet to retain his composure and calm. The world was and, since the Fall, had always been in the grip of fools and criminals, but some men went to heaven.

Well before being taken in hand by Roman poets, satire had been, among the Greeks, a vehicle for popularizing moral ideas.[391] It was no less so for Gregory. The satirist, sustaining the miscellaneity of his work by the force of his fictional personality, orders its contents in keeping with his ideas. What he writes is "a construct of symbols—situations, scenes, characters, language—put together to express some particular vision of the world."[392] As a chronicle of events in late-sixth-century Gaul, the *Histories* is less than comprehensive and balanced, but it leaves readers in little doubt as to what they should think of *gesta praesentia*. Gregory's choice of literary genre was well adapted to his goal of drowning out the *philosophans rethor* with the voice of Christian bluntness.[393]

9. *Historiae*: The Intellectual Pattern

In an extensive survey of heathen antiquity, Orosius's *Histories against the Pagans* judged the doings of non-Christians by a Christian standard, rewriting other peoples's past along lines they would not have chosen themselves. Gregory's very different history is, to all intents, the first Christian narrative of a Christian era.[394] No crisis comparable to the one inspiring Orosius set him to his task. Though Gregory suggests that the public wished to understand current events, he keeps us in the dark as to what these *gesta*

(Oxford 1981), pp. 106, 265; Laurence Durrell (1978), quoted in *Penguin Dictionary of Modern Quotations*, ed. J. M. and M. J. Cohen, 2d ed. (Harmondsworth, Middlesex 1980), p. 104. I came across the third quotation in the *Manchester Guardian Weekly*, where it was attributed to G. N. Clark.

[390] Quotation from Hodgart, *Satire*, p. 12.

[391] Paulson, *Fictions of Satire*, p. 42.

[392] Kernan, "Theory of Satire," p. 145; satire should not be mistaken for "a direct report of the poet's feelings and the literary incidents which aroused these feelings."

[393] Panegyric is at the opposite pole from satire; the rhetoricians of Gaul used to be its most celebrated practitioners: Chadwick, *Poetry and Letters*, p. 54; Galletier, *Panégyriques latins* I, xv-xvi.

[394] Perhaps the qualifier "in Latin" should be added, but Socrates, Sozomen, and Theodoret are, I believe, the only potential rivals; and, besides being mainly retrospective, they are historians of the Church rather than of an era.

might contain that was other than self-explanatory.[395] We may speculate that his public believed the current régime to be worse than any other within memory, as men often do, or that anachronistic longings had been nourished by the spectacle of Justinian's Western conquests, or that the standards and categories inculcated by traditional education were distressingly irreconcilable with current realities. Misconceptions of some sort were at large for Gregory to rectify. A different sound from his emerges from the only contemporary Gallic chronicler. Monod said, "One would believe, in reading Marius [of Avenches], that the Empire had endured no setback and that Gaul was still subject to its power."[396] Gregory's implied public might have included Marius. Whatever the stimulus, Gregory felt called upon to expound, through the *gesta* within his reach, a Christian interpretation of history at a level that he took care to keep modest and unassuming. Unlike Orosius, he was not called upon to answer and outbid the promise of *Roma aeterna*.[397] On a scale of a few decades, there was neither need nor room for God's providential plan. Although Gregory's times, like all others, obviously moved between Creation and Final Judgment, the world he portrayed might as well have been indeterminate or timeless. Almost the only span within it that mattered was the very short one of individual existence.

Gregory's remoteness from a providential vision of history is best measured by the verticality of his organizing principle: a panorama whose scenes are hierarchically ordered in relation to the Almighty. In a providential scheme, time plays a purposive part, drawing men closer to their Creator. For Orosius (and not him alone), the Incarnation was a historical turning point, paralleled by the institution of the Roman Empire, itself an improvement in the condition of humanity.[398] Gregory, by contrast, not only wiped out the Roman side of the Incarnation, but presented Jesus Christ as a theological fact (the fulfillment of biblical prophecy) and as the prototype of miracle-working saints.[399] Biblical history as well as the persecutions are in

---

[395] Above, nn. 185-96.

[396] Monod, *Études critiques*, p. 155. Marius is cited above, n. 35.

[397] Paschoud, *Roma aeterna*, and the works he cites at pp. 7-8 n. 3. Lacroix, *Orose et ses idées*, pp. 183-87. Despite the sack of 410, Orosius still had to reckon with the deeply entrenched idea (propagated, e.g., by Virgil) that Rome had discovered the secret of at least collective eternity and could rise above troubles that leveled other states. For whatever reasons, Gregory did not.

[398] For Orosius's teaching, see, typically, *Hist.* 6.1. On the providential interpretation of history, e.g. Patrides, *Grand Design of God*, pp. 7-9, 13-19; Hanning, *Vision of History*, pp. 5-43; Keen, "Medieval Ideas of History," pp. 296-97, 299-301; Coopland, "Medieval View of History," pp. 39, 41, 304-305.

[399] *Hist.* 1.19 (birth, wise men, massacre of the innocents), 20 (life, miracles, and death), 22 (resurrection), 24 (ascension). Readers' attention is not drawn to the coincidence between the establishment of the Roman imperial régime (1.18) and the Incarnation; above, ch. II n. 155.

book I, not as constituents of a broad, advancing sweep of time, but as exemplifications of timeless conditions. When we are told that hatred of Christians began because the senators resented Pilate's sending his report about Christ to the emperor instead of to them, or that senators and other leading men of Bourges were impervious to Christian evangelization, we know that these are not stages from benightedness to enlightenment: they are monitory tales, the first of many, addressed by Gregory directly to the senatorial descendants in his audience.[400] Only one fragment of divine foresight is drawn to our attention: namely, that the Merovingians were raised up by God's mercy as *viri fortes*, reminiscent of Old Testament kings, to save Catholic Gaul from Arian heresy.

Gregory's subordination of history to moral instruction is well illustrated by his famous admonition to the Franks in the preface to book V.[401] Because historically minded, we tend to infer that he considered his own generation of Merovingians to be worse than preceding ones. He says so clearly enough in the preface in question.[402] Yet, if he sought to trace deterioration, the high point from which it sets in can be little else than Clovis's attack on the Visigoths, a brief moment in his reign. Gregory is probably misunderstood if supposed to dispense good or bad grades to whole generations of kings. What he sets out instead is a timeless lesson—the consequences of social discord and its remedy. The ideas of this preface recur in the *Histories* in several guises and through two mouths besides Gregory's own. Clovis personifies the ideal of social leadership when defeating the Arian Visigoths, but only then; Gregory personally bemoans the ills of Frankish society, first briefly, then in the preface to book V; Fredegonde takes up the same themes in self-accusation; and King Guntram chimes in, after the failure of his Visigothic campaign, only to be answered in kind by his generals.[403] Though adapted to particulars, the ideas are always the same, so obviously so that Fredegonde and Guntram are clearly mouthpieces for the author. Actions convey the same message in Clovis's campaign. The angry exchange be-

---

[400] *Hist.* 1.24, 31: timeless conditions, such as the outbreak of crime in the human race (Cain and Abel), the transitoriness of human endeavor (Babylon), etc. Pilate's report: *Hist.* 1.24; Bourges: 1.31.

[401] *Hist.* 5.*praef.*, K-L p. 193: "Taedit me bellorum civilium diversitatis, que Francorum gentem et regnum valde proterunt, memorare [in which we glimpse a foretaste of the prophesied Last Days, when son rises against father etc.]. Debebant enim eos exempla anteriorum regum terrere, qui, ut divisi, statim ab inimicis sunt interempti. Etc." The "former kings" are obviously biblical and not Frankish, as Thorpe, p. 253, mistakenly translates. The Romans and Carthaginians are also called on in the preface for examples of the disastrous consequences of internal conflict.

[402] K-L p. 193: "Utinam et vos, o regis, in his proelia, in quibus parentes vestri desudaverunt, exercimini. . . . Recordamini, quid capud victuriarum vestrarum Chlodovechus fecerit . . . ! Et cum hoc facerit, neque aurum neque argentum . . . habebat." Oldoni tr., I, xxxix-xl, was not alone in basing a schema of deterioration on these sentiments.

[403] *Hist.* 2.37, 4.48, 5.*praef.*, 34, 8.30.

tween Guntram and his generals abruptly dissolves; nothing comes of it or was meant to. The actors did their part by showing that the causes of social impotence were simple and self-evident.

The theology underlying Gregory's satire need not again be detailed. He presupposed that the governance of God, the proved ability of human beings to follow the path He traced, and the eternal reward of those who did so were all facts within reach of everyone's experience. Here lay sense and sanity. But this fallen world had other attractions, for the mind groping for certainty among the vanities of philosophers as well as for the flesh seeking immortality in biological progeny. In and among these, the dissolute vainly struggled, striving after goods not worth having: here was the domain of the absurd. Ordered and portrayed by Gregory in the light of this vertical pattern, historical events—even those of yesterday—might be not only explained but also endured with confidence and hope.[404]

The consequences of these principles, as worked out in the *Histories*, are not overtly theological and have practical consequences for the writing of history. Gregory seems, for a start, to have turned his back on any other than a chronological notion of historical continuity. The "inner" connection between stories that Ebert failed to find in him was purposely effaced.[405] Gregory was not unacquainted with other methods. Buchner drew attention to the characteristics of Sulpicius Alexander and Renatus Frigeridus, the two lost fifth-century historians whom Gregory read and quoted: they had a lively and informed sense of politics and campaigning, a completely this-worldly concern with human drives, passions, and forces; and these preoccupations informed their understanding of events.[406] One has only to list these (laudable) traits in order to realize that such an approach was irreconcilable with Gregory's vision of events.

The activities of fallen humanity could have no rational sense except in the language of "philosophers"; these were base strivings after worthless goals and had to be portrayed in their senselessness. Gregory implemented this belief by dispensing with the connectedness that events tend to assume. Modern readers, wishing to learn Frankish history or whatever, have understandably striven to reassemble Gregory's pieces and to perceive through them the "linear" motives and policies that they were certain lay behind the incidents reported. Their varied successes attest to Gregory's inability to be quite fragmentary enough.[407] He usually respected chronolog-

---

[404] Above §§ 3 and 6.

[405] Above, n. 16.

[406] Buchner, Einleitung, pp. xv-xvi. Also see n. 216 above.

[407] Among the many possible examples, Dalton I, 8-135 and *passim*; Lot, Pfister, and Ganshof, *Destinées de l'Empire*, pp. 254-63. I also engaged in this exercise: "Byzantine Policy in the West under Tiberius II and Maurice (579-585)," *Traditio* 13 (1957) 73-118.

ical order—how precisely he did so within annalistic segments cannot be measured—but though chronology sometimes orders a meaningful progression, such as the developing intrigues surrounding Gundovald, it also allowed Gregory to separate related subjects and in this way to efface the links between them.

One incident out of many—an innocuous one—illustrates his practice. Because drawn from one of the introductory books rather than from a contemporary one, it is not entirely typical, but its fame in literary studies makes up for this defect. Early in book III, we are told of a raid by Danes on Frisia. Theuderic, in whose realm Frisia lay, sent his son, Theudebert, against the raiders with a strong force. They were beaten and their king, Chlochilaicus, killed. The raid is often mentioned in the great Old English poem, *Beowulf*.[408] In Gregory's *Histories*, the Viking-like descent lacks any wider context; it occupies a thematic void. Fortunatus informs us, incidentally to a eulogy, that Danes attacked Frisia in Gregory's adult lifetime. For all we know, such raids were intermittent occurrences.[409] In Gregory, however, the rationale for the chapter is not the condition of the northern frontier or a comparably long-term consideration, but rather the (understated) role of one man. Theuderic's son, Theudebert, is the commendable king of book III, which ends with his death. It was in keeping with Theudebert's role that he should make a memorable early appearance, as the obedient son valorously carrying out the needed task of ridding the kingdom of marauders.[410] No doubt the Danish raid is a historical event (its approximate date is perhaps not quite so certain as it has seemed), but Gregory detached it from any context of foreign relations and northern defense. Instead, he presented Theudebert to us in a setting that would persuade us to keep him in mind until his return, seventeen chapters later.[411]

The isolation of subjects, and the omission of essential details, such as family relationships, are complemented, in Gregory's striving after fragmentation, by the intensity of individual scenes. His dramatizations have already been briefly examined. Between summary accounts of the Passion and Resurrection, Gregory interjects a story circling around Joseph of Arimathea. For having taken Jesus off the cross and honorably buried Him, Jo-

---

[408] *Hist.* 3.3. For bibliography and discussion, see Goffart, "*Hetware* and *Hugas*." Gregory refers to the slain northerner as a Dane, whereas the *Beowulf* poet calls him a Geat; the discrepancy is comparable to classifying Alexander the Great as a Greek rather than a Macedonian. For the view that Gregory's "Dane" excludes "Geat," see Curt Weibull, *Die Geaten des Beowulfsepos und die dänischen Trellenborg*, Acta Regiae Societatis Scientiarum et Litterarum Gothoburgensis, Humaniora 10 (Göteborg 1974), pp. 16-19.

[409] Fortunatus *Carmina* 7.7; cf. Goffart, "*Hetware* and *Hugas*," p. 86 with n. 17.

[410] He is one of the three Merovingians of whom Gregory approved; below, nn. 490-94.

[411] Typically, Theudebert returns in a domestic context (*Hist.* 3.20, 22). For a correct approximation of the date, see Zöllner, *Gesch. d. Franken*, p. 86 n. 5. The temptation to date the raid near 515 should be resisted.

seph was more hated by the high priests than Jesus himself. They imprisoned him; but, after Jesus rose from death, an angel came and miraculously freed Joseph from jail. When the priests accused the guards of having allowed Jesus' body to be removed, they confounded the priests by replying, You give us Joseph and we'll give you Jesus.[412] The mocking dialogue of Gregory's first dramatization typifies the many other self-contained, morally instructive, and entertaining scenes that, by drawing the reader within their small compass, tend to divert him from whatever the "line" of the narrative might be. The account of King Theuderic's ravaging of Auvergne ends with his appointing Sigivald to head the Frankish garrison. Before going on with Sigivald's doings, Gregory successively inserts the story of Munderic and, in the contrasting romantic mode, the touching adventures of Attalus and Leo the Cook.[413] One has no trouble finding justifications for these and other means of interrupting the narrative with diversions. The story of Munderic is, among other things, a commentary on Theuderic's treachery (he eventually kills Sigivald), whereas that of Attalus celebrates the triumph, with divine help, of innocence over politics. Yet these self-contained tales, though apt, stand apart from the main events and contribute to keeping the story sketchy and superficial. That was the idea. Gregory encourages us by a variety of devices to look for suggestive links between chapters, often by way of contrast or complement. But the surface connections, notably the tendency of politics and war to assume the form of impersonal "policy," were mutilated almost beyond recognition.

Gregory did not foster nostalgia of the sort that opposes a bad present to a good past. Despite the preface to book V, the Merovingians are not so much a lineage experiencing deterioration as a uniform pack of reprobates, forming a backdrop against which the virtues of three kings (Clovis, Theudebert, and Guntram) stand out. The longer course of time is even more plainly uniform. Gregory had no place for a secure, still less a glorious, Roman Empire. The emperors appear mainly as persecutors of the Church. What we call the barbarian invasions takes the form, in his pages, of a continuation of these Roman persecutions under different auspices.[414] The non-Arian Huns offer an occasion to dramatize God's punishment of unforgivably sinful Gaul, as well as the power of Sts. Peter and Paul; Attila, totally overshadowed, barely materializes, and Aëtius fares little better.[415] The events of the present were just like those of the past. The high priests

---

[412] *Hist.* 1.21. The story presupposes that (as in Roman law) guards bore personal responsibility for the custody of their prisoners.

[413] *Hist.* 3.13 (Theuderic and Sigivald), 14 (Munderic), 15 (Attalus).

[414] Above, n. 235.

[415] *Hist.* 2.5-7. Little more than five short sentences in these long chapters are concerned with the Huns and Attila. About Aëtius, see below, n. 458.

and soldiers of Jesus' Palestine, a fourth-century bishop and his wife, a fifth-century Arian impostor in Carthage, and an episcopal couple at Le Mans in the 580s could uniformly be brought to life in dramatic scenes that differed in details but might all belong to the same moment.[416] History was both varied and ever the same.

Less predictably, except from a perspective of satire, the actors in the *Histories* are seen in domestic settings, in company with their women and children, almost as often as in public roles. Gregory rarely descends to denunciation or fails in decorum, but the dignity that many of his characters might lay claim to, on the strength of their high stations, dwindles to common humanity or less when their domestic lives are bared. Writing about the super-rich of second-century Rome, the satirist Lucian illustrated the implications of delicate concealment: "these great men are for all the world like handsomely bound books. Outside are the gilt edges and the purple covers. . . . [T]heir brilliancy attracts all eyes, but between the purple covers lives many a horrid tale."[417] Privacy sustained the majesty of imperial rule and lofty status. Perhaps domestic misadventures were more publicly aired in Frankish Gaul than they had been in an earlier age, yet the decision to set them down in black and white had much to do with the sort of history one wrote.[418] The fondness of the Merovingians for their servingwomen prolonged practices that, to hear Salvian and Caesarius of Arles, were hardly unprecedented among the Christian grandees of late Roman Gaul.[419] What made a difference was whether to treat such lapses from monogamous virtue as abstract sins, as Salvian and Caesarius did, or to spell them out in inglorious detail. Gregory had no reservations. From the moment in book I that we encounter Bishop Urbicius roused up by his wife to readmit her to his bed, canons or no, we are rarely left to speculate on the role of sex and family cares in the course of events.[420]

The Merovingians come before us in the *Histories* under the auspices of the most elemental virility. Childeric, Merovech's son, was so profligate that he made free with the daughters of his subjects. Incensed by this behavior, they deposed him. He fled to exile with the Thuringian king Bisinus

[416] *Hist.* 1.21, 44, 2.3, 8.39.

[417] Lucian of Samosata *The Dependent Scholar*, tr. H. W. and F. G. Fowler, *The Works of Lucian of Samosata*, 4 vols. (Oxford 1905) II, 25: tragedies worthy of Sophocles and Euripides take place behind serene and ornate façades, and the familiar who is cast out is feared lest he should disclose the secrets of the household.

[418] Outside the royal family, the conspicuous case involves Eulalius and Tetradia: *Hist.* 10.8.

[419] Salvian *De gubernatione Dei* 7; Caesarius of Arles *Sermons* 41.3, 5, 43.4-5, ed. and tr. Marie-José Delage, Sources chrétiennes 175, 243 (Paris 1971, 1978) I, 132-33 (editor's summary), II, 284-88, 290-92, 316-20. Strict monogamy did not sit easily with houses staffed by slave women.

[420] *Hist.* 1.44, 3.4-5, 4.3, 25-28.

and his wife, Basina. The Franks, after eight years under a Roman king, were ready to call Childeric back. He returned, and Basina left Bisinus in order to seek him out. She told Childeric that she knew he was very *utilis* and admired his *strenuitas*, but that if she heard of anyone more *utilis* than he across the seas, she would assuredly seek out his bed. She did not have political virtues in mind. From their union, Clovis was born.[421] The adventuress Basina is even more down to earth than the merely lustful Childeric. Gregory was not partial to kings who debauched their subjects' daughters or to wives who left their husbands.[422] The story is not meant to excite admiring wonder. It sets the scene for the conduct seen among Clovis's descendants. Such, he tells us, were their origins on both sides; take them for the voluptuaries they were.

Domesticity not only punctures the dignity of individuals but also levels the pretensions of their public actions. The clash of Cain and Abel was the model: "From that moment onward the entire human race never ceased to commit one execrable crime after another."[423] With Gregory, feuds inside families and out are not an exotic import, acclimatized to Roman Gaul by Visigoths, Burgundians, and lately Franks. They are the customary expression of human aggression, ranging from public wars between Franks and Thuringians to petty quarrels between fellow townsmen and kindred joined by marriage. Gregory's brother, Peter, was the victim of a feud involving a strictly Gallo-Roman cast of characters, and God Himself righteously avenged wrongs done to His servants.[424] Gregory's insensitivity to the "barbarian" origin of feud poses a problem to any student of the early Middle Ages. Was everyone as forgetful as he of the presumably more refined procedures of Roman law? Does his predilection for exceptional incidents illuminate the margins rather than the norm of contemporary legality?[425] Whatever the case may be, the prominence of domestic passions and motives, and the absence of distinctions between private revenge and public war, are additional steps in Gregory's elimination from the *Histories* of anything resembling decorous politics. It need not have been less possible to portray the Merovingians as far-sighted statesmen than it was for Procopius to evoke a suitably emperorlike Justinian. But, whereas the Greek historian exposed the underside of the reign in a separate book, Gregory made one

[421] *Hist.* 2.12.

[422] *Hist.* 2.42; 3.22, 5.32, 9.33, 10.8.

[423] *Hist.* 1.3.

[424] *Hist.* 3.4, 7-8 (Franks and Thuringians), 7.47, 10.27 (in cities), 5.32 (possibly a deliberate account of Frankish behavior), 5.5 (Gregory's brother), 3.33, 35 (other Gallo-Romans); GM 79 (God). Wallace-Hadrill, "Bloodfeud of the Franks," remains the classic exposition.

[425] Scholars are beginning to abandon the assumption that feud was strictly a "Germanic" import and are turning their attention instead to the variety of ways in which criminal offenses were dealt with in Roman law.

choice and stuck to it: royal and episcopal actions were private conduct writ large.[426]

Gregory rarely mentions the mighty for any other reason than to abase them.[427] Besides, he reserves special animus for social climbers, ever a target for satirists. Andarchius and Leudast, two slaves whom royal favor elevates to great power, earn the grim rewards of their temerity. They are not alone.[428] Humble men who stay in their place occur chiefly as innocent victims of "slaughters" occasioned by others. An unnamed pauper reenacts the story of the widow's mite, and the slave cook Leo stars in one of Gregory's most lyrical tales (closely allied to the repertory of ancient romance).[429] Gregory, himself a senatorial descendant, did not spare his peers. Just before portraying Childeric's sexual prowess, he alleges, typically, that the emperor Avitus, most illustrious of fifth-century Gallic senators, was deposed "for wishing to act licentiously (*luxuriosae*)"; and he compliments Sidonius Apollinaris, a paragon of fine writing, by portraying him in the role of an underdog, deprived of all his powers as bishop by rebellious clergy.[430]

Gregory's care to strip away finery and leave men bare suggests a final observation. Many modern accounts of the passage from Rome to Middle Ages stress the encounter between barbarism and civilization, sometimes called "the clash of civilizations."[431] That there were cultural differences between the established population and the newcomers is self-evident; but is it certain, as our accounts take for granted, that these cultures may truly be said to have met, locked horns, or engaged in any other sort of collective encounter?[432] A demurral, not lacking pertinence by way of analogy, comes

---

[426] In the *Wars*, Procopius portrayed a statesmanlike Justinian (not without occasional touches of criticism); while composing his decorous history, he simultaneously vented his bile in the scurrilous *Anecdota*. See now Cameron, *Procopius*, pp. 49-83.

[427] For laymen, the eulogistic obituary of Duke Chrodinus is unique (*Hist.* 6.20). This is not because other estimable laymen were lacking; Fortunatus found many who merited complimentary poems.

[428] *Hist.* 4.46, 5.48-49, 6.32.

[429] See above, nn. 280, 282.

[430] *Hist.* 2.11 (Avitus), 22-3 (Sidonius). See above, n. 346.

[431] "Le heurt des civilisations": Lucien Musset, *Les invasions. Les vagues germaniques*, Nouvelle Clio 12 (Paris 1965), p. 177; cf. Paolo Brezzi, *L'urto delle civiltà nell'alto medioevo. Dagli stanziamento barbarici all'unificazione carolingia* (Rome 1971).

[432] The existence of a clash between two cultural levels has been taken for granted rather than demonstrated. In its original sense *barbarus* was contrasted as *un*civilized to civilized, the "other" *vis-à-vis* the "one." A gap of this sort may endure without limit of time, or it may be bridged overnight. The Greeks, after they were incorporated into Rome's empire, did not stop calling the Romans "barbarians"; some Jews remained alien to Hellenism, others were Hellenized. What one people called the next depended on their respective ways of life, not on whether one was objectively more or less civilized than the other. Our notion of passing through "levels" of civilization, however, implies a gradual or evolutionary process, presumably accompanied by the same tensions and conflicts that accompany the rearing of a child. This idea was foreign to classical antiquity and arose largely in the European Enlightenment; cf. Breisach, *Historiography*, pp. 205-209. To find clashes between "high" Romans and "low"

from more recent observations of the convergence of cultures deemed to contrast sharply with one another:

> In the colonial experience, the image is not that of a world of science confronting the world of magic. Very often it is only that of mediocrity encountering superstition, since "the closest contact often occurs at the least desirable level." . . . "Civilisation" does not contact "barbarism." . . . What happens is, that men make contact with other men. . . . The processes of colonisation are thus all on the personal level.[433]

This point of view has obvious relevance to the understanding of so major, and detailed, a source for the invasion period as Gregory's narrative. The *Histories*, instead of documenting the encounter of Romanity and barbarism that moderns postulate as having taken place, portrays all events in personal terms, and allows no whisper to be heard of cultural contrast, conflict, or enrichment. Ferdinand Lot, who carefully traced the presumed processes by which barbarians "fused" with the Roman population, pointed to Gregory as prime witness to the fusion of Gallo-Romans and Franks.[434] Lot may be right, but Gregory does not himself intimate that the Gaul of his time stood at the end of such a process. Nothing in the *Histories*, other than Clovis's baptism, suggests that a cultural rapprochement had taken place or, what is more important, that any was needed. Gregory attests to a state of mind very much attuned to the "personal level" of the quotation—a valuation of men, negative and positive, based on criteria far simpler than their cultural backgrounds.

Hardly anything contributes more to Gregory's implication of cultural homogeneity than his disregard, earlier observed, of ethnic differences.[435] There are references, of course, to Franks, Huns, Thaifals, Syrians, Jews, Bretons, and several others, including Persarmenians. The word "barbarian," though infrequent, is not avoided. Yet, the many pages of the *Histories* leave these ethnic names almost bereft of content. There is supposed to be something definitely Frankish about axes cleaving skulls, especially from behind. Gregory makes the point as a grim joke, by repetition. (Every satire

---

barbarians, one is best advised to read such classics of Romanticism as Thierry's *Récits* (above, n. 8) or its source of inspiration, Chateaubriand's prose epic *Les martyrs* (1809), bks. V-X. The same modern ideas, in more respectable dress, appear in, for example, Marc Bloch's suggestion that Rome and the Germans represented "two types of societies that had each attained unequal levels of evolution," and that antagonism between them resulted when "more archaic institutions" came into contact with "des institutions d'un modèle plus évolué": "Sur les grandes invasions. Quelques positions de problèmes," (1940-45), in Bloch, *Mélanges historiques*, 2 vols. (Paris 1963) I, 104.

[433] Thornton, "Jekyll and Hyde in the Colonies," pp. 226-27; this is an extended review of the English tr. (1964) of O. Mannoni, *La psychologie de la colonisation* (1950), from which the internal quotations are drawn.

[434] Lot, *Invasions germaniques*, pp. 165-276.

[435] See above, n. 223.

needs a central image, often of cannibalism, as in Swift's *Modest Proposal*.)[436] Merely colorful ethnic traits are few: Frankish kings wore their hair long (were short haircuts the rule for all other males?); at the end of Frankish meals, the tables were removed; barbarians were partial to sweetened wine flavored with wormwood (like our vermouth?); consecrated wands were the Frankish sign of diplomatic safe conduct; Bretons were distinctive in costume and hair style (the distinctiveness of their Church goes unmentioned). These five items come close to being the total harvest.

Even the intrusive problem of language, soon to be interestingly aired by Bede, is all but ignored. When Spanish Goths turned up in Tours, Gregory engaged them in theological debate without apparent linguistic difficulty. Perhaps there was none, but how can we be sure?[437] Gregory conspicuously lacks a collective label for persons of the same background as himself. Goths, he says, call persons of our faith *Romani*. It is not his word; he is an Arvernian. Other men are also tagged by their home towns, as the alternative to the ethnic labels Frank, Saxon, etc. But nothing in Gregory's usage corresponds to our term "Gallo-Roman." Predictably, the cultural traits of the Romance majority are taken for granted.[438] Ethnicity is incidental to the *Histories*, far more incidental than it probably was in the daily lives of Gregory's contemporaries or even in that of the bishop himself. His systematic insensitivity to ethnic differences went hand in hand with the leveling of earthly dignities and pretensions. The presence among his featured holy men of a Thaifal, a Breton, a Lombard, and a Thuringian showed, if illustration were needed, that God took no account of tribal origins in choosing His friends.[439]

In contrast to ethnicity, the defense of orthodoxy attracts a great deal of Gregory's attention. Its prominence as a theme in the *Histories* is not self-explanatory. For more than a half-century, Arian kings had been cleared from all but a small part of Gaul and, for good measure, from Italy and Africa as well.[440] Gregory had resided since birth in a land safe for Catholicism, in which even a memory of persecution at the hands of heretics would

[436] *Hist.* 2.27, 40, 42 (all three associated with Clovis), 7.14, 8.30, 36, 10.27 (Fredegonde). On central images, Paulson, *Fictions of Satire*, p. 9.

[437] Goffart, "Foreigners," pp. 80-81, 83-84, 96 n. 2; on language, 87-88.

[438] *Ibid.*, pp. 86-87. Thorpe tr., p. 433, has "Gallo-Roman" where Gregory's word is "Latin."

[439] *Ibid.*, pp. 91-92.

[440] The Gallic domination of the Visigoths of Toulouse was reduced to Narbonne and its hinterland (Septimania) after 507. The Burgundians were conquered in 533-34; they had not remained Arian to the last. By the early 530s, the Arian rulers of Africa, by the 550s those of Italy, had been overcome by Justinian's armies. Gregory was born in 538. The Visigoth Euric, apparently the only Arian persecutor in Gaul, died in 484. It would have been hard, under the circumstances, for normal Catholics of Gregory's generation to look around and regard Arianism as an active menace.

not easily have been come by, except in written form. The Spanish Goths, who still held a Gallic enclave, were more threatened in their Arianism than threatening to the Catholics north of their borders. To be sure, the Frankish king Chilperic toyed for a moment with the idea of imposing an Arian-leaning definition of faith, but all it took to discourage him from this plan was a show of temper by a bishop of noted saintliness.[441] From the 550s on, Latin Christendom was genuinely menaced by the schism that separated much of the North Italian Church from the Roman See; it was the first breach since the fourth century in the resolute unity of the Latin Church. Gregory says nothing of it, though his friend Fortunatus ought to have been well informed.[442] The place that Arianism holds in Gregory's preoccupations is hard to account for on the assumption that this tired heresy continued to endanger the Church of Gaul.

The situation Gregory faced may have been that, in the minds of his public, orthodoxy was so unquestioned and unthreatened as no longer to matter enough. The Merovingian kings took no account of it in arranging their marriages. Women from among the pagan Lombards and the Arian Burgundians and Visigoths were married to Frankish kings, and Frankish princesses went in return to the Arian kings of Italy and Spain, as well as to the pagans of Saxon Kent. Catholicism, if not wholly disregarded in these alliances, was a subsidiary consideration.[443] Indifference of another sort showed itself among Gallo-Roman Catholics. Under the year 588, Gregory relates a story mainly situated about twenty years earlier. Pronimius was a native of Bourges, who, for some reason not known to Gregory, emigrated to Gothic Septimania. He was well received there by the (Arian) king and was made (Catholic) bishop of Agde. Pronimius earned a place in the *Histories* by later giving religious offense to his patrons and being forced to return to Frankish territory. His initial emigration is more striking.[444] Were there more subjects of the Catholic kings of the Franks who shared Pronimius's preference for life under Gothic kings, however Arian? Though un-

[441] On the Spanish situation, Thompson, *Goths in Spain*, pp. 29-51. Chilperic dabbles in heresy, *Hist.* 5.44. Gregory portrays himself first trying to talk Chilperic into theological reason, as usual without success.

[442] On the Three Chapters, in general, see Fliche and Martin, *Histoire de l'Église* IV, 476-82, 493-96; Amann, "Trois-chapitres"; Pavan, "Invasioni barbariche," pp. 88-90. Fortunatus appears to have associated with the schismatics: Stein, *Bas-Empire* II, 672-73, 833-34.

[443] Respectively, *Hist.* 3.20, 27, 4.9, 3.5, 4.27-28; 3.31, 1, 10, 5.38; 4.26, 9.26. Gregory often leaves out the nationality. Whether the Lombards were pagans or something else is not specified; they were not Catholic (below, n. 450). Bede informs us that Charibert's daughter in Kent was assured freedom to practice her religion and had a personal bishop (*H.E.* 1.25). Gregory shows three Frankish princesses resisting conversion to Arianism (below, n. 447), and indicates that the third among them was encouraged to retain her faith (next note).

[444] *Hist.* 9.24; Leuvigild learned that Pronimius had urged Ingund to resist conversion to Arianism.

answerable, the question invites us to wonder how nostalgic the denizens of southern Gaul—Gregory's audience—might have been for the Burgundian and Gothic régimes that the Franks had displaced. Neither line of Arian kings was wholly beyond memory or blackened by famous crimes. Both might, in receding into the past, have gained luster by comparison with the Frankish present. Even Gregory acknowledges, though not in the *Histories*, that one Burgundian king, a victim of Frankish brutality, had won veneration as a martyr.[445] The *Histories* is far from idealizing the current dynasty. Nevertheless, Gregory leaves us in no doubt that the Franks were an improvement over their predecessors: they brought security to Catholicism from Arian mischief.

Book II, which narrates the advent of the Franks and Clovis's life, also contains our introduction to Arianism. Nothing is said earlier about the origins of the heresy in Roman Alexandria or its history in the fourth-century Empire. At Adrianople in 378, Valens earns death for having drafted monks into the army, not (as Orosius specified) for infecting the Goths with Arian error. The closest Gregory comes to mentioning Roman Arianism is to refer to Hilary of Poitiers being exiled by the doing of unnamed heretics.[446] Though Gregory obviously knew better, he reserved Arianism for the blackening of certain lines of kings. Book II supplies a catalogue of their atrocities: Vandals brutally torturing a young Spanish girl (as a lead-off, nicely anticipating the fate of the Frankish princesses Chlothild the Younger and Ingund); further Vandal horrors and an attempt to fake a miracle; an early (pagan) Gothic king associated with persecution by heretics; King Euric cutting off Catholic heads and blocking church doors with briars; a bishop dragged off from Tours to Spanish captivity; the Burgundian Arian Gundobad teetering on the brink of orthodoxy, but too obstinate to take the plunge.[447] Arianism occasions what may be Gregory's most credulous statement: the Ostrogothic princess Amalasuntha, to avenge her slave-lover, murdered her mother by pouring poison into the communion

---

[445] GM 74. Cf. *Hist.* 3.5-6. Sigismund, a convert to Catholicism with the murder of his son to atone for, founded the great monastery of Agaune.

[446] Orosius *Hist.* 7.33. About all this, see above, n. 207.

[447] *Hist.* 2.2 (cf. 3.10, Chlothild; 5.38, Ingund; both cases feature physical abuse of the resisting Catholic), 3.4 (Athanaric associated with heresy by implication and never qualified a pagan), 24 (Gregory cites as evidence Sidonius *Epist.* 7.6, whose account is largely at odds with his), 26, 34.

In 2.28, the Burgundian king Gundioc is said to be "ex genere Athanarici regis persecutoris, cui supra meminimus" (K-L p. 73). This is often taken to be genealogical information, establishing a blood tie between Visigothic kingship and the Burgundian dynasty; e.g. Wolfram, *Gesch. d. Goten*, p. 28 with n. 23. Gregory's meaning probably is less factual and more tendentious. He meant that the Burgundian king belonged to that tribe of persecuting heretical kings about whom he had been talking. Since none of the Burgundians was reputed a persecutor of Catholics, Gregory had to blacken them by association.

chalice; only the devil could have allowed this to happen, Gregory comments, for if we Catholics drank poison in the name of the coequal Trinity, we would come to no harm.[448] The *Histories* gives little support to the idea that the Arian Visigoths had at least saved Gaul from Attila's Huns. Yes, they were at the battle, aiding Aëtius, but the real action belonged to Sts. Peter and Paul, as well as to Bishop Anianus of Orléans; the Hunnic army was routed by Catholic prayers, regardless of who did the actual fighting. Besides, Arian persecution was not just a matter of ancient history. It made victims of two Merovingian princesses and was loosed only yesterday by King Leuvigild upon the Catholics of Spain, whom he tried to win over to an insidious profession of faith. The Arians were obstinate; no torrent of biblical truth would sway them from error.[449] Arianism had ceased to be a threat to anyone by the time the *Histories* ends (591); even the Spanish Goths, prompted by King Reccared, had abandoned the heresy.[450] Meanwhile, Gregory had it play a decisive part in imparting to *gesta praesentia* a religious sense that others might have been less sensitive to than he.[451] Gregory's forgetful audience was reminded that the Catholic Church of Gaul had been fiercely assailed by Arian attacks and had been saved by the pagan convert Clovis. Whatever other virtues the Merovingians lacked, they had gotten where they had by God's nurturing, to preserve His Church from enduring foes.

What had they made of themselves after expelling the Arians? The Fredegar chronicle, dated ca. 660, includes a famous legend prophesying Merovingian decline. Clovis's parents, on their wedding night, saw apparitions indicating that their son would be like a lion, his sons like leopards and unicorns, theirs like bears and wolves, and the fourth generation like dogs and lesser beasts.[452] Gregory is unlikely to have directly inspired this legend: his good words for the second and third generations of Merovingians are too few. But the *Histories* does tend to leave the impression that, after Clovis, the course was downhill. Normal expectations are that the first herolike layman encountered in a historical narrative (with another century to go before the end) should not also be the last. Because we find no heroic Franks beyond book II, we suspect something is seriously wrong.

[448] *Hist.* 3.31. The misrepresentation of Amalasuntha is somewhat more extreme than that of Theodoric, GM 39 (portrayed as the martyrdom of Pope John). Cf. the Italian versions: *Excerpta Valesiana* 2.83-95; Gregory the Great *Dial.* 4.31 (GM 39 contains elements of both).

[449] Repulse of the Huns, *Hist.* 2.7. The princesses, n. 447 above. Leuvigild's attempted compromise, 6.18. Arian obstinacy, 5.43, 6.40.

[450] *Hist.* 9.15-16. Gregory seems unaware that some Lombards were Arian; but we, too, are poorly informed of religious conditions among the Lombards at this time; see Fanning, "Lombard Arianism Reconsidered."

[451] Thompson, *Goths in Spain*, pp. 26-27, rightly emphasizes that political and religious sympathies normally did not coincide. Gregory evidently wanted them to.

[452] Fredegar *Chron.* 3.12.

The answer has sometimes been thought to be straightforward: the Merovingians precipitously declined from early valor; "Clovis was the only moment of light before the long darkness into which his descendants led the Frankish kingdom and people."[453] Vinay developed the alternative possibility that Gregory continued after Clovis to find embodiments of Frankish heroism: several major characters whom Gregory deplored nevertheless excited positive emotions in him for expressing the barbaric energy and forcefulness Clovis had exemplified; it was typical that the most criminal moment of Fredegonde's career occasions no avenging thunderbolt, or even a verbal explosion from Gregory; the historian's silence (Vinay concluded) signified his renewed acknowledgment of Frankish instincts and uncontrollable impulses as a constructive force. Other *miseri*, such as the patrician Mummolus, are argued to have aroused the same response from Gregory.[454] However provocative Vinay's suggestion is as an alternative to the objective character of Merovingian decline, it arises from a misreading of Gregory's irony. Accounts of misconduct that omit statements of outrage do not express the author's tacit wonder at elemental energies. Rather, they understate deliberately and invite readers to supply whatever amplifications the text implies.[455] There is no getting away from the dearth of heroic prowess in the *Histories*.

Ulfilas, the fourth-century apostle of the Goths, is said to have omitted the books of Kings from his translation of the Bible, so as to avoid stoking the aggressive disposition of a war-loving people. Without resorting to the same expedient, Christian authors addressing fellow Romans had long been just as emphatic as Ulfilas in denying applause to the military virtues.[456] The scarcity of these virtues in Gregory's *Histories* may be observed even before the Franks come onto the scene. The Israelites spend forty years in the desert learning the law, but no attention is paid to their conquest of the Promised Land. The *viri fortes* who periodically freed them from alien subjection are never named. Gregory's closest approximation of a Roman hero is Theodosius I: his weapons were vigils and prayers rather than the sword.[457] Aëtius, whose name surely retained luster in Gregory's Gaul, is neatly disposed of: Bishop Anianus of Orléans calls him out of Arles to deal

[453] Oldoni tr., I, xliv.

[454] Vinay, *San Gregorio*, pp. 88-100.

[455] A good example of Gregory's understatement is the account of the sack of Convenae, cited above, n. 285.

[456] Philostorgius *H.E.* 2.5. In addition to the obvious Orosius, a striking example is the *Epitome de Caesaribus* 1, 13, 15, in which neither Augustus nor Trajan (though called *bellicosus*) is singled out for military exploits, and Antoninus Pius earns special praise for maintaining peace.

[457] *Hist.* 1.11 (the Israelites simply cross the Jordan and "receive" the Promised Land), 12 (*viri fortes*), 42-43 (twice mentioned that Theodosius put all his hope in God).

with the Huns; the bishop's prayers win the battle; the prayers of Aëtius's wife in Rome save him from death; Aëtius tricks his Gothic and Frankish allies away from the scene of victory, collects all the booty from the battle-field, and goes home; only then is he properly introduced, not in Gregory's words but in an excitedly admiring quotation from the contemporary historian Renatus Frigeridus, at once followed by Gregory's report of the great general's murder and its violent revenge.[458] In this assemblage of fragmentary frames, the need to satisfy the expectations of the audience for praise of Aëtius's heroic stature is combined with the resolve to cut a *vir fortis* down to merely human size.

Where Clovis is concerned, the portrayal of "an ideal figure" realizing the divine plan to convert the Franks and rid Gaul of Arianism is far more deeply shadowed by heinous crimes than any comparable narrative in Bede.[459] When Clovis first comes before us, he is helped by Ragnachar, his fellow king, in overcoming the Roman Syagrius. Just before book II ends with Clovis's death, Ragnachar returns, to be killed in the last of three brutally vivid stories of how Clovis did away with his royal Frankish relatives. There is no mistaking the mode of these stories. They are all ironic encounters of bad with worse, leaving it for us to decide whether Clovis or his victims were more depraved.[460] Gregory's supposedly naïve line about Clovis—"For daily God laid low his enemies before his hand and augmented his kingdom, for he walked before Him with an upright heart and did what was pleasing in His sight"—occurs as a comment at the end of the first in this unedifying series.[461] If really meant to justify Clovis's murderous duplicity, its purpose would have been better served by quietly glossing over this phase of the reign. Gregory took the opposite course, intensifying the horror beyond any need of relating the facts. His comment, in conspicuously biblical language, casts our minds back to the Old Testament and its highly ambiguous kings who walked before God with an upright heart but

[458] Treatment of Aëtius, *Hist.* 2.7-8. It cannot be accidental that the only action of his that Gregory reports is vaguely discreditable.

[459] Cf. Bede *H.E.* 3.1-3, 6, 9, 12 (Oswald), 3.14, 24, 4.5 (Oswy), 4.12, 15, 16, 5.7 (Cædwalla). Oswy comes closest to Clovis in having negative traits, but he is not presented in such a way as to shock readers' sensibilities. Cædwalla is safely pagan throughout the violent phase of his career. Edwin, the first Northumbrian royal convert, reminds one of Clovis, but is consistently laudable: *H.E.* 2.9-14; cf. below, ch. IV nn. 290-92.

Wood, "Gregory of Tours and Clovis," is primarily concerned with the historical Clovis, about whose career he says much of importance. He is tempted (p. 272) by the idea of seeing Bede's account of Edwin as dependent on Gregory's of Clovis.

[460] Ragnachar, *Hist.* 2.27, 42, (the two other crimes) 40, 41. Paulson, *Fictions of Satire*, p. 43, points out that real satiric action is a movement from bad to worse. The three Clovis crimes have this pattern, characteristic of Gregory's storytelling as seen above, nn. 284, 286.

[461] On this line, Kurth, "De l'autorité," pp. 201-202. Traditionally, it has been taken to characterize Gregory's peculiar tolerance for crime provided it was carried out by the right person.

who were hardly Christians. Louis Halphen observed that the very chapter
to which these words are appended evokes the unsavory stratagem by which
Ehud, savior of the Children of Israel, slew the king of Moab (Judg. 3:15-
26).[462] Though there was heroism of a sort in Clovis, as in the biblical prototypes, no one was to blind himself to the profound defects of the prowess
they and he embodied. For him to be called a new Constantine at baptism
was qualified praise, since that emperor had killed his wife and son.[463]
Clovis was no *roi très chrétien* himself, but he at least made it possible for his
descendants to learn this role, by gaining the enlightenment he and the
biblical heroes lacked.

In two prefaces, Gregory holds up Clovis as model, once of God's reward
to champions of orthodoxy, the next time—to current kings—of achievement in battle against foreign peoples.[464] Nevertheless, the contemporary
books contain very little that might serve to arouse the Merovingians to
martial endeavors. Childebert II made war on the (non-Catholic) Lombards; they had formerly invaded Gaul and, though repulsed, had never
been counterattacked. Gregory utters no words of approval, still less of
praise. On the contrary, he takes every opportunity to spell out the losses
and futility of Childebert's campaigns.[465] Was Gregory more amenable to
military action against the Arian Goths, who still held a part of Gaul and
had lately harmed a Catholic Frankish princess? One would not think so
from his account of the expedition ordered by King Guntram. The staunch-
est opponent of the campaign could not have more effectively described its
squalor and ridiculed its sequels.[466] As bishop of Tours, Gregory was very
conscious of Breton border raiding, yet Frankish countermeasures are
scathingly portrayed. The usurpation of Gundovald was a grave danger to
social order. What defeated him was not the incompetent attacks of the
army sent against him, but the cowardice and treachery of his supporters.
Again, the patrician Mummolus proved very effective in defending the
kingdom against Lombard invaders and their Saxon allies; he gained his position by deceiving his father, soon defected from his king, and ended his
life as the strong arm of a rebel, whom he betrayed.[467] King Sigibert earns
more praise for extricating himself from defeat by the Avars than for pre-

[462] Halphen, "Grégoire de Tours," pp. 36-37.

[463] The Constantine whom Gregory mentions in connection with Clovis is the one of the
Sylvester legend (*Hist.* 2.31). The main reference to Constantine (1.36) mentions his killing
of son and wife, but not his conversion; Helena overshadows her son. Clovis's mother, however, was the lustful Basina, hardly a Helena.

[464] *Hist.* 3.*praef.*, 5. *praef.* (quoted above n. 402).

[465] *Hist.* 6.42, 9.25, 29, 10.3.

[466] *Hist.* 8.30, also 8.45 (Desiderius), 9.31-32.

[467] *Hist.* 5.29, 10.9 (Bretons), 7.38 (Gundovald), 4.42, 6.1, 7.38 (Mummolus).

viously vanquishing them.[468] The inglorious flavor of all these stories cannot be ascribed only to the military incompetence of Gregory's contemporaries. Gregory abhorred civil conflict, but had no more liking for war of any other sort. Committed to the peaceful resolution of disputes, avoiding the ways of Cain, he was not the sort of author from whom a gallery of great captains might be expected, even if they had lived within his sight.

Gregory made no secret of where heroism was located. It was exemplified by the two unnamed lovers who disappointed the expectations of their families and remained chaste throughout marriage, and by Leo the Cook, who extricated Attalus from captivity. Hospicius of Nice was a hero, and so were Salvius of Albi, the Lombard Vulfolaic, Aredius of Limoges, and many others.[469] Real *virtus* emanated daily from the miracle-working tombs of the Christian world. The models of heroism were the martyrs and confessors hierarchically ordered in the *Wonders*. A history that proceeds by juxtaposing the *virtutes sanctorum* to the *excidia miserorum* has no place for heroism in any but a religious setting. Clovis did not perform posthumous miracles. As a pagan, he had had the merit of respecting bishops and listening to his Catholic wife. So disposed, he had gained divine help in battle and been converted with his people. He had not only championed Catholicism against the Arians but had also taken care to safeguard the possessions of St. Martin in the ensuing war.[470] These acts were highly commendable, and they had won Clovis and his descendants great earthly rewards. As to whether Clovis had also gained admittance to heaven, there was no information.

Alongside the authentic heroism of the *amici Dei*, the deeply flawed Clovis subsides into being merely the heaven-blessed founder of a royal line within which rulers of comparable merit were rare but not wholly absent. For the attribute of empire building that makes Clovis so outstanding a Merovingian in our eyes counts for Gregory only to the extent that empire was given by God. The qualities to be sought among kings were not efficiency, farsightedness, enterprise, or military leadership, but moral excellence, gained (as Gregory once said, adapting St. Paul) by internal struggle of the spirit against the flesh and liberation from the bondage of avarice.[471] Even in Orosius's *Seven Books*, Theodosius I is far more exemplary than

----

[468] *Hist.* 4.29, 23.

[469] *Hist.* 1.47 (the Two Lovers), 3.15 (Leo), 6.6 (Hospicius), 5.44, 50, 7.1 (Salvius), 10.29 (Aredius).

[470] *Hist.* 2.27, 29-31, 37; 3.*praef.* For the biblical reminiscences in this narrative (Moses crossing the Red Sea, the pillar of fire, the overcoming of Pharaoh, the walls of Jerico), see Pietri, *Ville de Tours*, pp. 774-76.

[471] *Hist.* 5.*praef.*, K-L p. 194: "Si tibi, o rex, bellum civili delectat, illut quod apostolus in hominem agi meminit exerce, ut spiritus concupiscat adversus carnem et vitia virtutibus caedant."

Constantine. Gregory agreed. Among recent emperors, he all but omitted Justinian and was hardly displeased that Justin II, grasping and suspected of heresy, went insane.[472] There was a model emperor in Gregory's day, one even preferable to Theodosius. Tiberius II was a true Christian, of surpassing openhandedness, who had no need to fear his enemies because he had put his faith in God; "so long as he continued to take pleasure in distributing alms to the poor our Lord went on providing him with more and more to give." The resounding victory of his forces over the Persians was an incidental consequence of his virtues.[473] As God's generosity lavished miracles upon humankind through His saints, so was the pre-eminent royal virtue heedless giving to relieve the wants of the needy, and cupidity the pre-eminent sin. The descendants of Clovis could not shine in the *Histories* by offering proofs of temporal success. What there was of that—an appreciable quantity—has to be gathered indirectly from Gregory's narrative and other sources. Gregory measured their greatness, if any, by the same standard of unworldliness that made a model of Tiberius II.

One would like to know what reputation the Merovingians had among Gregory's contemporaries, for it seems certain that some at least of his portrayals do not reflect what was generally thought. The two other kings in whom he found virtue—Theudebert and Guntram—might be held back for a moment. Those lacking redeeming qualities are nevertheless differentiated. Among the sons of Clovis, it is hardly surprising that Chlodomer, butcher of Sigismund of Burgundy, and Theuderic, ravager of Auvergne, should be uniformly dark.[474] Childebert I called for more complex treatment. In Gregory's telling he wholly lacks qualities. He pretends to compassion and delicacy of feelings while continually dabbling, unsuccessfully, in the same power games as his brothers.[475] Fortunatus, a friend of Gregory's, calls Childebert "gentle, wise, good, treating all alike" and uniquely concerned with "the glory of bishops," altogether an outstanding exemplar

---

[472] Orosius *Hist.* 7.35 (cf. Augustine *Civ. Dei* 5.26). On Gregory's neglect of Justinian, n. 208 above. On Justin II, *Hist.* 4.40.

[473] Quotation, *Hist.* 5.19; victory over the Persians, 4.40, 5.19, 30. A Byzantine history of Heraclian date is also positive though more restrained: Theophylact Simocatta *Historiae* 1.2. 3-7, tr. M. and M. Whitby (Oxford 1986), pp. 22-23. Tiberius does not have a comparably good press with modern historians; e.g. Bury, *History of the Later Roman Empire from Arcadius to Irene*, II, 79-82. About both him and Justin II, Cameron, "Early Byzantine *Kaiserkritik*."

[474] *Hist.* 3.6 (Chlodomer), 3.2, 7, 8, 9, 11-15, 23, 34-35 (Theuderic I). Neither one is taxed with sexual irregularity. It was hardly necessary.

[475] *Hist.* 3.9-10 (conspires to seize Auvergne, then runs away), 15 (makes and breaks alliance with Theuderic), 18 (plays a heinously hypocritical part in the murder of his nephews), 23-24 (flip-flops again), 28 (engages in civil war), 31 (cheats Chlothar but is outdone in cheating), 4.16, 17, 20 (incites Chramn against his father, then dies), 6.29 (welcomed Chlothar's repudiated bastard Gundovald). On the plus side, 3.10 (distributed to churches the church plate looted in Spain), 28 (did penance for civil war when it was stopped by a divinely occasioned storm).

of the "king benefactor of the Church."[476] Others agreed. As late as 575, almost two decades after Childebert's death, his former subjects remained attached to his name.[477] Gregory thought it important, on the contrary, that Childebert should look especially contemptible.

Another candidate for public applause was Chlothar I, the last of Clovis's sons, who reunited the entire kingdom in his last years. Three decades after his death, when Chilperic's infant successor was baptized, it was deemed a great compliment for the child to be named Chlothar after his grandfather.[478] Gregory's Chlothar, however, is not someone whose name one should be pleased to bear. In addition to the faults he shared with his brothers, he could not control his troops and let them blunder into disaster; he tried to mulct the Church and backed down; his domestic life was extraordinarily irregular; he let his son Chramn carry on at such lengths as to have to be suppressed in regular war; on his deathbed, he finally realized that God was powerful enough to kill someone as great as himself.[479] Though free of Childebert's hypocrisy, he surely lacked merit of any kind.

The third generation from Clovis lost two of its four members by 575. Charibert, the eldest, is a fleeting figure in the *Histories*, seen mainly as a sensualist. Sigibert, whose widow Brunichild lived when Gregory wrote, emerges in his account as a man of military ability, with the ambition such talents encourage. His restless and unrestrained aggressiveness, typified by the recruitment of wild men from beyond the Rhine for his civil war, outweighed the apparent austerity of his sex life.[480] Gregory flanks Sigibert, at the moment of his murder, with a Gothic adviser and a parvenu chamberlain, who are killed or wounded with him. Instead of being invited to mourn the king, we are told of the chamberlain's misdeeds.[481] Sigibert's main rival, Chilperic, is so prominent as Gregory's leading royal villain as

[476] Reydellet, *Royauté*, pp. 322-28; cf. Collins, "Theodebert I," pp. 32-33; Brennan, "Image of the Frankish Kings," p. 7.

[477] *Hist.* 4.51.

[478] *Hist.* 4.21 (Gregory draws no attention to the reunification of the kingdom, usually applauded in our books, e.g. Lot, *End of the Ancient World*, pp. 321-22), 10.28 (Guntram stresses that Chlothar II has been named after his grandfather).

[479] *Hist.* 3.18 (combines with Childebert to murder his nephews), 4.2 (abortive attempt to tax the Church), 3 (sex life), 13 (does not control his troops), 13, 16-17, 20 (Chramn), 21 (deathbed). Reydellet, *Royauté*, p. 411, points out that Chlothar's are the only "last words" recorded by Gregory; he oddly concludes that the deathbed scene reveals "un homme d'une rare élévation spirituelle."

[480] Charibert: *Hist.* 4.26. Sigibert: 4.23, 29, 30 (aggression against Guntram), 47 (dispute with Guntram), 49, 50 (tribes from across the Rhine, which he cannot control; bullies Guntram), 51.

[481] *Hist.* 4.51; "Gothic" was not a neutral nationality in Gregory's vocabulary because of its association with Arianism. Nie, "Roses in January," p. 287, thinks Gregory admired Sigibert; Dalton I, 60-61, classes him among the "better Merovingian kings." Sigibert tends to be appealing to modern authors; this is not the impression Gregory wishes to convey.

to need special comment. To complete the catalogue, one might mention Sigibert's son, Childebert II, after whose years Gregory dates books V-X. A child in 575, Childebert II was over twenty-one by the end of the *Histories*. He remains a shadow in Gregory's narrative, giving orders when too young to do so personally, and never seeming to take command, though he may eventually have done so. His mother, Brunichild, also fails to gain firm shape despite an appreciable series of appearances.[482] Could Gregory risk speaking his mind about them? He would probably have been more forthcoming if either one had given signs of Christian rulership.

Chilperic has proved fascinating to modern readers of Gregory. E. K. Rand even presented him as a "brighter aspect" of Merovingian times.[483] None of Gregory's kings attracts more attention to himself. Chilperic appears by turns as a would-be poet and theologian, who rebuilt amphitheaters to hold games, added letters to the alphabet, and had a realistic view of how much money and power was flowing to the Church. He was the only sixth-century Merovingian who forcibly converted Jews. He cultivated diplomatic relations with Byzantium and with the Byzantine-influenced Visigoth, Leuvigild, and gives the impression of having himself aped Byzantine rulership.[484] Everything that has given Chilperic modern appeal made him loathsome to Gregory, who has nevertheless won credit for "supplying all the elements . . . of a just appreciation of [Chilperic's] character and ideas."[485] Gregory even includes moments when Chilperic, without doing

[482] Childebert II is the subject of verbs of action when far too young to make decisions: *Hist.* 6.1, 11, 42, 7.6. After he comes of age (7.33), his main activity is to preside over a purge (8.34, 9.8-10, 12, 14, 10.19). He intercedes in favor of Theodore of Marseille (8.13) and acts wisely concerning the alleged culprits sent by Maurice (10.24). Gregory observes him up close (8.14), but has nothing to report.

Brunichild marries her nephew (5.2); welcomes a refugee from the Gundovald debacle (7.43); Guntram is suspicious of her (7.33, 8.4, 9, 28, 31); she does not replace Childebert's *nutritor* (8.22). All these are ambiguous, but tilting slightly toward the negative. Other ambiguous facts have a positive slant: she was scorned by the nobles after Sigibert's death (6.4, 9.8-9), and was the target for many of Fredegonde's attempts at assassination (7.20, 8.29). These and other items have nourished modern historical imagination; there are many assessments of Brunichild (the most comprehensive is Kurth, "Reine Brunehaut"). But Gregory himself seems to be resolutely noncommittal. The one certainty is that he does not credit her with the virtues he prizes (and applauds in women like Chlothild, Radegund, and Ingoberga).

[483] Rand, "Brighter Aspects." Chilperic is usually thought to be worthier of esteem than Gregory makes him out to be. Cf. Reydellet, *Royauté*, p. 419, "La puissante originalité du roi de Neustrie lui [i.e. to Gregory] a, semble-t-il, échappé"; Dalton I, 62, 66.

[484] *Hist.* 5.17 (circus), 44 (theology, poetry, and new letters), 6.5, 17 (forcible conversions), 46 (poetry and realism about the Church). Relations with Byzantium, 6.2; with Leuvigild, 6.18, 33, 34, 40, 45. Chilperic's Byzantine tendencies are suggested by his concern with circus games, magnificence (6.2), and theology (5.44). For interpretation of the passages about Chilperic and the Jews, see Goffart, "Conversions of Bishop Avitus," pp. 480-86.

[485] Reydellet, *Royauté*, p. 419, echoing Buchner, Einleitung, pp. xxx-xxxi. Cf. Kurth, "De l'autorité," pp. 192-94 (stresses how the portrayal of Chilperic documents Gregory's "perfect sincerity").

anything extraordinary, merits sober approval: he (momentarily) lavishes alms upon churches and the poor, acts against a corrupt count, delivers to Gregory the men who had robbed St. Martin's tomb, hearkens to the advice of wise counselors, is moved by compassion and behaves with restraint, and releases prisoners in honor of the birth of a son.[486] Some hold it to Chilperic's credit that, when Gregory stood accused of having maligned the queen, he was allowed to exonerate himself and escape scot free.[487]

Gregory did not expect that the information he supplied about Chilperic would ever be understood otherwise than as intensifying his verdict that this king was "the Nero and Herod" of the age. Chilperic was the murderer of at least two of his own sons, and of two wives into the bargain. His conduct had, in Gregory's view, unleashed a plague upon the kingdom, massacring innocent babes (it was no excuse that they included Chilperic's own infants). He organized a gratuitous war against a peaceable brother and, in this way, occasioned many thousand more victims, to no purpose.[488] No good came from anything he did. Outwitted at an episcopal council, Chilperic asked in despair, "What may I do that the queen's wishes in this matter might be carried out?" He was a pretentious coward, saved more than once from disaster by a savage but resolute wife, Fredegonde, whose special prominence by Chilperic's side serves above all to demean him.[489]

Two grandsons of Clovis, Theudebert and Guntram, shared in the family faults but, in Gregory's view, also showed something of the founder's true qualities; that is, openness to divine grace. Contemporary sources about Theudebert are more plentiful than about any other Merovingian in the *Histories*, and they assure us that Gregory's portrait, though not necessarily untrue, falls far short of being comprehensive. Theudebert was an active and enterprising warrior, closely engaged for fifteen years in the turbulence arising from Justinian's Western conquests. Agathias called him a bold and restless spirit, who loved danger more than he need have. First of the Frankish kings to strike gold coins, he occasioned great relief in Constantinople by dying before he could pursue his designs for eastward expansion.[490] Foreigners report all this and more, and Marius of Avenches calls

[486] *Hist.* 5.34, 47, 6.10, 19, 22, 23.

[487] *Hist.* 5.49; Kurth, "De l'autorité," p. 194, "incontestable noblesse."

[488] *Hist.* 5.18, 39 (sons), 4.28, 5.39 (wives), 5.34 (epidemic), 6.31 (gratuitous war). Chilperic brought the Merovingians to the brink of biological disaster: at his death, only one grown-up member of the dynasty survived. Gregory was sensitive to considerations of this sort (7.8).

[489] Quotation, *Hist.* 5.18. Chilperic's cowardice, 4.51, 5.34, 6.41. Fredegonde as villainess is larger than life—a satirist's creature and, typically, the most memorable woman in the *Hist.* It is highly doubtful that Gregory admired her in spite of himself, but one easily understands how Vinay came to conclude that he did (above n. 454).

[490] Zöllner, *Gesch. d. Franken*, pp. 87-95; Stein, *Bas-Empire* II, 325-28. Justinian checked his eastward expansion by giving lands to the Lombards and subsidizing them.

him *rex magnus Francorum*.[491] Gregory, without hiding Theudebert's martial valor, scales down his enterprises to a single prudent foray into Italy, yielding great booty but called off as soon as the climate proved unhealthy to the troops. Later successes were won by proxy and wasted by Theudebert's unworthy son.[492] Gregory stresses Theudebert's greatness—he is the unrivaled hero of book III—but its basis, according to him, was anything but military:

Once he was firmly established on the throne, Theudebert proved himself to be a great king, distinguished by every virtue. He ruled his kingdom justly, respected the bishops, was liberal to the churches, relieved the wants of the poor and distributed many benefits with piety and friendly goodwill. With great generosity he remitted to the churches in Clermont-Ferrand all the tribute that they used to pay to the royal treasury.[493]

The historian's approval is unfeigned. Of course, Theudebert also had an unsavory wife, a Gallo-Roman version of Basina, whose bold advances he succumbed to; and a grasping official of his was suitably lynched as soon as Theudebert died. It is predictable that Theudebert's excellence should be qualified.[494] The remarkable thing is Gregory's care to reorient his fame from expansionism by armed force and diplomacy to the tranquil beneficence of a genuine Christian. The few lines just quoted are more likely to encapsulate Gregory's prescription for Merovingian kingship than does his account of Clovis's dazzling success.

Last but not least, Guntram earned the epithet *bonus* from Gregory because he, too, lived up to a model of tranquil beneficence. Gregory's portrayal of Guntram, extending over seven books, is the most detailed and complex in the *Histories*. Vinay gained the impression that, at one time, Gregory rested great hopes in him, but ultimately changed his mind. Oldoni says, "Guntram was Gregory's greatest disapointment."[495] The abundance of material invites exegesis of this sort. Yet Gregory did not long for dynamic kings and expected no consistency in their behavior. What he found in Guntram was an enduring quality of innocence, undimmed by in-

[491] Marius of Avenches *Chron.* 548, ed. Mommsen, p. 236. Collins, "Theodebert I," pp. 7-33.

[492] *Hist.* 3.32; loss of his conquests, 4.9. Gregory's account is a faint shadow of what we know from Byzantine sources.

[493] *Hist.* 3.25, tr. Thorpe, p. 185.

[494] *Hist.* 3.22 (Deuteria abandons her husband to take up with Theudebert), 26 (she arranges her grown-up daughter's death for fear that Theudebert might desire her); 3.36 (the greedy official; see above, nn. 211-12). Deuteria seems to be a cross, in miniature, between Basina and Fredegonde.

[495] Vinay, *San Gregorio*, pp. 135-43; Oldoni tr., I, lx. Reydellet, *Royauté*, wisely concludes (p. 420): "les témoignages sont trop nombreux pour qu'il soit possible de nier que Gontran ne soit, sinon le roi idéal, du moins celui qui s'en raproche le plus aux yeux de Grégoire."

termittent excesses. Guntram listened to bishops; he could be merciful and was certainly open-handed. He had not been a promoter of civil war. He welcomed peace and came closer to caring for his nephews than to dispossessing them.[496] Paul the Deacon, in adapting the *Histories* to his purposes, saw how readily Guntram might be developed into a Frankish counterpart of Tiberius II.[497] Guntram is the only Merovingian whom Gregory credits with miracles.[498] Gregory's approval could hardly have been unanimously shared by public opinion. Guntram, a mere survivor among seven siblings, must have been regarded by many as the most contemptible of Chlothar's sons.[499] All the more reason for Gregory to insist. Christian kingship was not to everyone's taste, but it was through rulers who showed a trace of disinterestedness—something transcending the scuttlings of the *civitas terrena*—that a flicker of divine grace could be seen to infuse the leadership of society.

Gregory's *Histories* are not oriented to our expectation, or even to a Eusebian or Orosian model, of what a history should look like. Their order has to be sought outside the riotous diversity of their contents, in the consequentiality of Gregory's dominant ideas. History, as he portrayed it, did not "go anywhere." It simply was, and had to be narrated as a succession of moments that time itself helped to disconnect from each other. Some moments attested to God's care for mankind and glorified His friends, the saints. Others illustrated the merited end of those who strove after false riches and, more sadly, of their victims. The *Histories* is not a philosophical treatise, but an explanation of current events for the sake of a needful public. Bewildering as present times were they might be confronted calmly if a few notions were kept in mind: that no significant distinction existed between the slave and the bishop, the family and the polity, the bedroom and the council chamber; that ethnicity was an incidental detail; but, on the other hand, that the Catholic Church mattered very much; that sainthood

---

[496] Guntram's excesses: *Hist.* 4.25 (marital irregularities), 26 (tricks Charibert's widow), 5.16 (arbitrary execution), 35 (carries out his late wife's criminal wishes), 10.10 (unjust killing of a chamberlain). Gregory's main disagreement with Guntram was over the treatment of Bishop Theodore of Marseille (6.11, 24, 7.5, 8.12, 20).

Guntram's good points: relations with bishops, *Hist.* 5.20, 6.22 (a bishop bemoans falling from his rule to Chilperic's), 8.1-7, 27; mercy, 8.6, 27; generosity, 7.40, 8.3, 9.20-21; avoids civil war, peaceable, 4.30, 47, 49, 50, 6.19, 31; cares for his nephews, Childebert II, 5.17, 6.11-12 (quarrel), 33 (makes amends), 41, 7.8, 8.4, 13, 45, 9.10-11, 20; Chlothar II, 7.5, 7, 8, 14, 8.9, 31, 9.18, 20, 10.28.

[497] Below, ch. V n. 219.

[498] *Hist.* 9.21.

[499] Guntram has no exploits to his credit; his conduct on several occasions was not just unheroic, but feeble. The behavior of Childebert II's emissaries toward him is tinged with contempt, *Hist.* 7.14. The conspiracy surrounding Gundovald in 584 must have founded its hopes in part on the assumption that the last surviving adult Merovingian was a surmountable obstacle.

was the only heroism; and that kings deserved praise only for exemplifying Christian virtues. When spelled out as stark lessons, these ideas have all the charm and persuasiveness of pious generalities. One easily understands why Gregory, a solicitous teacher, preferred to express them in the shimmering technicolor of his ten books.

10. Conclusion

In the last centuries of the Roman Empire, Clio lost her voice among Latin Christians. The likelihood that this would happen was foreshadowed by St. Jerome when he outlined the history of the Church that he planned to write but never did: "how and through whom, from the coming of the Savior to our day—that is, from the apostles to the dregs of our time—the Church of Christ was born and matured, waxed in persecutions, was crowned with martyrdoms, and, after the coming of Christian emperors, became greater indeed in power and riches but meaner in virtues."[500] The program for Jerome's account was in keeping with the pessimistic masters of Latin historiography. The *Chronicle* of Sulpicius Severus went some way toward carrying it out and, as a result, almost failed to come down to us.[501] The Church histories that found ready ears, Rufinus's translation of Eusebius and Orosius's *Seven Books*, were encouraging tales of a benign Providence. Jerome's gloomy outline, like its profane precursors, would have needed continuing stability and triumphs to sustain its pessimism. After 395, amidst usurpations, heresies, and barbarians, no Christian had any interest in illustrating how "the dregs of our times" might be traced from "the coming of the Savior." Orosius's charge—to show, on the contrary, how well Christian times compared to the past—was a somewhat unsatisfactory alternative and, in any case, dealt with general history rather than with the Church.[502] Unless very carefully tailored (and correspondingly questionable), no serious history of the Church could end on a note of corporate self-satisfaction. Realism and even religious humility recommended the sober schema Jerome proposed. Yet that outline demanded the desolating confession that the glories of the apostolic age were growing ever more remote from the iniquities of the present day. A history that, far from strengthening the Church, could only comfort its enemies was better not written. Nor was it.

Gregory broke the silence by being above all a contemporary historian. It was a choice arising from considerations that are best called philosophical, in however qualified a sense. Gregory proceeds methodically and sup-

[500] Jerome *Vita Malchi, praef.*, *PL* XXIII, 55.
[501] It survives in a unique eleventh-century ms (Halm ed., pp. v-vii) and gained popularity only in the sixteenth: Bernays, "Über die Chronik des Sulpicius Severus," pp. 191-95.
[502] *Hist.* 1.prolog.9-14.

plies adequate clues to his reasoning. The Word made Flesh, the surpassing event of world history, had stripped language of its one-time function as the organizer of sense impressions and reduced it to being a mere instrument of description, requiring no art or sophistication. The written word was de-valued. Meaning was no longer to be sought by meditation upon phenom-ena or abstraction from them. It was apprehensible to everyone, even the uneducated, in the visible and experienced operations of God in the world. Miraculous events, within the historian's purview to record, were the ground of meaning, and the task of a religious teacher was primarily to con-vey to his public a world that, on a day to day basis, made sense in the light of Christian truth. Gregory's goal was pastoral, and contemporary history was his means of persuasion, the only means that, in his view, retained ef-fectiveness when experience alone, rather than words, had the capacity to elicit belief.[503]

The *Wonders* was Gregory's "abstract" work, affirming by sheer repeti-tion those countless individual occurrences of the improbable that rendered vain the systems and abstractions of "the philosophers." But the eight books also embodied an answer to the problem of Church history as ex-pressed by St. Jerome. Undismayed by the glories of any past, Christian or profane, Gregory celebrated the active presence in the here and now of Christ, the Virgin, the Precursor, the apostles, martyrs, early and later con-fessors, and holy men lately deceased. All of them were not just figures out of a bookish past, but perceptible to anyone's senses in the miracles their *virtus* on earth continually performed. A history of Christian growth and evangelization was implicit here, although not spelled out in the order of events, and there was no doubt about its being open-ended: relics, shrines, and miracles could multiply indefinitely in the same way that Gregory showed them to have multiplied in the recent past. They were a cumulative resource. If anyone still yearned for Virgil's "empire without end," here was the one Christ bestowed on His Church, exceeding anyone's greediest ex-pectations. Gregory's *Wonders* are our guide to the rock on which the Church was built and thanks to which it endured the abundant failings un-avoidable in its earthly existence.

This transposition of the golden age of the Church to the everyday of Merovingian Gaul is the foundation of confidence that sustains the pessi-mism, outrage, and irreverence of Gregory's *Histories*. Gregory went straight to the moral heart of Jerome's unwritten history, "the dregs of our time," the subject everyone wanted to hear about; and he got there neither by the dismal route Jerome prescribed nor by Salvian's wholesale avoidance of historical circumstances. Instead, Gregory conjured up a perennial his-

[503] Above, nn. 140-66.

tory reaching back to Adam and Cain and forward to the end of time, a muddle of miraculous blessings and brutal horrors, ever changing and ever the same. Gregory saw no route or direction embedded in the chaos of events. As free from Orosius's ascending line as from Jerome's descending one, he simply took upon himself a personal role as spokesman for his society, responsible for selecting *facta* and transmuting them into meaningful *dicta*.

Whereas the *Wonders* refuted "the philosophers," the *Histories* was Gregory's alternative to the narrative no *philosophans rethor* could be found to write. Indifferent to the novelty of Frankish manners, his muse was stirred by the persistence of an old and fundamentally un-Christian intellectuality. The past mattered enough not only to arouse Gregory's pastoral eloquence but most of all, to force him to devise a mode of persuasion certain to outshine the rhetor's beguiling fluency. Gregory was conscious of a definite public at least in Clermont and Tours. He identified with it, spoke in its name, and filled the *Histories* with matters that it would find topical.[504] As a storyteller surrounded by an audience as concrete as he could conjure up, he held the *Histories* together without need of a plot. His milieu stimulated him to create a work of art.

Precisely how Gregory gained familiarity with prescriptive satire may be beyond our power to determine, but too many of its distinguishing features are in the *Histories* for the resemblance to be coincidental. If, as Gregory urged, the events of the distant and near past had the objective character of being "mixed and muddled," no literary form was more appropriate for their narration than the *satura*; and he, as the unassuming but continually prominent spokesman expounding the moral sense of *gesta praesentia* to a needy public, was perfectly suited to adopting the blunt, antirhetorical, truth-speaking persona of the satirist. Gregory's concept of the past, though partly Orosian, strikes an unexpectedly original note. Its irony foreshadows the Voltairian idea that history depicts only crimes and calamities, but Gregory, not stopping there, found room for the countervailing *virtutes sanctorum*: the mad world castigated by the holy prophet also contained its critic and what he stood for. Though nourished by the Bible, Gregory's idea of history as a mixture of opposites could hardly have arisen independently of the literary genre in which it found expression.

Readers go to the *Histories* for something else than prodigies, saints, and Gregory's life story. Turbulent and gaudy Merovingian personalities and events not only fill most of the work but also account for its unfailing appeal. Never had conditions in a Christian land been described so freely and scathingly as they were by him. Gregory's unflinching irony in discoursing

[504] Above, nn. 347-52.

about "the dissolute" was intimately related to his miracle-centered theology. Credulity toward the holy and irreverence toward the profane were opposite sides of the same bluntly rustic refusal to cater to "philosophic" susceptibilities or to bow to polite standards of verisimilitude and restraint. Gregory affirmed that the martyrs and confessors were the only heroes of the Church and that, far from populating a mythical past, they existed in the here and now. The Constantines and the Clovises had honorable places in the course of events, but no one had ever heard of their performing posthumous cures. Earthly glory and riches had nothing in common with the superior humanity embodied in the friends of God. Thanks to the security given exclusively by the saints, one could contemplate "the dregs of our times" with open eyes and call what one saw by the proper names. In these terms, Gregory conjured up the *civitas terrena* in his own and his audience's backyard. Contemporaries, far better placed than we to recognize Gregory's irony, were given a jolting lesson in Christian values. The first thing they were to understand about profane *gesta praesentia* was that, almost without exception, they were crimes and follies expressive of empty and futile cravings.

Gregory's account of the *excidia miserorum* was meant to inspire contempt of the world, not to denounce, still less to celebrate, the Franks or anyone else. Simultaneously, more particular lessons were imparted. Gregory's advocacy of generosity as the pre-eminent royal virtue, of orthodoxy as being important even when it seemed safe, of mercy and nonviolence, and of other matters can be easily inferred from his presentation. The perennial history he evoked is a gallery of pictures with a narrator to guide us among them. The features on the canvasses are sometimes indistinct, but the moral colors are invariably clear. Gregory's artistry resides in making us forget that the *Histories*, in format as in contents, is didactic literature.

One cannot leave Gregory without recalling the part he has played, as "l'Hérodote de la barbarie," in documenting a nadir of civilization following the end of the Roman Empire.[505] Tradition maintains that, in the early centuries of the Christian era, the Roman Empire declined and was, in the West, overrun by primitive aliens, the Germanic barbarians. The alleged result was that the level of civilization plummeted, except to the limited extent that the Christian Church was able to cushion the collapse. Gregory's *Histories* is taken to mark something like the lowest point in this sharply descending curve. Not only are the practices he wrote about supposed to illustrate the savagery of the age, but his own unabashed and boundless faith in miracles is deemed to show that the Gaul he lived in

---

[505] Ampère, *Hist. lit.* II, 300; the evocation of Herodotus is unimportant by comparison with the circular contention that Gregory's epoch was one of "barbarie" and that, because every epoch finds its historian, Gregory was its spokesman (II, 292).

stood closer to the Haitian hinterland than to the fellowship of decorous Christians. Gregory holds a uniquely underprivileged place among Latin authors between, say, Sidonius Apollinaris and Alcuin. Other figures, such as Boëthius, Gregory the Great, Isidore, and Bede, are portrayed as rays of light brightening their possibly gloomy environs. Gregory of Tours, on the contrary, is considered both to describe barbaric backwardness and to attest to it personally by the language and disposition of his writings. He certifies to modern men that the Dark Ages were, at least for a moment, authentically dark.

This idea of early medieval gloom resulting from Rome's fall has a strong hold on the European historical imagination and shows no sign of losing its appeal.[506] Gregory still stars as witness to deepest darkness. Yet, as much as need be said about the documentary value of the *Histories* was said by Kurth, many decades ago, when he pointed out that Gregory illustrated the high and low extremes and took ordinary life for granted.[507] The horrors and crimes found in the *Histories* can be multiplied outside Merovingian times and are all too easily duplicated in any fifteen-year period of newspaper reading in the twentieth century.[508] Bondage, frustration, and absurdity belong to every age and tend to wear similar masks. Gregory's preference for the spectacular was recognized by others, such as Albert Hauck; but they, like Kurth, were pragmatic observers, with no explanations for Gregory's selection of material. Why should his scenes be exceptional? The general view continued to prevail that Merovingian normality, portrayed with unflinching realism, sprang before our eyes from Gregory's pages ("suspect the worst").[509] But Hauck and Kurth had pointed in the right direction. Gregory's conscious literary design juxtaposed the vain strivings of the earthbound with the fellowship of the saints. The *Histories* is religious literature and conveys meaning, not knowledge. It has the realism of caricature. Far from documenting gloom, it forces us to reorient our thinking toward a late-sixth-century Gaul that appears to have generated a satire only

---

[506] For its beginnings, ch. I n. 41 above. For better or worse, "Dark Ages" now has a neutral sense, meaning "early Middle Ages," and is used by historians, especially in England, who do not believe in gloom (e.g. Llewellyn, *Rome in the Dark Ages*). The pejorative sense of the phrase remains vigorous; e.g. Robert Jackson, *Dark Age Britain* (Cambridge 1984), defines the period as extending between the Romans and the Normans and believes it must be defended from being thought an abyss.

[507] Kurth, cited above, n. 271.

[508] In a curious, isolated effort to show that Merovingian behavior was not unique, Thorpe, p. 458 n. 41, quoted a dispatch concerning punishment for petty theft in a central African republic in 1972. Cf. the more sensible comment of Rand, "Brighter Aspects," p. 181: "And I think I could undertake to compile from one year of the most proper of American newspapers, the *Boston Transcript*, a record of diversified crime in my own country that would make Gregory's assortment, culled from the preceding 168 years, tremble for its laurels."

[509] Wallace-Hadrill, as above, n. 201.

marginally less accomplished and sophisticated than those of Juvenal's Rome and Swift's England.

However original Gregory is as a Christian historian, he invites even more attention as a "philosopher," the spokesman for a science or system of thought that seemed to him to surpass in truth and certitude anything that the past had to offer. We are accustomed to brush aside Gibbon's line about the "triumph of superstition," on the grounds that it is an exaggerated statement about a cultural decline that Christians strove to avert, or at least to counteract, rather than to bring about.[510] The allegation of Ludwig Dindorff in 1830 that "we owe barbarity not so much to the barbarians as to the Christians" seems to be another chip off Gibbon's block and equally contrary to what we have come to understand about the cultivation and transmission of the classical heritage by medieval Christians.[511] In the words of Christopher Dawson, "it was the Latin tradition that was victorious throughout the conquered lands, and the survival of the classical tradition was of vital importance for the future of Europe and the birth of mediaeval culture."[512]

These statements are too simplified to be worth weighing against each other. But if Gibbon and Dindorff deserve to be recalled with respect in the present context, it is for demanding that we should recognize an emphatic Christian opposition to classical rationality, an opposition that Gregory of Tours was not alone in embodying and that Dawson with many other moderns tends to understate. Gregory was an enthusiastic subverter of "the classical tradition." He did not hail the "triumph of religion" or of "barbarity," but neither did he conceive of himself as the spokesman of a "Church [that] remained as the representative of the old tradition of culture."[513] On the contrary, he spoke for something new, different, and assertive. He forces us to confront the possibility that the "triumph of superstition" had a positive face, whose existence and worth in the history of thought deserves acknowledgment even, perhaps especially, outside a confessional context. For the future of European intellectual development did not hinge only on successive "renaissances" of the classical tradition. Something other than a profitless detour in the history of thought was involved in such non-Hellenic improbabilities as an omnipotent and incarnate God, creation out of nothing, and daily miracles.

---

[510] Gibbon's precise words (*Decline and Fall*, ch. 71, ed. Bury, VII, 308) are: "I have described the triumph of barbarism and religion." The familiar or vulgar version that I quote is documented, e.g., by J. M. Roberts, review of Franco Venturi, *Settecento reformatore*, in *Times Literary Supplement* (March 21, 1986) 309 col. 1: "Gibbon unrolled a story of barbarism and superstition (as he saw them)."

[511] Preface to John Malalas *Chron.* (above, ch. II n. 233), p. vii.

[512] Dawson, *Making of Europe*, p. 98.

[513] *Ibid.* p. 99.

Gregory of Tours, living after more than two centuries of Christian subversion of the old and affirmation of the new, had little reason to doubt the blessedness of his days. He filled many pages celebrating the main evidence for it—the wonders that took place unceasingly in the shrines dotting the by no means small world that he and his audience inhabited. Byzantine armies were mercifully distant. Lombards, Saxons, and Avars posed no pressing dangers. Arian heresy had been expelled. Hundreds of churches, great and small, had been built and staffed.[514] They enclosed treasures of relics beyond price, from which divine blessing poured in an inexhaustible stream.

To this considerable extent, the Church Gregory belonged to was secure and in good working order. On the other hand, the context it lived in was Christian in little else than baptism. Christ's offer of new life to all continued to have a low rate of acceptance. The imperfections of the present were not the result of unwelcome recent developments. One might hardly look back from Merovingian Gaul and glimpse an epoch in which better conditions had prevailed. The mass of perdition was tenacious and ever reluctant to change its ways. Its members bore no single ethnic or cultural stamp. They included many ecclesiastics as well as laymen, and they came from every walk of life. The Old Testament account of the stiff-necked Chosen People accurately foreshadowed current conditions.

What had changed was that now there was the certainty of an alternative to the ceaseless cycle of faithlessness and remorse. The task of a practical bishop was to get on with the job of shaping his surroundings into a Christian society. To this end, Gregory held up a mirror to recent history, reflecting the leading figures of his age, and not a few lesser ones, in the colors appropriate to their conduct. The *Histories* was not likely to win the *miseri* to better ways, but at least it might clear the air and suggest to the not yet committed where, in a safe Church, the line lay between right and wrong.

Gregory was not cut off from the last centuries of the Roman Empire. The ills he exposed as a churchman were directly bequeathed by ancient society,[515] and the literary genre in which he cast the *Histories* was as much a creation of classical rhetoric as was the sophistry he claimed to eschew. The continuing hold of antiquity on him and Frankish Gaul is predictable. If he strikes us as novel and radical, it is for espousing a post-patristic Chris-

---

[514] N. D. Fustel de Coulanges, *Monarchie franque*, p. 583, "Il est certain que les évêques du sixième siècle dépensèrent beaucoup en constructions. Je ne pense pas qu'à aucune autre époque on ait élevé autant d'églises"; for details, see Vieillard-Troïekouroff, *Monuments religieux*.

[515] In other words, one would be hard put to identify any conditions Gregory deplored that resulted specifically from the substitution of barbarian for Roman rule.

tianity that turned its back remorselessly on "the vanity of earthly wisdom" and presented Catholicism as empirically verifiable truth. Gregory's religion, the condition for the masterful hold he had on his present, is the most unsettling phenomenon he offers to our attention, and no one concerned with the Middle Ages can afford to pass it casually by.

Bede and the Ghost of Bishop Wilfrid

1. *Historia ecclesiastica gentis Anglorum*: Detachment or Advocacy?

"**h**appy youth," Alexander the Great exclaimed at the tomb of Achilles, "to have Homer as herald of your valor"; happy England to have Bede as its first historian.[1] Gregory of Tours is sometimes dubbed the "father" of French history and Paul the Deacon that of the history of post-Roman Italy; Jordanes's *Getica* has, in some circles, commanded almost religious respect for its pioneering account of the Germanic *Völkerwanderung*. But fatherhood is no substitute for historiographic merit; the historians of the Goths, Franks, and Lombards have all been judged variously flawed and inadequate to their great tasks. Their works pale alongside the array of virtues that all agree are found in Bede's *Ecclesiastical History of the English People*: a tale of origins framed dynamically as the Providence-guided advance of a people from heathendom to Christianity; a cast of saints rather than rude warriors; a mastery of historical technique incomparable for its time; beauty of form and diction; and, not least, an author whose qualities of life and spirit set a model of dedicated scholarship. Bede may even be oversold, as when he is called "the greatest of all historians of a barbarian conversion" without it being observed that he alone accorded conversion more than passing attention.[2] A more fitting eulogy is James Campbell's remark that "Bede defies patronage."[3] Modern scholars have often felt superior to other early medieval historians, but not to Bede.

If England has been lucky in what Eleanor Duckett called its *Aeneid*, so has its Virgil been well treated by posterity.[4] The textual transmission of Bede's *History* is excellent, and so is the scholarship it has inspired. Continuously read for twelve centuries, it survives in more than one hundred fifty manuscripts and was still being copied by hand when first printed.[5] Better yet, the manuscripts include several dating from a few years after the author's death; thanks to their meticulous copyists, the text of the *History*

---

[1] The anecdote occurs in the preface to Jerome's *Vita s. Hilarionis*, PL XXIII, 29. A more remote source is Cicero *Pro Archia poeta* 10.24. The passage in Jerome is a crux in the dating of the H.A.; see Alan Cameron in *Journal of Roman Studies* 55 (1965) 244-45, and 61 (1971) 257-59.

[2] Mayr-Harting, *Venerable Bede, Rule of St. Benedict, and Social Class*, p. 1.

[3] Campbell, "Bede," p. 184.

[4] Duckett, *Anglo-Saxon Saints*, p. 320.

[5] Blair, "Historical Writings," p. 221.

is almost as problem-free as a modern book.[6] It is beautifully edited.[7] Besides, a student of the *History* has access to a full and admirable commentary, by Charles Plummer, and to an equally full concordance, by Putnam Jones, advantages that our other three authors lack.[8] These resources have not lain fallow. Books and articles on or involving Bede abound, some occasioned by anniversary celebrations in 1935 and 1973, others by an annual lecture at Jarrow, many more by initiatives of other kinds (of course, they are not exclusively concerned with the *History*).[9] For all these reasons, Bede holds a privileged and unrivaled place among the first historians of Christian Europe.

The many excellent studies of Bede's great *History* make it superfluous to treat him on a scale comparable to that of our three other authors. One subject, however, invites attention; namely, the immediate and local circumstances that gave rise to the *History*. In the life of early Northumbria, the composition and issuance of a work so largely concerned as Bede's is with local developments was itself a historical event. Though we might take pleasure in imagining that the *History* flowed disinterestedly from Bede's pen for our enlightenment and edification, it is more likely to have had a narrower context. At a minimum, Bede probably had reasons for taking time out of a busy life to assemble and shape so ambitious a work. The hypothesis, so easily entertained from a modern perspective, that Bede wrote aloofly, *sub specie aeternitatis*, should be avoided until more plausible possibilities are exhausted.

To several recent commentators, Bede has seemed to have had an uncomfortable relationship to the world in which he lived; his outlook, they suggest, was austere and abstract. "Bede's dynamic," according to Patrick Wormald, "was neither learning nor common sense but idealism. It was

[6] Mynors, *OMT*, p. xxxix: "Bede's reader has little more need to trouble himself with the details of textual criticism than the reader of Gibbon and Macauley."

[7] See List of Abbreviations, under Plummer and Colgrave, *OMT*. In the *OMT* volume, the edition and textual introduction are by Mynors; the Latin text is complemented on facing page by Colgrave's not-altogether-reliable translation; Colgrave also supplied a historical introduction and the annotation. In Mynors' opinion (p. lxxiii), Plummer's text may be "fairly described as final"; his edition has the added value of identifying and italicizing known borrowings (such as from Gildas).

[8] Plummer's commentary is in vol. II of his edition (n. 7 above). (A supplement to Plummer's commentary was completed by Professor J. M. Wallace-Hadrill before his untimely death.) Jones, *Concordance*. It is to be hoped that the recent concordance to Gregory of Tours' *Histories* (above, ch. III n. 1) will render comparably valuable services. Another precious resource is Laistner and King, *Hand-list*, which is undergoing revision.

[9] *Bede: His Life, Times and Writings*. Bonner, ed., *Famulus Christi*. Jarrow Lectures, annually since 1958. Note, also, Bolton, "Bede Bibliography," and the comprehensive bibliography by Musca, *Venerabile Beda*, pp. 400-36, supplemented in the review by Wormald in *Durham University Journal*. Among recent continental studies of Bede, see Davidse, "Sense of the Past" (the essentials of an Amsterdam doctorate of 1976).

idealism which dictated his conception of the past, just as it coloured his opinion of the present."[10] James Campbell observed that the *History* was focused on "an idealized past, rather than a devalued present." On Wormald's reading, this orientation reflects Bede's inner disposition: "socially speaking, Bede was without a background. . . . [His] personal history cut him off from contemporary aristocratic society and its values, and buried him, from boyhood, in books."[11] That the atmosphere of the *History* is the direct outcome of the author's biography as known to us is most clearly asserted by David Kirby:

Bede . . . lived all his life from the age of seven in a monastery, in cloistered seclusion. . . . It is not likely . . . that he ever witnessed an act of real violence and inconceivable that he experienced royal wrath. . . . [He] was a monk, a scholar, a quietly devout and pious man, writing of a lay world he hardly knew, in praise of kings who appeared to him, from what he was told, to possess definite virtues as rulers and individuals. . . .

The serenity which Bede brings to the ecclesiastical personalities of the period of the Conversion . . . is a mirror of the peace and charity of Bede himself and of the timeless quiet of his own life, the melodious unison of plainsong and the contemplative observation of the canonical hours. . . .

Bede glides pleasantly over the peaceful waters of what was for him essentially the golden age of Christianity in England.[12]

In much the same spirit, Bede is described by D. H. Farmer as a "detached scholar . . . out of touch with the power struggles of contemporary politics."[13] To hear Wormald again, Bede was an "isolated figure"; he was representative of his society in crystallizing "the enthusiasm with which the Anglo-Saxons, like other early Germanic peoples, threw themselves into the balance of the old Romano-Christian world," and at the same time anomalous in being exclusively absorbed in that book-learned past.[14]

Bede may finally be experiencing the fate of his fellow early medieval historians. Patronizingly or not, his *History* is certainly enduring a romantic interpretation of the same sort as that which derived the disorder of Gregory of Tours' *Histories* from the turbulence of the world Gregory depicted and presumably lived in.[15] With Bede, in a neat reversal, the order and sanctity he evoked in the English past are taken to have been projected from his experience of monastic calm. The middle term of the argument,

[10] Wormald, "Bede and Benedict Biscop," p. 155.

[11] Campbell in his *Anglo-Saxons*, p. 84; Wormald, "Bede, *Beowulf*," p. 62.

[12] Kirby, "Northumbria in Time of Wilfrid," pp. 2-4 (in the order of Kirby's argument, my third extract comes first). In a later study, Kirby acknowledged that Bede did not write "in an obscure cell," but had many links with the outside: "Ceolwulf of Northumbria," p. 171.

[13] Farmer, "St. Wilfrid," p. 37.

[14] Wormald, "Bede, *Beowulf*," pp. 68-69.

[15] Above, ch. III nn. 7-17.

in his case as in Gregory's, is naïveté: unable to distinguish the world out-side the monastery walls from that within, Bede was the unconscious play-thing of his circumstances and environment. In properly romantic fashion, the artist is deemed to mirror his world, which with Bede was the very shel-tered, atypical community of Wearmouth-Jarrow or, even more austerely, that of the books imported from the Mediterranean by its founding abbot, Benedict Biscop.[16]

There is a more creditable basis than romanticism for the recent emer-gence of these views. The course of historical research into Anglo-Saxon England has had the predictable effect of detracting from the authoritative-ness of Bede's narrative. Whereas accounts of early England were once little more than enhanced rewritings of the *History*, a substantially modified im-age has been and is continuing to be pieced together from the fragments of all sorts that scholars make it their business to accumulate and analyze; what Bede did not say has come to weigh heavily alongside his testimony.[17] Assuming that he wished to be a source—that he meant to supply an ac-curate, comprehensive, and circumstantial account of the early English Church "for the enlightenment of future times (*ad instructionem posterita-tis*)"[18] —one may feel forced, sooner or later, to ponder Bede's inadequa-cies, and even to look for answers to the unutterable question, Why was he so bad?

No one has called Bede bad or come near to doing so, even in intention. Bede's fame is not in danger. But he seems well on the way toward gaining an aura of secluded naïveté that might have made him shudder. Before this conception hardens into orthodoxy, second thoughts might be given to an aspect of the *History* that is generally taken as self-evident, or approached from a very lofty angle; namely, Bede's reasons for composing it. One of his last works, the *History* was long deemed the culmination of his labors, the summit toward which he had been working all his life—an account of the Christian beginnings of his people.[19] Few believe this patriotic scenario any longer; biblical commentary, not history, was the privileged focus of Bede's scholarship, and presumably he would have gone to his grave without re-grets even if his fellow countrymen had not been furnished with an account

[16] Mayr-Harting, *Coming of Christianity*, p. 40: "To Bede, the real world was to a consider-able extent the world of books."

[17] E.g. Wallace-Hadrill, "Rome and the Early English Church"; Kirby, "Bede's Native Sources"; Campbell, "Observations on the Conversion of England." Cf. Wormald, "Bede, *Beowulf*," p. 58, "The quest for 'alternative perspectives' on the Age of Bede is perhaps char-acteristic of modern studies"; p. 68, "Historians are now readier to admit that [Bede's] is only one view of what happened in seventh-century Britain."

[18] The quotation is from his preface, Mynors, OMT, p. 6. Cf. Blair, "Historical Writings," p. 201.

[19] E.g. Levison, "Bede as Historian," p. 132.

of their conversion.[20] As an alternative, his introduction to the *History* sets out several of the motives historians generally give for their labors: to supply models of good and bad conduct, to inform posterity, to oblige esteemed patrons.[21] Bede's statements need not be doubted, but neither do they have to be considered exhaustive. A history of one's land, the first of its kind, makes a strong and even a political statement. Bede's *History*, one suspects, had a place in the Northumbria of 730.

Campbell's comment that Bede evokes an idealized past and devalues the present has precise implications for the place the *History* occupied in its time. Bede, in the final months of his life, sent a pamphlet-length letter to Egbert, bishop of York. He expressed deep misgivings about the condition of the Northumbrian Church and spelled out remedies that should at once be instituted.[22] These same criticisms are perceptible in the *History*, usually in reverse, as an image of the preferable conditions that had once prevailed.[23] However far or near Bede stood *vis-à-vis* contemporary aristocratic society, he was not detached at least from his ecclesiastical surroundings; no reader of the *Letter to Egbert* can doubt that the *History* bore a relationship to the times when it was written. But what sort of relationship? If it is assumed that Bede, as a critic of his day, was out of touch with what lay beyond the monastery gates, that he dreamt of a golden age, idealizing the past and devaluing the present, then it appears to follow that both the *History* and the *Letter* are jeremiads.[24] Bede, presumably, was a mournful voice in the wilderness, crying to ears deservedly deaf because their possessors were in closer touch with social reality than the would-be prophet of Jarrow. Perhaps this was so, as many current commentators believe; but why should it have been? No evidence compels us to think of Bede as an isolated, impractical, and sorrowing critic. Instead, he might have been, in concert with others, a forceful advocate rectifying the past as a model for action in the present. The *History* and the *Letter to Egbert* lend themselves

[20] Jenkins, "Bede as Exegete and Theologian," p. 152; Meyvaert, "Bede the Scholar," p. 44. This is reflected in his medieval reputation: Brunhölzl, *Gesch. d. lat. Lit.* I, 220; Ray, "What Do We Know about Bede's Commentaries?"; Laistner and King, *Hand-list*, p. 10: one must inventory Bede's theological works in order to appreciate the extent to which he became a "classic" author. The more traditional view of the H.E. is espoused by Musca, *Venerabile Beda*, p. 104, and Cowdrey, "Bede and the 'English People,' " p. 503.

[21] For the first two, Mynors, *OMT*, pp. 2, 6. The third is most explicit: "Denique hortatu praecipue ipsius Albini [abbot of St. Augustine's, Canterbury], ut hoc opus adgredi auderem, provocatus sum" (p. 4).

[22] *Epistola ad Ecgbertum episcopum*, ed. Plummer, I, 405-23; tr. Dorothy Whitelock, *English Historical Documents* I, 2d ed. (London 1979), pp. 799-810. The letter is more fully discussed below, n. 101.

[23] See below, nn. 102-103.

[24] The term is used in connection with the *Letter to Egbert* by Bolton, *History of Anglo-Latin Literature*, p. 181.

just as readily to this interpretation, and perhaps more so, than to the supposition of helpless idealization and elegiac lament.

Bede's *History*, in spite of its title and grandiose incorporation of the English microcosm into the macrocosm of providential time, is predominantly concerned with Northumbria. Book I ends on a Northumbrian note, and, from the time of the mission of Paulinus to King Edwin in book II, the focus moves northward and stays there to the end.[25] Bede's interest in other kingdoms and in Canterbury is genuine, but subordinate to his narrower homeland.[26] No doubt this limitation results from the constraints within which he worked and the information he could acquire.[27] But, from another standpoint, it was entirely fitting that Northumbria should supply the core of a history of the English Church. In no other kingdom, so far as we may tell, had serious steps been taken to commemorate the local past. Northumbria was precocious.[28] Contemporary fellow countrymen of Bede's composed accounts of the Gregorian mission, of Iro-English sanctity, and of Rome-trained episcopacy well before he took these subjects in hand.[29] Not all these works were written in a serene and impartial spirit; one of them, the most ambitiously historical, is an unblushing piece of special pleading, designed to vindicate a controversial bishop, recently deceased. The Northumbrian Church was not a haven of tranquillity; one uproar or another punctuated its existence throughout Bede's life. It offered an excellent terrain for the birth of historical writing. As Kirby has rightly said, "The key to unlocking the process of writing the HE may still lie concealed in the tensions of the time in which Bede wrote."[30]

2. The Background and Foreground of the *Ecclesiastical History*

Like all authors lapsing into autobiography, Bede portrayed himself as he wished to be seen and remembered. Jordanes detailed his Gothic

[25] The sudden switch to Northumbria in *H.E.* 1.34 is conspicuous. The pagan king Ethelfrith is evidently portrayed as a counterpart of Augustus in Orosius's narrative: as the birth of Christ coincided with the institution of the *pax Romana*, so the implanting of Christ among the *Angli* coincided with their acquisition of security from the Britons. The mission of Paulinus begins to be narrated in *H.E.* 2.9.

[26] For documentation, see below, nn. 81, 89.

[27] Kirby, "Bede's Native Sources," p. 341. It is important to observe, however, that these constraints are a consideration of ours only. Bede himself is not a witness to a shortage of sources. His preface to the *History* deliberately vaunts the many trustworthy authorities on whom the narrative is based. He sees no need to apologize for shortcomings or gaps in his gathering of information.

[28] To the contrary, Blair, *Introduction to Anglo-Saxon England*, p. 321: "There is no reason to suppose that the writing of hagiography was peculiar to Northumbria." This makes too little allowance for the evidence.

[29] Respectively, the Whitby anonymous *Life of Gregory the Great*, the anonymous *Life of St. Cuthbert*, and Stephen's *Life of St. Wilfrid*. Much more about these will presently be said.

[30] Kirby, "Bede, Eddius Stephanus," p. 114.

ancestry; Gregory of Tours insisted on his local attachments, faulty Latin, and blunt wisdom; Paul the Deacon, most reticent of all, supplied little more than a formula of humility.[31] Bede presented himself as a lifelong monk and Christian scholar: born on the monastery lands, given over to its abbots for rearing at age seven, "from then on I have spent all my life in this monastery, applying myself entirely to the study of the Scriptures; and, amid the observance of the discipline of the Rule and the daily task of singing in the church, it has always been my delight to learn or to teach or to write."[32] More follows, but largely in a statistical vein.

No one would wish to detract from so moving a self-portrait. This is the real Bede, but is it the only one? There is additional information. Bede was incensed at having ideas of his impugned for heresy; well aware of the quality of his scholarship, he did not shrink when necessary from pointing out the ignorance of others; he was impatient with Isidore of Seville and with a poor translation from Greek into Latin; his famed discretion slips readily into *suppressio veri*; he was not altogether satisfied with his working conditions; the celebrity he came to enjoy was not merely posthumous; and he died in an aura of sanctity, captured in a pupil's beautiful account of his last days.[33] These fragments add something to his autobiographical comments, but not nearly enough for full disclosure of the personality of a complex and many-sided man. The truth is, unsurprisingly, that we know very little about Bede and that, because of our ignorance, we are well advised not to accord his deliberate self-portrait undue weight in our reading of the *History*.

Bede died in 735, a few years into his sixties. On the Continent, Charlemagne's grandfather had recently stemmed the western tide of Islam.[34]

---

[31] Above, ch. II nn. 100-101, ch. III nn. 341-59, 362-63; below, ch. V nn. 23-24, 251-52.

[32] *H.E.* 5.24, tr. Colgrave, OMT, p. 567. For an appropriate illustration of how this passage may be taken too absolutely, Quentin, "Bède le Vénérable," col. 632, "rien n'est plus simple que sa vie"; likewise Raby, "Bède le Vénérable," col. 395, "voilà le caractère de Bède, le savant paisible."

[33] Accusation of heresy: for a full account, see Charles W. Jones, *Bedae Opera de temporibus* (Cambridge, Mass. 1943), pp. 132-34. Ignorance of others: on his deathbed he corrected a treatise on nature, saying, "nolo ut pueri mei mendacium legant" (*Epistola de obitu Bedae*, ed. R.A.B. Mynors, OMT, p. 582). Concerning his relations to Isidore (whom he normally used without acknowledgment), see Meyvaert, "Bede the Scholar," pp. 58-60, and Ray, "Bede's *vera lex*," pp. 15-17. Poor translation from Greek, *H.E.* 5.24 (concerning the *Passio s. Anastasii*). *Suppressio veri*: very apparent in what he does with the *Vita Wilfridi*, as we shall see (below, § 5) and as noted by Plummer II, 315, and Campbell, "Bede," 189 n. 76. Working conditions: he points out that he had to be his own secretary and copyist (Plummer I, xx). Celebrity: his fame while alive had to have been more than local if Nothelm, priest of London, sought answers from him on biblical questions (ca. 725, Laistner and King, *Hand-list*, p. 62) and if Abbot Albinus of Canterbury encouraged him to write a history (n. 21); Quentin (as n. 32) stresses that he was already famous while alive. Death: Cuthbert *Epistola de obitu Bedae*, ed. Mynors, OMT, pp. 580-86.

[34] His death was noted (sometimes under the wrong year) in continental annals: MGH SS.

Most of Bede's works are undated, but he cannot have begun writing much before 700. His first treatise on time reckoning dates from 703, the year in which Bishop John of Hexham ordained him priest.[35] From then on, a stately succession of biblical commentaries proceeded from his pen. The *History* came late in his life; 731 is its official date, but a continental event of 732 seems to be recorded.[36] Although Bede's birth (673) occurred within a decade after the Synod of Whitby (664), and his ordination as deacon (692) within two years after Archbishop Theodore's death (690), little more weight should be attached to his youthful memories than to our own.[37] The period of his maturity, the one he knew from thoroughly conscious personal experience, is almost entirely excluded from his *History*. No reversal of emphasis could be more marked than that between Gregory of Tours' accent on the present and Bede's on the past.[38] This fact need not imply anything specific about Bede's knowledge of, or feelings about, the events of his mature lifetime. The one certainty is that he chose not to write about them.

Two of our authors have little but histories to their name, and even Paul the Deacon would dwindle in stature if limited to the nonhistorical items of his bibliography. Bede, however, would be a giant in medieval thought

---

I, 24-25, 64, 67, 73, 114. The victory of Charles Martel is the latest event alluded to in the *H.E.*; see n. 36. For a good recent survey of Bede's life and work (and Northumbrian hagiography), see Michael Lapidge in Greenfield and Calder, *New Critical History*, pp. 15-22.

[35] Laistner and King, *Hand-list*, p. 144; ordination: *H.E.* 5.24; for its date, Plummer I, xi.

[36] In *H.E.* 5.23-24, Bede clearly presents 731 as the closing date of his work, but 5.23 contains a reference to the Saracens ravaging Gaul "et ipsi non multo post in eadem provincia dignas suae perfidiae poenas luebant." Because *non multo post* means "soon after 729," the Arab defeat must be that of 732; cf. Wallace-Hadrill, "Bede's Europe," p. 73. Kirby, "Ceolwulf of Northumbria," p. 170, shrewdly notes that Bede's reference to troubled times in the same chapter was probably written toward 733; i.e. after Ceolwulf's brief deposition in 731.

Everyone proceeds as though it were certain that Bede finished the *H.E.* in 731, the date universally assigned to the work. Plummer (II, 339) and Colgrave (*OMT*, p. 557 n. 5) therefore agree that if Bede refers to Charles Martel's victory of 732, his words had to be a later insertion. Kirby (as above), owing to the discrepancy of dates, spoke about "editions" of the *H.E.* and ("Bede, Eddius Stephanus," p. 108) emphasized that Bede added to the *H.E.* in 732-33; Wormald, review of Musca, p. 233, even has Bede write somberly about *advancing* Arabs and "only later" add the fact of their defeat.

The logic of these inferences is not compelling. Bede never announces the date when the *H.E.* left his hands. Like any author, ancient or modern, he was free to choose a cutoff point that did not precisely coincide with the instant when he ceased dictating. His brief and undated reference to the Saracen defeat in Gaul (which helps to give 5.23 its generally positive tone and in no way suggests a later insertion) justifies the conclusion that he completed the *H.E.* later than 731, i.e. in 733 or 734; there is no certain way to be precise. The interesting question arising from this chronology of composition is why Bede chose 731 as his "official" date and why, besides, he chose to ignore those events of 731 that are noted in the annalistic continuation (nn. 174, 178).

[37] Plummer I, xi. I have rounded off Plummer's more carefully stated dates 672-73, 691-92; cf. below, n. 115.

[38] Cf. Wormald, "Bede, *Beowulf*," p. 59.

and letters even if he had never written a line of history: "Among the artists, statesmen, missionaries, athletes of the spiritual life, who proliferated
in England in the late seventh and eighth centuries, he was the most unexpected of all products of a primitive age, a really great scholar."[39] His
works on grammar and chronology, and most of all his biblical commentaries, were brought to the Continent by Anglo-Saxon missionaries and
teachers and had an unequaled impact on the Carolingian revival of learning. Side by side with Isidore of Seville, of whom he was well aware but did
not esteem, he was instrumental in reshaping the heritage of late antiquity
and the patristic period into forms that facilitated their absorption into a
totally Christian culture. Almost all his output is extracted from earlier authorities; its derivative character used to be deprecated while its pedagogic
creativity went unnoticed. More patient assessments are beginning to do
justice to Bede's deftness of selection, combination, and rearrangement.[40]
The extraordinary clarity of his mind and the elegant simplicity of his Latin
suggest an intellectual capacity that might have won attention in any epoch.

However distinguished in other endeavors, Bede did write history and,
typically, he ranged more widely and comprehensively over the field than
any of his peers. Before examining these works, it is appropriate to ask,
more generally, whether or not Bede labored in a historiographic desert.
Wilhelm Levison's justly celebrated study, "Bede as Historian," gave this
question a somewhat misleading turn. "When Bede began to write," he said
in opening, "there was a decline of historiography everywhere in the western world; the historical heritage of Antiquity was not only diminishing
but, moreover, had ceased to be productive."[41] Levison carefully traced the
decline he had in mind, with special reference to the seventh century, and
concluded that Bede marked a new departure. More or less direct echoes of
Levison's opinion occur in appreciations of Bede, but its premises seem
never to have been reconsidered.[42] Bede does not need praise for reanimat-
ing Latin historiography unless the compliment is deserved.

For a start, Levison's reference to the "heritage of Antiquity" and its decline suggests that the seventh-century writings he discussed next were the
last gasps of a production that had been lively and continuous to that point.
The distant background had not been quite so rosy. Histories on the ambitious scale of the *Ecclesiastical History* had not been common in the Latin
world after the start of the Christian era; typically, Tacitus and Suetonius

[39] Southern, "Bede, Monk of Jarrow," p. 268.
[40] Laistner, *Thought and Letters*, p. 163.
[41] Levison, "Bede as Historian," p. 111.
[42] Echoed by Colgrave, OMT, p. xxx; also Barnard, "Bede and Eusebius as Church Historians," p. 106.

are separated from Ammianus Marcellinus by more than two centuries, with nothing in between (if transmission may be trusted) on a scale comparable to theirs.[43] Christianity made little difference; the fathers of the Latin Church, though very productive in other respects, generated few histories. The largest chronological gap in the composition of such works lies, as we have seen, in the one hundred fifty years between Orosius and Gregory of Tours, and was not occasioned by a "diminishing classical heritage"; on the contrary, what allowed Gregory to find his voice as a historian was a determination to be liberated from antiquity.[44] The breakthrough his work signified benefited Bede even if Gregory's influence on him was small.

From Gregory onward, historiography was a growth industry among Westerners. Levison gave the evidence a dimmer cast. His demonstration begins, "There had been several continuations of Eusebius' Chronicle as translated by Jerome: hardly one was added after the sixth century."[45] This semblance of exhaustion is more than offset by facts Levison omitted. Rather than simply add to the continuations of Eusebius-Jerome, Isidore of Seville compiled a completely new world chronicle, as Bede himself was to do again; besides, the Frankish chronicle of Fredegar is as much a continuation of Eusebius-Jerome (with Isidorian touches) as it is of Gregory of Tours.[46] Levison continues: "In Italy, only the *Liber pontificalis*, the official collection of the Lives of the Popes, put forth new germs."[47] "Only" is an undeserved qualification; for better or worse, no history of Italian origin since Constantine (at least) can compare in importance with the *Liber pontificalis*, of which Bede had a copy.[48] The pattern of gratuitous depreciation is unrelieved: the Briton Gildas was "no historiographer at all" (Bede thought otherwise); Isidore's historical writings "mark the end of historiography," and Julian of Toledo's *Historia Wambae regis* merely illustrates that history was not wholly extinguished in Spain; Gregory of Tours is mentioned mainly in order that the Fredegar chronicler, his first continuator, might rank "on a lower level" and his second should be "even poorer."[49] No

---

[43] Tacitus, ca. A.D. 110; Suetonius, ca. 130; Ammianus Marcellinus, ca. 390. Besides, regardless of the language in which Ammianus wrote, it may be more proper to classify him as a Greek historian than as a Latin one (above, ch. I n. 17).

[44] Above, ch. III at nn. 24-26.

[45] As n. 41.

[46] On the relations to Eusebius-Jerome of the major chronicles of Isidore and Bede, see above, ch. I nn. 23-24. The Fredegar chronicle is visibly developed out of that of Eusebius-Jerome (consulted by the chronicler in its fifth-century version continued by Hydatius); the core (bk. II) is preceded by a statistical prologue (bk. I), then augmented by a variety of continuations, including a summary of Gregory of Tours and an original account from 580.

[47] As n. 41.

[48] See above, ch. I n. 27. On Bede and the *Liber pontificalis*, Levison, "Bede as Historian," p. 120.

[49] On Gildas, ch. III nn. 252-55. Bede: *H.E.* 1.22, *historicus eorum* (i.e. of the British, an interesting sign of the association of a historian with the people whom he chronicled—the

one could tell from Levison's account that all these works compare well in historical interest, if not in style, with the Latin writings of the fifth and sixth centuries, and that as a cluster they form as rich an aggregate of historiography as had occurred for a long time. Whereas Gregory of Tours avoided making the Franks his subject, Isidore celebrated the Spanish Goths, Gregory's continuators provided the Franks with the history he had eschewed, and an anonymous Italian briefly narrated the origin of the Lombards.[50] In other words, the century that brought papal history to fruition also generated the first "national" histories (owing very little to Jordanes) and had the confidence to recast Eusebius's universal chronicle in an updated form. Levison's assessment of the history of Western historiography needs to be stood on its head. Bede, far from bestriding an arid landscape, follows upon more than a century of self-assured activity.

The list of Bede's historical writings given here includes a hagiographic component. Levison's study—whose virtues far outweigh the shortcomings criticized here—endorses the standard distinction between hagiography and history; Bede, he said, was specially remarkable for writing history in an age of ubiquitous hagiography from which history had almost vanished.[51] Such a comment takes little account of the part Bede allocated to saints and miracles in the *History* or the proportion of hagiography among its sources. With him, as with Gregory of Tours (and many more), the differentiation is otiose. St. Jerome said he had put himself into training for the Church history he meant to write by composing the *Life of St. Malchus*.[52] Saints were historical personages, their miracles and the adventures of their relics were historical events. Hagiography has as much claim to be integrated in a medieval historian's output as biography in a modern one's. Bede himself, in listing his works, enveloped his chronicles with the rubric "books on the reckoning of time" but aligned the "histories of saints" before the "history of the Church."[53]

On this understanding, Bede's historical writings may be broken down into five categories:

—chronicle, or universal history: one very brief, the other a *Major Chronicle* as extensive as that of Eusebius-Jerome;[54]

---

same reflex that, in Paul the Deacon, made Gregory of Tours the historian of the Franks, ch. III n. 62). On the question whether he is a historian, see Thompson, "Gildas and the History of Britain," p. 203.

[50] Above, ch. I nn. 34, 36, 29; below, ch. V n. 163. Levison, "Bede as Historian," p. 133, established that Bede was unacquainted with Isidore's *Historia Gothorum*; cf. Wallace-Hadrill, "Rome and the Early English Church," p. 130.

[51] As n. 41.

[52] Jerome *Vita Malchi praef.*, PL XXIII, 55.

[53] H.E. 5.24. Also along these lines, Schoebe, "Was gilt im frühen Mittelalter als Geschichtliche Wirklichkeit?" pp. 625-51.

[54] Ed. Mommsen, MGH AA. XIII, 247-321. Though soon detached in textual transmis-

—saints' lives: a prose adaptation of Paulinus of Nola's verse *Life of St. Felix*, an improved Latin translation of the Greek *Passion of St. Anastasius*, a rendering into verse of the anonymous *Life of St. Cuthbert*, and a prose revision and expansion of the same *Life*;[55]

—a chronicle of saints, or narrative *Martyrology*;[56]

—an account of the foundation of his monastery: the *History of the Abbots of Wearmouth-Jarrow*;[57]

—and the *Ecclesiastical History of the English People*, cited hereafter in the abbreviated form *H. E.*

The longest of these, and the most ambitious, is without doubt the last. In the homogeneous format of the Penguin translations, the roughly three hundred pages of Bede's *H. E.* compare to the four hundred of Eusebius's *History of the Church* and the five hundred forty of Gregory of Tours.[58] Plummer's great edition of Bede's historical works, which lacks many of the items just listed, includes the *Letter to Egbert of York* whose contents were indicated above. Though not a history, but a critical account of contemporary conditions in the Church, this document has abiding interest for historians and students of the *H. E.*[59]

Bede's very considerable historical production may be usefully divided into works that are and are not addressed to English subjects. There is no lack of merit in the non-English histories. Although Bede could not have known that the Eusebian *Chronicle* had originally been the complement to an elaborate treatise on scientific chronology, his own *Major Chronicle* was

---

sion, the two chronicles formed the chapters "De mundi (*or* sex huius saeculi) aetatibus" in Bede's short and long treatises *De temporum ratione*. The latter are edited, without the chapters of chronicle, by Jones, *Bedae Opera de temporibus*.

[55] See Laistner and King, *Hand-list*, pp. 87-90. On the identification of Bede's version of the *Passio s. Anastasii*, see Franklin and Meyvaert, "Bede's Version."

For Bede on St. Cuthbert, see the List of Abbreviations, under *Verse Cuthbert* and *Prose Cuthbert*. For the earlier account on which Bede depended, see under Anon. *Cuthbert*. On the shortcomings of Colgrave's Latin text of Bede *Prose Cuthbert*, see Laistner's review in the *American Historical Review*.

[56] Identified by Quentin, *Martyrologes historiques*, pp. 16-56. Also see Jacques Dubois and Geneviève Renaud, *Édition pratique des martyrologes de Bède, de l'Anonyme lyonnais et de Florus* (Paris 1976).

[57] The ms title is *Vita beatorum abbatum Benedicti, Ceolfridi, Eosterwini, Sigfridi, atque Hwaetberhti*. For Bede's title (*H. E.* 5.24), see the List of Abbreviations. The abbots take precedence over the abbey; this preference is not peculiar to Bede; e.g. the *Liber pontificalis* is about the popes, not the Roman Church.

[58] Leo Sherley-Price, tr., *Bede, A History of the English Church and People* (Harmondsworth, Middlesex 1955); G. A. Williamson, tr., *Eusebius, A History of the Church from Christ to Constantine* (Harmondsworth, Middlesex 1965); for Thorpe's Gregory of Tours, see the List of Abbreviations.

[59] Above, n. 22. Raby, "Bède le Vénérable," col. 399, includes Bede's little treatise *De locis sanctis* (parts of which are copied into the *H. E.*) among his *opera historica*. This classification is defensible but not compelling.

integrated within a larger work on chronological questions.[60] He followed the lead of Isidore of Seville in totally recasting the *Chronicle* of Eusebius-Jerome. Fifth- and sixth-century authors had simply re-edited and continued Jerome; Isidore, then Bede each rewrote the entire work in an original form. This comparatively sudden need to give universal history a different shape from the one imprinted upon it in the fourth century is a historiographic fact that merits observation and study, but not here.[61] Bede's *Major Chronicle* circulated widely on the Continent, inside and apart from the treatise to which it was originally attached, and had a great future, like Jerome's before, as the trunk on which continuations were grafted.[62]

His *Martyrology*, the first compilation of its kind, is little known, at present, outside specialized circles. It is a chronicle of saints, based on the existing *Martyrology* ascribed to St. Jerome and, like it, built on a calendar year running from 25 December rather than on the annalistic framework normally used for chronicles of ordinary events.[63] Opposite many but not all days of the year, Bede listed the appropriate saint's feast and—his special innovation—supplied a précis of the history of each one. The ratio of martyrs to confessors is tipped heavily in favor of the former, and Bede's preference in summarizing his sources went to the grim circumstances of martyrdom.[64] What resulted was a compact catalogue of Christian heroes and heroines, together with a monotonous but impressive reiteration of the imprisonments, tortures, and executions they endured for their belief. The martyrs were not meant to be seen as pitiable victims of religious persecution; Christianity embodied what was most modern and desirable in Bede's society, whereas the "classical heritage" was something to be shunned. The heroes of Christianity symbolized the triumph of the enduring faithful over the coercive apparatus of the state, the power of motivated guerrillas over ponderous and soulless armies. Bede might, with reason, have regarded himself as an authority on the meaning of barbarity and heroism. The martyrs focused attention on the values that were worth dying for and helped one to recognize those that were not. Bede's *Martyrology* provided in brief a record of Christian heroism that could otherwise be found only in bulky

[60] Barnes, *Constantine and Eusebius*, pp. 111-15. Bede's treatise surveys every aspect of the computation of time, whereas Eusebius's *Chronography* was addressed to the specific problem of reconciling historical dates. *Pace* Jones, *Saints' Lives and Chronicles in Early England*, pp. 17-18, no Latin chronicle until Bede's was "the practical part of a textbook."

[61] Cf. above, ch. I n. 24.

[62] For appreciative words, see Brincken, *Weltchronistik*, p. 113, according to whom all chronography in the Carolingian and Ottonian ages was dominated by Bede's influence.

[63] *Martyrologium Hieronymianum*, ed. H. Quentin and H. Delehaye, *Acta sanctorum*, November vol. II, part 2 (Brussels 1931). See Quentin, "Bède le Vénérable," coll. 636-41; important remarks on Bede's copy of the Hieronymian Martyrology, col. 644.

[64] Quentin, *Martyrologes historiques*, pp. 57-111; martyrs outnumber confessors by a large multiple. Cf. ch. I, n. 32.

tomes of collected *passiones.*[65] Even more seminal than the *Major Chronicle,* it was not only welcomed by continental scholars but was augmented and worked over so intensely as to result, within one hundred fifty years, in the definitive *Martyrology* of Usuard, a basic book of medieval Christendom.[66]

Bede's *Major Chronicle* dates from 725; the *Martyrology* is believed to be even later.[67] His hagiographies are comparatively early works.[68] The piece on St. Felix illustrates Bede's interest in the *opus geminatum* form—verse and prose on the same subject—which re-emerges in his work on St. Cuthbert. (Near the end of the eighth century, the same idea inspired Alcuin to set the *H.E.* to verse in his *Poem on the Saints and Bishops of York.*)[69] Bede's improved translation of the *Passion of St. Anastasius,* long believed lost, is just beginning to be better known.[70] Anastasius was a recent martyr, recalling the great war between Byzantium and Persia in the early seventh century. Even more to the point, the saint had, since midcentury, acquired a cult in Rome, to which his head had been brought from Palestine; the relics were venerated in a Greek monastery near St.-Paul's-outside-the-Walls.[71] The cult gained a special dimension because two men named Anastasius were prominent in Rome's doctrinal resistance to Constantinople over Monotheletism and somehow became associated with the martyr.[72] At least in Rome, therefore, Anastasius was a topical saint, and it does not seem far-fetched that Bede's impulse to improve the Latin text of the *Passion of St. Anastasius* was a distant reverberation of the martyr's current Roman fame.

Among Bede's works on English subjects, the *H.E.* towers over its companion pieces. There is no need at present to discuss the verse and prose *Lives of St. Cuthbert* or the *History of the Abbots;* their subjects are Northumbrian, and they will be examined in relation with contemporary Northumbrian works by other authors.[73] The *H.E.,* though well known, calls for a few words of introduction.

---

[65] See, *Edda, Saga, Skaldendichtung,* pp. 181-82. Wormald, "Bede, *Beowulf,*" pp. 36, 39, 46, 50, 53, 55, 57-58, suggests that the early Middle Ages had only lay models of heroism.

[66] Dubois, *Martyrologes du moyen âge latin,* pp. 37-56. More than fifty years passed, however, until Bede's martyrology attracted attention and was amplified.

[67] *Ibid.* p. 91.

[68] *Ibid.* p. 87, as an opinion, with emphasis on the lack of evidence for dating.

[69] On *opus geminatum,* Peter Godman, in Alcuin *The Bishops, Kings, and Saints of York,* ed. P. Godman, Oxford Medieval Texts (Oxford 1982), pp. lxxviii-lxxxviii.

[70] As above, n. 55.

[71] Bede *Chron. maius* 537, 539-40; this martyrdom is the only incident of the war recorded by Bede; he also notes the translation of relics to Rome. The very next event in the *Chron.* is the conversion and glorious reign of Edwin of Northumbria—a nice contrast of conditions at the two extremities of the Christian world. On the historical circumstances, Kaegi, "Some Seventh-Century Sources on Caesarea."

[72] Llewellyn, *Rome in the Dark Ages,* pp. 164, 118, 143-44.

[73] For an able discussion of the writings in question, including Bede's (and the *Life of Guth-*

In five books, evocative in number of the Pentateuch and the five languages of Britain, Bede narrates the fall of Britain into the hands of the Anglo-Saxon invaders; how Christianity came to the latter through the Gregorian mission; the setbacks this mission suffered, and the countervailing
action, in Northumbria, of missionaries from Irish Iona; the restoration of
Roman order (notably in the reckoning of Easter) through the Synod of
Whitby and the coming from Rome of Archbishop Theodore; the golden
age that ensued; and, ultimately, the winning by the English of their Ionan
friends to the observance of the proper Easter. This last event, in 716, is
followed by a tour d'horizon of the English Church at the time of writing
(731), but it is fair to say that the attention Bede pays to the last decade of
the seventh century and the first three of the eighth is extremely scanty and
selective.

Whether as grammarian, computist, exegete, or historian, Bede's genius
did not extend to conceiving novel literary designs. He adapted, corrected,
and improved the work of others even when writing about St. Cuthbert and
about the origins of his own monastery; he honored St. Ethelthryth with a
poem but did not try his hand at her life; all his non-English histories,
though sometimes drawing on a remarkable range of sources, owe their
plans to identifiable models.[74] In light of this record, the *H.E.* has the
anomalous distinction of appearing to be Bede's most original work. Whatever relation it may have to Eusebius's *Church History* or to Gregory of
Tours, neither the Greek nor the Gallo-Roman historian supplied its underpinnings.[75] Should the *H.E.* be assumed to have been drawn freehand,
as it were, and not to have been borne aloft by one or more earlier writings?
In view of Bede's consistent practice, it would be risky to draw this conclusion without giving serious thought to other possibilities. Gildas had
sketched a history of Britain down to Saxon times; hagiographers contemporary to Bede, but earlier than the *H.E.*, anticipated his efforts to narrate
the course of Christian conversion in England. If models were a normal aid
to Bede's authorship, there was no lack of appropriate ones for the *H.E.*[76]

A little effort is needed to grasp the coherence of the *H.E.*; the work

---

lac, disregarded here because Northumbrian only in authorship), see Thacker, "Social Background."

[74] The *Verse* and *Prose Cuthbert* are based on the Anon. *Cuthbert* (above, n. 55). Bede's
poem on St. Ethelthryth, *H.E.* 4.20. The chronicles are modeled on those of Eusebius-Jerome
and Isidore; the *Martyrology* is developed out of the Hieronymian *Martyrology*; the *Vitae* of St.
Felix and St. Anastasius are both adaptations of earlier hagiographies. The same may be observed in regard to his other works: the biblical commentaries have models; the works on time
and *De natura rerum* derive in the first instance from Isidore (Manitius, *Geschichte d. lat. Lit.*
I, 77-78).

[75] Campbell, "Bede," pp. 162-63; Wallace-Hadrill, "Gregory of Tours and Bede," p. 96;
Wallace-Hadrill, "Bede and Plummer," p. 79.

[76] This is more fully dealt with below, § 4.

might well seem fragmented at first reading. Quite a few chapters, some very long, look as though they were isolated from the main line of narrative development and from each other. The vision of St. Fursey, the miracles at Barking, the *Libellus responsionum* of Gregory the Great, and the extracts from Bede's *Holy Places*, stand out as examples in a list of apparent digressions that is easily lengthened.[77] The *H.E.* as a whole does not advance briskly on a straight chronological track. Posthumous miracles are narrated on the occasion of King Oswald's death and a later translation of relics on that of Queen Ethelthryth's; Gregory the Great's life is recapitulated as part of his obituary, and later obituaries (of Abbess Hild of Whitby, Bishop Wilfrid of York, and others) have the same retrospective character.[78] Time moves backward and forward rather freely on either side of the span confining the material of each book.

In these ways, the *H.E.* shares the episodic character of the histories of Eusebius and Gregory of Tours, but a large part of the modern appeal of Bede's work comes from its perceptible and unusual dramatic unity. What palliates its episodicity is that the attentive reader becomes aware of a compact, unfolding, and concluded story: the Britons, who lost God's favor by their sins, compounded their guilt by denying the Gospels to the English, God's righteous scourge upon them; first the emissaries of Gregory the Great, then the Irish brought to the English the priceless seed of God's Word, which they prudently tended into vigorous growth; and the grateful converts repaid not only Rome, by missions to the continental heathen, but also their Irish benefactors by winning them to the Roman Easter.[79] As a fragment of the larger tale of the Almighty's salvific purpose, nothing so poetic and pleasing had ever been written in any language, or would be.

In spite of the admiration rightly aroused by Bede's art, it should not go unobserved that the dramatic framework that sustains and animates his narrative embodies a contrast in perspective that affects the *H.E.* as a whole. From one standpoint, the *H.E.* concerns the entire English Church. Gregory the Great was responsible for giving the name *gens Anglorum* to all the pagan newcomers to Britain, and the term had currency in this sense before Bede.[80] Book I makes us particularly conscious of the broad perspective. Bede sets his stage in the opening chapter, describing Britain and its peoples, as well as Ireland; the Gregorian mission is narrated in the same spirit, and pains are taken throughout the work to supply information

[77] *H.E.* 3.19, 4.6-11, 1.27, 5.16-17.

[78] Oswald, *H.E.* 3.2, 9-13; Ethelthryth, 4.19; Gregory the Great, 2.1; Hild, 4.23; Wilfrid, 5.19. Also see *H.E.* 2.18, 4.3.

[79] Cf. Hanning, *Vision of History*, pp. 67-90.

[80] As we have recently been reminded by Wormald, "Bede, *Bretwaldas*, and Origins," p. 124.

about Christianity in the various Anglo-Saxon kingdoms. The *gens Anglorum* in the sense of Gregory the Great makes its presence felt.[81] On the other hand, as we have already observed, the *H.E.* has stronger claims to being mainly about Northumbria, on which the narrative focuses from book II, chapter 9, onward. The other Anglo-Saxon kingdoms seem to be almost as subsidiary to Northumbria as the Britons and Irish are to the English. The result of this dualism is that the drama that begins on a very lofty plane, with Providence and the merited punishment of the Britons through the worthy English, concludes in a strictly provincial fashion, with an Iro-Northumbrian mission to the Continent and the winning by a Northumbrian of Irish Iona to the Catholic Easter.[82] The gratifying concord of ending with beginning owes less to history than to our willing disregard of details.

There is no harm in what Bede does; the impact of the *H.E.* is not lessened by our noticing the disparity of scale between start and finish. But Bede's manipulation of his drama forces us to give thought to the way in which he designed the *H.E.* in the first place. Was the broad or the narrow perspective primary in his plan? The capsule characterizations of the *H.E.* often given in recent scholarship, while differing in details, seem to agree that the history is homogeneous and that Bede's aim may be inferred from its title as variously interpreted.[83] Such characterizations are based on what Bede succeeded in doing; they are an aid to our appreciation of the finished *H.E.*, but not necessarily of its genesis. No logic decrees that either the inception of Bede's project or the intent with which he set about his work should be directly reflected by the end-product. We do not know his point of departure, and we would be rash to think that it is revealed by the prefatory matter or by book I or by the title. The contents of the entire *H.E.* are the only secure basis of judgment.

As a finished text, without regard to its elaboration or sources, the *H.E.* gives the appearance of resulting from a rather delicate marriage of North-

---

[81] *H.E.* 1.1 (note also the careful identification of informants outside Northumbria in the preface); on the comprehensive orientation of the Gregorian mission, 1.29, 2.1; the progress of the Church outside Northumbria: 2.5, 15-16, 3.7-8, 18-22, 29-30, 4.1-3, 6-12, 14-17, 5.7-8, 20, 23.

[82] *H.E.* 5.9-10, 22; though these are not the last chapters, they appear to be the dramatic climax of the work.

[83] E.g. Hunter Blair, "Historical Writings," pp. 210-11; Colgrave, *OMT*, pp. xxx-xxxi; Campbell, "Bede," p. 182; Cowdrey, "Bede and the 'English People,' " pp. 501-502.

Wallace-Hadrill, "Bede and Plummer," pp. 89-90, recognized that, though the *H.E.* is "of the whole English people . . . it is not without a local slant"; saying no more than strictly necessary about Deira and Bernicia, Bede emphasized "the unity or at least the entity of Northumbria." Gransden, *Historical Writing in England*, pp. 16, 25, stressed the prominence of Northumbria and the disproportionate amount of space devoted to it in the *H.E.*; too hastily, Bede's course is attributed to sentimental reasons.

umbria with the wider *gens Anglorum*. The choice between the hypothesis of an unavoidably narrowed Church history of the English or that of a purposely enlarged Church history of the Northumbrians is not hard to make. Northumbria or its sons and daughters occupy ten of fifty-four chapters in books I-II (18 percent by chapter count, though not necessarily by lineage or words), and sixty-three out of eighty-six chapters in books III-V (73 percent). By the same rough measure, the entire *H.E.* is 52 percent Northumbrian.[84] Even its earliest and most consistently "Southern" book ends on a resoundingly Northumbrian note.[85] The missionary activity Bede records in Sussex and in Frisia is not by Englishmen in general but by Northumbrians; the continental enterprise of Boniface, proceeding from Wessex and well known to us, goes unmentioned.[86] Bede's best stories have the same parochial source: the slave boys in Rome, the tale of the sparrow flying through a hall, the nobleman whose chains fall off, the vision of Drycthelm, and Cædmon at Whitby are uniformly Northumbrian.[87] It seems only natural that the one of Bede's works dedicated to a layman should have been addressed to a king of Northumbria.[88]

If Bede's guiding thought had been to embrace all the English, few traces of such a plan have found their way into the finished work. As a result of the Roman and British preoccupations of book I, considerably less than half the *H.E.* is applied to chapters concerned with other Anglo-Saxon kingdoms.[89] To be sure, Canterbury holds a prominent place. Its association with the *H.E.*, clearly attested by Bede's prefatory acknowledgment that Abbot Albinus was his principal support and helper, is borne out by the account of the Gregorian mission and by the beneficent role assigned to Archbishop Theodore. Until the pope elevated York to metropolitan status in 735, Canterbury was the sole archbishopric in England, and Bede takes pains to treat it with affectionate respect.[90] But the role of Canterbury does

---

[84] Owing to overlaps, statistics of this sort cannot pretend to be exact. I take the following chapters of the *H.E.* to be Northumbrian (including events in other regions whose leading actors are Northumbrian, such as Wilfrid in Sussex): 1.34, 2.9-20, 3.1-6, 9-13, 14-17, 22-28, 4.3, 14-16, 18-32, 5.1-6, 9-15, 19-24.

[85] Above, n. 25.

[86] *H.E.* 4.13-16, 5.9-11. Similarly, an Irishman based in Northumbria, Cedd, is central to 3.22 (about Essex). About Boniface, see below, n. 92.

[87] Respectively, *H.E.* 2.1, 13, 4.22, 5.12, 4.24.

[88] Campbell, "Bede," p. 168.

[89] *H.E.* 1.2-14, 16-22, are situated in pre-English times; 2.1 is about Gregory the Great, and 5.16-17 about the Holy Places. The following chapters, comprising about 30 percent of the whole (by chapter count), appear to be concerned with England outside Northumbria: 1.1, 15, 23-33, 2.2-8, 15-16, 3.7-8, 18-21, 29-30, 4.1-3, 6-12, 17, 5.7-8.

[90] *H.E. praef.*, 1.23-33, 2.2-8, 3.29, 4.1-2, 12, 17, 5.8, 20. On Egbert of York receiving the *pallium* from the pope, see the annals in Plummer, I, 361; it cannot be coincidental that (as the annal records) Egbert's elevation from bishop to archbishop occurred in the same year Nothelm acceded to the see of Canterbury. Cf. below, n. 181.

not make up for the gaps in coverage outside Northumbria. A major achievement of recent scholarship has been to gather and assess the many traces of early English ecclesiastical activity that Bede omitted.[91] His widely noted lack of attention to the great kingdom of Mercia is hard to account for on the grounds that information was unavailable; Mercia was nearby and its clergy are unlikely to have been less communicative than those from elsewhere. The absence of any reference to Boniface's mission has always seemed strange, in as much as Daniel of Winchester, Boniface's patron, is cited by Bede as a correspondent and informant.[92] The silence of the *H. E.* on this subject and many others seems best accounted for by the premise that Bede's goal was never comprehensive coverage. The *H.E.* is what he wished it to be from the start—not a history of the English Church, but an account of the Northumbrian Church set in an all-English context, or a Northumbrian narrative enlarged to English dimensions.

As a work concerned with the whole of England, the *H.E.* would be necessarily Olympian. Power was so scattered in Bede's Britain that no history of the English Church could have readily advocated a cause or embodied an immediate political purpose.[93] In keeping with political circumstances and Bede's pervasive calm, the *H.E.* has generally been deemed to be addressed to posterity and not to have been a tract for its times. This view makes too little allowance for its provincial face. As a narrative of the Northumbrian Church dedicated to King Ceolwulf, the *H.E.* was well suited to pleading a cause and pressing a course of action. Nothing prevented the celebrated theologian and polymath Bede from being more actively engaged in his Northumbrian surroundings than the devout, secluded scholar whom he recommended to his reader's prayers.

The *H.E.* does not look as though it were a work of advocacy. It is about the past and effectively ends many years before the time of writing. The disputed issue to which it pays most attention, namely, the correct reckoning of Easter, cannot have been topical in the 730s; with minor exceptions, the Roman Easter had prevailed.[94] Bede preferred to inspire affection rather than to nourish hate; the *H.E.* is predominantly a gallery of heroes, many of them unforgettable. There are hardly any villains except the now

---

[91] Above, n. 17.

[92] Mercia: Kirby, "Bede's Native Sources," pp. 342, 368. Boniface: Wallace-Hadrill, "Bede's Europe," p. 74.

[93] Campbell, "Bede," pp. 168-69.

[94] Campbell, "Bede," p. 180, considers Easter dating still topical in 731 because the Britons persisted in rejecting the Catholic date (*H.E.* 2.4, 5.23). But the Britons' obstinacy was very different from the earlier crisis. The Easter problem had been critical in Northumbria because it divided friends from each other. This doleful schism was over. Where the Britons were concerned, disagreement over Easter was merely an aspect of an enduring hostility that would be settled, presumably, by armed force (e.g. the case of Aldhelm, next note).

dominated British.[95] Even the fierce king of Mercia, Penda, scourge of the first English converts to Christianity, is treated with restraint and credited with admirable sentiments.[96] The actions of the West Saxon king, Cædwalla, tag him as a savage brute, but Bede does not explicitly call him so.[97] His avoidance of blame and other criticism has been widely noted; this is his famous discretion. He is never more discreet than in respect to Wilfrid, the great Northumbrian bishop who died in 709. The spectrum of modern opinion bears out the ambiguity of the *H.E.*: Plummer, Colgrave, and many others have maintained that Bede disapproved of Wilfrid, whereas Marion Gibbs and Gabriele Isenberg hold that his feelings were positive.[98] On a more general plane, recent commentators have rightly stressed that the contrast between Bede's England and Gregory of Tours' Gaul is only apparent; enough may be read between the lines of the *H.E.* to suggest that an English Gregory would have found abundant turpitude and violence in Bede's "age of saints."[99]

The absence of Gallic turpitude from the *H.E.* is perhaps too hastily explained if attributed only to authorial sensitivity and temperament. Bede situates serenity and holiness in a bygone age beyond the reach of his audience's recollection: this is an argumentative thing to do. One of the greatest medieval works of advocacy, the *False Decretals* of Pseudo-Isidore (composed in France little more than a century after Bede), gives an appearance of serenity comparable to the *H.E.*'s; in the words of Schafer Williams, the *Decretals* conveys a "vision of the golden age of the church" under the pre-Constantinian popes.[100] The tale Bede tells is of the fast-receding golden age of the English Church. This angle of vision need not be attributed to idealism. What is a retrospective golden age if not a stick with which to beat the present?

[95] *H.E.* 1.22, 2.4, 20, 5.22. Aldhelm won some Britons to the Catholic Easter but they were subjects of the West Saxons (5.18).

[96] *H.E.* 2.22, 3.7, 9, 16-18, 21 (implied praise), 23.

[97] Cædwalla; see below, nn. 354-59.

[98] Plummer II, 316; he had predecessors in this view, but is held to be the fountainhead of the idea that Bede disliked Wilfrid. Along the same lines, e.g., Hunt, "Wilfrid," p. 242, "Bede evidently wrote in sympathy with Wilfrid's opponents" (an accurate assessment); Jones, *Bedae Opera de temp.*, pp. 134-35 (convinced that Bede was moved in part by personal considerations); Colgrave, "Bede's Miracle Stories," p. 206; Duckett, *Anglo-Saxon Saints*, p. 249. In a more qualified sense, Stenton, *Anglo-Saxon England*, 2d ed., p. 145: Bede treats Wilfrid "with a curious detachment." Whitelock, "Bede and His Teachers," pp. 32-33, turns sharply away from the idea that Bede had strong feelings about Wilfrid; before her, Kirby, "Bede's Native Sources," p. 356. Diametrically opposite to Plummer, Gibbs, "Decrees of Agatho," esp. pp. 242-46 ("Bede hoped to make Wilfrid better loved at centres in Northumbria antagonised by his quarrel with Aldfrith, as well as to please his spiritual sons at Ripon and Hexham, Selsey and Wight"); Isenberg, *Wurdigung Wilfrids*. Attention is drawn to Gibbs's positive view by Farmer, "St. Wilfrid," pp. 57-58.

[99] Campbell, "Bede," p. 182.

[100] Williams's thesis is entitled "Visio aetatis aureae ecclesiae Pseudo-Isidoriana."

Bede's *Letter to Egbert of York*, expressing his concern about the Northumbrian Church, allows us to detect several aspects of the *H.E.* that would otherwise be hidden from us or ambiguous. The *Letter* establishes that Bede cared very much about the provision of pastoral care to remote districts; he proposed that excessively large bishoprics should be broken up into dioceses small enough to permit each bishop to travel through the territory at least once a year in a round of pastoral visits. He urged that bishoprics should be established in monasteries, for lack of other suitable localities, and that episcopal households should be havens of religious life. The cost of these reforms should be met by the abolition of abusive family monasteries and the application of their endowments to the new monastery-bishoprics. In these ways, York would soon become a metropolis with twelve suffragan sees.[101]

The *Letter* lends a topical character to passages of the *H.E.* that might otherwise seem to be mere history. Bede must have thoroughly approved of Archbishop Theodore's division of the single Northumbrian bishopric, reported without comment; the pastoral rounds attributed to the Irishmen Aidan, Cedd, and Chad, and to the Irish-trained Northumbrian Cuthbert, all lovingly described, are not just manifestations of ancient saintliness, but models for present emulation; and the references to the monastery-bishoprics of Augustine at Canterbury and Cuthbert at Lindisfarne are meant just as much to set a living example as the Irish pastoral rounds.[102] As for the abusive monasteries, their fleeting appearance in book V of the *H.E.* would be hard to recognize without the *Letter*; on the contrary, we might easily reach the false conclusion that Bede foresaw an idyllic future in which all Northumbrians laid down their weapons in order to live as monks.[103] Bede's recommendations for reform matter less, for the moment, than the value of the *Letter* as a gloss to the *H.E.* For these few passages, at least, we know that the *H.E.* had direct bearing on Bede's time and place. Was all the rest mere history? Though the *H.E.* may seem straightforward, Bede's discretion assures us that it is anything but.

Bede is less isolated than he is sometimes thought to be. In the wider setting of Christian letters, his narrative reflects the condition of a branch of

---

[101] *Epist. ad Ecgbertum* 7-13, 3-4. Bede recalls that Gregory the Great had meant York to be the metropolis of a twelve-diocese province.

[102] Theodore's division, *H.E.* 4.12; pastoral rounds, 3.5, 23, 4.3, 27; monastery-bishoprics, 1.26, 27 (ch. 1), 4.27.

[103] *H.E.* 5.23: "Qua adridente pace ac serenitate temporum, plures in gente Nordanhymbrorum, tam nobiles, quam privati, se suosque liberos, depositis armis, satagunt magis, accepta tonsura, monasterialibus adscribere votis, quam bellicis exercere studiis. Quae res quem sit habitura finem, posterior aetas videbit." The irony of these lines is not easily grasped without outside assistance; cf. Davidse, "Sense of the Past," p. 667, who thinks Bede approves. An even more veiled reference to abusive monasteries occurs in the vision of Drycthelm (5.12).

literature that had thrived among Westerners for more than a century. As a historian of Northumbria, Bede was even less solitary than in a broader Latin context. Northumbria was a large kingdom, but its major religious centers were not far apart. If a signpost were erected at Bede's Jarrow to indicate (roughly measured) distances to comparable establishments, it would read: Hexham, 28 mi.; Lindisfarne, 53 mi.; Whitby, 53 mi.; Ripon, 66 mi.[104] The concentration of literate clergymen might be inconsequential but for one fact: in the generation immediately preceding Bede's, an exceptional and combative prelate, Bishop Wilfrid, had played a conspicuously positive or negative part in their existence and in that of the kingdom at large. His activity did not leave literary traces only in Bede. Levison spoke for more than himself in remarking, "We should like to hear more from [Bede] about the controversies and struggles of the last generation around the person of Wilfrid, about which he gives less but more discreet information than we have reason to believe he possessed."[105] In fact, a great deal more about Wilfrid may be discerned in Bede and others than any of them explicitly says.

Although Bede was unique among Northumbrian authors in not writing only about the illustrious churchmen of his land, he did now and then turn aside from biblical commentary and join his fellow countrymen in glorifying local heroes. This collective historiographic effort was unparalleled in early England. Its components are listed here in as strict a chronological order as information permits:

> Lindisfarne, *Life of St. Cuthbert*, 699-705[106]
> Whitby, *Life of St. Gregory the Great*, after 704[107]
> Bede, *Life of St. Cuthbert* (verse), before 716[108]
> Wearmouth, *Life of Ceolfrid*, after 716, 718?[109]

[104] I am very grateful to Lesley Abrams, doctoral candidate in the Centre for Medieval Studies, University of Toronto, for making these approximations of distance respectable.

[105] Levison, "Bede as Historian," p. 146.

[106] Cited above, n. 55. For the date, ed. Colgrave, *Two Lives of St. Cuthbert*, p. 33: at least a year after the translation of Cuthbert (698), but before the death of King Aldfrith (December 705).

[107] For the best edition, see the List of Abbreviations, under Whitby *Gregory*. The work was written after Ethelred ceased to be king of Mercia (704), while Ælffled was still abbess of Whitby (she died in 714), but after the death of Eanfled (born 626, still alive 685, death date unknown): Colgrave, *Two Lives*, pp. 47-49. Colgrave prefers a date nearer 714. The basis for any preference has to be the author's mention of "diebus Edilredi regis illorum [i.e. the South English]" (Whitby *Gregory* 18, p. 102). If this could have been written by a Northumbrian on the morrow of Ethelred's resignation (as well as somewhat later), an early date within the span 704-14 is equally justifiable.

[108] Cited above, n. 55. King Osred, who was killed in 716, is referred to as living: *Verse Cuthbert* 552-55, ed. Jaager, pp. 99-100.

[109] See *VCeolf* in the List of Abbreviations. For its date, n. 195 below.

"Eddius Stephanus," *Life of Wilfrid,* before 720[110]

Bede, *Life of St. Cuthbert* (prose), before 721[111]

Bede, *History of the Abbots,* after 725[112]

Bede, *H.E.,* 731

One way to react to this list is to acknowledge that Bede had minor contemporaries, just as he himself composed minor histories, and then to disregard their writings as well as all of his except the *H.E.,* on the grounds that they are minor. Another possibility is to blend the minor works with the *H.E.* into a comprehensive "harmony of the Gospels," dovetailing bits from each relevant text into a composite narrative. As a small illustration of this procedure, one might note that the *Life of Wilfrid,* but not Bede, has King Oswy "smile" when asking the Council of Whitby whether Columba or Peter was the greater saint; the next step is to insert the appealing personal detail into an account of the incident closely based on Bede's, on the premise that the addition is a justified improvement.[113] Harmonization is particularly attractive when one's aim is to compose a balanced modern account of the early English Church, and not to grapple with the substance of each text.

The approach to be taken here stresses the distinctiveness of the various writings, their possibly abrasive relations to each other, the implications of the passage of time and sequentiality, and, not least, the accompanying course of events in the eighth-century kingdom. The hypothesis is that each of these Northumbrian narratives was a steppingstone toward the *H.E.* Together, they are the surviving traces of a very contentious tale capped, no less contentiously, by Bede's great work. The Northumbria of

[110] For editions and translations, see under *VW* in the List of Abbreviations; also Moonen, *Leven van sint Wilfrid;* its extensive notes thoroughly discuss modern differences of opinion concerning Wilfrid, regarded as the original apostle of the land now forming the Netherlands. For the common attribution to Eddius Stephanus (a master of chant mentioned in *VW* 14 and *H.E.* 4.2), see below, n. 210.

The absolute termini for the *VW* are 710/711 (a year after Wilfrid's death) and 731 (used by Bede in the *H.E.*). Ed. Colgrave, *The Life of Bishop Wilfrid by Eddius Stephanus,* p. x, considers "highly probable" composition within a decade of Wilfrid's death, "that is to say before 720." The best reason for agreeing with his approximation is that Bede's *Prose Cuthbert,* which was written by 721 (next note), was a response to *VW.* The matter is more fully discussed below, nn. 210-16.

[111] For the date, Colgrave, *Two Lives,* p. 16. Bishop Eadfrith, to whom the work is addressed, died in 721.

[112] Toward 725, Bede still used the *VCeolf* (*Chron. maius* 590, ed. Mommsen, p. 320); the date is inferred from this fact.

[113] Duckett, *Anglo-Saxon Saints,* p. 136. The passages in question are *VW* 10 and *H.E.* 3.25. Stenton, *Anglo-Saxon England,* p. 123, "the king gave his judgment with a smile"; in fact, Oswy's smile accompanies an earlier speech and clearly disparages Columba (below, nn. 326-27). Loyn, *Anglo-Saxon England and the Norman Conquest,* p. 228: "If King Oswy was smiling as he delivered his verdict." Along the same lines, Deanesly, *Pre-Conquest Church in England,* p. 89; Randers-Pehrson, *Barbarians and Romans,* pp. 323-24.

Bede's maturity had a history, though we know too little about it, and its literary remains, intent on rehearsing the past rather than disclosing the present, are the tips of an iceberg whose outlines and course need careful charting. Even if we care only moderately about Northumbrian happenings, our understanding of Bede's *H. E.* gains precision and concreteness from taking account of the circumstances that witnessed its birth.

3. The Genesis of Northumbrian Church History

For more than four decades, the ecclesiastical and political life of Northumbria was deeply affected, in one way or another, by the figure of Bishop Wilfrid, the first English-born bishop who, in Bede's careful phrase, acquired the training to instruct his countrymen in the ways of the universal Church.[114] When Wilfrid was elevated to episcopal dignity (665), Oswy, brother of the heroic Oswald, was king; when Wilfrid died in 709, the boy Osred, grandson of Oswy, occupied the throne and was indebted to Wilfrid for being there. Altogether, Wilfrid was bishop in Northumbria for about twenty years, in three periods punctuated by two long exiles. Twice he journeyed to Rome to obtain papal support for his reinstatement, with indifferent results at both ends.[115] His recoveries of power were almost as dramatic as his expulsions. Much of his most constructive work took place in Mercia and other parts of England, as well as on the Continent, in Frisia, during the intervals of exile.[116] He was a giant in the making of the English Church. Moreover, by dominating the horizon, generating hostility toward himself, and continuing to be an issue after his death, he incited the Northumbrian Church, alone in England, to provide itself with written history.

[114] *H. E.* 4.2: "primus inter episcopos, qui de Anglorum gente essent, catholicum vivendi morem ecclesiis Anglorum tradere didicit." Among modern historians, Wilfrid's standing has much improved in the past half-century; e.g. Wormald, "Bede, *Beowulf*," p. 55, "[Wilfrid] was the greatest, all things considered, of the early Anglo-Saxon saints"—an opinion that would have chagrined Bede.

[115] Oswy (642-70), Osred (706-16): Harrison, *Framework of Anglo-Saxon History*, p. 88. On Osred's indebtedness to Wilfrid, *VW* 59. Wilfrid's periods as bishop in Northumbria, according to Levison, MGH SRM VI, 168-72, 175, 177-78: 669-78, 686/87-691/92, 706-709/10. His journeys to Rome, 678-80, 704-705: *ibid.* pp. 172-74, 176-77. Neither papal decision in his favor was honored in Northumbria, *VW* 34, 58. His reinstatements came in the wake of political crises, *VW* 44, 59-60.

I am more concerned with relative chronology than with absolute dates, which have occasioned much controversy. My exposition is not affected if, e.g., Oswy died in 671 and Aldfrith in 704, or if the Synod of Austerfield occurred in 702. Modern authorities, like the sources themselves, tend to vary, especially by a margin of a year; see Wood, "Bede's Northumbrian Dates Again" (but her discussion stops short of the eighth century).

[116] Frisia, *VW* 26; Mercia, Sussex, Wight, *VW* 39-42; Mercia, *VW* 45 (cf. Plummer II, 318-19). For a fuller account of Wilfrid's Mercian interests, as reflected in Stephen's narrative, Kirby, "Bede, Eddius Stephanus," pp. 104-106.

The earliest Latin narratives composed in England are the anonymous *Life of St. Cuthbert*, the work of a monk of Lindisfarne between 699 and 705, and the likewise anonymous *Life of Pope Gregory the Great* by a monk of Whitby, presumably between 704 and 714.[117] Each of them refers to and, in some sense, results from a solemn transfer of holy relics, a ceremony designed to animate the liturgical cult of a personage closely associated with the communities in which the narratives arose. These incidents and two others like them should engage our attention before we turn to the writings in which they are recorded. There is a theory according to which myth originates in sacred ritual; in a manner reminiscent of this theory, Northumbrian history seems to descend from four elevations or translations of saints.[118]

Prior to the institution of canonization by the pope in the twelfth century, the medieval churches had no fixed procedure for declaring that their deceased son or daughter so-and-so was a saint. The cult "sprang spontaneously from the life of the Church. Local communities venerated their own heroes and other great men of whom they had heard." A favored context for instituting the celebration of a saint was a transfer of relics over a short or long distance, from one tomb to another, with perhaps a long intervening journey.[119] Canonizations of this sort stand behind the earliest Northumbrian hagiographies. In the case of Lindisfarne, the body of St. Cuthbert was raised from his grave on 20 March 698, precisely eleven years after his death, and given a new resting place. In that of Whitby, the remains of King Edwin, slain in 633, were uncovered in Lindsey, borne to Whitby, and reburied at some time between 680 and 704.[120]

The interest of these ceremonies is enhanced by our knowing from Bede's *H.E.*, though not from separate narratives, that a third event of the same sort and possibly a fourth occurred within the same period and honored

[117] Scholars hesitate over which Northumbrian hagiography is the earlier (cf. nn. 107-108). Colgrave, "Earliest Saints' Lives," p. 37, opts for the Anon. *Cuthbert*. Bullough, "Hagiography as Patriotism," pp. 341-42, prefers the Whitby *Gregory* (but cf. Bullough, "Columba, Adamnan, I," p. 129). There is no clear basis for choice. The most to be said, on the basis of the fixed termini, is that the Whitby *Gregory* may have been composed at the same time as the Anon. *Cuthbert* or later, but is unlikely to be earlier.

[118] Raglan, *The Hero*, pp. 141-72.

[119] Kemp, *Canonization and Authority*, pp. 21 (quotation), 29, and (in general) 3-35. On early translations, Aigrain, *Hagiographie*, pp. 186-89; and especially Heinzelmann, *Translationsberichte*. Graus, "Sozialgeschichtliche Aspekte der Hagiographie," pp. 140-41, cautions against assuming that every translation made a saint; more than this ceremony was needed to ensure the continuity of a cult.

[120] Anon. *Cuthbert* 4.14 (after the monastery elders held council and by permission of Bishop Eadberht). Edwin: Whitby *Gregory* 18-19 (the result of a miraculous discovery). The termini for its occurrence are 680 (the death of Abbess Hild of Whitby) and 704; but it took place in the lifetime of Eanfled, still alive in 685 but who must have been getting on, since she was born in 626 (above, n. 107). The 690s are possible.

Northumbrian saints outside Northumbria. In 695, the body of the virgin-queen Ethelthryth (better known to us as Audrey), once wife of King Ecgfrith of Northumbria, was elevated at Ely, perhaps in the presence of the exiled bishop Wilfrid.[121] The fourth incident occurred at an indeterminate time between 679 and 697; the remains of the Northumbrian king Oswald were translated to the monastery of Bardney, in Lindsey, at the behest of Queen Ostryth of Mercia, a Northumbrian princess.[122] Oswald had been venerated, at least outside Mercia, before his translation to Bardney; the canonizations of Ethelthryth, Edwin, and Cuthbert were new.[123]

Unlike the annual cycle of saints' feasts, the ceremonial elevation, dis-covery, or translation of holy relics occurred only once, as an event charged with significance for the living participants. The proceedings often had po-litical content. There could hardly be a more impressive way for a faction within the Church to sustain its conviction that God blessed the cause it championed than to enlist one of His saints on its side. The discovery of the martyrs Gervasius and Protasius by Bishop Ambrose of Milan is a justly famous illustration of the political uses of the cult of saints; the late fourth and fifth centuries were rich in comparable episodes.[124] Their emergence in England in the 690s is a sign of Christian maturity.

In view of the political potential of canonizations, it is hardly surprising that Bishop Wilfrid should be associated with the elevation of the relics of Queen Ethelthryth, who had died at Ely in 679. The ceremony of 695 oc-curred three years after Wilfrid had been forced to leave Northumbria for the second time and had exiled himself to Mercia.[125] When Ethelthryth

---

[121] *H.E.* 4.19. Bede does not say that Wilfrid was present, only that he was among the many who could attest that the queen's body was free of decay when she was unearthed (cf. *VW* 19); his presence seems implied, though stated in such a way as not to be obvious. Instead, Bede specially emphasizes the testimony of the physician Cynifrid, who was present at both Ethelthryth's death and her exhumation.

[122] *H.E.* 3.11. The chronological proximity of these translations is masked in the *H.E.* Even the elevation of Cuthbert, reported closest to its actual occurrence (*H.E.* 4.30), should, if entered in order, fall somewhat after the death of Theodore (5.8). Bede scattered these com-paratively recent events as postscripts to incidents of the past (just as, in hagiography, post-humous *miracula* are often narrated immediately after a saint's *vita*).

[123] Bede's most clearly dated reference to the early cult is in *H.E.* 3.12; also see 3.6. The indications in 3.2, 9-10, might be earlier than the translation to Bardney, but need not be.

[124] On the attachment of translations to concrete events, Heinzelmann, *Translations-berichte*, p. 57. Ambrose's translations: Paulinus *Vita s. Ambrosii* 13-15 (Gervasius and Protas-ius), 27-29 (Vitalis and Agricola, with transfer to Florence), 32-33 (Nazarius and Celsus), ed. and tr. M. S. Kanieka, Catholic University, Patristic Studies 16 (Washington 1928), pp. 50-54, 68-70, 74-76; Dudden, *Life and Times of St. Ambrose* I, 291 with n. 4, 298-319. For some other early translations, see Sozomen *H.E.* 7.21, 29, 9.2, 16-17. The political aspect of the latter two is clearly spelled out (one occurs as a result of a dream of the Augusta Pulcheria). The repatriation of the corpse of John Chrysostom (438)—also a saint-creating translation—was a deliberate measure of pacification; Socrates *H.E.* 7.45, Theodoret *H.E.* 5.36.

[125] *VW* 45-46.

had been Ecgfrith's queen and he sole bishop of Northumbria (670-78), he had been her spiritual counselor, perhaps to his detriment; it had been a time in which the kingdom had enjoyed a prosperity long since lost.[126] The queen's uncorrupted remains, unearthed in 695, gloriously attested to her virginity, but they also dramatized and honored the epoch that Wilfrid had shared with her.

The translation of the relics of King Oswald to Bardney, if it took place in the 690s, would have been no less relevant than Ethelthryth's to the exiled bishop, whose base for episcopal activity from 692 to 703 was Leicester, in Mercia.[127] Without ever saying so, Bede's *H.E.* invites the inference that Wilfrid was the principal promoter of the cult of Oswald. The main focus of the cult was Wilfrid's foundation at Hexham, endowed by none other than Queen Ethelthryth: reports of miracles by the martyred king came from both lands that Wilfrid had evangelized.[128] If Oswald was peculiarly Wilfrid's saint, any extension of the cult was, simultaneously, a celebration of the great bishop's contribution to English Christianity. Bede, who almost wholly obscured Wilfrid's presence at the elevation of Ethelthryth, accorded him no place at all in the undated translation to Bardney.[129] The silence of the *H.E.* cannot be considered a bar to the possibility that Wilfrid had a hand in the ceremony. Among other things, the implanting of Oswald at Bardney recalled that, when Wilfrid had been bishop, Lindsey had belonged to Ecgfrith's realm; it had been lost to Northumbria within a year after Wilfrid's first expulsion.[130]

The translations of relics that took place in Northumbria in the same years as those at Bardney and Ely were just as topical. Hild, the formidable abbess of Whitby, had sent an envoy to plead against Wilfrid before the pope (680), and several priests trained in the male branch of her monastery

---

[126] *VW* 19-22; *H.E.* 4.19. One of Wilfrid's main antagonists was to be Erminburg, Ethelthryth's successor as queen, *VW* 24, 34.

[127] Leicester is a guess: Poole, "St. Wilfrid and Ripon," p. 73.

[128] Kirby, "Northumbria in Time of Wilfrid," pp. 26-28. Hexham, *H.E.* 3.2 (its foundation, *VW* 22). Miracles out of Frisia (3.13) and Sussex (4.14). Kirby is right to regard Wilfrid's cultivation of Oswald as paradoxical at first sight, but it is not "peculiar" (p. 28). Wilfrid as a champion of Roman observance had an excellent reason to promote a cult of King Oswald: the "martyr" king, a Northumbrian convert to Christianity only indirectly and involuntarily implicated with the "poisonous weeds" of the Irish, was admirably suited to be the symbolic link between the innocently Hibernicized Christians of Northumbria and their reordering along Roman lines by Wilfrid. Wilfrid hoped, by magnifying Oswald, both to overshadow the memory of Aidan and his peers and to retain the benefits of their evangelization.

[129] *H.E.* 3.11. Wilfrid makes his unobtrusive début in 3.13. The translation occurred between the Mercian reconquest of Lindsey (679) and the murder of Ostryth (697): Plummer II, 154-55. Ostryth's hostility toward Wilfrid in 680 (*VW* 40) is no obstacle to her amicable cooperation with him in the 690s; circumstances had changed.

[130] *H.E.* 4.21; *VW* 24 (no reference to loss of territory).

had been ordained in the sees that, in Wilfrid's view, were rightfully his.[131] A part of King Edwin's body—his head—lay buried at York; it was not a focus of public worship. The translation of his other remains to Whitby, more than a half-century after his death, when a miracle was needed to locate his remains, had a somewhat desperate and speculative character; it is hardly accidental that Bede, three decades later, says nothing of the Whitby cult of Edwin or of any other Edwin cult.[132] But, back toward 690, the Whitby translation had a conspicuous motive. Edwin epitomized the earliest Roman evangelization of Northumbria (he was also grandfather of the abbess of Whitby). His cult, if only it took hold, would overshadow by priority the acts of Wilfrid, the merely second spokesman in Northumbria for Roman customs, or, perhaps more simply, might aspire to rival with the Wilfrid-sponsored cult of King Oswald.[133]

Cuthbert belonged to a more recent and controversial past. As a symbol to others rather than by his own desire, he was directly involved in the opposition to Wilfrid. Cuthbert was drawn from his hermitage in 684 by the joint entreaties of King Ecgfrith and Archbishop Theodore so as to assume the see of a deposed Wilfridian. Within months, his royal sponsor was fatally defeated in the military disaster at Nechtansmere (685). Cuthbert died soon after (687), but was not discredited by his ill-chosen period of episcopate; on the contrary, his eccentrically ascetic way of life and irresistible fame as a wonder worker sustained the hold of the Church over the remote lands that Northumbria ceased to control in the wake of the Picts' victory over Ecgfrith.[134] The needs of the Church in the reign of the latter's

[131] VW 54; Whitby priests: Bosa at York and John of Beverley at Hexham (then York), H.E. 4.12, 23, 5.2-6, 20.

[132] Edwin died in 633; the translation took place after 680, before 704. Whitby Gregory 18-19 (summary below, n. 146): the finding of the relics has the normal trappings of a translation narrative, but then the discoverer, Trimma, unceremoniously dug up the remains and took them to Whitby. He might almost be a relic dealer, though not presented in this way by the hagiographer.

Bede first states that Edwin's head was buried on the porch of the church at York (H.E. 2.20) and, much later, that his body lay at Whitby along with other royalty (3.24); no reference is made to the circumstances in which Edwin came to rest there. Cf. Wallace-Hadrill, Early Germanic Kingship, pp. 80-83.

[133] H.E. 3.24 (her mother Eanfled, Oswy's wife, was Edwin's daughter and Wilfrid's patron when he was very young, VW 2-3). Ælffled was not a staunch friend of Wilfrid's (so Mayr-Harting, Coming of Christianity, pp. 150-51, 167). She is spoken of warmly in VW 59-60, but in the special circumstances of 705-706 (see below, n. 166). Archbishop Theodore urged her in the 680s to make peace with Wilfrid because she was a leading enemy of his (VW 43).

Faced with an overbearing figure identifying Rome with himself, Whitby had reason to dramatize the earlier roots of Rome in Northumbria; Edwin was better suited for this role than the Roman missionary Paulinus.

[134] Cuthbert's episcopacy, H.E. 4.27. Ecgfrith's defeat and death resoundingly vindicated Wilfrid, implicitly shaming churchmen such as Cuthbert who were parties to the replacement

successor, Aldfrith (685-705), were different from those of the prosperous years that ended in the defeat of 685. Cuthbert, whose holiness had wide appeal, was the hero suited to Aldfrith's circumstances. After death, though probably not in life, he became the alternative focus of enthusiasm, the symbolic anti-Wilfrid, recognized as such by Wilfrid's partisans and cultivated in this role by everyone else, including Bede.[135] When Cuthbert was elevated from his first tomb in 698, three years after Ethelthryth had been elevated at Ely, his body proved to be as free of corruption as hers.[136] This first declaration of Cuthbert's cult cannot have wholly lacked the symbolism it was to have in the decades to come.

Wilfrid was still alive when the first *Life of St. Cuthbert* was written, and it is possible, though less certain, that the Whitby *Life of Gregory the Great* also appeared in his lifetime.[137] If a moment suitable for their composition were to be chosen out of the available years, it would fall in the months immediately following the abortive Council of Austerfield in 703. About ten years into Wilfrid's second exile, Archbishop Berhtwald of Canterbury was prompted by papal command to summon a council at the southern edge of Northumbria in the presence of King Aldfrith; Wilfrid was given safe conduct to attend. The latter's biographer, our sole informant, supplies a credible report but leaves out too much to convey a comprehensive sense of the gathering. Though presumably called in a spirit of conciliation, the entire assembly, including bishops from Mercia, somehow turned against Wilfrid. The outcome, for reasons not easily discerned, was a paroxysm of hostility directed against not only Wilfrid but also his formerly undisturbed followers, who were excommunicated and scattered; from distant Malmesbury, Aldhelm wrote them a letter enjoining fidelity to their leader and fortitude in their trials.[138] Whatever the cause, the result spelled out by Wil-

---

of deposed Wilfridians. But though Cuthbert retired from active episcopacy late in 686 and resumed eremitic life in preparation for death, his popularity—and Lindisfarne's—seem to have been undimmed. On the disaster at Nechtansmere, n. 161 below.

[135] By annexing significant portions of the Anon. *Cuthbert*, Stephen's *VW* documents the Wilfridian recognition of Cuthbert's role. Cf. Colgrave, *Life of Bishop Wilfrid*, p. x, and below, nn. 218-19.

[136] Anon. *Cuthbert* 4.14; Bede *Verse Cuthbert* 38-39, *Prose Cuthbert* 42, H.E. 4.30. In addition to St. Ethelthryth's body, the arm and hand of King Oswald, in a reliquary at Bamburgh, were also reputed to be untouched by decay: H.E. 3.6.

[137] See above n. 117. Wilfrid died in 709; the Whitby *Gregory* dates from before 714.

[138] *VW* 46-49. Thacker, "Social Background," p. 271, believes that the *VW* contains "official accounts" of the councils of Austerfield and at the Nidd—a difficult opinion to substantiate. The accounts are unique and not visibly flawed, but do not pretend to be official and are unverifiable. Bede's failure to include a report of this council, even one borrowed from *VW*, is perhaps the clearest instance of *suppressio veri* in the H.E.

Aldhelm *Epistolae* 12, ed. Rudolf Ehwald, MGH AA. XV, 500-502, tr. M. Lapidge and M. Herren, *Aldhelm, The Prose Works* (n.p. 1979), pp. 168-70. Neither Ehwald (n. 1) nor

frid's biographer is clear: the Council of Austerfield brought anti-Wilfrid sentiment to its highest pitch and occasioned the aged bishop's last trek to the Holy See. But the storm was unexpectedly brief. At Aldfrith's death (705), a dynastic crisis forced a rapprochement between Wilfrid's enemies and him, and made possible the bishop's third and final return to Northumbria.[139]

Wilfrid resoundingly defended his forty-year episcopate before the Austerfield council. The terms he used, as known to us, may belong to his biographer rather than to him, but in one form or another he called history to the assistance of his cause; to oppose him was, he suggested, an act of infidelity toward all the wholesome and Catholic improvements he had brought to the Northumbrian Church.[140] The sensitivity to the past that Wilfrid thus aroused, and the period of inflamed feelings following this council, furnish a motive—the only one open to documentation—for the writing of the Whitby *Life of Gregory* and the first *Life of St. Cuthbert*. The evidence bearing on the date of these earliest of English hagiographies is too thin to permit certainties, but their contents sustain the idea that disinterested piety did not alone give them birth.

The Whitby *Life of Gregory the Great*, though quaint and entertaining, is an exceptionally crude hagiography. Its enduring value is as an example of authentically naïve, half-educated writing.[141] The author makes no secret of the community on whose behalf he worked. He was given a complicated directive—to narrate the first evangelization of Northumbria in the context of a celebration of the pope—and he had no very clear notion of how to go about this awkward task. There were serious problems. Whitby had an altar of St. Gregory but no wonder-working relics of the pope; King Edwin, recently reburied near this altar after his translation, had apparently occasioned no cures or other prodigies. Historical documentation was all but nonexistent.[142] The author was not without schooling; several of Pope Gregory's works were familiar to him, and he succeeded in extracting the

---

Herren (pp. 150-51) has convincing grounds for dating Aldhelm's letter to another time than after the Austerfield council; cf. Thacker, p. 239.

[139] VW 58-60. About the dynastic crisis, nn. 165-66 below.

[140] VW 47 (Wilfrid's speech of justification). Also see below, n. 304.

[141] Blair, *World of Bede*, p. 278; Thacker, "Social Background," p. 70, considers it very atypical. Ed. Colgrave, *The Earliest Life of Gregory the Great*, pp. 48-49, attributes most responsibility to the author's ignorance of hagiographic form. The dominant impression is of ignorance inelegantly coexisting with knowledge: considerable acquaintance with biblical exegesis and Gregory's works side by side with receptivity to legends that are unseemly in a Christian context (Whitby *Gregory* 15, 28, 29). By comparison, the Lindisfarne Anon. is an artist. The Whitby author lacked the "Hibernian background" that Bullough discerned in the Anon. *Cuthbert*: "Columba, Adamnan, II," p. 27; but cf. Thacker, pp. 98-100.

[142] Whitby *Gregory* 19. No miracles are credited to Edwin. A somewhat wondrous occurrence at the site of the king's first burial is reported, but it is only edifying, not thaumaturgic.

passages of autobiography they contain.[143] But he had no hagiographic models, or at least none he found useful. He felt bound to apologize at great length for Gregory's lack of miracles; they were not, he argued, indispensable for sanctity. Yet he managed, paradoxically, to report miracles of Gregory's all the same.[144] And what miracles! The unrestrained deployment of folklore motifs in the Whitby *Life* is far out of line with every other Northumbrian hagiography in the age of Bede.[145] Sedate hagiographic commonplaces are reserved only for the discovery of King Edwin's corpse; its credibility gains little as a result.[146]

A central issue in the study of the Whitby *Life* has been whether or not it was known to Bede. The *H.E.* contains two stories found also in the *Life of Gregory*, the main one being that of the English (more precisely, Deiran) boys in Rome who inspired the pope's mission.[147] Bede's ignorance of the *Life* is the currently preferred, though not the unanimous, position. That Bede does not acknowledge its existence or make verbal extracts is agreed to be unimportant. The main argument, devised eighty years ago and repeated ever since, is that Bede would surely have used more than two of the Whitby stories if he had known them.[148] "Surely" is a risky modifier. The

[143] Colgrave, *Earliest Life*, p. 53; the use of Gregory's writings is carefully itemized in Colgrave's annotation.

[144] Problem of miracles: Whitby *Gregory* 3-5; ch. 5 is very heavy going (Colgrave, *Earliest Life*, p. 56, "It is when our author seeks to comment or to put forward theological and philosophical theories that he becomes involved and turgid"). Miracles nevertheless: 20-23, 26, 28-29.

[145] The shocking ones are Whitby *Gregory* 28-29, and perhaps 22. Folklore motifs occur mainly in other miracles than Gregory's: 10 (the crowd dividing into three groups), 15 (Paulinus and the crow), 17 (Paulinus's soul in the form of a swan; cf. ed. Colgrave, p. 150 n. 68), 26 (the dove on Gregory's shoulder).

[146] Whitby *Gregory* 18-19, ed. Colgrave, pp. 100-105. The location of Edwin's bones was revealed in a dream to Trimma, a Northumbrian priest living in a monastery of the South English; he was to go to a village and ask a certain *ceorl* who knew the precise spot; it took two repetitions of the dream, the last with a whipping, for Trimma to obey; the relics were located in " 'such and such a village in Lindsey' (our brother who told me the story and who was a kinsman of the priest [Trimma] could not remember its name)." These motifs are precedented in translation narratives; the threefold vision derives indirectly from the famous *Epistola Luciani de revelatione corporis Stephani martyris primi* (Heinzelmann, *Translationsberichte*, p. 79). Otherwise, however, the translation of Edwin lacks saintly attributes, such as the occurrence of miracles on the journey and after reburial.

The design of the Whitby *Gregory* betrays greater acquaintance with hagiography than its contents suggest. It is ordered along the standard lines of *vita* followed by *miracula* (from ch. 20 on). But the *vita* ends with the translation of Edwin, not Gregory, whereas the *miracula*, which normally relate to the translated saint, switch back to the main subject.

[147] *H.E.* 2.1 (= Whitby *Gregory* 9-10, longer than Bede), 12 (= *ibid.* 16, shorter). Also see below, nn. 286-98.

[148] Bede's knowledge of the Whitby text is strongly denied by Colgrave, "Earliest Saints' Lives," pp. 50-51; "Earliest Life," pp. 133-36; *Earliest Life*, pp. 56-59. Limone, "Vita di Gregorio Magno," also endorses the thesis of independence. To the contrary, Richter, "Bede's Angli," pp. 101-102.

On the course of this discussion, see Wright, *Cultivation of Saga*, pp. 43-45. To account for

argument takes too little account of Bede's critical acumen, especially in confronting a text written fifty miles south of Jarrow in his own adulthood. He need not have been less sensitive than we are to the farrago of the Whitby *Life*. A connoisseur of hagiography, he was well aware that there was skepticism at large. The Whitby *Life*, whose precise origins he probably knew, is likely to have seemed to him even more flawed by pious invention and other shortcomings than it does to us; it could, in his eyes, have typified the ignorance of Northumbrians about the Gregorian mission until his own acquisition of documentation from Canterbury. [149] He treated the *Life* accordingly, extracting the two stories he could use, noting that King Edwin was buried at Whitby but not venerated as a saint, and skipping the rest as unworthy of repetition once the letters of Pope Gregory had been acquired.

Yet the flaws we observe in the Whitby *Life*, and Bede's marked restraint in using it, have no relevance at all to the moment in the early eighth century when it was initially composed. Together with the anonymous *Life of Cuthbert*, it marks the genesis of written history among the Anglo-Saxons, a milestone in their cultural development. The Whitby *Life*, however

---

the absence in Bede of much that is in the *Life of Gregory*, Thurston, "Oldest Life," argued that the Whitby text derived from Bede. Reaffirming the priority of the Whitby text, Butler, "Hagiographica (Chronicle)," pp. 312-13, nevertheless endorsed Thurston's opinion that "it seems inconceivable . . . that Bede, if the *Vita Antiquissima* was before him, would have neglected so much attractive material" (p. 313); Butler concluded that Bede and the Whitby *Life* were independent of each other. Cf. Moretus, "Deux anciennes vies." Thurston, whose main argument was unanimously rejected, unduly influenced the discussion. After him, only Colgrave (*Earliest Life*, as above) spelled out what "attractive material" Bede would have appropriated if he had had it: e.g. the continuation of the angels-not-Angles story, featuring "locust" interpreted as *sta in loco*, and the account of Paulinus's soul going to heaven in the shape of a swan. I would suggest that *sta in loco* was one pun too many, and that Paulinus as a swan is cruder than any of Bede's hagiography (Thurston's selection, which includes the swan, is no better founded). Bede was not an indiscriminate collector of "picturesque stor[ies]," as Thurston and Colgrave imply, nor did he have unlimited space for Gregory. Thacker, "Social Background," p. 78, makes much of Bede's failure to mention the name of Gregory's mother, originally attested by the Whitby *Life*. Would Bede have accepted the name on such authority? Should we?

[149] A naïve Bede and a Northumbria without contacts among monastic centers are prerequisites for Bede's ignorance of the Whitby *Gregory*. On a more credible view of the circumstances, it is improbable that the *Life* should have passed him by. Nothing it says about Gregory the Great had reason to appeal to him, except the passage he appropriates (with suitable changes) and presents as a beautiful story that did not have to be believed (*H.E.* 2.1). The omission of material about King Edwin is more disquieting; cf. Wallace-Hadrill, *Early Germanic Kingship*, p. 82, "It seems extraordinary that Bede should not have known of the cult of Edwin at Whitby, or, if he knew it, should not have reported it." This view seems extreme. Edwin's "cult" bore no resemblance to Oswald's, let alone Cuthbert's; even the Whitby *Gregory* does not credit him with miracles; if he had any celebration, it could have been only a local one at Whitby. Bede might have championed his sanctity if it had been expedient to do so, but in fact the *H.E.* had no more room for a sainted Edwin than for a sainted Ethelbert: he would have detracted from St. Oswald, patron of the Irish mission.

clumsy and amateurish in execution, was adequate for the purposes its sponsors intended; namely, to fill out the image of Pope Gregory as apostle of England. Distant memories, unless actively cultivated, tend to be crowded out by more recent ones. Everyone knew that Deiran Northumbria owed its first evangelization to the "men" of Pope Gregory or to the "dignitaries" whom he had sent, but these were misty generalities.[150] Paulinus, the Gregorian emissary to the north, and Edwin, the king whom he converted, were less shadowy, but not by much.[151] Pope, missionary, and king were all overlaid in their Roman associations by the more easily remembered events of later decades, at whose center, epitomizing Rome in Northumbria, stood the commanding figure of Bishop Wilfrid.

The task of the Whitby *Life* was to redress this imbalance. One step had been to transfer the remains of King Edwin to Whitby. The next was to seize upon the only personage involved in the earliest conversion whom one might hope to write about in suitably emphatic terms. The *Liber pontificalis* supplied a meager biography of Gregory, his works contained additional information, and the enterprise he had launched was momentous enough to fire literary imagination.[152] Twenty-odd years later, with help from Canterbury, Bede would do it all incomparably better. Nevertheless, the Whitby *Life* took the first, halting step, shortsightedly portraying Gregory as though he were almost exclusively the apostle of Northumbria, but nevertheless giving a density and detail to the initial mission that it could not possibly have retained in oral memory. However unanswerable Wilfrid's claims to historical significance might be, he was merely the second propagator of Roman customs. Sustained by the *Life of Gregory*, Whitby and its friends could now orient their reverence toward the first.[153]

The earliest *Life of St. Cuthbert* is a far more talented and convincing hagiography than the Whitby *St. Gregory*. One reason for its artistic success, but probably a secondary one, is that the anonymous monk of Lindisfarne

---

[150] Whitby *Gregory* 11 (*venerandae memoriae viros*); VW 47 (*proceres*). On the cursory nature of the former, see Colgrave, *Earliest Life*, p. 146 n. 50. The other reference is cited in context below, n. 304.

[151] According to Bede, at least one member of Paulinus's mission lived continuously in Northumbria till the late seventh century, but his existence has no independent attestation (*H.E.* 2.20). See below, n. 312.

[152] *Liber pontificalis*, ed. Duchesne, I, 312. Known to the hagiographer: Colgrave, *Earliest Life*, p. 37.

[153] Bullough, "Hagiography as Patriotism," p. 342, suggests that the Whitby *Gregory* was oriented against Aidan; the Roman pope was celebrated in order to offset the Irish mission. This seems unlikely owing to the eighth-century date of composition and the absence of any allusion to Irish Christianity. Rather than opposing the Irish, the Whitby text is well designed to undermine a rival "Romanity": the original Roman mission was celebrated so as to counteract Wilfrid's latecoming, secondary, but loudly advertised introduction of Roman customs.

was widely acquainted with such hagiographic classics as Sulpicius Seve-rus's *Life of St. Martin*.[154] His curious division of the *Life* into four books, excessive for so brief a work, possibly points in the direction of Gregory the Great's *Dialogues*.[155] Though such models helped, the essential difference was Cuthbert himself, an authentic holy man, the object of an established cult, about whom there was no lack of edifying information. This is why the *Life* consists of an almost uninterrupted succession of miracle stories, enclosed within only the sketchiest biographical framework. With so rich a vein of certified holiness, extended attention to historical context was su-perfluous.[156]

Although the cult of St. Cuthbert could look after itself, its cultivation was not detached from the aftermath of the Council of Austerfield. Wilfrid, the living giant of the Northumbrian Church, incited his adversaries to unite in celebrating heroism of a kind contrasting to his—the same eccen-trically humble and ascetic sanctity that, in a great biography, had made St. Martin of Tours a reproach to the Gallic episcopate.[157] The first *Life of Cuthbert* is sensitive to Wilfridian themes. It specifies, without details, that Cuthbert obtained the Roman tonsure at Ripon and that the rule of life he taught was observed at Lindisfarne to this day "with the rule of Bene-dict."[158] These are fuzzy statements; whether Cuthbert himself had any-thing to do with the Benedictine Rule is left vague, and his Roman tonsure

[154] Cf. Wallace-Hadrill, "Bede and Plummer," p. 91; Bullough, "Columba, Adamnan, I" p. 130; II, pp. 21, 27. For a very full discussion, Thacker, "Social Background," pp. 87-100.

[155] The Anon. *Cuthbert* is no longer than the single-book Whitby *Gregory*, *VCeolf*, or *VW*. But the Anon., unlike Bede, makes no direct use of the *Dialogues*. A more appropriate model may be the three books of Adamnan's *Life of Columba*: Bullough, "Columba, Adamnan, I," p. 126.

[156] Thacker, "Social Background," p. 80. In lieu of biography, the four books of the Anon. *Cuthbert* outline stages of the saint's life. The most enchanting miracles are in bk. II; as in bk. I, many of them are not acts of Cuthbert's but divine favors (notably, food when in need or visions). He becomes an assiduous healer after episcopacy (4.3-7, 12) and translation of his relics (4.15-17). His retirement to a hermitage, though by no means unique in Britain, is the most individual feature of his asceticism (3.1-7, 4.11-13).

[157] Mayr-Harting, *Coming of Christianity*, p. 97. Cf. Stancliffe, *St. Martin and His Hagiog-rapher*, pp. 265-312. The Anon.'s most notable debt to Sulpicius Severus identifies Cuthbert with Martin as an ascetic miracle worker who is reluctantly made bishop: Anon. *Cuthbert* 4.1; *Vita s. Martini* 10. (Similarly, Cuthbert as hermit is identified with St. Anthony.) Bede, though using Martinian literature, does not seem to have recognized any affinity to St. Martin. The list of great saints in *Prose Cuthbert praef.* lists Cuthbert for Britain and Hilary of Poitiers for Gaul. On this curious feature, see Thacker, "Social Background," pp. 119, 123-24.

[158] Roman tonsure, Anon. *Cuthbert* 2.2. Benedictine Rule, 3.1: "nobis regularem vitam pri-mum . . . constituit, quam usque hodie cum regula Benedicti observamus" (ed. Colgrave, pp. 94-96). For the special association of the Benedictine Rule with Wilfrid, see *VW* 14 and 47. Possibly, he himself imposed it in the months that Lindisfarne was in his charge (below, nn. 191-92). An even clearer symptom of sensitivity is the oversimplified assertion that Cuthbert was chosen as bishop of Lindisfarne (4.1). Cuthbert was originally elected to Hexham in re-placement of an expelled Wilfridian (below, n. 161).

is, on the basis of what we know about early Ripon, improbable. Both facts were excised in Bede's revision of the *Life*.[159] But, when written, they conveyed the unmistakable meaning that Cuthbert was respectable in Wilfridian terms.

A third detail of Cuthbert's biography struck at a historical memory, already mentioned, that must still have been fresh enough in the early 700s to comfort Wilfrid's partisans. Ecgfrith had been king during Wilfrid's best years as bishop of Northumbria; the falling-out of king and bishop had occasioned Wilfrid's first appeal to Rome and a harsh reception on his return.[160] Yet even after Wilfrid was driven into exile, Ecgfrith remained friendly enough toward his followers to permit one of them, Tunberht, to be made bishop of Wilfrid's cherished foundation at Hexham (681). Three years later, however, Tunberht was deposed by Archbishop Theodore. The incident is hard to interpret otherwise than as a sign of the king's complete alienation from Wilfrid's adherents. To give maximum legitimacy to the withdrawal of royal favor, the saintly Cuthbert was sought from his hermitage at Farne and made bishop of Hexham in Tunberht's place.[161] This dubious promotion brought little honor to the holy man. Soon after it took place, the king responsible for it was struck down; in less than a year, as we have seen, Ecgfrith was dead at Nechtansmere.

Ecgfrith's violent end was, unmistakably, a vindication of Wilfrid; God had intervened to avenge the king's insults to His champion. Yet there is no text in which the calamity is portrayed in these colors. We know only that, as soon afterward as could be arranged, Wilfrid was restored to Northumbria.[162] The reason Ecgfrith's death lacks the Wilfridian sense it must have had in life is that the first written record of Nechtansmere occurs in

---

[159] Cuthbert and Eata were expelled from Ripon so that Wilfrid might make it a house of Roman observance: Bede *Prose Cuthbert* 8; *H.E.* 5.19. The statement of the Anon. *Cuthbert* about the tonsure need not be fanciful unless Bede gives the full story. Whether the line is true or not matters less than what it tells us about the Lindisfarne anonymous: he made a point of showing conformity by Cuthbert to the norms of Christian life that Wilfrid had implanted in the Northumbrian Church.

Bede's excisions: tonsure at Melrose, *Prose Cuthbert* 6; nothing at Ripon, 7-8; at Lindisfarne, 16, he converted even reluctant brothers from *prisca consuetudo* to *regularis custodia* (this may allude to a change from Irish customs, but vaguely and without reference to the Benedictine Rule).

[160] *VW* 19-40.

[161] *H.E.* 4.12, 27-28. Cuthbert was elected late in 684; consecrated 26 March 685; Nechtansmere, 21 May 685. On residual sympathies toward Wilfrid in Northumbria, Kirby, "Northumbria in Time of Wilfrid," pp. 26-27. On Tunberht's ties to Wilfrid, *VCeolf* 2-3. Bede specifies that Cuthbert was elected to Hexham, but exchanged it with Eata for the latter's see at Lindisfarne (*H.E.* 4.28). No time, however, is specified for the exchange. The Anon. *Cuthbert* 4.1 knows the saint only as bishop of Lindisfarne (above, n. 158), but 4.5 leads one to believe that Cuthbert effectively served as bishop of Hexham. Bede *Prose Cuthbert* 25 muddies the waters.

[162] *VW* 43-44. On these chapters, see below at nn. 237-40.

the anonymous *Life of Cuthbert* and is surrounded there by an aura of providential inevitability, directly associated with Cuthbert's reluctant elevation to episcopacy. No sooner does the *Life* begin than we are told of a prediction made to Cuthbert by a child-playmate that he would be a bishop.
When, already aged, he was consulted as a seer by Abbess Ælffled of
Whitby, he foresaw Ecgfrith's death, the accession of Aldfrith, and his own
episcopate. As a bishop in spite of himself, he was at Carlisle when Ecgfrith
campaigned in the north, "to be overcome and slain in accordance with
God's predestined judgment"; and Cuthbert announced the disaster long
before news arrived.[163] On the testimony of the *Life of Cuthbert*, the king's
death was without significance in the ecclesiastical politics of Northumbria;
unalterably determined by God, and foreseen by St. Cuthbert, the events
had simply taken their course. The reinterpretation proved effective, the
more so as none other had yet been set down in writing.

To sum up, the first and probably the second earliest English ventures
into literary composition were carried out at the opening of the eighth century in monasteries playing a leading part in the ecclesiastical life of Northumbria. These hagiographies are unlikely to have originated for no other
reason than to satisfy the spiritual needs of the communities in which they
were created. A giant had long cast his shadow over the Northumbrian
Church; whether in residence or exiled abroad, Wilfrid stood for the most
vividly memorable forty years conceivable by contemporaries; namely,
those they had personally experienced. The hold Wilfrid had on memory
was a monopoly that, in the eyes of some, deserved to be broken. While he
was still alive, two other heroes were set before the limited reading public,
each one a giant in his way, offering an alternative to the self-advertisement heard at Austerfield. Far from being a dim shade, Pope Gregory was
the true fountainhead of Northumbrian Christianity; and Cuthbert of Lindisfarne, "the holy martyr of the Lord, in whose honor He granted health
to many men after his death,"[164] was destined in short order to be the sin-
gular patron of his land. In promoting these *Lives*, Whitby and Lindisfarne
effectively solicited the past to redress the balance of the present.

Aldfrith was king of Northumbria when the anonymous *St. Cuthbert* was
written and when Bede was ordained priest. He died in December 705. At

---

[163] Anon. *Cuthbert* 1.3 ("spiritalem Dei electionem predestinatam," ed. Colgrave, p. 64),
3.6 (the saint's predictions a year before the event); 4.8 ("Eo tempore quo Ecgfridus rex Pic-
torum regionem depopulans, postremo tandem secundum praedestinatum iudicium Dei super-
andus et occidendus vastabat," p. 122). The Anon. *Cuthbert* is distant from Bede's retributive
version of Nechtansmere, *H.E.* 4.26. Modern assessments of the event: Stenton, *Anglo-Saxon
England*, 2d ed., p. 88, "This disaster marks the end of the English ascendancy in northern
Britain"; Mayr-Harting, *Coming of Christianity*, pp. 117-18.
[164] Anon. *Cuthbert* 4.15.

once, a rival arose to contest the succession of his eight-year-old son, Osred. Tradition favored the adult claimant; father-to-son inheritance was the exception among English royalty rather than the rule.[165] When Wilfrid heard that Aldfrith, his implacable enemy, had died, he left Mercia, entered Northumbria, and made overtures to the pretender, Eadwulf. Surprisingly, Eadwulf ordered him to decamp within six days on pain of death. The pretender overestimated the strength of his position. His summary rejection of Wilfrid brought about a realignment of factions that would have been impossible in settled circumstances. Together with Ælffled, abbess of Whitby, the supporters of the boy Osred quickly made up their differences with the exiled prelate. Between the forces they could summon up, Eadwulf vanished without trace, and Osred improbably gained the throne.[166] A council of reconciliation took place at the river Nidd in 706. The timely demise of the bishop of York made it possible to transfer the bishop of Hexham and vacate his see. Wilfrid, a septuagenarian in failing health, contented himself with Hexham, whose monastic core he had founded, and the Abbey of Ripon.[167] On these terms, he returned to live out his last years without disturbance. In 710, on the first anniversary of the great man's death, the abbots of his many monasteries in and out of Northumbria gathered at Ripon and celebrated the almost miraculous peace that, unexpectedly, his holy patronage still allowed them to enjoy.[168]

So, at least, says Wilfrid's biographer, leaving us more certain of the note of serene vindication on which he wished to end his narrative than of the condition of Wilfrid's spiritual descendants. More than twenty years separate the death of Wilfrid from the completion of Bede's *H.E.* We are far worse informed about them than about the seventh century. One of many important facts of this period about which too little is known is the date of the *Life of Wilfrid*. Failing a history of Northumbria in these decades, one must be content with a bare outline of names and dates.[169]

[165] Kirby, "Northumbria in Time of Wilfrid," pp. 10, 20.

[166] *VW* 59. *VW* 43 refers to a letter of Theodore's to Ælffled of Whitby (presumably the sponsor of the Whitby *Gregory*) urging her to make peace "unreservedly (*sine dubio*)" with Wilfrid. Her relations with Wilfrid between 686 and 705 are undocumented. Stephen suggests that her alliance with Wilfrid came about only in resistance to Eadwulf and in support of Osred (as Oswy's daughter, she had reason to champion her near kin even if he were only eight). Thacker, "Social Background," p. 47, recognizes that Ælffled became friendly to Wilfrid only late in life, but believes that the esteem for her shown by the *VW* reflects the collective feelings of the Wilfridians. Other interpretations are possible. The *VW* speaks respectfully of all Wilfrid's royal enemies and probably had political reasons for doing so.

[167] *VW* 60 (sketchily summarized by Bede, *H.E.* 5.19). On the dates, Harrison, as above n. 115; a year earlier, Kirby, "Bede, Eddius Stephanus," p. 113.

[168] *VW* 68.

[169] The essentials are very well presented by Kirby, "Northumbria in Time of Wilfrid."

Among the Northumbrian kings, the years prior to the *H.E.* witnessed the momentous transfer of power from the descendants of Oswy to a collateral branch of the extended royal family. Oswy's line was exceptionally enduring by Anglo-Saxon standards, and the transition was not easy. Its point of departure was Eadwulf's abortive challenge to Osred, which should have succeeded; we saw why the improbable accession of an eight-year-old ruler came about.[170] The boy Osred, whom Bishop Wilfrid is said to have adopted as his son, occupied the throne long enough to be accused by St. Boniface of making free with nuns and by Ethelwulf of murdering his nobles. He was assassinated in 716.[171] The circumstances of his death are veiled in silence, and nothing is known of Coenred, who followed him, except that he was a very distant cousin and ruled for a mere two years (716-18).[172] Just as Coenred's preferment over nearer kin puts one in mind of violent change, so his replacement within two years by Osred's brother, Osric, suggests a legitimist reaction, comparable to the one that safeguarded Osred in 706. Again, there are no details. In a reign of more than a decade (718-29), Osric gained no reputation, good or bad. But his succession is arresting: by his choice, the throne passed to the brother of Coenred, Ceolwulf.[173] In other words, the tumultuous change of 716 was re-enacted sedately in 729. Ceolwulf's reign was disputed in 731—he was tonsured—but only momentarily; between him and the near cousin Eadberht, who took the place he vacated by withdrawing to Lindisfarne in 737, Northumbrian kingship held firm until 758.[174] Ceolwulf, then, was the king in whom a new régime that had sought to gain control of Northumbria for almost a quarter century since 705 finally achieved stability. Bede's disciple Egbert,

[170] Above, n. 166.

[171] *VW* 59: "sancto pontifici nostro filius adoptivus factus est" (ed. Levison, p. 254). Stephen's "our" may associate Wilfrid's spiritual family in the adoption. Precisely what the "adoption" amounted to is left unclear. On Osred's mischief, Kirby, "Northumbria in Time of Wilfrid," pp. 15-16, 20. His violent end: *H.E.* 5.24.

[172] For his family, see the table in Kirby, "Northumbria in Time of Wilfrid," p. 21. Kirby, "Bede, Eddius Stephanus," p. 106, considers Osred's assassination as "the great political divide in early eighth-century history"; cf. "Northumbria in Time of Wilfrid," p. 20, "The monopoly of royal power by the descendants of Æthelfrith had at last been broken." Northumbria undoubtedly experienced great change in the early eighth century, but Osred's murder may have been just a step (like Eadwulf's contestation in 704) in a process completed only in 729.

[173] *H.E.* 5.23. Bede does not state whom Osric was related to (later annals, considered trustworthy, identify him as Osred's brother), but he takes pains to specify that he designated Ceolwulf, brother of Coenred, as his successor. On the annal indicating Osric's family ties, Kirby, "Northumbria in Time of Wilfrid," p. 33 n. 86; Blair, "Some Observations on the *Historia regum*," pp. 82-83.

[174] *Bedae Continuatio*, ed. Plummer, I, 361. Kirby, "Northumbria in Time of Wilfrid," p. 21. On the favorable condition of Northumbria till 758, Stenton, *Anglo-Saxon England*, 2d ed., pp. 91-92. Kirby's idea ("Ceolwulf of Northumbria," p. 168) that Ceolwulf abdicated in 737 one step ahead of deposition or assassination seems unnecessarily speculative.

who became bishop of York in 732, belonged to this branch of the royal kin (his brother became king in 737).[175] Ceolwulf is best remembered as the monarch to whom Bede dedicated the H.E.

For most of these years, the shaky condition of the kings was not paralleled by the episcopate. When Wilfrid died (709), a monk of Whitby, John of Beverley, was bishop of York, and the see of Lindisfarne was held by Eadfrith, Cuthbert's successor but one. John died in 721, a few months after having resigned from York and having (irregularly) ordained another Whitby monk, Wilfrid II, in his place. At Lindisfarne, Eadfrith, a monk before becoming its bishop, is thought to have personally executed the magnificent Lindisfarne Gospels; like John of Beverley, he died in 721. Bede's prefatory letter to the revised *Life of St. Cuthbert* is addressed to him and his monks. Another monk of Lindisfarne, Æthilwald, replaced him (721-40).[176] At Hexham, the see passed at Wilfrid's death to Acca, long his faithful companion, who, in our scanty evidence, looks like the outstanding Northumbrian bishop of Bede's maturity. A builder, book collector, and connoisseur of chant, he sponsored many of Bede's biblical commentaries, the core of his contribution to Christian learning. Acca, together with the abbot of Ripon, Tatbert, also commissioned the composition of a *Life of Wilfrid*.[177] It is a perplexing fact that Bede had the same patron as Wilfrid's biographer.

The apparent calm of the Northumbrian bishoprics was broken in 731: in the same year that Bede chose for ending the H.E. and in which King Ceolwulf was briefly dethroned, Acca was permanently driven from Hexham.[178] A few months later, the ex-monk of Whitby, Wilfrid II, resigned from York, and Egbert took his place (732).[179] Bede's famous letter of ad-

[175] Plummer II, 378; Alcuin *Bishops, Kings, and Saints of York*, ed. Godman, pp. xlv, lvi. Note, also, the genealogical table in Kirby, "Northumbria in Time of Wilfrid," p. 21. Egbert's father (Eata) and brother (Eadberht) each bears the name of a bishop of Lindisfarne; Egbert himself is the namesake of one of Bede's special heroes, a Northumbrian voluntarily exiled in Ireland.

[176] John of Beverley, H.E. 5.3, 6. Cuthbert's successors at Lindisfarne: Eadberht, Anon. *Cuthbert* 4.14, Bede *Prose Cuthbert* 40, 42, 43, H.E. 4.29-30; Eadfrith, Anon. *Cuthbert praef.*, Bede *Prose Cuthbert praef.*, Plummer II, 297 (curiously, he is absent from the H.E.); Æthilwald, H.E. 5.12, 23. On Eadfrith and the Lindisfarne Gospels, Blair, *Northumbria in Days of Bede*, p. 193; for a different account, Thacker, "Social Background," pp. 81, 84.

[177] Acca: H.E. 5.20; VW 22, 57, 64. Stephen oddly refers to Acca as *beatae memoriae*; because Acca died only in 740, the words cannot be posthumous unless interpolated by a later hand; use of this formula for the living is not unique with Stephen, see Levison, MGH SRM VI, 217 n. 3. Patronage of Bede's work, Plummer I, xlix, 329; Manitius, *Gesch. d. lat. Lit.* I, 73-74. Patronage of Wilfrid's biography: VW *praef.* On Bede's feelings toward him, see below, n. 261.

[178] *Bedae Continuatio*, ed. Plummer, I, 361.

[179] Resignation: Alcuin *Bishops, Kings, and Saints of York*, lines 1248-50 (Alcuin improbably

monition and advice to Egbert followed within two years.[180] In 735, almost the exact centenary of Paulinus's episcopate, Egbert received the *pallium* from Rome, and York gained rank alongside Canterbury as the metropolis of a second English ecclesiastical province.[181] The passage of political power from one to another branch of the royal family was evidently accompanied by a no less momentous change in the organization of the Northumbrian Church.

Gaining familiarity with the chronology of royal and episcopal events is a steppingstone toward the chronology of historical writings, already outlined a few pages ago. Bede is responsible for most, but not all, of the literature on topical subjects composed in the decades between Wilfrid's death and his own (709-35). Within the reign of Osred (705-16), he wrote the verse *Life of St. Cuthbert*, announcing the intention of devoting a second opus to the miracles of Cuthbert that he had had to omit. He said nothing about rewriting the *Life* in prose.[182] The year of Osred's assassination witnessed the resignation, departure for Rome, and death in France of Abbot Ceolfrid of Wearmouth-Jarrow (716). The two events need not have been unrelated. Not long afterward, as it seems, an anonymous monk of Wearmouth wrote the *Life of Ceolfrid*, an account of the founding years of Wearmouth-Jarrow, in which Ceolfrid had participated from the very beginnings in 674. A more political biography than Ceolfrid's was that of Wilfrid, commonly attributed to Eddius Stephanus but more certainly the work of the priest Stephen, a monk of Ripon. Its date calls for separate attention. Bede's prose *Life of St. Cuthbert*, completed before 721, when he was in his forties, might almost be called an anticipation of the *H.E.* History of another sort occupied him in the *Major Chronicle* of 725 and the *Martyrology*; but the same period also witnessed his *History of the Abbots of Wearmouth-Jarrow*, a revision of the anonymous *Life of Ceolfrid*. Then, in 731 (or a few years thereafter), he completed the *H.E.*, for which he had already been gathering material at the time of the *Major Chronicle*. In more than one passage, as we have seen, the *H.E.* anticipates Bede's *Letter to Egbert of York*; the letter was sent in November 734, a scant year before Bede's

---

suggests that Wilfrid II chose his own successor); Plummer I, 278. He lived until 745. Egbert directly succeeded him in 732, but was consecrated only in 734.

[180] The *Letter to Egbert* is dated 4 November 734 (Plummer I, 423; II, 388).

[181] On the meaning of the *pallium* in England, Brooks, *Early History of Canterbury*, pp. 66-67; the pope granted it to Paulinus in 634, after the Northumbrian mission had already been ruined, *ibid.* pp. 64-65. For the event of 735, Plummer I, 361; the annal in question also records the advent of Nothelm to the see of Canterbury. That the papal grant to Egbert coincided with a succession at Canterbury can hardly be accidental. As a courtesy, a sitting archbishop would have been spared having his province curtailed, but an incoming one (provided he consented) would merely enter upon a redefined office.

[182] See below, nn. 223-24.

death and Egbert's receipt of the *pallium*. Bede was well aware that the elevation of York to archiepiscopal rank was about to take place.[183]

The *Major Chronicle* and the *Martyrology* have been mentioned only in order to suggest the extent to which Bede's histories are concentrated in the last decades of his life. Another trait mentioned earlier is that all Bede's works concerned with English history, except the *H.E.*, are obvious adaptations or revisions of earlier writings.[184] But the need for adaptations is more self-explanatory for some subjects than for others. Bede's *Martyrology* and the writings on the *Reckoning of Time*, for example, markedly improve upon the works from which they were compounded. But precisely why did he have to rewrite the Lindisfarne *Life of St. Cuthbert* and Wearmouth *Life of Ceolfrid*?

No problem of this sort affects Bede's transposition of the *Life of Cuthbert* from prose to verse. His initiative falls in the same order of hagiographic activity that led him to cleanse the botched translation of the *Passion of St. Anastasius* and to turn Paulinus's verse *Life of St. Felix* into prose.[185] (Even so, as we shall see, the additions Bede made to the Lindisfarne *St. Cuthbert* are not limited to previously unrecorded miracles.) With Bede's rendering of the *Life of St. Cuthbert* into prose, however, merely hagiological explanations cease to be adequate. The prose *Life* is not the work recording omitted miracles that Bede announced in the poetic version; rather, it is a very self-conscious revision of the Lindisfarne *Life*, carried out with the approbation and assistance of the saint's monastery.[186] Bede's transformation of the *Life of Ceolfrid* into the *History of the Abbots* could scarcely have been a private impulse either. What need was there for these efforts? The Lindisfarne *Life* and the *Life of Ceolfrid* were comparatively recent compositions; neither is deficient in the way that the Whitby *Life of Gregory the Great* is flawed. We prize them for more than antiquarian reasons, and we are thankful that they somehow managed to survive.[187] Nor does Bede himself, to the extent that he mentions models, impugn their quality, as he does

---

[183] The grant of the *pallium* cannot have been a casual matter, determined in the year it took place. It required negotiations with Canterbury as well as Rome. On Nothelm's probable role in the process, see below, nn. 265-66. If the Northumbrian dioceses were to be increased from three or four to twelve or thirteen, the change had grave political implications. In writing to Egbert, Bede was well aware that the pope had acted, although his act had yet to take official effect (above, n. 181).

[184] Above, n. 74.

[185] The closest parallel is with Bede's prose *Life and Passion of St. Felix*, a complement to the verses of Paulinus of Nola. With Cuthbert, he was supplying a verse complement to the prose of the Anon. *Cuthbert*. Cf. above, n. 69.

[186] Below, nn. 223-26.

[187] Plummer I, xlvi-vii; Colgrave, *Two Lives*, pp. 3-4, 15; Blair, *World of Bede*, p. 279. The best explanation for the *Prose Cuthbert* as a hagiographic enhancement of Anon. *Cuthbert* is given by Lapidge, in Greenfield and Calder, *New Critical History*, pp. 19-20.

that of the *Passion of St. Anastasius.* Substance rather than style is likely to have been at issue: some statements had to be changed. How Bede altered the original narratives holds the part of the answer accessible to us; if, in a busy existence, he took the trouble to recast them, it was out of urgent concern—surely not his alone—that certain facts should or should not be in the written record.

These considerations have taken us farther in time than is yet appropriate. Bede's prose *Life of St. Cuthbert* was completed before 721, and the *History of the Abbots* between 725 and 731; in other words, the anxieties that occasioned their composition fall roughly within the decade that closed with the *H.E.* The first work of a topical nature originating in Wearmouth-Jarrow—namely, Bede's verse *St. Cuthbert*—suggests greater calm. In setting the Lindisfarne *St. Cuthbert* to verse, Bede condensed the prose but retained most of the miracles and other incidents. Among the omissions are the references to Cuthbert's Roman tonsure and to the observance of the Rule of St. Benedict at Lindisfarne, neither of which would be reinstated in Bede's prose *Life*.[188] Three of Bede's nine additions have interest for more than edification. After the story of Cuthbert seeing Aidan's soul going to heaven, Bede insists on Aidan's glory (*gesta sacerdotis huius veneranda per orbem*) and relates a miracle of his. (The episode is not in Bede's prose *Life*, but resembles a passage of the *H.E.*[189]) He briefly introduces a new character in the form of Boisil, prior of Melrose, and, reinforcing a major theme of the original *Life*, has him predict Cuthbert's episcopacy.[190] Finally Bede devotes a full chapter—many more words than he would in the prose *Life*— to narrating the troubles that fell upon Lindisfarne after Cuthbert's death, and the return of peace, a year later, when Eadberht was elected bishop.[191] The source of these troubles is identified for us only by the *H.E.*, but it must have been common knowledge at the time: "The Reverend Bishop Wilfrid watched over the bishopric of that church for one year."[192]

These verses in honor of St. Cuthbert, penned while Ceolfrid was still

---

[188] *Verse Cuthbert* 6-7, proceed in such a way as to omit Anon. *Cuthbert* 1.7, 2.1 (tonsure); 13-15 omit much of Anon. *Cuthbert* 3.1-2.

[189] *Verse Cuthbert* 5; cf. *H.E.* 3.15. Bede's spontaneous expansion of the Anon. shows how deeply he approved of the Irish missionary. His feelings toward Aidan should not be equated with his disclaimer about the saint's Easter observance, as argued by Kirby, "Ceolwulf of Northumbria," p. 172. Little evidence sustains the opinion of Cosmos, "Oral Tradition and Literary Convention," that Bede used a pre-existing Life of St. Aidan.

[190] *Verse Cuthbert* 20.

[191] *Verse Cuthbert* 37, lines 786-812. The title of the chapter, "Quomodo iuxta prophetiam psalmi, quem eo moriente cantaverant, Lindisfarnenses sint inpugnati, sed domino iuvante protecti," is unambiguous in its sympathy for the victims ("nobilis illa . . . / Progenies . . . / Cedere iamque loco quam extrema subire pericli / Eligeret"). But the source and nature of the dangers are veiled in silence.

[192] *H.E.* 4.29.

abbot of Wearmouth-Jarrow, are Bede's inaugural contribution to the history of the English Church. They foreshadow the warmth toward Irish evangelists and aversion to Bishop Wilfrid that Bede's future writings would affirm. Nevertheless, the verse *St. Cuthbert* seems less political than the underlying Lindisfarne prose, whose sense Bede simply underlined without notable modifications.

The resignation and departure into voluntary exile of Abbot Ceolfrid in 716 marked the end of an era in the life of Wearmouth-Jarrow. Bede, writing his commentary on Samuel, interrupted the work with a little address to Bishop Acca, his patron, suggesting the "consternation" of his fellow monks at the abbot's sudden decision and his own relief at the orderly installation of a successor. [193] Ceolfrid had not just been sole abbot of the twin houses for twenty-seven years; he had participated in the foundation from its first days and, except for two brief absences, had been the resident leader of the community for more than four decades. [194] The special value of the Wearmouth *Life of Ceolfrid* lies in conveying this strongly contemporaneous sense of what the old abbot's leave taking meant. Yet to come was Bede's revision, the *History of the Abbots*, starring the remarkable but long-dead Benedict Biscop. When the original account was set down (that is, within a few years after Ceolfrid's departure and death) the entire existence of Wearmouth-Jarrow since 674 seemed to be summed up by the aged cofounder and abbot whose withdrawal and last months occupy a disproportionate share of the anonymous *Life*. [195]

The practical purpose of this narrative can only have been to record the delicate transition from the age of the founders to autonomous corporate life via a free election based on considerations of merit. Neither Pope Agatho's nor Pope Sergius's privilege authorizing free elections is copied

[193] Plummer I, xv-xvi.

[194] VCeolf 19, 7 (foundation), 8, 10 (absences).

[195] VCeolf 40 ends with wondrous occurrences at the abbot's tomb right after burial, as though the narrative had been written on the basis of reports by Ceolfrid's returned companions (37). As a result, it is often dated to the year after Ceolfrid's death; e.g. McClure (as below), p. 73, and Thacker, "Social Background," p. 141. The idea is attractive and not obviously flawed. The absolute termini are 717-25: Colgrave, "Earliest Saints' Lives," p. 58. Disproportion in contents: a little more than half (ca. 56 percent) concerns Ceolfrid's departure and final journey (ed. Plummer, I, 395-404).

McClure, "Bede and the *Life of Ceolfrid*," argues that the VCeolf is by Bede (I am very grateful to Dr. Ian Wood, of the University of Leeds, for drawing my attention to this article, and to Dr. Simon Keynes, of Trinity College, Cambridge, for lending me the journal). Some of her observations are useful and illuminating (see n. 197), but the argument suffers from a one-sided concept of the contents of the two texts. She maintains that, in the *Hist. abb.*, Bede's "views on Ceolfrid and on the most successful constitution for Wearmouth-Jarrow had not changed since he had worked them out during that troubled summer of 716" (p. 84). The *Hist. abb.* does agree with the VCeolf about the constitution of the monastery, but differs from it very much where Ceolfrid himself is concerned: too much of Ceolfrid's person is wiped out of the *Hist. abb.* for Bede to be plausible as his biographer.

into the *Life*; the fact is the more noticeable because Wilfrid's biographer also forgoes reproducing papal privileges for Ripon and Hexham.[196] Nevertheless, much attention is paid in the Wearmouth narrative to the transition from Ceolfrid to his successor, and even more to the organic bond between St. Peter's at Wearmouth and St. Paul's at Jarrow—"one monastery located in two places."[197] The beginnings of Wearmouth-Jarrow had been less than orderly. Owing to Benedict Biscop's restless absences, as many as three abbots had been in office at one time. Only at the death of Sigfrid and Benedict was the unity of the two establishments expressed in the single and long-lasting abbacy of Ceolfrid.[198] More than anyone else, including Benedict Biscop, he was the model. Monks from both establishments met after Ceolfrid's resignation and departure and freely elected Hwætbert to assume an abbacy identical to his. That orderly procedure, pursuant to the papal privileges and the Rule of St. Benedict, and duly approved by the ex-abbot, was more important as an accomplished fact and precedent than as the exemplification of written documents.[199] On this understanding, the disproportion between near and distant past in the *Life of Ceolfrid* loses some of its mystery. Although wondrous occurrences at the late abbot's grave are briefly noted, the biographer's purpose can hardly have been one of hagiography.[200] Ceolfrid's abbacy (regardless of anything he did) was a

[196] *VCeolf* 20, 25, and several places in the *VW* are suitable for entering copies of the papal privileges. Levison, *England and the Continent*, p. 24, refers to the privileges as "lost." It would be better to say that the early authors who could have preserved them by entering them in narratives did not do so, though both copied other documents into their writings. Perhaps someone will be able to explain what inhibited them.

[197] The quotation, *VCeolf* 19. McClure, "Bede and the *Life of Ceolfrid*," pp. 78-79, rightly stresses how concerned the biographer is to support the notion of a single abbot for both monasteries. The issue occurs in *VCeolf* 12, 16, 18, 19, 25, 29. In addition to these specific indications of concern, the biographer's subject, Ceolfrid, personally embodied over a quarter century in which Wearmouth and Jarrow were ruled as one.

[198] Multiple abbots, *VCeolf* 10, 12-13, 18. The Anon. comments apologetically on this situation, *VCeolf* 5-6, 12; so, to a lesser extent, does Bede, *Hist. abb.* 7. Single abbots begin only with Ceolfrid: *VCeolf* 15-18. If guided by Bede's *Hist. abb.*, one might agree with the account of Mayr-Harting, *Coming of Christianity*, p. 153: "Benedict Biscop founded these two monasteries . . . as one confraternity." Perhaps that had been Benedict's intention (the privilege he secured from Pope Agatho envisaged the union), but only Ceolfrid inaugurated the period in which Wearmouth and Jarrow were ruled in this way.

[199] *VCeolf* 28-30 (Acca's ratification is only in Bede *Hist. abb.* 20).

[200] *VCeolf* 40 intimates that a cult spontaneously arose at the abbot's grave at Langres, but no miracles are ascribed to Ceolfrid's relics. Even though little attention is paid to the details of Ceolfrid's long rule, the narrative has a notable biographic component: in addition to the account of Ceolfrid's early life at Gilling and Ripon, specially touching remarks are made about his father and about him as a baker at Ripon and as the sole survivor with a little boy after plague devastated Jarrow (*VCeolf* 34, 4, 14). The boy-monk is traditionally identified as Bede (Plummer I, xii, and many others). However that may be, no trace of personal warmth toward Ceolfrid infuses the *Hist. abb.* I find it hard to endorse the common view that Bede was devoted to him.

The claim of Bullough, "Alcuino e la tradizione culturale insulare," p. 578, that the *VCeolf*

vital precedent, and the free election of an abbot whose office was as exclusive as his marked a new start for the community. Both deserved commemoration.

Little is said of Ceolfrid's achievements, especially in the years of his sole abbacy; Bede would be slightly more informative.[201] On the other hand, Ceolfrid's beginnings are narrated in unique detail. Whereas Bede would dwell on Benedict Biscop's travels and imports from the Continent, the *Life of Ceolfrid* fills in the domestic background of Wearmouth-Jarrow. Ceolfrid was first a monk of Gilling, a royal foundation, which his brother, Cynefred, then headed; their relative, Tunberht, took charge when Cynefred withdrew to study in Ireland; after Cynefred died abroad of the plague, Tunberht, Ceolfrid, and other Gilling monks were invited by Wilfrid to Ripon, where Ceolfrid was ordained a priest; following a study journey to Kent and East Anglia, he stayed at Ripon until Benedict Biscop prevailed on Bishop Wilfrid to delegate him as an assistant in the establishment of Wearmouth; in the first period that Ceolfrid was left alone in charge of the new monastery, the resistance of noble inmates to his discipline led him to retreat to Ripon, but Benedict Biscop, back from the Continent, persuaded him to give Wearmouth a second chance; this time, the move was permanent.[202] The account has the special value of documenting the important contribution Wilfrid made to the establishment of Benedict Biscop's foundation. Not only was Ceolfrid trained and ordained at Ripon, but Tunberht, his relative, was the Wilfridian elected to Hexham in 681 and deposed in 684 to be replaced by Cuthbert of Lindisfarne.[203] Nowhere are we told to which faction Wearmouth-Jarrow inclined in the troubles of Wilfrid's lifetime; the *Life of Ceolfrid* at least allows us to guess. The details supplied by Ceolfrid's biography have value for another reason: Bede eliminated every one of them from his *History of the Abbots*. We could not possibly know, if the *Life of Ceolfrid* had not survived, that Wilfrid had a part in Benedict Biscop's enterprise.

By general consent, Ceolfrid's biography was composed soon after the abbot's death, but any consideration of its date forces us to cast an eye on political circumstances. Predictably, the *Vita Ceolfridi* presents the abbot's resignation as a spontaneous act. Yet its occurrence in 716 means that it coincides—how closely we cannot tell—with the violent advent of Coenred, a king who had no reason to look with favor and sympathy upon foundations instituted by Ecgfrith and his line and assisted by Bishop Wil-

---

and *VW* are new departures in hagiography, seems unlikely in light of Lotter, "Methodisches zur Gewinnung," pp. 310-14.

[201] See below, nn. 258-59.

[202] *VCeolf* 2-8. Cf. Mayr-Harting, *Coming of Christianity*, p. 166.

[203] *VCeolf* 2-3; above, n. 161.

frid, who since 706 had been a pillar of the old dynasty.[204] Ceolfrid was too long established and venerable an abbot to fear that the new régime would trouble him or his monastery. Danger would come if there were a vacancy, and Ceolfrid knew that his days were numbered. Under Coenred's unsympathetic rule, an interregnum at Wearmouth-Jarrow would tend to favor disaffected monks: royal support might be gained in the choice of a new abbot, or even of two abbots, dividing the monastery into its constituent parts. To avert this threat, Ceolfrid resigned and ensured that an election was held conforming to his wishes as founder-abbot and safeguarding the unity of the two houses. In all this, Ceolfrid—not Benedict Biscop—was the pivotal figure and the source of legitimacy.

The circumstances that (if these political conjectures are well founded) provoked Ceolfrid's resignation prevailed only as long as Coenred ruled. Already in 718 the "legitimate" Osric had replaced him, and one assumes that Osric was no less attached to the Wilfridians than his late brother had been. Regardless of who occupied the Northumbrian throne, Wearmouth-Jarrow had good reason to set down a written memorial of Ceolfrid's resignation, succession, and death. But the anonymous author would presumably have been inhibited about Ceolfrid at Ripon if a king hostile toward Wilfrid's party had been ruling. The cheerful account of Ceolfrid's days at Wilfrid's monastery evokes the mood and sympathies again prevailing, after Osric's advent, in the Northumbrian kingdom and Church. Bede's revised version, the *Historia abbatum*, would show how dispensable these details could be in a history of Wearmouth-Jarrow.

That there should have been close links between Bishop Wilfrid and the founders of Wearmouth-Jarrow is far from surprising. Wilfrid and Benedict Biscop were unique in their generation for the intensity of their continental and Roman experiences. That their activities in Northumbria should have been complementary is more likely than that they should have taken divergent tracks.[205] Ceolfrid's retirement and death ended this period of the monastery's history; so far as we know, the new abbot, Hwætbert, freely elected from among the six hundred monks, owed nothing to Ripon or to the great prelate now six or seven years dead.[206] But the *Life of Ceolfrid* was unconcerned to spell out Hwætbert's freedom from debts. Instead, it made clear without belaboring the point that, except for Wilfrid's generosity, there would have been no forty years of Ceolfrid at Wearmouth-Jarrow.

[204] Cf. above, n. 172.

[205] *VW* 3 points out that, in youth, Wilfrid and Benedict parted from each other after the first leg of their journey to the Continent. Their youthful bifurcation did not exclude later cooperation, as the *VCeolf* bears out. Only Bede's *Hist. abb.* presents Benedict Biscop as acting in a Northumbria ostensibly untouched by Bishop Wilfrid.

[206] On the other hand, he surely had to be acceptable to Ceolfrid, and was possibly his hand-picked choice.

What became of the Wilfridians after their leader's death? There is less to say about Tatbert of Ripon than about Acca of Hexham, whom Bede portrays as an enterprising and resourceful bishop on the scale of earlier giants. In his hands, the heritage of Wilfrid was not only secure but prospering.[207] What allows us to realize that Wilfrid's spiritual descendants remained a united force in Northumbria is the resplendent effort they made to cultivate their master's memory. They charged a monk of Ripon, the priest Stephen, to compose a *Life of Wilfrid*, and it turned out to be not only an outstanding biography but also the nearest thing to a history of the English church until Bede. Unlike the latter, Stephen condescended to realism, as when he said unblushingly that Wilfrid left his abbots valuables with which to secure royal and episcopal friendship. Stephen did not even avert his gaze from warfare.[208] Of course, he was a partisan; a priest from Wilfrid's burial place commissioned by his successors and addressing a Wilfridian audience could hardly have been anything else.[209] Yet the thrust of his apology or the interests it was meant to forward are not easily pinned down. The work is a fuller and more circumstantial biography than we are entitled to expect.

The *Life of Wilfrid* is usually dated between 710 and 720. A more precise approximation depends partly on its authorship. If, as is customary, the work is attributed to *Aeddi cognomento Stephanus*, a singing master Wilfrid brought from Kent to Ripon between 666 and 669, there would be a compelling reason to prefer an earlier date to a later one, for Eddius would have had to reach advanced old age in order both to survive Wilfrid and to write about him. But the attribution to Eddius has long been recognized to be more attractive than securely founded and can no longer be entertained.[210]

---

[207] Above, n. 177.

[208] VW 63 (Wilfrid tells his abbots why he is giving them treasures); 17 (British clergy driven out by the hostile swords of "our" people); 41 (conversion compelled by royal command). Warfare, VW 13, 19-20, 42.

[209] Below, nn. 211-12.

[210] On the date, n. 110 above. For a staunch defense of the attribution, Poole, "St. Wilfrid and Ripon," pp. 56-57, arguing especially against the reserve of Levison, MGH SRM VI, 179-80; with Levison, Colgrave, "Earliest Saints' Lives," p. 57. (In *Life of Bishop Wilfrid*, pp. ix-x, Colgrave admitted that "the actual evidence is far from strong," but adhered to tradition.) Besides reacting to the lack of positive proof, Levison was disturbed that Wilfrid's biographer, though capable of personal notes, failed to identify himself when referring to the singing master Ædde (VW 14). For a full discussion, deciding against identification with the singing master, see Kirby, "Bede, Eddius Stephanus," pp. 102-103 (among other things, Kirby works out Eddius's presumed age).

Kirby concludes (p. 106) that the VW "was written while Abbess Ælfflæd was living" and must antedate her death in 715. But VW 59-60, which are in question, contain nothing incompatible with composition after the abbess's death; Ælfflæd's testimony *nobis* is not a personal communication, but public witness (below, n. 215). The discrepancy between VW 59 and 60 that Kirby detects and stresses (p. 107) does not seem to me to be major and irreconcilable as it stands.

Yet the assignment of the *Life* to a different Stephen brings no immediate improvement to the problem of life spans. The biographer Stephen could not be much younger than Eddius if, as the text has been thought to imply, he had been with Wilfrid in Frisia in 678-79.[211]

A closer look at the *Life* makes one wonder whether its author was ever in Wilfrid's entourage. Much hinges on his usage of *nos* and *noster*, pronouns that the context rarely justifies construing in a personal sense. Stephen almost certainly had Ripon as his religious home; he may well have been among the many Wilfridians dispersed after Austerfield and joyfully restored two years later (ca. 703-705); and he was present at Ripon at the first anniversary of Wilfrid's death.[212] Whether any other "we" or "our" in the *Life* refers to him in particular is hard to determine. Stephen speaks explicitly to an audience of Wilfridians, which he associates in every "our."[213] He describes the collectivity of churches obeying Wilfrid (in 701-702) as "all our churches" and says "he established all our life" when he means that Wilfrid prescribed the rule of his monasteries.[214] When trusty witnesses "made known to us" the deathbed wishes of King Aldfrith, they did not take Stephen aside so as to speak to him but merely testified to all Northumbrians at the Nidd council.[215] Stephen does not spell out that he was with Wilfrid in Frisia in 679 or again in Rome in 704; instead, isolated instances of *nos* in the relevant chapters permit the inference that he was there. But, because he betrays no personal closeness to Wilfrid, the inference is hardly mandatory or preferable to a collective sense.[216] If Stephen is removed in

---

Jones, "Bede as Early Medieval Historian," p. 35, asserts that Bede did not know the *VW* when he wrote most of the *H.E.*, and was supplied with it only late in his labors. Kirby, "Bede, Eddius Stephanus," pp. 107-12, carefully develops a hypothesis that the *VW* had two editions, including one later than Acca's downfall (731), and that Bede saw only the first. Kirby's argument is more challenging than Jones's, but both solve fewer problems than they create. Their efforts arise from a correct sense that Bede's odd use of the *VW* needs explanation. Even so, no strong reasons exist for doubting that Bede had the *VW* in a form substantially similar to ours.

[211] Kirby, "Bede, Eddius Stephanus," p. 103 n. 7: "Despite R. L. Poole . . . there is no evidence that the author of the *Vita Wilfridi* accompanied Wilfrid on his first visit to Rome in 679." This is true where Rome is concerned, but, at first sight, *VW* 27 suggests that the author was in Wilfrid's party in Frisia in the preceding months.

[212] *VW* 17 (Ripon); 49-50, 60 (dispersal and restoration); 67 (anniversary). The authoritative, but too indiscriminate, interpretation of these passages is by Levison, MGH SRM VI, 180-81; e.g. the reference to *nostris* at Meaux (*VW* 57) does not have to include Stephen as he believed.

[213] Implied by the monotonous references to *pontifex noster* (i.e. Wilfrid), the audience is particularly indicated by the preacher's phrases of *VW* 1 (*nos autem, fratres, frequenter legimus*) and 8 (*ecce, fratres*).

[214] *VW* 45 (*omnes ecclesias nostras*), 61 (*omnem vitam nostram . . . constitueret*).

[215] *VW* 59 (*haec verba fidelissimi testes audierunt nobisque indicaverunt*), 60 (public testimony).

[216] *VW* 27 and 52-53. Here, forms of *nos* in a seemingly personal sense pop up in contexts

this way from Wilfrid's side in Frisia, he delays his appearance in the *Life* by a quarter century until 703, confirming the impression he otherwise gives (but Eddius Stephanus should not) of belonging to a later generation than his subject.[217] With a biographer named Stephen—of Ripon, for identification—who began observing events early in the eighth century, there is no age barrier urging that the *Life* should be written near 710 rather than near 720. The assignment of the *Life of Wilfrid* to that decade rather than a later one seems secure, for Stephen's use of the anonymous *Life of St. Cuthbert* was sharply reacted against before 721.

The prologue of the *Life of Wilfrid* is lifted bodily from the Lindisfarne *St. Cuthbert*. Admittedly, the latter was itself copied from ancient models, but Stephen made his borrowings from it, with the result that what was only the second biography of a Northumbrian bishop has the same beginning as the first.[218] The copying and emulation did not end there. Stephen characterized Wilfrid, upon his election as bishop, in the same Pauline words as are applied to Cuthbert at the same stage of his life; and, again, the parallelism is not accidental. Among the borrowings from St. Paul, the monk of Lindisfarne interpolated a phrase of his own: Cuthbert's "memory served him instead of books (*memoriam enim pro libris habuit*)." At the identical spot, Stephen adapted the phrase to his hero: Wilfrid "had an amazing memory for books (*memoriam enim miram in libris habuit*)."[219] Cuthbert's actions, especially in early life, are conspicuously likened to biblical incidents and personages; biblical parallels are even more often applied to Wilfrid.[220] Far more of the *Life of Wilfrid* is concerned with ecclesiastical affairs than with miracles, but the great prelate is not denied the conventional attributes of sanctity; his scattering of miracles, in life and after, bears more

---

that do not otherwise include Stephen. There is no sign of him in *VW* 25, 28, 29, 33, 34, or with Wilfrid in 50, 55, 56-57, all of which offer occasions for personal references. Two interpretations are therefore possible: that he inadvertently reveals his otherwise concealed presence or, more probably, that he uses *nos* loosely to mean "our party" or "fellow Wilfridians," as he does elsewhere.

[217] *VW* 11: "Qualem ergo illi tunc eum intellexerunt [i.e. in 684], talem adhuc et nos viventes novimus." It would be surprising if Eddius, who reached Ripon in 669 at latest, spoke in this temporally distant way.

[218] Levison marks the text: *praef.* (p. 193). For the sources of the Anon., see Colgrave, *Two Lives*, pp. 60-64. An additional and astonishing borrowing by Stephen is the Anon.'s description of the Roman tonsure: *VW* 6, from Anon. *Cuthbert* 3.1; cf. n. 159 above. Colgrave, *Life of Bishop Wilfrid*, p. x, recognized that Ripon looked upon Cuthbert as a rival to Wilfrid and that the *VW* probably responded to the Anon. *Cuthbert*.

[219] *VW* 11, ed. Levison, p. 205; Anon. *Cuthbert* 4.1, pp. 112-13. On this passage, Colgrave, *Two Lives*, p. 331.

[220] Anon. *Cuthbert* 1.3-5, 7, 2.1-4, 3.3, 4.1-3; *VW* 1-8, 12-14, 18-19, 23-24, 35, 37, 44, 56, 64. Mayr-Harting, *Coming of Christianity*, pp. 140-41, holds that Stephen makes "phenomenal" use of the Old Testament. Is it greater, allowing for length, than that of the Lindisfarne Anon.?

than a casual resemblance to a selection of Cuthbert's.[221] Of Cuthbert himself, Stephen of Ripon breathes not a word.

It may well be that the two greatest Northumbrian churchmen in the age of Oswy and Ecgfrith never came face to face, but the managers of their memories were highly conscious of their heroes' proximity. The Lindisfarne *Life of St. Cuthbert* took pains, as we have seen, to illustrate the respectability of its saint *vis-à-vis* Wilfrid's teaching and interests. Bede's *Verse Cuthbert* dispensed with some of these touches but introduced the new fact that Lindisfarne had been gravely disturbed after Cuthbert's death; though no one was named, the information was unambiguously to Wilfrid's discredit.[222] Against this backdrop of sensitivity, the plagiarism and imitation of the Lindisfarne *St. Cuthbert* in Stephen's *Life of Wilfrid* is difficult to explain away as harmless. Stephen seems, on the contrary, to have engaged in a rather gross rivalry, as though, scorning St. Cuthbert, he were saying: Let me illustrate the nature of real Northumbrian heroism. Whatever Stephen's program was, Lindisfarne took a very serious view of what he had done; it concluded that the original *Life of St. Cuthbert* had been soiled and devalued, and sought a replacement.

The first *Life* was the main source of Bede's prose *St. Cuthbert*, but he never mentioned it in the extraordinarily detailed prefatory account he gave of his process of composition.[223] Bede had more immediate reasons for supplying an elaborate preface than to show modern scholars how closely his methods and scruples approximated theirs. The bishop and monks of Lindisfarne had commissioned him (the same bishop had sponsored the original *Life*); the lengthy research and authentication Bede had undertaken with them in writing about the saint were worth describing in detail only insofar as they guaranteed complete authenticity to the biography that he now presented as though it had never been written before.[224] His version rubbed out the preface and other parts of the first *Life* that the *Life of Wilfrid* had appropriated, and it introduced another discreditable fact not previously committed to writing: Cuthbert and Eata had established the first

---

[221] *VW* 18 (cf. Anon. *Cuthbert* 4.6), 23 (4.10), 37 (4.3, 7), 66 (4.15).

[222] See above, nn. 158-59, 191.

[223] *Prose Cuthbert praef.* In the *Chron. maius* 570, ed. Mommsen, pp. 316-17, he also treats his verse and prose as the only available writings about Cuthbert. Bede's concealment of his main source needs to be taken seriously (cf. Ray, "Bede's *vera lex*," p. 18). This major omission means that the preface is a learned mask beguiling the reader with its sincerity. Bede had to have a good reason to engage in this exercise in persuasion.

[224] In *H.E. praef.* he finally acknowledges the Anon. *Cuthbert* as his source. Presumably, conditions had changed enough in ten years for its existence to be recognized. Even so, Bede treats it apologetically, "simpliciter fidem . . . accommodans." The Anon. survives only in continental mss (Colgrave, *Two Lives*, pp. 1-2).

monastery at Ripon; it was by expelling these holy men that Wilfrid had acquired his initial foundation.[225]

Bede's prose *St. Cuthbert* should not divert us much longer from Stephen's *Life of Wilfrid*. Yet it is essential, for an understanding of Stephen's work, not only to recognize its dependence on the Lindisfarne *St. Cuthbert*, but also to observe the vehement response it almost immediately provoked among the guardians of St. Cuthbert's memory. When, back in Osred's reign, Bede had set St. Cuthbert's deeds to verse, he had seen no need to rewrite the life in prose (his claims to the contrary in the introduction to the prose *Life* are a reinterpretation of his intentions rather than a statement of fact); toward 720, he willingly responded to the request of Lindisfarne that he should do so.[226] Only one event known to us in the interval helps to account for the change: Stephen had befouled the original *Life of St. Cuthbert* by placing it in the service of the very different sanctity Wilfrid had embodied.

The hostile reaction of Lindisfarne to the *Life of Wilfrid* is comparatively easy to detect, and so, as we shall see, is Bede's ultimate response to the version of English ecclesiastical history that, in Stephen's narrative, issued from Wilfrid's lips. Because the Wilfridian sponsors of Stephen have left fewer traces than his critics, it is more difficult to determine what advantage the *Life of Wilfrid* was supposed to procure for them in the late 710s. Whose opinion did they seek to sway by vindicating their spiritual father? In outline, the *Life* sets out a one-sided but not, for its time, obviously polemical story: Wilfrid, after a brief period at Lindisfarne, was trained in Gaul and Rome; he confuted the Irish "Quartodecimans" and won the Northumbrian kings to Catholic practices; elevated to the episcopate, he brought glory to the Northumbrian Church side by side with King Ecgfrith in the latter's best years; he was unjustly deprived and exiled, and twice journeyed to the Holy See, where the popes and their counselors found him innocent of any crime; at last reconciled to the Northumbrian court, he returned to spend his last years in peace.

Stephen's account is highly selective. Little over one-third of the *Life* is

---

[225] *Prose Cuthbert praef.*, 6 (tonsure at Melrose), 24 (becomes bishop); 8 (expulsion of Eata and Cuthbert from Ripon).

[226] *Verse Cuthbert, praef.*: "Si vero vita comes fuerit . . . spero me in alio opere nonnulla ex his, quae praetermiseram, memoriae redditurum" (ed. Jaager, p. 57). The context is one of miracle only, not biography: Bede has not been able to expound all of Cuthbert's *gesta*; daily his relics carry out new ones, and men who know newly reveal old ones. But cf. *Prose Cuthbert praef.*: "Sciat autem sanctitas vestra quia vita eiusdem . . . heroicis dudum versibus edidi. . . . In cuius operis praefatione promisi me alias de vita et miraculis eius latius esse scripturum. Quam videlicet promissionem in praesenti opusculo . . . adimplere satago" (Colgrave, p. 146).

concerned with Wilfrid's Northumbrian achievements; the balance mainly portrays his efforts at rehabilitation. Although, for five years under King Aldfrith, he enjoyed a second period as bishop of York, Stephen ascribes no initiatives to him in its course; Wilfrid, once alienated from King Ecgfrith, worked constructively only in Frisia, Sussex, and Mercia.[227] Even so, his many years of activity in Mercia, with whose kings he was on good terms, are inadequately described; one ten-year stretch all but vanishes.[228] The *Life* is an obstinately Northumbrian narrative. For whose sake? There is no easy way to tell what meaning contemporary readers were intended to extract from the great bishop's biography.

Stephen's decidedly anti-Irish sound is more obtrusive than eloquent. His scorn would have given offense in certain quarters and comfort in others, but the quarrels between Irish and Roman usage seem, by the 710s, to have been more relevant to the periphery of Northumbria than to its core.[229] The lengthy account of Wilfrid's Roman appeals is not much more obviously related to problems at the time of writing. That Stephen pays much attention to these efforts, especially the second one, is perhaps predictable, but puzzling in light of the qualified results they attained. Modern readers observe that, to go by the transcribed documents and Stephen's narrative, the papacy remained unfailingly circumspect, lacking illusions about exerting power at a great distance and unwilling to circumvent its local representative, the archbishop of Canterbury.[230] Regardless of qualifications, however, Rome did invariably find in Wilfrid's favor. Several kings, as well as Archbishops Theodore and Berhtwald, made Wilfrid suffer, but Rome never failed to vindicate him. If there were any lesson in this tale, it would seem to be that the Northumbrian Church had a great interest in being directly subordinated to the Holy See, as it would be if it had an archbishop of its own.

The early chapters interestingly anticipate this conclusion. As Stephen's narrative approaches the Synod of Whitby, the Irishman Colman is pre-

[227] VW 1-23 (achievements), 26-34, 43, 50-58 (efforts at rehabilitation), 45 (restored under Aldfrith); for activity outside Northumbria, n. 116 above. The claim of Thacker, "Social Background," p. 250, that the VW mainly concerns Wilfrid as the leader of a great monastic *paruchia*, has little apparent basis.

[228] References to Mercia hint at Wilfrid's extensive activity and interests, but details are skimpy (VW 14, 15, 40, 43, 45, 47, 48, 57, 64); ten years of exile there are silenced in the passage from VW 45 to 46. On Wilfrid and Mercia, see John, "Social and Political Problems of the Early English Church," pp. 51-52. Wilfrid's attachment to his homeland is further illustrated by his refusal of attractive offers in the Frankish kingdom (VW 4, 28) and his evasion of Theodore's suggestion that he should be the next archbishop of Canterbury (43).

[229] British and Irish schismatics or Quartodecimans: VW 5, 10 (sneering reference to St. Columba), 12, 14-15, 47 (*Scotticae virulenta plantationis germina*). Only one reference to *Scotti* is neutral (21). On the topicality of the Easter question by the early 700s, see above, n. 94.

[230] Poole, "Wilfrid and Ripon," pp. 67-68, 77-78; Farmer, "St. Wilfrid," pp. 48-49, 53-54, 55-56.

sented as "metropolitan bishop of York."[231] An immediate consequence of the synod, in Stephen's telling, was Wilfrid's election as bishop in place of the departing Colman; the bishop-elect went to Gaul for ordination and was then destined for "the episcopal see of the city of York," the see to which, in his absence, Chad was irregularly elevated and in which, after the latter's deposition, Wilfrid was installed by Theodore.[232] Stephen, after having finally moved Wilfrid into Colman's place, supplies him with the same title; he was "established as metropolitan bishop of the city of York." The term "metropolitan" never appears again in the *Life*, but one is reminded of it a few chapters later:

As the religious King Ecgfrith expanded his realm to the north and south by triumphs, so Bishop Wilfrid of blessed memory enlarged the realm of the Churches (*regnum ecclesiarum*) to the south over the Saxons and to the north over the Britons, Irish, and Picts; loving and kindly to all nationalities (*gentes*), he zealously carried out ecclesiastical duties.[233]

These words are as close as Stephen comes to evoking a Wilfridian golden age, and one cannot help inferring that it had something to do with Wilfrid's being both ordained to York and sole bishop of Northumbria.

What strikes the eye in these passages is not so much that the title "metropolitan bishop of York" was anachronistic in the 660s, though it was, than that it became a reality in 735, only about fifteen years after Stephen of Ripon wrote. Although next to nothing suggests that Wilfrid himself wished York to be archiepiscopal, its status might have become topical by the time Acca and Tatbert commissioned the *Life of Wilfrid*.[234] Toward 720, the kingdom was organized into three coequal sees. As a result, a position

---

[231] VW 10.

[232] Wilfrid elected and goes to Gaul, VW 11-12; elevation of Chad, 13; Wilfrid installed, 15.

[233] VW 21. In recent literature *regnum ecclesiarum* is customarily taken out of context and construed as something belonging to Wilfrid; namely, his large collection of churches and monasteries: Wallace-Hadrill, "Rome and the Early English Church," p. 128; Gibbs, "Decrees of Agatho," p. 233; Isenberg, *Würdigung Wilfrids*, pp. 89-102 (elaborately glosses the term before citing the passage in which it appears); Brooks, *Early History of Canterbury*, p. 74; Thacker, "Social Background," p. 236 ("the great *r.e.* of the master"). Stephen's context, however, is unambiguous: as Ecgfrith expanded his realm, Wilfrid extended the sway or domain of Christian communities, in a wholly impersonal sense. The author's meaning is faithfully rendered by Webb's translation, p. 153: "enlarged the field of Wilfrid's ecclesiastical jurisdiction." The only oddity is Stephen's use of the plural *ecclesiarum*, but no specifically Wilfridian sense can be given to that. Stephen did not express his pride in Wilfrid's far-flung possessions, followers, and riches through the phrase *regnum ecclesiarum*.

[234] On the event of 735, nn. 181-83 above. Acca belonged originally to the clergy of York and stayed there in passing from Bosa's entourage to Wilfrid's: H.E. 5.20. Gibbs, "Decrees of Agatho," argues at length that the creation of an archbishopric was an issue in Wilfrid's time; Brooks, *Early History of Canterbury*, p. 72, rightly stresses that no evidence points in this direction.

comparable to the dominance that Colman and Wilfrid had enjoyed as sole bishop in the kingdom under Oswy and Ecgfrith might be re-created in only one way: by prevailing on the pope to elevate York to be the metropolis of a province. The *Life of Wilfrid* would have been worth writing by way of example if its sponsors nursed ambitions of this kind.

Stephen of Ripon ascribes an astonishing level of militance to his hero: Wilfrid, when young, offered himself to martyrdom; he led his followers, though without personally wielding arms, in successful battle against pagan robbers; he caused a royal reeve to hunt down a child whom he had cured and who had been promised to him as a monk; he supported King Ecgfrith in victorious combat against the Picts and the Mercians; not quite so forthrightly, he assisted Cædwalla of Wessex in his astonishing rise to power.[235] These passages are comparatively few, mainly in the "prosperous" third of the *Life*, and somewhat offset by Wilfrid's saintly endurance of the injustices heaped on him; yet, the contrast they make with a figure like Cuthbert or with the whole tenor of Bede's *H.E.* is glaring. If there is a message in the portrayal of Wilfrid's forcefulness, its appeal seems to be to the Northumbrian kings.

Wilfrid's main difficulties were with Kings Ecgfrith and Aldfrith; Ecgfrith's second wife, Erminburg, was also a source of active hostility.[236] Stephen's *Life* spells out their responsibility but remains remarkably well disposed toward them and their descendants. Erminburg, felled by illness for her bad treatment of Wilfrid, becomes the occasion for his liberation; bad as she was then, she eventually became an exemplary abbess. God's revenge for Wilfrid's expulsion was quickly exacted: Ecgfrith's brother, Ælfwine, was killed in battle against the Mercians (679).[237] Stephen, perhaps inhibited by the first *Life of St. Cuthbert*, completely avoided painting Ecgfrith's death in the same retributive colors as Ælfwine's. In a unique instance of reversed chronological order, he described the reconciliation of Archbishop Theodore with Wilfrid and Theodore's plea to Aldfrith of Northumbria to make peace with the exiled bishop (686); only then, after anticipating Wilfrid's restoration, did he mention the "most wretched slaughter" in which Ecgfrith lost his life (685). No more than a faint hint of a relation between the king's death and Wilfrid's fate is given by Theodore's statement that Aldfrith, by reinstating Wilfrid, would contribute to the redemption of Ecgfrith's soul.[238] Aldfrith himself is even more gently treated. Although he was responsible for the second expulsion and, in part,

[235] Martyrdom, *VW* 6; battle against pagans, 13; hunts down child, 16; support of Ecgfrith in combat, 19-20; assistance to Cædwalla, 42.
[236] *VW* 24, 34, 36, 38-40, 45, 47, 58-59.
[237] *VW* 24 (Erminburg as abbess; Ælfwine), 29 (Wilfrid's liberation).
[238] *VW* 43-44.

for the shameful doings at Austerfield, it is his unnamed counselors who are blamed for refusing reconciliation, whereas the king himself, mortally stricken by God for scorning the papal decrees of restitution, is shown repenting on his deathbed, promising amendment if he should recover and, for the good of his soul if he should not, appealing to his successor to make peace with Wilfrid. Again, after Aldfrith's death, anonymous royal counselors obstructed Wilfrid's return, but with the accession of the child Osred, better sentiments prevailed, thanks, in part, to the royal lady, Abbess Ælf-fled of Whitby.[239]

However famous Bede's discretion may be, the *Life of Wilfrid* is almost more discreet in bearing no malice to the family of King Oswy. The feelings shown are far more positive than the circumstances would normally warrant, for heredity within a single branch was not the rule in Anglo-Saxon monarchy.[240] To hear Stephen, however, Ecgfrith, the outstanding member of the line, experienced his best days side by side with Wilfrid; and the great bishop, unembittered by intervening troubles, ended his life as adoptive father to Oswy's direct descendant, the boy Osred. It does not help to maintain that Stephen simply told the truth; the same facts might be presented in a variety of ways depending on the impression to be made. Dynastic conditions in the span within which Stephen wrote should be briefly recalled: Osred was murdered in 716; a distant collateral, Coenred, ruled from 716 to 718; and he was replaced from 718 to 729 by Osred's brother, Osric—again a descendant of Oswy. It seems unlikely that the *Life of Wilfrid* was written in the two years of interrupted continuity between Osred and Osric; Stephen of Ripon is best described as a "legitimist," and one expects that his sentiments were shared by Acca of Hexham and the other Wilfridians who commissioned his work. The teaching of the *Life of Wilfrid* is, at its simplest, that great advantage might accrue to a king from having a bishop in Wilfrid's mold by his side and even greater if that prelate should gain immediacy to Rome by papal elevation of his see to archiepiscopal rank. Such lessons would not have been inappropriate for King Osric, who, at his accession in 718, need not have been foreordained to be the last and most obscure of Oswy's line.

If it were not for Bede's *H.E.*, our accounts of the conversion of England would be built around the *Life of Wilfrid*. It is among the finest in the impressive series of episcopal biographies composed since the third century, when this type of narrative, often richer in ordinary events than in mira-

---

[239] *VW* 44 (Aldfrith called *sapientissimus*), 58-59 (councilors blamed), 60 (Ælffled elaborately praised). Thacker, "Social Background," p. 243, understates the case when saying that "Eddius" is fair to Wilfrid's enemies: he is much friendlier than a partisan of Wilfrid should normally be.
[240] Kirby, "Northumbria in Time of Wilfrid," p. 17.

cles, began to be written. Few equal it within a century except the Gallic *Life of Desiderius of Cahors*.[241] Gregory of Tours, we saw, set about composing the *Histories* within a long-standing historical vacuum. Bede, with Stephen's biography behind him, had no such handicap; a one-dimensional account of the English Church offered a far better surface to lean upon than none at all.

Stephen of Ripon gave immediate offense. We are especially aware of this because the outlook of the offended soon prevailed and overshadowed the claims of the *Life of Wilfrid*. In the 710s and 720s, however, the future was still open. Stephen's sponsors, Acca and Tatbert, were great dignitaries of the Northumbrian Church. Their ascendancy had been endangered by the assassination of Osric and the advent of Coenred, and though the latter proved to be a mere interlude, the sense of Wilfridian security was bound to have been shaken. In these circumstances, almost certainly after Coenred's passing from the scene, Acca and Tatbert may well have thought it desirable for all Wilfrid's spiritual progeny that the figure of their master, whose best years must now have been largely forgotten, should be evoked in circumstantial detail and presented as the one example of Catholic excellence that England had generated. When the tenor of Stephen's account is related to the political conditions at the time of writing, some inferences may be tentatively made concerning the more particular destination of the *Life of Wilfrid* and the special ambitions of its Northumbrian sponsors. The issuing of Stephen's *Life* was meant to strengthen and enhance the existing strength of the Wilfridians; though provoked by defensive instincts, it was an aggressive step, raising the temperature of ecclesiastical politics. Wilfrid had been controversial when alive; as the hero of a biography, he became the stalking-horse for the strivings of other men.

Bede is at the center of the response to the *Life of Wilfrid*. How Lindisfarne at once enlisted him to rewrite the *Life of St. Cuthbert* has already concerned us and presently will again. As the 720s wore on, Stephen's work would impinge on Bede as he wrote the *History of the Abbots of Wearmouth-Jarrow* as well as the *H.E.* Before turning to these literary reactions, another possible trace of the impact of the *Life of Wilfrid* should be noted. An odd, irregular incident occurred at York in 721: the saintly and aged bishop, John of Beverley, resigned and, before withdrawing to monastic peace, carried out by himself the consecration of the successor he had chosen, presumably with royal consent; the new bishop, Wilfrid II, had been trained, like John, as a monk of Whitby.[242] Saintly or not, John of Beverley acted

---

[241] *Vita s. Desiderii ep. Cadurcensis*, ed. Bruno Krusch, Corpus Christianorum, ser. Lat. 117 (Turnhout 1957), pp. 345-401. It is likely to be rather near the *VW* in date.

[242] *H.E.* 5.6 (Bede presents the facts without trace of disapproval); 4.23 (Whitby).

in violation of the canons. Might he have been anxious about whom York would fall to if it became vacant without someone of his prestige to influence the succession? Designs on the bishopric of York are, as we saw, implicit in Stephen's *Life of Wilfrid*. The fear it provoked offers a motive for the otherwise puzzling accession of Wilfrid II.

No later than 721, Bede composed a new *Life of St. Cuthbert* and described it to the bishop and monks of Lindisfarne, in the introductory letter, as though it were the uniquely authoritative account of the saint. The reasons for his action, and the eager support Lindisfarne gave him, should not again detain us.[243] Bede's work on the *Life* is suggestive of the directions in which the existence of the *Life of Wilfrid* turned him. As Levison observed, "He relates the progress of Cuthbert's life more clearly than his predecessor, noting in due order [the various stages of Cuthbert's career]."[244] The explicit chronological progression of Bede's version does not necessarily improve the model; more than once, order is achieved by arbitrarily reshuffling chapters.[245] Nor does the agent of change have to have been Bede's "historical sense," which, in the *H.E.*, often favors skewed chronology. The chances are that Bede simply strove, with success, to equal Stephen's stately advance through Wilfrid's life.

In the course of "straightening" Cuthbert's biography, Bede gave prominence to two facts that had no place in the older version: that the saint had, with Eata, established a colony of Melrose at Ripon and was driven out to make room for others; and that, at Cuthbert's death, a "storm" descended upon Lindisfarne, threatening to disperse the community until the election of Bishop Eadberht restored calm. Wilfrid, though not named, bulked large in both incidents (as the *H.E.* would point out).[246] In a death-

[243] Above, n. 125.

[244] Levison, "Bede as Historian," pp. 127-28, attributes these merits to Bede's "historical sense." Thacker, "Social Background," p. 116, also seems to approve of change in the direction of "historicity"; his view (p. 115) that Lindisfarne wanted a *Vita* of its saint in keeping with the latest fashion is not very convincing (but cf. above, n. 187). In a different sense, Rosenthal, "Bede's *Life of St. Cuthbert*," pp. 604-605 (the rewriting is not always an improvement).

[245] *Prose Cuthbert* 3-6, clearly designed as a gradual progression toward the saint's becoming a monk; 8, smooths the transition from monk to prior of Melrose; 16, fills in his life at Lindisfarne before entering the hermitage; 18-20, intervert the information of Anon. *Cuthbert* for no clear reason; 29-33, miracles of healing, not before Ecgfrith's death, as Anon. 4.3-6, but after (30, someone shown in flight from fear of the barbarian enemy, as appropriate after Nechtansmere); 40, interverts Anon. 4.15 from after to before the saint's translation.

[246] *Prose Cuthbert* 7-8 (Eata and Cuthbert at Ripon); tumult after Cuthbert's death (40, fulfillment of Ps. 59, "Siquidem sepulto viro Dei tanta aecclesiam illam temptationis aura concussit, ut plures e fratribus loco magis cedere, quam talibus vellent interesse periculis"); *H.E.* 4.29, "episcopatum ecclesiae illius anno uno servabat venerabilis antistes Vilfrid." It is typical of Bede in the *H.E.* that, unless readers also consult the *Verse* and the *Prose Cuthbert*, they

bed scene again new to Bede's version, Cuthbert enjoined the monks of Lindisfarne to have nothing to do with deviators from Catholic unity and from the proper time for celebrating Easter.[247] Aside from this brief line, no hint is given anywhere of tension between Roman usages and the Irish customs of Melrose and Lindisfarne; the references of the first *Life* to a Roman tonsure and the Rule of St. Benedict are not carried into Bede's revision. The two instances Bede mentions of monasteries passing from Irish to "Roman" hands—Ripon and one on the Tyne—are expressed in tones of resignation, "changed like all else by time" in the "frail and unstable state of the world."[248] That an improvement might be involved is never suggested. Throughout his account, Bede refused to contrast a lower to a higher tradition of religious life. The discipline Cuthbert practiced and taught bore no distinguishing label; it exemplified timeless Christian perfection.

Bede's farthest-reaching change of the first *Life of Cuthbert* gives a positive and almost institutional sense to the tradition Cuthbert embodied. Now and again, the first *Life* shows Cuthbert preaching in the countryside, but its main focus is the saint's miracles.[249] Bede, without neglecting the miracles, developed Cuthbert into a paragon of pastoral care, bringing the Gospels in great simplicity to remote villages. He also associated Cuthbert's exemplary practices with the institution of a monastery-based episcopal see, whose incumbent lived in common with the monks, after the fashion, Bede maintained, of Christ's apostles in Jerusalem and of Augustine and the other emissaries of Pope Gregory in Canterbury.[250] It is here, in short, that Bede first set out the ideas found, invariably in a context of Irish monk-pastors, in some of the most lyrical passages of the *H.E.* (some simply taken over from his *Life of Cuthbert*) and advocated with vehemence in the *Letter to Egbert of York*.[251]

The appeal of Bede's carefully crafted presentation has proved difficult to

---

would conclude that Wilfrid's tenure of Lindisfarne was thoroughly creditable (cf. n. 103).

Bede's homily for the feast of Benedict Biscop (whose date cannot be determined) seems to refer indirectly to the dubious way Wilfrid acquired Ripon: the *reges saeculi* "locum ei [i.e. Benedict Biscop] monasterii construendi non ab aliqua minorum personarum ablatum sed de suis propriis [i.e. the kings'] donatum dare curabant"; ed. D. Hurst, Corpus Christianorum, ser. lat. 122 (Turnhout 1955) 91 lines 113-16.

[247] *Prose Cuthbert* 39. The deathbed scene (37-39) is said to be based on the report of Abbot Herefrith. Bede also portrayed the death of Boisil (18) and added a deathbed scene to his adaptation of the *VCeolf*, i.e. *Hist. abb.* 11-14. Gregory the Great's *Dialogues* gave popularity to deathbed scenes.

[248] *Prose Cuthbert* 3, 8. A veiled allusion to Irish usages in reference to Cuthbert's teaching of regular life, n. 159 above.

[249] Anon. *Cuthbert* 2.5-6, 4.5 (incidental to main subject).

[250] *Prose Cuthbert* 9 (*erat quippe moris eo tempore*), 14, 16. Contrary to the Anon. *Cuthbert*, Bede also ascribes miracles of healing to Cuthbert before his episcopate (16).

[251] Cf. above, nn. 101-103. Rosenthal, "Bede's *Life of St. Cuthbert*," pp. 605-607.

resist; it takes the tough-mindedness of a Dorothy Whitelock to contrast Bede's barefooted preachers unfavorably to Wilfridian prelacy.[252] From his prose *St. Cuthbert* onward, Bede repeatedly proposed that there was something of incalculable value, and urgently needed at present, in the evangelization of the countryside by monk-priests reared in the ways of the Irish fathers. As redesigned by Bede, St. Cuthbert changed from an eccentrically holy wonder worker into a model pastor, losing much of his primitive charm but becoming instead the grounds for militant advocacy of the (basically Irish) institution to which he had belonged and which Lindisfarne perpetuated. Cuthbert had tramped the hills of Northumbria saving souls while Wilfrid raised dust on the roads to and from Rome.

One last point about the new *Life of St. Cuthbert*. Bede's assent to the request of Lindisfarne that he should undertake this commision cannot have been a wholly individual decision. Wearmouth and Jarrow were "Roman" foundations, whose first years Wilfrid had assisted; they were situated in the diocese of Hexham, which Wilfrid had helped to create and which his leading disciple, Acca, continued to head; and Acca had long been a leading patron of Bede's biblical scholarship. Yet Bede responded to Lindisfarne's request with more than a mechanical execution of literary labor. Though he deleted many of the proper names of informants recorded in the old *Life of Cuthbert*, he saw to it that the few new ones should include the very aged priest Ingwald, monk of Wearmouth; the almost-dying Sigfrith, monk of Jarrow; and, for recent information, an unnamed priest of Jarrow.[253] A reader of the new *Life* was reminded near its start and finish of Bede's monastery. And Bede asked, in the introductory letter, to be enrolled in the Lindisfarne register and remembered in the prayers of the congregation. In several ways, he drew attention to the ties uniting his community with Lindisfarne.

More explicit evidence suggests that Wearmouth-Jarrow may have been reorienting its ecclesiastical affinities. Bede's verse celebration of St. Cuthbert, written before the departure of Abbot Ceolfrid, had had no institutional implications; his prose *St. Cuthbert* emphatically did. Without ceasing in the 720s to compose biblical commentaries on Acca's behalf, Bede also thought it proper to provide Wearmouth-Jarrow with a new and much changed account of its foundation.[254]

The anonymous *Life of Ceolfrid*, which we examined above, was briefly cited by Bede in the *Major Chronicle* of 725, about five years, therefore,

---

[252] Whitelock, "Bede and His Teachers," p. 33.

[253] Bede *Prose Cuthbert* 5, 6, 46.

[254] At least *De templo*, *In Ezram et Neemiam*, and *In Marcum*: Laistner and King, *Hand-list*, pp. 75, 39, 50.

after he had written the prose *St. Cuthbert*. It is plausibly inferred that
Bede's *History of the Abbots of Wearmouth-Jarrow*, which is in effect a major
revision of the *Life of Ceolfrid*, dates from between the *Major Chronicle* and
the *H.E.*[255] There is no way to fix upon a more precise date within the span
725-31. Plummer, who thought Bede's prose *St. Cuthbert* had not "bettered
the original," came close to saying the same thing about what Bede made
of the *Life of Ceolfrid*: "he more often abbreviates than expands . . . [and]
sacrifices some interesting details."[256] Plummer helps us to realize that, in
both cases, the revisions cannot be convincingly related to qualitative defects in the prototypes. Bede, in the *History of the Abbots*, adds little to the
factual content of the *Life of Ceolfrid*. What he does do—surely not as a private initiative—is to turn the account of the foundation of Wearmouth-
Jarrow in a new direction.

Benedict Biscop is the unrivaled star of the *History of the Abbots*. He, the
first sentence tells us, founded Wearmouth and ruled it for sixteen years.
Not only is pride of place in the first of the two short books given to his
continental travels, and to his imports of manuscripts, valuables, paintings,
and craftsmen, but his death is held over to occupy the opening chapter of
the second.[257] The *Life of Ceolfrid*, as we have seen, reflects the emotions of
716; Bede's narrative, separated by almost forty years from Benedict Biscop's death (689), is a cool historical reconstruction, paying to the four earliest abbots the attention each was due. It is an excellent record of the
founding years of the monastery, an improvement to that extent over the
Life of Ceolfrid. But there is a conspicuous loss. The earlier account told us
much of Ceolfrid's origins and life at Ripon, and it showed that Bishop Wilfrid had helped Benedict Biscop by letting him have Ceolfrid as assistant.[258]
All this Bede blotted out. One even suspects that the attractive image of
Ceolfrid as a priest joyfully laboring in the bakery at Ripon is transmuted by
Bede into the equally attractive image of the ex-thane Eosterwine thresh-
ing and milking at Wearmouth.[259] In Bede's portrayal, Benedict Biscop
acted on his own initiative, supported by land grants from King Ecgfrith.

[255] Levison, "Bede as Historian," p. 129 n. 1.

[256] Plummer I, xlvi-vii.

[257] Benedict Biscop is the solitary hero of *Hist. abb.* 1-6, 9, 11-13 (in illness, overshadows
his fellow victim, Sigfrid); 14 (his death occupies the initial chapter of the second *libellus*).

[258] Above, n. 202. Bede's Ceolfrid materializes only at the foundation of Jarrow (*Hist. abb.*
7) and does nothing noteworthy until made sole abbot (13). He is strictly pigeonholed as
Benedict's *a primis exordiis adiutor* (7, 22). The account of his rule (15) exceeds the *VCeolf* in
as much as it records donations, but anything anecdotal or personal is missing; the memorable
figure of the chapter is the benefactor Witmær.

[259] *VCeolf* 4; *Hist. abb.* 8. Even if Bede did not "substitute" Eosterwine for Ceolfrid, the attractive anecdote assigned to the former could, if Bede had wished, have been joined by something appealing about Ceolfrid.

The solitary prominence given to Benedict was partly at Ceolfrid's expense but also, glaringly, at Wilfrid's. We are left to understand that Wearmouth-Jarrow owed its character as a "Roman" monastery to Benedict alone.

Bede's concern, in the later 720s, is unlikely to have been to pass a personal judgment upon the late bishop Wilfrid; as a monk of Jarrow under the rule of an abbot, he was better suited to contribute, as spokesman for those whose sympathies he shared, to an opposition to Wilfrid's living successors. Before entering upon the *H.E.*, he composed works on behalf of Lindisfarne and his own monastery that indicate, overtly or by omission, just how topical the figure of Wilfrid still was as an issue in current arguments.

Unfortunately, the details of these disputes wholly escape us. Only the barest external facts are known. In 729, Osric, the last descendant of Oswy, yielded the kingship to his distant cousin, Ceolwulf, brother of the ephemeral king of 716-18. It was to Ceolwulf that Bede dedicated the *H.E.* Stenton's opinion that Bede "clearly mistrusted [Ceolwulf's] political capacity" puts a more negative construction on his comments than they will bear when related to their prototype in Jerome's *Chronicle*; to advert to the turmoil of the present as an excuse for not writing about it need only, as with Jerome, express the conviction that calm will return and afford a better occasion for historical record.[260] Although Ceolwulf was briefly dethroned in 731, the same year saw Acca of Hexham permanently driven from his see. Not many months later, Bede's disciple, Egbert, near cousin of the king, replaced the irregular Wilfrid II as bishop of York.[261] When these facts are added together, the possibility arises that Bede, his community, and Lindisfarne inclined toward the ascendant branch of the royal kin, and that the

---

[260] Stenton, *Anglo-Saxon England*, 2d ed., p. 91. Bede, as usual, uses his own words, but the similarity of idea is obvious: *H.E.* 5.23, ed. Plummer, p. 349, "cuius regni et principia et processus tot ac tantis redundavere rerum adversantium motibus, ut, quid de his scribi debeat, quemve habitura sint finem singula, necdum sciri valeat"; Jerome *Chron. praef.*, ed. Helm, p. 7, "Quo fine contentus reliquum temporis Gratiani et Theodosii latioris historiae stilo reservavi . . . quoniam dibacchantibus adhuc in terra nostra barbaris incerta sunt omnia." In other words, things have to settle down before they may be written about. The same passage also bears on the date of the *H.E.* (above, n. 36): Bede may have referred to *rerum adversantium motus* fully aware of Ceolwulf's temporary dethronement, but resolved to keep these troubles out of his serene history.

[261] Above, nn. 174, 178, 179 (175). Acca lived to the end of the decade, but was replaced at Hexham by Frithbert in 734 or 735: Plummer II, 330. Kirby, "Bede, Eddius Stephanus," p. 107, believes that the expulsion of Acca "must have been traumatic . . . for Bede, who was devoted to Acca as his diocesan." Bede's warm feelings toward Acca are inferred from a long series of dedications ("dearest so-and-so"); most of all, "dearest of all prelates on earth" (Plummer I, xxxiii, xlix; II, 329). Six of Bede's sixteen surviving letters are to Acca. Cf. Whitelock, "Bede and His Teachers," pp. 26-27. The problem is whether written formulas (*dilectissime*) are a reliable measure of friendship. Bede hoped that Ceolwulf and Egbert would reform the Northumbrian Church (cf. Bullough, "Hagiography as Patriotism," p. 346); these were probably the men chiefly responsible for unseating Acca.

leading Wilfridian, Acca, lost his see for having abortively challenged the new régime.[262]

4. Bede's Three Models for the *Ecclesiastical History*

ar from being an isolated masterpiece, Bede's H.E. ends an intramural argument that the Northumbrian Church had engaged in since the last decade of the seventh century. The motives generally offered for its composition leave out of account the competitive context in which Bede worked. Plummer's opinion, almost concealed in his notes, was that Bede, a solicitous teacher, wrote for "the edification of his readers." Levison believed that, though invited to write by Albinus of Canterbury, he also was spontaneously inspired by "a kind of national feeling" that had long brought the idea of such a work to the forefront of his thoughts. In Stenton's view, Bede seized the "great opportunity" afforded by an audience, such as King Ceolwulf, ready "for a work of erudition devoted to the growth of the English church."[263] These and other suggestions, though grounded in Bede's prefatory remarks, presuppose an atmosphere of monastic serenity and dispassionate scholarship, rather than the many years during which history had been a topical issue in Northumbria. Bede capped a series of fragmentary essays on local Church history, some of them his own, and summed them up in a grandiose but hardly dispassionate synthesis.

What we know best of the setting of the H.E. is its Northumbrian past, to which we shall presently return in order to examine the use Bede made of the Whitby *Life of Gregory the Great* and especially of Stephen of Ripon's *Life of Wilfrid.* Where the immediate and direct motivation of the H.E. is concerned, the most telling fact is Bede's contact with Canterbury, attested by the patronage of Albinus, whom he acknowledged to have incited the work, and by the role of Nothelm, priest of London, as the physical link between Bede and vital documentation from Canterbury and Rome. The importance of this literary association has long been noted.[264] At simplest, it explains why Bede's account strives to embrace the whole English Church and is not addressed only to that of Northumbria, which had been the sole concern of his predecessors and himself until now. Also obvious are the amity and deep respect shown in the H.E. for Canterbury, especially in the person of Archbishop Theodore.

Yet it seems naïve to imagine that the H.E. was the casual outcome of momentarily converging scholarly interests. Nothelm, Bede's contact man, made two journeys to Northumbria and, in between, went all the way

[262] Cf. Kirby, "Northumbria in Time of Wilfrid," p. 24.

[263] Plummer I, xxii n. 5; Levison, "Bede as Historian," p. 133; Stenton, *Anglo-Saxon England*, 2d ed., p. 187.

[264] Wallace-Hadrill, "Bede and Plummer," p. 90, and "Gregory of Tours and Bede," p. 104.

to Rome. His travels were important for Bede's documentation, but their sole purpose could hardly have been to supply a historian with sources. The same Nothelm became archbishop of Canterbury in 735, and the start of his pontificate precisely coincided with the elevation of York to archiepiscopal status.[265] Is this mere chance? Greater justice is done to what the *H.E.* meant for the English Church by regarding it as proof of active cooperation between North and South for more than literary reasons. We do not know the identity and rank of the Northumbrians who, with Bede, took pains to ingratiate themselves with the see of Canterbury; their reasons for doing so also elude us. The most plausible circumstances are suggested by the immediate future of the *H.E.*; namely, that its publication virtually coincided with the papal grant of the *pallium* to Egbert of York and the completion of the Gregorian plan for a second English archbishopric and province. That this momentous step called for cooperation between King Ceolwulf and the archbishop of Canterbury, as well as for the assent of Rome, offers a more serious perspective on Bede's celebration of the English church than the conventional reasons given in his introductory letter.[266]

How did Bede go about presenting his various patrons' case for the creation of a second province of the English Church? Certainly without vehemence or argument. He intimated, as gently and serenely as he knew how, that the time for implementing this Gregorian idea had come. But to conceive of Bede's enterprise in this way either proposes one more interpretation of the *H.E.* after many others or outlines the program Bede was called upon to translate into words. There is a more practical side, already encountered some pages ago, to the question how Bede went about his task. Though learned, and brilliant in literary composition, he was not in the habit of creating original designs for books: he normally used models. Where, then, did the structure of the *H.E.* come from?

The introductory letter does not tell us and was not meant to. Bede has received more than his share of credit, with respect to the prose *St. Cuthbert* as well as the *H.E.*, for baring his methods in exceptional detail. He has even been thought to anticipate the modern reverence for explicitly acknowledged documentation.[267] There is just enough similarity to justify the

[265] See above, nn. 181, 183. Also Meyvaert, "The *Registrum* of Gregory the Great and Bede." Nothelm's first visit to Jarrow was before 725; he could supply Bede with papal letters about the English mission only after his journey to Rome. Bede mentions Nothelm's two trips not only in *H.E. praef.*, but in the prefatory letter to Albinus of Canterbury.

[266] The more so if one considers that the *H.E.* was completed later than 731 (n. 36), and that the grant of the *pallium* was decided before 735 and was known to Bede as imminent in November 734.

[267] Stenton, *Anglo-Saxon England*, 2d ed., p. 187; Blair, "Historical Writings of Bede," p.

rapprochement. Bede's orientation, however, was not toward disclosure of how he worked but toward authentication of the finished product. To disarm those inclined to doubt his words, Bede listed his many *auctores*, not books or documents but living men ready to vouch for his credibility; as a last resort, they rather than Bede bore responsibility for the information they supplied and he reproduced. Bede's alignment of oath-helpers lacks neither candor nor respectability, but its context is medieval.[268]

Whatever its intentions, Bede's introduction is a valuable guide to his oral informants, and it is not without relevance to the problem of how the *H.E.* was planned. Bede draws attention to two blocks of information that stand out clearly in the finished work. "From the beginning of this book (*volumen*) to the time when the English people received the faith of Christ, we learned what we report mainly from ancient writings collected from all directions."[269] This refers unmistakably to book I, chapters 1-22; but Bede does not specify which one of the "ancient writings" supplied the framework for organizing the information supplied by the others. The second block concerns "all that the disciples of St. Gregory had done in the kingdom of Kent or in the neighboring kingdoms" and the supplementary papal letters obtained by Nothelm in Rome; for all this, Bede warmly thanked the latter and, primarily, Abbot Albinus, who had gathered the information Canterbury could supply.[270] The materials in question are (with rare exceptions) entered from book I, chapter 23, to the end of book II of the *H.E.*—the span devoted to the Gregorian mission. The balance of the *H.E.*, even reaching back to embrace Paulinus's share of the mission from Rome, is predominantly concerned with Northumbria; from book III onward, whatever information Bede obtained from elsewhere, including Canterbury, was fitted into the interstices of a basically regional history.

Bede's introductory account of his authorities implies that the *H.E.* is in three parts, of which the last far exceeds the others in length. But, just as in introducing the *Prose Cuthbert* he made no reference to his written (and principal) source, so in the *H.E.* he said nothing of the earlier narratives

---

199. But cf. Ray, "Bede's *vera lex*," p. 11: "The sheer size of the discussion of sources is an idiosyncracy."

[268] "Lectoremque suppliciter obsecro, ut, siqua in his, quae scripsimus, aliter quam se veritas habet, posita reppererit, non hoc nobis imputet"; he had only striven to commit to letters *simpliciter* what he had gathered *fama vulgante*. See the important discussion of Ray, "Bede's *vera lex*," pp. 13-14.

[269] "A principio itaque voluminis huius usque ad tempus, quo gens Anglorum fidem Christi percepit, ex priorum maxime scriptis hinc inde collectis ea, quae promeremus, didicimus" (Plummer I, 6). In this context it is impossible (but unimportant) to determine whether *volumen* denotes the whole history or book I.

[270] "Omnia, quae in ipsa Cantuariorum provincia, vel etiam in contiguis eidem regionibus a discipulis beati papae Gregorii gesta fuere" (*ibid.*; the passage is a few lines earlier than the one in n. 269).

that, as it appears, gave his history its pattern. One of them is widely acknowledged and beyond dispute; namely, Gildas's *Ruin of Britain* (or *De excidio*), which we have already met in a different context.[271] It underlies the
first of Bede's three divisions. Bede's use of the other two in this structural
fashion has not yet been recognized, but the part they play is thoroughly
similar. They are the Whitby *Life of Gregory the Great*, for the period of the
Gregorian mission, and, for all the rest, Stephen of Ripon's *Life of Wilfrid*.
Bede did not cherish these texts; they served his purposes, and served them
well, by providing him with a ready-made substratum for correction, expansion, and rectification.

Having one or more texts to react against is a help to invention even today; often, words to object to or contradict prove a greater spur to eloquence than words one respects. It is not as though new Church histories
could have been generated by dispensing copies of Eusebius's prototype (in
Rufinus's Latin rendering) and prescribing imitation. At the edge of the
civilized world, Eusebius might have proved more demoralizing than encouraging.[272] A new Church history had a better chance of being called
into existence—as by Abbot Albinus—when its outlines were already
formed in the prospective author's head. It took a good library and rare skill
for Bede to bring the *H.E.* to its high polish and artistic refinement. Its
core, however, was insular. Bede first improved the historical chapters of
Gildas, then the Whitby *Gregory*, finally Stephen of Ripon, not the least
of whose contributions was the base line determining when the *H.E.* would
end. Bede's adversary relationship to Stephen's *Life of Wilfrid* is central to
the *H.E.*; if Orosius wrote seven books *adversum paganos*, Bede wrote no
fewer than three, perhaps not against the long-dead Wilfrid, but certainly
adversum Stephanum. We shall soon turn to that. Something should first be
said about Bede's use of the two other literary models.

Bede's attachment to Gildas in *H.E.* 1.1-22 is traced with ease. His dependence is expressed far less in unattributed quotations, however lengthy,
than in a precise retracing of Gildas's topics. From the description of Britain
paralleling *De excidio* 3 to the condemnation of the Britons paralleling *De
excidio* 26, he repeatedly drew upon different sources, such as Orosius, and
complementary ones, such as the *Passion of St. Alban* and the *Life of St. Germanus*, but deployed them for no other purpose than to retell, augment, or

[271] Plummer I, xxiv n. 1 (noting the lack of acknowledgment); esp. Hanning, *Vision of History*, pp. 69-78, noting that Edmond Faral first drew attention to the importance of Gildas for
Bede.

[272] Any reader of Eusebius quickly realizes the riches of documentation available to him,
including, besides the New Testament, more than sixty named authors. (Rufinus's translation
does not precisely correspond to the Greek, but the general impression of a wealth of evidence
cannot be far different.) For a would-be imitator in Bede's position, the example need not
have been encouraging.

modify Gildas's narrative.[273] In a Britain that Gildas reserved to the British, Bede found room for the Picts and the Irish; for a Roman conquest hinging on the rebellion of Boudicca (whom Gildas never named), he substituted the plain facts of invasion by Caesar and Claudius extracted from Orosius and others; in place of an abandonment of Britain by the fourth-century tyrant Maximus, he properly ascribed the evacuation to the fifth-century usurper Constantine.[274] Gildas supplied the melody for Bede's variations.

A complex instance of Bede's relationship to his model best rewards study. His attention was caught by a passage of Gildas concerning the building across the island of a barrier against northern barbarians. In the *De excidio*, the context for this incident is that the Romans withdrew their army and rule from Britain owing to exigencies on the Continent, leaving the natives to suffer severely from attacks by Irish and Picts; the Britons appealed for help to the Romans, who sent an expeditionary force that cleared out the invaders and ordered the Britons to build a wall. In Gildas's words (they must be cited in Latin in order to illustrate what Bede did with them):

Quos iussit construere inter duo maria trans insulam murum, ut esset arcendis hostibus turba instructus terrori civibusque tutamini; qui vulgo irrationabili absque rectore factus non tam lapidibus quam cespitibus non profuit.[275]

In Gildas's view, effective walls were built of stone (*lapides*), whereas those built of turf (*cespites*) were worthless. Bede reproduced this instance of wall building in *H.E.* 1.12, with direct quotations from Gildas. But he

---

[273] The quotations are concentrated in *H.E.* 1.12-16, 22. Gildas's guidance reaches much further back when measured by topics: description of Britain (*De excidio* 3 = *H.E.* 1.1), inhabitants of Britain (4 = 1.1 later part), Caesar (5 = 1.2), Roman conquest (6-7 = 1.3), Christian conversion (8 = 1.4), Diocletian's persecution (9 = 1.6), St. Alban (10-11.1 = 1.7), Arianism (11.2–12 = 1.8), Maximus and the abandonment of Britain (13 = 1.9, 11), Britain after Rome (14-19 = 1.12), appeal to Aëtius (20 = 1.13), sufferings of the Britons (20-23 = 1.14), coming of the Saxons (23-25 = 1.15), Ambrosius (25-26.1 = 1.16), condemnation of the Britons (26.2-4 = 1.22). Of Bede's seven chapters without counterparts in Gildas, *H.E.* 1.5 prepares a rectification of Gildas in 1.15 (as we shall presently see); 1.10 concerns Pelagianism, and lays the ground for the mission of St. Germanus; and 1.17-21 are largely drawn from the *Vita s. Germani episcopi Autissiodorensis* (by Constantius of Lyon, ed. W. Levison, MGH SRM VII, 247-83) and deliberately framed by separated parts of *De excidio* 26 (see below, n. 283).

[274] *De excidio* 4 evokes the pagan Britons as though indigenous; in their place, *H.E.* 1.1 carefully itemizes all the pre-Saxon inhabitants and even presents the Britons as immigrants (but the Irish seem to be indigenous). Roman conquest, as n. 273. Relying on Orosius, Bede separated the usurpation of Maximus (1.9) from the usurpation that occasioned the abandonment of Britain (1.11); *De excidio* 13 had conflated them. Miller, "Bede's Use of Gildas," claims that Bede thought more highly of Gildas when writing the *H.E.* than in 729, when writing the *Chronicon maius*; the distinction is shaky.

[275] *De excidio* 15.3, ed. Winterbottom, p. 93. Gildas's account of the walls has been much censured. For a plausible and sympathetic discussion, see Thompson, "Gildas and the History of Britain," pp. 206-207. (Thompson is not concerned with Bede's transformation of the passage.) Also sympathetic, Stevens, "Gildas Sapiens," p. 358.

almost certainly had the same passage of the *De excidio* in mind in H.E. 1.5, when he related, mainly after Orosius, that the emperor Septimius Severus, after triumphing in civil wars, was obliged to attend to disorders in Britain (Orosius is italicized; the words of Vegetius, the second authority Bede quotes, are set off by braces):

Ubi magnis gravibusque proeliis saepe gestis receptam partem insulae a ceteris indomitis gentibus, non muro, ut quidam aestimant, sed *vallo distinguendam putavit.* Murus etenim de lapidibus, vallum vero, quo ad repellendam vim hostium castra muniun- tur, fit de {cespitibus, quibus circumcisis}, e {terra velut murus exstruitur altus supra terram, ita ut} in ante sit {fossa, de qua levati} sunt cespites, {supra quam sudes de lignis fortissimis praefiguntur}. *Itaque* Severus *magnam fossam* etc.²⁷⁶

What provoked Bede into supplying a long, scholarly clarification of these ancient events? As it happens, Aurelius Victor's *Caesares* and the anonymous *Historia Augusta* furnish a basis for Bede's "as some believe (*ut quidam aestiment*)"; but it would be astonishing if he had consulted them for this one passage and thought they needed correction.²⁷⁷ The alternative is that Bede had more respect for earthworks than Gildas did and took this occasion to present readers with a little learning out of Vegetius's military treatise substantiating his point of view: Gildas erred in distinguishing good walls of stone from worthless ones of turf; each material might supply effec- tive fortifications. When the H.E. reaches Gildas's "profitless" wall, Bede is far from dismissing the earthwork in the manner of his source (Gildas in italics):

eosque [= Brittones] interim a dirissima depressione *liberatos,* hortata est [legio] in- struere *inter duo maria trans insulam murum,* qui *arcendis hostibus* posset esse praesidio [Gildas 15.3]; sicque *domum cum triumpho magno* reversa est [Gildas 16.1]. At in- sulani murum, quem iussi fuerant, *non tam lapidibus quam cespitibus* construentes [Gildas 15.3], utpote nullum tanti operis artificem habentes, ad nihil utilem sta- tuunt. [Bede's free continuation need not be quoted in Latin.] However, they built it for many miles between the two above-mentioned estuaries or inlets, hoping that where the sea provided no protection, they might use the rampart to preserve their border from hostile attack. Clear traces of this wide and lofty earthwork (*vallum*) can be seen to this day. It begins about two miles from the monastery of Aebber- curnig at a place which the Picts call Peanfahel and the English Penneltun, and runs westward to the vicinity of the city of Alcluith.²⁷⁸

Gildas emphasized the incompetence of a leaderless British mob. Instead, Bede, by evoking the lack of craftsmen, provided the Britons with an ex-

---

²⁷⁶ H.E. 1.5, ed. Plummer, I, 16-17. Vegetius *Epitoma rei militaris* 1.24, ed. Lang, p. 26.

²⁷⁷ Aurelius Victor *Caesares* 20.18, ed. Dufraigne, p. 28, and H.A. *Sept. Sev.* 18.2, ed. Hohl, I, 150. Plummer II, 15, heads a rich collection of material with the remark, "I do not know to whom Bede is alluding here." Gildas is likely.

²⁷⁸ H.E. 1.12, ed. Plummer, I, 26; tr. Sherley-Price, p. 52.

cuse that readers whom stone churches still amazed would understand, and he invited admiration for the remains of the grandiose *vallum* that, though "uselessly (*ad nihil utilem*)," had nevertheless been built.[279]

The story went on. Gildas related a second expedition in assistance of the British; the Romans cleared out the Picts and Irish but explained that they really could not come again; as a parting gift, they erected a proper stone wall across the island. Bede followed where Gildas led, and, having prepared the ground, added that the rampart the Romans built, still grandly standing in his time, was reared over the *vallum* of Septimius Severus.[280]

By modern standards, Bede got it all wrong. The stone remains he ascribed to the fifth century were Hadrian's Wall (parts of which stood not far from Jarrow), and the allegedly British earthwork farther north was the later Antonine Wall.[281] He could hardly have known better. Fully exploiting the means at his disposal, he intelligently integrated into Gildas's account the evidence of his supplementary sources, Orosius and Vegetius, and the knowledge he had of surviving Roman ruins. It was, though wrong, a creditable piece of historical reconstruction.

Bede did not set out simply to improve the record. One has only to read the *H.E.* alongside the *De excidio* to observe differences of orientation. Bede used his British guide, himself harshly critical of his fellow countrymen, in such a way as to shape a far more damning and enduring indictment of the Britons. Nowhere is this more apparent than when Bede nears the end of Gildas's historical introduction. The part of the *De excidio* that Bede retraced closes on a note of triumph over the Saxons: there was a battle at *mons Badonicus*, securing a long breathing space, but the Britons, far from abstaining from wickedness, turned from external to civil wars.[282] Bede broke this account in two, pausing at the victory. He then inserted a parenthesis no less than five chapters long, closely based on the *Life of St. Germanus of Auxerre* and narrating Germanus's two saving visits to the Britons. Next comes the conclusion, completing Bede's Romano-British section and picking up the balance of Gildas's paragraph. We are to understand that, in spite of St. Germanus's visits, the British did not abstain from wickedness, and even compounded their sins.[283] The passage is exception-

[279] Blair, *World of Bede*, p. 166.

[280] *De excidio* 18; *H.E.* 1.12, ed. Plummer, I, 27.

[281] Colgrave, OMT, p. 26 n. 1, 42 n. 1, 44 n. 2, sets the record straight concerning Roman walls, but he does not seem to understand what Bede was doing. Bede's reconstruction of the events (with modern equivalents): a Roman turf wall by Septimius Severus (the substructure of what we know to be Hadrian's Wall), 1.5; then, a British turf wall (the Antonine Wall to us), 1.12; finally, a Romano-British stone wall (Hadrian's Wall to us), *ibid.*

[282] *De excidio* 26.

[283] Pause: *H.E.* 1.16. St. Germanus: 1.17-21. Closing of the parenthesis opened at 1.16: 1.22 (the British grow more wicked and even deny the Word of God to the English). Bede is establishing a theme that runs through the *H.E.* and gives it a good part of its dramatic effect.

ally important for the dramatic flow and providential dimensions of Bede's history, as Robert Hanning has shown.[284] Yet it is also clear that the effect was achieved at the expense of chronological fidelity; Bede's own *Major Chronicle* establishes that St. Germanus could hardly have turned up in Britain after the battle of *mons Badonicus*.[285] Here, as in other cases, Bede the advocate had the better of Bede the historian.

Of the three models underlying the *H.E.*, none is followed so closely as Gildas's *De excidio* and none more distantly than the Whitby *Life of Gregory the Great*. Its role was rather to illustrate Northumbrian ignorance about the authentic circumstances of the Gregorian mission than to serve as Bede's guide. In the spirit of the etymological *lucus a non lucendo*, Bede availed himself of the Whitby *Life* as much by not reproducing its colorful stories as by substituting for them the information and letters supplied to him from Canterbury by Albinus and Nothelm. The main segments of *H.E.* 1.23 to 2.30 have shadowy counterparts in the model, but in very different proportions and sequence. The Whitby *Life* narrates the mission to Kent, disposed of in a sentence; the life of Gregory the Great, assembled from the *Liber pontificalis*, from a superficial gleaning of autobiography out of the pope's writings, and from fanciful legends; and the mission of Paulinus to Northumbria, centering on the conversion of King Edwin and inelegantly dividing the account of Gregory into two ill-joined halves. Bede straightened all this into chronological order, enriched it beyond recognition, and discarded almost all the legends, as well as the account of the later translation of Edwin's relics to Whitby.[286]

---

[284] Hanning, *Vision of History*, pp. 76-78.

[285] Bede's *Chron.*, which extensively uses Gildas, situates the mission of Germanus of Auxerre (§§ 491-92) in the reign of Valentinian III and Marcian (A.D. 451-55; § 488), after the advent of the Saxons (§ 489) and before the death of Aëtius (§ 493); on the other hand, the victory of Ambrosius Aurelianus is set as the last item in the reign of Zeno, more than thirty years later (§§ 504, 498). Bede was acquainted with Prosper's *Chronicle*, which, if he could translate consular dates, would have situated Germanus's mission in the equivalent of A.D. 429 (ed. Mommsen, MGH AA. IX, 472).

Plummer I, 32, disputed the idea that Bede misplaced Germanus's mission: "The phrase 'ante hos annos' may well cover a period of twenty years, 429-49." This saves appearances but misses the spirit of what Bede was doing: he had a reason to deal loosely with a chronology that he could have corrected.

[286] *H.E.* 1.23-26 parallel Whitby *Gregory* 11-12 (first sentence); *H.E.* 1.27-32, written sources, new with Bede; 1.33, probably Canterbury tradition; 1.34, Northumbrian affairs, possibly as a substitute for Whitby *Gregory* 12 (second sentence, i.e. an immediate jump from the conversion of Kent to that of Northumbria).

H.E. 2.1, Gregory's death, common source with Whitby *Gregory* 32; his apostleship, parallels Whitby *Gregory* 4, 5, and esp. 6 (cf. below, n. 295); parentage, parallels Whitby *Gregory* 1; monastic life and regretful assumption of pastoral duties (to "magisque successus") parallels Whitby *Gregory* 1-2; writings, substitutes for concern about the lack of miracles, in Whitby *Gregory* 3-5, 7 (on the writings, see also Whitby *Gregory* 24-27); burial and epitaph, again parallel Whitby *Gregory* 32; postscript, parallels Whitby *Gregory* 9-10. The parallels and "substitutions" do not prove dependence or utilization, but do enhance its possibility. The se-

The conspicuous traces of the Whitby *Life* in the *H.E.*—the basis for maintaining that Bede used it at all—are the story of the Deiran boys in Rome who inspired Gregory's initiative, and that of the vision which decisively influenced Edwin's conversion. Both were much changed (as the *Prose Cuthbert* shows, Bede did not hesitate to alter legendary material). The first, deprecated as an *opinio*, was deployed as an epilogue to Gregory's biography, a poetic summation of the pope's apostolate rather than an authentic incident in his life. (We could hardly do better.[287]) The second, however, became history; it was integrated into the account of how Edwin was won to Christianity.[288]

If one were guided by a concern for sources, Bede's narrative of Edwin's conversion might seem "somewhat confused," the result of an effort to combine "three versions current in Northumbrian tradition."[289] But Bede was acquainted with Gregory of Tours, even if the *Histories* never directly enters the *H.E.*, and through Gregory with the arduous steps by which another pagan king was finally brought to the baptismal font with all his people: goodwill toward Christian teachers, a Catholic marriage, the wife's exhortations, permission for their children to be baptized, a miracle (in battle) as the decisive step toward conversion, a baptism voluntarily imitated by the leading subjects, and earthly prosperity and might through the true faith.[290] The slow advance to conversion of Gregory's Clovis does not exactly match the outline of Bede's account of Edwin, but the parallels are so close that the possibility of accidental resemblance seems improbable. Bede knew how to make a story his own by amplifying it; he did so at least three times, as we shall see, in relation to Stephen's *Life of Wilfrid*.[291] Even more so here, the Whitby author's pitifully inadequate account of Edwin's

quence of topics in Gregory's biography is remarkably close. More about Edwin's conversion presently.

[287] Meyvaert, *Bede and Gregory the Great*, pp. 7, 11, conjectures that the story, originally in a different place, was moved after Bede acquired new source material. Where processes of composition are concerned, many things are possible. But the placement of the story hardly seems awkward; its presentation as a poetic summation of Gregory's life illustrates Bede's delicate sense of the difference between story and history. A conspicuous instance of Bede's free handling of legend occurs in *Prose Cuthbert* 5, corresponding to Anon. *Cuthbert* 1.6. Cf. above, n. 245.

[288] *H.E.* 2.9-14; the Whitby story enters into 1.12.

[289] Colgrave, *OMT*, p. 182 n. 1.

[290] On Bede's use of Gregory of Tours, see Levison, "Bede as Historian," p. 132 with n. 4 (cited once, outside the *H.E.*; perhaps the model for the autobiographical chapter *H.E.* 5.24); Cook, "Bede and Gregory of Tours" (rather thin). Gregory *Hist.* 2.27-31, 37, 3.*praef.*; cf. above, ch. III n. 459. Wallace-Hadrill, "Gregory of Tours and Bede," p. 113 n. 55, and *Early Germanic Kingship*, p. 80 n. 36, draws attention to the parallel between Edwin's promise of conversion in return for victory over his enemy (*H.E.* 2.9) and Clovis's words at Tolbiac (*Hist.* 2.30). A more striking parallel is that between the long course of Clovis's conversion and Edwin's no less leisurely pace. For the view of Wood, see above, ch. III n. 459.

[291] Below, nn. 326-28, 338-42, 350-60.

conversion is grandly enlarged into a demilitarized counterpart of the miracle in battle that sent Clovis to the font. And from the first lines of the Northumbrian conversion story, as Plummer noticed, Bede's evocation of Edwin's temporal success anticipates the report, in the climactic chapter, of the divine spirit's promise to him.[292] To interpret Edwin's repeated hesitations merely as a literary device, designed to sew together three equivalent traditions, underestimates Bede's talent and faith in the possibility of historical reconstruction.[293] From beginning to end, and including the two papal letters, we are dealing with a carefully integrated design. The Whitby St. Gregory was not so much used as grandly outdone.

It might be argued that the Whitby *Life* contributed nothing more to the H.E. than these stories. Even less has been claimed; some argue that, because Bede's details differ from those of the *Life*, the legends reached him by parallel transmission.[294] There is no way to be sure that the *Life* led Bede to narrate the Gregorian mission as he did, complete, notably, with a biography of the pope whom the Whitby author was first to call "our apostle."[295] Nevertheless, the Whitby *Life* seems to impinge on a few more passages of the H.E. Skipping lightly over Ethelbert of Kent, it specifies that Edwin of Northumbria was the most *singularis* in power among the kings since the advent of the English; Bede almost certainly echoed and amplified this statement, and may have been prompted to fill in corresponding details about Ethelbert.[296] In place of the excised translation of Edwin to Whitby, Bede drew attention to the burial of the king's head at York, without intimations of sanctity.[297] A final parallel is hard to resist. Birds are prominent in the legends of the Whitby *Life*, as when Paulinus's soul is seen going to

[292] The decisive element is that, in both cases, the conversion is brought about by direct divine intervention, i.e. miracle. All previous steps had lacked that essential ingredient, reserved for the climactic chapter.

Plummer, who believed that Bede was acquainted with the Whitby *Gregory*, drew attention (II, 94) to the link between beginning and climax: (H.E. 2.9), "Cui videlicet regi, in auspicium suscipiendae fidei et regni caelestis, potestas etiam terreni creverat"; (2.12) the divine spirit's promise, "ut . . . omnes qui ante te reges in gente Anglorum fuerant, potestate transcendas" (Mynors, *OMT*, pp. 162, 178).

[293] Colgrave, as n. 289.

[294] Above, n. 148.

[295] H.E. 2.1: "quem recte nostrum appellare possumus et debemus apostolum" (Plummer I, 73). This novel concept seems to belong to the Whitby anonymous: 4, "virum sanctum Gregorium . . . et ut ita dicam, apostolicum" (ed. Colgrave, pp. 76-78); 5, "apostolicum nostrum sanctum Gregorium virum" (p. 82); finally, a long explanation in 6 (pp. 82-84), including, "quomodo omnes apostoli, suas secum provincias ducentes . . . ostendent, . . . nos ille, id est gentem Anglorum, . . . credimus . . . adducere" though not physically present. But Thacker, "Social Background," p. 41, rightly draws attention to Aldhelm *De virginitate* (prose) 55; cf. 42, *pastor et pedagogus noster* in reference to Gregory.

[296] Whitby *Gregory* 12; H.E. 2.9 (Edwin); 1.25 (Ethelbert).

[297] H.E. 2.20. Edwin is said to be buried at Whitby (3.24), but as the father of an abbess, and like the royal father of another abbess, rather than by reason of holiness.

heaven in the form of a swan. Bede's account of the Northumbrian conversion contains a beautiful parable featuring a sparrow. It is attractive to
think that Bede's enchanting sparrow stands in place of all the questionable
bird stories of the Whitby *Life*.[298]

From the Gregorian mission, Bede passed to all intents directly into the
golden age of the English Church. No sooner are we in book III than we
encounter the miracles procured by the relics of King Oswald and the exemplary lives and pastorate of Irish saints. Dark intimations of confusion in
the Church are not heard prior to the Synod of Whitby; Bede insists that
the faulty Easter, however deplorable in itself, detracted not at all from the
radiant merits of Aidan and his cohorts. It is after the synod that sadness
intervenes, in the form of a lamentable plague.[299] Bede knew too little
about the Gregorian mission, let alone about earlier centuries, to be
thought to have idealized them; a realistic alternative was beyond reach.
The past that Bede may rightly be said to have endowed with artificial perfection comes afterward, from book III on. For him as for any reader of the
H.E., its start is situated many years before the arrival from Rome of Archbishop Theodore, who perfected what was already good. Bede's golden past
is just as Irish as it is Roman, and Columba of Iona receives no less reverent
attention than Pope Gregory of Rome.[300]

For this period in the history of the English Church, as for the earlier
parts of the *H.E.*, there was a narrative pre-existing Bede's, namely Stephen's *Life of Wilfrid*; and, unlike the other two models, it embodied a comprehensive alternative to Bede's outlook. There had been the Gregorian
mission, it implied, and then collapse into confusion, from which the
Church had been saved by the Roman teaching newly brought by Wilfrid.[301] Ten years or so before the *H.E.*, Stephen invited his readers to recognize that an error-filled past might be redeemed by a Wilfridian future.
The *Life of Wilfrid* gave focus to the vision of the English Church that Bede

[298] The account of the assembly at which Edwin's followers abandoned paganism features a
parable with a memorable sparrow (*H.E.* 2.13); it may stand in lieu of Whitby *Gregory* 15: the
appalling story of Paulinus and the crow, in a gathering of Edwin's still-heathen people. For
the other bird stories, see above, n. 145. The only one that met with enduring success was
Pope Gregory's dove (Whitby *Gregory* 26).

[299] The Easter dating of Columba and Aidan (*H.E.* 3.3, 17) is mentioned after line upon
line of praise, including two miracles. Bede's words are better designed to justify than to blame
them: the Irish evangelists celebrated Easter as they had learned, i.e. in good faith; 3.5, they
celebrated Easter according to poor calculations, but lived by prophetic and gospel words;
3.16, they celebrated with the same intention as we and not as Quartodecimans.

[300] Mayr-Harting, *Coming of Christianity*, p. 69. Pepperdene, "Bede's *Historia ecclesiastica*,"
completely misapprehends Bede's account of the Irish.

[301] *VW* 47: "Necnon et ego primus post obitum primorum procerum, a sancto Gregorio di-
rectorum, Scotticae virulenta plantationis germina eradicarem, . . . secundum apostolicae
sedis rationem totam Ultra-Umbrensium gentem permutando converterem?" (ed. Levison, p.
242). The passage is translated below at n. 304.

most fervently opposed. Yet it was history—a clear, chronological narrative of events that, to be refuted, had to be met on its own grounds. How Bede did so is our next concern.

5. The Abasement of Bishop Wilfrid

Bede's obituary of Wilfrid in the final book of the *H.E.* is an unavowed summary of Stephen's *Life*, but Stephen's impact on the *H.E.* goes so far beyond this passage as to exceed the contribution of Gildas and the Whitby *Gregory* put together. Wilfrid appears time and time again in books III-V, yet manages to escape any suspicion of greatness until his obituary notice, if there. He held Bede's attention not so much as a result of personal memories, though there were some, as by grace of Stephen's account.

One event Bede left out of the *H.E.*, except for the merest hint, was the Council of Austerfield in 703, an omission not easily attributed to discretion.[302] It is an appropriate point of departure for an attempt to examine the *Life of Wilfrid* through Bede's eyes.

Stenton remarked, "The ultimate significance of [Wilfrid's] work lies in the achievements which he claimed for himself at the council of Austerfield."[303] We do not know what, in fact, Wilfrid said there; we cannot even be entirely certain that he was given an occasion to justify himself. What we have and can prize is the speech Stephen of Ripon ascribed to Wilfrid. More than a personal apologia, it is almost a counteroutline of large stretches of the *H.E.*:

After the death of the first dignitaries sent by Pope Gregory [Wilfrid says] was I not the first to root out the poisonous weeds planted by the Irish? [Did I not] bring the Northumbrian people completely in line with the Holy See, by converting it to the true Easter and to the tonsure in the form of a crown, instead of the former way of shaving the back of the head from the top down? [Did I not] teach you to chant according to the practice of the primitive church, with a double choir singing in harmony, with reciprocal responsions and antiphons? [Did I not] establish the life of monks according to the rule of father Benedict, which no one before introduced here?[304]

If these are Wilfrid's claims to "ultimate significance"—and Stenton is surely right that this is what they must have been in the eyes of the Wilfridians—it remains to be seen how many of them retain their integrity after Bede filtered them through the *H.E.*

[302] Above, n. 138. The theme of the pages to come was stated by John, "Social and Political Problems of the Early English Church," p. 44: "It looks in more than one place as though Bede is going out of his way not to contradict Eddius whilst conveying a totally opposed version of the same facts."

[303] Stenton, *Anglo-Saxon England*, 2d ed., p. 145.

[304] VW 47, tr. Webb, p. 181, modified from tr. Colgrave, p. 99.

Wilfrid's brightest years were those that first brought him to the see of York and witnessed his achievements in the course of its tenure, such as the foundation of Hexham. They should not be overlooked. Stephen of Ripon dwelt on these events, though not in the Austerfield speech. As we have seen, the Wilfridian golden age he evoked was never recovered after the expulsion of 678.[305] The silence by which Bede responds to these parts of Stephen's narrative is eloquent.

Five more parts of Stephen's *Life* proved especially provocative to Bede. In keeping with the idea of planting poisonous weeds, Stephen bracketed the Irish with the Britons and flatly called both "schismatics." He even supplied an ancient name for their schism. They were Quartodecimans, agreeing with a condemned group of early Christians who celebrated Easter on the fourteenth day of the lunar month Nissan regardless—the crucial point—of whether it was a Sunday or not. By Stephen's account, the insular Quartodecimans unreconciled to Roman reckoning after Whitby formed the party that brought about the elevation of Chad to York while Wilfrid was on the Continent (665), and the defect of Quartodeciman orders eventually brought about Chad's deposition.[306] In a different vein, but also of interest to Bede, Stephen vaunted Wilfrid's contribution to the evangelization of Frisia and Sussex. Not only was Wilfrid the pioneer of Christianity in Frisia, but the foundations he laid were built upon by "his son . . . Willibrord, who was nurtured at Ripon."[307] As for Sussex, Wilfrid was the first to preach the gospel in these wilds, winning over the king and queen as point of departure. He was also guided by God to the side of King Cædwalla of the Gewisse to assist his famous exploits.[308] Wilfrid's apostolate to the heathen in Frisia and Sussex did not pass untarnished into Bede's H.E. Finally, one should observe Stephen's treatment of Archbishop Theodore. He is cast in a friendly light as the authority who opened the way for Wilfrid to mount the see of York and again as the aged penitent who strove almost *in extremis* to make up to Wilfrid for earlier wrongs. But when not forwarding Wilfrid's interests, Theodore is among his leading enemies. Stephen asserted that he took bribes from King Ecgfrith, and that his iniquitous "decrees of the dissension" exacerbated Wilfrid's troubles. Although Stephen was no less magnanimous toward Theodore than toward the Northumbrian descendants of Oswy, the conduct ascribed to the arch-

[305] VW 15-23. Stephen never again mentions successes in Northumbria (cf. above, nn. 227-28).

[306] VW 5, 12, 14-15. On the Quartodecimans, ed. Colgrave, *The Life of Bishop Wilfrid by Eddius Stephanus*, p. 157; Cross, ed., *Oxford History of the Christian Church*, 2d ed.

[307] VW 26: "fundamentum fidei . . . quod adhuc superaedificat filius eius, in Hripis nutritus, gratia Dei Wilbrordus episcopus." (ed. Levison, p. 220).

[308] VW 41-42.

bishop did him so little credit that readers cannot gauge Theodore's significance for the English Church in any but a negative way.[309] Bede took notice and expressed different opinions.

Bede did not depend on Stephen's *Life* as he did on Gildas to supply the skeleton of his narrative. From Edwin onward the succession of Northumbrian kings was available as a chronological framework. Stephen's more valuable contribution was the history of error and injustice out of which Bede, in reaction, painted his golden age. And when Stephen stopped, so did he. The relationship of the two narratives can be traced in detail, as a succession of responses by Bede to Stephen's statements.

"*After the death of the first dignitaries sent by Pope Gregory.*" The phrase might be deemed innocuous in itself and merely suggestive of innocent ignorance. Yet a hostile reader like Bede had occasion to consider it vague, hasty, and dismissive. Contrary to Stephen's implication of interruption and a new beginning, he illustrated the continuity of Roman influence. By his account, the Gregorian masters were sent to Canterbury as well as Northumbria, and the Canterbury mission endured long after that to the north; Wilfrid himself consecrated Putta, a man trained in chant by Gregory's "disciples."[310] There was no call, therefore, for exaggerating the gap between the Gregorians and later times.

As a further sign that the thread was unbroken, Bede insisted on the concreteness of the memory left by the northern mission: the physical appearance of Paulinus, first archbishop of York, was still, it seems, remembered. Of all the characters in the *H.E.*, his features alone are detailed.[311] Bede produced even more gripping proof of continuity in the form of the deacon James, a Roman-trained teacher of chant, who survived in Northumbria from Paulinus's days to the Synod of Whitby.[312] Astonishment has been recently expressed that the prodigious deacon James did not become "one of the great legendary figures in the Northumbrian church."[313] The plausible reason for his not doing so is best left unstated. James's first appearance in the *H.E.* comes right after the physical description of Paulinus.

"*The poisonous weeds planted by the Irish.*" On a strict reading of Stephen's *Life*, this phrase need refer only to the Irish tonsure and computation of Easter. A less friendly reader might notice that nothing but weeds are mentioned in relation to the Irish. Their period of dominance is implicitly a

[309] VW 15, 43 (forwards Wilfrid's interests), 24, 29, 30 (acts against Wilfrid).

[310] *H.E.* 4.2.

[311] *H.E.* 2.16. This has attracted favorable notice from commentators.

[312] *H.E.* 2.16, 20, 3.25, 4.2 (very often for so minor a character).

[313] Kirby, "Bede's Native Sources," pp. 342-43.

blot on Northumbrian Christianity, and they are classed as "Quartodeci-man heretics."[314] As we shall soon see, Bede explicitly tagged Wilfrid with contempt for the Irish.

Bede's own response is too fervent and lengthy to need tracing in detail. The *H.E.* leaves us in no doubt about the magnitude and beauty of the Irish contribution. The Irish not only worked in England but welcomed English-men in Ireland and trained them. Their salutary influence continued long after Whitby; as Bede took pains to show, Cuthbert was their chief disciple. It is no accident, besides, that the English priest Egbert, first heard of in Bede's eulogy of Aidan, was responsible for the conversion of Iona to the Roman Easter that constitutes the dramatic climax of the *H.E.*[315] Seen in relation to the figure of Wilfrid and the design of the *H.E.*, the priest Egbert has the same prodigious quality at the end of the work as the deacon James has for the beginnings of Northumbrian Christianity.

Quartodeciman schismatics. Bede carefully refuted the charge. A letter from the papal court in the 630s to certain Irish bishops bore out that there had been some insular Quartodecimans. Bede emphasized that, by this tes-timony, the heinous practice was a recent vagary and implicated only a few.[316] Twice more, in connection with Iona and Aidan, he insisted that the Irish, however faulty their Easter observance, never deviated from cel-ebrating on Sunday. They did not "as some think" or "as some falsely sup-pose" hold Easter on whatever day of the week 14 Nissan fell.[317] Bede is unlikely to have been thinking of Aldhelm's half-century-old letter men-tioning British Quartodecimans in Cornwall.[318] The "false supposition" was that of Stephen's *Life of Wilfrid.* Bede returned to the charge with ref-erence to the bishops who consecrated Chad, whom Stephen specifically called Quartodecimans. These two Britons, Bede said, "contrary to canon-

---

[314] Note that, in Irish tradition, Saxon Christianity began only with Oswald and those bap-tized with him: Bullough, "Hagiography as Patriotism," p. 343.

[315] Cf. n. 299 above. Bede's disavowals of Irish Easter dating are sometimes overstressed by commentators; e.g. they and Aidan are the only aspects of the Irish in Bede mentioned by Campbell, "Bede," pp. 175, 179-81. In reality, Bede's loving treatment of the Irish reaches right back to his inclusion of Ireland in the opening chapter (*H.E.* 1.1). Typically, he coun-teracts the Synod of Whitby by an immediate eulogy of the Irish and their contribution to Northumbria (3.26). He was first to introduce Boisil and Melrose into any narrative of Cuth-bert's life (*Verse Cuthbert* 20, line 485) and stressed Cuthbert's association with both Boisil's Melrose and Aidan's foundation, Lindisfarne (4.27). The same links are essential to Bede's advocacy of pastoral rounds in the countryside and monastery-bishoprics (above, n. 102). An-other aspect of the matter is the contrast between good Irish and bad British in the dramatic design of the work (above, n. 79). On Egbert, *H.E.* 3.4, 27, 4.3, 26, 5.9-10, 22-24; his ap-pearances are out of proportion with his historical importance.

[316] *H.E.* 2.19.

[317] *H.E.* 3.4, 17.

[318] Aldhelm *Epist.* 4, ed. Ehwald, pp. 480-86; dated 680.

ical custom, [kept] the Sunday of Easter from the fourteenth to the twentieth day."[319] Though misguided, they celebrated on a Sunday.

To judge from the amount of space Bede devoted in the *H.E.* to the correct reckoning of Easter, one might infer that the issue was one that personally engaged him as a matter of grave ecclesiastical concern. Another and perhaps more satisfying possibility is that Easter dating was the choicest jewel in Wilfrid's crown and that, for this reason, Bede had to be more Catholic than the pope, even if, toward 730, divergent reckonings had ceased to be topical in the practical life of the English Church.[320]

"[I brought] the Northumbrian people completely in line with the true Easter and to the tonsure in the form of a crown." Stephen of Ripon did not stress the tonsure; neither did Bede, whose lengthiest passage on the subject, couched in very conciliatory language, occurs in the letter of 710 from Abbot Ceolfrid to the king of the Picts.[321] The date of Easter was the main point of contention, and Wilfrid's springboard to fame.

His role as the Roman spokesman at Whitby is no less marked in Bede's *H.E.* than in Stephen's account. His remarks are longer than in Stephen's version and do much greater credit to Wilfrid's scholarship. He was, Bede said, a *vir doctissimus* and King Alchfrid's master of *eruditio Christiana*.[322] The outline of the Whitby synod remains Stephen's, but profound changes are made by amplification. It seems now that the departure of Paulinus did not terminate the observance of Roman Easter dating in Northumbria, that the first attack on Irish dating was by a Roman-trained Irishman, that Wilfrid became prominent at Whitby owing to the inability of the Gallic bishop

[319] *H.E.* 3.28.

[320] Against the suggestion that Bede's talk about the date of Easter was topical (also Mayr-Harting, *Coming of Christianity*, pp. 111-12), see above, n. 94. Plummer is thought to have been too impatient with Bede's attention to Easter; Wallace-Hadrill, "Bede and Plummer," p. 83, stresses that if Bede was obsessed with Easter dating, it was as a symbol of unity of discipline which, in his view, was with unity of doctrine "a condition of survival for the Church" (similarly, Mayr-Harting, p. 43).

Plummer's instincts may have been sound and Bede out of line. Once past the early fourth century, divergences over Easter dating elsewhere, though numerous, tended to lack the doctrinal seriousness that, to go by Bede, they had in England. Yet Gregory the Great set an example of tolerance for diversity. Perhaps the reality reflected by the *H.E.* is not that of current feelings about Easter dating (literally or as a symbol), but of something much narrower: namely, the needs of Bede's argumentation; he had to outdo the Wilfridians, so as to take the wind out of their sails. Stephen's account of Whitby is about Wilfrid; Bede's is about Easter dating.

[321] *VW* 47 (the passage quoted at n. 304 above) and 6 (Wilfrid's own tonsure, acquired in Gaul and in the Roman manner). *H.E.* 5.21, ed. Plummer, I, 342-44 (playing down its theological significance). For a full discussion, James, "Bede and the Tonsure Question": a matter of organization, not of doctrine.

[322] *H.E.* 3.25, ed. Plummer, I, 182.

Agilbert to speak English rather than to his great eloquence, and that he (unlike his biographer) was learned enough to recognize the difference between Irish computation and Quartodeciman heresy.[323] Stephen's account was subverted by the addition of new facts and modified circumstances.

What Bede decisively undermined was the notion that Wilfrid had any sort of exclusive credit in the controversy ("Was I not the first?"). Instead, "the most violent defender of the true Easter was Ronan, Irish indeed by origin"; the deacon James was also of this discipline and had continually celebrated the true Easter since the days of Paulinus, lastly in Queen Eanfled's service; many others had been aware that Aidan's practice was questionable but had tolerated it out of love for him.[324] As a proper revisionist, Bede took the wind out of the "great man" interpretation of Whitby. The foundation for instituting Roman Easter reckoning in England had been laid by others. Without initiating anything, Wilfrid gained an occasion to shine from Bishop Agilbert's foreignness. And he was well aware, contrary to the loose talk of his biographer, that the Irish computation of Easter was free of the error of the Quartodecimans.[325]

As Bede appropriated the story of the boys in Rome from the Whitby *St. Gregory*, so he took from Stephen of Ripon the story of how King Oswy decided the issue at Whitby by preferring to have St. Peter, keeper of the keys of heaven, on his side when he reached the gates. Stephen's details differ from Bede's, but never more so than in the opening line: "Then King Oswy, bidding the holy priest Wilfrid to be silent, smiled and questioned all those present, saying, 'Tell me, which one is greater in the kingdom of

---

[323] *VW* 10, ed. Levison, pp. 202-204. *H.E.* 3.25: for every point except Agilbert, see the next notes. Agilbert's inability to speak English had already been memorably related (3.7); he asks King Oswy that, for this reason, Wilfrid should speak in his stead (Plummer I, 184). Stephen's version: "Inperatum est ab Aegilberchto episcopo . . . sancto Vilfrido presbitero et abbati suaviloqua eloquentia in sua lingua Romanae ecclesiae et apostolicae sedis dare rationem" (ed. Levison, p. 204); the accent is on *eloquentia* rather than *sua lingua*. Cf. below, n. 351.

[324] For continuity since Paulinus, Ronan, and tolerance of Aidan's practice, see Plummer I, 181-82. Bede implies that tolerance of diversity had been the norm until the waters were troubled by an *acerrimus* defender of Roman practice and his opponent Finan, *homo ferocis animi*; they were more troubled still (*gravior controversia*) after Colman became bishop, but Bede lowers a veil over the details. Is Wilfrid implied? He materializes a few lines later, untainted by any part in the prehistory of the synod. Cf. Stephen's view of the matter: "De conflictu Vilfridi presbiteri contra Colmanum episcopum de ratione paschae" (ed. Levison, p. 202).

[325] *H.E.* 3.25, ed. Plummer, I, 186: "Iohannes enim ad legis Mosaicae decreta . . . nil de prima sabbati curabat; quod vos [i.e. Colman and the Irish] non facitis, qui nonnisi prima sabbati pascha celebratis"; Wilfrid reproaches Colman for being mistaken on both counts and for differing from both John and Peter. It is a wonderfully backhanded way of rectifying Stephen's slur on the "schismatic" Irish. Cf. Farmer, "St. Wilfrid," p. 39, who thinks Bede wrote the truth about the incident whereas Stephen erred. How can one know? Also judging the *VW* by the standard of the *H.E.*, Thacker, "Social Background," p. 262, calls its account of Whitby "perfunctory" and considers "Eddius" poorly informed. Bede's abundance is not a guarantee of greater authenticity or trustworthiness.

heaven, Columcille [= Columba of Iona] or the apostle Peter?' "[326] Stephen's Oswy smiled because he knew the answer to his own question: Who was this paltry Columba anyway? The word *subridens* is an insidious touch, and Bede knew what to do with it. In his version of Oswy's intervention, all trace of condescension toward Columba is removed. The great Irishman is treated with complete respect by king and synod. Stephen's *subridens* is transposed to an earlier point and Wilfrid's own lips: "About your father Columba . . . I might reply that at the Judgment many will say to the Lord that they prophesied in His name . . . and that the Lord will reply that He never knew them [Matt. 7:22-23]. But far be it from me to say this of your fathers, since it is much fairer (*iustius*) to believe good rather than evil about unknown men."[327] Plummer commented on these lines under the heading, "Insolence of Wilfrid."[328] The words Bede placed in Wilfrid's mouth epitomized the contempt for the Irish that he discerned in Stephen's *Life*.

Besides diverting credit from Wilfrid in the Easter controversy, Bede also denied that the synod was the end of the story. Converting the king and the Northumbrians to the correct Easter was well and good, but there were others to be won, no less dear to God. Bede marked their entrance into the fold. The Britons, to their lasting shame, had hoarded the Word of God and tried to keep it from the pagan English; the latter, however, once saved from error in Easter dating, did not rest until they won their Irish coreligionists to correct belief. The ultimate goal of Bede's narrative was the conversion of Irish Iona, the source of so much profit to Northumbria, and he prepared us for this event from the start of book III (even before the Whitby synod). The acceptance of the Roman Easter by Iona in 716 is, in effect, the happy ending of the *H.E.*, and its agent is the priest Egbert.[329] Bede's implied lesson that it is more blessed to be last than first is not wholly detached from the undermining of Wilfrid, whose priority matters so much to Stephen and who seems not to have cared at all for the fraternal extension of Roman customs to the Irish.[330]

---

[326] VW 10: "Tunc Osviu rex . . . subridens interrogavit omnes, dicens: 'Enuntiate mihi, utrum maior est Columcille an Petrus apostolus in regno caelorum?' " (ed. Levison, p. 204).

[327] *H.E.* 3.25, ed. Plummer, I, 187. The meaning is that Columba's sanctity and miracles are open to doubt, as Wilfrid later repeats (p. 188) in a speech referring to *ille Columba vester*— a speech in which Bede precisely transfers to Wilfrid, as a declarative statement, Oswy's question in VW (n. 326 above).

[328] Plummer II, 191.

[329] On the Britons, *H.E.* 1.22 and nn. 94-95 above; English efforts to convert the Irish to the proper date of Easter, *H.E.* 5.9, 15, 22.

[330] Whereas Stephen passes directly from Whitby to the victor Wilfrid's election as bishop (VW 11), Bede eulogizes Colman and his kind (above, n. 315), then—surprisingly—tells of the plague that struck England and, less surprisingly, of Egbert, future savior of Iona (*H.E.* 4.27). Only then do we hear of Wilfrid's being chosen bishop (4.28).

The teaching of chant in the Roman style. The claim laid in the *Life of Wilfrid* is related to the beginning of the sentence, that Wilfrid was the first to do so after the death of Pope Gregory's missionaries.[331] Bede's response in the *H.E.* is a model of alteration for the worse. Chant is mentioned in the context of Archbishop Theodore's epoch-making prelacy, when all sorts of splendid things happened in England. "From that time also the knowledge of sacred music, which had been known only in Kent, began to be taught in all the English churches. In the churches of Northumbria, the first master—except for James, whom we spoke of above—was Aeddi, surnamed Stephen, who was invited by the very reverend Wilfrid."[332] Wilfrid's claim to priority is explicitly recorded by Bede, but because squeezed between Theodore and the wonderful deacon James (whose continual teaching of chant after 633 gives a memorable note of calm to the end of *H.E.* 2), it dwindles to insignificance. Stephen of Ripon portrayed matters differently. He had Wilfrid bring the singing master Aeddi to Ripon before Theodore reached England.[333]

As for authentically Roman chant, Bede recorded it as reaching Northumbria with John, archchanter of St. Peter's, Rome, whom Benedict Biscop escorted to Wearmouth.[334] By then, Wilfrid was in exile.

Introduction of the Rule of St. Benedict. In addition to having Wilfrid include the Rule in his apologia at Austerfield, Stephen of Ripon refers to this, together with the import of teachers of chant, in connection with the running of Ripon Abbey between 666 and 669: "[Wilfrid] much improved the ordinance of the churches by means of the Rule of Benedict."[335] To our astonishment, Bede's response to this claim is silence. The Rule of St. Benedict is wholly absent from the *H.E.* As we saw, the reference to this rule in the Lindisfarne *Life of St. Cuthbert* does not survive in either Bede's verse or his prose version. The Rule is mentioned in the *Life of Ceolfrid* and in Bede's *History of the Abbots*, but for no more than one of its clauses: the provision for abbatial elections by merit. As far as the inner life of Wearmouth-Jarrow was concerned, Bede insisted (like the anonymous writer be-

---

[331] VW 47: "quomodo iuxta ritum primitivae ecclesiae asono vocis modulamine, binis adstantibus choris, persultare responsoriis antifonisque reciprocis instruerem" (ed. Levison, p. 242).

[332] *H.E.* 4.2: "Sed et sonos cantandi in ecclesia, quos eatenus in Cantia tantum noverant, ab hoc tempore per omnes Anglorum ecclesias discere coeperunt; primusque, excepto Iacobo, de quo supra diximus, cantandi magister Nordanhymbrorum ecclesiis Aeddi cognomento Stephanus fuit, invitatus de Cantia a reverentissimo viro Vilfrido" (Plummer I, 205; my translation borrows from both Colgrave and Sherley-Price). James's teaching of chant: 2.20.

[333] VW 14 (between his return from Gaul after ordination as bishop and his installation in York by Theodore).

[334] *H.E.* 4.18; cf. Bede *Hist. abb.* 6; VCeolf 10.

[335] VW 14: "cum regula Benedicti instituta ecclesiarum Dei bene melioravit" (ed. Levison, p. 209).

fore him) that the teaching of Benedict Biscop, on which it was based, arose from experience gained in seventeen monastic houses.[336] Nothing could be clearer than Bede's refusal to favor a single rule. The curious thesis recently elaborated with great learning—that Bede imbibed an outstandingly concentrated "dose of Benedictinism"—goes about as far as an argument from silence can.[337] One would dearly like to know what everyone concerned, including the Wilfridians, thought about monastic organization. The probability is that, because the Rule of St. Benedict was synonymous with Wilfrid, Bede's writings maintain a resolute distance from it, except for its electoral clause in an electoral context.

Wilfrid's accession to York and years of achievement. As an example of *suppressio veri*, Bede's perfunctory treatment of this subject deserves more attention than it gets. The retrospective obituary notice of Wilfrid near the end of the *H.E.* tells us in one breath of his becoming bishop "of the whole Northumbrian province" and in the next of his being driven from office in Ecgfrith's reign.[338] The same dismissive leap occurs in the chronological narrative. After having gone to Gaul, been consecrated bishop, and returned to teach many rules of Catholic observance, Wilfrid materializes without proper explanation "guiding the bishopric of the Church of York." He is asked to escort King Oswy to Rome, but the king dies. He sends representatives to the Synod of Hatfield. And, owing to a quarrel with King Ecgfrith, he is expelled.[339] Bede cannot be expected to have followed Stephen in celebrating Wilfrid's share in the martial triumphs of King Ecgfrith, but it is astonishing, to say the least, that the *H.E.* gives no hint of Wilfrid's stone churches at York and Ripon, or of his foundation at Hexham, in Bede's back yard.[340]

What Bede does say is almost more pointed than his omissions. Wilfrid's accession to York was impeded by the ordination of Chad in the too long interval during which Wilfrid was away in Gaul being canonically consecrated. Stephen and Bede agree on the facts but not on their presentation.

---

[336] On the Benedictine Rule in the *Vitae* of Cuthbert, nn. 158-59 above. Bede *Hist. abb.* 11, 16, just like *VCeolf* 16, 25, refer only to ch. 64 of the Rule. According to both accounts, Benedict Biscop prided himself that the rule observed at Wearmouth-Jarrow derived from his experience with the rules of seventeen different monasteries: *VCeolf* 6; *Hist. abb.* 11.

[337] Wormald, "Bede and Benedict Biscop," p. 144.

[338] *H.E.* 5.19: "Ceadda vir sanctus . . . curam secessit, accipiente Vilfrido episcopatum totius Nordanhymbrorum provinciae. Qui deinde regnante Ecgfrido, pulsus est episcopatu, et alii pro illo consecrati antistites, quorum supra meminimus" (Plummer I, 326).

[339] *H.E.* 3.28, 4.2 (to Gaul and back), 4.3 (guiding York), 4.5 (asked to escort Oswy to Rome; is represented at Hatfield), 4.12 (quarrel and expulsion). A clear echo of the important *VW* 21 (quoted above at n. 233) appears in *H.E.* 4.3: Wilfrid administered the bishopric of York, indeed of all the Northumbrians and of the Picts, "quousque rex Osviu imperium protendere poterat." But Chad is the subject and hero of the chapter.

[340] *VW* 19-21 (triumphs), 16-17, 22 (church constructions). The substance of *VW* 21 is relegated by Bede to a participial clause (n. 339 above).

The *Life of Wilfrid*, however scathing about Chad's backers, is cordial to Chad himself, whose personal holiness is acknowledged. It adds that Theodore's removal of Chad made way for Wilfrid, who generously helped Chad to obtain the new see of Lichfield in Mercia.[341] Bede simply eliminated Wilfrid's troubled accession from the *H.E.* If attentive, we might suspect that something went amiss, but the details are bathed in silence. Instead, Bede turned the circumstances inside out, shifting the spotlight from Wilfrid to his rival and, again, as with the Synod of Whitby, filling in many hitherto unrecorded details. We are told a touching, and long, story: how Chad was named to York while Wilfrid was abroad; was poorly consecrated; overcame this impediment by the goodness of Archbishop Theodore; withdrew to the monastery of Lastingham (his brother's foundation); and, by the request of King Wulfhere of Mercia to King Oswy (without any help from Wilfrid), finally gained the see of Lichfield.[342] These incidents form the outline of a memorable narrative, not lacking characteristic notes of Irish simplicity and holiness. Chad, another of Bede's genuine heroes, is not alone in gaining his prominence primarily at Wilfrid's expense.

Archbishop Theodore. The contrast between Stephen and Bede on this subject is both self-evident and self-explanatory. If books III-V of the *H.E.* are conceived of as an extended "rectification" of Stephen's *Life of Wilfrid*, the part Bede assigned to Theodore resembles what he made of Benedict Biscop in the *History of the Abbots*. Just as, in relation to the *Life of Ceolfrid*, Benedict took over the starring role from Ceolfrid and even intruded his death scene into the second *libellus*, so Theodore both looms over the years of Wilfrid's maturity, blotting out the latter's splendor, and has his death projected into the same book in which Wilfrid dies.[343] Of course, Theodore was not magnified only in order to contradict the *Life of Wilfrid*. His epis-

---

[341] VW 14-15. Chad came from Ireland, a *servus Dei religiosissimus et admirabilis doctor*; his good faith was plain; he was completely gentle (*mitissimus*) and humble when faced with his misconduct. Although the story illustrates Wilfrid's magnanimity (*bonum pro malo reddens*), Stephen dwells longer on Chad than one would expect.

[342] Chad *qui postea episcopus factus est* is introduced as brother of Cedd, in the context of Lastingham; he procures a miracle, *H.E.* 3.23; listed, by anticipation, as the third bishop of Mercia, 3.24; he is chosen by Oswy to be bishop and poorly consecrated, but is an outstanding pastoral bishop, *erat enim de discipulis Aidani* (Wilfrid is mentioned here as though Chad were not occupying his see or otherwise his rival, 3.28); Archbishop Theodore notifies Chad of his poor consecration and, though the latter humbly volunteers to resign, Theodore reconsecrates him and tells him to stay, 4.2; it seems, though, that Chad withdraws to Lastingham while Wilfrid takes over as bishop of Northumbria, 4.3; Chad is invited to Mercia and leads a thoroughly edifying life, *ibid.* That he and his brother were *de Hibernia* is never said, though possibly implied by the reference to Aidan.

[343] See above, n. 257. Bede has no objective reasons for reporting Theodore's death (690) in *H.E.* 5.8. The translation of Cuthbert in 698 closes the previous book (4.30-32), and most of the interval is occupied by miracles of John of Beverley, who died in 721 (5.6). A single book for the period of Theodore's archiepiscopate would have been a tidy alternative.

copate was as crucial as the Gregorian mission to Bede's Canterbury connection.[344] But to the extent that the *H.E.* reflects a contemporary argument between ecclesiastical factions in Northumbria, the alternative— Theodore or Wilfrid?—may take us to the symbolic heart of the debate. In any case, it has long been observed that whereas the Northumbrian interventions of Theodore are execrated by the *Life of Wilfrid*, they earn Bede's quiet applause.[345]

The Frisian mission. Bede did not contradict Stephen of Ripon concerning Wilfrid in Frisia: "he was the first to begin the work of evangelization in that place." But there are two qualifications. Bede said so only in Wilfrid's obituary notice, at the year 709, rather than in 678, when Wilfrid's winter in Frisia took place; and he added the factual but not innocuous statement that the task was "later completed with great devotion by Willibrord, the very reverend bishop of Christ." The corresponding clause in Stephen specified that Willibrord was "[Wilfrid's] son . . . nurtured at Ripon."[346] Bede's reinterpretation of the continental mission wiped Wilfrid out of it except as a casual afterthought.

Wilfrid enters the *H.E.* very early and quietly. A flash forward from 642 to 703 (a frequent device in the *H.E.*) portrays him with his disciple Acca, traveling to Rome and pausing with Willibrord in Frisia. Acca was Bede's informant for this chapter. He supplied Willibrord's account of miracles of St. Oswald in Germany (merely alluded to) and in Ireland. The featured miracle involves the cure of a repentant Irish scholar who had allied biblical studies with a life of vice. In the scene, Wilfrid is a silent bystander and no hint is given of a link between him and Willibrord; he looks like an appendage to Acca. We do learn something about Willibrord, however. Nothing is said of his association with Ripon or Wilfrid, only that, when still a priest, he had been in Ireland "living a pilgrim's life out of love for his eternal fatherland."[347]

This early chapter foreshadows the design of Bede's main account of in-

[344] Above, nn. 89-90.

[345] Plummer II, 316. For Stephen's views, *VW* 24, 29, 30, 45, 46, 54, 60. What Gibbs, "Decrees of Agatho," calls the "decrees of the dissension" (cf. *VW* 45) were Theodore's doing and at the heart of Wilfrid's troubles. Farmer, "St. Wilfrid," p. 37, observes Bede's preference for Theodore over Wilfrid, whom Farmer thinks Bede should have held dear.

[346] *H.E.* 5.19: "et quod postmodum Vilbrord, reverentissimus Christi pontifex, in magna devotione conplevit, ipse primus ibi opus evangelicum coepit" (Plummer I, 326). A.D. 679 corresponds more or less to *H.E.* 4.12. *VW* 26 is quoted above, n. 307.

[347] *H.E.* 3.13. This corresponds in time to *VW* 50, Wilfrid going to Rome to appeal against his treatment at the Council of Austerfield (on this journey, Acca is prominent at Wilfrid's side, *VW* 57). Willibrord: "Sed et in Hibernia cum presbyter adhuc peregrinam pro aeterna patria duceret vitam" (ed. Plummer, I, 152). There is no way to tell whether the fable of the repentant Irish scholar is somehow targeted at Wilfrid, whose early education and first steps in religion were at Lindisfarne (*VW* 2-3).

sular efforts on the Continent. According to him, Willibrord's background was not Ripon, but Ireland, and his spiritual father not Wilfrid, but the priest Egbert, who later won Iona to the Roman Easter. A reader of the *H.E.* is left in no doubt about the origins of the continental mission. It was conceived in Ireland by the English voluntary exile, Egbert, whom visions and prophecies (some by Cuthbert's master, Boisil of Melrose) reserved for a greater task, but who sent Irish-trained substitutes, among them Willibrord. They established a strong foothold.[348] Wilfrid, stripped of his bond to Willibrord, receded to the margins of the missionary effort. He was a casual bystander, the ordinand in Mercia of a missionary bishop, and, when all was done, an incidental precursor.[349] The mission, in the *H.E.*, was an Anglo-Irish accomplishment. It is hard to believe that Bede's account is truer to fact than Stephen's, which it surely does not complement.

Wilfrid in Sussex and by Cædwalla's side. As in the case of the Synod of Whitby, a comparison of Bede's account with Stephen of Ripon's reveals a considerable expansion. No other episodes of Wilfrid's career hold a larger place than these in the *H.E.* In Alcuin's *Poem on the Bishops of York*, a verse condensation of the *H.E.*, Wilfrid is most praised for his exploits in Sussex.[350] But Bede's lengthy narrative redounds to Wilfrid's credit only if held far away from Stephen's *Life*.[351]

For a start, Bede issued the usual *démentis*. Wilfrid was not the first evangelist in Sussex. There had long been an Irish monastery at Bosham, though without influence on the natives. Nor did Wilfrid have to convert the royal couple: the king, Æthelwealh, had previously been baptized in Mercia, in the presence of King Wulfhere; and Æthelwealh's queen, so far from needing conversion, had been born to Christian parents. Wilfrid's mission worked from the ealdormen downward.[352] (Bede's stories of the

---

[348] *H.E.* 5.9-11. On Egbert, n. 315 above. For a good illustration of Bede's success in writing Wilfrid out of the Frisian mission, see Hanning, *Vision of History*, p. 88.

[349] *H.E.* 5.11; this was in 692-93. Bede's account makes it sound as though Willibrord had no part in sending Suidbert to Wilfrid for consecration. Berkum, "Willibrord en Wilfried," typically prefers Bede's account of the origins of the Frisian mission to Stephen's.

[350] Alcuin *Bishops, Kings, and Saints of York* 577-645, here 579-605, ed. Godman, pp. 48-50. Alcuin's account of Wilfrid consists of only three incidents: the evangelization of Sussex, that of Frisia, and the vision at Meaux. Although Wilfrid is praised, dependence on Bede's account effectively expels him from Northumbria: Alcuin's readers (and Bede's for that matter) find no achievement of Wilfrid's in the land that the VW cherishes.

[351] VW 41: "ad illos paganos in Suthsexun . . . sanctus episopus noster confugit. . . . primum regi et reginae verbum Dei . . . praedicare coepit; deinde postea . . . gentes, quibus ante praedicatum non erat, et numquam verbum Dei audierunt, congregatae sunt" (ed. Levison, p. 234). Thousands of conversions ensue; the king is made meek and pious by the Lord; and Wilfrid's *suaviloqua eloquentia* proves effective (as at Whitby, n. 323 above).

Mayr-Harting, "St. Wilfrid in Sussex," p. 5, claims that "Eddius was trying to magnify Wilfrid's achievement." Not having read Bede's *démentis*, Stephen may only have been badly informed.

[352] *H.E.* 4.13, ed. Plummer, I, 230-31.

famine and fishing lessons may be imaginatively transposed from Stephen's account of Wilfrid in Frisia.)[353] The chapter in which these incidents are related ends with Wilfrid's baptizing two hundred fifty slaves whom King Æthelwealh had given him and at once delivering them from slavery. At the close of the next chapter, Cædwalla both kills Æthelwealh and subjects all Sussex to "a worse condition of servitude." The ironic parallel cannot be unintentional.[354] Bede did not mean that Christianity had enervated Æthelwealh and his people. The irony depends on our sharing with him the unstated knowledge that Stephen extolled Cædwalla as Wilfrid's protégé.

Ostensibly naïve, Bede's entire treatment of Cædwalla in *H.E.* 4.15-16 is ironic. Its sense becomes apparent only in the light of the corresponding chapter of the *Life of Wilfrid*. Stephen was totally enthusiastic, stressing Wilfrid's influence: "Our holy bishop helped and supported Ceadwalla in all kinds of ways . . . until he was in a strong enough position to . . . establish his sway. . . . God exalted our bishop through Ceadwalla's victory."[355] But Stephen preferred generalities to an account of Cædwalla's specific exploits. Bede took the opposite course. All is martial detail, and for a while Wilfrid is wholly absent. Cædwalla killed Æthelwealh, wasted his kingdom with fierce slaughter, reduced it to slavery, oppressed it harshly, deprived it of episcopal care. He then turned his attention to the Isle of Wight, earnestly trying to clear out all the natives by massacre. To this point, Cædwalla is reminiscent of his hated Welsh namesake, the Christian ally of Penda and slayer of Edwin, who wished to wipe out the whole English nation.[356] Bede then surprises us: "[Cædwalla] bound himself by a vow, even though—they say (*ut ferunt*)—not yet reborn in Christ, to give the Lord a fourth part of the island and its booty if he should conquer it."[357] Stephen had kept incautiously silent about Cædwalla's lack of baptism, of

---

[353] *Ibid.*, pp. 233-34. Cf. *VW* 26, ed. Levison, p. 220: "Et doctrinam eius secundum paganos bene adiuvavit; erat enim in adventu eorum eo tempore solito amplius in piscatione et in omnibus frugifer annus, ad Domini gloriam reputantes, quem sanctus vir Dei praedicavit." Of course, transpositions of this sort are unprovable. For parallels, see above, nn. 259, 298, and below, n. 364.

[354] *H.E.* 4.13, ed. Plummer, I, 232: all the inhabitants of Selsey are baptized, "inter quos, servos et ancillas ducentos quinquaginta; quos omnes ut baptizando a servitute daemonica salvavit, etiam libertate donando humanae iugo servitutis absolvit" (these are the last words of the chapter). Cf. 4.15, p. 236: "provincia graviore servitio subacta."

[355] *VW* 42, tr. Webb, pp. 174-75; ed. Levison, pp. 235-36, "Nam sanctus antestis Christi in nonnullis auxiliis et adiumentis sepe ancxiatum exulem adiuvavit et confirmavit, usque dum corroboratus . . . regnum adeptus est . . . Tunc vero rex Cedvalla triumphalis, sancto pontifico nostro per Deum elevato."

[356] *H.E.* 4.15-16. The British namesake, 2.20, 3.1.

[357] *H.E.* 4.16, ed. Plummer, I, 237: "voto se obligans, quamvis necdum regeneratus, ut ferunt, in Christo, quia, si cepisset insulam, quartam partem eius simul et praedae Domino daret."

which Bede was aware from the king's famous withdrawal to Rome in 688. When that subject came up, in the next book, Cædwalla emerged from a Roman font suitably washed of his many sins and promptly died.[358] Bede's earlier evocation of him, however, was as a blood-soaked, would-be Constantine and was meant to horrify, not to redound to his credit. When Cædwalla took his vow, Wilfrid turned up: "happening to come (*superveniens*) there," he was just in time to collect the premium vowed to God.[359] Stephen of Ripon had said that "God directed [Wilfrid's] way" to the Sussex heathens. Bede's ungodly coincidence (*superveniens*) looks like a pointed reinterpretation of Stephen's phrase. The chapter ends with a long, uplifting tale of two princes from among the vanquished "who were specially crowned by God's grace." The victims, not the blasphemous conqueror or his bishop, engaged Bede's sympathies.[360]

THESE ten points do not exhaust Bede's response to Stephen's *Life of Wilfrid* or the passages of the *H. E.* in which Wilfrid is mentioned. Yet they suggest how profound and wide-ranging an effect Wilfrid's biography had on the construction of Bede's work. Far more than just being a source, the *Life* impelled Bede to seek information from elsewhere that would contradict, dilute, or reorient Stephen's claims for his hero. Much of what might be called Bede's main line of narrative, from the Gregorian mission through the Synod of Whitby to the evangelization of Frisia is stamped by this spirit of active refutation. As we shall see in a moment, the influence of the *Life of Wilfrid* on Bede is nowhere more marked than in determining where the *H. E.* would end. Before turning to that, other passages in which he came into contact with Wilfrid or Stephen's *Life* will be surveyed.

When narrating the death of King Ecgfrith at Nechtansmere, Bede did not need to react against Stephen's version of the tragedy. The incident had, as we saw, been drained of its emphatically Wilfridian overtones long before the *Life of Wilfrid* was written.[361] Bede restored moral content to the disaster, but for a reason diametrically opposite to Wilfrid's interest. King Ecgfrith, Bede maintained, had without provocation sent an army against Ireland in 684, spurning the appeal of the holy man Egbert not to do so. The year after, again contrary to friendly advice (notably St. Cuthbert's),

[358] *H.E.* 5.7. Stephen (*VW* 42) both overlooked Cædwalla's paganism and placed Wilfrid's activity in a context of conversions and glorification of the Lord.

[359] As n. 357, continuing the quotation: "Quod [i.e. the vow] ita soluit, ut hanc Vilfrido episcopo, qui tunc forte de gente sua superveniens aderat, utendam pro Domino offeret." Stephen on Wilfrid (*VW* 41), "ad illos paganos in Suthsexun, Deo dirigente viam" (ed. Levison, p. 234). Bede's *superveniens* echoes Cædwalla's first entrance, as slayer of Æthelwealh, at the opening of *H.E.* 4.15: "Interea superveniens cum exercitu Caedualla."

[360] *H.E.* 4.16: the boys' execution was delayed until they could be taught to be Christians; as soon as they were baptized, the execution took place. This is a suitably understated horror story.

[361] Above, nn. 161, 163, 237-38.

he marched against the Picts and suffered the divine punishment of being destroyed with his army. The raid upon the inoffensive Irish, unrecorded before the *H.E.*, was the occasion of the king's punishment. Cuthbert's counsel, absent from his three *Lives*, is also new to the *H.E.*[362] At the time when it occurred, the disaster at Nechtansmere had vindicated Wilfrid and gained his reinstatement in Northumbria, but thanks to reinterpretation over the next forty years, the incident gained its final form in the *H.E.*, as an illustration of God avenging the injured Irish and their unheeded friends.

In the *Life of Wilfrid*, the death of Ecgfrith's brother, Ælfwine, in 679 and of King Aldfrith in 705 are both portrayed as divine retribution for wrongs done to Wilfrid. Bede drained the first of these of Wilfridian content partly by adjusting the apparent chronology. The battle of 679 in which Ælfwine was killed is placed much later than Wilfrid's destitution; Wilfrid had already evangelized Sussex by the time we hear of the battle.[363] Besides, Ælfwine's death is mentioned as though it had been almost a mistake, occasioning as deep sorrow in Mercia, whose queen was the victim's sister, as in Northumbria. The sacrifice of his life, somewhat like that of Romeo and Juliet, facilitated the making of peace beween the two camps. The same battle also gives rise to Bede's famous story of the captured nobleman whose shackles persistently fall off as the miraculous result of Masses for his soul. The tale looks suspiciously like a replacement for a miracle in Stephen's *Life* involving shackles that fall off Wilfrid.[364] As for the death of King Aldfrith, Bede abridged Stephen's account but left its core intact: "Aldfrith . . . scorned to receive [Wilfrid] and did not long survive."[365] Sparing the memory of Oswy's later descendants may not have ranked high in Bede's priorities.

Earlier commentators have observed Bede's enthusiasm for persons in bad odor with Wilfrid or the Wilfridians, such as Theodore and Chad.[366] In a Wilfridian interpretation, Cuthbert was an "intruder" at Hexham in 684, and John of Beverley a somewhat less flagrant intruder at Hexham and York a little later. The former dominates the end of Bede's fourth book, and John the beginning of the fifth. In an astonishing series of consecutive

[362] *H.E.* 4.26. More than any other, this chapter suggests that Bede meant the *H.E.* to demonstrate Northumbrian amity toward the Irish. The paradoxical outcome is that Stephen's Ecgfrith, Wilfrid's persecutor, is more kindly portrayed than Bede's, the benefactor of Wearmouth-Jarrow. The reason is that Stephen and his patrons bolstered the family of Oswy, whereas Bede favored the line that replaced it.

[363] *VW* 24, 59; *H.E.* 4.13 (Wilfrid destituted), 4.13-16 (Wilfrid in Sussex), 4.21 (Ælfwine killed).

[364] *H.E.* 4.22; shackles falling off Wilfrid, *VW* 38.

[365] *H.E.* 5.19, ed. Plummer, I, 329. Bede recognized Aldfrith's scriptural learning (4.26, 5.12), but had nothing good to say of his reign (5.18).

[366] Above, nn. 341-45. Stephen, though kindly disposed toward Chad, did not mean him to be the hero of Wilfrid's delayed accession to York, as he is in the *H.E.*

chapters, each is credited with remarkable miracles, whereas Wilfrid, in his obituary, is left with nothing more miraculous to his credit than the vision at Meaux that promised him four more years of life.[367] Abbess Hild of Whitby is noted by Stephen to have sent an emissary to Rome to argue in opposition to Wilfrid's first appeal. Bede does not mention that fact but extolls Hild and her monastery. Another royal abbess, Æbbe of Coldingham, is reported by Stephen to have intervened with King Ecgfrith to procure Wilfrid's release from imprisonment. Bede speaks kindly of Æbbe, but not without qualification. In the *Life of St. Cuthbert*, Coldingham is the scene of the saint's enchanting encounter with the sea beasts who dried his feet. In the *H.E.*, Æbbe's monastery is most memorable for grave misconduct among its nuns.[368]

Bede records one face-to-face encounter between Bishop Wilfrid and himself. It must have taken place between 706 and 709, when Wilfrid held the see of Hexham and was the ordinary of Wearmouth-Jarrow; perhaps he visited Bede's monastery. Their talk was detached from the incident often thought to have alienated Bede from Wilfrid, in which his chronological writings were impugned before the old bishop as being heretical. Nothing about this is mentioned in the *H.E.*[369] Instead, the subject of conversation was the celebrated Queen Ethelthryth, who died as abbess of Ely in 679 and was elevated from her tomb in 695; she had remained a virgin through twelve years of marriage to successive husbands. Bede breaks into the first person: "When I inquired, because certain persons doubt whether this [= her abstinence] was so, Bishop Wilfrid of blessed memory replied to me, saying that he was the most certain witness to her untouched condition, in as much as [King] Ecgfrith promised to give him lands and much money if he were able to persuade the queen to have intercourse with him, for [Ecgfrith] knew that of all men she held [Wilfrid] in greatest affection."[370] Bede adds, a few lines later, that Wilfrid veiled Ethelthryth as a nun when she finally retired from court, and that later still he was among those persons who could testify to the incorrupt condition of her corpse when she was elevated from the tomb.

[367] Cuthbert and John of Beverley: *H.E.* 4.27-32, 5.1-6 (twelve consecutive chapters warmly applauding contemporaries of Wilfrid presumably in bad odor with him and his partisans).

[368] Hild: *VW* 54; *H.E.* 4.23-24. Æbbe of Coldingham: *VW* 39; Anon. *Cuthbert* 2.3; Bede *Prose Cuthbert* 10; misconduct at Coldingham, *H.E.* 4.25 (the only other reference to Æbbe, 4.19, seems neutral).

[369] Above, n. 33.

[370] *H.E.* 4.19, ed. Plummer, I, 243: "sicut mihimet sciscitanti, cum hoc, an ita esset, quibusdam venisset in dubium, beatae memoriae Vilfrid episcopus referebat, dicens se testem integritatis eius esse certissimum; adeo ut Ecgfridus promiserit se ei terras ac pecunias multas esse donaturum, si reginae posset persuadere eius uti conubio, quia sciebat illam nullum virorum plus illo diligere."

Although Bede referred to doubters of Ethelthryth's virginity, he is unlikely to have been among them. He considered the queen's restraint wholly admirable and extolled her in an abecedary poem.[371] What, then, is the point of his conversation with Wilfrid? Two subsidiary facts worth ascertaining would have been how the queen's retirement to monastic life was arranged and how Ecgfrith obtained permission to remarry. Unasked, both questions remain unanswered. Bede was not wrong, however, to focus on the central issue when facing the aged Wilfrid. The bishop, a rare survivor from Ecgfrith's early reign, had directly observed the queen's behavior in married life. He had been so close a confidant of hers that the king engaged his good offices to change her mind. By his admission, Wilfrid was a *testis certissimus* because if he failed to sway her no one else could have. His comment does honor to the virgin queen's unshakable determination. Yet Wilfrid's reply, as reported by Bede, reflects on the bishop as well as the queen. It gives the curious impression that Wilfrid had taken the king's side: even the prospect of a large bribe did not arouse Wilfrid to enough eloquence to talk Ethelthryth into the royal marriage bed. To hear instead of his strengthening her resolve would better accord with our expectations. Bede may have taken the occasion to respond at Wilfrid's expense to Stephen's allegation that Archbishop Theodore was bribed.[372]

One last passage of the H.E. in which Wilfrid casually occurs lends itself to a similar suspicion of malice. When taking note of the death of King Oswy (670) Bede related that Oswy, out of deep love of Roman and apostolic customs, decided to leave for Rome if he could, to end his days there; he offered Bishop Wilfrid much money to escort him.[373] But Oswy died and nothing came of his plan. We are left to wonder why Bede allocated precious words to this trifle. If Oswy had realized his wish, he would have been the first English king to make this one-way journey, which Bede considered salutary to English kingship (it made room for younger men). That the king present at the Synod of Whitby should have harbored this ambition had value as an example. Where he is concerned, well and good.[374] But did

[371] H.E. 4.20.

[372] Bribery, VW 24. Another possibility is that Bede parodied Stephen's "realism"; above, n. 208.

[373] H.E. 4.5. If Oswy had realized his wish, he would have been the first English king to accomplish this pilgrimage, anticipating Cædwalla (5.7) by almost two decades. Even Oswy was not quite the first: Bede reports that Alchfrid, Oswy's son and co-king, wished to have Benedict Biscop escort him to Rome (only for a visit), but was prevented from going by his father (*Hist. abb.* 2).

[374] With a full list of examples, Wallace-Hadrill, "Gregory of Tours and Bede," pp. 109-10: "it can hardly be supposed that such resignations made in general for political stability." They might if they dampened or prevented intrafamily conflicts. Also see Krüger, "Königskonversionen," pp. 171-83. Neither the VW nor Bede substantiates Krüger's claim that Cædwalla, like Oswy, was encouraged (*angeregt*) by Wilfrid.

Oswy really need to strip his kingdom of its vigorous new bishop into the bargain? Wilfrid's place in the story is a little odd. His association with "a large gift of money," though eye-catching, is too vague to dwell on. Because the *H.E.* denies Wilfrid any achievements as bishop of Northumbria, Bede's meaning may go beyond the intimations of a hunger for riches. The message is, rather, that much turbulence and grief would have been avoided if someone as enamored of the Holy See as Bishop Wilfrid had, in his second year at York, accompanied Oswy to Rome, and stayed there.[375]

From book III onward, Stephen of Ripon's *Life of Wilfrid* lurks behind the main narrative of the *H.E.* as the rival to be rectified or contradicted, the mirror whose image must be meticulously reversed. Stephen's influence is most conspicuous in defining when "the ecclesiastical history of the English people" would end. Of course, Bede leaves us in no doubt that the English Church was a body whose life was nowhere near reaching its term on earth.[376] But he does finish the *H.E.*, in a climax that is much more definite and dramatically satisfying than Gregory of Tours' ending of the *Histories*, yet also—unlike Gregory's—falls very far from the time at which he admits to be writing. However beguiling on an artistic plane, Bede's termination so oddly curtails recent times that it seems arbitrary and puzzling, until the antagonistic relationship of the *H.E.* to the *Life of Wilfrid* is taken into account. Predictably, in this light, the close of Stephen's biography governs the end of Bede's refutation and dispenses him from going on. Wilfrid dies and is duly celebrated. The obituary of Abbot Hadrian comes next, together with appreciative words about Wilfrid's successor at Hexham, Acca: the age of Theodore had ended but a standard-bearer for the Wilfridians lived on at Hexham.[377] Then, after an abrupt seven-year leap, comes Bede's climax. Anticipated since the chapter on St. Columba, it narrates the conversion of Iona by the priest Egbert to the Roman Easter.[378] The great Irish saint whose name, in Stephen's *Life*, had provoked Oswy's contemptuous "smile" was resoundingly vindicated in the reconciliation of his spiritual heirs to Catholic unity. After this, barring factual odds and ends, the program of the *H.E.* had been completed and, though the life of the English Church went on, there was nothing more to be said about its history.

---

[375] In other words, a transposition to a much earlier period of his life of the intentions advertised in *VW* 55 (Wilfrid's desire in 704 to stay in Rome as a penitent till death). Bede begins the comprehensive chapter on Wilfrid (*H.E.* 5.19) with notices of an English king and a prince (*iuvenis amantissimae aetatis et venustatis*) who abandoned everything for lifelong pilgrimage in Rome: Wilfrid kept coming back.

[376] E.g. *H.E.* 5.23; in any case, the climax in 5.22 marks the end only of a regrettable discord and presupposes continuity in improved conditions.

[377] *H.E.* 5.19-20.

[378] *H.E.* 3.4, 5.22.

6. Conclusion

B ede's neglect of contemporary events in the *H.E.* should not discourage us from trying to restore his great work to its immediate and local circumstances. When this is done, Bede can no longer be conceived of as a solitary genius fed on books and detached since boyhood from his social milieu; his evocation of a golden age loses the appearance of a jeremiad and acquires that of vigorous advocacy. In its time, the *H.E.* continued a debate concerning the past that Wilfrid and his Northumbrian opponents had pursued ever since the 690s. Whatever the issues of this argument may have been at earlier stages, when Bede wrote they focused on the elevation of York to metropolitan status, a cause that involved a range of parties extending from Bishop Acca of Hexham, and others nearby, to the archbishop of Canterbury and the pope in Rome. The politics of the Northumbrian Church offer a more plausible point of departure for the *H.E.* than Bede's spontaneous initiative or the unmotivated incitement of Abbot Albinus.

Metropolitan status for York was not itself controversial. It had been anachronistically transposed by Stephen of Ripon to Wilfrid's heyday, and its impending arrival was welcomed by Bede in the *Letter to Egbert.* The disputed question was which faction in Northumbria would effect the change and to what end. By the time the *H.E.* was composed, politics uninfluenced by the written word had in all likelihood decided that question in favor of the persons in whose behalf Bede worked. The passing of Osric in 729 and his replacement by Ceolwulf removed the kingdom from the descendants of Oswy and transferred it to the royal line that, in the next decades, occupied not only the throne but also the see of York, and achieved its elevation to archiepiscopal rank. These leaders saw to it that the division of the English Church into two provinces took place on terms of amicable cooperation with Canterbury.

Bede's sympathies are apparent from the royal dedication of the *H.E.*, his relations to Egbert, and his Canterbury connection. According to Bede, the "bad" past began at the death of King Aldfrith in 705; the pullulation of abusive monasteries thereafter coincided with Wilfrid's last restoration and with the power of his principal successor, Acca of Hexham.[379] The latter's expulsion in 731 was as positive a sign for the future as Egbert's elevation to York the next year. Thanks to these changes, one might hope for fundamental reform in the Northumbrian Church—a return to the "good past" lovingly described in the *H.E.*

[379] *Epist. ad Egbertum* 13, ed. Plummer, I, 416: the bad past begins after Aldfrith's death, i.e. with the advent of Osred. The coincidence with Wilfrid's return and Acca's rule is left tacit.

Owing to the lack of detailed evidence about the 720s and 730s, some of this reconstruction is conjectural, the best approximation that may be attained from the few facts at our disposal. What seems beyond doubt is that the unique succession of ecclesiastical narratives in early-eighth-century Northumbria was occasioned by controversy. The efforts to mobilize the past for the uses of the present were set in motion by Wilfrid himself, if the Mercian translations of saints in the 690s were his doing, and the Wilfridian, Stephen of Ripon, brought them to a peak not exceeded until Bede composed the *H.E.* Bede defined his own position in the debate early in his productive career, when he set to verse the *Life of St. Cuthbert*; however discreetly, he was pro-Irish and anti-Wilfrid even before the death of King Osred in 716. He was the natural person for the bishop and monks of Lindisfarne to turn to after Stephen's *Life of Wilfrid* appeared. At their prompting, Bede composed a prose *St. Cuthbert* not only expurgated of those passages which Stephen had appropriated, but also straightened into chronological order and enriched with the two incidents in Cuthbert's life that told against Wilfrid. He took the occasion, besides, to outline the ideas on pastoral care and monastery-bishoprics that, in his *Letter to Egbert*, would become proposals for urgent action.[380] Under Abbot Hwætbert, Wearmouth-Jarrow was ready to detach the memory of its own beginnings from the prelate who had assisted Benedict Biscop.[381] Bede's account of the founder, in the *History of the Abbots*, is one of the many biographies called into existence by the urge to dilute and offset Wilfrid's solitary eminence; in the rewriting of the *Life of Ceolfrid*, Benedict Biscop not only overshadowed his follow founder, and allowed Ceolfrid's Ripon connection to be obliterated, but also rivaled his unnamed contemporary as a traveler to the Continent and Rome, and an importer to Northumbria of the riches of Mediterranean civilization. Bede had more than fifteen years of experience in partisanship by the time he launched into the *H.E.*

The issue that most sharply divided Bede, and presumably his patrons, from the Wilfridians was the Irish component of the Northumbrian past, and present. Nowhere does the *H.E.* farther depart from the *Life of Wilfrid* than in transmuting "the poisonous weeds planted by the Irish" into glowing images of Northumbria in flower. The paradoxical result is that the attention paid in the *H.E.* to the problem of Easter is in inverse proportion to the importance that Bede probably ascribed to it. Of course, the author of two works on the *Reckoning of Time* must have cared about proper Easter calculation; others, however, had made it a barrier between Christians and an occasion for allegations of heresy. A polarized past could not be effec-

---

[380] Above, nn. 101-102.
[381] Above, nn. 257-58.

tively argued with, but it could be rectified by the accumulation of additional evidence. Wilfrid, without being denied his glory at the Whitby council, was stripped of his solitary heroism, not least by being offset by the priest Egbert. The cost of eroding Wilfrid's eminence was that the Easter issue occupies more space in the *H.E.* than it objectively warranted. Bede had no choice except to affirm his detestation of Aidan's Easter observance and to deprecate that of Iona.[382] The obligatory professions of orthodoxy strike all the more jarring a note because they so markedly contrast with Bede's radiant portrayals of Irish evangelists and their pastoral methods, whose applicability to current needs was affirmed in the *Letter to Egbert*. More than sentiment and pastoral interests were at stake: the new province of York could grow to a full twelve dioceses only by drawing the Irish to the east within its fold. An English Church broadly welcoming to the Irish and Picts, and accepted by them, was the condition for creating a northern metropolis worthy of the name.

Restored to its local context, the *H.E.* furnishes an attractive illustration of the collective striving and pain out of which, with favoring circumstances, a great history may arise. Northumbria precociously experienced the acrimony and contentiousness that, as often elsewhere, enlivened and gave strength to the Christian Church. According to one modern theory, nonliterate societies reverently cultivate their historical memories through the ages, allowing fragments of them to pop up barely distorted after long passages of time.[383] The case of Northumbria suggests that the manipulation of the past, rather than a chaste fascination with it, animates the memory of a society. One sees this best in the canonizations of the 690s. The appearance in England of one Christian device for stimulating memory was followed, not long after, by the next—historical narrative. As an ultimate answer to Stephen of Ripon's narrowly Wilfridian account of the Northumbrian Church, nothing less would do than the "true" history of the *ecclesia gentis Anglorum*, provided of course that Bede was available to write it.

The laborious retracing of long forgotten quarrels gives an added dimension to the *H.E.* as "the masterpiece of Dark Age historiography."[384] The learning, research, and skill with words that have earned Bede this accolade continue to amaze and to present scholars with problems needing study. The *H.E.* can only gain from being restored to a collective effort by Northumbrians, prolonged over decades, to align the past of their Church with its present and, in this way, to define its nature. Bede's genius, like anyone else's, is beyond explanation, but it had the advantage of being har-

---

[382] *H.E.* 3.13 (Aidan), 3.4 (Iona).

[383] E.g. Bullough, *Age of Charlemagne*, pp. 117-18; Eis, "Origins of German Language and Literature," pp. 77-79.

[384] Campbell, "Bede," p. 160.

nessed to an undertaking whose limits were more precisely defined than if he had been a secluded monk bent on impartially commemorating the English past. Clearly, he was "someone ready to get his hands dirty on the issues of [his] time."[385] The *H.E.*, like his other works, was developed from existing models; and the program Bede set himself for outdoing his predecessors was not so much to retrace the English conversion for the instruction of posterity as to supersede the rival accounts of the same period. The qualities we still admire in his narrative stem from the controversialist's certainty of his goal. What became of the objectives Bede sought, other than Egbert's *pallium*, is anybody's guess. The *H.E.*, fortunately, took on a life of its own and endowed the beginning of Christianity in England with a brilliance that has never failed to excite the admiration of posterity.

[385] Blake Morrison, in *Times Literary Supplement* (April 11, 1986), p. 382 (about John Le Carré).

Paul the Deacon's Interpretation of Lombard History

1. The *Historia Langobardorum*: Disappointment and Promise

Paul the Deacon is the most distinguished Italian author of the eighth century and the first to write at any length since Pope Gregory the Great (d. 604). When young, he frequented the court of Ratchis, king of the Lombards (744-49); his earliest poem bearing a date (763) was addressed to Adalperga, daughter of another Lombard king as well as duchess of Benevento; Paul's *Historia Romana*, his initial venture into history, was also dedicated to her; and in the early 780s Paul was one of the scholars at Charlemagne's court. Perhaps destined for the Church from birth and long a deacon, his association with the ducal house of Benevento coincided with his membership in the nearby monastery of Monte Cassino. This was where Paul died, probably in the 790s, leaving unfinished his most famous work, the *History of the Lombards*.[1]

This narrative, hereafter abbreviated *H.L.* (for *Historia Langobardorum*), was extraordinarily popular in the Middle Ages. Well over one hundred manuscript copies survive. Georg Waitz believed that no medieval history surpassed its success except the thirteenth-century *Chronicle* of Martin the Pole.[2] Paul's reputation in modern times is much higher than Martin's. He is liked for many qualities, including "sincere affection for his people," and invariably praised for preserving information that would otherwise be lost.[3] But Paul the historian is not spoken of with the respect reserved for Bede or Gregory of Tours. Something seems to be missing.

Paul was conspicuously well-read, not perhaps in ancient literature but in most of the historical classics from the fourth century onward and much else. He wrote poetry and is regarded by Dag Norberg as a key figure in the fashioning of medieval Latinity.[4] Yet the *H.L.*, when laid alongside these

---

[1] For details, see § 2.

[2] Bethmann, "Paulus Diaconus," pp. 309-10, 316-18; Waitz in MGH SS. *rer. Lang.*, p. 28; Laistner, *Thought and Letters*, p. 271; Guenée, *Histoire et culture historique*, p. 302. Rhee, "Germanischen Wörter," p. 272, estimates 200 full or partial mss.

[3] Sestan, "La storiografia dell'Italia Longobarda," p. 374; Brunhölzl, *Gesch. d. lat. Lit.* I, 264; Frederichs, *Gelehrten um Karl dem Grossen*, p. 17 (an extreme statement of the position). For an admirable discussion of this aspect of Paul, see Menghini, "Stato presente," pp. 237-40; Mommsen, for one, could not envisage Paul as a patriot (as below, n. 17).

[4] Norberg, "Développement du latin en Italie," pp. 497-98, 501, 503; stressing the literary movement in northern Italy in Paul's formative years, Norberg states that Paul's genius gave

accomplishments, is found wanting. Echoing the views of Gian Piero Bognetti (the leading figure in recent Lombard studies), Chris Wyckham concluded that Paul "had a fairly simplistic sense of the past. What passes for such in his history is mostly pride in Lombard prowess."[5] To J. M. Wallace-Hadrill, Paul's theme was the victory of Catholicism; intent on the past rather than the present, he was deeply interested in the impact of Rome and Christianity on his ancestors.[6] According to Robert Hanning, Paul lacked "a central concern with the importance of national conversion for national history"; mixing secular with Christian interpretations, he practiced a historiography in which merely "national interests [are] occasionally colored by Christian concerns."[7] These scholars, while moderately differing over the main lines of Paul's preoccupations, seem to agree that the *H.L.* is perplexing and fails to fulfill legitimate expectations. As Leicht put the matter, "it has to be confessed that [Paul] does not provide a history that satisfies our demands."[8] The Lombards were worse served than the Franks and Anglo-Saxons had been.

Many commentators consider the *H.L.* to be redeemed by some of its components. Thanks to it, we retain at least fragments of such otherwise lost sources as the chronicle-history of Secundus of Trent.[9] Gibbon, without giving reasons, already asserted that "[Paul's] pictures of national manners, though rudely sketched, are more lively and faithful than those of Bede or Gregory of Tours."[10] In the perspective of nineteenth-century romanticism, Paul played the invaluable part of a collector of Germanic legends: "he drew from the living tradition of his people, which he reproduces with such charming simplicity that we may confidently infer the fidelity of his version and his abstinence from personal amplifications"; in the *H.L.*, "we possess the legendary tradition of the Lombard people in its widest form and continual development." The *H.L.* supplied a whole set of stories to the Brothers Grimm.[11] Paul's language "allows the original storytelling

---

order to disparate elements and in this way created a new, personal, and cultivated style. On Paul's language, also see Rhee, "Germanischen Wörter," pp. 273-92.

[5] Bognetti, "Processo logico e integrazione delle fonti," p. 159; Wyckham, *Early Medieval Italy*, p. 29. The same already in Wattenbach, *Deutschlands Geschichtsquellen*, 5th ed., I, 161.

[6] Wallace-Hadrill, *Barbarian West*, pp. 43-44.

[7] Hanning, *Vision of History*, p. 96.

[8] Leicht, "Paolo Diacono," p. 74. G. Pontoni, *Introduzione alla* Historia Langobardorum *di Paolo Diacono* (Milan 1940) and *Introduzione agli studi su Paolo Diacono storico dei Longobardi* (Naples 1946) are not at the Bodleian Library or in the National Union and British Library catalogues; but see *Revue d'histoire ecclésiastique* 42 (1947) bibliog. no. 3894, and 43 (1948) bibliog. no. 2062. They have eluded me.

[9] Del Giudice, "Storico dei Longobardi," p. 42. Laistner, *Thought and Letters*, p. 271; Bognetti, as n. 5.

[10] Gibbon, *Decline and Fall*, ch. 45, ed. Bury, V, 5 n. 10.

[11] Bethmann, "Paulus Diaconus," p. 337; Del Giudice, as n. 9. That Paul collected Germanic legends is taken for granted by See, *Germanische Heldensage*, p. 74.

tone of these Germanic tales to sound through."[12] The *H.L.* was, as a result, "the first fully accomplished attempt to combine a delight in Germanic individuality with the cultural ideal of antiquity."[13] Even in recent decades, the "poetry" thought to be embodied in his retelling of legends is considered, apart from any other aspect of the *H.L.*, to have crucial importance for a positive appreciation of the author: "With this [capacity to relate Lombard tales] he resolves and overcomes in his person the problem of the fusion of Germanism and Romanity."[14] It seems as though the margins of the *H.L.* make up for what is lacking at the core.

Under Paul's pen, the phrase "about this time" can refer to spans of as much as thirty or forty years; he has long been noted for defects in chronology. But, among premodern historians, this failing is hardly unique with him. The traits that most detract from the *H.L.* are a lack of external motivation and of inner coherence. The history appears to hang in the air, without discernible objective and purpose. In the view of Brunhölzl, "Paul does not write . . . out of the needs of daily life or for a practical purpose. . . . [H]e takes position in the most reticent manner toward the . . . [historical] developments of his day."[15] Sestan stated the same view in positive

---

Jakob and Wilhelm Grimm, *Deutsche Sagen* (1816-18), 3d ed., II, 21-37, nos. 388, 390-404, 406-408, 410; tr. Ward, *German Legends of the Brothers Grimm* II, 20-38. Leyen, *Heldenliederbuch*, p. 113, regarded himself as one of their continuators; on Paul the Deacon, "Ihm verdanken wir, wie man weiss, besonders wertvollen Übersetzungen [!] einiger alten Heldenlieder."

[12] Brunhölzl, *Gesch. d. lat. Lit.* I, 264; Bethmann, "Geschichtsschreibung der Langobarden," p. 337, endorsed the view of the Grimms that the Lombards were the great source of Germanic legends. The quotation: Hampe, "Paulus Diaconus," p. 398. Cf. Wattenbach, *Deutschlands Geschichtsquellen*, 5th ed., I, 162: "We owe to him the preservation of that rich treasure of sagas unfalsified by any later erudition . . . [all this written down by] the hand of the old monk . . . with loyal love." The notion has been tenacious; Grundmann, *Geschichtsschreibung*, 2d ed., p. 15: Paul ekes out his written sources "durch eine Fülle langobardischer Sagenüberlieferung, die seinem Werk einem besonders ursprünglischer Klang gibt." The yardstick of *Ursprünglichkeit* is unspecified. According to Gardiner, "On Translating Paul the Deacon," p. 46, Paul "caught" the Lombard legends just when they were losing their significance.

[13] Hampe, "Paulus Diaconus," p. 399. Gschwantler, "Heldensage von Alboin," p. 245, maintains that medieval authors regarded heroic legends as totally credible sources about the past; a prime example cited is Paul "der den heroischen Sagen uneingeschränktes Vertrauen schenkt." The evidence is less clear: because the raw *Sagen* are lost, what Paul did with them is unverifiable. As for his being "trusting," few would claim that he was more critical—at least overtly—with other categories of sources than this one.

[14] Vinay, "Paolo Diacono e la poesia," p. 113. For a sense of the importance acquired by Paul's legends in recent German historiography, see Hauck, "Heldendichtung und Heldensage als Geschichtsbewustssein," and Jarnut, "Frühgeschichte," pp. 2-4, 15-16, with special reference to the theory of Reinhard Wenskus about *Traditionskerne* and origin legends, which Jarnut treats as established certainty. To the contrary, with special reference to Paul, see Graus, review of Wenskus, p. 189.

[15] Brunhölzl, *Gesch. d. lat. Lit.* I, 267. Paul as a nostalgist with no sense of the present, Vinay, as below n. 20, p. 127.

terms: "Until the contrary is proved, [the *H.L.*] may be considered as born of the spontaneous initiative of its author."[16] Paul composed it at Monte Cassino, after the fall of the Lombard monarchy (774) and after returning from the Carolingian court (ca. 785). Nostalgia, a desire to portray the old Lombards as very ferocious, or simple emulation of Jordanes, Gregory of Tours, and Bede—these and the like are the motives proposed for his writing. It seems as though Paul had little intellectual or historical awareness.

The greatest shortcoming of the *H.L.* is considered to be a lack of structure and design. Mommsen said that Paul "formed his history out of the most disparate sources into a formal unity with complete stylistic mastery"; but Laistner voiced the more general view that Paul's narrative is "sometimes exceedingly confused."[17] At best, according to Sestan, he is a chronicler, competent enough to handle discrete events seriatim but unable to grasp long-term processes such as the Christianization and Latinization of the Lombards.[18] In the words of Heinz Löwe, "it is unmistakable that Augustinian thinking" did not give "unity to [Paul's] vision of history (*Geschichtsbild*)"; the narrative is lively and picturesque, but the most it achieves is to align individual episodes in chronological order.[19] The *H.L.* is an assemblage of "real and legendary facts," often superficially connected, and more commendable for "freshness" and "the author's profound sense of participation in the subjects he narrates" than for the guidance of a powerful intellect.[20]

Opinions so negative as these are best deemed provisional. Although representative of current assessments, they help most to suggest that Paul deserves more searching study than he has yet received. In fact, a rehabilitation of the supposed defects of the *H.L.* is in such easy reach, at least as a hypothesis, that it may be sketched in a few lines.

When Paul returned to Monte Cassino from Charlemagne's court and composed the *H.L.*, his near-neighbor as prince of Benevento was Grimoald III (788-806), son of Paul's one-time patron, Adalperga, herself the daughter of the last king of the Lombards. Benevento lay far enough to the south to have escaped the fate that the Lombard kingdom endured at the hands of Charlemagne. It was the one part of Italy in which Lombard history could be written without nostalgia, as a profitable subject of instruction

[16] Sestan, "Storiografia dell'Italia Longobarda," p. 372.
[17] Th. Mommsen, "Die Quellen," pp. 486-87; Laistner, *Thought and Letters*, p. 269.
[18] Sestan, "Storiografia dell'Italia Longobarda," p. 385.
[19] Heinz Löwe in Wattenbach-Levison, *Geschichtsquellen*, p. 214.
[20] Balzani, *Early Chroniclers of Europe*, p. 75; Morghen, "Paolo Diacono"; Brunhölzl, *Gesch. d. lat. Lit.* I, 263-64; Sestan, "Storiografia dell'Italia Longobarda," pp. 379, 384 (essentially a chronicler). For a comparable but different view, see Vinay, "Un mito per sopravvivere," pp. 125-49.

for a Lombard prince. Now, the most glowing and chivalric king in the *H.L.* is Grimoald I (d. 671); in more space than is devoted to any other Lombard monarch, Paul lovingly traces Grimoald's career from romantic origins in Frioul through glorious reigns at both Benevento and the royal capital of Pavia. The absence of a connection between the heroic Grimoald of Paul's history and his namesake, the reigning prince of Benevento, would be more surprising than its presence. It is not far-fetched to conjecture that the *H.L.* had as its immediate purpose to edify and instruct young Grimoald III.[21]

Not only is a purpose for the *H.L.* within reach, but its inner structure is more coherent than generally supposed. Book III of the *H.L.* has a happy ending comparable to that of Jordanes's *Getica*; like tales with such endings, it culminates in a marriage that repairs and regenerates Lombard society. The whole third book is governed by a plot with characters and formal features similar to those observed in the *Getica*.[22] The adjoining book II closes with the famous episode of Rosamund murdering Alboin at the height of his success as conqueror of Italy. Alboin's tragic death is not just a historical fact providing the book with its climax; all the chapters, although often seeming to be disconnected, are affected by the conventions of a tragic scenario. These two books furnish the most conspicuous instances of a practice of deliberate plotting, or literary design, that Paul implemented in every book of the *H.L.* and in other of his works as well. When Paul's narrative is subjected to literary analysis, it turns out to be not a haphazard assemblage of historical extracts and barbarian legends, but an instructive and eminently Christian interpretation of the Lombard past.

2. Frioul, Pavia, Benevento, and Charlemagne's Court

Paul the Deacon did not wholly efface himself behind his writings. He attached an account of his ancestry to the tale of the first Grimoald's heroic beginnings in Avar captivity; when evoking the fateful skullcup that occasioned Alboin's murder, he recalled having been at court when King Ratchis personally displayed the grisly relic; one of his best poems pleads with Charlemagne for generosity toward his brother's starving wife and children; and, out of sympathy for a fellow Italian practicing his craft among Frankish royalty, he drew attention to the sixth-century poet Ve-

---

[21] The Beneventan side of Paul, including the idea that the *H.L.* was destined for Grimoald III, is well brought out by Krüger, "Beneventanischen Konzeption," p. 34. Paul's orientation toward Benevento comes near to being as obtrusive as Bede's toward Northumbria. Leicht, "Paolo Diacono," pp. 70-72, already saw the probable connection of the *H.L.* to Grimoald III.

[22] Above, ch. II nn. 259-61 and *passim*.

333

nantius Fortunatus and wrote him an epitaph.[23] Even the insistent manner in which the *H.L.* passes back and forth between Frioul, Pavia, and Benevento seems guided less by any inherent rhythm in Lombard affairs than by the poles of Paul's existence and the palaces of his patrons.

Nevertheless, there is no autobiographical intent; Paul's personal revelations are incidental to different purposes. None of our authors is more determined than he to conceal his presence and, in the manner of ancient historians, to impart an objective character to his writings. One result is that the traces he leaves of himself are frustratingly free of dates. The long, unresolved debate among scholars over his biography almost entirely concerns the chronology of his life rather than its stages, which are well enough documented. The main point of uncertainy is the date of what Italians call his *monacazione*—his withdrawal into Monte Cassino. Paul was either a lifelong courtier who sought refuge at the tomb of St. Benedict when already middle-aged, or a lifelong monk who often secured court patronage for his scholarship.[24] On balance, as we shall see, the evidence tips in the latter direction.

Paul came from Frioul, the border duchy at the head of the Adriatic that defended Italy from invasion by Slavs and Avars. His home town probably was Forum Iulii itself, the modern Cividale. He could not have been born earlier than 720 or later than 730; unless we make him very old when he wrote the *H.L.*, the second half of the 720s is more believable for his birth than the first. Paul's own claim to nobility, and that made for him in his epitaph, seem confirmed by his early association with the court of the Lom-

---

[23] *H.L.* 4.37 (Paul's ancestor), 2.28 (Ratchis and the skullcup), 2.13 (Fortunatus); for the poem to Charlemagne, n. 45 below.

[24] Hodgkin, *Italy and Her Invaders* V, 72, set out the two possible political reasons. The more popular theory is that either Charlemagne's conquest or Rodgaud's Frioulan rebellion (776) drew or drove Paul into Monte Cassino: Dahn, *Paulus Diaconus*, pp. 23-25; Crivellucci, "Alcune questioni," pp. 4, 10, 16-17; and many more (the idea goes back to the literary historian Tiraboschi). The alternative is that the abdication and withdrawal to Monte Cassino of Ratchis (749) inspired Paul to do likewise: Waitz, in MGH *Script. rer. Lang.*, p. 14; Menghini, "Stato presente," 263-66, 274, 366.

The ancient, circumstantial account of Paul's life is in *Chronicon Salernitanum* 9-10, ed. Ulla Westerbergh, Studia Latina Stockholmiensia 3 (Lund 1956), pp. 9-13, a narrative of the third quarter of the tenth century. Modern biographers have had to clear away the enduring legends stemming from this text; see, e.g., n. 34 below. After the pioneers Bethmann and Dahn, Menghini's is the best attempt to reconstruct Paul's life. Also important, owing to the documentary value of his poetry and letters, is Karl Neff, *Die Gedichte des Paulus Diaconus. Kritische und erklärende Ausgabe*, Quellen und Untersuchungen zur lateinische Philologie des Mittelalters, ed. Ludwig Traube, 3, fasc. 4 (Munich 1908); but Neff is mediocre as a biographer. Paul's poetry and associated items are cited here as Neff followed by a number in Roman numerals. Also see, for Paul's works rather than his life, the introductory survey of Engels, *Observations sur le vocabulaire*, pp. 1-3. The suggestive study of Taviani, "Dessein politique du *Chronicon Salernitanum*," is concerned with the chronicler's perception of Paul and the *H.L.*, not with Paul himself.

bard kings at Pavia. The same is suggested by the exile and confiscation of property meted out to his brother, Arichis, in 776, after the rebellion of Duke Rodgaud against Frankish rule had failed.[25]

His parents, whatever their social standing, may have destined Paul at birth for an ecclesiastical career. His father was called Warnefrid, and his brother bore the same Lombard name as Warnefrid's father; Paul, however, was singled out to receive a Christian name, and his sister became a nun when young. Paul's epitaph associates his sacred studies with the Pavian period of his life.[26] When he left home for the royal capital, he probably moved in the direction his family had always intended him to take.

Frioul, because of its strategic location, was no ordinary duchy. In Paul's lifetime, its ducal family supplied one Lombard king in Ratchis (744-49) and, after Ratchis's retirement to Monte Cassino, another in his brother Aistulf (749-56), who provoked the papacy into securing the first Carolingian intervention in Italy (755-56). Ratchis even returned briefly to Pavia from Monte Cassino after Aistulf's accidental death, in an abortive effort to regain his throne (December 756–March 757). The Frioulan origins of Ratchis help to explain why Paul came to the royal capital in the 740s, when perhaps still an adolescent, and was educated by a grammarian whose uncle had been honored for his learning by an earlier king.[27] There was no contradiction between studies of this sort and the pursuit of an ecclesiastical career.

The direct evidence for Paul being at Ratchis's court is slight enough to have nourished skepticism about his having had any substantial association with this or any other Lombard king. Yet Paul knew Pavia well; he writes of it with authority in the *H.L.* and had no other occasion than these years for acquiring familiarity with it. He was also acquainted with the palace of Monza, north of Milan. Perhaps his earliest surviving composition is a

[25] Del Giudice, "Storico dei Longobardi," p. 9, preferred 720-25; Bethmann, "Paulus Diaconus," p. 255 with n. 2, favored ca. 730; Waitz, in MGH *Script. rer. Lang.*, p. 13, also inclined to the late 720s. The only basis for conjecture is that Paul had to have been at least a youth in Ratchis's reign (744-749) and died in the 790s. Dahn, *Paulus Diaconus*, p. 2, underscored that Cividale as birthplace is just a guess.

Paul's epitaph by his pupil Hilderic, in MGH *Script. rer. Lang.*, pp. 23-24 (his nobility, lines 11-14); the epitaph wrongly has Paul enter Monte Cassino after his return from Francia (error noted by Bethmann, "Paulus Diaconus," p. 259). Dahn was particularly intent (pp. 2, 4-5) on playing down Paul's alleged nobility, on which see now Krüger, "Beneventanischen Konzeption," p. 20 n. 16.

[26] The father was called Warnefrid, the brother Arichis (*H.L.* 4.37). Paul's nun-sister is mentioned, but not named, in the petition-poem to Charlemagne (below n. 45). The idea that he was destined for the Church was denied, for no apparent reason, by Bethmann, "Paulus Diaconus," p. 256, and plausibly urged by Menghini, "Stato presente," p. 93.

[27] Wyckham, *Early Medieval Italy*, pp. 45-46. Ratchis tries to recover the throne: Krüger, "Königskonversionen," pp. 171-72; Hallenbeck, *Pavia and Rome*, pp. 51-52. For Paul's teacher, Flavian, and his uncle, *H.L.* 6.7.

poem about nearby Lake Como that suggests personal knowledge of the site rather than a school exercise. Though more facts would surely be welcome, there is no serious reason to doubt that Paul spent an appreciable period in Pavia under Ratchis and, possibly, under Aistulf as well. It is also tempting to guess that this was where he was ordained deacon and started upon the path of ecclesiastical preferment.[28]

Paul's dated writings begin in 763 with a poem on the ages of the world addressed to King Desiderius's daughter, Adalperga. By then, Paul was a deacon and lived far to the south, in the Duchy of Benevento, within which Monte Cassino was located.[29] The segment of his life that most completely eludes us extends from the end of Ratchis's reign (749) to his completion of the *Historia Romana* (ca. 770). In the latter, he signs himself *exiguus et supplex*, a formula that he often uses again; its emphatic humility almost certainly identifies him as a monk.[30] The issue, much debated, is when and in what circumstances Paul left the world for monastic seclusion.

Two of the three views that have been advocated still merit consideration. In 749, King Ratchis abdicated and withdrew, perhaps reluctantly, to Monte Cassino. This incident has been taken to provide a likely psychological moment for Paul to follow his king into the cloister. The alternative date proposed is 775 or 776; on this hypothesis, Paul fled to or was forced into Monte Cassino in the wake of Charlemagne's conquest of the Lombard kingdom (774) or the suppression of Rodgaud's Frioulan rebellion (776).[31] The earlier date implies a very different Paul from the one whom only politics drove into monastic refuge. If he waited till the 770s, he would have

---

[28] Dahn, *Paulus Diaconus*, pp. 9-12, radically minimized Paul's contact with the Lombard court; he was too skeptical, but preferable to the undocumented exaggerations of, e.g., Viscardi, *Le Origini*, 4th ed., pp. 41-42; not much better, Belting, "Beneventanischen Hof," pp. 168-69, who alleges that Paul was at the Pavian palace school and served there as Adalperga's tutor; along the same fanciful lines, Rhee, "Germanischen Wörter," p. 271. Paul certainly not a lifelong servant of the Lombard monarchy, as claimed by Löwe, in Wattenbach-Levison, *Geschichtsquellen*, p. 223; cf. below, n. 34. For his knowledge of Pavia, Monza, and Lake Como: Menghini, "Stato presente," p. 98.

[29] Neff, no. II. Although to write it Paul did not have to live in Benevento, the hypothesis that he did is preferable to any other. Arichis and his wife are central to the poem, and there is no trace of Paul outside Benevento except for his few years with Charlemagne's court.

[30] *H.R. praef.*, ed. Crivellucci, p. 3. Del Giudice, "Storico dei Longobardi," p. 25, concluded from this that the *H.R.* was written in a monastery; also, Menghini, "Stato presente," p. 235 (cf. below, n. 33). For comparison, letter to Abbot Theodemar, *pusillus filius supplex* (MGH EE. IV, 507); letter to Adalhard, *Paulus supplex* (*ibid.*, 509); dedication of the epitome of Festus, *ultimus servulus* (*ibid.*, 508); poem praising St. Benedict, *dedi famulus supplex* (Neff, no. VI); dedication of the homiliary, *famulus supplex* (Neff, no. XXXII); letter in the name of Theodemar accompanying the Rule of St. Benedict, *supplex* (MGH EE. IV, 510). Bethmann, "Paulus Diaconus," p. 258, pointed out that Paul's being called *diaconus* does not exclude his already being a monk, for Charlemagne's circular about his homiliary, which definitely dates long after his monastic profession, calls him *diaconus*, not *monachus* (MGH *Capitularia* I, 81).

[31] See above, n. 24.

been a courtier for some twenty years, with the kings at Pavia or the ducal couple at Benevento, and would presumably have abandoned a worldly life for the safety of the cloister only with deep regret. A line from a poem of his in honor of St. Benedict, in which he qualifies himself as *exul, inops, tenuis, is* taken to document the politically caused wretchedness that drove him into Monte Cassino.[32]

Neither reason suggested for Paul's *monacazione* is wholly satisfactory, and the second may be definitely excluded. The exile and wretchedness Paul refers to in verse are not a personal condition; he shared them with all other Christians here below. Besides, the dedication of the *Historia Romana*—with Paul qualified as *exiguus et supplex*—provides a probable *terminus ante quem* for his becoming a monk. Everyone agrees that this history must antedate the fall of the Lombard kingdom in 774. It is dedicated to the same duchess whom Paul hails in 763 as having one child; now she has three.[33] Pregnancies are an imprecise time scale, but 770 is not an unreasonable inference from the circumstances. One more step backward may be permissible. The poem of 763 is on a historical subject; it is addressed to the eventual dedicatee of the *Roman History*, a work whose composition called for monastic tranquillity and resources. It would hardly be surprising if, by 763, the first moment when Paul the Deacon addresses the duchess of Benevento, he already belonged to the congregation of Monte Cassino.

The idea that he followed Ratchis there in 749 is more romantic than compelling. If political circumstances influenced his decision, there were other incidents to motivate him than only Ratchis's abdication. In the H.L., Paul implies disapproval for Ratchis's brother Aistulf (749-56), whose rough handling of the papacy in the early 750s resulted in Frankish intervention and the beginning of the end for the Lombard kingdom. The accession of Desiderius, after Aistulf's accidental death, was challenged by Ratchis himself (756-57). If local ties mattered, Paul may not have expected the same favors from the Brescian Desiderius, former duke of Tus-

---

[32] Neff, no. VI. Dahn, *Paulus Diaconus*, pp. 24-25, first claimed that these words testified to Paul's own misery; endorsed by Neff, pp. 23-33; exaggerated by Viscardi, *Le Origini*, p. 43. For the correct interpretation, Menghini, "Stato presente," pp. 233-34.

[33] The dating was set out by Dahn, *Paulus Diaconus*, pp. 14-15, 20: Paul would not have promised Adalperga to continue the history down to "our times" if the continuation were bound to culminate in the downfall of her father's kingdom; therefore, the H.R. must antedate 774. Without being ironclad, the argument is more convincing than not. Del Giudice, "Storico dei Longobardi," pp. 22-27, tried to date the H.R. later than 774; though unsatisfactory, his reasoning merits attention. Like him, Waitz in MGH *Script. rer. Lang.*, p. 14, believed that sources for the H.R. would have been more easily found in a monastery than in a palace.

Adalperga's children: one, on the basis of Neff, no. II, according to Del Giudice, p. 22, and Menghini, "Stato presente," p. 248 (I am less certain); three and another on the way, H.R. *praef.*, ed. Crivellucci, p. 4; cf. Dahn, *Paulus Diaconus*, p. 78.

cany, as from the Frioulan dynasty.[34] These external events offer little more than vaguely possible reasons for Paul to become a monk. We are well advised also to give a hearing to his personal and private considerations. By about 755-60, he was reaching age thirty and faced a career decision: Did he wish ecclesiastical preferment, or would he rather be a teacher and scholar? For someone aspiring to be a man of letters, there were advantages that only a monastery could confer. Nowhere does Paul suggest anything but deep attachment to Monte Cassino and its patron saint. Pavian vicissitudes may have disappointed him, but unless his withdrawal to St. Benedict's monastery is dated after the Carolingian conquest, it marked the beginning of his productive life. For all one knows, Paul's decision was spontaneous and wholly unrelated to politics.[35]

Except for about four years in the Frankish kingdom (781-85), Paul was at Monte Cassino until his death. But he had not run out of Frioulan connections. In 757, the newly installed king Desiderius took vigorous steps to suppress resistance to himself in the powerful duchies of Spoleto, in central Italy, and Benevento, to the south. In the latter, the young duke Liutprand, a relative of the great king Liutprand (d. 744), despised the upstart Desiderius and threatened to place himself under the protection of the Carolingian Pepin. Desiderius obtained naval help from the nearby Byzantines and so abruptly ended Liutprand's defiance that he vanished from history. The vacant dukedom was given to a Frioulan, Arichis, then only twenty-three years old.[36] The new duke was the namesake of Paul the Deacon's grandfather and brother. A much earlier Arichis had, according to the *H.L.*, been tutor to the children of the first duke of Frioul before being appointed by King Agilulf to be duke of Benevento (ca. 591-641).[37] History had, to some extent, repeated itself. No one knows what family the eighth-century Arichis originated from or what decided Desiderius to entrust this major responsibility to him, but Desiderius chose well. Soon afterward, per-

---

[34] Aistulf, *H.L.* 6.51, 56 (harsh, impulsive). The origins of Desiderius, Krüger, "Beneventanischen Konzeption," p. 34. Except for *Chronicon Salernitanum* 9, ed. Westerbergh, pp. 10-11, there is no evidence that Paul had ties to either one. To the contrary, the claims of Corbato, "Paolo Diacono," p. 11, and Wyckham, *Early Medieval Italy*, p. 39, who makes Paul a grammarian under Desiderius toward 760; also Brunhölzl, *Gesch. d. lat. Lit.* I, 257, alleging that Desiderius made Paul Adalperga's tutor. These statements cannot be disproved, or substantiated. For what it is worth, a Brescian, Petronax, refounded Monte Cassino (early in the century): *H.L.* 6.40.

[35] An early date for Paul's *monacazione* seems mandatory: the poem to Adalperga is religious; the dedication of the *H.R.* uses a formula of humility that Paul favored throughout his life (above, n. 30). To the hypothesis that Paul was moved to imitation by Ratchis's withdrawal, I prefer the alternative that he entered Monte Cassino for his own reasons. The lack of evidence encourages guesses, such as Wattenbach's that Paul followed Arichis and his wife to Benevento and there became a monk (*Deutschlands Geschichtsquellen*, 5th ed., I, 136).

[36] Hodgkin, *Italy and Her Invaders* VII, 256-58; Gay, *Italie méridionale*, pp. 28-29.

[37] *H.L.* 4.18-19, 39, 43-44.

haps by prearrangement, he gave Arichis his daughter Adalperga in marriage. Although Paul's poem of 763 and the *Roman History* are both addressed to her, the Frioulan Arichis, whom Paul calls wiser than any other prince of the age, may have had more to do than she with mobilizing the pen of his countryman in Monte Cassino and placing it at the service of his culturally ambitious reign.[38]

Paul's production in these years was destined for his monastery as well as for Benevento. He set to verse the miracles of St. Benedict and, possibly, composed a *Life of St. Gregory the Great*, the least studied of his four historical works. His verses to an unnamed friend, some of whose lines are echoed in a later letter to Adalhard of Corbie (a cousin of Charlemagne), may have been addressed to this distinguished Frank in connection with his brief stay at St. Benedict's (before 780).[39] The devoted teaching for which Paul would later be praised at Charlemagne's court surely had a background in these monastic years. Toward 767, Duke Arichis developed Salerno as a coastal fortress and secondary capital. Paul wrote at least one poem to adorn the duke's constructions. In the Orosian way, Paul's verses contrast the pagan structures reared in Rome from the plunder of the world (*externis rapinis, exuvia miserorum*) to those built by a Christian prince. The historical sense shown here had further scope in Paul's verses of 763 to Adalperga (which we prize for containing a precise date) and, of course, in the *Historia Romana*, also written for her and the major work of this period of his life.[40]

Completed when Adalperga was the mother of three, the *Historia Romana* was well suited to the needs of a ducal couple who, in emulation of Justinian, adorned their capital with a church of Holy Wisdom (St. Sophia). Paul's statement that the *History* was designed to forward Adalperga's cultivation need not have been the sole consideration behind his work, nor she his only patron.[41] The book itself and its dedication conclude with

[38] Paul's dedication of the H.R. to Adalperga need not imply closeness. If Frioulan origins and, possibly, blood linked him to Arichis, the latter's patronage would have been more certain than that of the royal daughter, Adalperga; hence, Paul needed to court her with literary offerings.

[39] St. Benedict, H.L. 1.26; for the *Life of St. Gregory* and its uncertain date, see below, § 5. Verses to a friend, Neff, no. VIII and p. 128.

[40] Neff, no. XII, pp. 56-62, by Peter of Pisa; the text (with facing translation) is in Godman, *Poetry of the Carol. Ren.*, pp. 82-86. A little treatise on grammar also documents his teaching: Manitius, *Gesch. d. lat. Lit.* I, 271-72; Löfstedt, "Notizen," pp. 81-82 (the work establishes a connection between Paul and Peter of Pisa). The verses for Salerno, Neff, no. IV, pp. 14-18. The poem on the ages of the world, above n. 29. On the H.R., see below, § 3. Paul's prefatory letter to Adalperga was not discovered until 1835: Bethmann, "Paulus Diaconus," p. 308.

[41] Hodgkin, *Italy and Her Invaders* VIII, 60-66; Gay, *Italie méridionale*, pp. 29-34. Further on the Beneventan court, Belting, "Beneventanischen Hof," pp. 141-93; he argues that Arichis, in emulating Byzantium, competed with the Byzantine cities of southern Italy, such as Naples, and did not distance himself from Pavia—interesting, but far from certain. Belting

the promise of more: Paul would carry on from 552 to current times. He even gave clear signs of what the early parts of the continuation would look like. Yet it took more than twenty years for this sequel, the *H.L.*, to be composed, and not in full even then. For this reason, Del Giudice urged that the date of the *Roman History* should be set later than it normally is.[42] Although he was right to see an improbability in the long postponement of Paul's confidently announced continuation, any displacement of the *Romana* to a point appreciably closer to the *H.L.* is barred by the reference to Adalperga's three children (by 787, she had five, all grown).[43] The *H.L.* cannot antedate the later 780s. The long interval, though real, is not perhaps quite so puzzling as Del Giudice thought, provided Paul is understood to have had a stable base in his monastery. There was no obstacle to his beginning the *H.L.* on the morrow of completing the *Historia Romana*. Notes, sketches, drafts might pile up year after year. They were still at Monte Cassino, decades later, when Paul was finally able to take the project in hand and bring it as close to completion as it came.

The Lombard kingdom fell to Charlemagne in 774, and Arichis of Benevento, whom the conquest did not directly affect, took the occasion to elevate his territory from a duchy to a semiroyal principality. The next year, Pope Hadrian warned Charlemagne of a conspiracy involving Frioul, Spoleto, and Benevento, together with the Byzantines and the refugee Lombard king Adalchis (brother of Adalperga of Benevento). If there was substance to this allegation, the combination was undone by the death, in August 775, of the able Byzantine emperor Constantine V. Charlemagne's only response was to attack the duke of Frioul, Rodgaud, who in fact rebelled and declared himself king. Charles fell upon Rodgaud with a small force in early 776, killed him, recovered all the cities that had defected, installed Frankish counts, and returned home soon after Easter (14 April) to deal with a Saxon rising. Rodgaud's revolt probably explains why Paul's married brother, Arichis, had all his property confiscated at about this time and was exiled to Francia, leaving his family destitute.[44]

(pp. 168-69) and others extract more from Paul's preface to the *H.R.* than he says; Dahn, *Paulus Diaconus*, p. 14 n. 5, comments sensibly. Paul never intimates that he was, or had been, Adalperga's tutor. He was, at best, an informal literary adviser and did not have to be present at the Beneventan court; cf. Dahn, p. 19, after Mabillon.

[42] The *H.R.* unmistakably points to the *H.L.*: in the preface and *H.R.* 16.23 (ed. Crivellucci, pp. 4 lines 14-18, 238 lines 8-9), Paul declares he will continue. Bethmann, "Paulus Diaconus," pp. 272, 314, and Waitz, review in *Göttingische gelehrte Anzeiger*, p. 597, concluded that the *H.L.* continues the *H.R.* only "to some extent." Mommsen, "Die Quellen," pp. 487-88, regarded the link between the two works as important and often overlooked. For an attempt to date the *H.R.* after 774, see above, n. 33.

[43] For Adalperga's five children at Arichis's death, Bethmann, "Paulus Diaconus," p. 297, on the authority of *Chronicon Salernitanum* 5, ed. Westerbergh, p. 25.

[44] Gay, *Italie méridionale*, pp. 29-30, 34-35; Bertolini, "Carlomagno e Benevento," pp. 612-

Paul's appeal to Charlemagne to free his brother and to restore some of his property is set out in a poem—perhaps the best verses Paul ever composed—that must have been written within the year ending in April 783, the seventh of Arichis's exile. Traditionally, Paul is thought to have sent this poem to Charles from Monte Cassino and to have thus earned an invitation that brought him to the Frankish court by the winter of 782-83. This chronology of events, though logical, is somewhat unimaginative.[45] A more satisfactory account of Paul's Frankish stay, and the works associated with it, becomes possible if he is assumed to have gone north a year earlier. The poem of 782 does not have to have been Paul's first approach to Charlemagne. It might just as plausibly be regarded as a formal presentation piece, written not to convey information but to express artistically a petition made long before. On this hypothesis, Paul could already have been in Francia when he composed the poem. To explain how he left Monte Cassino in the first place, one would look instead to Charlemagne's Italian journey of 781. In April of that year, the Frankish king brought much of his family to Rome to celebrate Easter with Pope Hadrian; for dynastic reasons, it was an important moment in the reign. It would hardly be surprising if, on this occasion, Paul sought out Charlemagne in Rome, not far from Monte Cassino, and, more expeditiously than in formal verse, obtained permission to plead for his brother. Paul was already a distinguished scholar. The interview presumably resulted in an invitation to join the Frankish court and continue pressing the brother's cause. Within the same year, Paul followed Charles to his winter quarters at Quierzy-sur-Oise (781-82). Charlemagne's Italian journey of 781 is, in any case, a memorable stage in the formation of his learned circle. On the way to Rome, he met Alcuin at Parma and induced him to join the royal entourage as soon as he could.[46]

---

20. Also on Arichis's new title, Krüger, "Beneventanischen Konzeption," pp. 18-19 (with bibliog.). The fall of the Lombard kingdom, Bullough, *Age of Charlemagne*, pp. 49-50. The events of 775-76: Böhmer and E. Mühlbacher, *Regesten des Kaiserreichs*, 2d ed., nos. 198a, 200a-f, 203a (cited hereafter as B-M plus a number or page); Classen, "Karl der Grosse, das Papsttum und Byzanz," pp. 555-56.

45. Menghini, "Stato presente," pp. 321-22; Neff, no. XI, pp. 51-53, dated May 782; most lately, Godman, *Poetry of the Carol. Ren.*, p. 82, "shortly before Paul joined Charlemagne's court circle." The poem, admirably translated by Godman, might just as well have been written by Paul within the court circle as from outside. I am not certain that, in it, Paul "abandons all artifice" (Godman, p. 9, and others). The reference to his sister who "has almost lost her sight through crying" is hyperbolic, and hyperbole may tinge the description of the sister-in-law's begging for food beside the highway to feed four children.

46. B-M 291b (Easter, 15 April); Bullough, *Age of Charlemagne*, pp. 99-101; Bertolini, "Carlomagno e Benevento," pp. 424-25; Classen, "Karl der Grosse, das Papsttum und Byzanz," pp. 558-59. Charles's invitation to join the court was conveyed by Peter of Pisa: Fleckenstein, "Karl der Grosse und sein Hof," p. 47 n. 190. I think Paul approached Charles in Rome and joined his court late in 781. Possibly, he was recommended by knowledge of Greek, for whose

341

Paul's journey to Francia looms large in his literary production, but most of the works it occasioned were composed after he had returned to Monte Cassino. Securely into his fifties, he was conscious of the weight of years he bore and did not stay away long.[47] The writings, largely verse, directly associated with his northern sojourn may be satisfactorily assigned to winter 781-82 (Quierzy Palace), summer 782 (Poitiers), winter 782-83 (Thionville Palace), and 783-84 (Metz or its environs). There is no clear sign that Paul was with the court at Herstal (winter 783-84), and the following year Charlemagne wintered uncomfortably in Saxony with a limited entourage. If summer 784 was when Paul wished to visit Abbot Adalhard at Corbie, but could not, then he would have been incapacitated by illness from September to Christmas of that year.[48] Early spring 785 might already have seen him on his way back to his monastery, with a stop in Rome to convey a request from Charlemagne to Pope Hadrian.[49] Whatever the details may be, there is no positive reason for locating Paul in Francia after 784. He may have been back in his monastery for as long as two years when Charlemagne made his third journey to Italy and Rome (786-87) and visited Monte Cassino.

However brief, Paul's stay at the Frankish court was a professional and personal success. His teaching was praised. The commission to compose the *Deeds of the Bishops of Metz* entrusted to his pen a delicate task of importance to the royal family, as we shall see. Much work was given him to be carried out at Monte Cassino. And his brother, Arichis, who occasioned the journey, was presumably freed.[50]

The final segment of Paul's life is no richer than the earlier ones in chron-

---

(faint) traces, see below; Charles had just arranged a Byzantine marriage for his daughter Rotrud.

[47] Godman, *Poetry of the Carol. Ren.*, p. 88 (stanza 12): "iam gravante senio." This is taken seriously by Waitz, in MGH *Script. rer. Lang.*, p. 13 n. 1; but the poem is playful.

[48] Neff, no. XII-XIII (781-82), petition (no. XI, 782), epitaph of Fortunatus (no. XXIX, 782), poetic exchanges (no. XV-XXIII, 782-83), letter to Theodemar (XIV, Jan. 783), Metz epitaphs (no. XXIV-XXVIII, 783); *Gesta episcoporum Mettensium*, 784. Visit to Adalhard that does not take place: Neff, no. XXXI.

Charlemagne spent the winter of 781-82 at Quierzy-sur-Oise, 782-83 at Thionville, 783-84 at Herstal; he was in Saxony, roughing it, for most of 784-85, then at Attigny and Aix, winter 785-86: B-M pp. 102-103, 106-107, 108-109, 109-10, 111. On wintering in Saxony, cf. Bullough, *Age of Charlemagne*, pp. 60-61.

[49] *Codex Carolinus* 89, MGH *EE*. III, 626; Vogel, "Réforme liturgique sous Charlemagne," p. 224; he favors Paul returning before 786. According to Dahn, *Paulus Diaconus*, p. 55, and others, Paul accompanied Charlemagne in 786; against this view, Menghini, "Stato presente," pp. 352-53 (Paul was back in Monte Cassino, ready to greet Charlemagne on his visit in 787). Bullough, *Age of Charlemagne*, p. 102, brings Paul north in late 782 and keeps him there for as many as six years.

[50] Freeing of Paul's brother: Bethmann, "Paulus Diaconus," p. 262, on the basis of the poem *Paule sub umbroso*, Neff, no. XXI (782-83); no. XXII also points in this direction. Dahn, *Paulus Diaconus*, p. 36, is more guarded, but the poems are good evidence.

ological details. We know what he did rather than when. Frankish commissions resulted in three major editorial enterprises: a selection of fifty-four letters of Gregory the Great for Adalhard of Corbie (with a particularly warm dedication); the epitome of an ancient glossary, Festus's *De verborum significatu*, addressed to Charlemagne to enrich the classical rarities in the palace library; and, by special royal request, a collection of homilies for the night office throughout the year. Nothing may be said about the *Collectio Pauli* of Gregory's letters until someone studies it. The epitome of Festus establishes Paul's claim to attention among classical philologists. As for the homiliary, prescribed by Charlemagne for use throughout his lands, it is Paul's contribution to the Carolingian basic books and one of two or three fountainheads of medieval sermon collections.[51] Charlemagne, when visiting Monte Cassino in 787, asked Abbot Theodemar for a copy of the autograph of the Benedictine Rule. Modern research has shown that the version Monte Cassino gloried in had not quite been written out in the saint's hand. All the same, the text was duly transcribed and sent northward with authentic measures of monastic food and drink. In the name of his abbot, Paul composed a long letter to accompany the package.[52]

Paul's continuing association with Prince Arichis and his family is documented by the admiring and friendly epitaph Paul wrote at Arichis's death (26 August 787). The poem was influenced by models he had come to know in Francia. He was also called on to write an epitaph for Ansa, mother of Duchess Adalperga and widow of the last Lombard king.[53]

[51] Letters of Gregory the Great: Ewald, "Studien zur Ausgabe des Registers Gregors I," pp. 472-84 (Ewald doubted that the Paul in question was ours). Also see Posner, "Das Register Gregors I," pp. 248-65, and Norberg, *In Registrum Gregorii Magni studia critica* II, 31-32. In the H.L., Paul used the 200-letter collection, not the one to Adalhard; but the former always travels with his in mss. Paul's, however, is separate and exists by itself in five mss. Posner and Norberg agree that the *Coll. Pauli* has two parts copied from the Lateran register at different times.

Sextus Pompeius Festus *De verborum significatu cum Pauli epitome*, ed. W. M. Lindsay (Leipzig 1933); dedication to Charlemagne, ed. Lindsay, p. 1, and Neff, no. XXX; appreciative comments, Manitius, *Gesch. d. lat. Lit.* I, 264-66. Dedication of the homiliary, Neff, no. XXXII; on its importance, in brief, see Gatch, *Preaching and Theology in Anglo-Saxon England*, pp. 28-29.

[52] Covering letter: MGH *EE*. IV, 510-14; Bethmann, "Paulus Diaconus," p. 298, dated between 789 and 797. On the text of the Benedictine Rule sent north on this occasion, Bischoff, "Hofbibliothek Karls des Grossen," p. 45. The commentary on the Rule of St. Benedict often ascribed to Paul is not his work; see Hafner, "Paulus Diaconus."

[53] Arichis epitaph: Neff, no. XXXI; affected by Paul's acquaintance with models found in Frankish kingdom, *ibid.*, pp. 110-11. Epitaph of Ansa: Neff, no. IX. Ansa still lived after Charlemagne married Fastrada (autumn 783): MGH *Necrologiae Germaniae* II, 12 no. 29. Krüger, "Beneventanischen Konzeption," p. 30 n. 76, sets the epitaph before Paul's northern sojourn (774-782); so did Waitz, in MGH *Script. rer. Lang.*, p. 191. Dahn, *Paulus Diaconus*, p. 68, and Abel and Simson, *Jahrbücher* II, 506 n. 1, agreed that the epitaph belongs to Ansa's lifetime because Paul refers serenely to the marriage of her daughter to Charlemagne (she was repudiated in less than a year, 770-71); Neff, p. 46, held that epitaphs written in the subject's

His main "Beneventan" project, however, was the all-important *H.L.* According to Erchempert, a ninth-century historian of the Lombard South, Paul carried his narrative down only to King Liutprand's death in 744 because he could not bear to speak of the last thirty years of the independent kingdom. Other commentators down to our times have endorsed variations of this view, believing Paul to have despairingly ended the *H.L.* with its sixth book.[54] It is understandable that the somewhat sentimental idea of a deliberate termination in 744 should have continuing appeal, but the alternative of an unintentional interruption occasioned by Paul's death is more probable. In three earlier historical works, Paul clearly announced his ending; not so in the *H.L.* The lack of a dedication and introduction is no less conspicuous. Even if he had contemplated post-Liutprand Italy with a heavy heart, his patron or patrons deserved acknowledgment and an explanation of the author's scope and intentions similar to that heading the *Historia Romana*. Besides, the attention Paul paid in *H.L.* 6 to the Frioulan Pemmonids, who succeeded Liutprand, and his explicit promise to relate a miracle later, "in its proper place," offset the terminal implications of Liutprand's death. *H.L.* 6 has even been found to contrast in stylistic finish with the earlier books.[55] As we shall eventually see, there are reasons to believe that Paul planned the *H.L.* to have two more books than the six he managed to complete. To die near age seventy in the eighth century was to exceed one's life expectancy. The *H.L.*, continually postponed since the 770s by other occupations, needed more time for full elaboration than Paul was allotted.

Paul should not be buried before a word is said about Beneventan affairs in these last decades and his hypothetical part in them. Speculation about his role as an intermediary between Charlemagne and the princes of Benevento, though impossible to substantiate, is too important for assessing

---

lifetime are not unusual, but doubted that such was the case here. The epitaph of Ansa challenges one's ingenuity (and notion of Paul's political sympathies). Ansa died while exiled in Francia with her husband, the deposed King Desiderius: Abel and Simson, *Jahrbücher* I, 194-95. Yet, Paul's poem treats the failed marriage to Charles just like the very fruitful one of Adalperga to Arichis of Benevento, and it refers to Ansa's son, Adalchis, a refugee in Byzantium after 774, as "Bardorum spe maxima" (though Paul was not hostile toward the Franks). In view of the contents, one would like to date the epitaph to early 771, but only Dahn's rather desperate hypothesis of composition in Ansa's lifetime makes this possible.

[54] Erchempert *Historia Langobardorum Beneventanorum*, ed. G. H. Pertz and Georg Waitz, MGH *Script. rer. Lang.* p. 234: Paul intentionally omitted his times "quoniam in eis Langobardorum desiit regnum." Against Erchempert, Bethmann, "Paulus Diaconus," p. 313. With him, for various reasons, Waitz in MGH *Script. rer. Lang.*, p. 25 (the work was planned for only six books); Löwe in Wattenbach-Levison, *Geschichtsquellen*, p. 223; Vinay, *Alto medioevo latino*, p. 127; Brühl, "Langobardische Königsurkunden als Geschichtsquellen," pp. 53-54; Brunhölzl, *Gesch. d. lat. Lit.* I, 263; and others.

[55] For all these points, Krüger, "Beneventanischen Konzeption," p. 18; they make the hypothesis of accidental interruption far more probable than that of intentional ending.

the *H.L.* to be considered otiose. From the fall of Pavia onward (774), Arichis and his duchess had become the pillars of the Lombard cause in Italy, backed by Byzantium and viewed with suspicion by the pope and the Frankish court. The danger they represented was neutralized in 781 by the turn of Constantinople toward Charlemagne. A few years later, after Charles's victory over the Saxons, the aloofness of Arichis became obtrusive and annoying to the Franks. The main objective of Charles's journey across the Alps late in 786 was to impose his dominance over southern Italy. During winter 787, Arichis sent his grown-up son and co-ruler, Liutprand, to Charles in Rome as a virtual hostage and emissary of peace. Charles, though inclined to accept Arichis's terms, was pressed by the pope and by his Frankish entourage to advance into Beneventan territory (this was the occasion of his coming to Paul's monastery). Arichis offered no resistance and fortified himself in Salerno. At Capua, where Charles stopped his progress, Arichis's younger son, Grimoald, joined him with more generous terms of peace. At the same time, Charles's entente with Constantinople came apart. By April, the Frankish king had reached agreement with Arichis, returned Liutprand to him, and taken away Grimoald with twelve other distinguished Beneventans as hostages for the prince's good behavior. Arichis's peaceful course had saved his principality from devastation and resulted in no noticeable curtailment of his autonomous rule. Pope Hadrian was not pleased.[56]

As Charlemagne withdrew across the Alps, the Byzantines prepared a major attempt to wrest Italy from the Franks. The Lombard pretender Adalchis now sported a Greek name and a Byzantine dignity; he was counted on by his sponsors to win local assistance. The role of Benevento in these plans is hard to assess. Arichis's co-ruler, Liutprand, only twenty-five, died in July 787; little more than a month later, the father also expired. Because Arichis's last surviving son, Grimoald, was a hostage in the Frankish kingdom, the Beneventan succession was at Charlemagne's mercy. Awaiting his decision, the dowager princess Adalperga took affairs in hand with the assistance of Beneventan dignitaries. Pope Hadrian urged Charlemagne not to send Grimoald home; because Adalperga was the sister of Adalchis, it was easy to suspect nefarious dealings between Benevento and the Byzantines. Two groups of Frankish *missi* were in the area, but ineffectual in the pope's opinion.[57]

Charlemagne took months to make up his mind but eventually disre-

---

[56] Hodgkin, *Italy and Her Invaders* VIII, 60-71; Abel and Simson, *Jahrbücher* I, 543-70; Gay, *Italie méridionale*, pp. 35-37; Classen, "Karl der Grosse, das Papsttum und Byzanz," pp. 559-60; Bertolini, "Carlomagno e Benevento," pp. 631-36.

[57] Abel and Simson, *Jahrbücher* I, 604-606, 612-15, 617-18; Bertolini, "Carlomagno e Benevento," pp. 637-55.

garded Pope Hadrian's advice. In March 788, young Grimoald III was sent home under obligation to honor Arichis's undertakings of the previous year. He was, besides, to place Charles's name on his charters and coinage and to style his hair in the Frankish fashion. The Byzantine preparations were going ahead anyway, more or less known by Charlemagne's court. A Benevento grateful for receiving its rightful prince was deemed more reliable in opposing Byzantine ambitions than one in the care of Adalperga. Events bore out the wisdom of this reasoning. When, late in 788, the Byzantines and Adalchis attacked, the newly installed Grimoald called out the Beneventans to resist; a Frankish *missus*, Winigis, arrived with a small force to supervise operations, and the invaders suffered a costly defeat. Retreating to Constantinople with his protectors, Grimoald's uncle had seen the last of Italy.[58] The exploit that Paul attributes in the *H.L.* to Grimoald I on first becoming duke of Benevento is that this "very warlike man . . . overthrew with the utmost slaughter" the Greeks who came to plunder the shrine of St. Michael at Mt. Gargano.[59] The past did not too inaccurately reflect the first months of the current prince.

After this resounding start as a defender of Frankish hegemony, Grimoald was eventually tempted to greater independence. By 791, Charles's name dropped from his coins. He acquired a Byzantine bride but did not long keep her. There was inconclusive skirmishing between him and Charlemagne's sons; the Frankish conquest of the Avars left him dangerously exposed as one of the few remaining rulers inadequately submissive to the great northern king. Nothing decisive happened. Grimoald predeceased Charlemagne and left no heir (806).[60] Paul the Deacon may have died a decade or more before him, though the year moderns prefer is 799. His pupil Hilderic, who became a reputed grammarian, furnished his grave with an admiring if inaccurate epitaph.[61]

There is no way to establish what part, if any, Paul played in Beneventan-Frankish relations from 785 to his death. No personage known to us,

[58] Hodgkin, *Italy and Her Invaders* VII, 71-82; Abel and Simson, *Jahrbücher* I, 630-35; B-M p. 122 (also no. 296a). Krüger, "Beneventanischen Konzeption," pp. 29-30, rightly concludes that Paul did not hope for Adalchis's return (as the epitaph of Ansa seems to imply, n. 53 above).

[59] *H.L.* 4.46.

[60] Belting, "Beneventanische Hof," pp. 147-50; Classen, "Karl der Grosse, das Papsttum und Byzanz," pp. 560-61; also, Classen, "Italien zwischen Byzanz und dem Frankenreich," p. 93 (originally in *Spoleto Settimane* 27, 1981).

[61] Epitaph: above, n. 25. Paul's works never allude to Charlemagne's imperial proclamation of December 800. Mabillon was the first of many to infer his death in 799 from this observation: Dahn, *Paulus Diaconus*, p. 73; Menghini, "Stato presente," p. 366; Löwe in Wattenbach-Levison, *Geschichtsquellen*, p. 223. Menghini, pp. 362, 364, aware that the date of death cannot be fixed, suggested that Paul, if alive in 797, would have written an epitaph for his abbot, Theodemar. On Hilderic's grammar (more interesting than his teacher's), see Löfstedt, "Notizen," pp. 82-83.

however, enjoyed closer and more confidential relations than he with both courts. He was determinedly anti-Byzantine, and his sympathy for the papacy was by no means unqualified.[62] That Byzantium and Rome should have been the losers in the power game of the late 780s, out of which both the Franks and Benevento did well, might simply be coincidental, but it is too interesting a coincidence to be overlooked. The author of the *Historia Romana*, the *Gesta episcoporum Mettensium,* and the *H.L.* is unlikely to have been indifferent to the course of contemporary events. Nor did he need to worry that such interests might be out of keeping with his monastic profession. There was nothing improper about a teacher of grammar conveying lessons in Christian rulership.[63] Grimoald III, taking command of the threatened but surviving bastion of Lombard autonomy, could hardly afford to forget that the most learned Italian of the age, an old family friend, lived nearby. Though the new prince may not have taken the aged monk's advice, the likelihood is that Paul destined the *H.L.* for his eyes.

3. *Historia Romana*: Italy from Janus to Justinian

The dedicatory letter of the *Roman History* opens with the affirmation that Duke Arichis of Benevento has almost sole claim to the palm of wisdom among the princes of the age, and that his duchess, Adalperga, for whom the history is meant, strives to imitate him. Paul explains the genesis of his work. In his continual efforts to promote Adalperga's cultivation, he had proposed that she should read the *Roman History*, or *Breviary*, of Eutropius; Adalperga perused it keenly, as she was wont, but besides finding its brevity excessive, she regretted that the pagan author had left out all reference to divine history and Catholic religion; she therefore commissioned Paul to expand Eutropius at suitable points and to make insertions from Holy Scriptures so as to give greater clarity to the original author's chronology. Presenting the finished product, Paul says that, in addition to harmonizing Eutropius with Scriptures and providing appropriate expansions, he had begun the narrative somewhat before Eutropius and extended it beyond his ending, from the emperorship of Valentinian I (364) to the times of Justinian. In closing the letter he resolves to persevere; with God's protection, if the duchess so desires and if both his health and the source material (*maiorum dicta*) do not fail, he will in another *libellus* carry the history "down to our age."[64]

---

[62] As will be seen in the analysis of the *H.L.*

[63] Cf. Wallach, *Alcuin and Charlemagne,* pp. 31-82.

[64] "Cum . . . historiis etiam seu commentis tam divinis inhaereas quam mundanis, ipse, qui elegantiae tuae studiis semper fautor extiti, legendam tibi Eutropii historiam tripudians optuli. Quam cum avido, ut tibi moris est, animo perlustrasses, hoc tibi in eius textu praeter immodicam etiam brevitatem displicuit, quia utpote vir gentilis in nullo divinae historiae cultusque

347

It is risky to judge a book only by the description its author provides. Paul's lines to Adalperga are neither inaccurate nor misleading, but they need interpretation in the light of what he does.

The sixteen books of the *Historia Romana* break down into three parts of unequal length: a short prelude, situated without numbering before Eutropius's first chapter; then the ten books of Eutropius; and finally an original continuation in six books, each of about the same length as the previous ten. Except for exactly copying the Eutropian *Breviary*, Paul was active throughout in selecting and styling the contents.

In a few pages somewhat reminiscent of the "Summary of the Ages" with which Jordanes began his *Romana*, Paul gave a backward extension to Eutropius's beginning. Whereas the latter's *Breviary* starts at the first year of the Roman era—the foundation of the city (A.U.C.)—Paul preferred a different frame: "The first to rule Italy, according to some, was Janus." He went on to the next Italian kings, from Saturn to Latinus, the arrival of Aeneas, the rule of his son over the Latins, and the other legends, until the link was made with Romulus founding Rome.[65] The adoption of an Italian focus places Paul in good company among Christian historians. The Christian universe of Orosius begins in timeless geography; Gregory of Tours narrows the scope of his *Histories* to Christian Gaul by the middle of his first book and stays there; Isidore of Seville introduces his *History of the Goths* with a celebration of Spain; Bede's *History* opens with a description of the British Isles and an account of their original inhabitants.[66] Like these predecessors, Paul anchored history in geography. His work, however "Roman" in title, begins with the earliest Italian rulers, and, at the close of book XVI, it is Italy, not Rome, that Justinian's forces conquer from the Goths. The narrative that Paul would homogeneously continue from Justinian's conquest to the Lombard eighth century could be only Italian, not Roman.

The few pages of pre-Eutropian history suffice to define the limited ex-

---

nostri fecerit mentionem; placuit itaque tuae excellentiae, ut eandem historiam paulo latius congruis in locis extenderem eique aliquid ex sacrae textu Scripturae, quo eius narrationis tempora evidentius clarerent, aptarem. At ego, qui semper tuis venerandis imperiis parere desidero, utinam tam efficaciter imperata facturus quam libenter arripui. Ac primo paulo superius ab eiusdem textu historiae narrationem capiens eamque pro loci merito extendens, quaedam etiam temporibus eius congruentia ex divina lege interserens, eandem sacratissimae historiae consonam reddidi" (ed. Crivellucci, pp. 3-4). For Paul's continuation and the promise to provide a complementary history *ad nostram aetatem*, see below.

[65] "Primus in Italia, ut quibusdam placet, regnavit Ianus" (ed. Crivellucci, p. 5); the prologue, *ibid.* pp. 4-10. The skeleton is from the Eusebius-Jerome *Chron.*, additional information from the fourth-century *Origo gentis Romanae* and *De viris illustribus* (which accompany Aurelius Victor in the text tradition and are in Pichlmayr's edition of Victor, Leipzig 1911), and Virgil.

[66] For Orosius, above, ch. II n. 326; Gregory, above, ch. III n. 200; Bede, above, ch. IV n. 273; Isidore *Historia Gothorum*, ed. Mommsen, MGH AA. XI, 267 ("De laude Spaniae").

tent of Paul's additions from Scriptures. The prominence they are given in the dedication is open to misunderstanding. Although Adalperga had found Eutropius pagan, which he was, his *Breviary* is mainly noteworthy for lacking religion of any kind. Even Jordanes, because dependent on the pre-Christian Florus, allowed more space to pagan cults in his *Romana* than Eutropius did. After all, the *Breviary* had been written for the Christian emperor Valens; its nonsectarian quality is precisely what recommended it to a Christian posterity. Paul had no intention of baptizing Eutropius. What mattered was that Adalperga and Paul's other readers were versed in sacred history and more familiar with its chronology than with any other. The obscurity that needed clarification was the equivalence of Eutropius's Roman dates to biblical ones. This "harmony," easily achieved by the intermittent insertion of lines from Jerome's *Chronicle*, is all that Paul deemed it necessary to supply. His *Roman History*, unlike Eutropius's, is not indifferent to religion, but neither does it Christianize Italy before its time.[67]

The Eutropian part of Paul's *Romana* is basically a ten-book quotation, copied so faithfully as to include obviously obsolete phrases, such as a direct address to Valens (d. 378). Sestan once surveyed the histories among which Paul might have chosen a model and concluded that Orosius was the only possible alternative to Eutropius, but clearly less satisfactory for a narrative of Paul's scope.[68] Although not wrong, Sestan's finding leaves out of account the likelihood that Paul's choice was foreordained. Eutropius's had long been the Roman history par excellence.[69] The fidelity of Paul's transcription testifies to the respect with which the *Breviary* needed to be treated. Paul capitalized on its currency not only by quoting the text in full, but also by labeling the whole of his sixteen books with a title far better suited to Eutropius's subject, Rome, than to his own, Italy.

In keeping with the faithful copy, Paul tailored his amplifications in such a way as to avoid modifying the Eutropian core. The beginning of every book except the first, and the ending of six, are unaltered. Book VIII is reproduced intact. Many additions are very short, and few cover as much as a page of the latest edition. Insertions with specifically Christian content

---

[67] Jordanes *Rom.*, e.g. ¶¶ 91, 94, 95, 99, 106, 133, 164, 174, 179. On the nonsectarian quality of Eutropius, above, ch. I n. 18. The obtrusive date in the prologue is the conventional one of the fall of Troy (ed. Crivellucci, p. 6 line 11 to p. 7 line 2). In Eutropius ch. 1, Paul emends the date with reference to Jerome and supplements it with a biblical hitching post: "sive, ut placet Orosio, .CCCCIIII., ante sex annos, quam decem tribus Israel a Sennacherib, rege Chaldeorum, transferrentur in montes Medorum" (p. 10). The other insertions before Christ: *H.R.* 1.3, 5, 6, 7, 8 (bis), 13, 20; 2.9, 14, 21, 26, 27; 3.7, 18; 4.5, 17, 27; 5.3, 9.

[68] Sestan, "Qualque aspetti," pp. 58, 56-57.

[69] That was why Paul gave it to Adalperga; cf. above, ch. I n. 14 (two translations into Greek; well represented in Latin ms collections).

are limited to the birth and passion of Jesus Christ and the martyrdom of Sts. Peter and Paul. As just said, they and the antecedent items of Jewish history were meant to furnish chronological guidance rather than to convey information. Paul's objective, according to the dedication, was to relieve Eutropius of the curse of excessive brevity. Although many sources are used, the recurrent ones are Jerome's *Chronicle*, mainly for sacred chronology; the anonymous late-fourth-century *Epitome de Caesaribus* for the emperors; and, most of all, Orosius.[70]

Besides borrowing information, Paul seems to have selected passages in such a way as to give a recognizably Orosian coloring to the *Breviary*, baptizing it in spirit rather than substance. Eutropius, without going out of his way to distort the record, had set out a positive account of Roman expansion, whereas Orosius (who used Eutropius) stressed the costs of imperialism to conqueror and victim alike. Orosian accounts of defeats and assorted horrors are numerous among Paul's additions. It is specified that the Carthaginians excised Regulus's eyelids preparatory to torturing him to death; the cruelty of Sulla is heightened; a gladiators' rebellion inflicts terrible damage in the region of the future principality of Benevento. Paul looks ahead to the circumstances of Alboin's murder in the *H.L.* when he picks up Orosius's reference to a Balkan people so savage that they turned the skulls of their enemies into drinking cups. There is more in the same vein, including several passages about women that will be examined shortly. In the Orosian spirit, which saw improvement in history after Christ was born a Roman subject, Paul's expansions are fewer for the age of the emperors.[71]

Various personalities have anecdotes added to their entries. Sestan considered it exceptionally odd that Philip the Arab and his son, whom Christian tradition commemorated (however wrongly) as the first Christian emperors, are singled out only for the son's lifelong abstention from laughter (an addition from the *Epitome*). Paul, in this case, saw to it that an expansion of the Eutropian core should not clash with Eutropius's religion.[72] Although a few details augment the lines about Pompey, and a long eulogy out of the *Epitome* those about Augustus, the most noteworthy expansion of a biography concerns Julius Caesar. Late antiquity preferred to deplore Caesar as a conqueror than to recommend him as a model; Eutropius, for one, carefully measured the attention paid to Caesar, and Jordanes simply

[70] Paul's additions are very visible in Droysen's edition, as footnotes to Eutropius; in Crivellucci's they are less obtrusive, in angle brackets within the text. The Christian additions: *H.R.* 7.8, 11, 15.

[71] *H.R.* 2.25, 5.8, 6.10; the imperial period occupies books VII-X.

[72] Sestan, "Qualque aspetti," p. 63. Eutropius even skips Constantine becoming a Christian, and Paul leaves the blank.

passed him by. With Paul, the tide of Caesar's popularity had turned. Out of Orosius, long extracts are added about his Gallic and Alexandrian wars, along with a flattering eulogy out of the rarely used Solinus. The Alexandrian extract shows that Caesar's fame with Paul came not just from being an Italian who had subjected the lands where the Franks now dwelt, but from prowess itself. Paul was Christian enough to subscribe to the Orosian horror of war, but Augustine's choice of Caesar to exemplify the reprehensible lust for domination seems to have lost its attraction. In the court circle of Charlemagne, the nickname "Julius" would be borne by his son, Pepin of Italy.[73]

In analyzing the additions to Eutropius, Sestan was most struck by those that he believed were meant to appeal to feminine taste, primarily Adalperga's. Such passages in Paul's writings are by no means confined to the *Historia Romana*. Women, especially bad ones, are conspicuous in the H.L., and even his *libellus* on the bishops of Metz is decorated with epitaphs of Carolingian ladies.[74] The taste for history in which women play a part may have been as much Paul's own, or the wider public's, as Adalperga's.

The stories in question are more random than Sestan thought. A Sabine girl turns up in order to explicate a common bridal acclamation; Tarpeia has more to do with the topography of Rome than with treason; a young lady traveling to Apulia earns mention from being curiously killed by lightning. Women are only passively relevant to Maxentius's licentiousness and to Mithridates's poisoning of his harem; almost the same is true of the Spanish captive who occasions Scipio's gallantry in a famous story.[75] Female initiatives meet with unfailing disapproval: Cleopatra hopes to save herself by trying to add Augustus to her long chain of seductions, but to no avail; with feminine folly, the wife of the last Carthaginian ruler hurls her children and herself into a pyre; feminine folly again accounts for suicidal conduct, this time by the women of the Cimbri and Teutons.[76] What women do in all these passages may be less noteworthy or unique than that the female presence in Eutropius is enlarged.

Another set of additions concerns places and peoples. Samnium and its

[73] Pompey, H.R. 6.14, 19; eulogy of Augustus, 7.10; Caesar, wars, 6.17, 22 (omitting minor insertions), eulogy, 6.25. Augustine on Caesar, *Civ. Dei* 5.12. For another fifth-century detractor, see Fulgentius *De aetatibus mundi et hominis* 11 (published among the works of Fulgentius the mythographer, ed. Rudolf Helm, Leipzig 1898, despite doubt about the attribution; also see *Fulgentius the Mythographer*, tr. Leslie George Whitbread, n.p. 1971. The date of the tract might be ca. 460). On Pepin of Italy as "Julius," see Fleckenstein, "Karl der Grosse und sein Hof," pp. 43-44.

[74] Sestan, "Qualque aspetti," pp. 56-57.

[75] Respectively, H.R. 1.2 (the Sabine girl and Tarpeia), 4.27, 10.4, 6.12, 3.15. On death by lightning as a form of heroization, see Cerfaux and Tondriau, *Culte des souverains*, p. 107.

[76] Respectively, H.R. 7.7, 4.2, 5.2.

inhabitants are considered the ancient counterpart of Arichis's duchy and subjects. Hence the Roman wars against the Samnites receive special attention, with sympathy for the losers as well as a characterization of their presumably enduring flaws. The foundation of Benevento is also mentioned. For similar reasons, Paul took an interest in the Gauls and Ligurians—considered synonymous—who had once populated the North Italian plain. They are credited, among other things, with the building of Pavia and with many successes against the Romans. The *H.L.* confirms that Paul regarded these Cisalpine Gauls as precursors of the Lombards.[77] Among the Italian places dear to him, only Frioul is left out until the non-Eutropian books, perhaps for lack of opportunity to mention it.

Sestan found no way to classify all of Paul's expansions. In general, Paul seemed to him to disregard Central Italy, to manifest no solidarity with Germans and other northern barbarians, to refer to many fewer great authors than occur in Jerome's *Chronicle* (which contributed the information he has), and to reveal a taste for marvels and portents.[78] Although the last of these might result from planning rather than personal fancy, Sestan's observations are basically correct. Paul's additions to the *Breviary* establish several features of his thinking that the later writings confirm, but no strong pattern emerges. In Christian fashion, he mixed in enough Orosius to temper the Eutropian note of continual Roman triumph. This did not prevent him from also restoring heroic stature to Julius Caesar. In small ways, Paul enhanced the appeal of the *Breviary* to his Beneventan patrons without altering the substance of what had long been a classic.

The final part of the *Historia Romana*—Paul's six-book continuation from 364 to 552—not only develops the Italian orientation foreshadowed in the prelude to book I, but also, as we shall see, exemplifies the style of narrative that would reappear in the *H.L.* Paul's originality in these books can obviously not be measured by the provision of firsthand information. In a handful of cases, Paul reports facts that seem accurate and for which he is the sole authority, presumably on the basis of writings since lost.[79] For much the most part, however, Paul used a wide array of known sources, sometimes with significant departures from the model. What he made of them was a story that no Westerner had ever told before. Although existing chronicles reported fifth- and sixth-century events, only the *Romana* of Jor-

---

[77] Samnium, *H.R.* 2.8-9, 16; northern Italy, 3.2, 6, 9 (a battle with Hannibal near Ticinum), 4.2-4; cf. *H.L.* 2.23. In the latter, the reference to Gauls invading Italy might anticipate the Franks as well.

[78] Respectively, Sestan, "Qualque aspetti," pp. 71-72, 75, 72, 68.

[79] *H.R.* 12.7 (ed. Crivellucci, p. 167, Greek source?), 14.19 (p. 203, n. 82 below), 15.4 (pp. 208-209, Greek source?), 15.7 (p. 213 lines 1-2).

danes, with its obviously Constantinopolitan outlook, supplied a consecutive account in Latin of what we call "the decline and fall of the Roman Empire." Paul had the choice of stringing Jordanes after Eutropius, but took an independent course. Gregory of Tours had given no thought to what happened to the Empire; Bede had been more interested in the subject, but from a remote, provincial perspective. Paul, about two-thirds through the eighth century, was the first Westerner to attempt an interpretation of the end of the Empire and the establishment of the successor-kingdoms. He elaborated the theme in a more personal manner than is generally acknowledged.

The major departure of the *Historia Romana* from Eutropius, as observed before, is that Paul's scope is not Rome. At the beginning of book XVI (the last), he stated that, because the empire of the city of Rome ended in the previous book, it seemed appropriate to him to change the dating from the Roman era to the years of the Lord's Incarnation.[80] The *Romana* of Jordanes, whose endpoint falls less than a year before Paul's, carries on emperor by emperor, in a sequence that, from Augustus, could be easily prolonged to the last Byzantine *basileus*. Jordanes, without sounding like Eutropius, resembled him and late Roman historians generally, by narrating imperial history as serial biography. Paul started his continuation in this manner but soon broke away. On the model of Jerome and Orosius, he numbered the emperors; at the death of Honorius (423), when the numbered sequence switches to Constantinople, he lost interest in the principals and said little, besides, about the unnumbered Western emperors.[81] From the middle of book XIII to the end of XV, the Roman Empire is incidental to a narrative better called (after Thomas Hodgkin's multivolume work) "Italy and Her Invaders." If, in the final book, the emperors Anastasius, Justin, and Justinian win attention, it is as players in Italian politics and surely not, in Justinian's case, for bringing about a Roman restoration. Long before ending the *Historia Romana*, Paul regained the Italian track on which, with the two-faced Janus, he had begun.

The dominant preoccupation of a history is often best revealed by its

---

[80] *H.R.* 16.1: "Cessante iam Romanae urbis imperio utilius aptiusque mihi videtur ab annis dominicae incarnationis supputationis lineam deducere, quo facilius quid quo tempore actum sit possit agnosci." The idea of A.D. reckoning must come from Bede: it was hardly common in Italy; the papal chancery adopted it only toward 970. *H.R.* 16 contains three A.D. dates. Although *H.R.* 15 ends with Zeno's death (491), Paul's reference to the end of Rome's empire reaches back to 15.10, where Jordanes's statement about 476 is recorded.

[81] Emperors were not officially numbered, and many unnumbered lists exist (MGH AA. XIII, 415-37). Paul chose to follow Orosius as far as he went. Different numbering is found in the chronicles of Prosper and his continuator, Victor of Tunnuna, as well as in Cassiodorus; no numbers in Jordanes, Isidore, and Bede.

most fictional pages. In the case of the *Historia Romana*, the fictions are concentrated in books XIV and XV, amplifying the theme of the invasions of Italy.

The remarkably short frame of book XIV is the seven-year reign (450-57) of Marcian, successor of Theodosius II. Paul had no interest in Marcian (a hero to Jordanes) except for saying, wrongly, that he died the victim of a palace conspiracy.[82] The real subject is Attila's devastation of North Italy and Gaiserich's attack on Rome and points south, together with the interventions of Pope Leo the Great to prevent both invaders from causing greater damage. Notably clarifying Jordanes (the source), Paul spelled out how Aëtius's fears of Visigothic strength after their joint victory over the Huns in Gaul had the unintentional result of unleashing Attila upon Italy. Paul stretched the ensuing siege of Aquileia to three years (exactly the same span as Theodoric's siege of Ravenna and Alboin's of Pavia), and he added the tale of an Aquileian lady appropriately called Digna who, in preference to Hunnish captivity, chose to drown herself in the moat lying conveniently beneath her window.[83] Besides making Attila's invasion memorable, Digna's choice of death over dishonor is an inverted anticipation of the treason in the *H.L.* of Romilda, who betrayed nearby Frioul to the Hunlike Avars out of lust for their king.[84] By a series of city names and additional provinces, Paul filled out Jordanes's sketchier catalogues of places afflicted by Hunnish devastation. His final contribution to the saga of Attila involves the latter's interview with Leo the Great: the Hun agreed to everything not because won by the pope's eloquence, but because threatened

[82] H.R. 14.19, "facta suorum conspiratione peremptus est" (ed. Crivellucci, p. 203). For the correct account, see Croke, "Date and Circumstances." Several rulers in the *H.L.* die in more suspicious circumstances than otherwise attested; e.g. Childebert II, *H.L.* 4.11. Jordanes on Marcian, *Romana* ¶¶ 332-33: Might Paul have wished to undercut his effusive praise? Paul's alteration has no obvious motive. Possibly, it distantly influenced Zonaras's twelfth-century story of a conspiracy; see Crivellucci's note to this passage.

[83] H.R. 14.8-10. The sieges of Ravenna (*H.R.* 15.18) and Pavia (*H.L.* 2.27).

[84] H.R. 14.10. Romilda, *H.L.* 4.37. Digna prompts the observation that suicide to escape rape has a place in Christian tradition; see Michel, "Suicide." Ladies who drowned themselves were celebrated as martyrs at Antioch: Domnina and her daughters (Eusebius *H.E.* 8.12. 3-4) and Pelagia (Ambrose *De virginibus* 3.32-34). Also see Procopius *Wars* 2.8.35: ladies drowning in the Orontes in 540 to escape indignities at the hands of the Persians. According to Joannes Malalas *Chron.* 11, ed. Dindorff, p. 277, the emperor Trajan, when at Antioch, readied a furnace and invited Christians who so desired to throw themselves into it; many became martyrs in this way, including St. Drosina and other virgins (here, no danger of rape is mentioned). A more credible martyr-suicide by fire is Apollonia, an aged virgin of Alexandria, whose end is related by Eusebius, *H.E.* 6.41.7. Eusebius also reports a case in Rome clearly modeled on that of Lucretia, with Maxentius (soon to fall before Constantine at the Milvian Bridge) in the role of Tarquinius Superbus (*H.E.* 8.14.16-17). The three stories from Eusebius's *H.E.* are in the Latin translation of Rufinus, ed. Mommsen, *Eusebius Werke* II part 2, Die griechische christlicher Schriftsteller (Leipzig 1908), pp. 603, 767-79, 787. Much of this information was supplied by Dr. Ian McDougall, of the *Dictionary of Old English*, University of Toronto, for whose help I am very grateful.

with death by an old man with a drawn sword seen only by him—obviously St. Peter.[85] In Paul's portrayal, the Italian portion of Attila's Western campaign is not, as normally, a damaging epilogue, but the main event.

We are then shown that the Hunnic ravaging of the North was not isolated. Although Rome was saved from Attila by the intervention of St. Peter, it did not escape the seaborne attack of Gaiserich, accompanied by Moors as well as Vandals. Paul's addition to this sack of 455 is a spoliation of the area south of Rome. His source of inspiration was an apocryphal tale about Paulinus of Nola, recorded in Gregory the Great's *Dialogues*, but this story serves as an anchor for Paul's imaginative expansion rather than as its basis. A Vandal descent merely on Rome would not have been nearly so effective in complementing Attila's wasting of the North as was a further destructive foray into the lands of the future Duchy of Benevento.[86]

By boldly amplifying scrappy facts, Paul was as eloquent as any modern historian in expressing the idea that barbarian invasions inaugurated a new era. The last clear-cut Roman success he portrays occurs in book XIII, brought about on Honorius's behalf by Count Constantius;[87] by book XIV, as we have seen, the initiative has passed out of Roman hands, except for Pope Leo and the force he spoke for; and, in XV, the Western Empire falls, decades after its effectiveness had ceased. Paul's personal contribution to this last act was to turn Odoacer's coup d'état into a conquest comparable to the invasions of Attila and Gaiserich, and prepared by a gathering of ferocious barbarians in Pannonia. Again, Paul had authorities to uphold this version of the events. Jordanes spoke of Odoacer "invading" Italy supported by hordes of tribesmen; he probably meant *invadere* in the sense of "to seize (from within, as by coup d'état)." Besides, Eugippius's *Life of St. Severinus of Noricum* relates an interview between Odoacer and the saint, which Paul took the liberty of situating during the (fictional) march of Odoacer's forces from Pannonia to Italy.[88] All in all, the underpinnings for "Odoacer's barbarian conquest of Italy" were less flimsy than those for the lady Digna and the Vandal plunder of the Campania.

No sooner had Odoacer swept away the anachronism of Roman sover-

[85] *H.R.* 14.11-12. The basic source for Leo's interview with Attila is Prosper *Epitoma Chronicon* 1367, ed. Mommsen, MGH AA. IX, 482 ("ita summi sacerdotis praesentia rex gavisus est" that he withdrew). In Paul's version, the pope is overshadowed by the apparition.

[86] *H.R.* 14.16-19. Gaiserich's sack of Rome is famous, but there was no simultaneous Vandal foray to the south. The legend about Paulinus: Gregory the Great *Dial.* 3.1; his account, presupposing one of the various Vandal coastal raids on Italy, calls for Paulinus to outlive his death in 431.

[87] *H.R.* 13.1-3.

[88] *H.R.* 15.8. Jordanes *Rom.* ¶ 239 ("Odoacer . . . turbis munitus Italiam invasit"). *Regnum* or *imperium invadere* was a standard phrase for a usurpation, or "to seize power," as in Jerome *Chron.*, ed. Helm, p. 228, "Constantinus . . . regnum invasit." Paul knew the idiom: *H.R.* 15.1. Eugippius *Vita s. Severini* 7, ed. Hermann Saupe, MGH AA. I part 2, p. 11.

355

eignty in Italy than Paul's attention veered to the Balkans, in order to trace the next conqueror, Theodoric the Ostrogoth. He even managed to anticipate Theodoric's invasion by playing on the ambiguity of "the city"— Rome or Constantinople—and thus inventing a preliminary Ostrogothic raid into central Italy.[89] After Theodoric prevailed, he in turn proved less interesting in book XVI than the circumstances leading to the next conquest, by the Byzantine generals Belisarius and Narses. No reader of Paul's *Historia Romana* can retain the belief that there was anything novel about the invasion of Italy by the Lombards, or that they had less right to be in the peninsula than anyone else.

Paul, however, did not identify himself primarily with the nationality of his ancestors. A special value of the *Historia Romana* resides in documenting the priority of Italy in his thinking. Paul was not alone in thinking of Italy in this way. As Peter Classen has shown, the idea that Italy was a unit was unaffected by the Lombard invasion and the long coexistence within it of Byzantine and Lombard territories.[90] (One is reminded of the persistence in Bede of the idea that Britain remained one despite the heterogeneity of its residents.) For Paul's purposes, geography underlay the community of his Lombard audience with the historical personages about whom he discoursed—Aeneas, Romulus, the Scipios, Theodosius I, Leo the Great, Theodoric, and many others, including the Cisalpine Gauls. His attitude did not change when he went on to write about the Lombards themselves.

On a rapid reading, the features of Paul's continuation of Eutropius that stand out are the passages concerning the Huns and Vandals, Odoacer and the Ostrogoths, that are marked by his personal touch. By gradually detaching the narrative from the Roman emperors, Paul effectively provincialized his subject: Italy remained, broken from its imperial past by successive invasions whose intensity and frequency are stressed. Yet our grasp of Paul's historical vision owes more to comparisons of his account with its sources than to explicit signals from him, which no effort has yet been made to detect. He remained true to Eutropius in aligning a succession of facts as though they illustrated a tale already familiar to the audience. The difference is that, in his six-book complement, he was the pioneer who gave Eutropian shape to events that no Westerner had yet interpreted. Here, in the original part of his first history, Paul implemented the complex narrative method that, with modifications, he used in the later ones. His method merits separate attention.

---

[89] H.R. 15.6: a raid by the forces of Theodoric Strabo "usque ad quartum Urbis miliarium . . . , nulli tamen Romanorum noxius"; they returned to Illyricum. The source is Jordanes *Rom.* ¶ 346, but readers of Paul would have been hard put to recognize *urbs* as Constantinople.

[90] Classen, "Italien zwischen Byzanz und dem Frankenreich," pp. 85-115 (texts illustrating the concept of Italy as a unit, pp. 111-14).

4. Narrative Continuity in the Original Books of the *Historia Romana*

Paul's brief descriptions of how his continuation of Eutropius was conceived do not go very far. By his account, the six *libelli* were drawn "from the statements of the ancients in my own style [and are] scarcely different from the foregoing [ten books]"; they were "woven together . . . from various authorities in [my] own style."[91] Once past the copy of Eutropius, the reader would encounter a different manner of writing, but he might rest assured that the contents came from the *maiores* (we would say "primary sources") and that a close resemblance to Eutropius was retained. Paul made no allowance for being novel in any other respect than style. Yet, as has just been seen, books XI-XVI differ markedly, on occasion, from the sources on which they are based. Even Paul's general interpretation of the age, in playing down the Empire well before 476 and in emphasizing foreign invasions, more closely resembles what is found in our manuals than any authority he could have read.

Paul's originality, though sometimes obtrusive, has been largely unrecognized. Hans Droysen, editor of the *Romana*, argued that, for the last books, Paul must have used a single lost work similar to Eutropius's *Breviary*. An author who relied as heavily as he did on direct quotation in books I-X could not, Droysen believed, be responsible for the liberties taken from book XI onward with Jordanes and other sources.[92] Georg Waitz made short work of the hypothesis of a lost source, but he spoke of Paul's initiatives only in the negative terms of "chronological and factual errors brought about by careless use of sources [and] false combinations." Waitz agreed with Wilhelm Oechsli that Paul, to his discredit, had been uncritical and had rashly joined facts that should have been kept apart. These defects, Waitz pointed out, also characterized his use of sources in the *H. L.*: "Carelessness of various kinds, misunderstandings [and] chronological errors are demonstrable right down to [the reports of] his own age"; in trying to solve the problem of extracting a coherent narrative out of varied material, Paul's process of compilation was marked in both histories by somewhat arbitrary combinations as well as by retouchings and, here and there, expansions.[93]

---

[91] *H. R. praef.*: "Ego deinceps meo ex maiorum dictis stilo subsecutus sex in libellis, superioribus, in quantum potui, haud dissimilibus, usque ad Iustiniani Augusti tempora perveni" (ed. Crivellucci, p. 4); "Hucusque historiam Eutropius composuit . . . ; deinceps quae secuntur idem Paulus ex diversis auctoribus proprio stilo contexuit" (pp. 149-50). The second passage seems influenced by Jerome's transition from Eusebius's *Chron.* to his continuation (ed. Helm, p. 231).

[92] Droysen, "Zusammensetzung der *Historia Romana*" (still a useful study).

[93] Waitz, review of MGH AA. II, pp. 596, 599. He criticized Droysen for italicizing passages as though Paul copied them verbatim when he did not (p. 594).

The esteem Paul was denied in such negative appraisals was presumably offset by his being absolved of ever consciously saying something untrue. Waitz pointed out, rather stiffly, that no one had yet accused Paul of falsification, the implication being that no one should start doing so. To avoid the slightest hint of intentional invention, even the lady Digna, or Paul's startling allegation that the (calamitous) expedition of Basiliscus against Vandal Carthage was a success, had to be ascribed to "carelessness" or another venial sin. Rashly combining sources was judged to be more creditable than the composition of deliberate fiction.[94]

Such views have tended to inhibit study of the novel elements in the *Historia Romana*. Yet there is no reason to fear that Paul will suffer from being allowed to be conscious of what he was doing. The idea of a dazed Paul vaguely unaware of his faulty methods does not even have the lady Digna's compensatory virtue of being *ben trovato*. Paul's continuation of Eutropius is remarkably perceptive, as we have seen. There is more of him in it than he confessed to when modestly saying that he had imposed a homogeneous manner of expression upon a variety of authorities. The scale and extent of what he did repays examination.

Paul learned much from Eutropius and retained books of the same length, but he made no attempt to structure his continuation in precisely the same way. The ten books of the *Breviary* embody a periodization of Roman history closely corresponding to that of our multivolume equivalents; each division is remarkably self-contained.[95] Paul's approach, contrary to Eutropius's, was to establish conspicuous bridges between his books. Theodosius I and the usurper Maximus lead from book XI to XII; Honorius and another usurper draw together XII and XIII, Valentinian III and Gaiserich the next pair; the somber book XIV, covering a mere seven years, is connected to XV by Gaiserich again and, very artificially, by the short-lived emperor Avitus; Theodoric the Ostrogoth and Bishop Epiphanius of Pavia (whose *Life* by Ennodius is a major source) furnish the links between XV and XVI; and, at the end, Justinian, St. Benedict, the Lombards, and their leader, Alboin, are well established as bridges to Paul's next continuation

[94] *Ibid.* p. 596 (forgery). For the lady Digna, n. 84 above. Basiliscus, *H.R.* 15.2. Crivellucci (pp. 206-207) is puzzled about how Paul went wrong. Finding a motive for deliberate alteration is not easy.

[95] Eutropius *Breviarium* 1: founding of Rome through its capture by the Gauls and their repulse; 2: to the end of the First Punic War; 3: to the end of the Second Punic War; 4: from the Macedonian War to the Jugurthine; 5: from the invasion of the Cimbri and Teutones to the supremacy of Sulla; 6: from Sulla to the assassination of Caesar; 7: from the advent of Augustus to the end of Domitian, i.e. the Julio-Claudians and Flavians; 8: Nerva through Alexander Severus, i.e. the Antonines; 9: Maximinus to the retirement of Diocletian, i.e. the soldier-emperors; 10: from Diocletian's successors through Jovian, i.e. the Constantinian dynasty.

358

whenever he should happen to supply it. Though properly concluded, the *Historia Romana* ends with thirteen years still to run in Justinian's reign.

These links counteracting the emphatic formal divisions in the *Historia Romana* imply a radical change in the relationship of chronology to books. Book XI, from the advent of Valentinian I to the overthrow and death of his son, Gratian, retains a certain dynastic homogeneity of the Eutropian kind, but by the end of book XII, which separates one part of Honorius's reign from the next, it becomes obvious that Paul has abandoned the co-incidence of books with historical periods. Even its retention in book XI is more apparent than real. The span from Valentinian I to Gratian could not have been an epoch to the author who was aware of the dynasty continuing in Gratian's brother, Valentinian II, and who deliberately split the crucial reign of Theodosius I between books XI and XII.[96] In other words, Paul ceased to coordinate books with the chronological articulation of the narrative as soon as he began to extend the *Breviary*. By bridging the book divisions, he instituted a purely linear chronology, lacking any significantly periodic subdivisions.

Paul's detachment of book divisions from periods was akin to his insertion into Eutropius of hitching posts from sacred chronology. His readers, unlike many ancient and modern ones, were presumably not instructed in the epochs of Roman history, but they were equipped and familiar with universal chronicles. Paul could take it for granted that, as soon as the Eutropian books were left behind, these handbooks of dates—Bede's was the latest to become available—would continue to satisfy the readers' need, if any, for a rigid sequence of events.[97] His own task was to supply a narrative whose coherence had a more ambitious basis than chronology. In any case, there was no agreed-upon periodization of the years 364-552 for him to conform to. He was forced to break new ground.

For us, however, it is no easy matter to determine Paul's alternative basis of coherence. Aside from the length of the books, he most closely agrees with Eutropius in composing a narrative of discontinuous, chapter-length segments. The reader advances from one autonomous chapter, or even paragraph, to the next and rarely finds any overt effort made to ease the transition. A chronicle like Jerome's, though similar, externally unifies the abrupt blocks of narrative by means of an uninterrupted succession of dates.[98] In Eutropius's *Breviary*, when originally composed, the effect of fragmentation was largely tempered by strong unifying elements that the

---

[96] Valentinian II, *H.R.* 12.3; Theodosius II, 11.14-16, 12.1-2, 4-8.

[97] Bede's *Chronicon maius* is much used by Paul from *H.R.* 13.5 to the end; see ed. Crivellucci, p. xxxviii. He also drew on Bede's *H.E.*

[98] Paul availed himself of an "external" element for the integration of a history in the *Gesta episcoporum Mettensium*—a sequence of bishops rather than of dates (below, § 5).

359

author did not need to spell out; Eutropius's focus was a living Rome: its era, its notorious conquests, its succession of emperors. The periods covered by each of the ten books had a unity of theme or dynasty that Eutropius had not had to devise. The readers he addressed were being reminded of what they vaguely knew already. Even in the years nearest to Eutropius's writing, and therefore hardest to periodize, book X ranged precisely from the first to the last Constantinian emperor, with only the isolated and conveniently short-lived Jovian as an unavoidable afterthought. Channeled by these extrinsic aids and by a subject matter narrowly limited to politics and war, the fragmentary chapters of the *Breviary* created the illusion of flowing narrative. The same effect could not long be achieved by a continuator.

Predictably, the further Paul advanced from the fourth century, the less Eutropian he seems to be except in the retention of books and in an increasingly obtrusive fragmentation of the story. For example, the part of Honorius's reign contained in book XII is formed of a sequence of six virtually self-contained calamities: chapter 10, Gildo's rebellion; chapter 11, the treasonable collusion of Rufinus and Stilicho with barbarians (not self-contained because Stilicho's fate is put off); chapter 12, the invasion of Radagaisus; chapters 13-15, the Visigoths from Alaric's entrance into Italy to Wallia; chapter 16, the end of Stilicho; chapter 17, out of Britain, the usurpation of Constantine.[99] Translated into the chronology of our manuals, the six calamities trace a zigzag course—397-98, 395, 405, 402-15, 408, 407-409—but Paul did not provide dates or believe that his readers begrudged him some flexibility in this respect. In the Eutropian manner, his chapters concerning Honorius are supposed to be selected illustrations of the reign, but what they look like is an accumulation of great, yet miscellaneous, misfortunes. For this puzzling character, the course of events is partly at fault. A crumbling empire, assertive churchmen, and barbarians who occupied provinces were facts of a kind that Eutropius had been spared. The device Jordanes had resorted to in his *Romana* to integrate the kaleidoscopic events of the fifth century was to center his account on the emperors of Constantinople. This option was not available to Paul in Lombard Italy. Nevertheless, he was too inventive an author to have lost control of his material so much that he would take "dramatic and picturesque events" and string them together into a sequence "without really digesting them into a whole."[100]

What he appears to have done instead was to conceive of a scenario or plot for each book and to organize the fragmentary paragraphs or chapters in accordance with this tacit design. Since his procedure can be docu-

[99] Ed. Crivellucci, pp. 168-75.
[100] Sestan, "Storiografia dei Longobardi," p. 364; Dahn, "Paulus Diaconus," p. 247.

mented only by internal evidence, it is hardly possible to determine whether, for example, he worked out a detailed scheme as a preparatory step to composition or, more cursorily, devised a mental simplification of the events he was concerned with while familiarizing himself with the sources. However achieved, the existence of conscious plotting is implied by several traits: the uneven time span of the six books; their invariably bipartite structure, grouping information into contrasting or complementary halves; and the consistent occurrence near the end of each book of a "prophetic" passage announcing the theme of the next. The effects we have already seen Paul produce could not have been achieved by a random assemblage of borrowings; Droysen, though mistaken about a lost source, was on the right track in sensing the presence of a guiding hand. There had to have been a method by which Paul was able to take many accurate extracts from sources and to combine them harmoniously with material that, in Waitz's guarded words, he retouched and expanded.[101]

Paul did not carve the period from Valentinian I to the reconquest of Italy (364-552) into even segments. Books XII, XIII, and XV approximate a standard duration of thirty-three years; but book XIV, as we saw, involves only seven, whereas book XVI, the last, encompasses no fewer than sixty-two. (Book XI, to complete the tale, covers a shade less than two decades.)[102] A factor of eight separates the longest span from the shortest. Other considerations than chronology were applied in Paul's choice of events. Although precise dates are stated at infrequent intervals, passing time is continually implied by the phrases, already common in Eutropius, that connect each paragraph to the next: *eodem anno, interea, hoc anno, anno deinde sequenti, dum haec geruntur,* and many more. These transitions point insistently to a time relationship between the events reported, but that is merely their literary function; no precise track may be traced from the information they provide. The passage of time was allowed only a subordinate part in the ordering of Paul's story. Transitional phrases evoking chronological relationships are on the same plane as dramatic juxtapositions and literary patterning as devices controlling the narrative.

At three points, Paul leaned noticeably backward to retrieve information out of the past. In the first, the omission of dates allowed him to behave as though chronological order were not violated (this is the opening of book XIV): Marcian becomes emperor (450); Valentinian III makes peace with Gaiseric (442); Attila rules with his brother, whom he kills (444). By the end of the next chapter, the events move past 450, and the time sequence

---

[101] Droysen, as above, n. 92; Waitz, n. 93 above, p. 600.
[102] Time spans, H.R. 11: 364-83, 12: 383-410?, 13: 411-50, 14: 450-57, 15: 457-91, 16: 491-52.

is regained.[103] Paul evidently designed the narrative in such a way as to pick up Attila at an earlier stage of his career than 450, preparatory to having him join battle with Aëtius and the Goths in Gaul. His inconspicuous contrivance for doing so—possibly inspired by the opening of book III of Bede's *History*—is an editorial announcement right after Marcian's accession, that the years of Valentinian III were assigned to the reign of Marcian or of his (Eastern) predecessor. Behind this smoke screen, Paul backtracked to the treaty of 442, from which point the motion was again forward.[104] In book XV, Paul openly gave directions, once to explain from fourth-century events why there were two varieties of Goths ("It is now necessary to explain . . ."); the next time, uniquely, to advertise backward motion: "But so that it might be fully known why and whence [the Ostrogothic conquest of Italy] came about, it is necessary to return for a while to earlier matters." Despite the prominent introduction, no notice was given when the main time sequence was regained.[105] In order to introduce Theodoric and the Ostrogoths Paul departed from his practice of not overtly filling in background. The first book of the *H.L.* would, on a larger scale, perform the same retrospective task for the Lombards, preparatory to carrying forward the course of Italian events in book II.

As we saw, *Historia Romana* 14 portrays a devastation of North Italy by Attila that is paralleled, after a transitional passage, by Gaiserich's ravaging of the South. Bipartite structures of this kind recur in all six books. Normally, the transitional passage delimiting halves consists of a change of reign: Theodosius I dies and his sons succeed him; Honorius dies leaving Theodosius II as sole emperor; Theodoric the Ostrogoth dies and Justinian becomes emperor.[106] In book XI, the midpoint features the admission of the Goths into the Empire, the disaster at Adrianople, and the death of Valens, whereas in book XV a transition is effected from Odoacer to the Ostrogoths.[107]

Each half of a book has its thematic identity. In book XII, for example, the admirable exploits of Theodosius are balanced by a succession of calamities under Honorius. In book XIII, each half is itself bisected so that years of recovery alternate with years of disaster in an A-B-A-B pattern. Paul had

---

[103] *H.R.* 14.1 (Marcian's accession and Valentinian's peace), 2 (Attila), 3 (Attila's Western campaign, 451).

[104] *H.R.* 14.1, "Coeterum Valentiniani tempora huius vel superioris imperatoris curriculis adscribuntur." One suspects, but cannot pin down, a connection to a similar remark of Bede's in *H.E.* 3.1, ed. Plummer, I, 128.

[105] *H.R.* 15.6, "Exigit nunc locus dicere" (cf. *H.L.* 4.37, n. 251 below); 15.10, "Sed ut ad liquidum quam ob causam vel unde advenerit possit agnosci, necesse est aliquantisper ad superiora repedare." The main sequence is regained at 15.15.

[106] Respectively, *H.R.* 12.8-9, 13.8-9, 16.10-11.

[107] *H.R.* 11.10-11, 15.10-11.

a sense of the dramatic value of contrasts; the books have inner shape and tension.[108] Bipartite plans are a widespread phenomenon in narrative and often reappear in medieval literature.[109] They are common to all Paul's histories, including the *H. L.*

Paul made no secret of his intention to continue at some future time beyond the limit chosen for the *Historia Romana*, but the most precise anticipation of his plan occurs, without being drawn to our attention, near the end of book XVI. Delicately poised between Belisarius's partial conquest of Italy and Narses's completion of the task, there appears a conspicuous pause in the action:

In these same times, the most blessed father Benedict, after a period as a solitary, lived in the holy monastery at Cassino and, besides foreknowing the future, shone with amazing miracles.

This was also when the tribe of the Lombards, then a friend of the Roman people, lived in Pannonia under the royal rulership of Audoin. He fought at this time with Turisind, king of the Gepids, and gained the victory through Alboin, his youthful and energetic son. For Alboin personally sought out Turismund, Turisind's son, in the battle line and boldly attacked and killed him. In this way he cast the Gepids into confusion and gained the victory for his people.[110]

Paul wrote these lines as many as twenty years before setting to work on the *H. L.*, but two high points of its first book are foreshadowed. Alboin's youthful exploit was the start of his brilliant career, and St. Benedict's miracles are extolled soon afterward, not least in order to contrast Alboin's martial valor to authentically Christian heroism.[111] The prophetic St. Benedict, who, in Gregory the Great's famous account, foresaw the destruction of Monte Cassino by the Lombards, gave Paul an occasion to insert a synopsis of his next, yet-to-be-written installment.[112]

Book XVI is not alone in having a "prophetic" passage in near reach of its ending. The subject featured in earlier books is Britain. Paul's string of

---

[108] For the calamities in *H. R.* 12, n. 99 above. The pattern of *H. R.* 13: A, 1-3; B, 5-7; A, 9-12; B, 13-18. The eulogy of Honorius in 13.8 seems curious, but follows in the footsteps of Orosius *Hist.* 7.35.9, 37.11, 42.15-16.

[109] Clover, *Medieval Saga*, pp. 42-44.

[110] *H. R.* 16.20: "His ipsis apud Cassinum temporibus post solitariam vitam sancto degens cenobio stupendis beatissimus pater Benedictus nec minus futurorum praescius radiabat virtutibus.

"Hac etiam aetate gens Langobardorum amica tunc populi Romani apud Pannonias degebat, quibus in regni gubernaculo Audoin praeerat. Is eo tempore cum Turisendo Gepidarum rege confligens per Alboin suum filium iuvenem strenuum victoriam nanctus est. Denique inter ipsas Alboin sese acies Turismodum Turisendi regis filium appetentem alacriter aggressus extinxit perturbatisque hac occasione Gepidis suis victoriam peperit" (ed. Crivellucci, p. 236).

[111] *H. R.* 1.23, 26.

[112] Gregory the Great *Dial.* 2.17.

isolated entries concerning Britain, most of them without direct bearing on
Italy or even the Empire, is an oddity well designed to attract the notice of
attentive readers. For Britain, through its notorious association with St.
Benedict's biographer, Pope Gregory, was not so remote from Monte Cassino as geography suggests.[113] The apparent function of each entry is, as
type to antitype, to offer a capsule summary of the next book. The British
event anticipates in miniature what would take place on a large scale in the
heartland of the Empire (see Table 1). The British passages might be read
in isolation, as an extended, otherwise unparalleled strand of provincial
history. A more likely possibility is that each one is a thematic transition
to the next book, similar to the chronological bridges already observed.

Once attention is paid to formal features in the *Historia Romana*, Paul's
guiding hand gains firmer contours. Unlike Eutropius, he could not count
on a framework of agreed upon periods. The common ground between him
and his audience was the flowing, neutral time of universal chronicles,
which he took pains to affirm in the *Historia Romana* by counteracting the
tendency of divisions between books to coincide with meaningful moments. On the other hand, Paul was not a chronicler but a historian, engaging in the normal task of interpretation. The six time spans he selected,
the bipartite structure of each book, and the regular occurrence of "prophetic" passages all point to a systematic shaping of the material. But Paul
kept any explicit interpretative statement to himself. As a narrator, he invariably proceeded by indirection, demanding that his sense be arrived at
by attentive reading. The surface of his account is a patchwork of discon-

Table 1

Anticipation	Fulfillment
(H.R. 11.16) A usurper out of Britain kills Gratian	(H.R. 12) A plague of usurpers
(12.17) A usurper out of Britain leads unwittingly to the coexistence of Hispano-Romans with barbarians	(13) Romans and barbarians coexist
(13.17) The Saxons invited into Britain set the island aflame	(14) Attila and Gaiserich set Italy aflame
(14.14) St. Germanus in Britain triumphs by miracle over the Saxons	(15) Sts. Epiphanius and Severinus dominate the barbarians by moral force
(15.19) In Britain, Aurelius Ambrosianus overcomes the barbarians for a while	(16) Justinian gains Italy from the barbarians for a while

[113] For an interesting list of Anglo-Saxons at Monte Cassino in the eighth century (though
somewhat earlier than Paul's presumed time there), see Krüger, "Königskonversionen," p.
222.

nected fragments. How they join into something more eloquent than a chronicle of events may be grasped only by deliberate effort.

The previously examined book XIV, with its very short time span and unusual concentration of new material, is perhaps the most transparently structured of Paul's additions to the *Historia Romana*. Its subject, foreshadowed in the British passage of the previous book, was the Italian equivalent to Bede's *adventus Saxonum*. This compact theme, which we might call "The End of the Safety of the Western Empire," is elaborated in five symmetrically balanced groups of chapters (see Table 2). The two devastations, as noted before, owe much to Paul's creativity. It was by his doing, rather than by the testimony of authorities, that they gained a vivid resemblance to Bede's account of the Saxons.[114] The two-chapter entr'acte, composed of faithful source extracts, has special value for illustrating Paul's method. The immediate background is that Attila, scourge of Italy, duly died (ch. 13). As though to complement the near miracle of his death, but with scant relevance to anything else (and two decades out of place), we are told that Bishop Germanus of Auxerre went from Gaul to Britain to overcome heresy and procured the wondrous Hallelujah victory over the Saxons and Picts (ch. 14).[115] This brief, glowing vision of the next world leads directly into its demonic contrast: Valentinian III envied Aëtius, murdered him, thus ending the safety of the Western Empire, and was himself murdered in revenge (ch. 15). The devastation of Italy thereupon resumed. Symmetrical effects like these did not spring naturally from Paul's reading, still less from the muddle of events.

The final book of the *Historia Romana*—at sixty-one years the longest in duration of Paul's set—was laid out like book XIV in a pattern of two complementary stories punctuated by subsidiary paragraphs. Book XV ends with Theodoric in control of Italy and strengthening his position by diplomacy. Its British passage leads us to anticipate an Italian counterpart to the exploit of Ambrosius Aurelianus in mastering the Saxons but not permanently. Paul could count on its being known that, though Justinian over-

Table 2

    1. Chronological setting (Valentinian III, Gaiserich, accession of Marcian)

2-13. North Italy devastated by Attila

14-15. Entr'acte

16-18. South Italy devastated by Gaiserich's Vandals

    19. Chronological setting (Gaiserich, Avitus, death of Marcian)

---

[114] Above, nn. 82-89.

[115] Paul's chronological displacement of St. Germanus was, of course, anticipated by Bede, as above, ch. IV nn. 283-85.

came the Goths, the Lombards soon undid his conquest by establishing themselves in Italy. The scenario of book XVI is outlined in Table 3. There is nothing here comparable to the inventiveness of book XIV. The authorities, though paraphrased and combined in various ways, are faithfully rendered. Paul's interpretation of the events is also subtler and more complex.

The external simplicity of the two-part scheme may be arrived at only after reflection. Paul distracts us from it while shading and enriching it by many internal effects. The initial blurring results from a basically topical narrative that jumps from subject to subject. The first of the two story segments is composed of seven topics, none of which proceeds continuously for more than three paragraphs at a time. The emperor Anastasius, introduced in chapter 2, returns and dies in chapter 5; the praiseworthy Theodoric of chapter 4 re-emerges as the bad Theodoric of chapters 8-9, then becomes momentarily praiseworthy again in chapter 10 (on the basis of information displaced by many years), only to revert at once to wickedness that leads to his death;[116] the accession of a Catholic Vandal in Africa (ch. 7) terminates the persecutions previously described (chs. 3-4) but is wholly divorced from Belisarius's African conquest, to which no religious motives are assigned (ch. 14). By our standards of composition, Paul seems to be trying to make a topical account look chronological only to fail on both counts. Yet, when clarified by a scenario whose logic overrides the detailed course of events, his narrative gains firmness, as that of an author who proceeds by studied indirection.

Paul's obscurity urges the reader to keep asking himself what the story is, and rewards him by not blurring its edges to such an extent that the focus cannot be regained. Once the pattern of long story segments and transitional paragraphs is grasped, it is a comparatively simple task, but still a task, to transpose indirection into continuity. On a smaller scale, the reader is invited to hunt for significant juxtapositions and running subplots. It hardly seems accidental, for example, that Paul, after terminating the

Table 3

  1. Chronological setting (the Incarnation style will now replace the Roman era)
  2-9. Heresy and Catholicism contend
  10-11. Transition (Theodoric dies, Justinian becomes emperor)
  12-19. Byzantine conquest of Italy, first phase
  20. Pause (prophecy of Italy's future: St. Benedict and the Lombards)
  21-23. Conquest of Italy, concluding phase

[116] H.R. 16.8-9 are concerned with the years 519-24. Theodoric's praiseworthy action in 16.10 belongs ca. 507.

Western Empire in the middle of the previous book, delayed abandoning the Roman era until he could imply an association with the accession of a heretic, Anastasius, to the Roman imperial throne.[117]

As one block of events follows the other, the story of heresy contending with Catholicism is so structured that an opening alignment of heretic emperor, heretic Vandal king, and good Theodoric gives way to one of Catholic emperor, Catholic Vandal king, and wicked Theodoric. In an obvious contrast, two miraculous punishments of Arian Vandals in Africa are situated just before Theodoric's beneficent building of palaces in major Italian centers. As a further reinforcement of the message, the preceding chapter balances dark and light in exactly the same fashion. Paul well knew that it took more than Arianism to make a ruler bad (Rothari in the *H.L.* illustrates the point).[118] Although Catholics were persecuted and Theodoric even put Symmachus and Boëthius to death, the initial story segment is free of military activity, and contrasts with the segment involving Justinian, which relates not just abstract conquest, but many horrors of war, perpetrated by the imperial forces as well as by the Goths.[119] In order to underscore this difference, the transitional chapters draw attention, just before noting Theodoric's death, to his martial success against the Franks, and they associate Justinian's advent with aggressive ambitions: he immediately sent off Belisarius to triumph over the Persians. Since no sustained attention is given otherwise to Theodoric's foreign policy, still less to the Franks, the reference at this point to his military effectivenes seems best understood as a compact illustration of the security of Italy under him—a note of wry nostalgia to carry over into the era, however Catholic, of Justinian.

Book XVI is unusual for containing a gallery of popes and incidents of papal history. The earlier books refer only to Leo the Great; here, Paul included seven popes out of the possible ten. In the opening story segment, papal incidents provide general assistance to the course of the narrative. While the heretic Anastasius was emperor, Rome was bloodied by strife between the contending popes Laurence and Symmachus; Symmachus succored African Catholics; the envoys of Hormisdas were received badly by Anastasius and well by the Catholic Justin; John was imprisoned by Theodoric after an embassy to Constantinople on his behalf. The one point emphasized is that both Anastasius and Theodoric incurred the divine retribution of death as a consequence of their bad treatment of papal

---

[117] H.R. 16.1-2; cf. above, n. 80. Like consular, imperial, and royal years, A.D. dating is also a ruler list—that of God's governance on earth. This made it convenient for use by the Church amidst the many kings of England, in France in the waning days of the Merovingians, and by Paul in the circumstances he describes. The change in dating style is Paul's only first-person intervention in the H.R.

[118] H.R. 16.3-4. Rothari, H.L. 4.42, 45, 47; see below, nn. 243-45.

[119] Horrors of war, H.R. 16.16 (highly colored), 18, 22.

ambassadors.[120] In the second story segment, a much tighter relationship is suggested between the popes and Justinian's conquest of Italy. The Gothic king Theodahad aroused Justinian's anger by murdering the latter's protégée, Amalasuntha; he therefore sent Pope Agapitus to Constantinople to obtain the emperor's forgiveness. The pope on arrival found the court infected with Eutychian heresy. He succeeded in bringing Justinian back to orthodoxy and both excommunicated the patriarch Anthimus and had him exiled. Agapitus then died, without fulfilling his mission on Theodahad's behalf.[121] Once Rome was under imperial control, Belisarius, under orders, exiled Pope Silverius for refusing to rehabilitate the patriarch Anthimus; Silverius died in exile. For also refusing rehabilitation, his successor Vigilius was taken to Constantinople and exiled. The information comes from the *Liber pontificalis*, but the interweaving with the political situation was Paul's doing. His achievement in developing this subplot resides in associating the popes more closely with Justinian's Italian conquest, and in a more effectively ironic manner, than is generally equaled by modern narratives.

One thing learned from reading between the lines is that Paul's sympathies are elusive. "As soon as [Justinian] undertook the imperial prerogative, he bent his mind to restoring the condition of the state." Paul later refers to Justinian's *felicitas* and provides him with a notable eulogy in the *H.L.* He even manifests emphatic approval for Belisarius, whose exploits culminate in the presentation of a magnificent gold cross to St. Peter.[122] Yet Paul certainly does not invite us to applaud the conquest of Italy or the treatment of Popes Silverius and Vigilius. Pope Agapitus pursues heresy in Constantinople, but, by Paul's handling of the story, the reader is left wondering, in the end, whether the pope might not have done better to carry out the mission with which Theodahad had charged him. Theodoric, though "polluted by the Arian plague" and responsible for wicked acts, is conspicuously constructive and a sturdy defender of Italy. Paul's successive nuggets of fact are simply stated; taken individually, they suggest naïve approval or disapproval. What Paul thinks may be got at mainly by observing the subtleties of his narrative and taking them into account.

By Eutropian standards as well as ours, book XVI leaves much to be desired as a plain report of sixty-one years of Italian history. Paul's goal was something else; namely, to convey in an impersonally objective manner what was in fact a pioneering and individual interpretation of the events.

[120] H.R. 16.2, 3, 5, 6, 8-10.
[121] H.R. 16.12-13 (Agapitus), 18 (Silverius), 21 (Vigilius). Paul's source on papal matters: *Liber pontificalis* 53-61, ed. Duchesne, I, 260-98.
[122] H.R. 16.11 ("ad reparandum statum rei publicae"); *felicitas*, 16.23; account of the reign, *H.L.* 1.25. Belisarius: H.R. 16.19.

The hasty reader was offered little more than miscellaneous fragments of information succeeding each other in the temporal alignment of a chronicle. But someone willing to make the effort to meditate over the text would arrive soon enough at the ideas giving shape to these fragments and, if attentive enough, would grasp several layers of meaning. The scenario underlying book XVI stressed the ironies of Justinian's Western expansion: the perils Catholics formerly endured at the hands of Arians and Eutychians were slight by comparison with the horrors of war and hectoring of the popes that accompanied a conquest destined anyway not to be enduring. Report was intertwined with commentary, but only for the attentive reader.

In the *Historia Romana*, the basic unit of discourse is the book. The full work came into being in the same way as many medieval narratives: a prelude and continuation were given to a borrowed core, here consisting of Eutropius's *Breviary*.[123] Despite a scattering of additions to the latter, the larger assemblage does not appear to cohere on a more ambitious basis than Paul's focus on Italy and all its peoples, superseding Eutropius's Rome. From the point where Paul left Eutropius behind, he strove to carve the years into intervals delimiting incidents that lent themselves to the unobtrusive telling of intelligible and memorable stories. Book by book, he turned the past into dramatic units, each one a "present" that might be grasped as a whole.

The analyses given of books XIV and XVI might be repeated four more times without substantially adding to what has already been learned of Paul's narrative method. Not surprisingly, his interpretation of the age owes much less to the Byzantine Jordanes than to the testimony of the Christian Westerners Prosper of Aquitaine, Ennodius of Pavia, Eugippius, Bede, and the *Liber pontificalis*. More personal to Paul, as we have seen, was the dramatic role of barbarians in books XIV and XV. However plausible it may seem that Paul as a Lombard should have identified with earlier invaders of Italy, his words offer little support to such a view.[124] The figures to whom he ascribed heroism were not Attila, Odoacer, or Theodoric, but Pope Leo, Bishop Epiphanius, and St. Severinus, the churchmen whose moral force tamed the invaders' fury. (His view of the early Lombards would be no different.) What Paul saw and enhanced was the possibility of casting Attila's Huns and the others as a caesura between one epoch of Italian history and the next, in the manner of the Saxons in Bede's *History*. He was among the first to arrive at this idea and hardly the last to express it.

The six original books of the *Historia Romana* may be savored in their own right. They are as ambitious an exposition as the Carolingian age

---

[123] Cf. Clover, *Medieval Saga*, p. 40-41: sagas develop by the addition of ancestors before, progeny or other kin afterward.

[124] As observed by Sestan, "Qualque aspetti," pp. 74-75.

would witness of the theme "The End of the Ancient World and the Beginning of 'Our Times.'" Their special value, for purposes of studying Paul, resides in illustrating that he was a deliberate and painstaking narrator, shaping the sources he drew upon into new forms and more intent than Jordanes, Gregory of Tours, or Bede to lend an appearance of objectivity to his words. His first work embodies the devices that reappear, as we shall see, in all his future histories.

5. Minor Works: Gregory the Great and the Bishops of Metz

Owing to the brevity of Paul's northern sojourn, the *Deeds of the Bishops of Metz* is the one of his historical writings whose date may be most precisely approximated, whereas the time when he composed the *Life of Gregory the Great* is almost impossible to pin down. Presumably Paul wrote about Pope Gregory after becoming a monk of Monte Cassino. St. Benedict, its founder, owed his posthumous fame to the biography forming book II of Gregory's *Dialogues*; the connection between Monte Cassino, St. Benedict, and Pope Gregory best accounts for Paul's biography. Its normal assignment to the period after Paul's journey to the Frankish kingdom depends in part on an argument from silence. Paul's *Historia Romana* contains no borrowings from the *Histories* of Gregory of Tours, but Gregory was used in the Metz narrative and the H.L., and in the papal biography as well. [125] Since the one work unaffected by Gregory of Tours dates from before the northern voyage, it is a plausible inference that Paul first encountered Gregory's *Histories* in the Frankish kingdom and wrote the *Life of Gregory* only after coming back. [126] Yet the silence of the *Romana* is not perhaps quite so eloquent as this reasoning requires. Is there anything in Gregory's *Histories* that Paul would have had to copy into the *Romana* if the *Histories* had been available to him? [127] Until such passages are given a credible basis, the argument from silence remains indecisive. If one could assume that Paul knew Gregory of Tours before going to Francia, then the hypothesis that his biography of Pope Gregory preceded even the *Romana* might be preferred to the alternative that it was among his last works. Whatever its place in Paul's bibliography, it will occupy us before the *Bishops of Metz*.

[125] On the text of Gregory's *Hist.* used by Paul, see Krusch, "Handschriftlichen Grundlagen," pp. 707-708 (the *Vita s. Gregorii* is not taken specifically into account); it resembled C1 (called the "Carolingian edition," see above, ch. III n. 63).

[126] Dahn, *Paulus Diaconus*, p. 56; Manitius, *Gesch. d. lat. Lit.* I, 259; Brunhölzl, *Gesch. d. lat. Lit.* I, 262.

[127] Sestan, "Qualque aspetti," p. 52 n. 5, says that Paul had Bede, but not Gregory, when composing the H.R.; yet he made no attempt to explain what, if anything, Paul would have taken from the *Histories* if he had had Gregory's work on hand. Paul's familiarity with Bede at so early a date is itself surprising and attests to the presence of northern books at Monte Cassino (cf. above, n. 113).

Not surprisingly, the Whitby *Life of Gregory the Great* was unknown to Paul.[128] Regardless of whether he decided spontaneously to write about the pope or, as is more likely, responded to a request, he could regard himself as composing the first proper commemoration of Gregory, superseding the inadequate entry of the *Liber pontificalis*.[129] Paul's admiration for the great pope was no less than Bede's; the *H.L.* would accord him a starring role. A Lombard resident in the duchy of Benevento had reason to know what sort of pope he deplored; Gregory was the positive ideal. Paul conceived of his task as that of a redactor rather than of a searcher after new information. His main sources were the brief biographies of Pope Gregory embedded in the *Histories* of Gregory of Tours and Bede, supplemented by the *Liber pontificalis* and the pope's works.[130] The *Dialogues* and one letter supply the entirety of what Paul drew from Gregory himself. No search for biographical details was made through the fourteen books of letters.[131]

The *Life of the Very Blessed Gregory, Pope of the City of Rome* (as its full title runs) is one in a long chain of Latin hagiographies of notable bishops by identified authors. From the third-century *Life of St. Cyprian*, the series descends through the fifth, sixth, and seventh centuries, and keeps going. Paul, in the last part of the *Historia Romana*, drew heavily on Ennodius's *Life of St. Epiphanius of Pavia* and Eugippius's *Life of St. Severinus* (in the class, though not of a bishop). The Northumbrian examples of the *Lives of St. Cuthbert* and Stephen of Ripon's *Life of Wilfrid* have recently detained us.[132] Although these narratives vary in many respects, their common aim is to celebrate Christian leadership—pastorate in its many forms, a type of magistracy specific to the Church. They are more recognizable to modern eyes as biography than hagiographies often are.

Besides embodying the same literary patterning observed in the *Historia Romana*, Paul's account of Gregory the Great affords an almost too perfect illustration of his predilection for bipartite and symmetrical composition, as an outline shows (see Table 4). Various devices are used to integrate the two halves. A first-person discourse by Gregory on the delights of monastic life (I, 2) is complemented by his allocution to the people of Rome in time

[128] On the Whitby *Life*, see above, ch. IV nn. 107, 141-53. It was later combined with Paul's narrative and known only in this contaminated form (*PL* LXXV, 41-59) until properly published by H. Grisar, "Die Gregorbiographie des Paulus Diakonus in ihrer ursprünglicher Gestalt, nach italienischen Handschriften," *Zeitschrift für katholische Theologie* 11 (1887) 158-72. An improved text is given by Walter Stuhlfath, *Gregor I. der Grosse. Sein Leben bis zur seinen Wahl zum Papste nebst einer Untersuchung der ältesten Viten*, Heidelberger Abhandlungen zur mittleren und neueren Geschichte 39 (Heidelberg 1913), pp. 98-108.

[129] Cf. above, ch. IV n. 152.

[130] Gregory of Tours *Hist.* 10.1; Bede *H.E.* 2.1.

[131] Stuhlfath's edition (above, n. 128) systematically indicates the sources.

[132] Cf. ch. I n. 33. *H.R.* 15.3, 5, 9, 17-18 (*V. Epiphanii*); 15.8 (*V. Severini*). About St. Cuthbert and Wilfrid, see above, ch. IV nn. 110, 155-57, 208-41.

of plague (II, 2). The rescue of the patriarch of Constantinople from heresy (I, 3) anticipates the rescue of England from paganism (II, 3), which is further heralded by a reference to Pope Gregory's charitable concern for distant Christians, such as the monks of Mt. Sinai (II, 2). Again, half the account of the mission—the famous slave boys episode—is said to occur in the pre-pontificate period, as Bede specified, but the story is told among the English chapters in the later part of the *Life*. The reference to Gregory's posthumous achievements (such as the growth of the English Church) comes before, not after, his death, in the bridging position Paul normally reserved for prophecy.[133]

Further analysis would probably reveal additional refinements. Paul reconciles simplicity of manner, including a mainly linear chronology, with dramatic effects attained by parallelism, contrasts, juxtapositions, and very occasional manipulations of time.[134] By comparison with Paul's *Life*, Bede's account of Gregory sounds argumentative and hortatory, while that of Gregory of Tours accumulates concrete details, twists chronology, and features visual effects. It merits notice that the three finest historians of the early Middle Ages lavished attention on Gregory the Great. For anyone wishing to take the opportunity, this common topic offers a practical basis for drawing them together in a conversation about how to compose historical prose. On a less technical note, all three shared the inclination to see Pope Gregory primarily as exercising a pastorate, a model of episcopacy to his fellow bishops. Without doubting, still less contesting, the Petrine tradition, none of them attached to Gregory any reference to primacy or other attributes of the papal office. Bede's insistence that Gregory was the apostle of the English dwindled in Paul's hands into quiet praise for a job well done,

Table 4

   I. Before pontificate (chs. 1-9)
      1. Birth and life in the world (chs. 1-3)
      2. Ascetic-monastic life (chs. 4-6)
      3. In Papal service in Rome and Constantinople (chs. 7-9)
  II. Pontificate (chs. 10-17)
      1. Plague and election (chs. 10-11)
      2. Writings, health, pastorate, especially charity (chs. 12-14)
      3. English mission (chs. 15-16)
      4. Impact on the future and death (ch. 17)

[133] On "prophetic" passages, nn. 110-13.
[134] Cf. Stuhlfath, *Gregor der Grossen*, p. 76: "One may admire the smooth (*schlichte*) art with which Paul took the colored stones and fashioned a mosaic giving a united effect."

and the honorific *consul Dei*, from Bede's transcript of the papal epitaph, was avoided.[135]

If the *Life of Gregory the Great* is a particularly transparent example of Paul's narrative style, the *Deeds of the Bishops of Metz* is perhaps the subtlest of his works, and only ostensibly concerned with its advertised subject. The problems it raises reach into the history of the Carolingian dynasty and are peculiar to the circumstances of its composition. A full discussion would be out of place here.[136] Only enough will be said to suggest the importance of the work in Paul's bibliography and to illustrate his techniques.

While Paul was in the Frankish kingdom, Angilram, the incumbent bishop of Metz, commissioned him to write about his predecessors. The treatise is not long and survives in very few manuscripts. Its full title, *Brief Account of the Number or Series of Bishops Who Succeeded Each Other from the Very Beginning of Evangelization in the City of Metz*, is usually shortened to *Gesta episcoporum Mettensium*; it will be referred to here mainly as the Metz *Gesta*.[137] The account Gregory of Tours gave of his predecessors in closing the *Histories* is the first northern example of an episcopal history comparable to the Roman *Liber pontificalis*. Paul appears to have been uninfluenced by this part of Gregory's work; and though, as we shall see, the Roman *Liber* served him as a model, his use of it was very limited.[138]

As an episcopal history compared to others of the type, Paul's work is skeletal, unsatisfactory, and almost wholly untainted by archival and other local information. Yet it would be hasty to ascribe these flaws to poor research. Angilram was a court bishop, whom Charlemagne appointed to the key office of archchaplain in 784, the year in which Paul composed the Metz *Gesta*. The city of Metz had close associations with the Carolingian house. Arnulf, the sainted ancestor of the line (d. ca. 640), had been its bishop before withdrawing to the rigors of a hermitage. The longest segment of Paul's *Gesta* associates Arnulf with Charlemagne and with the latter's wife, Hildegard, the mother of his three legitimate sons. Hildegard had

---

[135] Paul *Vita s. Gregorii* 16: "deservedly should be called apostle by the English." In closing, Paul adverts to the same subject that exercised the Whitby monk, but in very different tones: "Iam vero utrum aliquibus vir iste tanti meriti miraculis claruerit, superfluo queritur, cum luce clarius constet, quod is qui virtutum signa suis meritis valuit aliis quoque Christo largiente adquirere, si exegisset opportunitas, facilius poterat hec etiam ipse promereri" (ed. Stuhlfath, p. 108). For *consul Dei*, Bede *H.E.* 2.1, ed. Plummer, I, 79.

[136] See Goffart, "Early Design."

[137] The standard edition, based on one ms and three early editions from lost mss, is ed. G. H. Pertz, MGH SS. (in folio) II, 261-68.

[138] On Gregory, above, ch. III n. 318. Paul is invariably credited with the first northern example of an episcopal history on the Roman model. The Metz *Gesta* cannot be disposed of so easily. Paul used the *Liber pontificalis* in one of the four main segments, not in his overall design. Besides, his *Gesta* had no influence: Hermann, "Zum Stande der Erforschung," pp. 134-35.

just died (April 783) and had been buried near the tomb of St. Arnulf (other members of the family were there, too). What Angilram asked of Paul was more than a local history. The Metz we are invited to contemplate is not a humdrum diocese, but the ecclesiastical symbol of the new Frankish régime.[139]

Paul's design of the *Gesta* superimposes two ideas. The continuity of the work comes from the list of thirty-seven bishops, most of them merely numbered names. There is no attempt to mask the dearth of information. Onto this very spare episcopal chronicle, four developed scenes are hung, each as a unit with its internal sense and plot. They concern Clement, the first bishop of Metz; Bishop Auctor at the time of Attila's Western campaign; St. Arnulf, the Carolingian ancestor; and finally Chrodegang, the immediate predecessor of Paul's patron. The utilization of the episcopal chronicle as a framework for separate stories is the mechanical aspect of Paul's plan. Simultaneously, he gives meaning to the entire treatise by relating each of the four scenes to a literary prototype. Scenes I, II, and III re-enact in the context of Metz the tales of the Creation, the Deluge, and the Blessing of Jacob, out of the book of Genesis, whereas the "modern" scene IV is couched in the characteristic formulas of the Roman *Liber pontificalis*. Only in this final section does Paul adopt the accents and subject matter of conventional episcopal history on the Roman model. The results may be set out in schematic form, as in Table 5.

In the closing lines, Paul reminded the incumbent bishop, Angilram, that his achievements would eventually be entered at this point.[140] He

Table 5

PROTOTYPE	GESTA EPISCOPORUM METTENSIUM
Creation	1. (Scene I) Apostolic foundation of the see of Metz
	2-12. Names of bishops
Deluge	13. (Scene II) Bishop Auctor and the church of St. Stephen weather the Hunnic storm
	14-28. Names of bishops
Isaac blesses Jacob	29. (Scene III) St. Arnulf and his descendants, the Carolingians
	30-36. Names of bishops
Liber pontificalis	37. (Scene IV) Bishop Chrodegang and Roman renewal at Metz

[139] See the study cited above, n. 136. The obituary year of Arnulf of Metz is unknown; the year generally given comes from Sigibert of Gembloux (d. 1111); see Krusch in MGH SRM II, 427.

[140] Ed. Pertz, p. 268 lines 33-35. The passage is reminiscent of Eutropius's dedication of the *Breviarium*.

showed, in this way, that the episcopal chronicle was open-ended. As bishop yielded to bishop, Angilram and his successors would be added one by one, presumably on the uniform Roman pattern applied to Chrodegang. The longer part of the *Gesta* reflects the Old Testament, and only the last section is modeled on the *Liber pontificalis*, but if the extensions fell into place as intended, this disproportion would be temporary and soon reversed. In any case, the *Gesta* has the bipartite plan customary in Paul's books. Here, old dispensation gives way to new, foreshadowing to fulfillment. Paul implied that the prolonged infancy of the diocese had recently been superseded by its regenerated maturity.

When Paul reaches Bishop Chrodegang, conventional history begins. In the familiar phrases of the *Liber pontificalis*, he narrates how Roman liturgy, chant, and cults were introduced into the Frankish Church. Metz had evidently returned to the sources of its foundation. The earlier scenes are handled in a uniform but very different way. Paul composes each one on three levels, in which a fragment of Genesis is mirrored in a moment of the history of Metz that, in turn, portrays or speaks to eighth-century conditions. The Creation scene traces Bishop Clement's evangelization of Metz back via St. Peter to the Ascension of Jesus Christ. As spelled out by Paul, the details of St. Peter's making of the Western Church lead us to understand that the Church at its origin incorporated the same pattern of metropolises and suffragan sees that was currently being striven for in the Frankish Church.[141]

The Deluge scene that comes next dispenses with aquatic imagery, but explicitly evokes universal ruin. Paul took it for granted that, in the imagination, barbarians such as the Huns would be associated with destructive water—waves, tides, floods—as they are in modern usage.[142] Whereas Metz was destroyed, the ark of the Church guided by its Noah, Bishop Auctor, rode out the devastation. But survival was not identical to continuity. The Hunnic flood explained how the northern Church lost touch with its Roman point of departure and became disorganized. To situate the breach of continuity in the fifth century had topical implications at the time of writing. From our perspective, informed by such contemporary observers as St. Boniface, the Church in Gaul flourished under the Merovingians and seriously deteriorated in the decades during which Charlemagne's predecessors, notably Charles Martel, rose to power.[143] Paul, working on behalf of a court bishop in a period of reform, was expected to counteract this vi-

---

[141] Goffart, "Early Design."

[142] And already were in classical times: "Cimbros inundasse Italiam," Justin *Epitome* 38.4.15; Salvian *De gubernatione Dei* 6.67, "inundarunt Gallias gentes barbarae." The same expression is found in the Old Testament.

[143] Goffart, "Early Design."

sion of the situation; he supplies an innocent reason for the Frankish Church to need reordering along Roman lines. Attila and the Huns were unobjectionable culprits.[144]

If the opening scenes suggest that the *Gesta* might be about something larger than Metz, certainty is achieved in the section about St. Arnulf, the longest of the four. Not only is the Church of Metz incidental to the story, but even Arnulf, the main actor, plays a subordinate part. A detailed interpretation of the scene, published elsewhere, will not be repeated here. Suffice it to say that its theme appears to be the succession of Charlemagne, as he and his court had resolved upon it not long before Paul's writing. The choice of Isaac's blessing of Jacob as prototype of the scene is the main clue to its meaning. As far as may be known, the historical St. Arnulf effortlessly regulated his inheritance. If Paul called upon him and his two sons to re-enact the roles of Isaac, Jacob, and Esau, it may have been as stand-ins for living eighth-century actors.[145] In 781, the younger sons of Charlemagne by Hildegard were crowned by the pope as kings of Italy and Aquitaine. Two years later, Hildegard died. Charlemagne remarried in less than five months. Hildegard had borne him nine children in twelve years— Would he now engender a whole new collection of sons to vie with hers for fragments of the kingdom? Charlemagne's near-childlessness in the next decades offers one answer to the question. Paul's *Gesta* complements it with another, far more detailed.[146] It even distorts history to the extent of portraying descent from Arnulf of Metz as though it had invariably been from father to one son (the truth was multiple succession). From the figural tale of Arnulf/Isaac and his sons, we learn that Charlemagne was resolved to have no more male heirs; that Charles the Younger, his eldest son by Hildegard, was designated as sole heir to the Frankish kingdom (the equivalent of being Jacob); and that Pepin, son of Himiltrude—Charlemagne's very first son, but out of Christian wedlock—was excluded from a share of the inheritance (the equivalent of being Esau). The scene appropriately closes with a celebration of the late queen Hildegard, whose sons alone were now established to be throne-worthy. She is associated in death with St. Arnulf to seal Charlemagne's radically new ordering of his succession.[147]

[144] Paul's own *H.R.* 14 pointed the way. In *Gesta*, ed. Pertz, p. 262 lines 29-30, he reproduced a few words from *H.R.* 14.5, in which a passage from Prosper's *Chron.* about the year 435 is carried over to the account of Attila's attack on Gaul in 451, so that the Hunnish destruction of the Burgundian king Gundicarius and his forces coincides with Attila's campaign (perhaps an important step toward the legend intertwining the Burgundians with Attila).

[145] The account of Arnulf preferring his younger son over the elder is wholly contrived. Not only is it undocumented, but also the Merovingian context suggests that the elder son, who duly became bishop of Metz, was in fact preferred.

[146] As we saw (nn. 45-48), Paul's sojourn at Charles's court coincided with these events.

[147] Goffart, "Early Design."

The sound Petrine beginnings that were swept away by the Hunnic flood and were then promised a new start in the choice of Arnulf's seed (in the junior line) ripen to maturity in scene IV. Bishop Chrodegang restores Roman ecclesiastical forms to the see of Metz, and is seen to do so, significantly, in the stereotyped language of the Roman *Liber pontificalis*. On this positive note, symbolic of what was happening to the entire Frankish Church after Chrodegang, Paul brought the *Gesta* to a close. Of course, the work was ended only for the time being. As the episcopal line of Metz continued, so—it was hoped—would the episcopal record, emulating in this way as otherwise the practices and regularity of the see of St. Peter. In the perspective of a long, untroubled future of ecclesiastical order, Paul the Deacon had merely supplied the sketchy beginnings of the proper "bishops' book" that, from Chrodegang onward, would commemorate each leader of the Church of Metz.

Commissioned and sponsored by a court bishop, the Metz *Gesta* is a document of Charlemagne's early reign, indicative of its achievements and hopes. The ideas it embodies probably came to Paul from Bishop Angilram. His task was to embed them in a many-layered narrative, evoking a past that, in the microcosm of Metz, mirrored the current conditions of the Frankish kingdom. The office of archchaplain, or head of the royal *capella*, which Angilram assumed in 784 (and possibly exercised *ad interim* in the months before his formal entrance upon the charge), might be translated into our language as "minister of religious affairs," but only on the understanding that few affairs were more important than religious ones at Charlemagne's court.[148] Disguised as local history, the Metz *Gesta* sought deliberately to be a programmatic statement concerning the current Frankish Church and its royal defender. The achievement of institutional regularity and permanence is the dominant idea of this memorandum that Angilram brought with him into Charlemagne's *capella*.

So understood, the Metz *Gesta* is less relevant to Paul as a historian than as a man of letters. The treatment of the Huns in scene II echoes the *Historia Romana*; as there, barbarian invaders draw a line of demarcation between one epoch and the next. But in the three scenes modeled on Genesis, Paul's concern is not to recapture the real past. What the *Gesta* vividly illustrates is Paul's ability to write parables of a special kind, stories that reveal their meaning only after a process of reflection and meditation. More than the *Historia Romana*, the *Gesta* reveals Paul's gift for fable, somewhat similar to that of Gregory of Tours inasmuch as the reader is drawn inward by the details of what he is told and distracted in this way from the relations of one tale to the next. The account of the Huns at Metz unable to pene-

---

[148] *Ibid.*

trate the church of St. Stephen is a notable instance of the type, and so, most of all, is the story of St. Arnulf's ring, cast into the Moselle and returned years later by a fish.[149] Each tale, complete in itself, invites acceptance as an isolated entertainment, from which one passes to something else. Where Paul differs from Gregory is that the fragmentation is only ostensible. The biblical prototype of each scene hovers in the background as an incitement to the careful reader to link the separate fables into longer narrative entities. Paul strove to reconcile simplicity of language and tone with the expression of complex and subtle meaning. The colorful fable had as much a part in this quest as the avoidance of complicated vocabulary and syntax. Paul's last work was composed in the same way.

6. Preliminary to the *Historia Langobardorum*

After returning from Charlemagne's court, Paul the Deacon eventually had time to continue the history whose first installment had appeared in the far off days when young children gladdened the ducal house of Benevento. The question, still raised in 1975, whether the *H.L.* is the sequel announced in the *Historia Romana* or a wholly new conception may be answered without qualification.[150] As Paul's first installment is Roman mainly because of Eutropius, so the Lombards of the second installment are prominent rather than fundamental: the subject of both is Italy. That is the sense of the elaborate description of the peninsula in *H.L.* 2, Paul's equivalent to the geographic introductions of Orosius and Bede.[151] In a few chapters of *Historia Romana* 15, Paul reached back to retrace the pre-Italian adventures of the Ostrogoths; in the whole of *H.L.* 1, the same thing is done for the Lombards.[152] Only these preliminaries are strictly ethnic. Where the main narrative is concerned, the welds between the "Roman" and "Lombard" installments are easy to identify. The thematic notes on which the earlier history closes, especially in its "prophetic" chapter, are picked up and amplified as *H.L.* 1 nears its end. But the precise junction between the *Historia Romana* and its sequel occurs at the start of *H.L.* 2. Paul had interrupted the narrative of Italian events after Narses's successful conquest of the Goths, and it is with Narses ruling the peninsula that the action resumes.[153]

---

[149] The Huns at Metz, *Gesta*, ed. Pertz, p. 263 lines 2-8; Arnulf's ring (cf. the ring of Polycrates and other tales of lost objects returned in a fish), p. 264 lines 15-36.

[150] Corbato, "Paolo Diacono," p. 21; cf. above, n. 42.

[151] *H.L.* 2.14-24; cf. above, n. 90.

[152] Above, n. 105.

[153] *H.L.* 2.1: Narses, ruling Italy and preparing for war against Totila, calls on the Lombard king Audoin for assistance (Paul does not have Narses's expedition come from outside; he is shown sharing Italy with the Goths in the same way that a Byzantine exarch shared it with the Lombards). The overlap with the ending of the *H.R.*, which notes Totila's defeat, amounts to about three lines (ed. Crivellucci, p. 238 lines 5-7).

Paul had made Italy the historical substratum of the *Romana* in order to integrate the eighth-century Beneventan present with all its pasts. His longstanding program was so well adapted to a succession of invaders and régimes, that, when he launched into his continuation, the Frankish conquest of 774 imposed no change of design.

The *H.L.* is formed of six books. The first is an ethnic prologue, as just seen, and the last ends with the death of Liutprand, greatest of the Lombard kings, in 744. Like the original books of the *Historia Romana*, those of the *H.L.* are distributed in such a way as to bridge rather than to interrupt the flow of time. Invariably, a very conspicuous feature of one book carries over to the next: Alboin (*H.L.* 1-2); the Lombards without a king (2-3); Agilulf and Theudelinda (3-4); Grimoald I (4-5); Cunicpert (5-6); Ratchis and Aistulf (6-[7]). The work was not meant to proportion historical coverage to roughly equivalent periods. The span of book VI is twice that of book V, and books II and III together cover little more than half that of book IV.[154] Paul is more detailed, paradoxically, about events most distant from his lifetime. But there is no way to tell how circumstantially the years after 744 would have been narrated. The work has no conclusion and lacks the introduction that might have told us for whom Paul wrote and what were his intentions and methods. As earlier shown, the *H.L.* was probably left unfinished because Paul died.[155] It differs fundamentally from the other "barbarian histories" in being incomplete. The unavoidable question is what length Paul meant it to have.

His resort to bipartite books and fondness for symmetrical order are a help in divining the original plan. The Lombard kings of the *H.L.* include only one unambiguous model of conduct. Many fail to qualify. Alboin is a tragic hero; Authari is unbaptized and Agilulf unmourned; Liutprand is admirable but attended by elegiac notes. The ideal hero is Grimoald I, son of a Frioulan duke, successor of his brother as duke of Benevento, and, by invitation, king of the Lombards at Pavia. The romance of his origins and royal reign extends from the middle of *H.L.* 4 far into the fifth book, and it incarnates the geographic triangle so dear to Paul's heart. Grimoald not only is the most exemplary king of the Lombards, but occupies more space than any other. If he were the pivot figure of a bipartite *H.L.*, Paul's plan would have called for eight books, half the number of the *Romana*.

An additional clue to this design occurs in Paul's opening book. At the precise center of *H.L.* 1, we encounter a legendary Lombard king named Lamissio, whose exploits are largely Paul's invention.[156] Lamissio is almost

---

[154] *H.L.* 1: 4th century?–567; 2: 551-72; 3: 572-90; 4: 590-662; 5: 662-90; 6: 688-744. Only a meaningless guess may be made about the opening date of the *H.L.*

[155] Above, n. 55.

[156] Below, n. 175.

a miniature Grimoald. As the latter when very young escaped the Avar flood, so the infant Lamissio was saved from untimely death in a pond (his name is allegedly the Lombard equivalent of Moses). His mother, like Grimoald's, was a whore; Grimoald had seven siblings, Lamissio six. Both won one great victory in youth, another after circumstances brought them to the royal throne.[157] Lamissio does not just happen to fall in the middle of the opening book; he is the leader under whom the Lombards changed from a poor people striving to maintain their existence, to a race of conquerors gaining wealth and renown. As turning point for the first book, Lamissio seems to herald the part assigned to the no-less-epic Grimoald I in the entire *H.L.*; namely, to be the hinge of a projected eight books.

The major event that the *H.L.* omits by ending with Liutprand is, of course, Charlemagne's conquest of the Lombard kingdom, as well as its preliminaries under Pepin I. An eight-book *H.L.* would undoubtedly have included these events, and various indications, in the Metz *Gesta* as well as in *H.L.* 6, suggest that Paul's account of the Frankish seizure of Lombardy would not have been hostile.[158] Neither did he have to approve. The hand of Providence was there to be invoked as a neutral cause for ambiguous occurrences.[159] Italy had endured so many invasions that singling out a notably bloodless one for censure would have been churlish, and certainly out of character with Paul.

In any case, the events of 774 were not predestined to conclude Paul's narrative. The *H.L.*, as sequel to the *Historia Romana*, was necessarily oriented toward the principality of Benevento. Adalperga, the dedicatee of the first installment, was still alive. A place of honor in the projected book VIII was probably reserved for the glorious reign of Prince Arichis. However dim the unwritten books of the *H.L.* are fated to remain, their broad outlines are not wholly unknowable. Paul could have gone about his task in an optimistic and not a mournful frame of mind. The young Grimoald III ruled Benevento. Under this energetic son of a great prince, Lombard history continued to have relevance for the present. Besides, Paul's invar-

---

[157] Lamissio's origins, *H.L.* 1.15; Grimoald's, 4.37. Lamissio's name: "et quia eum de piscina [= fish pond], quae eorum lingua 'lama' dicitur, abstulit, Lamissio eidem nomen inposuit" (ed. Bethmann-Waitz, p. 55); cf. Exod. 2:10, "Vocavitque nomen eius Moyses, dicens: Quia de aqua tuli eum." Not surprisingly, Paul's etymology proves to be more convenient than accurate. On the word "lama," see Engels, *Observations sur le vocabulaire*, pp. 83-84. First exploit, Lamissio *H.L.* 1.15 (overcomes an Amazon), Grimoald 4.46 (defeats Greeks). Victory after kingship, Lamissio 1.17; Grimoald 5.7-10 (repels Constans II).

[158] Paul unreservedly praises the Carolingians, and even Charles's conquest of the Lombard kingdom: *Gesta episcoporum Mettensium*, ed. Pertz, p. 265. The same praise is echoed (of course without the conquest, thirty years beyond the last events noted) in *H.L.* 6.16, 23, 37, 42, 46, 53-54.

[159] See below, nn. 190-91, on the role of Providence in the Lombard conquest of Italy (a way to detach painful events from human causation).

iable concern was Italy rather than a single people. There was much in the past for Grimoald III to learn with profit as he matured in his role as the remaining native sovereign in the peninsula.

The *H.L.* is less of a patchwork of source extracts than the *Historia Romana*, but the number of borrowings is high. Some of the originals are known to us, such as the *Origo gentis Langobardorum*, the *Histories* of Gregory of Tours, and the *Liber pontificalis*. Others are lost but identified, such as, most notably, the seventh-century *Historiola de gestis Langobardorum* by Secundus, bishop of Trent; and others still may be only suspected.[160] Paul did not lack for books and made good use of them. Besides, any reader of the *H.L.* quickly realizes that dry reports suggestive of a chronicle alternate, at no set intervals, with passages of a very different kind, relating colorful legends, similar to the tale of Digna in the *Romana* and of St. Arnulf's ring in the Metz *Gesta*.[161] Paul, as usual, left rough edges between his chapters. Time moves onward; but, other than that, the continuity of the narrative is rarely overt. And owing to the intermittent legends, which focus attention inward upon their intricacies, readers are strongly drawn toward the fragments and away from the unfolding of a continuing story. Paul's diversionary tactics, which we have come to know, have been exaggerated rather than counteracted by the modern interest in the detection of sources and by fascination with Paul's legends. The latter have often been taken to be, not integral components of the *H.L.*, but faithful renderings of ancient tales circulating orally among the Lombards, and therefore freely detachable from their context in Paul.[162] The outcome has been that the *H.L.* tends to be a mine of material rather than a narrative; it is regarded as a succession of fragments of widely varying value, assembled by a naïvely patriotic redactor incapable of forming an organic whole out of the information he gathered.

The *H.L.* regains literary integrity if read in the same way that has proved effective in approaching Paul's earlier histories. The work holds together better than first impressions suggest. Because only a fraction, however large, was completed, whether Paul subordinated the entire work to an overarching idea similar to that of the (much shorter) Metz *Gesta* cannot be known. The intelligible unit of the *H.L.*, as of *Historia Romana* 11-16,

---

[160] Mommsen, "Die Quellen" (above, n. 17), is still the best account. An English adaptation is in the original edition of Foulke's translation (Philadelphia 1907), unfortunately omitted from the 1974 reprint.

Paul acknowledges his debt to Secundus of Trent (*H.L.* 3.29, 4.27, 40), but not in detail. For a full discussion of their relations, see Ken Gardiner, "Paul the Deacon and Secundus of Trent." For the *Origo*, see § 7.

[161] As examples of this contrast: *H.L.* 1.14-15, 22-24; 2.10-13 (the last is not a legend, but a digression about Fortunatus), 28-32 (the last two look like chronicle); 3.27-30, 32-35.

[162] On the legends, see, as above, nn. 10-14, and below, nn. 310-20.

is the individual book. Not time, but an unstated scenario, gives each book its coherence. That some chapters look like chronicle whereas others beguile with legend is an incidental consideration. All chapters, regardless of origin and sound, work together in the elaboration of an integrated theme. By making the effort to determine Paul's plot, one may keep clear of his diversions and false trails and establish how he meant his words to be understood.

7. *H.L.* 1: The Nonprovidential Origin of the Lombards

Paul's main source for Lombard beginnings was the same as ours: namely, the *Origo gentis Langobardorum*, an anonymous narrative probably of the seventh century that he found affixed as prelude to the Lombard law code, as it still is in surviving manuscripts.[163] Although he was bound to treat this text as authoritative, not least because it was surely familiar to his audience, he could be selective about which portions to appropriate or reject. The *Origo* begins with a miracle featuring the Germanic gods Freya and Wodan, whose supernatural intervention gave the Lombards their first victory. Paul was too well schooled a Christian to attribute divine powers to such creatures: "At this point," he says, "the men of old tell a silly story . . . ," and he reproduces it with suitable commentary.[164] But the *Origo* was more profoundly and pervasively flawed than by this tale. As prelude to the Lombard laws, it was placed in the same relationship as the tale of Hebrew origins is to Mosaic law; its narrative was perilously close to the book of Genesis in intimating that the pre-Christian Lombards were as divinely chosen a people as the Chosen People of the Bible. That (in Paul's view) false implication of the *Origo* was what he set out to eliminate and to replace with a merely human tale. Like the *Origo*, *H.L.* 1 traces the Lombards from insignificance to greatness, but Paul portrayed the Lombards as a merely human phenomenon. The providential hand did not foster their beginnings.

H.L. 1 is more diverse in contents than the later books. It opens on a note that still seemed so scientific in the nineteenth century that Felix Dahn rewrote its substance, with a few modifications, into the modern ex-

---

[163] Ed. Waitz, MGH *Script. rer. Lang.*, p. 26; cf. the editor's comment, p. 1, "Extat in tribus edicti [Rothari] codicibus." Paul says that almost all codices of the Edict of Rothari (the basic Lombard legal collection) contain the *Origo*: *H.L.* 1.21. For a good discussion of the *Origo*, see Gschwantler, "Heldensage von Alboin," pp. 221-25. He argues that an earlier, slightly fuller version of the *Origo* than the one available to us was utilized by both Paul and the anonymous *Historia Langobardorum codicis Gothani* (ed. Waitz, MGH *Script. rer. Lang.*, pp. 6-11). This may be the case, and deserves serious attention, but Gschwantler takes too little account of the possibility that the expansions in the ninth-century *Codex Gothanus* derive, however indirectly, from Paul.

[164] *H.L.* 1.18.

planation of the causes of the "Migration of Nations" (*Völkerwanderung*).[165]
The scientific prelude is no sooner over than we encounter such creatures
of legend as the Seven Sleepers (traditionally of Ephesus), Cynocephali
(dog-headed men traditionally associated with the ends of the earth), and
Amazons, whose historicity Paul goes out of his way to defend.[166] The second half of the book features some of Paul's best Lombard tales, among
them the wicked princess Rumetruda, and the boldness of Alboin and gallantry of his Gepid host. Their profane impact is offset by no fewer than 194
lines of verse relating the miracles of St. Benedict.[167] However varied, the
components of Paul's narrative are not haphazardly assembled.

The structure of *H.L.* 1 is notably symmetrical. The book contains two
long digressions: one near the beginning, the other just before the end (in
the same "prophetic" position detected in the *Historia Romana*). The first
evokes extremes of undesirability. Paul successively unfolds images of
Christianity frozen in sleep, a beastly way of life deprived of the sun's
warmth, and watery abysses at the ends of the earth.[168] The second portrays
an extreme of desirability in idealized images of Christian rulership and holiness: Justinian's triumphs, laws, buildings, and wise men; St. Benedict,
the miracle worker, and his holy fortress. These are the poles, North (in-
fernal) and South (celestial), between which the action flows. The Lombards advance from Scadanan in six steps. Three obstacles in their way are
successively overcome, after which three victories over more powerful foes
continually increase their wealth and greatness. The hero Lamissio, Paul's
own creation, forms the link between these triads. Lamissio personally masters the third obstacle and then leads the people to their first victory. Midway between his exploits, the Lombards are said to cross a river, the symbolic dividing line between, one might say, their mythical and their heroic
periods. (See Table 6.)

[165] Dahn, "Ursachen der Völkerwanderung." Retaining Paul's emphasis on overpopulation,
Dahn substituted a new scientific reason: the Germans' attainment of the "stage" of settled
agriculture occasioned a surplus of people. Two recent studies are committed to the historicity
of the migration legend: Frölich, "Herkunft," and Jarnut, "Frühgeschichte."

[166] Gregory of Tours wrote about the Seven Sleepers of Ephesus (above, ch. III n. 72); Paul's
are in a seaside cave in the Far North, venerated by the ignorant heathen and perhaps preserved by God for the eventual conversion of the northerners (*H.L.* 1.4). Cynocephali, 1.11:
a false rumor launched by the Lombards to frighten their enemies. Amazons, 1.15.

On these creatures, see Müller, *Gesch. d. antiken Ethnographie* II, 305-306. Müller points out
that Paul is thoroughly classical in his ethnographic ideas (II, 321-22). Also see Lecouteux,
"Cynocéphales." Paul was only the second author (after the Ethicus *Cosmography*, possibly of
the same century) to situate the Cynocephali in the North.

[167] Rumetruda, *H.L.* 1.20; Alboin and his host, 1.23-24; St. Benedict, 1.26.

[168] *H.L.* 1.4-6. Jordanes's *Getica*, much used in the opening chapters, supplies his account
of Scandza (*Get.* ¶¶ 16-24; in Paul's rendering, might simply be Germania) and inspires reflections about the effect of latitude on the length of daylight. On Paul's early chapters and
Jordanes, see Hachmann, *Goten u. Skandinavien*, pp. 24-25.

Once entered the second phase of Lamissio's career, Paul's Lombards are and remain in the equivalent of historical territory, fighting against known peoples and touching the edges of documented time. The epoch that needed to be cleansed of religious overtones lay in the dimmer past. Paul's device for expurgating the *Origo* was to explain the Lombard migration by an unbroken chain of rational causes and effects.

The seventh-century *Origo* portrays the Lombards as being in Scadanan (presumably Scandinavia) when challenged by the Vandals. An alterative, earlier version—that of the Frankish Fredegar chronicle, possibly known to Paul though never acknowledged—has the Lombards already moved south and across the Danube when the Huns block their advance.[169] Although the Vandals are a literary borrowing from Jordanes's account of the Gothic migration, neither the *Origo*, Fredegar, nor Paul attempts to harmonize Scadanan with Jordanes's Scandza. No reference is ever made to the Lombards' crossing by ship to the mainland (to Fredegar, Scathanavia is on the mainland).[170] Paul, for his part, takes pains to locate the Lombards' original home in a vast Germania, the land of human germination, so prolific in men, owing to the northern latitude, that it could not feed its teeming masses. This is the main part of his scientific prelude, rooted in Hippocratic climatic and medical theory.[171] Scadanan, besides sharing the Malthusian

Table 6

   I. Mythical period (chs. 1-3 [scientific prelude, 1-2])
  II. (North) Pole of undesirability (chs. 4-6)
 III. Mythical period, concluded (chs. 7-14)
 IV. Lamissio (chs. 15-17 [river crossing, 16])
  V. Heroic period (chs. 18-24)
 VI. (South) Pole of desirability (chs. 25-26)
VII. Heroic period, concluded (ch. 27)

[169] *Origo* 1 (the subject of the story is "How the Lombards Got Their Name"), ed. Waitz, pp. 2-3; Fredegar *Chron.* 3.65, ed. Krusch, p. 110 (the same story of how they got their name is localized after, rather than before, their migration). Whether or not Paul consulted Fredegar is a difficult question in the study of his sources (disregarded by Mommsen, as above, n. 17). The best comments are by Monod, review in *Revue critique d'histoire et de littérature*, p. 276.

[170] Jordanes *Get.* ¶ 26: on landing on the Continent, the Goths first drove the Ulmerugi from their homes, then "subjugated" the neighboring Vandals. Reversing roles, the Vandals of the *Origo* were cast as the aggressors. Fredegar: "Scathanavia, que est inter Danuvium et mare Ocianum" (as n. 169).

See above, ch. II n. 394. Both Frölich, "Herkunft," p. 4, and Jarnut, "Frühgeschichte," p. 3, stiffly reject Hachmann's association of the *Origo*'s legend of Lombard beginnings with Jordanes's legend. They espouse Wenskus's theory about the constitutional role of origin legends—a theory requiring that legends should be authentically ancient.

[171] *H.L.* 1.1. Paul owed to Isidore the idea of Germany as the land of human germination

misfortune of Germania, had the particular disadvantage of being an island so flat as to be almost indistinguishable from the waves of the sea that invade its shores.[172] The harshest of natural circumstances, then, occasioned the initial Lombard migration. Those sent to wander formed the third part of a small people, chosen by lot, in a manner consecrated by ancient historiography. By the time Paul began to paraphrase the *Origo*, he had turned the first Lombards into a band of needy refugees, selected by a human contrivance and sustained by merely human leadership.[173]

If scientific reading nourished the opening chapters, more conventional literature carried the story forward. Paul did not go out of his way to make the first phase of Lombard migration look historical. The geography is vague to say the least. One rival people, the Assipiti, defies identification; another, the Amazons, is so fabulous that Paul expressed critical doubts and resolved them by the recollection of being told about the existence of such creatures in the recesses of central Europe.[174] The *Origo* lists a certain Laiamicho in the ordinary line of earliest Lombard kings. Paul turns him into Lamissio, a Lombard Moses saved from the waters and reared by King Agio, with all the attributes of archetypal heroism. As noted above, he plays the pivotal part in the Lombard migration.[175]

By modern standards of history, the narrative is no improvement on the *Origo*, but no one could mistake Paul's earliest Lombards for a divinely chosen people. Driven south by famine and flood, they were threatened by the Vandals and vanquished them out of a desire for the glory of freedom. Again hungry, they moved, were blocked by the Assipiti, and gained passage thanks to the single combat of a slave who sought liberty. As they reached the river whose crossing (as we know) led them into history, the

---

(*Etymologiae* 14.3.4). His source for the fully formed ancient climatic theory has not been identified. On the theory, in brief, see See, "Germane als Barbar," p. 50; further, Müller, *Gesch. d. antiken Ethnographie* I, 137-44; Helms, "Zur Wandlung des Germanenbild."

[172] *H.L.* 1.2.

[173] Third part of a small people, *H.L.* 1.7; selection by lot, 1.2. Cf. Herodotus *Hist.* 1.94 (driven by famine, the Lydians draw lots and half emigrate to northern Italy); Jordanes *Get.* ¶ 283 (choice by lot in a slightly different context). Beginning of the paraphrase of the *Origo*, *H.L.* 1.3.

[174] On a premise of historicity, scholars have supplied all Paul's names of places and peoples with identifications if at all possible. Assipiti, *H.L.* 1.11. Amazons, 1.15; as a general rule, Paul materializes in the first person so as to give credence to what might be disbelieved (such as 1.4-6, 2.28, 4.37). The Assipiti have, in fact, been identified as Usipites by Wenskus, *Stammesbildung*, p. 444; cf. Frölich, "Herkunft," pp. 8-9, and Jarnut, "Frühgeschichte," p. 9. But Wenskus's argumentation suggests that the earlier position of learned doubt is preferable.

[175] Above, n. 157. *Origo* 2, ed. Waitz, p. 3: "fecerunt sibi regem nomine Agilmund, filium Agioni, ex genere Gugingus. Et post ipsum regnavit Laiamicho ex genere Gugingus. Et post ipsum." On the characteristics of archetypal heroes, Raglan, *The Hero*, ch. 16. For the interpretation of Lamissio along the lines of Höfler and K. Hauck, see Moisl, "Anglo-Saxon Royal Genealogies," p. 227.

hero nurtured in their midst won a watery contest with the Amazon delegated to block them.

Along the way, Paul spelled out the "silly" ancient legend featuring Freya and Wodan—an obligatory component of early Lombard history, expected by the public. Paul's exegesis surrounds it with the learned trappings of Euhemerism. Wodan was Mercury, who originated in Greece, and of course the story was untrue: "For victory is not granted to the power of man but rather given from heaven." Because Wodan, like all pagan gods, was just a man deemed divine by deluded men, he could not possibly have brought about the Lombard defeat of the Vandals.[176] Paul did not have the option of substituting history for the *Origo*'s myth. Instead, he made every effort to neutralize a tale that he considered theologically dangerous by rewriting it in a fuller, logically consistent, and innocuous manner.

The second half of *H.L.* 1, after the Lombards' fateful river crossing, opens with successive setbacks: a Bulgarian sneak attack and the failure of a riposte under Lamissio's leadership. The hero then mustered every resource of eloquence, appealed to the people's love of freedom, liberated all slaves capable of bearing arms, and led them to a great victory over the Bulgarians, out of which they emerged not only richer, but also readier for warlike enterprise.[177] As the successes of the Lombards unfold, Paul balances their exploits with negative touches. Their utter defeat was prevented only by the foundling hero; the Rugians were cleared from their path by a Christian saint and an Italian king; the dastardly deed of their own king's daughter provoked the war with the Herules that the latter lost out of their king's overconfidence. A shadow fell even over Alboin's final destruction of the Gepids when their slain king's skull was turned into the drinking vessel that, in *H.L.* 2, would trigger Alboin's catastrophe.[178]

---

[176] *H.L.* 1.8, "Haec risui digna sunt et pro nihilo habenda. Victoria enim non potestati est adtributa hominum, sed de caelo potius ministratur." Paul tells the story as though Wodan were a man living in a house rather than, as in the *Origo*, from an Olympian standpoint. On Wodan's identity, 1.9. On gods as men elevated to divinity by other men, see above, ch. II n. 280. To complete the refutation, Paul supplies an alternative account of how the Lombards got their name: not from women using their long tresses to disguise themselves as men, but from men wearing their beards bushy and never trimmed (1.9; from Isidore *Etymologiae* 9.2.95). Paul was not alone in believing that the *Origo* needed alteration; see the *Hist. Lang. cod. Gothani* (composed ca. 807-10; n. 163 above).

[177] *H.L.* 1.16-17. In the first assault, the Bulgarians carry off the only daughter of King Agelmund (the capture of princesses is a recurrent motif in the *H.L.*; see below, n. 269). The victory over the Bulgarians as a turning point: "[Langobardi] ex illo iam tempore ad expetendos belli labores audaciores effecti sunt" (ed. Bethmann-Waitz, p. 56).

[178] *H.L.* 1.17, 19, 20, 27. The Herule war and Alboin's visit to Turisind have been recently discussed by Gschwantler, "Heldensage von Alboin," pp. 241-43, and "Versöhnung als Thema einer heroischen Sage"; Wagner, "Alboin bei Turisind"; also see Leyen, *Heldenlieder-*

Is *H.L.* 1 about the rise of the Lombards? The general thrust of the narrative certainly moves in this direction. By its close, the Lombards have
become a great people and are ruled by the celebrated hero who would soon
lead them into Italy. But Paul's negative touches are there for a reason, and
so is the second digression, abruptly extolling Justinian's reign as an ideal
of Christian society (no Western historian had done this before) and celebrating St. Benedict at Monte Cassino as an active link between earth and
heaven.[179]

There was as much point in injecting these incongruous figures into the
tale of Lombard origins as in denying the divinity of Wodan. The first
digression, emphasizing the repellent nature of the North, is balanced by
the second, foreshadowing the redeemed Christian future from which Alboin's Lombards were still appallingly distant. By means of the digressions,
Paul formed *H.L.* 1 into a contrast epic, "where one pole is the ironic human situation and the other the origin or continuation of a divine society."[180] The flight of the Lombards from the miseries of Germania and Scadanan ensured them an existence that was merely human; their increase in
numbers and enrichment were real but morally indifferent. Alboin's feat in
killing the Gepid king's son was outdone by the king's gallantry in respecting the duty of hospitality; Alboin's next exploit yielded the skullcup that
would be his downfall and that of many others.[181] The action of the book,
however adventurous, exemplifies the ironic round of merely human success and failure. The Lombards were on a treadmill. Their epic had motion
only in as much as the demonic North receded and they drew nearer to the
establishment of a "divine society" that, at the least, presupposed their
conversion to Christianity. Justinian and St. Benedict were the yardstick
by which to measure the "rise" of the Lombards. Paul's heathen ancestors
had got somewhere but had far to go, in a different direction.

The *H.L.* never refers in so many words to the conversion of the Lombards to Catholicism (or, for that matter, to Christianity of a less orthodox

---

buch, pp. 5-7, 11-18. The tales are treated as isolated fragments; no thought is given to
whether they are related to the entire book.

[179] *H.L.* 1.25-26. Jordanes spoke approvingly of Justinian, but did not deliver a comprehensive eulogy; Gregory of Tours and Isidore of Seville (*Chron.* 397-400) left him unmentioned
or unremarkable, except for heresy; Bede did a little better, actually mentioning the promul-
gation of the code, but came nowhere near portraying a great reign (*Chron.* 515-20); Fredegar
Chron. 2.62, supplies only a romance of Justinian and Belisarius (ed. Krusch, pp. 85-88).
With Paul, one again suspects a Greek source (as above, nn. 79, 82, and below, n. 214).

[180] Frye, *Anatomy of Criticism*, p. 317.

[181] On the visit to the Gepid king, see the articles listed above, n. 178. Paul probably depended on an oral narrative of some sort, but no one can affirm that it was a *Heldenlied* as
commonly defined by modern Germanists.

kind). Commentators have understandably censured the omission.[182] Paul's avoidance of the subject contrasts with Gregory of Tours' account of Clovis and, much more glaringly, with Bede's *H.E.* Familiar with both, Paul did not follow suit, but was hardly indifferent to the religious dimensions of the Lombard past. From the perspective of 790, so preliminary a step as baptism was a matter of merely historical interest, in whose portrayal one would have to vie with the enchantments of Bede. Paul, intent on the immediate audience, saved his advocacy for more urgent religious goals. Narrating a conversion was not the only way one could be a concerned Christian historian. *H.L.* 1 illustrates his alternative course.

8. *H.L.* 2: The Tragedy of Italy

A brutal murder and the fragmentation of the Lombards bring *H.L.* 2 to a close; the return of the Lombards to security and cohesion is traced in *H.L.* 3, which ends in a marriage and enthronement. Whereas the plots of the other books are rarely obvious, these two may be rapidly identified from their final episodes as being tragic and comic, respectively. The tragedy is not strictly Lombard. With *H.L.* 2, Paul picks up the history of Italy at the point where it was interrupted in the *Historia Romana*, and carries it forward.[183] The argument conveyed by his plot is that the tragedy of Italy was not the Lombard invasion, as many might imagine, but the murder of Alboin and its consequences. Except for its opening segment, *H.L.* 2 is concerned with only a halfdozen years. It has five parts, as shown in Table 7.

It was common knowledge before the *H.L.* that the Lombard invasion came about as a result of the invitation of Narses, the imperial governor. His betrayal was in revenge for being recalled and threatened with humiliation by the empress Sophia. Paul agrees with an anonymous seventh-century chronicler in associating this consecrated tale with strong approval of

Table 7

    I. Narses and the Romans (chs. 1-5)
   II. Alboin's conquest (chs. 6-14)
  III. Italy and its provinces (chs. [14] 15-24)
  IV. Alboin's conquest, concluded (chs. 25-27)
   V. The tragedy of Alboin, the Lombards, and Italy (chs. 28-32)

---

[182] Above, nn. 7, 19. On the problem of determining early Lombard religious affiliations, see Fanning, "Lombard Arianism Reconsidered."
[183] Above, n. 153.

Narses's government of Italy.[184] Highly effective against the Goths, Franks, and other enemies, Narses was also outstandingly pious, a rebuilder of churches who, like the exemplary Christian emperor Theodosius I, "obtained victory more by supplication . . . to God than by the arms of war." He employed Lombards against the Goths and had friendly relations with them. Of course, his activities brought him riches, but the complaints of the Romans about his greed were captious; they were moved by envy.[185]

Between Narses's service to Italy and the Romans' ingratitude, Paul inserted a plague, describing it in vivid detail: "And these evils happened to the Romans only and within Italy alone, up to the boundaries of the nations of the Alamanni and the Bavarians." Paul not only made the plague symbolically selective, but also displaced it to the vicinity of Justinian's death (565), about four years before its actual outbreak.[186] So positioned, the plague gives us to understand that the Romans proved blind to a manifest sign of God's anger before they yielded to envy and agitated for Narses's dismissal. The crowning folly came when the empress Sophia threatened the well-deserving governor with ignominy. In sum, an act of God and human sinfulness delivered Italy to the Lombards at the same time as the ill-used Narses caused some of its fruits to be taken to them, as a magnet, perhaps, but almost as a legal token of transferred dominion.[187]

Paul was surely aware of the potential parallelism between the first and

[184] Marius of Avenches *Chron.* a.568 (removal of Narses), a.569 (invasion, with no overt link to the foregoing); Gregory of Tours *Hist.* 4.41 (invasion, but no Narses); *Liber pontificalis* 63 (in revenge for envious Roman complaints, Narses betrays); Isidore of Seville *Chron.* 402 (betrays, terrified by Sophia's threats); Fredegar *Chron.* 3.65 (like Isidore); *Continuatio Havniensis Prosperi* ¶ 4, ed. Mommsen, MGH AA. IX, 337 (like Isidore, but in a context of meriting well). Paul *H.L.* 2.1-3 is most reminiscent of the *Continuatio Havniensis*, but the *Liber pontificalis* points in the same direction. Isidore wrote about fifty years after the events; a new edition of the *Liber pontificalis* may date from about the same time. Cf. Hodgkin, *Italy and Her Invaders* V, 60-65.

The legend of Sophia's humiliation of Narses has an interesting parallel in that of the destitution of the Persian general Bahram toward 580: Anastasii Bibliothecarii *Historia tripartita*, ed. C. de Boor, in Theophanes *Chronographia*, 2 vols. (Leipzig 1885) II, 161.

[185] *H.L.* 2.5; the source is *Liber pontificalis* 63, ed. Duchesne, I, 305.

[186] *H.L.* 2.4 (the death of Justinian and succession of Justin II are noted toward the end). For the correct date, Marius of Avenches *Chron.* a.570, 571 (very clearly after the invasion) and *Excerpta Sangallensia* 570 (MGH AA. XI, 238; IX, 336). Also see MGH *Script. rer. Lang.*, p. 74 n. 1.

[187] *H.L.* 2.5: "Simulque multimoda pomorum genera aliarumque rerum species, quarum Italia ferax est, mittit, quatenus eorum ad veniendum animos possit inlicere" (ed. Bethmann-Waitz, p. 25). The editors (n. 5), claiming that Paul followed a "folk tradition," point to a parallel in Constantine Porphyrogenitus *De administrando imperio* 27, ed. Gy. Moravcsik and R.J.H. Jenkins, new ed., Corpus fontium historiae Byzantinae 1 (Washington 1967), p. 114 (this tenth-century work situates the incident in the eighth!). But cf. *H.L.* 2.23, about the ancient Gauls: "Causa autem cur Galli in Italiam venerint haec fuisse describitur. Dum enim vinum degustassent ab Italia delatum, aviditate vini inlecti ad Italiam transierunt" (ed. Bethmann-Waitz, p. 85). The Gauls, who built Ticinum-Pavia, were the proto-Lombards; as above, n. 77.

last parts of *H.L.* 2. The Narses chapters contain the ingredients of tragedy: riches, envy, folly, and, most of all, revenge. From the *Liber pontificalis*, Paul reproduced Narses's bitter, punning response to those scheming to have him recalled: "If I have done evil to the Romans, I shall incur/devise evil."[188] Paul took pains, however, to muddy the waters. Narses is an admirable Christian magistrate. The great plague, an unmotivated divine visitation, simply happens. With these facts neutralizing the tragic elements, the passage of Italy from Narses to Alboin cannot be interpreted as a tale of catastrophe.

Any doubts one might have about the course of Paul's reasoning evaporate when the details of Alboin's invasion unfold. The Lombards are so far from engaging in armed conquest that the narrative is free of any trace of death and destruction. (Gregory of Tours, a contemporary of the events, told a different story, disregarded by Paul.)[189] The Lombards entered Italy "without any hindrance"; Alboin set his nephew over an unresisting Frioul; no sooner did he encounter a bishop than he confirmed the property of his Church; most of Venetia came into his possession; moving on to Liguria, he entered Milan, "deserted" by its archbishop. Pavia endured a three-year siege, but for all we may tell no one was hurt in its course; no hint of an assault or slow starvation darkens the stately pageant. The closest Paul comes to bloodshed is in relating how a miracle induced Alboin to break his vow to massacre all the Pavians.[190] There was an easy explanation for the Lombard promenade: "the Romans had then no courage to resist because [of] the pestilence that occurred in the time of Narses." The Providence absent from *H.L.* 1 ruled Italy in *H.L.* 2. God's design was manifest in the selective plague that particularly afflicted Liguria (the future Lombardy) on the eve of Alboin's invasion.[191] One does not argue with divine providence.

Paul drew attention to the limits of the initial Lombard conquest; the "regions which Alboin had taken" are even singled out in the final chap-

[188] "Si male feci cum Romanis, male inveniam" (ed. Bethmann-Waitz, p. 75). Neither Hodgkin, *Italy and Her Invaders* V, 61, nor Foulke, p. 59, does well with this sentence (Hodgkin: "I shall find myself in an evil plight"). For the story to work, *inveniam* has to be open to radically opposed meanings.

[189] *Hist.* 4.41.

[190] *H.L.* 2.9, 12, 14, 25, 26, 27. The miracle that confirms the bloodlessness of the conquest is particularly effective; in its wake "ad eum omnis populus in palatium quod quondam rex Theudericus construxerat, concurrens" began to hope for the future (ed. Bethmann-Waitz, p. 87). *Omnis populus* joins the Italians to the Lombards; Theodoric was the last memorable king of all Italy. For an analogous tale of the sparing of a city, see *H.A. Aurel.* 22.5–24.9.

[191] *H.L.* 2.26, "Nec erat tunc virtus Romanis, ut resistere possint, quia et pestilentia, quae sub Narsete facta est, . . . [and a later famine] universam Italiam devastabat" (ed. Bethmann-Waitz, pp. 86-87). This idea is also found in the *Hist. Lang. cod. Gothani*, ed. Waitz, p. 9 line 32, whether independently of Paul or not is hard to tell (above, n. 163).

ter.[192] Had only these parts of the peninsula been deeded to the Lombards by unmotivated divine decree? In *H.L.* 2, the role played in *H.L.* 1 by the negative and positive poles has its counterpart in a lengthy catalogue of the Italian provinces, including Sicily. It ends with the phrase, "Italy then, which contains these provinces. . . ." The digression is inserted halfway through the account of Alboin's conquest, so that his invasion frames or encloses the provincial catalogue.[193] In the few years he had until tragedy struck, Alboin was able to take amicable possession of only a small part of the land that Providence seemed to have destined for the Lombards.

The Alboin of *H.L.* 1 engages in strenuous personal exploits; that of *H.L.* 2 is only the tragic hero at the top of Fortune's wheel. To underline the point, Paul has him pause at the edge of Pannonia, climb a mountain, and look out as far into Italy as he could see.[194] Alboin behaves in consistently statesmanlike fashion, securing the friendship of the Avars, winning allies from among the Saxons, guiding many other non-Lombards into Italy, and treating the victims of his invasion as though he were already their merciful ruler.[195] As the digression implies, all Italy lay open to him.

Then human frailty intruded. A chronological note at the start of the tragic action sums up what is to come. Far gone in an evening's merriment, Alboin forces his wife, Rosamund, to drink a toast from the cup he had made of her slain father's skull, and the expulsion from paradise gets under way. Rosamund plots revenge, gains the help of Alboin's foster brother, Helmechis, and, with more difficulty, that of the *vir fortissimus* Peredeo. A trap is laid and sprung, and Alboin dies, bringing disaster to all concerned.[196]

Contemporaries like Gregory of Tours reported Alboin's murder in considerable detail. They substantially confirm the acts of Helmechis and Rosamund, including their flight to Byzantine protection after the crime.[197]

---

[192] *H.L.* 2.32.

[193] *H.L.* 2.14-24; the digression starts after the first sentence of 2.14, which mentions Alboin's conquests in Venetia. On one aspect of this catalogue, see above, n. 66. For an interpretation of the catalogue similar to the one argued here, see Vinay, "Un mito per sopravvivere," p. 131.

[194] *H.L.* 2.8. Paul, in a personal intervention, shows *bisontes* grazing on this mountain; what is one to make of this?

[195] *H.L.* 2.6, 7, 8, 26; Paul approves of these immigrants as replenishing a population wasted by plague and famine.

[196] *H.L.* 4.28. The scene of Alboin's murder is very reminiscent of Jordanes's account of the death of the Visigoth Thorismund (*Get.* ¶ 228), as pointed out by Leyen, *Heldenliederbuch*, p. 9. Gschwantler, "Heldensage von Alboin," p. 227, sees a similarity to the death of the false Smerdys in Herodotus, but the parallel escapes me.

[197] Rosamund's name does not appear until well into the seventh century: *Continuatio Havniensis Prosperi*, ed. Mommsen, pp. 337-38. Considerably earlier, John of Biclar *Chronica*, ed. Mommsen, MGH AA. XI, 213, specified that Alboin was killed by his familiars (*a suis*) at his wife's instigation; but the genuinely contemporary Marius of Avenches *Chron.* a.568, MGH

Two features of the story are new with Paul: the skullcup, and the role of Peredeo (he appears fleetingly in the *Origo* under the name Peritheus). The skullcup first turns up in Paul's *Historia Romana* as an Orosian horror practiced by the barbarians of the Rhodopian Mountains (modern Macedonia). Its part in Alboin's fate—comparable to the apple in Genesis—is so novel that Paul intrudes authenticating words right after Rosamund's forced toast: no one should doubt the tale, for Paul personally saw King Ratchis displaying the very object. In view of Ratchis's role in the waning years of the kingdom, the skullcup instrumental in the Lombard tragedy loses none of its fatefulness for being placed in his hands.[198] This wonderful symbol associating original sin with ancestral barbarity may already have been current coin in the 740s, as Paul claims. If not, he can only be applauded for inventing it.

AA. XI, 238, reverses the initiative: Alboin was killed *a suis*, i.e. Helmechis, with the consent of Alboin's wife, whom Helmechis later married. In the state of our evidence, the first witness to the classic story is Gregory of Tours *Hist.* 4.41: Alboin married the daughter of a man he had killed; she waited for an occasion to take revenge; enamored of one of Alboin's servants, she poisoned the king and fled with her paramour; both were caught and killed (an earlier Italian story of Gregory's, *Hist.* 3.31, is comparably melodramatic and more certainly false). Fredegar *Chron.* 3.65 merely abbreviates Gregory. Gregory's ending varies markedly from Marius, John of Biclar, and the *Continuatio Havniensis*, who agree that the queen and Lombard treasure were received in Ravenna. Cf. Gschwantler, "Heldensage von Alboin," pp. 216-21; he deems Gregory's account to be "heroic" because involving revenge for slain kin, but then to shift into an "unheroic" mode. These categories are of doubtful relevance to Gregory's narrative; he was telling a suitably ironic tale of the doings of depraved humanity.

No Western author is aware of the story told by Theophylact Simocatta (ca. 630) *Historiae* 6.10.7-12, tr. Whitby, pp. 174-75, according to which Alboin courted Cunimund's daughter and, when spurned, seized her by force, occasioning war between the Lombards and Gepids; he then married her (long before Cunimund's death) so as to obtain peace. Gschwantler, p. 244, wrongly infers that the *Origo* (ed. Waitz, p. 4 line 13) was aware of "the rape of Rosamund." It says that Alboin, after his victory, took Rosamund as booty—a story incompatible with Theophylact's.

[198] Andree, "Menschenschädel als Trinkgefässe," though naïve and uncritical, contains a rich collection of ancient and medieval references to skullcups; the alleged practice tends to be concentrated in the Balkans (and almost always, in the eyes of the reporter, documents barbarian ferocity). Also see Orosius *Hist.* 5.23.17-18; *H.R.* 6.10 (the locale is modern Macedonia). "Skull" is cognate with "shell," Germ. *Schale*, Fr. *écuelle*; the meaning "vessel" is common to them. To that extent, "skullcup" is tautological, in the same way as "The Los Angeles Angels." According to Andree, p. 18, Jakob Grimm "showed" that the making of cups out of the skulls of defeated enemies and some other persons was an ancient and early medieval custom.

The *Oxford English Dictionary*, s.v. "skull," lists a single sixteenth-century instance of skull meaning "cup"; under 5c, it supplies a surprising set of texts dating from 1825 to 1856 that illustrate skullcups as prized, but nevertheless readily procurable, items of contemporary table furnishing. A similarly benign usage is described by Andree, p. 1: at a Bavarian church, miracles were procured by drinking out of the skull of St. Sebastian.

One does not quite know what to do with Paul's report (*H.L.* 2.28) that Alboin was buried under a staircase in the palace, "sub cuiusdam scalae ascensu"—*scala* in another guise. Paul's authenticating words, *ibid.* On Ratchis's reign, Hallenbeck, *Pavia and Rome*, pp. 51-52; he sought good relations with the pope.

The name Peredeo, slightly different from the *Origo*'s Peritheus, evokes the Romance word meaning "lost." Paul must have known that, in the report of earlier witnesses, all Alboin's followers were parties to his death, not just the queen and a henchman.[199] Peredeo absorbs this social dimension of the king's downfall; he stands for a collectivity of "lost" Lombards. He also makes up in human interest for an Alboin who, like a proper tragic hero, neither says nor does anything between the drinking bout and the sword-play of his murder. Around Peredeo, Paul develops a secondary tragedy, in which Rosamund plays Delilah to his Samson, with the Byzantines as the Philistines. The identification is not left to the reader's imagination but is spelled out. Decoyed into the queen's bed, Peredeo is tricked into the plot by the threat of exposure and passively consents to the murder.[200] He joins in the flight to Byzantine territory, wins admiration in Constantinople for his strength, is blinded by the emperor's order, and redeems his honor by cutting down two valued court dignitaries.[201] After Alboin's murder and the sinister mutual killing of Rosamund and Helmechis, the heroic end of Peredeo restores calm to the narrative.

Despite the drama and movement surrounding Alboin's death, the climax of *H.L.* 2 comes only in the last chapter. The Lombards broke apart under the rule of dukes, a form of government that they had outgrown as far back as in their mythical period. The Roman *potentes*, whom Alboin's short-lived successor started to butcher, were harried and made tributaries, and the Italian clergy and people underwent the sufferings of armed subjugation, which Alboin had spared them.[202] Paul, by involving us in the individual tragedies of Alboin and the others, saw to it that the initial Lombard invasion should be totally disconnected from the ravaging of Italy. A

[199] *Origo gentis Langobardorum* 5, ed. Waitz, pp. 4-5: "occisus est in Verona in palatio ab Hilmichis et Rosemunda uxore sua per consilium Peritheo" (Peritheo's role is played by Alboin's wife in Marius, n. 197 above). On figures in tragedy comparable to Peredeo, see Frye, *Anatomy of Criticism*, p. 218. Many authorities specify that Alboin was killed *a suis*; in addition to those cited above, n. 197, *Excerpta Sangallensia* and Agnellus, in MGH AA. IX, 336.

[200] Cf. Gschwantler, "Heldensage von Alboin," pp. 228-35. He leaves out of account the likelihood that Peredeo's role was developed by Paul. Gschwantler claims that Rosamund sleeping with Peredeo was a "tiefster Selbsterniederung" (p. 233). It is hard to know why.

Leyen, *Heldenliederbuch*, p. 11, speaks for a substantial group of scholars who consider the sequel to the killing as different in kind from the killing proper: the end of Rosamund, Helmechis, and Peredeo "klingt nach byzantinischem Intrigenspiel und hinterhältigen Verbrechen, das ist vom germanischen Heldenlied weit entfernt."

[201] *H.L.* 2.28 (Peredeo is the lover of Rosamund's maid). Peredeo as Samson, 2.30. Cf. Gschwantler, "Heldensage von Alboin," p. 224; it need not follow that his liaison with Rosamund's maid, or his role in the conspiracy, authenticates the claim of the *Hist. Lang. cod. Gothani* that Peredeo was a *cubicularius* rather than a *vir fortissimus*, as Paul asserts. Peredeo's fight with a lion at Constantinople resembles the much longer and more fabulous combat of Smbat Bagratuni, narrated by Sebeos *Histoire d'Héraclius*, tr. Frédéric Macler (Paris 1909), pp. 38-39.

[202] *H.L.* 2.32; cf. 1.14 (the idea that proper peoples are ruled by kings is biblical).

seventh-century chronicler had preceded him in this vision of the events. The invasion did no harm; bloodshed and robbery began only after Alboin's murder.[203] God's decree and Byzantine folly had transferred the land to its new ruler in peace and amity; all would have been well. The skullcup occasioned a social as well as personal catastrophe, unloosing the horrors that ultimately tore apart the Lombard people and the whole peninsula.

9. *H.L.* 3: The Lombards Reborn

Comedy calls for a special character, on the Roman stage a tricky slave, who engineers the dénouement, often by an act of humility or self-deprecation. Justinian's strong right arm, Belisarius, has this part in Jordanes's *Getica*.[204] In *H.L.* 3, the role is played by Authari, the restorer of Lombard kingship. Impatient to see his Bavarian bride-to-be, Theudelinda, Authari dons disguise, joins an embassy concerned with the marriage, and makes believe he is viewing the bride on the groom's behalf. The irony is that this assumed role proves to be real. Theudelinda and Authari are duly married, but a recognition scene at once allows us to realize that he is no more than a transitory husband; death soon claims him. He had, as pretended, inspected the bride on behalf of another husband, Agilulf. The latter's marriage to Theudelinda, and his elevation to kingship as Authari's successor, give the book its festive happy ending.[205]

The rationale of this scenario cannot come from the profane history of the Lombards or Italy. About midway through *H.L.* 3, the régime of ducal fragmentation is superseded by the monarchy of Authari, who, at least according to Paul, restored legality, order, and good government.[206] He and his generals defended the land against Frankish invaders. Authari even made progress to the far south, symbolically completing the conquest of the peninsula and distantly supervising the foundation of the duchy of Benevento. By his doing, overtures were made for an enduring peace with the

---

[203] *Continuatio Havniensis Prosperi* ¶ 5, MGH AA. IX, 337: "postquam . . . Longobardis quiete post proelia Italiae insedentibus ius regale rite [Alboaenus] administraret, [he was killed]." Marius *Chron.* a.573, MGH AA. XI, 238, says that "plures seniores et mediocres ab ipso [Alboin's short-lived successor] interfecti sunt." Are these Italo-Romans or Lombards (the latter owing to the king's insecurity)?

[204] For Belisarius's relation to the happy ending, see ch. II, n. 286. On the *servus dolosus*, Murray, *Aristophanes*, pp. 224, 260-61; Harsh, *Handbook of Classical Drama*, pp. 317-19. The wily slave was Plautus's favorite character: Beare, *Roman Stage*, p. 51; Segal, ed., *Plautus*, p. xv; for a fuller account, Fränkel, *Elementi plautini in Plauto*, pp. 223-41. "Comedy" is used here as the generic term for stories with happy endings, not as a class of stage play.

[205] Authari's embassy, his marriage, and the recognition scene (a servant of Agilulf's magically knows how to interpret portents, and prophesies to him that the king's bride will be his wife): *H.L.* 3.30. The pithy detail that Agilulf learns of his future while relieving himself might be transposed from Fredegar *Chron.* 4.34. Authari's death and succession, *H.L.* 3.35.

[206] *H.L.* 3.16. It complements the last chapter of *H.L.* 2. For commentary on both, see Goffart, *Barbarians and Romans*, pp. 177-88 (written before I was aware of Paul's literary design).

Franks.[207] Paul is very generous in crediting Authari with accomplishments. But Authari loses out in the main plot. Not he, but the colorless Agilulf, emerges as the true hero.

The marriage of Agilulf and Theudelinda is a traditional happy ending —a family festival marking the birth of a new or reconstituted society. The *Getica* has familiarized us with the historical uses of such events.[208] What is in our minds after the close of *H.L.* 2 is the lapsed monarchy and fragmentation of the Lombards. But Paul wants us to think of more than political disorder. *H.L.* 3 is full of religious events, some only tenuously relevant to Italy. Its opening chapters feature a holy man in Provence; the bad, possibly heretical emperor Justin II is contrasted to his totally exemplary successor, Tiberius II, whose extraordinary generosity was divinely rewarded by greater riches, internal security, and foreign success; the see of Aquileia is torn between Roman and Byzantine obedience in the matter of the Three Chapters; Gregory the Great becomes pope; we hear of the conversion of the Spanish Goths from Arianism and of the papal mission sent to convert the English.[209] Social integration has more profound aspects than earthly kingship, and Paul forces us to focus on them. Christianity touches Authari only to the extent that, when he tried to get a Frankish bride, he was refused on religious grounds.[210] Agilulf and Theudelinda, however, were the embodiment of Lombard conversion. Paul does not say so; he expects it to be known.[211] In their marriage, we are meant to recognize the union of the Lombards with their supernatural ruler. Paul took care not to vie with Bede in narrating the passage of a people to Catholicism, but in the scenario of *H.L.* 3 he manifested that "central concern with the importance of national conversion for national history" which he has been thought to lack.[212]

The chapters of *H.L.* 3 do not fall into a pattern quite so clear-cut as those of *H.L.* 1-2, even after the focal point of the plot is determined. The likelihood is that the institution of Authari as king divides the book into two parts: a phase of deteriorating fortune for the Lombards followed by a phase of recovery. Almost all the characters customary in comic plots are introduced before Authari makes his dramatic entrance and turns the action in a more positive direction. Among the helping figures, the Frankish King Guntram and the future Gregory the Great pass by fleetingly in the

---

[207] Defense against the Franks, *H.L.* 3.17, 22, 29, 31; the South and Benevento, 32-33; overtures to the Franks, 28, 34.

[208] Frye, *Anatomy of Criticism*, p. 43; cf. above, ch. II nn. 259-61.

[209] Holy man, *H.L.* 4.1-2; Justin II and Tiberius II, 11-12, 15; Aquileia, 20, 26; Gregory the Great, 24; conversions in Spain and England, 21, 25, 28.

[210] *H.L.* 3.28.

[211] Their Catholicism is presupposed in *H.L.* 4; see below, n. 224.

[212] Hanning, *Vision of History*, p. 96.

first half; the prominent part is played by the emperor Tiberius II, for no other apparent reason than to exemplify rulership of a distinctively Christian kind. King Guntram no sooner appears than he withdraws; his long return engagement late in the action associates him with the open-handed charity of Tiberius and offsets the merely terrestrial exploits of Authari.[213] Another helper is, of course, Authari himself, whom we mistake for the hero until almost the end. The main obstructors are Maurice, the "first Greek emperor," and the Frankish king Childebert, whom Maurice incites into repeatedly attacking the Lombards. Childebert is Paul's equivalent of the stock *miles gloriosus*; the four ever-larger and invariably abortive expeditions that he orders into Italy approximate a running joke.[214]

After Agilulf and Theudelinda are recognized as a personalization of Lombard conversion, one realizes that the holy man Hospicius, who opens *H.L.* 3, prophesies the whole of the action in an apocalyptic moment. The only glimpse Paul gives of the Lombards on scattered rampages under their many dukes involves their invasions of Frankish Gaul recorded by Gregory of Tours.[215] Hospicius, borrowed from Gregory in this connection, explains that God, for reasons of His own, allowed the Lombards to act as scourges of the wicked, but they could not fatally harm the good. When a Lombard tried to cut down Hospicius with a sword stroke, his arm was paralyzed in midair; his companions cried for mercy, and Hospicius freed the arm; not

[213] Guntram, *H.L.* 3.3; the future Pope Gregory, 13. Euin, duke of Trent, another helpful figure, appears here and continues into the next book: *H.L.* 3.9, 10 (marries a daughter of Duke Garibald of Bavaria), 27 (commands a royal army against Byzantine territory); by his marriage, prefigures Authari and Agilulf. The return of Guntram, 3.34; on this type of character, Frye, *Anatomy of Criticism*, pp. 174-75.

[214] Maurice: *H.L.* 3.15, 17 (incites Childebert), 22 (again, but with his sister as basis of blackmail), 29 (Childebert announces cooperation to him), 31 (more Frankish cooperation). Childebert, in addition to the foregoing, 3.10, 21 (his sister captured by Byzantine soldiers), 28, 34, 35.

Concerning Maurice as a "Greek" emperor, Goubert, *Byzance avant l'Islam* I, p. 41, attributes the label to Paul's doing; he would have inferred Maurice's Greekness from his being born in Cappadocia rather than in a European province. The contemporary Evagrius, *H.E.* 5.19, makes him a Roman but from a family resident in a Cappadocian town. I am not convinced that the reasoning Goubert attributed to Paul was within his power. Earlier Westerners had called Eastern emperors "Greek" as a pejorative term, but Paul is apparently stating neutral fact. The Eastern sources deserve a second look, for Maurice might well have been regarded by some contemporaries as the first Greek emperor.

H.L. 3.29 involves a rare piece of historical criticism. Paul confronts Gregory of Tours *Hist.* 9.25 and Secundus of Trent and exclaims: Why does Secundus pass over so great a Lombard victory as this one, when the destruction of the Franks is recorded in "their own" history (ed. Bethmann-Waitz, p. 108)? Gregory is more likely than Secundus to be at fault.

[215] This may be well chosen. The seventh-century *Continuatio Havniensis Prosperi* notes only one major event during the interregnum: "inter quos [i.e. duces] primus Zafan Ticinensium dux, qui Gallias aggredi conatus est et maximum robur Langobardorum super amnem Rodanum . . . amisit et cum paucis, qui ex fuga remanserunt, Italiam repetit" (MGH AA. IX, 338).

only was the healed Lombard converted, but he became a monk in Hospicius's monastery. Some dukes listened reverently to Hospicius and returned safely home, others despised his words and perished miserably.[216] The lesson of this parable seems to be that, after Alboin's murder, the Lombards were fallen humanity with the possibility of redemption. Their problem was not that they lacked an earthly monarch, but that they had yet to acknowledge the Lord of the universe. The absurd condition that the plot would resolve was their godlessness.[217]

The first part of *H.L.* 3 documents the impotence of the unleashed Lombards. Opposed by Hospicius and the generals of good king Guntram, their attacks on Gaul petered out. Elsewhere, the virtues of the emperor Tiberius II were so outstanding that the Byzantines prospered. Lombard wickedness alienated the Saxons whom Alboin had brought to Italy; they seceded, trekked back to Germany, and came to grief.[218] Successively, the dangerous figures of the Frankish king Childebert and the "Greek" emperor Maurice became prominent. The Lombard monarchy was restored none too soon.

Authari is highly rated as a king. Ending the ducal régime, he defended and expanded Lombard rule. Paul insists on the completeness of his achievement. The acquisition of a Bavarian bride was also to his credit; after he married Theudelinda, the largest Frankish invasion was repelled, and rumor had it that he extended Lombard dominion southward—a matter of special interest to the Beneventan audience. Where rulership is concerned, however, Paul is sturdily Augustinian in maintaining that temporal effectiveness was not enough. The point is made not only by having Agilulf emerge as the true hero, but also by flanking the good Authari with the better Tiberius and Guntram. Their exceptional liberality, unearthing buried treasure and pouring it out for Christian purposes, suggests the nonsexual fruitfulness that issues from an earthly kinship married to true belief.[219] Authari, in short, was just as limited a foreshadower in ruling the Lombards as he was in marrying Theudelinda.

In the second half, Paul needed to express hostility toward the Christian

[216] *H.L.* 3.1-2; cf. Gregory of Tours *Hist.* 6.6. The borrowing is very literal, but Gregory narrates Hospicius's miracles in connection with his death in the 580s, rather than simultaneously with the Lombard invasions (in *Hist.* 4).

[217] About the absurd law at the center of comic plots, see above, ch. II nn. 281-82.

[218] For all three, Gregory of Tours is the source. Paul's major addition is a reason for the Saxons' secession: though they had accompanied Alboin with the intention of settling in Italy, the Lombards now alienated them by refusing them the right to live by their laws. In view of their sad fate, their departure might have been made to seem foolish, but is not.

[219] The motif of recirculating buried treasure is pressed very hard. *H.L.* 3.11-12 (largely based on Gregory of Tours *Hist.* 4.40, 5.19, 30), 34 (the story of Guntram and buried treasure is unprecedented). However admired Narses may be in *H.L.* 2.1-3, 5, he is evoked here burying his treasure and killing all who knew the secret except one man (cf. Alaric's burial in Jordanes).

rulership embodied by the emperor Maurice and King Childebert while nevertheless suggesting a turn by the Lombards toward Catholicism. (A possible parallel is Bede's contrasting treatment of the British and Irish.) Childebert is discredited by simple incompetence. He was a good Christian, whose Spanish brother-in-law suffered martyrdom and whose sister died in Byzantine custody;[220] but Childebert was also Maurice's errandboy, ordering ineffectual Frankish armies against the Lombards and refusing overtures of peace. The "Greek" Maurice never nears the front of the stage. The Christianity he represented is impugned in connection with the schism of Aquileia. Paul, in a complete, perhaps unwitting misrepresentation of the condemnation of the Three Chapters, portrays the situation in such a way that Byzantium condemned the chapters (true), whereas the papacy upheld them (not true). A papal letter, drafted by the future Gregory the Great, is said to have urged Aquileia to approve the chapters; soon after, the imperial exarch fell violently upon the Aquileian clergy and forced its adherence to the condemnation.[221]

In this way, Paul extended to the Three Chapters the familiar historical pattern of the papacy being doctrinally at odds with Constantinople. The election of Pope Pelagius II, which is specified to have been "without the authority of the emperor" because Rome was beset by a Lombard siege, might even be more to the Lombards' credit than not.[222] We are to understand that orthodox Rome was the sole source of Italian Christianity, while at the same time the Lombards were the papacy's shield against Byzantine heresy. Paul affirmed the connection in an account of sympathetic calamity that is the more effective for being repeated in H.L. 6. Venetia and Liguria, the original Lombard conquests, suffered a deluge unparalleled (it was thought) since Noah; and Verona, where Alboin was murdered, endured both water and fire. In the same flood, the Tiber overflowed into Rome, plague struck down many Romans, including Pope Pelagius, and the dea-

---

[220] H.L. 3.21. The chapter begins with Childebert II winning a battle against the Spanish Goths; Paul then explains the reason. He also specifies that Childebert's sister was brought to Sicily and died there (she is the second example of the captured princess motif, n. 177 above). These amendments are probably Paul filling out of information in Gregory of Tours, but it is hard to tell why he thought the changes desirable.

[221] At the Second Council of Constantinople (553), Pope Vigilius subscribed to the condemnation of the Three Chapters, and his successors stood by his decision, which was very unpopular in the West. On Paul and this council, see below, n. 281. H.L. 3.20, refers to "tria capitula Calchidonensis synodi" (ed. Bethmann-Waitz, p. 103). In fact, the Three Chapters became an issue long after Chalcedon, and, in the eyes of opponents of Justinian's council, they detracted from the definition of Chalcedon. (On the Three Chapters, see above, ch. III n. 442.)

The exarch's violence, H.L. 3.26. This refers to the so-called Istrian Schism, which was in defense of the Three Chapters and against Constantinople as well as Rome.

[222] H.L. 3.20.

con Gregory was elected to the see of St. Peter.[223] As Adam's fall was a *felix culpa*, the condition for eventual redemption, so this flood that made Gregory pope was a fortunate calamity. Its waters are as much as we ever see of a collective Lombard baptism.

10. *H.L.* 4: The Lombards Prosper, Fall from Righteousness, and Find a Savior

Without spelling out a Lombard conversion, Paul proceeded as though the deed were done. He used the past tense in *H.L.* 4 to refer to the time when the Lombards were pagan, and he specified that Agilulf "holds the Catholic faith" without marking a moment of initiation.[224] In Christian symbolism, the crossing of the Red Sea signifies baptism. Paul omits the Lombards' crossing, but as book IV opens, he shows them having attained their promised land and entering upon their book of kings—what we would call ordinary history. *H.L.* 4, for much of its course, looks like a chronicle, and it spans the record number of seventy-two years, fifty of which are bunched up in the last eleven chapters, whereas fifteen are strung out in the opening thirty. To interpret this long span, Paul adopted a well-known Old Testament pattern of action: the Chosen People prosper; they lapse into the worship of false gods and are punished; and Providence mercifully raises up a hero to save them.[225]

As usual, the book is bipartite. Lombard prosperity in the days of Agilulf, Theudelinda, and Gregory the Great is the theme of the opening half. Gregory the Great's death is elaborately dated and marked by a sympathetic crop failure. This is the turning point from prosperity to the worship of false gods.[226] In the second segment, the theme of precipitate decline alternates with the romantic origins of Grimoald, the Lombard savior. We pass from one thread to the other and back again until, in the last chapter, the two converge. The sinning Lombards, though scourged by the advent of an Arian ruler, do not mend their ways. They even engage in the folly of dividing the monarchy between brother-kings and are duly visited with the punishment of civil war. The two brothers are swept away; the evil genius of the civil strife is assassinated; and Grimoald, the shining hero from Benevento, mounts the Pavian throne unstained by the crimes attending his accession.[227]

The prosperous years during which the reign of Agilulf and Theudelinda

---

[223] *H.L.* 3.23-24. For the repetition in *H.L.* 6, n. 281 below.
[224] Both in *H.L.* 4.6: "Langobardi, cum adhuc gentilitatis errore tenerentur"; by Theudelinda's entreaties, "rex permotus, et catholicam fidem tenuit" (ed. Bethmann-Waitz, p. 118).
[225] Cf. Frye, "History and Myth in the Bible," pp. 7, 9.
[226] *H.L.* 4.29.
[227] *H.L.* 4.51.

coincided with the pontificate of Gregory the Great are presented, like much of the *H.L.*, as a succession of miscellaneous facts, often disconnected from each other in time and place. We have to stand far from the page in order to discern what Paul wished us to see. The unifying pattern comes from a drumbeat of commendable actions on the part of the main actors. Agilulf made peace with the Franks and repatriated Italian captives; he established friendly relations with the Avars, even helping them against the Byzantines. Continuing to treat the latter as the great enemy, Agilulf narrowed their Italian districts and carried on a successful feud when his daughter was captured. He wielded a firm hand over turbulent Lombard dukes. When Benevento fell vacant, he appointed the Frioulan Arichis to the southern duchy.[228]

Theudelinda was Gregory the Great's pipeline to Pavia; through her, Agilulf not only entered into a firm peace with the pope, but also put the Church in Lombard territory back on its feet. At Monza, once developed by Theodoric the Ostrogoth, Theudelinda built up the royal complex with a church to John the Baptist (again a motif of conversion) and with a palace whose walls portrayed Lombard achievements. Pope Gregory's letters to her and Agilulf are quoted in full, much as Bede had transcribed the papal letters to Ethelbert of Kent and to the king and queen of Northumbria.[229] Also reproduced is a letter of Gregory's to Arichis of Benevento, whose Catholic friendship constrasts markedly with the pagan obstinacy, despite a helping miracle, of Duke Ariulf of Spoleto (to Paul, Spoleto is bad news). Even the destruction of St. Benedict's foundation at Monte Cassino seems less calamitous when immediately paired with the cordial relations between Duke Arichis and Pope Gregory.[230] Paul's accumulation of details remains cool and detached. Only its substance allows us to realize that Lombard affairs were in good hands.

No fewer than five entries in the opening segment report natural occurrences—drought, severe cold, plague, and the like. Such events were often noted in chronicles and were probably drawn by Paul from the *Historiola* of Secundus of Trent, his main source for Agilulf and Theudelinda.[231] These reminders of the severity of nature, distributed among the many positive

[228] *H.L.* 4.1, 13 (Franks); 12, 20, 24 (Avars); 3, 13, 27 (dukes); 8, 20, 22, 28 (Byzantium); 18 (Benevento).

[229] *H.L.* 4.5-6, 8 (restoration of the Church, peace with the papacy); 21-22 (building at Monza); 9 (letters of Gregory the Great).

[230] *H.L.* 4.16 (ed. Bethmann-Waitz, pp. 121-22): Ariulf finds out how the martyr-bishop Savinus has helped him in battle, but not the slightest change is observed in him (cf. the behavior of Peter of Pavia toward the same martyr, *H.L.* 6.58). Spoleto is rarely mentioned, and never approvingly. Monte Cassino and Arichis of Benevento: 4.17-18 (monastery and duchy are again paired in *H.L.* 6).

[231] *H.L.* 4.2, 4, 10, 14, 15. On Secundus of Trent, 27 (godfather to the son of Theudelinda and Agilulf); 40 (his death in 612).

actions we have seen, inject a note of realism and counteract any impression of panegyric; readers needed to be told that, even in an era of prosperity, this world was not safe from epidemics and cruel weather. Besides, a close look at the individual incidents suggests that no more than one has ominous implications for Lombard affairs. Rains of blood and bloody signs in the heavens are associated with damaging civil wars among the Franks; the drought is counterbalanced by locusts that, amazingly, avoid field crops and content themselves with marsh grasses; the comet marks the passing of Duke Euin of Trent, established in earlier chapters as a commendable man; plague rages, but in imperial territory.[232] The exception involves a recurrence of plague. It again ravages Byzantine Ravenna, but Lombard Verona is affected the next year.[233] There is something disturbing about this, for the sharing of a calamity tends, in Paul's narrative, to be a sign of rapprochement. In this case, though, the implication is not clear.

The lapse of the Lombards from virtue is marked, at its culminating stage, by a civil war between two brothers sharing the monarchy. Paul prepared this climax by a trail of reports of internal dissension that runs through the entire book. It begins, appropriately, with civil wars among the Merovingian Franks, whose practice of sharing kingship among the qualified heirs was notorious for its violent sequels. Thirty thousand men died in a conflict between one Frankish king and his royal cousin; the kingship fell to two little boys in the charge of their grandmother, who had to buy off the Avars; another war pitted two Frankish cousin-kings against each other. Even Lombard territory witnessed such conflicts. In Spoleto, two brothers contended for succession to their father's duchy, and one emerged as victor. That Merovingian and Spoletan behavior should eventually be transposed to Pavia measured the depths to which the Lombards would descend.[234]

The first half of *H.L.* 4 ends with the death of Pope Gregory. His greatness as a Christian magistrate is best documented, in Paul's account, by a declaration he made in a letter to the emperor Maurice: if he had chosen to take a hand in the death of Lombards, they would now be split up in the utmost confusion without leaders; but, because he feared God, he refrained from having a part in bringing death to anyone. Upon his passing, the vines died of cold and the crops failed: "indeed the world was then bound to suffer from famine and drought when, upon the departure of so great a teacher, a lack of spiritual nourishment and the dryness of thirst attacked the souls of men."[235] With these words, Paul set the theme for the next installment.

[232] Blood, *H.L.* 4.4, 15; locusts, 2; comet, 10 (on Euin, see above, n. 213); plague, 4.

[233] *H.L.* 4.14; cf. 3.23-24, 6.5.

[234] Frankish civil wars, *H.L.* 4.4, 11, 15; Spoleto, 16; the climax, 51.

[235] *H.L.* 4.29, tr. Foulke, p. 172, ed. Bethmann-Waitz, p. 126. If one counts by chapters, more than half the book is over, but only 604 has been reached.

Agilulf and Theudelinda continued to reign, but were adrift without their anchor. The alternative to the Catholicism Gregory embodied was that of Byzantium. The Lombards, in their slide toward the Empire, entered figuratively upon the worship of false gods.

In the next-to-last chapter, Paul related a story whose only apparent goal is to sum up the Lombard decline in allegorical form. The fable, whose setting and actors have no relation to Lombard history, seems to be harmlessly edifying. One day, the wife of the Persian king turned up incognito in Constantinople and obtained imperial sponsorship for her baptism; when an embassy arrived to bring her back to Persia, she refused to share her husband's bed again unless he joined her in Christianity; in haste, the Persian king came peacefully to Constantinople with sixty thousand of his people, was baptized in their company with the emperor as godfather, and, having regained his wife, headed back joyfully to his country.[236] It looks, at first glance, as though readers were also meant to rejoice at the winning of souls to Christ. Casual readers were bound to interpret the story in this obvious way.

The implied date is very odd, however, and urges us to look again. Paul, in order to place the tale where it is in *H.L.* 4, situated the incident after the advent of the Byzantine emperor Constans II (641). The Fredegar chronicle, the only source for this story known to us, associates it with the emperor Maurice (d. 602) and the year 588. Although Paul kept the emperor and everyone else anonymous, his version merely simplified Fredegar's and almost certainly derived from it. Paul was well aware of the chronological implications of the name Maurice and surely did not need a second informant in order to transfer the huge Persian baptism from Antioch, its location in the chronicle, to the emperor's presence in Constantinople.[237]

Paul's chronological displacement of the tale, to suit the flow of his narrative, forces us to reconsider its lesson. Conversion is a blessing, of course, but not all roads to the font are equally commendable. There was nothing wrong in making conversion a condition for marriage (even a besotted suitor retains his free will), and Gregory the Great himself urged the Catholic wives of pagan kings to evangelize their husbands. But Paul's Persian queen falls into neither of these slots. Already married, she spontaneously leaves her husband, pursues her own wishes (however holy), and forces her spouse, by sexual blackmail, to undergo with his people a baptism that,

---

[236] *H.L.* 4.50.

[237] By 641, the Persian Empire had been overcome by the Moslems. The historical kernel of the conversion story involves persons and incidents of the later sixth century, as in Fredegar *Chron.* 4.9. Paul's understanding of Maurice's regnal years is illustrated in *H.L.* 3.15 and 4.26 (his death is recorded before Gregory the Great's). Monod (above, n. 169) was convinced that Paul took this story from Fredegar.

though welcome to Christians, involves him in submission as man to wife and as godson to the Byzantine emperor. What makes this conversion story reprehensible is that the queen's blackmail works; only after baptism, confirmation in Catholicism, and receipt of imperial gifts does the Persian king recover his wife. [238] Paul may have narrated the Persian fable when he did, and in the way he did, as a figural commentary on the political influence of Theudelinda. After the death of Gregory the Great, the Catholic wife led her infatuated husband into amicable relations with a Byzantine Empire whose designs on the Lombards were anything but friendly.

In view of the five-decade span from 604 to the accession of Grimoald, which ends the book, Paul ascribed extraordinarily few actions to the kings of Pavia. Only two activities are prominent: in the case of Agilulf, a succession of truces with the Byzantine exarch, followed by a peace embassy to Constantinople; in the case of the kings issuing from Theudelinda or related to her, the building, endowment, and decoration of churches. Agilulf also has the seizure of two cities to his credit; the other kings confine themselves to church construction. [239] What we are to think of such government is suggested by associated events. When relating the coming to Italy of the Irish holy man Columbanus, Paul made a point of detaching him from Agilulf, whose patronage he in fact enjoyed; Columbanus arrives in a chronological no man's land after Agilulf's death, and Bobbio is founded with the aid of an anonymous king. [240] In an evidently symbolic episode, Peter, the cantor of St. Peter's in Pavia, is struck down by lightning. No more is heard thereafter of a connection between Lombard kings and the Petrine see until *H.L.* 6. Abandoning Gregory the Great's concern for Pavia, the popes appear to be won or bribed into exclusively Byzantine sympathies by the emperor Phocas's endorsement of papal claims to ecclesiastical supremacy and his cession of the Pantheon for conversion into a church. The problem of Aquileia, introduced in *H.L.* 3, returns only to solidify into an enduring schism between the old metropolis and the new, Byzantine-controlled patriarchate of Grado. [241] Matters come to such a point of degradation that, after Theudelinda's daughter is accused and cleared of sexual misconduct,

---

[238] " 'Ite, renuntiate regi vestro . . . nisi . . . ipse in Christum crediderit, me iam ultra consortem thori habere non poterit.' . . . Qui nihil moratus . . . pacifice ad imperatorem venit. . . . Qui . . . ab augusto de fonte levatus, catholica fide confirmatus est; multisque muneribus ab augusto honoratus, accepta sua coniuge, . . . ad suam patriam repedavit" (ed. Bethmann-Waitz, p. 137).

[239] *H.L.* 4.32 (includes seizure of two Byzantine cities), 35, 40; churches, 41, 47, 48.

[240] *H.L.* 4.41, specified to be at least ten years after Agilulf's death. Cf. Jonas of Bobbio *Vita s. Columbani* 1.30: "ab Agilulfo . . . honorifice receptus est" (MGH SRM IV, 106).

[241] The cantor Peter, *H.L.* 4.31; favors of Phocas toward the Church of Rome, 36 (from the *Liber pontificalis* 68-69, ed. Duchesne, I, 316-17); Aquileia, 33.

her royal husband is murdered by a victim of his adulteries. Paul noted Agilulf's death, not Theudelinda's. Neither one earns an obituary comment.[242]

The only king whom Paul approved of in this long period was Rothari.
He "was brave and strong and followed the path of justice"—compliments
rarely found anywhere in the *H.L.* Rothari was the first to codify the Lombard laws; he seized Byzantine cities and won a great pitched battle with the
imperial forces.[243] Paul makes a rare intervention in the narrative in order
to vouch personally for the authenticity of the miracle that defended the
king's tomb from would-be defilers.[244] But Rothari, for all his merits, was an
Arian heretic; under him, almost every city had two bishops.[245] Great monarch though he was, the kingdomwide schism he provoked was a deplorable
development. No Catholic could suppose otherwise. Rothari, in short, was
an instrument of God's wrath, both a reprieve from Catholic misgovern-
ment and a punishment visited upon the Lombards for their sins.

Meanwhile, the salvation of the Lombards was being prepared. As in
none of the earlier books, Paul needed to establish a secondary stream of
narrative in the second half of *H.L.* 4 and to move it forward as a distinct
entity until the final chapter. His point of departure was the extraordinary
chapter featuring Romilda of Frioul.[246] A reader of this chapter eventually
realizes, by focusing on the subject of enduring interest, that its real center
of gravity must be, not Romilda, but the wondrous beginnings of Grimoald.
In *H.L.* 1, the hero Lamissio, one of a brood of seven, is born of a common
whore, doomed by her to die of exposure, and saved by giving a sign of life
when the king passed by. Grimoald's beginnings echo these motifs. He was
one of eight children, his mother an "abominable harlot," though a duchess; her depravity doomed him until the child-hero, by a desperately bold
stroke, won his freedom from Avar slavery.[247] In retrospect, these were the
first steps of a prodigious destiny. But there could be no development of
Grimoald's story if he starred in the tale of his origins. The lust of Romilda
and her gruesome punishment furnish an appropriate distraction.

The artificiality of the Romilda legend stems not only from its function,
but also from the villainess herself and the context of Avar invasion. Up to
this point in the *H.L.*, as well as later, the Avars were on good terms with
the Lombards. Their invasion of Frioul, killing Duke Gisulf and many
others in pitched battle and besieging the fortified cities, was an isolated

[242] Theudelinda's daughter and her husband, *H.L.* 4.47-48. Agilulf's death, 41. The same
chapter reports that Theudelinda ruled with their underage son, who eventually went insane;
it is the last we hear of her.
[243] *H.L.* 4.42; quotation tr. Foulke, pp. 193-94; success against the Byzantines, 4.45.
[244] *H.L.* 4.47.
[245] *H.L.* 4.42.
[246] *H.L.* 4.37.
[247] Above, n. 157; *H.L.* 1.15.

instance of hostility, without yesterdays or tomorrows in Avar relations with the Lombard kingdom—at least as portrayed by Paul.[248] Romilda was Gisulf's widow, the bearer of his eight children; for all we are told, her life until widowhood was blameless; her four daughters proved determined and resourceful in saving their virtue from Avar assault.[249] As though unhinged by the invasion and her husband's death, Romilda behaved like a second Tarpeia.[250] She betrayed Forum Iulii to the Avars out of lust for the youthful vigor of their king. The Avar king promised Romilda marriage to win entrance into the city; after herding hundreds of Lombard captives northward, he rewarded her with a hideous and fatal quenching of her lust.

As intended, Romilda's depravity overshadows the exploit of her youngest son, Grimoald, in managing to escape from the Avars with his three brothers. This diversion is soon accompanied by another, closing the long chapter and featuring Paul's own ancestors: "At this point (*locus*) general history must be postponed so that I, the author, might relate a few things of a private character concerning my genealogy."[251] It is the closest Paul comes to autobiography. In fact, the account of his ancestry adds nothing to the tale of Romilda and her children that would warrant a postponement. We are merely told, as if it mattered, that Paul's great-grandfather was captured in this Avar raid, and that he, like the sons of Gisulf, successfully escaped and made his way back to Frioul. The romance of the fugitive guided by a wolf and befriended by a Slavic woman is only a little less arresting than the lust of Romilda. Again diverted from the main course of the narrative, we are left wondering what pertinence the tale of Paul's ancestor might have.

Paul's intrusions into the *H.L.*, most often for purposes of authentication, are no more candid or naïve than the rest of his work. The miracle at Rothari's tomb that he vouched for, the skullcup that he saw in King Ratchis's hands, and the Amazons fought by Lamissio whom he thought possibly real, are far too symbolic for Paul's comments about them to be taken as statements of literal fact.[252] Paul's ancestor, named Lopichis, is helped by a wolf (*lupus*), and chronology is skewed by the telescoping of time, since four generations, from Paul to his great-grandfather, normally span far fewer than the two hundred years implied here. Because the recital

[248] Cf. above, n. 228; the rest of the *H.L.* tells basically the same story (an advantageous one from Paul's perspective: the Avars were not conquered by Charlemagne until 796; their independence from the Frankish Empire paralleled that of Benevento).

[249] Grimoald's sisters adopted a memorable stratagem to discourage Avar sexual advances: *H.L.* 4.37, ed. Bethmann-Waitz, p. 130 lines 26-33.

[250] The very opposite of Digna at nearby Aquileia in the *H.R.*; above, n. 84.

[251] "Exigit vero nunc locus, postposita generali historia, pauca etiam privatim de mea, qui haec scribo, genealogia retexere" (ed. Bethmann-Waitz, p. 131).

[252] *H.L.* 4.47, 2.38, 1.15.

of Paul's progenitors, which ends the story, tells us no more than their names, it is hard to believe that the aim was self-advertisement, except in a very special sense. Paul's great-grandfather remotely sharing the fate of the first Grimoald foreshadows the association of Paul himself to Grimoald III. Paul's intrusion was an unusually direct device for suggesting the figural dimension of the first Grimoald's adventures.

Conspicuously launched, the second narrative strand alternates thereafter with the course of Pavian events. Gisulf's sons survived the Avar raid on Frioul, escaped from their captors, and returned home. The two grown ones took charge of the paternal duchy but, like their Pavian counterparts, were deluded by pretenses of Byzantine friendship; they perished in a trap. When they were replaced in Frioul by Gisulf's brother, the younger sons, Rodoald and Grimoald, rowed away in disgust to join their one-time fosterer, the duke of Benevento, Arichis.[253] For a second time, Byzantine treachery then impinged on their destiny. Arichis's son, on the way to visit Pavia, was driven mad in Ravenna by a mysterious potion. Although the aged Arichis commended Rodoald and Grimoald to the Beneventans as their protectors, the Frioulan brothers faithfully served Arichis's crazed son when he succeeded his father. Within a year, the son was killed fighting Slavic raiders whom Rodoald defeated in a counterattack. He died after five years as duke of Benevento. Grimoald succeeded him; a "very warlike man, outstanding in every respect," he inaugurated his rule with a great victory over the Greeks.[254]

If all the details were historical, the resemblances to eighth-century circumstances would be astonishing. Both the old Arichis and Paul's patron of the same name were Frioulans and direct royal appointees to Benevento. Rodoald preceded Grimoald I as duke, just as—in the 780s—Grimoald III was preceded by his brother Liutprand, co-ruler with Arichis II, and, like his namesake, inaugurated his rule by defeating a Greek invasion.[255] The hostility to Byzantium discreetly expressed in Paul's narrative of Pavian events is emphatic when Benevento is in question. Paul sounds as though he were saying something to the reigning Grimoald. The *H.L.* discourages any designs that involved cooperation with the Greeks.

When Paul portrayed Rodoald and Grimoald rowing away from Frioul toward Benevento, he evoked more than the flight of two boys from their uncle's suspect guardianship. Benevento became the sole home of Lombard sovereignty after Charlemagne conquered the Pavian monarchy in 774. Paul's *History* is one sign of this shift; another is the autonomous de-

---

[253] *H.L.* 4.38-39.
[254] *H.L.* 4.42-44, 46.
[255] Cf. above, nn. 57-58.

velopment of Lombard law in the South long after the eighth century.[256] A southward *translatio regni* took place. Written history sometimes assuages the sting of painful events by prefiguring them. The centrality of Grimoald I in the *H.L.* displaces elements of the eighth-century *translatio regni* by more than a century, comfortably earlier than the Frankish conquest. Already with the first Grimoald, the true hope of the Lombards took up residence in Benevento. The rowboat crossing the Adriatic has much the same positive significance as the pivotal river crossing in *H.L.* 1.

In the final chapter of *H.L.* 4, the Pavian and Beneventan strands converge. We see the descendants of Theudelinda ruining themselves in an abrupt tragedy, engineered by a Machiavellian villain, Duke Garipald of Turin.[257] Two brothers, with capitals in Pavia and Milan, respectively, shared the monarchy in Merovingian fashion. No sooner did this happen than evil men aroused enmity between them. Duke Garipald urged King Godepert to seek the help of Grimoald of Benevento against King Perctarit. Sent to Benevento on this mission, Garipald persuaded Grimoald to seize royal power from the worthless brothers. Grimoald marched north, gaining strength along the way, but Godepert was still unaware of the usurpation when the Beneventan reached Pavia. By Garipald's treachery, Grimoald was admitted to the Pavian palace and, as an unwitting actor in the villain's ultimate contrivance, killed Godepert in what was to have been an unarmed interview. King Perctarit fled from Milan to the Avars; other members of the royal family were variously exiled or spirited away. When the archfiend Garipald entered the church of St. John to celebrate Easter, the dwarf of the murdered Godepert lunged down from the baptismal font, decapitated him, and was himself at once cut down. So, on the feast of the Resurrection, the kingdom was in the power of its savior, Grimoald of Benevento.

11. *H.L.* 5: From Christian Kingship to Confusion and Anarchy

After a six-decade rush, *H.L.* 5 is assigned a rather short span, suited to the glorification of Paul's central hero. Two-thirds of it (counted by lines) are addressed to the nine years of Grimoald I's reign. The savior whose rise to kingship was traced in *H.L.* 4 is shown in the sequel engaging in admirable exploits; notably, the repulse of a Byzantine invasion and the snuffing out of a dangerous usurpation. But the intensity and dramatic interest of the book come from an extreme contrast between the chapters about Grimoald and the closing third, concerned with his immediate suc-

---

[256] Buchner, *Rechtsquellen*, pp. 36-37.

[257] For this character in drama, see Thorndike, *Tragedy*, pp. 95, 164-65, 190, 311. Cf. Frye, *Anatomy of Criticism*, p. 216: a "self-starting principle of malevolence whose motives never need to be spelled out."

cessors. After Grimoald's death, the dynasty of Theudelinda is abruptly restored in the person of Perctarit, the king whom Grimoald drove into exile. Perctarit and his son, Cunicpert, resume the feckless course of their line. Their weakness occasions a usurpation by Alahis, paragon of greed and anti-clericalism, who is defeated only by the direct intervention and death of a deacon disguised in Cunicpert's armor. To the exemplary rule of Grimoald there succeeds a king so incapable of fulfilling his duties that he must be saved by a churchman's heroic, but thoroughly uncanonical, sacrifice.[258]

Because of its unusual concentration on a single personality and theme, *H.L.* 5 is more linear and less fragmented in narrative than any other book. The usual bipartite and symmetrical structure is present (see Table 8). The second half is longer than the first, but not so much so by line count (237/300) as by chapters (14/25). Paul evidently intended that the division between the two halves should fall within Grimoald's reign and not at his death. In addition to the dramatic reversal from grandeur to degradation, three conspicuous contrasts are embedded in the narrative and serve to integrate it. A servant of Perctarit tricked Grimoald by masquerading as his master and was gallantly forgiven (I), but the deacon who disguised himself as King Cunicpert earned death as his reward (IV). For added emphasis, Grimoald's forgiveness of Perctarit's servant (I) is set off against the brutality of the Byzantines who executed a heroically loyal Lombard (II). Later, Grimoald disposed of a usurper without civil war among the Lombards (III), whereas in the usurpation of Alahis even the deacon's death in Cunicpert's place does not avert a general internecine battle (IV).[259] In a less obvious contrast, the Byzantine emperor Constans II strips the roof of a Roman church of its ornamental metal (II), and Pope Donus paves the area before St. Peter's in marble (III).[260] Paul plotted *H.L.* 5 as a romance that shifts abruptly into its ironic opposite after the central hero's death.

Table 8

   I. Grimoald's magnanimity (chs. 1-5)
  II. Grimoald repels the invading Byzantine Constans II (chs. 6-14)
 III. Natural events and return to Pavia (Entr'acte) (chs. 15-16)
 IV. Grimoald's prudent government and death (chs. 17-33a)
  V. Legitimist restoration and civil war (chs. 33b-41)

---

[258] *H.L.* 5.40. The deacon Seno stands in for Cunicpert to prevent his death, because Seno had "eiusdem statura et habitus" (ed. Bethmann-Waitz, p. 160), not because he was a better fighter; no indication that Seno stood a chance in battle. On clerics being forbidden to fight, Erdmann, *Entstehung des Kreuzzugsgedankens*, pp. 12-13.

[259] Respectively, *H.L.* 5.2-4, 40; 2-4, 8; 19, 40-41. On the switches of identity (including those of Rosamund in book II and Authari in book III), see Zurli, "Le 'proprietà' del motivo dello 'scambio de persona.' "

[260] *H.L.* 5.11, 31.

Above all, Paul's account of Grimoald exemplifies Christian heroism. Nowhere is Grimoald brought into relation with clergymen or ecclesiastical affairs; we learn only at his death that he built a church in Pavia.[261] But the first, very long incident of his reign allows him to display a quality of magnanimity reserved in the *H.L.* for only the most exceptional rulers. A treaty he makes with the Avars forces the deposed king Perctarit to abandon his refuge with them; apprised of Grimoald's gallantry, Perctarit asks to be allowed to return to Pavia in safety as a private citizen; Grimoald generously assents but, as support gathers around the returned ex-king, his courtiers persuade him to go against his word and kill Perctarit; the latter is extricated from this danger by two faithful friends, one of whom dons his clothes and takes Perctarit's place while he escapes; when the trick is discovered, and the accomplices are presented to Grimoald, the courtiers cry that they should be put to death, but Grimoald honors their loyalty, takes them into his service, and, when they express a preference for rejoining their exiled lord, allows them to leave with all their property.[262] Paul makes it clear that Grimoald was no saint. He let himself be talked into going against his word. But he was Christian enough to welcome and reward the stratagem that saved him from grave sin by extricating Perctarit from his grasp.

In a further development of the Christian theme, Grimoald's own heroism is expressed in cunning rather than in physical prowess, the wiles of Odysseus rather than the anger of Achilles. Early in the reign, he defeats a Frankish incursion by resorting to the ancient ruse of abandoning to them a camp full of food and wine and then catching them off guard. He later deals with the rebellious Duke Lupus of Frioul by inciting the Avars to attack him, thus avoiding civil conflict. When the Avars refuse to withdraw, he deceives their envoys into believing that his small army is enormous and gains their retreat.[263] The skillful avoidance of combat in mastering this rebel matters more to Paul than the successful outcome. There is no counterpart in *H.L.* 5 to the face-to-face killing by which Grimoald as a little boy saved himself from captivity. Even when he marches to Benevento against the Byzantines, he is portrayed hovering in the background and not personally fighting them.[264] Yet it is Cunicpert, renowned for boldness and great physical strength, who needs a deacon to die for him in battle. Reinforcing the lesson, the secondary heroes of the book earn their glory by the assumption of disguises and other tricks. The most applauded feat of arms

[261] *H.L.* 5.33.

[262] *H.L.* 5.2-4.

[263] *H.L.* 5.5 (Franks), 19-21 (Lupus). Paul spells out the idea of avoiding civil war by calling in foreign auxiliaries.

[264] *H.L.* 5.10; though intending to fight, Grimoald stands aside when told by his son, the duke of Benevento, that his participation is superfluous; the duke can handle the battle, and does.

involves a duke of Frioul who, instead of waiting for a full mobilization, advanced against attacking Slavs with so few men that he was at first mistaken derisively for the patriarch and his clergy.[265]

H.L. 5 straightforwardly narrates a model reign. The honoring of fidelity, the preference for guile over force, the avoidance of bloodshed, particularly between Lombards, are obvious lessons. But Grimoald did not shrink from the use of force. He indirectly repressed Lupus's rebellion—at great cost to the latter's Frioulan supporters, who were butchered in a great battle with the Avars; he punished Lombards who deserted the relief expedition to Benevento; and he took stern vengeance (including an attack on Easter Sunday) against Roman cities that had preyed on his lines of communication and otherwise harmed him.[266] Paul would not have us believe that Christian kingship was incompatible with severity. On a more amiable note, Grimoald welcomed Alzeco, a Bulgarian duke, and his people and provided them with settlements in Benevento. Alboin, in *H.L.* 2, had been similarly open to foreigners, such as the Saxons, whom the foolish Lombards had alienated after his death by denying them their customary laws. Paul approvingly adds that the descendants of Alzeco's Bulgarians continued to live in Benevento to his time, speaking their ancestral language as well as Latin.[267]

Paul credits Grimoald with two major exploits, one against a foreign enemy, the other against the usurping duke of Frioul, Lupus. Enough has been said about the latter. The first exploit involves the last appearance in the West of a lineal descendant of the emperor Augustus. As portrayed by Paul, Italy under the descendants of Theudelinda was an apple ready to be plucked by the Byzantines; but when the emperor Constans II arrived, Grimoald occupied the Pavian throne, and he succeeded in frustrating the Byzantine campaign by mustering an army and marching south. Paul seems to present Constans's invasion as a foreshadowing of Charlemagne's; a Frankish incursion is mentioned in the immediately preceding chapter. Constans, before setting out, visits a holy man to ask whether he will succeed; the holy man replies that he will not: the Lombards were safe so long as they honored the shrine of St. John the Baptist built by Theudelinda at Monza and thus enjoyed the saint's continual intercession. Paul intervenes to point out the fulfillment of the prophecy: "we have seen that before the ruin (*perditio*) of the Lombards" this church was given to worthless, greedy men. Unlike us, Paul's readers would have known well enough whether this after-the-fact prediction should be understood literally or metaphorically. Constans, fated to fail, invaded anyway and soon showed his base character

---

[265] Cunicpert's strength and boldness, *H.L.* 5.40; the resolute duke of Frioul, 23.
[266] *H.L.* 5.19, 26 (cf. 7), 27-28.
[267] *H.L.* 5.29 (cf. 2.6, 3.6).

by executing the brave Beneventan who carried word to Pavia and, by a trick, informed besieged Benevento of Grimoald's imminent arrival. By Paul's account, the royal army did little more than make an appearance. A battle eventually took place, at which both Grimoald and Constans were represented by proxies; Paul resolves it into a virtually symbolic encounter between Grimoald's spearbearer and a little Greek lifted bodily from his saddle. The serious point embedded in the tale is that Grimoald's presence at Pavia ensured a collective response to the Byzantine invasion. The northern Lombards were ready to leave Benevento in the lurch; many deserted Grimoald's relief army, claiming that he had simply stripped the palace at Pavia and was now going home. It took a figure of Grimoald's stature to rally the larger part against a danger that too few regarded as affecting them all. Another parallel may be intended here with the circumstances of 774.[268]

Paul's hostility to Byzantium—truer, one suspects, to the conditions of his lifetime than to those of the seventh century—reaches its acme in *H.L.* 5, in proportion with the danger he attributes to the invasion of Constans. After relating Grimoald's successful intervention, he takes pains to show Constans feeding like a scorpion on the body he had pretended to liberate. The emperor visited Rome and robbed its monuments of their metal ornaments; he moved on to Sicily and drove the population into slavery by extortionate taxes; his tyranny eventually invited assassination, followed in its turn by a usurpation, whose failure opened Sicily to a Saracen raid (the first appearance of the Moslems in the *H.L.* occasions no special comment). Symbolically, as well as for a touch of pathos, a daughter of Grimoald, held as a hostage, dies in Byzantine captivity; she is the third royal princess noted in the *H.L.* as suffering this fate.[269] Paul's concern with It-

---

[268] *H.L.* 5.6, Constans II "Italiam a Langobardorum manu eruere cupiens" (ed. Bethmann-Waitz, p. 146). The Franks, 5 (no king or other specific details are mentioned). Constans, the holy man, and Paul's comment, 6 (about Constans's consultation, cf. Theodosius I and the hermit John, *H.R.* 12.4). We lack the information needed to interpret Paul's comment. The brave Beneventan, 7-8. On the almost symbolic battle (10), see Hanning, *Vision of History*, pp. 98-99. Allegations of stripping the palace, *H.L.* 5.7.
Maisano, "Spedizione italiana," p. 147, points out that Paul's source, the *Liber pontificalis*, never intimates that Constans sought to seize Italy from the Lombards.

[269] *H.L.* 5.11-13. The princess, 8, 14; earlier ones: *H.L.* 3.21 (a Frank), 4.20, 28 (Agilulf's daughter; she is given back, but dies soon after release); in 1.16, Bulgarians carry off the daughter of King Agelmund.
Paul's hostility toward Byzantium is likely to have been political rather than emotional or religious in motivation. Benevento shared southern Italy with Byzantine enclaves. For anyone disposed as Paul was to good relations with the Franks and acceptance of their conquest of the Lombard kingdom, the obvious course to recommend for Benevento was one of amity toward the Franks and of completion of Lombard conquest by the expulsion of what remained of Byzantine rule from Italy (therefore, in Paul's perspective, Lombard conquerors continued to be topical).

aly, rather than specifically with the Lombards, helps explain his attention to the damaging outcome of Constans's campaign. Here, as in the post-Gregorian half of *H.L.* 4, papal Rome continues to be remote from the Lombards, but no longer wholly won by Constantinople. The contrast between Constans despoiling the Pantheon-turned-church of its metal roof and Pope Donus laying down a splendid marble pavement at least hints at a papacy shaken in its Byzantine allegiance and taking charge of its city.[270]

The romance of Grimoald ends as it must with the more than ordinary death called for by the hero's superhuman qualities. Nine days after being bled, he burst the weakened artery while shooting at pigeons with a bow; his doctors finished him off by applying poisoned medicine. Paul notes Grimoald's lawmaking and, as of no earlier king, describes his physical appearance: he was bald and wore a full beard (the association of baldness with heroic energy is pointed out a few chapters earlier). Though the throne passed to Grimoald's very young son, it was at once reclaimed by the deposed and exiled Perctarit.[271]

We learn soon enough that Paul deplored the restoration of Theudelinda's descendants. Characteristically, Perctarit's return is surrounded with the trappings of supernatural intervention. In a replay of Perctarit's expulsion by the Avars at the beginning of the book, he was forced to leave the Frankish kingdom by Grimoald's treaty with King Dagobert II; but while he was still on the ship taking him to England, a mysterious voice from shore, which could never be identified, announced that Grimoald had died. Perctarit headed for Pavia and effortlessly resumed the throne. In short, a mysterious decision of Providence determined the course of events.[272] The corpulent Perctarit, true to his dynasty, could think of nothing better to do on his return than to build churches. Seven years pass without another noted action except the deplorable installation of Cunicpert, his son, as co-king. The latter's poor judgment concerning the arrogant Duke Alahis—to try to animate his fidelity by forgiving past infidelities and promoting him from Trent to Brescia—was argued against by Perctarit but nevertheless assented to. Grimoald's successor died after eighteen years of inactivity. Paul's obituary remark that Perctarit was "mild and gentle" is only ostensible praise.[273] In the light of *H.L.* 4, the impression one gains is that Paul cast the line of Theudelinda as *rois fainéants* on the Merovingian pattern. It was an obvious association for a contemporary of Charlemagne's to make.

[270] As above, n. 260.

[271] *H.L.* 5.33. The poisoned medicines are in a class with Marcian's death (*H.R.* 14.19) and Childebert's (*H.L.* 4.11); cf. above, n. 82. Baldness, 5.23.

[272] *H.L.* 5.33; cf. 5.2. For a distant parallel, see Jonas of Bobbio *Vita Columbani* 1.23.

[273] *H.L.* 5.34-37. Typically, any casual reader of Perctarit's (brief) obituary would think that Paul thought well of him. Paul's discreet words have to be checked against his account of deeds.

The story of Alahis's rebellion against Cunicpert, which ends *H.L.* 5, reaches back into Perctarit's reign, as we have seen, in order to engage his responsibility in its outbreak. Paul's narrative is so absorbing and colorful—almost Merovingian in recalling Gregory of Tours—that its point tends to be lost unless carefully sought. In the final line, Cunicpert "returns to Pavia amidst everyone's enthusiasm and in the triumph of victory." The context seems plausible enough: Alahis is dead, his cause defeated; but Paul's words prove to be pure irony when restored to the full course of his tale.

Of course, Paul strips Alahis of any claim to sympathy, portraying him as an unrelieved villain. The saintly bishop of Pavia tried initially to remain impartial in the contest over the throne (Paul approves of this course), but Alahis greeted the bishop's emissary with gutter language and expressed such contempt for celibates that the clergy were forced to take sides; Alahis later vowed to fill a well with clerical genitals. Besides, he plotted to despoil his own supporters of their wealth as soon as he was able and, by the agency of a child, triggered their defection; and he forced unwilling cities to fight for him. He had no compensatory virtues. But neither did his opponent, Cunicpert, whose misplaced admiration and trust were responsible for forwarding Alahis's career in the first place.[274]

Paul's flow of entertaining details diverts attention from his implication that there was more than one villain. Cunicpert no sooner becomes sole king than he is shown engaging in amatory adventure. Deprived of the throne while absent from Pavia, he took refuge on a fortified island and made no countermove until invited to do so by Alahis's disaffected partisans. He did offer Alahis single combat but, when battle was about to be joined, yielded to the "prayers and tears" of his followers ("since he was of tender heart") and allowed the deacon Seno to don his armor, go into battle, and be killed in his place. Soon after, Alahis died in the mêlée, without Cunicpert affecting the outcome otherwise than by revealing that he was still alive. The Lombards on both sides suffered heavy loss of life.[275] Paul's intention at the end is that we should mourn rather than exult, for there had been no victory, only a wasting contest of bad with worse.

From a structural standpoint, *H.L.* 5 offers perhaps the best illustration

---

[274] *H.L.* 5.36, 38-41. The final line, "cum omnium exultatione et triumpho victoriae Ticinum reversus est" (ed. Bethmann-Waitz, p. 161). The bishop sends Alahis a specially pious deacon with the benediction of his Church, "ne quid ab eo ipse vel sua ecclesia adversi perpeteretur" (p. 157); in other words, the Church should protect itself and not take sides between claimants in a (civil) war.

[275] *H.L.* 5.37 (amatory adventure; somewhat similar to a story told about Valentinian I by Socrates *H.E.* 4.31, but radically abridged by Jordanes *Rom.* ¶¶ 310-11 and from there in Paul *H.R.* 11.7). *H.L.* 5.38 (Cunicpert flees to an island), 39 (called from there), 40 (accepts Seno's offer, "Victus tandem, ut erat pii cordis, eorum precibus et lacrimis," ed. Bethmann-Waitz, p. 160), 41 (Cunicpert shows himself to the troops, great loss of life).

of how Paul integrates ostensibly independent tales into a larger whole. In *H.L.* 2 and 3, the legends of Rosamund's revenge and of Theudelinda's marriage, each of which stands out from a drier context, may be shown easily enough to form part of a dramatic plot. The looser form of romance in *H.L.* 5 called for a somewhat different approach. The tale of Perctarit's escape from Grimoald's clutches at the beginning seems to have little in common with that of the usurpation of Alahis at the end, except for the accents and diverting details of legend. But in both, a crucial role is played by a secondary character who assumes royal clothes and masquerades as the king. The contrasting fate of these minor heroes epitomizes the main point of the book—what the passage from Grimoald to Cunicpert meant for the Lombard kingdom. In this way, two tales that seem wholly isolated from each other are shaped into a scenario that is articulated by the details they share.

12. *H.L.* 6: Italy in Transition

With *H.L.* 6, Paul moved into the eighth century and overlapped the years of his infancy. No other book is so rich in factual content or less enlivened by legend. After the unusual concentration of *H.L.* 5 on Lombard kingship, we are treated to no fewer than eight almost equally weighted themes, set out in a very fragmented way. *H.L.* 6 also happens to be the last book, though never meant to end the work as it does now. Had Paul completed it to his satisfaction, or did an amanuensis pull together an advanced draft into finished shape? Authors have no guarantee of dying at a convenient point in composition, precisely between books. The style of *H.L.* 6 has been found to be less polished than that of its predecessors.[276] Its narrative is also somewhat anomalous. There is no obvious caesura, just one effective parallel. What seems absent, for the first time in the *H.L.*, is the unifying force of a plot.

The one conspicuous structural feature of *H.L.* 6 is that Benevento opens the book on a very positive note, that Spoleto begins its second half, and that, in the last, rather ominous four chapters, both southern principalities intersect with King Liutprand (and the Frioulans who would succeed him).[277] The account of Benevento at the start is paired with a chapter on Monte Cassino, and the same pairing is later repeated immediately after a eulogy of King Liutprand. In the context of Paul's writings, such chapters have obvious relevance to himself and his Beneventan patrons. They recall

[276] Neff, *De Paulo Diacono Festi epitomatore*, pp. 31-33, argues a gradual weakening of Paul's style; Manitius, *Gesch. d. lat. Lit.* I, 268-69. Despite the force of Krüger's demonstration of incompletion (above, n. 55), it is odd that *H.L.* 6 itself survives as a completed book.

[277] *H.L.* 6.1-2, 30 (to my mind, this begins part two of the book; but the point is open to argument, for there are no obvious signposts here, or anywhere else for that matter), 55-57.

similar pairs in *H.L.* 4, in the second digression of *H.L.* 1 (Justinian followed by St. Benedict), and in the "prophetic" pause featuring the Lombards and St. Benedict just before the end of the *Historia Romana*.[278] Besides indicating extreme approval, these passages tend to have a more than
literal significance. The holy man Hospicius, who opens *H.L.* 3 and pro-
phetically announces its theme, is another case in point. Paul's care to associate Liutprand, Benevento, and Monte Cassino invites us, at the end,
to recall the opening Beneventan chapters as we read of the death of the
highly commendable king. In beginning the book, Paul evoked Grimoald
I's son, the admirable duke Rodoald of Benevento, who annexed Roman
cities while his wife built churches, and in whose principality, at Monte
Cassino, the dissolved flesh of St. Benedict continued to lie even though
his bones had been removed and translated to Francia.[279] That exemplary
principality and holy mountain still existed, not only at Liutprand's death
but at the time of writing. The intimation of a hopeful future balanced the
sadness of a regrettably isolated reign.

As implied by the Beneventan opening, hopefulness, or the turn of
events in promising directions, is the pervasive atmosphere of the first half.
The brief entry concerning Frioul initiates a chain of circumstances that,
owing to a calamitous defeat at the hands of the Slavs, results in the beneficent accession of Pemmo, the father of future kings, to the dukedom.[280]
But the most positive development involves the papacy. Alienated from
the Lombards—at least in Paul's account—ever since the death of Gregory
the Great, it now acted in concert with Lombard clergy in the repression of
Monotheletism at the Sixth General Council. Paul underscores the reconciliation by the earlier-used device of a sympathetic or shared misfortune: plague ravages both Rome and Pavia, making many victims, and is
allayed by the translation to Pavia of relics of the Roman martyr Sebastian.
At the next appearance of a pope, a solution is finally brought to the cen-
tury-old schism of the Three Chapters. Paul, never strong in the exposition
of theological controversy, portrays Pope Sergius winning back the dissi-
dent bishops of the Northeast (whose memory of the original difficulty cannot have been very vivid) by means of an explanation that made the Fifth
General Council sound identical to the Third. However that may be, Sergius shone, not least by the arrival in Rome of an English king to be baptized and live out his few remaining days. England is symbolic of a pastoral

---

[278] Liutprand, Benevento, refounding of Monte Cassino, *H.L.* 6.38-40. Earlier pairing:
4.17-18, 1.25-26, *H.R.* 16.20.

[279] Cf. Goffart, "Le Mans, St. Scholastica, and Literary Tradition"; I am no longer sure that
Paul closely agrees with the date 703 for the translation to Francia (p. 109 n. 7). See now
Hourlier, "Témoignage de Paul Diacre."

[280] *H.L.* 6.3, 24-26.

papacy in the style of Gregory the Great. An English note was struck in the second papal entry of *H.L.* 5 and now becomes dominant, as harmonious relations between the Lombards and the Holy See are re-established. As the first half of *H.L.* 6 closes, papal lands are spontaneously restored by the Lombard king, more English kings reach Rome as pilgrims, and ecclesiastical jurisdiction over Pavia is gained from Milan by Rome.[281]

The hopeful implications of the Beneventan beginning carry over even to grimmer subjects, for it is apparent that the dismal course of Byzantine developments and the equally dismal history of Cunicpert and his successors were not displeasing to Paul. The chapters concerning Byzantium narrate a continual round of usurpations, coupled with an abortive attempt by Justinian II to have the pope arrested and shipped to Constantinople. Paul's interpretation gains clarity in the second half: the internal instability of Byzantium and its quarrels with the papacy had the salutary effect of detaching it from Italy.[282]

The fate of the royal descendants of Theudelinda was no less to Paul's liking. As in the final line of *H.L.* 5, he took care that his sentiments should be discernible only to attentive readers. Cunicpert is called in his obituary "most beloved by all . . . conspicuous in every good quality and a bold warrior . . . buried with many tears." But deeds speak louder than words. Cunicpert's only positive action in *H.L.* 6 involves tearing out the eyes of a deposed duke of Frioul. Otherwise, he plots the unjust death of two holdovers from Alahis's rebellion and is cheated by a miracle out of implementing his design; and he supplies a saintly bishop who displeases him with an untamed horse, only to be again cheated by a miracle of the sought-after outcome.[283] With Cunicpert, Paul's comparison of Theudelinda's descendants to the *rois fainéants* is made almost explicit. The chapter before the one noting his death begins, "At this time in Gaul when the kings of the Franks were degenerating from their wonted courage and skill."[284] Cunicpert goes to his reward ironically mourned, and, in a splendid reprise of the end of *H.L.* 5, bad is followed by worse: Cunicpert's heir was quickly dislodged by a collateral, Aripert, who proved to be a facsimile of Alahis.

---

[281] *H.L.* 6.4-5, 14 (the synod in Justinian's time was against all those "qui, beatam Mariam solum hominem, non Deum et hominem genuisse, adfirmabant," ed. Bethmann-Waitz, p. 169), 15 (the coming of Cædwalla, from Bede *H.E.* 5.7), cf. 5.30; 6.27-29 (closing of first half). Paul can be reminiscent of Bede's discretion: in relating the recovery by Rome of jurisdiction over Pavia, he mainly stresses the holiness of the archbishop of Milan, who lost the suit.

[282] *H.L.* 6.9-10, 12-13 (usurpations), 11 (pope's arrest attempted), 31-34 (detachment), 35 (return of orthodoxy), 41, 49 (Leo III and iconoclasm).

[283] *H.L.* 6.17, tr. Foulke, p. 263; "cunctis amabillimus . . . omni bonitate conspicuus . . . cum multis Langobardorum lacrimis . . . sepultus est" (ed. Bethmann-Waitz, p. 170). *H.L.* 6.3 (tearing out eyes), 6, 8 (dirty tricks).

[284] *H.L.* 6.16, tr. Foulke, pp. 262-63: it is Paul's first notice of the Arnulfingians.

A bloody trail of civil war, executions, and gratuitous brutality brought him to the throne. Aripert II would be the last of Theudelinda's dynasty, but his end is reserved for the second half of *H.L.* 6. His advent provides our first glimpse of his successor. Cunicpert had left his son in charge of a fosterer, Ansprand, the father of Liutprand. Ansprand escaped the bloodbath, and King Aripert contemptuously released the boy Liutprand. The latter's reception by his father echoes that of young Grimoald I by his brothers. Paul even specifies that the boy's release "was done by the command of God Almighty who was preparing him for the management of the kingdom."[285] In Liutprand, the Lombards were assured of another savior, but not quite on Grimoald's scale.

The main point of Paul's chapter noting the degeneracy of the Merovingians is to hail the divine calling of St. Arnulf of Metz, the patriarch of Charlemagne's dynasty, who (it is said) was for a time steward of the Frankish palace. Arnulf, who died ca. 640, is mentioned some four decades out of chronological order, so that the rise of his line might coincide in narrative with the opposite movement among Theudelinda's descendants. Arnulfingian chapters straddle the account of Cunicpert's death and Aripert's brutal accession. The next passage after Arnulf's evokes the stewardship of his admirable son Anschis, named after Anchises, the father of Aeneas, in commemoration of the Trojan origin of the Franks. In the second half of *H.L.* 6, the elder Pepin and his son, Charles Martel, are both introduced with very flattering (if legendary or fictional) characterizations. Paul leaves us in no doubt about the divine election of the dynasty that would conquer the Lombard kingdom. Arnulf's descendants are even mentioned alongside a statement that all sorts of Anglo-Saxons kept coming on pilgrimage to Rome.[286] By thus aligning a papacy returning to Gregorian ways with the new Frankish dynasty and with the English as a current flowing between them, Paul showed his awareness of what we continue to regard as the dynamic forces of the age. The more remarkable fact is that the Arnulfingian phenomenon seemed to him to be a desirable turn of events even in the context of Lombard history. He had praised Charlemagne's family in the *Gesta episcoporum Mettensium*; in *H.L.* 6, he mentioned writing this work and remained consistent with the praise uttered there. However different the patronage and circumstances of the Metz *Gesta* had been from those of

[285] *H.L.* 6.18-22. Grimoald's flight, 4.37, ed. Bethmann-Waitz, p. 130 line 18, *inaestimabile gaudium*; Liutprand's release, 6.22, p. 172 line 11, the same phrase. Liutprand's providentiality, *ibid.*, tr. Foulke, p. 266; "Quod Dei omnipotentis nutu factum fuisse, qui eum ad regni gubernacula praeparabat" (ed. Bethmann-Waitz, p. 172).

[286] *H.L.* 6.16, 23 (the Trojan, i.e. Roman, name of Anschis-Anchises is ominous), 37 (the chapter about Pepin begins with a reference to the continual pilgrimages of Anglo-Saxons to the Holy See; from Bede *H.E.* 5.7, ed. Plummer, I, 294), 42 (Charles Martel). A story about Pepin in 6.37 is almost repeated in one about Liutprand in 6.38.

the *H. L.*, its views had not been forced out of him or expressed merely to win someone's favor. The account of the conquest of 774 in his never-written seventh book would probably have paralleled that of the peaceful invasion of Italy by Alboin in *H. L.* 2.[287]

In the second half of *H. L.* 6, a generally satisfactory present, typified by the exemplary reign of Liutprand, jostles with intimations of a troubled future. Paul's account, compressing more than thirty years, bears only a vague relationship to modern histories of the same period. A lack of information cannot have been the cause. The *Liber pontificalis* alone, with its detailed reports of meetings between King Liutprand and Pope Zachary, told him much that he chose to omit.[288] Liutprand marched south three times to break up rapprochements between Spoleto, Benevento, and Rome that threatened to detach the two southern duchies from the Lombard kingdom. In Paul's version, two of the campaigns are treated as one, and only Spoleto acts in concert with Rome. It had already been tagged in dark colors in *H. L.* 4 and now fulfilled the destiny foreshadowed there.[289] Meanwhile, Benevento retained its innocence: difficulties over its rulership occasioned Liutprand's interventions, but it stayed free of any suspicion of disloyalty.[290] Paul's aim was impressionistic interpretation rather than factual reporting; and, as we have already seen in connection with the holy man's prophecy to Constans II, some of what Paul wished to say necessarily eludes us for lack of the never-written books.

The narrative attains the satisfactory climax earlier prepared concerning Byzantium and the Lombard monarchy. Not only do the emperors continue to overthrow each other in rapid succession but, in Byzantine fashion, they dabble in heresy and, with Leo III, lapse into full-fledged iconoclasm. Italy unanimously resists. The same chapter that discourses on Leo's image-breaking also speaks of Liutprand conquering Classis (the port of Ravenna), and many other cities still under imperial rule, as well as of the Lombards resisting an emissary of the exarch sent to murder the pope.[291] Paul's implication that the end of Byzantium in Italy had come is very clear. The repulse of the Saracens besieging Constantinople is paired with Charles Martel's great defeat of the Saracens in Gaul. Typically, Charles's victory

[287] Cf. above, nn. 158, 190-91.

[288] *Liber pontificalis* 93, ed. Duchesne, I, 426-35; a crucial source for this period and almost certainly available to Paul with the rest of the *Lib. pont.*

[289] *H. L.* 6.55 (one campaign), 56-58 (the other); Spoleto with the Romans, 56. On Spoleto, n. 230 above; *H. L.* 6.44, showing the duke of Spoleto's son deposing his father is again, to Paul, characteristically Spoletan behavior. For Liutprand's campaigns as known to moderns, Wyckham, *Early Medieval Italy*, p. 44.

[290] In *H. L.* 6.55-58, Liutprand intervenes in Benevento only in order to regulate the succession and restore dynastic legitimacy; Benevento never conducts a foreign policy of its own or fails to defer to Pavia.

[291] Leo and iconoclasm, *H. L.* 6.49; also see above, n. 282.

is shown to have been lopsided in its losses, whereas the repulse of the Saracens in the East cost Constantinople three hundred thousand deaths from pestilence.[292]

The long-prepared end of Theudelinda's dynasty was equally to Paul's taste. King Aripert II is carried over into the second half of *H.L.* 6 only to perish. Attacked by Ansprand, he gained the advantage in a long, murderous battle, but inexplicably lost heart and left camp for Pavia, with the result that his army defected and forced his flight to exile in Francia. Weighed down by as much of the royal treasure as he could carry, he tried to swim the Ticinum and was dragged under by his burden of gold.[293] Paul stresses the qualities of Aripert's rule, much as he had had approving words for Perctarit and Cunicpert. Aripert was cautious and watchful, a churchgoer who gave many alms, and a lover of justice; "in his times the land was very bountiful." Paul then turns around and, departing from his usual reserve, pronounces a forthright condemnation: "but the times were barbarous (*tempora fuere barbarica*)." The barbarousness of Aripert's days had nothing to do with ethnicity, let alone with cultural backwardness. The good government, churchgoing, almsgiving, and fertility manifest in his reign were earthbound virtues. By being wantonly cruel in seizing power, senselessly covetous in his end, and merely terrestrial in between, Aripert II illustrated the reverse of Christian rulership. He was the worst of a bad lot. His brother with three sons, the last descendants of Theudelinda, escaped to Francia, Paul adds, where one of them could lately be found serving as count of Orléans.[294]

In view of Pope Zachary's several meetings with Liutprand, which Paul knew about but silenced, the absence of the popes from the second half is more noteworthy than the three passages mentioning them. Paul does little more in this respect than to nudge forward the ideas earlier stated. Anglo-Saxon pilgrims keep coming to Rome (here as earlier, Bede is the source); the Lombards defend the pope against Byzantine highhandedness while the emperor plunges into heresy; and Liutprand confirms Aripert's return of the Cottian patrimony to the Holy See. No suggestion is made that the popes might have combined with the southern Lombard duchies; the term used in this connection is "Rome," and the city or duchy is kept separate from its head.[295] The impression conveyed is that a papacy held in deep respect

---

[292] *H.L.* 6.45-47.

[293] *H.L.* 6.35.

[294] *Ibid.*, tr. Foulke, pp. 278-97; ed. Bethmann-Waitz, p. 176. Paul's sense is correctly conveyed if *barbarus* is understood as the opposite of "civilized," and if Grimoald I, especially at the opening of *H.L.* 5, is taken as the model of civilized conduct.

[295] Paul's silence about the popes, n. 288 above. Anglo-Saxons in Rome, *H.L.* 6.37 (above, n. 286), 49 (heresy), 43 (Cottian patrimony, also 28), 56 (southern duchies).

by distant northerners was drawing nearer to the Lombards, just as its detachment from Byzantium became more complete.

Liutprand's resemblance to Grimoald I is again apparent in the chapter characterizing the beginning of his reign. Grimoald, at the corresponding point, demonstrated his magnanimity; Liutprand's gallantry, exemplified in an anecdote, took the form of mercy toward offenders. The story begins, grimly enough, with an account of how a royal kinsman, Rothari, who schemed to assassinate Liutprand at a banquet, was killed at the palace; Rothari's four sons were also put to death. Paul passes without pause from this bit of realism to a second scene, in which Liutprand outfaced two (anonymous) armorbearers of his, whom he knew to be plotting his death; taking them alone into a forest, he drew his sword, dared them to do their deed, and when they confessed and begged for mercy forgave them.[296] In the closing obituary, Paul says much about Liutprand's construction of churches and monasteries. He also reports that Liutprand lavished money to rescue the relics of St. Augustine, resting in Sardinia and threatened by Saracen raids, and translated them to Pavia. Like Narses (and the emperor Theodosius I), he was a warrior who placed his trust in prayers rather than in weapons.[297] Nevertheless, the opening story seems to be central to Paul's concept of genuinely Christian rule: mercifulness gave Liutprand the New Testament stamp that distinguished a religious king.

So introduced, Liutprand's actions may be understood to meet with authorial approval. His main conquests of Byzantine cities in Italy are framed by reports of Leo III's iconoclasm; his interventions in Spoleto and Benevento are not only narrated at greater length than any other aspect of the reign, but are evidently applauded. Paul, consistent with his condemnation of joint kingship, specifies that Ansprand was on his deathbed when Liutprand was proclaimed co-ruler with him; and, later, that a gravely ill Liutprand, who was not expected to recover, was enough to explain the elevation of his nephew, Hildeprand, as co-king with him. The maintenance of friendship with the Franks and the Avars, Paul affirms, was Liutprand's special concern. He aided Charles Martel against the Saracens by supplying him troops. In a more ominous vein, Charles sent Liutprand his son, Pepin, so that the Lombard king "should take his hair according to custom." Young Alboin, in *H.L.* 1, had gone to the king of the Gepids for initiation to adulthood and had also, not long after, destroyed the Gepid kingdom.[298]

---

[296] *H.L.* 6.38. Presumably, the first story was historical and notorious (though it has traits in common with the killing of Godepert, 4.51); the second one, its pair, helps offset it.

[297] *H.L.* 6.58; translation of St. Augustine, 48.

[298] Conquests of Byzantine cities, *H.L.* 6.49; southern interventions, 55-58; co-rulership, 35, 55 (Paul's negative attitude is suggested in 4.30, 51; the *Gesta episcoporum Mettensium*, ed. Pertz, p. 265, celebrates succession from father to a single son); friendship with Franks and Avars, 6.58; aid to Charles Martel, 54; Pepin sent to Liutprand for initiation, 53 (cf. Alboin,

Liutprand's role *vis-à-vis* Pepin was as honorable as the Gepid king's toward Alboin; the omen pointed beyond his death.

Pepin's haircut is one of several suggestions of a troubled future that impinge on the latter half of *H.L.* 6. Liutprand's nephew, Hildeprand, was raised to kingship while his uncle was thought to be dying; during the enthronement ceremony, a cuckoo landed on his scepter. The ludicrous portent was duly noted at the time. (Hildeprand was in fact overthrown scant months after becoming sole king.) In Liutprand's obituary chapter, Paul mentions no fewer than three holy men, two of them with the gift of prophecy. The only call made on these powers involves the hermit Baodolinus and a hunting accident in which one of Liutprand's many nephews was wounded. A messenger, sent in haste to Baodolinus to ask prayers for the boy's recovery, was greeted with the words that what he had come to ask could not be done because the boy was dead. The incident not only underscores the inexorability of destiny or divine decree, but also foreshadows the similar accidental death of King Aistulf in 756.[299]

Even darker touches accompany the developing tale of Pemmo, duke of Frioul, and his sons. Pemmo's advent, in the first half, makes a very favorable impression, but it becomes apparent in what follows that our first acquaintance with Pemmo and his family is open to a more qualified reading if one consults information beyond the range of the *H.L.* Pemmo's sons, Ratchis and Aistulf, were both to be kings. The former overthrew Liutprand's nephew, threatened Rome, and, soon after the pope talked him into withdrawing, abdicated and entered Monte Cassino. Aistulf succeeded him as king and, by being very aggressive in his dealings with papal territory, provoked the northward journey of Stephen II and the first Frankish intervention—the beginning of the end for the Lombard kingdom. We have just seen how he died prematurely.[300]

Paul implies that Pemmo would not, in ordinary circumstances, have become duke of Frioul. The sole reason he did was that, in a battle against the Slavs whose deplorable foolishness is detailed, "all the nobility of the Frioulans perished"; Paul even extracts a line out of Eutropius to emphasize the magnitude of the disaster. Pemmo was a new man, the son of an exile from

---

[299] Liutprand's nephew, *H.L.* 6.55 (his overthrow, Wyckham, *Early Medieval Italy*, p. 45); holy men and a hunting accident, 58. On Aistulf's death, *Liber pontificalis* 94.48, ed. Duchesne, I, 454.

1.24; the substance of the ritual was different, but its goal the same). It seems doubtful that the haircutting mentioned by Paul was characteristically "barbarian"; a public celebration took place when the Byzantine emperor's son had his hair cut: Constantine Porph., *De caeremoniis* 2.23, ed. Reiske, I, 621-23; II, 731-32.

[300] On Pemmo's beginnings, next note. On Ratchis and Aistulf, Hallenbeck, *Pavia and Rome*, pp. 51-85. Conceivably, Ratchis's conduct as king would have appealed to Paul; cf. above, n. 198 *in fine* (conciliatory toward the pope).

another part of Lombardy, and he was married to a wholly unsuitable wife. Paul wins our sympathy for the pair by telling how the lowborn wife offered to withdraw so that Pemmo, now duke, might choose a more appropriate spouse, and how he staunchly refused, prizing her modesty and humility.[301] Such tales in Paul tend to be double-edged; the fundamental boorishness of the Pemmonids has been impressed upon us. Pemmo went on to do admirable things: he reared the sons of the massacred nobility as though they were his sons and, when they had grown up, led them to a great and almost bloodless victory over the Slavs. This victory is what we first hear about Frioul in part II of the book.[302] But the gears then shift. Pemmo shows another side of his nature by acting harshly in an ecclesiastical quarrel, forcing King Liutprand to intervene. The focus passes to his sons: Ratchis statesmanlike, Aistulf brusque and violent. A particularly vivid scene involving Liutprand at the palace in Pavia brings the character of the sons into the open. The same scenario is replayed as the Frioulans, forming the rear guard of the royal army, battle valiantly against the leagued Spoletans and Romans on Liutprand's second southern expedition: Ratchis "with his wonted magnanimity" allows his unhorsed opponent to crawl away to safety, whereas Aistulf takes on two men at once and sends both plunging to watery death.[303] Paul's sympathy for Ratchis is obvious, but he leaves us wondering whether the original disaster that brought the coarse Pemmonids to the fore might not have set in motion a chain of fatal circumstances.

The only happy ending in *H.L.* 6 involves Benevento, the principality that supplies the book with its happy beginning. In Spoleto, everything goes wrong. Two brothers ruled at once; a son, Transamund, revolted against his father and relegated him to the Church. Thus elevated to the dukedom, Transamund rebelled against Liutprand, fled to Rome when the king approached, returned when he withdrew, killed the man appointed to replace him, resumed rebellion, and allied with the Romans to harry Liutprand's southern expedition; Transamund then fell into the king's hands, was deposed, and suffered the same fate of being thrust into the Church that he had meted out to his father. Paul notes that a nephew of Liutprand was then appointed duke. He does not draw attention to what must have been obvious to his audience; namely, that the entrenched Spoletan dynasty ended with the deposed Transamund. Spoleto became a dependency

---

[301] *H.L.* 6.24-26. The Eutropian echo: 24, "Tantique ibi viri fortes per contentionis malum et inprovidentiam debellati sunt, quanti possent per unam concordiam et salubre consilium multa milia sternere aemulorum" (ed. Bethmann-Waitz, p. 173); *Breviarium* 10.12.1 (the Battle of Mursa) "ingentes Romani imperii vires ea dimicatione consumptae sunt, ad quaelibet bella externa idonea, quae multum triumphorum possent securitatisque conferre" (ed. Droysen, p. 178), cf. 6.21.1 (Pharsalia). Pemmo's origins and wife, *H.L.* 6.21.

[302] *H.L.* 6.45.

[303] *H.L.* 6.51-52, 56.

of Pavia and passed with the capital into Frankish hands. In Paul's time, it was the first point of contact between Benevento and Charlemagne's empire.[304]

The contrasting good fortune of Benevento is epitomized by the incident immediately preceding the report of Liutprand's death. As duke of "the Samnites" the king installed Gisulf, the legitimate heir whom he had undertaken to rear a decade earlier, when Duke Romuald, Gisulf's father, had died and Gisulf had still been too young to rule. Benevento was a model of orderly rulership. Father was succeeded by son, or older brother by younger, always one at a time. When Romuald died, leaving the child Gisulf, the ever faithful Beneventans rose up and slew conspirators against Gisulf's life. Liutprand intervened (he had come south to deal with Spoleto), took Gisulf honorably away to Pavia, and installed his own nephew Gregory as caretaker-duke. The latter's death brought a certain Godescalc to the dukedom (how is not quite clear). In the face of King Liutprand's advance, Godescalc tried to flee by ship to Constantinople and was seized and killed by the Beneventans, faithful as ever to the legitimate Gisulf, who thereupon came into his inheritance.[305] The dukes of Benevento who figure in *H.L.* 6 did not, in fact, belong to the same line as those of Paul's day, yet his insistence on the fidelity of the Beneventans is an obtrusive feature of the book. However Paul felt toward long-lived dynasties such as Theudelinda's, he applauded the loyalty of subjects toward their hereditary rulers.

Liutprand's obituary is the longest and most flattering in the *H.L.* It ends with the king's triumphing by prayers rather than arms; that and his maintenance of good relations with the Franks and Avars ring in our ears as salutary lessons of his reign.[306] The dynasty of Theudelinda and the Byzantine emperors had, by their faults, swept themselves from the Italian scene; the popes had drawn nearer to the Lombards, but not to them alone; Benevento and its holy mountain shone as beacons of a possible future; but the more certain future involved the ambiguous Pemmonids and the Providence-blessed Arnulfingians.

Paul gathered the pieces of a mosaic into *H.L.* 6. If he left out much that he knew, that too was in keeping with his normal manner. What one misses is a plot. Though Paul's sympathies are discernible on a small scale, they cannot be integrated into a coherent scheme embracing the book as a whole. Baodolinus and the other prominent holy men at the end, as well as

[304] Joint rule, *H.L.* 6.30; Transamund, 44, 55-57. On the outcome, Wyckham, *Early Medieval Italy*, p. 44.

[305] Accession of Gisulf, *H.L.* 6.58; death of Romuald, fidelity of the Beneventans, and installation of Gregory, 55; accession of Godescalc, 56; the latter, fleeing to the Byzantines from Liutprand, is killed by the faithful Beneventans, 57. The model of rulership in Benevento, 4.53-56.

[306] *H.L.* 6.58.

Monte Cassino at the beginning, raise the possibility that *H.L.* 6 was meant to be an ironic counterpart of the comic *H.L.* 3, preparatory to a replay in *H.L.* 7 of the Providence-willed invasion of *H.L.* 2. Along these or other lines, some ingredient would have been added to *H.L.* 6 that Paul lacked the time to supply. A discerning reader may eventually succeed in divining what it was.

13. Conclusion

Three of our authors make strong personal impressions. Rightly or wrongly, we have a sense of knowing Gregory of Tours because he tells us much about himself, Bede because of the consistency of his vocation and life work, Jordanes because he lives through his histories or not at all. Paul the Deacon is more elusive. He is so consistently reticent that the little of a personal nature that he discloses is better related to the momentary effect he seeks to produce than to any motive of autobiography. To interpret his reticence as extreme sensitivity, self-effacement, or shyness is surely an overambitious argument from silence.[307] We simply do not know how Paul appeared in life. The nearest we come to him may be in the playful poetry occasioned by his stay in Francia. The Paul who interests us most, namely, the Beneventan historian and would-be counselor to the ducal house, may be approached only through his writings. He attached weight to the appearance of objectivity.

Paul often used Jordanes, but never singled out his works for comment or acknowledged that the complementary *Romana* and *Langobarda* he himself undertook remarkably parallel his predecessor's *Romana* and *Getica*. The resemblance goes beyond the pairing of Roman with ethnic histories. Both authors, in the more novel of their works, utilize literary techniques of plotting to integrate their narrative and, in this way, to convey meanings that are not apparent to the casual reader. The *Getica*, once recognized to embody a love story of Romans and Goths with a happy ending, becomes a very different work from the clumsy but naïvely sincere abridgment of Cassiodorus that it otherwise seems to be.[308] Paul, even in the Metz *Gesta*, cannot be likened to Jordanes as a publicist for government policy. Though he, too, wrote for patrons, his voice was no less personal than Bede's. But the shaping of the past concerned him more than its investigation; and, like Jordanes, he yields his meaning more readily when approached from literary perspectives than if read with a historian's preoccupation for isolated facts.

[307] Brunhölzl, *Gesch. d. lat. Lit.* I, 258, 267.
[308] Above, ch. II §§ 8-11.

Paul is unequaled among our authors in the crafting of narrative. However simple in language, his prose writings called for as much attention to measure and arrangement as the meter of his verse. Devices greet us at every turn: the bridging of book divisions so as to flatten chronology, "prophetic" passages, bipartite books, parallelisms and contrasts of all sorts. He is full of surprises. One recalls in the *H.L.* alone: the Persian convert-queen presented as a warning exemplum, Lamissio as a miniature prefiguration of Grimoald, the admirable Authari turning into a mere *servus dolosus*, sympathetic calamities announcing political rapprochements, the heroic deacon Seno symbolizing a Church brought so low as to take sides and engage in combat. The main surprise is that the jagged fragments of which Paul's writings consist—"the defective inner linkage of individual stories"[309]—should be unified by discernible scenarios, and that even so unpromising a muddle as the Metz *Gesta* proves, on reflection, to convey a coherent synthesis of the aspirations of Charlemagne's court.

The legendary element of Paul's *H.L.* has always been regarded as something special.[310] He differs from his three principal predecessors in his choice of legends and in what he makes of them. Jordanes narrates facts having the appearance of legend, such as Ermanaric's punishment of Sunilda or the burial of Alaric, but he rarely breathes life into such scenes. Typically, in the account of migration from Scandinavia, Filimer stands out as a name rather than a personality. Jordanes possibly drew his tales from the same Germanic stock that Paul drew upon, assuming there was one, but there is no similarity to Paul in the way such tales are deployed.[311] The multiple dramatizations of Gregory of Tours are segments of a narrative that, unlike Paul's, does not aspire to survey a long span of time. Far from being uniform, they include romantic tales, such as the Two Lovers or Chlothild's evangelization of Clovis; grimmer episodes, such as the Thuringian queen inciting her husband to war; and genre scenes, such as the doings of Bishop Badegisel and his wife. There is no way to distinguish with precision which of these are legendary and which are not; Gregory is just as vivid and circumstantial in writing about Swabia or Persarmenia as when he writes about Tours.[312] In Bede's *History*, the many hagiographic legends are acceptable digressions or pauses in an overtly edifying account of God's salvific purpose. They are so well integrated into the whole as to make us doubt whether the term "legend" is appropriate to a context in which mir-

---

[309] Brunhölzl, *Gesch. d. lat. Lit.* I, 263.

[310] Above, nn. 10-14.

[311] Jordanes *Get.* 129-30 (Ermanaric), 157-58 (Alaric), 26-28 (Filimer).

[312] Gregory of Tours *Hist.* 1.47 (Two Lovers), 2.29 (Chlothild), 3.4 (Thuringian queen), 8.39 (Badegisel), 5.15 (Swabia), 4.40 (Persarmenia).

acles, prodigies of austerity, and visions are no less factual than episcopal successions.[313]

One should not stop at these three. The earlier author offering a decided foretaste of Paul's practice is the anonymous Frank customarily called Fredegar, who wrote toward 660 and is best known for being the first to derive the Franks from Troy. The legends Fredegar incorporates into his four-book narrative have a variety of origins. One—the Trojan story—is evidently "learned"; another is Lombard, several are Byzantine, others more local.[314] But provenance is a hazy and conjectural matter. It should not be taken to suggest that Fredegar's rendition faithfully corresponds to an exotic or native prototype. Unless frozen in writing, legends live by repetition, continually adapted to the audience, and are, as a result, more contemporary to the teller than to a posited original. To a historian like Fredegar, a legend was not a "source" to be treated with the respect owed to an authority bearing a name; even Bede made what he wished of the tale of the English boys in Rome.[315] Nor was Fredegar, or Paul, limited to adapting tales that had somehow reached his notice. It was a small step from adaptation to invention.

Fredegar, then, often adorned his narrative with legends. The more precise feature that draws him toward Paul is that the ground in which the legends are planted consists either of laconic chronicle or of a history (Gregory of Tours') boiled down to a chronicler's concision. The effect Fredegar produces is not precisely that of the *H.L.*; for one thing, Paul writes much better Latin. But the similarity is obtrusive. Again and again, flowing tales stand out against a backdrop of dryly abbreviated facts, inviting us to pause and listen closely.[316] The place of legends in the design of Fredegar's history and the possibility that it influenced Paul are questions that cannot profitably be pursued here. For whatever the observation is worth, at least one earlier historian anticipated, perhaps only superficially, the alternation in Paul's *H.L.* of legends with humdrum historical reports. The *Origo gentis Langobardorum*, whose date is near Fredegar's, provides a comparable

[313] Bede *H.E.*, e.g. 3.2, 9-13, 15-17, 4.7-11, 27-32, 5.1-6.

[314] Fredegar *Chron.* 2.46, 8, 3.2 (Troy), 2.57 (Theodoric as a Byzantine), 62 (Justinian and Belisarius). Various: 3.7 (the emperor Avitus), 9 (origins of Merovech), 11 (Childeric and Wiomad), 12 (the birth of Clovis), 58-59 (Chrodinus and Gogo), 65 (similar to the *Origo gentis Langobardorum*), 70-72 (civil war), 4.9 (the Persian queen), 64-66 (Heraclius). This is not a full list. The special interest of Fredegar's legends was recognized in the nineteenth century. Giesebrecht supplied a generous selection of them as the appendix of his translation of Gregory of Tours (above ch. III n. 37). So had Ruinart in his edition of Gregory (1699).

[315] Above, ch. IV n. 287.

[316] E.g. MGH SRM II, 45-47 (the Trojan legend in context), 68 (Burgundian origins), 73-75 (Attila and Aëtius), 94-99 (from the emperor Avitus through Clovis's birth), 108-109 (Chrodinus and Gogo). In Fredegar's design, pp. 77-89 are an appendix to Hydatius, composed by stringing one legend to the next without guidance from a chronicle.

though more limited example of the same practice. So does the *Liber histo-riae Francorum*, written near Paris toward 727 and unlikely to have come to Paul's notice.

The astonishing feature of the *H.L.* is not that Paul periodically launches into a legendary tale, such as the dastardly deed of Rumetruda, Romilda's betrayal, or the escape of Lopichis, but that these legends, however con-spicuous and diverting in their own right, are integrated within the plot of each book. The disguised servant in the account of Perctarit's escape at the beginning of *H.L.* 5 points toward the disguised deacon Seno in the tale of Alahis's rebellion at the end; the skullcup accompanies Alboin's triumph over the Gepids at the close of *H.L.* 1 and his moment of hubris in *H.L.* 2, and it is found in the hands of King Ratchis as well; the treachery of Ru-metruda and gallantry of the Gepid Turisind work together, in *H.L.* 1, with the thoroughly historical evocations of Justinian and St. Benedict in cut-ting the early Lombards down to merely human size. The connection be-tween a legend and the book containing it is rarely more intimate than in the happily ending plot of *H.L.* 3: Authari's disguised visit to view Theu-delinda brings to light his true identity *vis-à-vis* the Lombards, and its sequel reveals Agilulf as the real hero. Paul's legends are not adventitious cullings, inserted here and there, as best as possible, in the ongoing course of Lom-bard history. They are tesserae of a special kind, distinct from references to natural calamities, extracts from Secundus of Trent or the *Liber pontificalis*, or other types of chapters, but like them in being components carefully se-lected to produce a unified mosaic.

Under these circumstances, the question of the origin of Paul's legends is even less important than that of Fredegar's. It has long been axiomatic that Paul borrowed "several of the familiar stories from the common stock of Germanic folk-tale," and that, as a result, the *H.L.* has the peculiar at-traction of "reproduc[ing] the legendary tradition of a Germanic people, undisturbed by learned criticism and rationalization (*Reflexion*), and also unfalsified by the misunderstandings of an alien (*volksfremder*) reporter."[317] These opinions, long cherished in a variety of formulations, as we have seen, would be easier to sustain if the linkage between Paul's stories were defective, and if the legends persisted in being refreshing oases in a desert of chronography. They are hard to reconcile with an *H.L.* ordered by de-liberate scenarios. It would be incautious to think that the Lamissio of the *H.L.* sprang from the imagination of anyone else than Paul, or that Rosa-mund's revenge was included complete with skullcup and Samson-like Pe-redeo in a fund of familiar tales before appearing in the *H.L.* Paul surely had oral sources, though they need not have been more Lombard than Italian,

---

[317] Bullough, *Age of Charlemagne*, p. 118; Brunhölzl, *Gesch. d. lat. Lit.* I, 264.

Frankish, or Byzantine. At least one "Germanic" motif found in his pages is already in the Talmud.[318] But sources of this sort supplied little more than raw material. Paul was a storyteller in his own right, not the unintrusive redactor of a "tradition." Historical writing as he practiced it called for the incorporation of legends adapted to or newly coined for the particular purposes he had in mind. They were an element of his rhetoric. The lady Digna had a vital role in the argument of the *Historia Romana*, Arnulf's ring in the Metz *Gesta*. The *H.L.* is special in Paul's production for the quantity of its legends, not for their presence or the place they hold in his exposition of the past.

The adaptation or composition of tales of the kind found in the *H.L.* is not extraordinarily demanding. In Paul's day, as for many centuries before and after him, storytelling was a common form of entertainment; its skills were not beyond his abilities to master. The dramatization of such incidents as Grimoald's accession to kingship or the Frioulan disaster of *H.L.* 6 was no harder for Paul than similar scenes had been for Gregory of Tours. The taxing aspect of Paul's work is what least strikes the eye, namely, the imposition of coherent interpretations upon the jumbled records of the past. Paul, who had few occasions to speak theoretically about his undertakings, appears to have distinguished history from chronography on the basis of the former's evocation of a meaningful story. He did not identify historical truth primarily with fidelity to fact or authoritative report; it mattered little if, as in the Metz *Gesta*, close to three-quarters of the narrative was more fictional than not. The historical past was not quite so malleable as the storyteller's raw material, but neither was it hard or inviolable; and the forms worth shaping it into were tales appropriate to the needs (or expressed wishes) of the audience.

Paul's legends are predominantly profane. This characteristic has given them much of the credibility they have enjoyed as authentic reflections of a "Germanic heroic age."[319] It is less obvious that the synthetic scenarios

---

[318] *H.L.* 1.20: the Herule lookout cannot announce what he sees because threatened with death by the king if he should report such news; he tricks the king into saying the words he is forbidden to utter. The story type is known to folklore studies as " 'You said it, not I' ": Thompson, *Motif Index of Folk-Literature*, no. J1675.2.1. Further see Gaster, "Zur Quellenkunde deutscher Sagen und Märchen," pp. 287-88: Paul's story agrees almost verbatim with the Talmudic tale of the death of R. Jehudah ha-Nassi. (The *terminus ante quem* of the Talmud lies within the sixth century.) Cf. Zachariae, "Ihr sagt er, nicht ich," who discusses later stories of the same type; on p. 402 n. 1, he emphatically denies the possibility of Paul's sharing a common source with the Talmud, on the grounds that he drew the story of the Herule king "aus dem Born der alten Volksüberlieferung"; but no indication is given of how this is known. Also see the addition to Zachariae by Rothbarth, "Ihr sagt er, nicht ich," drawing attention to another such story in Saxo Grammaticus *Res gestae Danorum*, ed. A. Holder (Strasbourg 1886), p. 321; it is paralleled by a vernacular version in the *Saga of King Olaf Trygvason*.

[319] Bethmann, as above, n. 12. The phrase in quotations belongs to Chadwick, *Heroic Age.*

beneath the surface of Paul's books, and within which the legends are integrated, are overwhelmingly Christian in substance. Because Paul paid no attention to the formalities of Lombard conversion or to the relationship of Arianism and Catholicism among the converts, he has been thought to take Christianity for granted and to be concerned above all (even more than Jordanes) with *Volksgeschichte*. Paul had, it is said, an inner attachment and warm love for the Lombard people.[320] If it were true that Christian themes left him indifferent, he would stand alone within our quartet of "barbarian historians" in deserving the label given to them all. But this monk of Monte Cassino is an improbable candidate for indifference toward religion. Like Gregory of Tours and Bede, he was a Christian historian, writing with didactic intent in a medium that, even in other hands than his, taught mainly by indirection.

Paul's sensitivity to Christian themes in history has frequently been noted in the previous pages. Those observed in his poem on the walls of Salerno, in *Historia Romana* 11-16, and in the Metz *Gesta* need not be reviewed. But the Christian look of the *H.L.* is unfamiliar enough to warrant a second glance. If Paul had a single guiding purpose, it was to place the Lombards in a Christian setting. He did not, like Bede, invoke an overarching theological framework within which his people were assigned a special place in God's scheme of salvation. The fixed point of his narrative is Italy, a place of earthly sojourn, rather than a single set of its residents. From this territorial perspective (already adopted in the *Historia Romana*), he consistently reinterpreted the Lombard past in such ways as to depreciate values that were merely human and to bring Christian ones to the fore. In each book, he went out of his way to undermine an obvious interpretation and, instead, to turn his readers toward a distinctively Christian vision of the past. In *H.L.* 1, the Lombard migration was not toward power and rich lands, but out of the ironic human condition and toward the values incarnated by Justinian and St. Benedict; in *H.L.* 2, the calamity was not that the Lombards invaded Italy, but that the murder of Alboin effaced the possibility of an orderly and bloodless change of régime; in *H.L.* 3, Lombard regeneration came not from a restored kingship, but from the accession of Christian royalty; in *H.L.* 4, 5, and 6, Lombard kings were shown to be admirable not on account of pious works and blood relation to Theudelinda, but for their accomplishments and Christian behavior. The negative sense that Paul attaches to the mere church constructions of Theudelinda's line, to Phocas's generosity to the popes, to the baptism of the Persian queen, and to Aripert II's charities attests to the sophistication of his religion, which surprises and delights. The Christian in him over-

[320] Brunhölzl, *Gesch. d. lat. Lit.* I, 263-64.

shadows the Lombard. His eulogies of Justinian, Narses, Tiberius II, and the Merovingian Guntram point in the same direction as the glowing accounts of Arnulf and his descendants: the quality of rule, measured by a religious standard, mattered more than its nationality. Among Lombard kings, no more than two, Grimoald and Liutprand, bear a New Testament stamp. Paul's didactic preoccupation helps to explain why the mere fact of Lombard conversion is alluded to rather than detailed.

What we do not know, of course, is the endpoint of Paul's narrative. How did he envision the relationship, after 788, of Lombard Benevento, which he cherished, to the Carolingian conquerors, to whom he was anything but hostile and whose power he portrayed as God-willed? Paul consistently favored the expulsion of the Byzantine Empire from Italy and must have been well aware that the heel and toe of the peninsula, on the southern border of the Duchy of Benevento, still were East Roman enclaves. Although the *H.L.* breaks off more than forty years before the time of writing, every sign leads us to expect that Paul would have advocated, however indirectly, that Grimoald III should cultivate good relations with Charlemagne. As a vassal of the Carolingian courts of Aachen and Pavia, and in harmony with a Church of Rome now oriented in the same northerly direction, Grimoald's Benevento (the refuge of Lombard autonomy) might confidently complete the great task of conquering Italy from the "Greeks" and making it secure from fragmentation and heterodoxy at their hands.[321]

As Paul's ancient history had been uncommitted to Rome, so his modern one could bear the end of the Lombard kingdom of Pavia with equanimity, but Paul was not indifferent to the course of events. It would have been pointless for him to distill and convey the lessons of the Italian past unless he saw promise in the possibilities of the moment. Paul sought to show that Beneventan submission to the Franks was not a defeat, but an opportunity; skillfully managed, it could be Grimoald's springboard toward the majestic Lombard goal that the skullcup had kept Alboin from attaining.

The idea that Paul died before being able to add the concluding books to the *H.L.* is uncomplicated and probable, but the alternative—that he deliberately abandoned the *H.L.*—cannot be cast entirely aside. Three years after becoming duke, Grimoald III detached himself from Frankish tutelage and strove after an independent course, not excluding amicable relations with Byzantium. Meanwhile, Charlemagne set about destroying the Avars, whose friendship with the Lombards the exemplary Liutprand had cultivated.[322] Even when written by an idealistic monk, a history designed to impart political instruction was subject to the whims of political change.

---

[321] Cf. above, n. 58; on the expulsion of Byzantium, see n. 269 above.

[322] Hodgkin, *Italy and Her Invaders* VIII, 85-86, 254-56; cf. Wyckham, *Early Medieval Italy*, p. 49.

Jordanes and Bede had had the security of knowing, when they wrote, that the side they favored had gained ascendancy and was likely to remain unshaken in the foreseeable future. Paul the Deacon, on the edge of Carolingian Europe, undertook the *H.L.* in a more delicate context. If death did not still his voice, the course of events may nonetheless have undermined the climax he was tending toward and dictated that his final work had a better chance of finding an audience if it remained an unfinished trunk.

Conclusion

Close study of our authors does not tend to confirm the idea that they were initiators and exponents of a "national" or "barbarian" history resulting from Germanic occupation of the West Roman Empire. *Gentes*, Roman or other, had long been a respectable subject for historians; *Volksgeschichte*, if it existed at all, did so as a loose subdivision of history in general. Josephus could not be denied a place of honor among its protagonists, and neither, *mutatis mutandis*, could Florus, Eutropius, and the other epitomators of the Roman past; even Dictys and Dares, in their Trojan fictions, purveyed the fate of nations. A special genre of "gentile" history did not need to be invented so as to accommodate the newcomers to the Western provinces. Goths, Franks, or whoever, once drawn within the ambit of Latin Christian culture, were admissible into written history, just as Gothic and Frankish laws were adaptable to the language of Roman jurisprudence. If Jordanes and Paul the Deacon come nearer than Gregory and Bede to exemplifying an "ideal type" of *Volks-* or *Stammesgeschichte*, it is because their accounts are more influenced by what might, with apologies, be called the Eutropian tradition.

Isolated from each other by place and time, living in unique circumstances and addressing dissimilar publics, our narrators, unsurprisingly, undertook very individual tasks:

—Jordanes wrote his little historical library so as to familiarize reconquered Italy with a past and present, Roman as well as Gothic, that the prospective audience might not otherwise have suspected but that, however contrived, encouraged the amicable fusion of both ethnic groups.

—Gregory of Tours portrayed at great lengths the miseries and the wonders of contemporary Gaul in order to illustrate *adversum philosophos* the perennial condition of humanity, fallen and redeemed.

—Bede traced the creation of the Northumbrian Church in such a way as to efface the dominant figure in its past and, in this cleansed perspective, to propose a plan of evangelical action for the nascent ecclesiastical metropolis of York.

—Paul the Deacon, if able to finish, would have composed a continuous history of Italy from pre-Roman to Frankish times, and so interpreted its Lombard segment as to suggest the course he thought best for the future of Italy at large and Lombard Benevento in particular.

None of them inquired disinterestedly into the past or desired to record it for a generalized posterity; the conditions for scholarship of this kind (problematic in the best of times) simply did not exist. History was the medium of their writings, not its goal, and their enduring interest for us is as practitioners of a form of sophisticated discourse whose vigor had evidently not been impaired by the retreat of Rome to the Bosphorus. Contemporary events play a much larger part in Gregory's pages than in the others'; that he is also the most abstract or religious in his message is only an apparent paradox. Events within living memory, because highly sensitive, could be effectively featured only as illustrations of timeless moral teaching, whereas the dim past, more malleable than the happenings of yesterday, was well suited to be grist for nonargumentative advocacy. Unlike the bishop of Tours, Jordanes, Bede, and Paul might, with exaggeration, be called political pamphleteers. Without saying so, each one was preoccupied with current problems and conjured up a past carefully tailored to bear on the local circumstances of his public and himself.

Jordanes and Bede, rarely linked, were most directly *engagés*. The latter differs from Jordanes in that he spent a lifetime in an atmosphere of controversy, in which the nature of the Northumbrian Church was repeatedly debated, often in writing; he capped an argument nearly four decades old. Jordanes, as far as he may be grasped, wrote the *Romana* and the *Getica* as an agent of public policy in the only existing state that had a clear sense of its interests and pursued them by the pen as well as the sword. The two authors most closely resemble each other in both being aligned with the winning side. They shared the considerable advantage of speaking on behalf of the ascendant cause and knowing that, regardless of the effect their writings might have, the fundamental change that they desired had already come about.

Paul the Deacon was an adviser rather than an advocate. Although his *Gesta* of the bishops of Metz is in the nature of a tract justifying the (securely entrenched) Carolingian régime, his other works do not promote a cause so much as offer counsel, reading the past as a guide to the future. Less a scholar than Bede and more a man of letters, he comes nearest of the four to resembling a conventional historian, especially if someone like Eutropius is taken as model for this role. As the latter had instructed the emperor Valens in the history of a Rome that he now ruled but had never seen, so Paul took up the more original task, in the *Historia Romana*, of providing the ducal couple of Lombard Benevento with an account of the wider context of their sovereignty. When he resumed the tale, for the sake of the same court, he again adapted the past, now directly Lombard, to the circumstances of his patrons. In both narratives, extraordinary liberties were taken

433

with evidence; but, for all that, Paul's vision of the past was less forcibly determined by partisanship than Jordanes's and Bede's.

As in all epochs, modern as well as remote, our historians cannot be detached from their audiences. If none of them was a Thucydides or a Sallust, so their times lacked the special societies—competitive political élites of imperial capitals—that had generated authors of that rare kind. The publics of our authors may be only faintly grasped; in some cases, the persons they addressed may have been very few. Apart from advertised patrons, their audiences exist for us most of all as inferences from the emphatic orientation of their works toward local problems and conditions. Paul made no apparent appeal to a faceless public—curiously so in view of his future popularity. Bede sought prayers as his reward from every satisfied reader "of this nation" whom the *H.E.* reached. Gregory perhaps and Jordanes certainly sought to influence the unseen, the former as a Christian teacher, the latter as a publicist aiding in the pacification of a distant Italy. For all three, the wider public did not exclude a nearer one, more immediately known and addressed. Our historians, monks included, assumed social roles comparable to those of their predecessors in antiquity.

Among them, Jordanes is least likely to attract enduring admiration. Although no longer overshadowed by Cassiodorus, he is less easily credited with personal convictions than with a voice of his own. Resident of a metropolis then rich in historical talent and productivity, and set to a task directly beneficial to the state, he recommends himself as an able craftsman rather than an imaginative shaper of the past. He is most original perhaps when likening the condition of the Empire to Adam's expulsion from paradise. The three Westerners outclass him. Undeterred by the comparative cultural poverty of their milieus, they produced works that, when better known, consolidate their claims to a place among historical classics.

Praise of Bede is so widespread and deserved that the special excellence of the *H.E.* hardly needs another airing. Paul's qualities, on the other hand, are still far from fully revealed and invite more attention than given here. He is extraordinarily interesting, not so much for reporting the past as for combining literary inventiveness with the interpretation of events. His modern fame has been as an unintrusive recorder of tales, a humble role that ill becomes him. He merits attention as, for example, the master storyteller of *H.R.* 14-15, expounding for the first time in Latin the theme of "the barbarian invasions," or that of *H.L.* 2, developing the thesis that Alboin's murder, not the Lombard invasion, was a calamity. The interpreter of the past even today is an intrusive creator; his ability to discern a plot in the jumbled happenings of yesteryear is closely allied to the storyteller's talent for breathing indeterminacy into characters, incidents, and outcomes that are wholly in his control. Paul is sometimes memorable for his plots and theses, and much more so for the devices and means by which he nudged his narratives along. He reserved plain cause-and-effect for the merely terrestrial course of Lombard origins, and generally preferred much subtler relationships, which invite further study. If, as Norberg held, Paul's language had a formative part in the shaping of medieval Latin, so his narrative methods seem assured of attention in accounts of medieval literature.

Gregory remains the most astonishingly original of the four. He was, to put it too simply, an entertaining edition of Salvian, a moralist who found a better way to persuade than repetitive exhortation. By affirming that profane common-sense wisdom still needed to be combatted, that artfully ordered words could no longer win conviction even for Christian truths, and that the persuasiveness of facts had to serve instead, his works force us to think hard of the discontinuities between Christian thought and the classical past and of the creative consequences of the tensions between them. His vision of the *series temporum*, "history," as a confused mixture of miracles and horrors that could not be separated from each other is a more arresting idea of the past than is found in Bede or Paul or many other Christian historians. That, moreover, this foe of philosophical "vanity" and record holder for the narration of miracles should have derived the form of his *Histories* from the Roman satires is a final measure of his fascination. The seventh century found in Gregory the historian of the Franks whom it sought, and initiated the long practice of making him more so. Unburdened of that mistaken identity, Gregory leaves much in eighteen books of *miracula* and *historiae* to be explored and learned.

The emphasis laid on our authors' individual goals, literary skills, and imaginations both diminishes and enhances the source value of their writings. Precise facts are a concern of ours, one that goes hand in hand with such technical innovations as the printed book, and with a confidence not many centuries old that the truth about the distant past is accessible and that events known only from faint traces may be faithfully reconstructed. Our quartet supply a great deal of information, some of it as direct witnesses, much more at second or more distant hand; in regard to this material, nothing has changed except the assumption that the authors preferred in principle to present a faithful account of events. In their scale of priorities, unintrusive fidelity to fact of the kind that modern researchers would like to find in them was a secondary consideration. To presume that they were either truth speakers or liars imposes on them a version of truth relevant to our goals rather than theirs. Various forms of record keeping were known to them: archives, calendars, most of all chronicles. Histories were too rare; their composition took too much energy, talent, and intelligence to be reduced to the same self-effacing role. If the information our authors

435

convey is detached from its context and appropriated for our purposes, it needs to be weighed by whatever means there are, in full awareness that our desire to dip into them as storehouses of neutral fact bears no relation to their own varied aspirations.

These differences aside, our authors, like narrative historians in general, are impeccable purveyors of opinions—opinions with a secure date and place. The substance of their statements may or may not prove accurate when checked, or may be impossible to verify, but there is no doubt that the statements were made. That the Goths came from Scandinavia lacks historicity in Jordanes's presentation; that he, in the 550s, said they did is a fact, and a precious piece of information for certain purposes. Paul the Deacon's account of the Three Chapters' controversy is much distorted; but he assuredly gave it, and in doing so testified to a late-eighth-century vision of the Fifth Council. The many miracles that Gregory and Bede report are concretely factual in the same sense; their accounts of supernatural occurrences may be pondered as stories, regardless of what one thinks of the supernatural.

Theoretically at least, one historian is as good as another where opinions are concerned. Superior technical resources do not make modern historians automatically wiser than their Dark Age forebears. Gregory of Tours' near-contemporary conviction that the Merovingian Chilperic was the Nero and Herod of his age is no less interesting than the conviction, widespread in our times, that Chilperic was strikingly original and outclassed his brothers. Bishop Wilfrid may deserve in our eyes to be considered the greatest of early Anglo-Saxon saints, but it also matters that Bede thought of him as a sidetrack in Northumbrian history. Jordanes's account of the Huns as a demonic offshoot of the Goths reveals deplorable ignorance of the difference between a Germanic people and one of Asiatic nomads, but it also exemplifies the systematizing tendency of ancient ethnography, which surely affected the view Constantinople took of its northern neighbors. The opinions of early narrators are a precious and abundant commodity, sometimes preferable to ours, often a useful check on our judgments, and for whatever purpose the most factual dimension of their testimony.

Our authors were deliberate creators. Their compositions were not reports for newspapers that would be pulped tomorrow, but works of art, born of the rarity of the written word. Bede's discretion cannot have been an inborn gift; it presumably resulted from a sustained and painful effort to say no more or less than had to be said. Jordanes's tailoring of Gothic history to the outlines of a tale ending happily was tinged with brilliance, and executed with admirable attention to detail. Paul not only pioneered the interpretation of the periods he discussed, but also devised unobtrusive ways to convey his views. By rejuvenating the biblical prophets, Gregory gave religious admonition an up-to-date voice, and he was concerned enough about his outspokenness to arrange for posthumous publication. The meticulously wrought indirections through which our narrators expressed themselves may prove, in the long run, to tell us more about the age they lived in than the information wrested from their pages.

Secondary Works Cited

Abel, Sigurd, and Bernhard Simson. *Jahrbücher des fränkischen Reiches unter Karl dem Grossen*, 2 vols. (Leipzig 1883-88)

Aigrain, René. *L'Hagiographie. Ses sources, ses méthodes, son histoire* (Paris 1953)

Allen, P. "The 'Justinianic' Plague," *Byzantion* 49 (1979) 5-20

Altaner, Berthold. *Patrology*, tr. H. C. Graef (Edinburgh-London 1960)

Amann, Émile. "Trois-chapitres," in *Dictionnaire de théologie catholique* 15 (1950) 1868-1924

Ampère, Jean-Jacques. *Histoire littéraire de la France avant le 12ᵉ siècle*, 2 vols. (Paris 1839)

Anderson, William S. "Roman Satirists and Their Tradition," in Fabian, ed., *Satura*, pp. 33-37

Andersson, Theodore. "Cassiodorus and the Gothic Legend of Ermanaric," *Euphorion* 57 (1963) 28-43

Andree, Richard. "Menschenschädel als Trinkgefässe," *Zeitschrift für Volkskunde* 22 (1912) 1-37

Antin, Paul. "Emplois de la Bible chez Grégoire de Tours et Mgr Pie," *Latomus* 26 (1967) 778-82

———. "Notes sur le style de Grégoire de Tours," *Latomus* 22 (1963) 273-84 (reviewed by P. Tombeur, *Moyen Âge* 72 [1966] 374)

Arcari, Paola Maria. *Idee e sentimenti politici dell'alto medioevo*. Università di Cagliari, Publicazioni della Facoltà di giurisprudenza, ser. II (Scienze politichi), vol. 1 (Milan 1968)

Arndt, Wilhelm. Review of Monod, *Études critiques*, in *Historische Zeitschrift* 28 (1872) 416-17

Auerbach, Erich. *Literary Language and Its Public in Late Latin Antiquity and in the Middle Ages*, tr. Ralph Manheim (New York 1965)

———. *Mimesis: The Representation of Reality in Western Literature*, tr. Willard Trask (Princeton 1953, reprinted Garden City, N.Y. 1957)

Badot, Philippe. "L'utilisation de Salvien et de la *Vita patrum Iurensium* comme sources historiques," *Revue belge de philologie et d'histoire* 54 (1976) 391-405

Baldwin, Barry. "The Purpose of the *Getica*," *Hermes* 107 (1979) 489-92

———. "Sources for the *Getica* of Jordanes," *Revue belge de philologie et d'histoire* 59 (1981) 141-46

Balzani, Ugo. *Early Chroniclers of Europe: Italy* (London 1883)

Banniard, Michel. "L'aménagement de l'histoire chez Grégoire de Tours: à propos de l'invasion de 451 (*H.F.* II 5-7)," *Romanobarbarica* 3 (1978) 5-38

Barnard, L. W. "Bede and Eusebius as Church Historians," in *Famulus Christi*, pp. 106-24

Barnes, Timothy D. *Constantine and Eusebius* (Cambridge, Mass. 1981)

Barnish, Samuel J. B. "The Anonymous Valesianus II as a Source for the Last Years of Theodoric," *Latomus* 42 (1983) 572-96

———. "The Genesis and Completion of Cassiodorus's *Gothic History*," *Latomus* 43 (1984) 336-61

Beare, W. *The Roman Stage* (London 1950)

Bede: His Life, Times and Writings. Essays in Commemoration of the Twelfth Centenary of His Death, ed. A. Hamilton Thompson (Oxford 1935)

Belting, Hans. "Studien zum beneventanischen Hof im 8. Jahrhundert," *Dumbarton Oaks Papers* 16 (1962) 141-93

Berkum, A. van. "Willibrord en Wilfried, Een onderzoek naar hun wederzijds betrekkingen," *Sacris Erudiri* 23 (1978-79) 347-415

Bernays, Jacob. "Über die Chronik des Sulpicius Severus," in his *Gesammelte Abhandlungen*, ed. Hermann Usener, 2 vols. (Berlin 1885) II, 81-200

Bernheim, Ernst. *Lehrbuch der historischen Methode und der Geschichtsphilosophie*, 6th ed. (1914, reprinted New York 1970)

Bertolini, Ottorino. "Carlomagno e Benevento," in *Karl der Grosse*, I, 609-71

———. "Il *Liber pontificalis*," *Spoleto Settimane* 17 (1970) 397-455

Bethmann, Ludwig. "Die Geschichtsschreibung der Langobarden," *Archiv der Gesellschaft für ältere deutsche Geschichtskunde* 10 (1851) 335-48

———. "Paulus Diaconus Leben und Schriften," *Archiv der Gesellschaft für ältere deutsche Geschichtskunde* 10 (1851) 247-334

Beumann, Helmut. "Gregor von Tours und der *sermo rusticus*," in his *Wissenschaft vom Mittelalter*, pp. 41-70

———. "Methodenfragen der mittelalterlichen Geschichtsschreibung," in his *Wissenschaft von Mittelalter*, pp. 1-8

———. *Wissenschaft von Mittelalter. Ausgewählte Aufsätze* (Cologne-Vienna 1972)

Bickerman, Elias. "*Origines gentium*," *Classical Philology* 47 (1951) 65-81

Birley, A. R. "The *Augustan History*," in T. A. Dorey, ed., *Latin Biography* (London 1967), pp. 113-38

Bischoff, Bernhard. "Die Hofbibliothek Karls des Grossen," in *Karl der Grosse*, II, 42-62

Blair, Peter Hunter. "The Historical Writings of Bede," *Spoleto Settimane* 17 (1970) 197-221

———. *An Introduction to Anglo-Saxon England* (Cambridge 1956)

———. *Northumbria in the Days of Bede* (London 1976)

———. "Some Observations on the *Historia regum* Attributed to Symeon of Durham," in N. Chadwick, ed., *Celt and Saxon*, pp. 63-118

———. *The World of Bede* (London 1970)

Blatt, Franz. *The Latin Josephus* I (Copenhagen 1958)

Bloch, Marc. *The Historian's Craft*, tr. Peter Putnam (New York 1962)

Blockley, R. C. *Ammianus Marcellinus: A Study of His Historiography and Political Thought*, Collection Latomus 141 (Brussels 1975)

BLTW. See *Bede: His Life, Times and Writings*

Boesch Gajano, Sofia. "Il santo nella visione storiografica di Gregorio di Tours," *Todi Convegno* 12, pp. 28-91.

Bognetti, Gian Piero. "Processo logico e integrazione delle fonti nella storiografia di Paolo Diacono," in his *L'età longobarda* III (Milan 1967) 159-84

Böhmer, J. F., and E. Mühlbacher. *Die Regesten des Kaiserreichs unter den Karolinger, 751-918*, 2d ed. (Innsbruck 1908)

Bollnow, Hermann. "Die Herkunftssagen der germanischen Stämme als Geschichtsquellen," *Baltische Studien*, N.F. 54 (1968) 14-25

Bolton, W. F. "A Bede Bibliography, 1935-1960," *Traditio* 18 (1962) 436-45

―――. *A History of Anglo-Latin Literature* (Princeton 1967)

Bonner, G. See *Famulus Christi*

Bonnet, Max. *Le Latin de Grégoire de Tours* (Paris 1890)

―――. Review of Arndt ed., *Revue critique d'histoire et de littérature*, N.S. 19 (1885) 161-74

―――. Review of Arndt-Krusch ed., *Revue critique d'histoire et de littérature*, N.S. 21 (1886) 147-54

Booth, Wayne. *The Rhetoric of Fiction* (Chicago 1961)

Borchardt, Frank L. *German Antiquity in Renaissance Myth* (Baltimore-London 1971)

Borst, Arno. "Das Bild der Geschichte in den Enzyklopädie Isidors von Sevilla," *Deutsches Archiv für Erforschung des Mittelalters* 22 (1960) 1-62

―――. *Der Turmbau von Babel. Geschichte der Meinungen über Ursprung und Vielfalt der Sprachen und Völker*, 4 vols. in 6 (Stuttgart 1957-63)

Bradley, Dennis R. "The Composition of the *Getica*," *Eranos* 64 (1966) 67-79

Braunfels, Wolfgang. See *Karl der Grosse*

Breisach, Ernst. *Historiography: Ancient, Medieval, Modern* (Chicago-London 1983)

Brennan, Brian. "The Image of the Frankish Kings in the Poetry of Venantius Fortunatus," *Journal of Medieval History* 10 (1984) 1-11

Brewer, E. Cobham. *A Dictionary of Miracles: Imitative, Realistic, and Dogmatic* (London 1884)

Brincken, Anna-Dorothee von den. *Studien zur lateinischen Weltchronistik bis in der Zeitalter Ottos von Freising* (Düsseldorf 1957)

Brooks, Nicholas. *The Early History of the Church of Canterbury* (Leicester 1984)

Brown, Peter. *Augustine of Hippo: A Biography* (Berkeley 1967)

―――. *Relics and Social Status in the Age of Gregory of Tours*, Stenton Lecture 1976 (Reading 1977)

―――. *The World of Late Antiquity* (London 1971)

Brühl, Carlrichard. "Langobardische Königsurkunden als Geschichtsquellen," *Studi storici in onore di Ottorino Bertolini* I (Pisa 1972) 47-72

Brunhölzl, Franz. *Geschichte des lateinischen Literatur des Mittelalters* I (Munich 1975)

Buchner, Rudolf. "Kulturelle und politische Zusammengehörigkeitsgefühle im europäische Frühmittelalter," *Historische Zeitschrift* 207 (1968) 562-83

―――. *Die Rechtsquellen* (Wattenbach-Levison, *Geschichtsquellen*, Beiheft, Weimar 1953)

―――. Review of K-L, in *Zeitschrift der Savigny-Stiftung für Rechtsgeschichte*, Germ. Abt. 62 (1942) 404-14; 68 (1951) 465-70; 72 (1955) 277-78

Bullitt, John. *Jonathan Swift and the Anatomy of Satire* (Cambridge, Mass. 1953)

Bullough, Donald. *The Age of Charlemagne* (New York 1966)

———. "Alcuino e la tradizione culturale insulare," *Spoleto Settimane* 20 (1973) 571-600

———. "Colombano," *Dizionario biografico degli Italiani* 27 (1982) 113-29

———. "Columba, Adamnan, and the Achievement of Iona, I, II," *Scottish Historical Review* 43 (1964) 111-31; 44 (1965) 17-33

———. "Hagiography as Patriotism: Alcuin's 'York Poem' and the Early Northumbrian *Vitae sanctorum*," in *Hagiographie, cultures et sociétés*, pp. 339-59

Burckhardt, Jacob. "On Fortune and Misfortune in History" (1871), in his *Force and Freedom: Reflections on History*, ed. J. M. Nichols (New York 1943), pp. 347-70

Burian, Jan. "Der Gegensatz zwischen Rom und den Barbaren in der Historia Augusta," *Eirene* 15 (1977) 55-96

Bury, J. B. *History of the Later Roman Empire from Arcadius to Irene*, 2 vols. (London 1889)

———. *History of the Later Roman Empire from the Death of Theodosius I to the Death of Justinian*, 2 vols. (London 1923, reprinted New York 1958)

Butler, Cuthbert. "Hagiographica (Chronicle)," *Journal of Theological Studies* 7 (1906) 304-15

C(hatillon), F. "L'illusoire *Mimésis* et les aléas d'une translation," *Revue du moyen âge latin* 24 (1968 [1977]) 91-97

Caeneghem, R. C. van. *Guide to the Sources of Medieval History*, Europe in the Middle Ages, Selected Studies 2 (Amsterdam 1978)

Callu, J.-P. "La première diffusion de 'L'Histoire Auguste' (VIe-IXe siècle)," *Bonner Historia-Augusta-Colloquium 1982-83*. Antiquitas Reihe 4, 11 (Bonn 1985), pp. 89-129

Cambridge Ancient History XI (1936)

Cameron, Alan. "Cassiodorus, Jordanes and the Anicii," unpublished communication, 11th Byzantine Studies Conference, Toronto, 25 October 1985

Cameron, Averil. *Agathias* (Oxford 1970)

———. "Cassiodorus Deflated," *Journal of Roman Studies* 71 (1981) 183-86

———. "Early Byzantine *Kaiserkritik*: Two Case Histories," *Byzantine and Modern Greek Studies* 3 (1977) 1-17

———. *Procopius and the Sixth Century* (London 1985)

Campbell, James, ed. *The Anglo-Saxons* (Ithaca, N.Y. 1982)

———. "Bede," in T. E. Dorey, ed., *Latin Historians* (London 1966), pp. 159-90; reprinted in his *Essays*, pp. 1-27

———. *Essays in Anglo-Saxon History* (London 1986)

———. "Observations on the Conversion of England," *Ampleforth Journal*, 78 (1973) 12-26; reprinted in his *Essays*, pp. 69-84

Canart, Paul. "Le nouveau-né qui dénonce son père. Les avatars d'un conte populaire dans la littérature hagiographique," *Analecta Bollandiana* 84 (1966) 309-331

Cappuyns, M. J. "Cassiodore," in *Dictionnaire d'histoire et de géographie ecclésiastique* 11 (1949) 1348-1408

Carnohan, W. B. *Lemuel Gulliver's Mirror for Man* (Berkeley 1968)

Caspar, Erich. *Geschichte des Pappstums* II (Tübingen 1933)

Cerfaux, L., and J. Tondriau. *Le culte des souverains* (Paris 1957)

Chadwick, H. Munro. *The Heroic Age* (Cambridge 1912)

Chadwick, Nora K., ed. *Celt and Saxon: Studies in the Early British Border* (Cambridge 1963)

———. *Poetry and Letters in Early Christian Gaul* (London 1955)

Chastagnol, André. "Le supplice de l'écartèlement dans les arbres (à propos d'H.A., Vita Aureliani, 7, 4)," *Colloque histoire et historiographie clio*, ed. R. Chevallier, *Caesarodunum* 15 bis (Paris 1980), pp. 187-201

Christ, Karl. "Römer und Barbaren in der hohen Kaiserzeit," *Saeculum* 10 (1959) 273-88

Christensen, Torben. "Rufinus of Aquileia and the *H.E.* lib. VIII-IX of Eusebius," *Studia Theologica* 34 (1980) 129-52

Chrysos, Evangelos K. "Gothia Romana. Zur Rechtslage des Föderatenlandes des Westgoten im 4.Jh.," *Dacoromania. Jahrbuch für östliche Latinität* 1 (1973) 52-64

Cipolla, Carlo. "Considerazioni sulla 'Getica' di Jordanes e sulle loro relazioni colla 'Historia Getarum' di Cassiodoro Senatore," Reale Accademia delle Scienze di Torino, *Memorie* (Scienzi morali, storiche et filologiche), 2d ser., 43 (1893) 99-134

Clark, Arthur Melville. "The Art of Satire and the Satiric Spectrum," in Fabian, ed., *Satura*, pp. 123-41

Classen, Peter. "Italien zwischen Byzanz und dem Frankenreich," in J. Fleckenstein, ed., *Ausgewählte Aufsätze von Peter Classen*, Vorträge und Forschungen 28 (Sigmaringen 1983), pp. 85-115

———. "Karl der Grosse, das Papsttum und Byzanz," in *Karl der Grosse* I, 536-608

Clover, Carol J. *The Medieval Saga* (Ithaca, N.Y. 1982)

Colgrave, Bertram. "Bede's Miracle Stories," in *BLTW*, pp. 201-29

———. "The Earliest Life of St. Gregory the Great, Written by a Whitby Monk," in Chadwick, ed., *Celt and Saxon*, pp. 119-37

———. "The Earliest Saints' Lives Written in England," British Academy, *Proceedings* 44 (1958) 35-60

Colish, Marcia L. "Historical Writing Then and Now: Against Exegesis," *Book Forum* 5 (1980) 270-78

Collins, Roger. *Early Medieval Spain: Unity in Diversity, 400-1000* (London 1983)

———. "Mérida and Toledo: 550-585," in Edward James, ed., *Visigothic Spain: New Approaches* (Oxford 1980), pp. 189-219

———. "Theodebert I, 'Rex Magnus Francorum,' " in *Studies Presented to J. M. Wallace-Hadrill*, pp. 7-33

Cook, Albert Stanburrough. "Bede and Gregory of Tours," *Philological Quarterly* 6 (1927) 315-16

Coopland, G. W. "The Medieval View of History," in his *The "Tree of Battles" of Honoré Bonet* (Liverpool 1949), pp. 38-47, 304-305

Corbato, Carlo. "Paolo Diacono," *Antichità altoadriatiche* 7 (1975) 7-22

Cosmos, Spencer. "Oral Tradition and Literary Convention in Bede's Life of St. Aidan," *Classical Folia* 31 (1977) 47-63

Courcelle, Pierre. *Histoire littéraire des grandes invasions germaniques*, 3d ed. (Paris 1964)

———. Review of Momigliano, "Cassiodorus and Italian Culture," in *Latomus* 16 (1957) 741-43

Courtois, Christian. *Les Vandales et l'Afrique* (Paris 1955)

Cowdrey, H. E. J. "Bede and the 'English People,'" *Journal of Religious History* 11 (1981) 501-23

Cracco-Ruggini, Lellia. "Pubblicistica et storiografia bizantine di fronte alla crisi dell'impero romano," *Athaenaeum*, N.S. 51 (1973) 146-83

Crivellucci, Amadeo. "Di alcune questioni relative alla vita di Paolo Diacono, storico dei Longobardi," *Studi storici* 9 (1900) 3-19

Croke, Brian. "A.D. 476: The Manufacturing of a Turning Point," *Chiron* 13 (1983) 81-119

———. "Cassiodorus and the *Getica* of Jordanes" (forthcoming)

———. "The Date and Circumstances of Marcian's Decease, A.D. 457," *Byzantion* 48 (1978) 5-9

———. "Mundo the Gepid: From Freebooter to Roman General," *Chiron* 12 (1982) 125-35

———. "The Origins of the Christian World Chronicle," in *History and Historians*, pp. 116-31

———. See also *History and Historians*

Curtius, Ernst Robert. *European Literature and Latin Middle Ages*, tr. Willard Trask (New York 1953)

Dagron, Gilbert. "Discours utopique et récit des origines: 1. Une lecture de Cassiodore-Jordanès: les Goths de Scandza à Ravenne," *Annales: Économies, sociétés, civilisations* 26 (1971) 290-305

Dahn, Felix. "Paulus Diaconus," *Allgemeine deutsche Biographie* XXV (Leipzig 1887) 245-48

———. *Paulus Diaconus*, Abt. 1. *Des Paulus Diaconus Leben und Schriften*, Lombardische Studien 1 (Leipzig 1876)

———. "Die Ursachen der Völkerwanderung," in E. von Wietersheim, *Geschichte der Völkerwanderung*, 2d ed., 2 vols. (Leipzig 1880) I, 1-17

Daiches, David, and Anthony Thorlby, eds. *The Medieval World*, Literature and Western Civilization (London 1973)

Dannenbauer, Heinrich. *Die Entstehung Europas. Von der Spätantike zum Mittelalter*, 2 vols. (Stuttgart 1959-62)

Davidse, Jan. "The Sense of the Past in the Works of the Venerable Bede," *Studi medievale*, 3d ser., 23 (1982) 647-95

Dawson, Christopher. *The Making of Europe* (London 1932)

Deanesly, Margaret. *The Pre-Conquest Church in England* (London 1961)

Dekkers, E. *Clavis patrum Latinorum*, 2d ed. (Turnhout 1961)

Del Giudice, Pasquale. "Lo storico dei Longobardi e la critica odierna (a. 1880)," in his *Studi di storia e diritto* (Milan 1889), pp. 1-43

Delehaye, Hippolyte. *Étude sur le légendier romain. Les saints de Novembre et de Décembre*, Subsidia hagiographica 23 (Brussels 1936)

————. *Les passions des martyrs et les genres littéraires*, 2d ed., Subsidia hagiographica 13B (Brussels 1966)

————. "Les receuils antiques des miracles des saints," *Analecta Bollandiana* 43 (1925) 5-85, 305-25

Demandt, Alexander. "Geschichte in der spätantike Gesellschaft," *Gymnasium* 89 (1982) 255-72

————. "Der spätrömische Militäradel," *Chiron* 10 (1980) 609-36

Demougeot, Émilienne. "Bedeutet das Jahre 476 das Ende des römischen Reiches im Okzident?" *Klio* 60 (1978) 371-81

Dill, Sir Samuel. *Roman Society in Gaul in the Merovingian Age* (London 1926)

Dobschütz, Ernst von. *Das Decretum Gelasianum*, Texte und Untersuchungen zur Geschichte der altchristlichen Literatur 3, 8, 3 (Leipzig 1912)

Doignon, J. "Tradition classique et tradition chrétienne dans l'historiographie d'Hilaire de Poitiers au carrefour des IVᵉ-Vᵉ siècles," in *Colloque histoire et historiographie clio*, ed. R. Chevallier, *Caesarodunum* 15 bis (Paris 1980), pp. 215-26

Dopsch, Alfons. *Wirtschaftliche und soziale Grundlagen der europäischen Kulturentwicklung aus der Zeit von Caesar bis auf Karl den Grossen*, 2d ed., 2 vols. (Vienna 1923-24)

Droysen, H. "Die Zusammensetzung der *Historia Romana* des Paulus Diaconus," *Forschungen zur deutschen Geschichte* 15 (1875) 167-80

Du Bos, abbé. *Histoire critique de l'établissement de la monarchie française dans les Gaules*, 3 vols. (Amsterdam 1734)

Dubois, Jacques. *Les martyrologes du moyen âge latin*, Typologie des sources du moyen âge latin, fasc. 26 (Turnhout 1978)

Duckett, Eleanor Shipley. *Anglo-Saxon Saints and Scholars* (New York 1947)

Dudden, F. Homes. *The Life and Times of St. Ambrose*, 2 vols. (Oxford 1935)

Dufourcq, Albert. *Étude sur les gesta martyrum romains*, 4 vols. (Paris 1900-10)

Dumville, David N. "The Chronology of *De excidio Britanniae*, Book I," in M. Lapidge and D. Dumville, eds., *Gildas: New Approaches*, pp. 61-84

————. "Gildas and Maelgwn: Problems of Dating," in *ibid.*, pp. 51-59

Ebert, Adolf. *Allgemeine Geschichte der Literatur des Mittelalters im Abendlande* I, 2d ed. (Leipzig 1889)

Eis, Gerhard. "The Origins of German Language and Literature," in Daiches and Thorlby, eds., *The Medieval World*, pp. 71-111

Eisenhut, Werner. "Spätantike Troja-Erzählungen—mit einem Ausblick auf die mittelalterliche Troja-Literatur," *Mittellateinische Jahrbuch* 18 (1983) 1-28

Elliot, Robert C. *The Power of Satire: Magic, Ritual, and Art* (Princeton 1960)

Engels, L. J. *Observations sur le vocabulaire de Paul Diacre*, Latinitatis Christianorum primaeva 16 (Nijmegen 1961)

Ensslin, Wilhelm. "Des Symmachus Historia Romana als Quelle für Jordanes," Bayerische Akademie der Wissenschaften, *Sitzungsberichte*, Phil.-hist. Abt. (1948), no. 3

————. *Theodorich der Grosse* (Munich 1948)

Erdmann, Carl. *Die Entstehung des Kreuzzugsgedankens* (Stuttgart 1935)

Erikson, Alvar. "The Problem of Authorship in the Chronicle of Fredegar," *Eranos* 63 (1965) 47-76

Ermini, Filippo. *Storia della letteratura Latina medievale dalle origini alla fine del secolo VII* (Spoleto 1960)

Ernst, Fritz. "Zeitgeschehen und Geschichtsschreibung. Eine Skizze," *Die Welt als Geschichte* 16 (1957) 137-89

Ewald, Paul. "Studien zur Ausgabe des Registers Gregors I," *Neues Archiv der Gesellschaft für ältere deutsche Geschichtskunde* 3 (1878) 433-660

Fabian, Bernhard, ed. *Satura: Ein Kompendium moderner Studien zur Satire* (Hildesheim–New York 1975)

Famulus Christi: Essays in Commemoration of the Thirteenth Centenary of the Birth of Bede, ed. G. Bonner (London 1976)

Fanning, Stephen C. "Lombard Arianism Reconsidered," *Speculum* 56 (1981) 241-58

Farmer, D. H. "Saint Wilfrid," in *St. Wilfrid at Hexham*, pp. 35-59

Fleckenstein, Josef. "Karl der Grosse und sein Hof," in *Karl der Grosse* I, 24-50

Fliche, A., and V. Martin. *Histoire de l'Église* IV (Paris 1948)

Foakes-Jackson, Frederick John. *A History of Church History* (Cambridge 1939)

Fontaine, Jacques. "Unité et diversité du mélange des genres et des tons chez quelques écrivains latins de la fin du IVᵉ siècle: Ausone, Ambroise, Ammien," Fondation Hardt, *Entretiens sur l'antiquité classique* 23 (1977) 425-72

Fornara, Charles William. *The Nature of History in Ancient Greece and Rome* (Berkeley 1983)

Fowler, Alastair. *Kinds of Literature: An Introduction to the Theory of Genres and Modes* (Cambridge, Mass. 1982)

Fränkel, Eduard. *Elementi plautini in Plauto*, tr. Franco Munari (Florence 1960)

Franklin, Carmela Vircillo, and Paul Meyvaert. "Has Bede's Version of the *Passio s. Anastasii* Come Down to Us in BHL. 408?" *Analecta Bollandiana* 100 (1982) 373-400

Frederichs, Hans. *Die Gelehrten um Karl dem Grossen in ihren Schriften, Briefen und Gedichten* (diss., Berlin 1931)

Friedrich, Johann. "Über die kontroversen Fragen im Leben des gotischen Geschichtsschreibers Jordanes," Bayerische Akademie der Wissenschaften, *Sitzungsberichte*, phil.-hist. Kl. (1907) 379-442

Frölich, Hermann. "Zur Herkunft der Langobarden," *Quellen und Forschungen aus italienischen Archiven und Bibliotheken* 55-56 (1976) 1-21

Frye, Northrop. *The Anatomy of Criticism* (Princeton 1956)

——. *The Great Code: The Bible and Literature* (New York–London 1982)

——. "History and Myth in the Bible," in Angus Fletcher, ed., *The Literature of Fact* (New York 1976), pp. 1-44

——. *The Myth of Deliverance: Reflections on Shakespeare's Problem Comedies* (Toronto 1983)

Fuchs, Harald. Review of Momigliano, "Cassiodorus and Italian Culture," in *Museum Helveticum* 14 (1957) 250-51

Fuhrmann, Manfred. "Die Mönchsgeschichten des Hieronymus. Formexperimente in erzählendes Literatur," Fondation Hardt, *Entretiens sur l'antiquité classique* 23 (1977) 41-89

Fustel de Coulanges, N. D. *La monarchie franque*, 3d ed. (Paris 1912)

Ganshof, F. L. *Een Historicus uit de VIe Eeuw. Gregorius van Tours*, Mededelingen van de Koninklijke Vlaamse Academie voor Wetenschappen, Letteren en Schone Kunsten van België, Kl. der Lett., XXVIII (1966), no. 5

Gardiner, K.H.J. "Notes on the Chronology of Fredegar IV," *Parergon*, no. 20 (1978) 41-42

———. "On Translating Paul the Deacon," *Parergon*, no. 21 (1978) 43-51

———. "Paul the Deacon and Secundus of Trent," in *History and Historians*, pp. 147-53

Gaster, M. "Zur Quellenkunde deutscher Sagen und Märchen," *Germania. Vierteljahrschrift für deutsche Altertumskunde* 25 (1880) 274-94

Gatch, Milton McC. *Preaching and Theology in Anglo-Saxon England: Ælfric and Wulfstan* (Toronto 1977)

Gay, Jules. *L'Italie méridionale et l'Empire byzantin*, Bibliothèque des Écoles françaises d'Athènes et de Rome 90 (Paris 1904)

Gibbon, Edward. *History of the Decline and Fall of the Roman Empire*, ed. J. B. Bury, 7 vols. (London 1896-1900)

Gibbs, Marion. "The Decrees of Agatho and the Gregorian Plan for York," *Speculum* 48 (1973) 213-46

Giordano, Oronzo. *Jordanes e la storiografia nel VI secolo* (Bari 1973)

———. "Sociologia e patologia del miracolo in Gregorio di Tours," *Helikon (Rivista di tradizione e cultura classica dell'Università di Messina)* 18-19 (1978-79) 168-209

Giunta, Francesco. "Considerazioni sulla vita e sulle opere di Jordanes," *Italica* 25 (1948) 244-47

———. *Jordanes e la cultura dell'alto medio evo* (Palermo 1952)

Godman, Peter. *Poetry of the Carolingian Renaissance* (London 1985)

Goffart, Walter. *Barbarians and Romans: The Techniques of Accommodation* (Princeton 1980)

———. "The Conversions of Bishop Avitus and Similar Passages in Gregory of Tours," in *"To See Ourselves as Others See Us": Christians, Jews, "Others" in Late Antiquity*, ed. Jacob Neusner and Ernest R. Frerichs (Chico, Calif. 1985), pp. 473-97

———. "Foreigners in the *Histories* of Gregory of Tours," *Florilegium* 4 (1982) 80-99

———. "The Fredegar Problem Reconsidered," *Speculum* 38 (1963) 206-41

———. "From *Historiae* to *Historia Francorum* and Back Again: Aspects of the Textual History of Gregory of Tours," in *Religion, Culture, and Society in the Early Middle Ages: Studies in Honor of Richard E. Sullivan*, ed. Thomas F. X. Noble and John J. Contreni (Kalamazoo, Mich. 1987), pp. 55-76

———. "*Hetware* and *Hugas*: Datable Anachronisms in *Beowulf*," in Colin Chase, ed., *The Dating of "Beowulf,"* Toronto Old English Series 6 (Toronto 1981), pp. 83-100

Goffart, Walter. "Le Mans, St. Scholastica, and the Literary Tradition of the Translation of St. Benedict," *Revue Bénédictine* 77 (1967) 106-41

———. "Old and New in Merovingian Taxation," *Past and Present* 96 (1982) 3-21

———. "Paul the Deacon's *Gesta episcoporum Mettensium* and the Early Design of Charlemagne's Succession," forthcoming, *Traditio* 42 (1986)

———. Review of Krautschick, *Cassiodor*, in *Speculum* 60 (1985) 989-91

———. "Rome, Constantinople, and the Barbarians," *American Historical Review* 86 (1981) 275-306

———. "The Supposedly 'Frankish' Table of Nations: An Edition and Study," *Frühmittelalterliche Studien* 17 (1983) 98-130

———. "The Theme of 'The Barbarian Invasions' in Late Antique and Modern Historiography," forthcoming in the Proceedings of the Dumbarton Oaks Symposium 1985, ed. Evangelos Chrysos

———. "Zosimus: The First Historian of Rome's Fall," *American Historical Review* 76 (1971) 412-41

Gooch, G. P. *History and Historians in the Nineteenth Century* (London 1913)

Goubert, Paul. *Byzance avant l'Islam*, I: *Byzance et l'Orient sous les successeurs de Justinien. L'empereur Maurice* (Paris 1951)

Gransden, Antonia. *Historical Writing in England c. 550 to c. 1307* (London 1974)

Grant, Robert M. *Miracle and Natural Law in Greco-Roman and Early Christian Thought* (Amsterdam 1962)

Graus, František. Review of Wenskus, *Stammesbildung*, in *Historica* 7 (1963) 185-91

———. "Sozialgeschichtliche Aspekte der Hagiographie der Merowinger- und Karolingerzeit," *Vorträge und Forschungen* 20 (1974) 131-76

———. *Volk, Herrscher und Heiliger im Reich der Merowinger* (Prague 1965)

Greenfield, Stanley B. See Lapidge, Michael

Grimm, Jakob. "Über Jornandes und die Geten" (1846), in his *Kleinere Schriften*, 8 vols. (Berlin 1864-90) III, 171-235

Grimm, Jakob, and Wilhelm Grimm. *Deutsche Sagen* (1816-18), 3d ed. by Hermann Grimm, 2 vols. (Berlin 1891); tr. Donald Ward, *The German Legends of the Brothers Grimm*, 2 vols. (Philadelphia 1981)

Grundmann, Herbert. *Geschichtsschreibung im Mittelalter. Gattungen–Epochen–Eigenart*, 2d ed. (Göttingen 1965)

Gschwantler, Otto. "Die Heldensage von Alboin und Rosimund," in Helmut Birkhan, ed., *Festgabe für Otto Höfler zum 75. Geburtstag*, Philologia Germanica, ed. H. Birkhan, 3 (Vienna-Stuttgart 1976), pp. 214-47

———. "Versöhnung als Thema einer heroischen Sage," *Beiträge zur Geschichte der deutsche Sprache u. Literatur (Paul und Braune Beiträge)* 97 (1975) 230-62

Guenée, Bernard. *Histoire et culture historique dans l'Occident médiéval* (Paris 1980)

Gutschmid, Alfred von. Review of Schirren, *De ratione*, in *Jahrbücher für classische Philologie* 8 (1862) 124-51

Hachmann, Rolf. *Die Goten und Skandinavien*, Quellen und Forschungen zur Sprach- und Kulturgeschichte der germanischen Völker, N.F. 34 (Berlin 1970)

Hafner, Wolfgang. "Paulus Diaconus und der ihn zugeschriebene Kommentar zur

Regula S. Benedicti," in Basilius Steidle, ed., *Commentationes in Regulam S. Benedicti*, Studia Anselmiana 42 (Rome 1957), pp. 347-58

Hagendahl, Harald. *Augustine and the Latin Classics*, Studia Graeca et Latina Gotheburgensia 20 (Göteborg 1967)

Hagiographie, cultures et sociétés, IVᵉ-XIᵉ siècles. Actes du colloque organisé à Nanterre et à Paris (2-5 mai 1979), ed. P. Riché and E. Patlagean (Paris 1981)

Hallenbeck, Jan T. *Pavia and Rome: The Lombard Monarchy and the Papacy in the Eighth Century*, American Philosophical Society, Transactions 72, part 4 (1982)

Halphen, Louis. "Grégoire de Tours, historien de Clovis," in his À travers l'histoire du Moyen Âge (Paris 1950), pp. 31-38

Hampe, K. "Paulus Diaconus," in J. Hoops, ed., *Reallexicon der germanischen Altertumskunde* III (Strasbourg 1915-16), 397-99

Hanning, Robert, *The Vision of History in Early Britain* (New York 1966)

Hansen, Günther Christian. "Sulpicius Alexander—eine Historiker nach Ammian," *Sitzungsberichte der Akademie der Wissenschaften der Deutschen Demokratischen Republik* 15G (1982) 89-91

Harrison, Kenneth. *The Framework of Anglo-Saxon History to A.D. 900* (Cambridge 1976)

Harsh, P. W. *Handbook of Classical Drama* (Stanford 1944)

Hauck, Albert. *Kirchengeschichte Deutschlands*, 9th ed., 5 vols. (Leipzig 1958)

Hauck, Karl. "Heldendichtung und Heldensage als Geschichtsbewustssein," in *Alteuropa und die moderne Gesellschaft. Festschrift für Otto Brunner* (Göttingen 1963), pp. 118-38

Heinzelmann, Martin. *Bischofsherrschaft in Gallien. Zur Kontinuität römischer Führungsschichten vom 4. bis zum 7. Jahrhundert. Soziale, prosopographische und bildungsgeschichtliche Aspekte. Francia* Beiheft 5 (Zurich-Munich 1976)

———. "Gallische Prosopographie, 260-527," *Francia* 10 (1982) 531-718

———. "Neue Aspekte der biographischen und hagiographischen Literatur in der lateinischen Welt (1.-6. Jahrhundert)," *Francia* 1 (1973) 37-44

———. "Une source de base de la littérature hagiographique latine: le receuil de miracles," in *Hagiographie, cultures et sociétés*, pp. 235-57

———. *Translationsberichte und andere Quellen des Reliquienkultes*, Typologie des sources du moyen âge latin, fasc. 33 (Turnhout 1979)

Heinzelmann, Martin, and Joseph-Claude Poulin. *Les vies anciennes de sainte Geneviève de Paris. Études critiques*, Bibliothèque de l'École des Hautes Études, Sciences hist. et philol. 329 (Paris 1986)

Hellmann, Siegmund. "Studien zur mittelalterliche Geschichtsschreibung, I. Gregor von Tours," *Historische Zeitschrift* 107 (1911) 1-43; reprinted in his *Ausgewählte Abhandlungen zur Historiographie und Geistesgeschichte des Mittelalters*, ed. Helmut Beumann (Weimar 1961), pp. 57-99

Helms, Hadwig. "Zur Wandlung des Germanenbild im 1. Jh. u. Z.," *Sitzungsberichte der Akademie der Wissenschaften der Deutschen Demokratischen Republik* 15G (1982) 29-32

Hendrickson, G. L. "Satura Tota Nostra Est," in Fabian, ed., *Satura*, pp. 1-15

Hermann, Hans-Walter. "Zum Stande der Erforschung der früh- und hochmittelalterlichen Geschichte des Bistums Metz," *Rheinische Vierteljahrsblätter* 28 (1963) 131-99

Hermann-Mascard, Nicole. *Les reliques des saints. Formation coutumière d'un droit,* Société d'histoire du droit, Collection d'histoire institutionelle et sociale 6 (Paris 1975)

Hillgarth, Jocelyn. "Historiography in Visigothic Spain," *Spoleto Settimane* 17 (1970) 261-352

———. "Ireland and Spain in the Seventh Century," *Peritia* 3 (1984) 1-16

Histoire littéraire de la France, 12 vols. (Paris 1733-63, reprinted 1866)

History and Historians in Late Antiquity, ed. Brian Croke and A. M. Emmet (Sidney 1983)

Hodgart, Matthew. *Satire* (London 1969)

Hodgkin, Thomas. *Italy and Her Invaders,* 8 vols. (London 1892-99)

Hohl, Ernst. "Die 'gotische Abkunft' des Kaisers Maximinus Thrax," *Klio* 34 (1942) 264-89

Hourlier, Jacques. "Le témoignage de Paul Diacre," *Studia monastica* 21 (1979) 205-11

Hunt, William. "Wilfrid," in *Dictionary of National Biography* XXI (London 1909) 242

Ideal and Reality in Frankish and Anglo-Saxon Society: Studies Presented to J. M. Wallace-Hadrill, ed. Patrick Wormald (Oxford 1984)

Iliescu, Vladimir. "Bemerkungen zur Gotenfreundlichen Einstellung in den *Getica* des Jordanes (I)," *XIIᵉ Conférence internationale d'études classiques Eirene (1972)* (Bucharest-Amsterdam 1975), pp. 411-27

Isenberg, Gabriele. *Die Wurdigung Wilfrids von York in der* Historia ecclesiastica gentis Anglorum *Bedas und die* Vita Wilfridi *des Eddius* (diss., Münster 1978)

James, Edward. "Bede and the Tonsure Question," *Peritia* 3 (1984) 85-98

———. *The Origins of France: From Clovis to the Capetians, 500-1000* (London 1982)

Jarnut, Jörg. "Zur Frühgeschichte der Langobarden," *Studi medievali,* ser. 3, 24 (1983) 1-16

Jeffreys, Elizabeth M. "The Attitudes of Byzantine Chroniclers toward Ancient History," *Byzantion* 39 (1979) 199-238

Jenkins, Claude. "Bede as Exegete and Theologian," in *BLTW,* pp. 152-200

John, Eric. "The Social and Political Problems of the Early English Church," *Agricultural History Review* 18 (1970) supplement (= Joan Thirsk, ed., *Land, Church and People: Essays Presented to H.P.R. Finberg*), pp. 39-63

Johne, Klaus-Peter. "Zur Problemen der Historia-Augusta Forschung," *Altertumswissenschaft mit Zukunft. Dem Wirken Werner Hartkes gewidmet.* Akademie der Wissenschaften der Deutschen Demokratischen Republik, Sitzungsberichte des Plenums und der Klassen, no. 3 (Berlin 1973), pp. 13-18

Jones, A.H.M. *The Later Roman Empire, 284-602* (Norman, Okla. 1964)

Jones, Charles W. "Bede as Early Medieval Historian," *Medievalia et Humanistica* 4 (1946) 26-36

———. *Saints' Lives and Chronicles in Early England* (Ithaca, N.Y. 1947)

Jones, Putnam Fennel. *A Concordance to the* Historia ecclesiastica *of Bede* (Cambridge, Mass. 1929)

Jungblut, Jean-Baptiste. "Recherches sur le 'rhytme oratoire' dans les 'Historiarum libri,' " *Todi Convegno 12*, pp. 325-64

Kaegi, Walter Emil, Jr. "Some Seventh-Century Sources on Caesarea," *Israel Exploration Journal* 28 (1978) 177-81

Kappelmacher, Alfred. "Iordanis," in Pauly-Wissowa, *Real-Encyclopädie der klassischen Altertumswissenschaft* 9 (1916) 1925-27

————. "Zur Lebensgeschichte des Iordanis," *Wiener Studien* 36 (1914) 181-88

Karl der Grosse: Lebenswerk und Nachwirkung, ed. Wolfgang Braunfels, 4 vols. (Düsseldorf 1965-67)

Keen, Maurice. "Medieval Ideas of History," in Daiches and Thorlby, eds., *The Medieval World*, pp. 285-314

Kemp, Eric Waldram. *Canonization and Authority in the Western Church* (London 1948)

Kermode, Frank. *The Sense of an Ending* (New York 1961)

Kernan, Alvin B. *The Plot of Satire* (New Haven–London 1965)

————. "Satire," in Philip P. Wiener, *Dictionary of the History of Ideas*, 4 vols. (New York 1966) IV, 211-17

————. "A Theory of Satire" (1959), reprinted in Fabian, ed., *Satura*, pp. 142-77

Kirby, D. P. "Bede, Eddius Stephanus and the 'Life of Wilfrid,' " *English Historical Review* 98 (1983), 101-14

————. "Bede's Native Sources for the *Historia ecclesiastica*," *Bulletin of the John Rylands Library* 48 (1965-66) 341-71

————. "King Ceolwulf of Northumbria and the *Historia ecclesiastica*," *Studia Celtica* 14-15 (1979-80) 168-73

————. "Northumbria in the Time of Wilfrid," in *St. Wilfrid at Hexham*, pp. 1-34

————. See also *St. Wilfrid at Hexham*

Köpke, Rudolf. *Deutsche Forschungen. Die Anfänge des Königthums bei den Gothen* (Berlin 1859), pp. 50-93

————. "Gregor von Tours" (1852), reprinted in his *Kleine Schriften zur Geschichte, Politik, und Literatur*, ed. F. G. Kiessling (Berlin 1872), pp. 289-321

Krautschick, Stefan. *Cassiodor und die Politik seiner Zeit*, Habelts Dissertationsdruck, Reihe Alte Geschichte, H. 17 (Bonn 1983)

Kries, C. G. *De Gregorii Turonensis vita et scriptis* (Bratislava 1839)

Krüger, Karl Heinrich. "Königskonversionen im 8. Jahrhundert," *Frühmittelalterliche Studien* 7 (1973) 169-222

————. *Die Universalchroniken*, Typologie des sources du moyen âge occidental, fasc. 16 (Turnhout 1976)

————. "Zur 'beneventanischen' Konzeption der Langobardengeschichte des Paulus Diaconus," *Frühmittelalterliche Studien* 15 (1981) 18-35

Krusch, Bruno. "Die handschriftlichen Grundlagen der Historia Francorum Gregors von Tours," *Historische Vierteljahrschrift* 27 (1932) 673-723

————. "Zu M. Bonnets Untersuchungen über Gregor von Tours," *Neues Archiv der Gesellschaft für ältere deutsche Geschichtskunde* 16 (1891) 432-34

Kurth, Godefroid. "De l'autorité de Grégoire de Tours," *Études franques* II, 117-206
———. *Études franques*, 2 vols. (Paris 1919)
———. "Grégoire de Tours et les études classiques au VIᵉ siècle," *Études franques* I, 1-29
———. "La reine Brunehaut," *Études franques* I, 265-356
———. "Les sénateurs en Gaule au VIᵉ siècle," *Études franques* II, 97-115
Lacroix, Bernard. *Orose et ses idées*, Université de Montréal, Publications de l'Institut d'études médiévales 18 (Montreal-Paris 1965)
Laistner, M.L.W. Review of Colgrave, *Two Lives*, in *American Historical Review* 46 (1941) 379-81
———. "Some Reflections on Latin Historical Writing in the Fifth Century," *Classical Philology* 35 (1940) 241-58
———. *Thought and Letters in Western Europe, A.D. 500 to 900* (London 1957)
———. "The Value and Influence of Cassiodorus' Ecclesiastical History," *Harvard Theological Review* 41 (1948) 51-67
Laistner, M.L.W., and H. H. King. *A Hand-list of Bede Manuscripts* (Ithaca, N.Y. 1943)
Lapidge, Michael. "The Anglo-Latin Background," in Stanley B. Greenfield and Daniel G. Calder, *A New Critical History of Old English Literature* (New York 1986), pp. 5-37
———. "Gildas's Education and the Latin Culture of Sub-Roman Britain," in Lapidge and Dumville, eds., *Gildas: New Approaches*, pp. 27-50
Lapidge, Michael, and D. Dumville, eds. *Gildas: New Approaches*, Studies in Celtic History 5 (Woodbridge, Suffolk 1984)
Latouche, Robert. "Grégoire de Tours et les premiers historiens de France," Association Guillaume Budé, *Lettres d'humanité* 2 (1943) 81-101
Le Bachelet, X. "Arianisme," in *Dictionnaire de théologie catholique* 1 (1923) 1848-49
Le Cointe, Charles. *Annales ecclesiastici Francorum*, 8 vols. (Paris 1665-79)
Lecouteux, Claude. "Les Cynocéphales: Étude d'une tradition tératologique de l'Antiquité au XIIᵉ siècle," *Cahiers de civilisation médiévale* 24 (1981) 117-28
Lecoy de la Marche, A. *De l'autorité de Grégoire de Tours. Étude sur le texte de l'Histoire des Francs* (Paris 1861)
Lefebvre, Georges. *La naissance de l'historiographie moderne* (Paris 1971)
Leicht, Pier Silvero. "Paolo Diacono e gli altri scrittori delle vicende d'Italia nell'età carolingia," Secondo congresso internazionale di studi sull'alto medioevo (1951), *Atti* (Spoleto 1953), pp. 57-74
Leonardi, Claudio. "L'agiografia latina dal tardantico all'altomedioevo," *La cultura in Italia fra tardo antico e alto medioevo*, Atti del Convegno tenuto a Roma, Consiglio nazionale delle ricerche 1979, 2 vols. (Rome 1981) I, 643-59
Levison, Wilhelm. "Bede as Historian," in *BLTW*, pp. 111-51
———. *England and the Continent in the Eighth Century* (Oxford 1946)
———. Review of Dalton, in *Historische Zeitschrift* 141 (1929) 180-82
Leyen, Friedrich von der. *Das Heldenliederbuch Karls des Grossen. Bestand, Gehalt, Wirkung* (Munich 1954)

Limone, Oronzo. "La vita di Gregorio Magno dell'Anonimo di Whitby," *Studi medievali*, ser. 3, 19 (1978) 37-67

Lipsius, Richard Adelbert. *Die apokryphen Apostelgeschichten und Apostellegenden. Ein Beitrag zur altchristlichen Literaturgeschichte*, 2 vols. (Brunswick 1883)

Llewellyn, Peter. *Rome in the Dark Ages* (London 1970)

Loebell, Johann Wilhelm. *Gregor von Tours und seine Zeit. Ein Beitrag zur Geschichte der Entstehung und ersten Entwicklung romanisch-germanischer Verhältnisse* (Leipzig 1839)

Lof, L. J. van der. "De san Agustín a san Gregorio de Tours sobre la intervención de los mártires," tr. José Oroz, *Augustinus* 19 (1974) 35-43

Löfstedt, Bengt. "Notizen zur mittelalterlichen Grammatiker," *Archivum Latinitatis medii aevi (Bulletin DuCange)* 42 (1979-80 [1982]) 79-83

———. "Zu Gregorius Turonensis *Hist. Franc.* 2.31," *Acta Classica* 21 (1978) 159

Lönnroth, Erik. "Die Goten in der modernen kritischen Geschichtsauffassung," in *Studia Gothica*, pp. 57-62

Lot, Ferdinand. *The End of the Ancient World and the Beginning of the Middle Ages*, tr. P. and M. Leon (London 1931)

———. *Les invasions germaniques. La pénétration mutuelle du monde barbare et du monde romain* (Paris 1945)

Lot, Ferdinand, Christian Pfister, and F.-L. Ganshof. *Les destinées de l'Empire en Occident de 395 à 888*, G. Glotz, ed., Histoire générale, Histoire du Moyen Âge 1 (Paris 1928)

Lotter, Friedrich. "Legenden als Geschichtsquellen," *Deutsches Archiv für Erforschung des Mittelalters* 27 (1971) 195-200

———. "Methodisches zur Gewinnung historischer Erkenntnisse aus hagiographischen Quellen," *Historische Zeitschrift* 229 (1979) 298-356

———. "Zu den Anredeformen und ehrenden Epitheta der Bischöfe in Spätantike und frühen Mittelalter," *Deutsches Archiv für Erforschung des Mittelalters* 27 (1971) 514-17

Löwe, Heinz. "Cassiodor" (1948), in his *Von Cassiodor zu Dante* (Berlin 1973), pp. 11-32

———. "Von Theoderich dem Grossen zu Karl dem Grossen," *Deutsches Archiv für Erforschung des Mittelalters* 9 (1952) 353-401

Loyn, H. R. *Anglo-Saxon England and the Norman Conquest* (London 1962)

Luiselli, Bruno. "Cassiodoro e la storia dei Goti," Accademia nazionale dei Lincei, Atti dei Convegni Lincei 45, *Convegno internazionale. Passagio dal mondo antico al medio evo da Theodosio a san Gregorio Magno (Roma, maggio 1977)* (Rome 1980), pp. 225-53

———. "Sul *De summa temporum* di Jordanes," *Romanobarbarica* 1 (1976) 81-133

Maenchen-Helfen, Otto J. *The World of the Huns*, ed. Max Knight (Berkeley 1973)

Maisano, Riccardo. "La spedizione italiana dell'imperatore Constante II," *Siculorum gymnasium*, N.S. 28 no. 1 (1975) 140-68

Manitius, Max. *Geschichte des lateinischen Literatur des Mittelalters* I (Munich 1911)

———. "Zur Frankengeschichte Gregors von Tours," *Neues Archiv der Gesellschaft für ältere deutsche Geschichtskunde* 21 (1896) 549-57

453

Markus, R. A. *Bede and the Tradition of Ecclesiastical History*, Jarrow Lecture 1975 (Jarrow 1976)

———. "Church History and Early Church Historians," *Studies in Church History* 11 (1974) 1-17

Marrou, H. I. *Histoire de l'éducation dans l'Antiquité*, 4th ed. (Paris 1958)

Martindale, John, ed. *Prosopography of the Later Roman Empire* II (Cambridge 1980)

Mascov, J. J. *Geschichte der Teutschen*, 2 vols. (Leipzig 1726-37), tr. Th. Lediard (London 1737-38)

Matthews, John. "Ammianus' Historical Evolution," in *History and Historians*, pp. 30-41

Mayr-Harting, Henry. *The Coming of Christianity to Anglo-Saxon England* (London 1972)

———. "St. Wilfrid in Sussex," *Studies in Sussex Church History*, ed. M. J. Kitch (n.p. 1981), pp. 1-17

———. *The Venerable Bede, the Rule of St. Benedict, and Social Class*, Jarrow Lecture 1976 (Jarrow 1977)

McClure, Judith. "Bede and the *Life of Ceolfrid*," *Peritia* 3 (1984) 71-84

McCulloh, John M. "The Cult of Relics in the Letters and 'Dialogues' of Pope Gregory the Great: A Lexicographical Study," *Traditio* 32 (1976) 145-86

Menghini, Evelina, "Dello stato presente degli studi intorno alla vita di Paolo Diacono," *Bolletino della Società pavese di storia patria* 4 (1904) 15-100, 231-85, 313-66

Meslin, Michel. "Le merveilleux comme langage politique chez Ammien Marcellin," in *Mélanges d'histoire ancienne offerts à William Seston* (Paris 1974), pp. 353-63

———. "Nationalisme, état et religions à la fin du IVᵉ siècle," *Archives de sociologie des religions*, no. 18 (1964) 3-20

Messmer, Hans. *Hispania-Idee und Gotenmythos. Zu den Voraussetzungen des traditionellen vaterländischen Geschichtsbildes im spanischen Mittelalters*, Geist und Werk der Zeiten 5 (Zurich 1960)

Meyvaert, Paul. *Bede and Gregory the Great*, Jarrow Lecture 1964 (Newcastle-on-Tyne 1964)

———. "Bede the Scholar," in *Famulus Christi*, pp. 40-69

———. "The *Registrum* of Gregory the Great and Bede," *Revue Bénédictine* 80 (1970) 162-66

———. See also Franklin, Carmella

Michel, A. "Suicide," in *Dictionnaire de théologie catholique* 14 (1941) 2739-40

Miller, Molly. "Bede's Use of Gildas," *English Historical Review* 90 (1975) 241-61

Misch, Georg. *Geschichte der Autobiographie* II, part 1, 2d half (Frankfurt 1955)

Moisl, Hermann. "Anglo-Saxon Royal Genealogies and Germanic Oral Tradition," *Journal of Medieval History* 7 (1981) 215-48

Momigliano, Arnaldo. "Biblical Studies and Classical Studies: Simple Reflections upon Historical Method" (1980), reprinted in his *Settimo Contributo*, pp. 289-96

———. "Cassiodoro" (1971), in *Dizionario biografico degli Italiani* 21 (1978) 484-504; reprinted in his *Sesto contributo*, pp. 487-508

———. "Cassiodorus and Italian Culture of His Time," British Academy, *Proceedings* 41 (1955) 207-45; reprinted in his *Studies in Historiography*, pp. 181-210, and in his *Secondo contributo*, pp. 191-230

———. *The Conflict between Paganism and Christianity in the Fourth Century* (Oxford 1961)

———. "Considerations on History in an Age of Ideology" (1982), reprinted in his *Settimo Contributo*, pp. 253-69

———. "L'età del trapasso fra storiografia antica e storiografia medievale, 300-550 D.C.," *Spoleto Settimane* 17 (1970) 89-118

———. "Historiography on Written Tradition and Historiography on Oral Tradition" (1961-62), reprinted in his *Studies in Historiography*, pp. 211-20

———. "A Medieval Jewish Autobiography" (1981), in his *Settimo contributo*, pp. 331-40

———. "The Origins of Universal History" (1981), in his *Settimo contributo*, pp. 77-103

———. "Pagan and Christian Historiography in the Fourth Century," in his *Conflict between Paganism and Christianity*, pp. 79-99

———. "Perizonius, Niebuhr and the Character of Early Roman Tradition" (1957), reprinted in his *Secondo contributo*, pp. 69-87

———. "The Place of Ancient Historiography in Modern Historiography" (1979), reprinted in his *Settimo contributo*, pp. 13-36

———. "The Rhetoric of History and the History of Rhetoric: On Hayden White's Tropes" (1981), reprinted in his *Settimo Contributo*, pp. 29-59

———. *Secondo contributo alla storia degli studi classici* (Rome 1964)

———. *Sesto contributo alla storia degli studi classici e del mondo antico*, Storia e letteratura 150 (Rome 1980)

———. *Settimo Contributo alla storia degli studi classici e del mondo antico* (Rome 1984)

———. "Some Observations on the *Origo gentis Romanae*," in his *Secondo contributo*, pp. 145-76

———. *Studies in Historiography* (New York 1966)

Mommsen, T. E. "Augustine and the Christian Idea of Progress," in his *Medieval and Renaissance Studies*, pp. 278-97

———. *Medieval and Renaissance Studies*, ed. Eugene F. Rice, Jr. (Ithaca, N.Y. 1959)

———. "Orosius and Augustine," in his *Medieval and Renaissance Studies*, pp. 340-45

———. "Petrarch's Conception of the 'Dark Ages,' " in his *Medieval and Renaissance Studies*, pp. 106-29

Mommsen, Th. *Die Provinzen von Caesar bis Diocletian* (*Römische Geschichte* V)(Berlin 1885)

———. "Die Quellen der Langobardengeschichte des Paulus Diaconus" (1880), reprinted in his *Gesammelte Schriften* VI (Berlin 1910) 484-539

Monod, Gabriel. *Études critiques sur les sources de l'histoire mérovingienne*, Bibliothèque de l'École pratique des hautes-études, sciences hist. et philol. 8 (Paris 1872)

———. Review of Bethmann, "Paulus Diaconus" *et al.*, in *Revue critique d'histoire et de littérature*, N.S. 7 (1879) 272-76

Moonen, Honorius. *Eddius Stephanus, Het Leven van sint Wilfrid, ingeleid, vertaald en van antiekeningen voorzien* ('s-Hertogenbosch 1946)

Moretus, H. "Les deux anciennes vies de Grégoire le Grand," *Analecta Bollandiana* 26 (1907) 66-72

Morghen, Raffaello. "Introduzione alla lettura di Gregorio di Tours," *Todi Convegno 12*, pp. 15-25

———. "Paolo Diacono," in *Enciclopedia italiana* 26 (1935) 232

Müller, Klaus Erich. *Geschichte der antiken Ethnographie und ethnologischen Theoriebildung*, 2 vols. (Wiesbaden 1972-80)

Murray, Gilbert. *Aristophanes: A Study* (Oxford 1937)

Musca, Giosuè. *Il Venerabile Beda, storico dell'alto Medioevo* (Bari 1973)

Navarra, Leandro. "Venanzio Fortunato: stato degli studi e proposte de ricerca," *La cultura in Italia fra tardo antico e alto medioevo, Atti del Convegno tenuta a Roma, Consiglio nazionale delle ricerche 1979*, 2 vols. (Rome 1981) I, 605-10

Neff, Karl. *De Paulo Diacono Festi epitomatore* (Erlangen 1891)

———. See List of Abbreviations, under Paul the Deacon

Nie, Giselle de. "Roses in January: A Neglected Dimension of Gregory of Tours," *Journal of Medieval History* 5 (1979) 259-89

Norberg, Dag. "Le développement du latin en Italie de Grégoire le Grand à Paul Diacre," *Spoleto Settimane* 5 (1958) 485-503

———. *In Registrum Gregorii Magni studia critica*, 2 vols. (Uppsala 1937-39)

O'Donnell, James J. "The Aims of Jordanes," *Historia* 31 (1982) 223-40

———. *Cassiodorus* (Berkeley 1979)

———. "Liberius the Patrician," *Traditio* 37 (1981) 31-72

O'Sullivan, Thomas D. *The "De excidio" of Gildas: Its Authority and Date*, Columbia Studies in Classical Tradition 7 (Leiden 1978)

Oldoni, Massimo. "Gregorio di Tours e i *Libri Historiarum*," *Studi medievali*, ser. 3, 13 (1972) 563-700

Olten, Michel. "Le rapport du texte à l'histoire," *Revue belge de philologie et d'histoire* 54 (1976) 374-82

Omont, Henri. "Manuscrits en lettres onciales de l'*Historia Francorum* de Grégoire de Tours," in *Notices et documents publiés par la Société de l'histoire de France à l'occasion du cinquantième anniversaire de sa fondation* (Paris 1884), pp. 3-18

Ong, Walter. "A Writer's Audience Is Always a Fiction," *PMLA* 90 (1975) 9-21

Opland, Jeff. *Anglo-Saxon Oral Poetry: A Study of the Traditions* (New Haven 1980)

The Oxford Anthology of English Literature, ed. Frank Kermode and John Hollander, 2 vols. (New York 1973)

Paschoud, François. *Cinq études sur Zosime* (Paris 1975)

———. "Influences et échos des conceptions historiographiques de Polybe dans l'Antiquité tardive," Fondation Hardt, *Entretiens sur l'Antiquité classique* 20 (1974) 305-37

————. *Roma aeterna: Études sur le patriotisme romain dans l'Occident latin à l'époque des grandes invasions*, Bibliotheca Helvetica Romana 7 (Rome 1967)

Patrides, C. A. *The Grand Design of God: The Literary Form of the Christian Views of History* (London 1972)

Paulson, Ronald. *The Fictions of Satire* (Baltimore 1967)

Pavan, Massimigliano. "Invasioni barbariche e conflitti religiosi nel tardo antico," *Cultura e scuola* 19, no. 74 (1980) 82-90

Payne, F. Anne. *Chaucer and Menippean Satire* (Madison, Wis. 1981)

Pepperdene, Margaret W. "Bede's *Historia ecclesiastica*: A New Perspective," *Celtica* 4 (1958) 258-62

Philippart, Guy. *Les légendiers latins et autres manuscrits hagiographiques*, Typologie des sources du moyen âge occidental, fasc. 24-25 (Turnhout 1977)

Pietri, Luce. *La ville de Tours du IVᵉ au VIᵉ siècle. Naissance d'une ville chrétienne*, Collection de l'École française de Rome 69 (Rome 1983)

Pinkus, Philip. "Satire and St. George," *Queen's Quarterly* 70 (1963-64) 30-49

Pizarro, Joachím Martínez, "A Brautwerbung Variant in Gregory of Tours," *Neophilologus* 62 (1978) 109-18

Poole, Reginald L. "St. Wilfrid and the See of Ripon" (1919), reprinted in his *Studies in Chronology and History*, ed. Austin Lane Poole (Oxford 1934), pp. 56-81

Posner, E. "Das Register Gregors I," *Neues Archiv der Gesellschaft für ältere deutsche Geschichtskunde* 43 (1921) 243-315

Press, Gerald A. "History and the Development of the Idea of History in Antiquity," *History and Theory* 16 (1977) 280-96

Quentin, Henri. "Bède le Vénérable," in *Dictionnaire d'archéologie chrétienne et de liturgie* 2 (1907) 632-48

————. *Les martyrologes historiques du moyen âge. Étude sur la formation du martyrologe romain* (Paris 1908)

Raby, F.J.E. "Bède le Vénérable," in *Dictionnaire d'histoire et de géographie ecclésiastique* 7 (1934) 395-402

Raglan, Lord. *The Hero: A Study in Tradition, Myth, and Drama* (London 1936, reprinted New York 1956)

Rajak, Tessa. *Josephus: The Historian and His Society* (London 1983)

Rand, E. K. "The Brighter Aspects of the Merovingian Age," Classical Association, *Proceedings* 18 (1921) 165-82

Randers-Pehrson, Justine Davis. *Barbarians and Romans: The Birth Struggle of Europe, A.D. 400-700* (Norman, Okla. 1983)

Randolph, Mary Claire. "The Structural Design of the Formal Verse Satire," *Philological Quarterly* 21 (1942) 368-84

Ranke, Leopold von. *Weltgeschichte* IV, part 2 (Berlin 1883)

Ray, Roger. "Bede's *vera lex historiae*," *Speculum* 55 (1980) 1-20

————. "What Do We Know about Bede's Commentaries?" *Recherches de théologie ancienne et médiévale* 49 (1982) 5-20

Reindel, Kurt. "Die Bajuwaren. Quellen, Hypothesen, Tatsachen," *Deutsches Archiv für Erforschung des Mittelalters* 37 (1981) 450-73

Reitter, Nikolaus. *Der Glaube an die Fortdauer des römischen Reiches im Abendland während des 5. und 6. Jahrhunderts* (Münster 1900)

Reydellet, Marc. *La royauté dans la littérature latine de Sidoine Apollinaire à Isidore de Séville*, Bibliothèque des Écoles françaises d'Athènes et de Rome 243 (Paris 1981)

Rhee, Florus van der. "Die germanischen Wörter in der *Historia Langobardorum* des Paulus Diaconus," *Romanobarbarica* 5 (1980) 271-96

Richards, Jeffrey. *The Popes and the Papacy in the Early Middle Ages, 476-752* (London 1979)

Riché, Pierre. *Éducation et culture dans l'Occident barbare, 6ᵉ-8ᵉ siècles* (Paris 1962)

Richter, Michael. "Bede's *Angli*: Angles or English?" *Peritia* 3 (1984) 99-114

Roberts, Michael. "Rhetoric and Poetic Tradition in Avitus's Account of the Crossing of the Red Sea ('De spiritalis historiae gestis' 5.371-702)," *Traditio* 39 (1983) 29-80

Rosenthal, Joel T. "Bede's *Life of St. Cuthbert*: Preparatory to the *Ecclesiastical History*," *Catholic Historical Review* 68 (1982) 599-611

Rothbarth, Margerite. "Ihr sagt er, nicht ich," *Zeitschrift für Volkskunde* 26 (1916) 88-89

Rouche, Michel. "Les baptêmes forcés des Juifs en Gaule mérovingienne et dans l'Empire d'Orient," in *De l'antijudaïsme antique à l'antisémitisme contemporain*, ed. Valentin Nikiprowitzky (Lille 1979), pp. 105-24

Rubin, Berthold. "Prokopios von Kaisareia," in Pauly-Wissowa, *Real-encyclopädie der klassischen Altertumswissenschaft* 23 (1957) 273-599

Šašel, Jaroslav. "Antiqui barbari. Zur Besiedlungsgeschichte Ostnoricums und Pannoniens im 5. und 6. Jahrhundert nach der Schriftquellen," *Vorträge und Forschungen* 25 (1979) 125-39

Saxer, Victor. "Reliques, miracles et récits de miracles au temps et dans l'œuvre de saint Augustin," in *Hagiographie, cultures et sociétés*, pp. 261-62

Schirren, Carl. *De ratione quae inter Iordanem et Cassiodorum intercedat commentatio* (diss., Dorpat [Tartu, Yuryev] 1858)

———. Review of Mommsen's edition of Jordanes, in *Deutsche Literaturzeitung* 3 (1880) 1422-23

Schlick, J. "Composition et chronologie des *Virtutibus sancti Martini* de Grégoire de Tours," *Texte und Untersuchungen zur Geschichte der altchristlichen Literatur* 92 (= *Studia patristica* 7) (1966) 278-86

Schmale, Franz-Josef. "Mentalität und Berichtshorizont, Absicht und Situation hochmittelalterlichen Geschichtsschreiber," *Historische Zeitschrift* 226 (1978) 1-16

Schnetz, Joseph. "Jordanes beim Geograph von Ravenna," *Philologus* 81 (1925) 86-100

Schoebe, Gerhard. "Was gilt im frühen Mittelalter als Geschichtliche Wirklichkeit? Ein Versuch zur *Kirchengeschichte* des Baeda venerabilis," in *Festschrift Hermann Aubin zum 80. Geburtstag*, ed. Otto Brunner *et al.*, 2 vols. (Wiesbaden 1965)

Schreckenberg, Heinz. *Die Flavius-Josephus-Tradition in Antike und Mittelalter* (Leiden 1972)

Schwartz, Jacques. "Jordanès et l'Histoire Auguste," *Bonner Historia-Augusta-Colloquium 1979/1981*, Antiquitas Reihe 4, 15 (Bonn 1983), pp. 275-84

Schwarz, Ernst. "Die Herkunftsfrage der Goten," in his *Zur germanischen Stammeskunde*, Wege der Forschung 249 (Darmstadt 1972), pp. 287-308

———. Review of Weibull, *Auswanderung*, in *Historische Zeitschrift* 190 (1960) 358-60

Scobie, Alex. "Storytellers, Storytelling, and the Novel in Graeco-Roman Antiquity," *Rheinisches Museum für Philologie* 122 (1979) 229-59

See, Klaus von. "Altnordische Literaturgeschichte als Textgeschichte," in his *Edda, Saga, Skaldendichtung: Aufsätze zur skandinavischen Literatur des Mittelalters* (Heidelberg 1981), pp. 527-39

———. *Deutsche Germanen-Ideologie von Humanismus bis zum Gegenwart* (Frankfurt 1970)

———. "Der Germane als Barbar," *Jahrbuch für internationale Germanistik* 13 (1981) 42-73

———. *Germanische Heldensage. Stoffe, Probleme, Methoden* (Frankfurt 1971)

———. *Kontinuitätstheorie und Sakraltheorie in der Germanenforschung* (Frankfurt 1972)

Segal, Erich, ed. *Plautus: Three Comedies* (New York 1969)

Sestan, Ernesto. "Qualque aspetti della personalità di Paolo Diacono nella sua *Historia Romana*" (1958), reprinted in his *Italia medievale* (Naples n.d. [1966]), pp. 50-75

———. "La storiografia dell'Italia Longobarda: Paolo diacono," *Spoleto Settimane* 17 (1970) 357-96

Simon, John L. "The Concept of Germanic Heroism in Felix Dahn's *Ein Kampf um Rom*," in *Iceland and the Medieval World: Studies in Honour of Ian Maxwell*, ed. G. Turville-Petre and J. S. Martin (Melbourne 1974)

Smalley, Beryl. *Historians in the Middle Ages* (London 1974)

Sordi, Marta. "Dalla storiografia classica alla storiografia cristiana," *Civiltà classica e cristiana* 3 (1982) 7-29

Southern, R. W. "Bede, the Monk of Jarrow," *The Listener* 71 (1964) 267-69

Spörl, Johannes. *Grundformen hochmittelalterlichen Geschichtsanschauungen* (Munich 1935)

Sprandel, Rolf. "Vorwissentschafliches Naturverstehen und Entstehung von Naturwissenschaften," *Sudhofs Archiv. Zeitschrift für Wissenschaftsgeschichte* 63 (1979) 313-25

St. Wilfrid at Hexham, ed. D. P. Kirby (Newcastle-on-Tyne 1974)

Staab, Franz. "Ostrogothic Geographers at the Court of Theodoric the Great," *Viator* 7 (1976) 27-58

Stancliffe, Clare. *St. Martin and His Hagiographer* (Oxford 1983)

Stein, Ernst. *Histoire du Bas-Empire*, 2 vols. (Paris 1949, 1959)

Stenton, F. M. *Anglo-Saxon England*, 2d ed. (Oxford 1947)

Stevens, C. E. "Gildas Sapiens," *English Historical Review* 56 (1941) 353-70

Sthamer, Eduard. "Eine neue Jordanes-Handschrift in Palermo," *Forschungen und Fortschritte* 5 (1929) 45

St.-Michel, Denise. *Concordance de l'*Historia Francorum *de Grégoire de Tours,* 2 vols., Collectum. Collection de listes et concordances de textes de l'Université de Montréal (Montreal n.d. [1979])

Stroheker, Karl Friedrich. "*Princeps clausus.* Zu einige Berührungen der Literatur des fünften Jahrhundert mit der Historia Augusta," *Bonner Historia-Augusta-Colloquium,* Antiquitas Reihe 4, 7 (Bonn 1970) 273-83

————. *Der senatorische Adel im spätantiken Gallien* (Tübingen 1948)

Studia Gothica: Die eisenzeitliche Verbindungen zwischen Schweden und Südosteuropa, ed. Ulf Erich Hagberg (Stockholm 1972)

Studies Presented to J. M. Wallace-Hadrill. See *Ideal and Reality*

Suerbaum, Werner. *Vom Antiken zum frühmittelalterlichen Staatsbegriff,* 2d ed., Orbis antiquus, H. 16-17 (Münster 1971)

Svennung, Josef. "Jordanes und die gotische Stammsage," in *Studia Gotica,* pp. 20-50

————. *Jordanes und Scandia. Kritisch-exegetische Studien* (Stockholm 1967)

Sybel, Heinrich von. *De fontibus libri Jordanis: De origine actuque Getarum* (diss., Berlin 1838)

Syme, Sir Ronald. "Controversy Abating and Credulity Curbed" (1980), reprinted in his *H.A. Papers,* pp. 209-23

————. "Fiction in the Epitomators" (1980), reprinted in his *H.A. Papers,* pp. 156-67

————. *Historia Augusta Papers* (Oxford 1983)

Taviani, Huguette. "Le dessein politique du *Chronicon Salernitanum,*" *Annales de Bretagne et des pays de l'Ouest* 87 (1980) 175-85 (= L'historiographie en Occident du Vᵉ au XVᵉ siècle. Actes du congrès de la Société des historiens médiévistes de l'enseignement supérieur, Tours, 10-12 juin 1977)

Teall, John L. "The Barbarians in Justinian's Armies," *Speculum* 40 (1965) 294-322

Thacker, A. T. "The Social and Continental Background of Early Anglo-Saxon Hagiography," D.Phil. thesis, Oxford 1976

Thierry, Augustin. *Récits des temps mérovingiens* (1840), 4th ed., 2 vols., in Thierry, *Œuvres complètes,* 8 vols. (Paris 1851) VII

Thompson, E. A. "Gildas and the History of Britain," *Britannia* 10 (1979) 203-26

————. *The Goths in Spain* (Oxford 1969)

Thompson, Stith. *Motif Index of Folk-Literature,* 6 vols. (Bloomington, Ind. 1955-58)

Thorndike, Ashley H. *Tragedy* (New York 1908)

Thornton, A. P. "Jekyll and Hyde in the Colonies," *International Journal* 30 (1965) 221-29

Thürlemann, Felix. *Der historische Diskurs bei Gregor von Tours: Topoi und Wirklichkeit,* Geist und Werk der Zeiten 39 (Bonn-Frankfurt 1974)

Thurston, Herbert. "The Oldest Life of St. Gregory," *The Month: A Catholic Magazine* 104 (1904) 337-53

Uytfanghe, Marc van. "Les avatars contemporains de l''hagiologie.' À propos d'un ouvrage récent sur saint Séverin de Norique," *Francia* 5 (1977) 639-71

————. "La controverse biblique et patristique autour du miracle, et ses répercussions sur l'hagiographie dans l'Antiquité tardive et le haut Moyen Âge latin," in *Hagiographie, cultures et sociétés*, pp. 205-33

———. "Latin mérovingien, latin carolingien et rustica Romana lingua: continuité ou discontinuité?" *Revue de l'Université de Bruxelles* (1977), no. 1, pp. 65-88

Vasiliev, A. A. *History of the Byzantine Empire*, 2d ed. (Madison, Wis. 1952)

Vieillard-Troïekouroff, May. *Les monuments religieux de la Gaule d'après les œuvres de Grégoire de Tours* (Paris 1976)

Vinay, Gustavo. *Alto medioevo latino. Conversazioni e no* (Naples 1978)

———. "Un mito per sopravvivere: l'*Historia Langobardorum* di Paolo Diacono," in his *Alto medioevo latino*, pp. 125-49

———. "Paolo Diacono e la poesia. Nota," *Convivium*, N.S. 1 (1950) 97-113

———. *San Gregorio di Tours (Saggio)*, Studi di letteratura medievale 1 (Carmagnola [Turin] n.d. [1940])

Viscardi, Antonio. *Le Origini* (Storia letteraria d'Italia), 4th ed. (Milan 1966)

Vogel, Cyrille. "La réforme liturgique sous Charlemagne," in *Karl der Grosse* II, 217-32

Vogüé, Adalbert de. "Grégoire le Grand, lecteur de Grégoire de Tours," *Analecta Bollandiana* 94 (1976) 225-33

Voss, Jürgen. "Le problème du moyen âge dans la pensée historique en France (XVIᵉ-XIXᵉ siècle)," *Revue d'histoire moderne et contemporaine* 24 (1977) 321-40

Vyver, A. van de. "Cassiodore et son œuvre," *Speculum* 6 (1931) 244-92

Wagner, Norbert. "Alboin bei Turisind," *Zeitschrift für deutsches Altertum und deutsche Literatur* 111 (1982) 243-55

———. "Germanische Namengebung und kirchliches Recht in der Amalerstammtafel," *Zeitschrift für deutsches Altertum und deutsche Literatur* 99 (1970) 1-16

———. *Getica: Untersuchungen zum Leben des Jordanes und zur frühen Geschichte der Goten*, Quellen und Forschungen zur Sprach- und Kulturgeschichte der germanischen Völker, N.F. 22 (Berlin 1967)

Waitz, Georg. Review of MGH AA. II, in *Göttingische gelehrte Anzeiger* (1879) 577-602

———. "Über die handschriftliche Überlieferung und die Sprache der *Historia Langobardorum* des Paulus," *Neues Archiv der Gesellschaft für ältere deutsche Geschichtskunde* 1 (1876) 533-66

Wallace-Hadrill, J. M. *The Barbarian West* (London 1957)

———. "Bede and Plummer" (1973), reprinted in his *Early Medieval History*, pp. 76-95

———. "Bede's Europe" (1962), reprinted in his *Early Medieval History*, pp. 60-75

———. "The Bloodfeud of the Franks," in his *Long-Haired Kings*, pp. 121-47

———. *Early Germanic Kingship in England and on the Continent* (Oxford 1971)

———. *Early Medieval History* (Oxford 1975)

———. "Fredegar and the History of France" (1958), reprinted in his *Long-Haired Kings*, pp. 71-94

———. "Gregory of Tours and Bede: Their Views on the Personal Qualities of Kings" (1968), reprinted in his *Early Medieval History*, pp. 96-114

———. *The Long-Haired Kings and Other Studies of Frankish History* (Oxford 1962)

Wallace-Hadrill, J. M. Review of K-L, in *English Historical Review* 67 (1952) 402-404

———. "Rome and the Early English Church: Some Questions of Transmission" (1960), reprinted in his *Early Medieval History*, pp. 115-37

———. "The Work of Gregory of Tours in the Light of Modern Research" (1951), reprinted in his *Long-Haired Kings*, pp. 49-70

Wallach, Liutpold. *Alcuin and Charlemagne: Studies in Carolingian History and Literature* (Ithaca, N.Y. 1959)

Walter, Emil H. "Hagiographisches in Gregors Frankengeschichte," *Archiv für Kulturgeschichte* 48 (1960) 291-310

Ward, Benedicta. *Miracles and the Medieval Mind: Theory, Record and Event, 1000-1215* (London 1982)

Wattenbach, Wilhelm. *Deutschlands Geschichtsquellen im Mittelalter*, 2 vols., 5th ed. (Berlin 1885), 6th ed. (Berlin 1893)

Wattenbach-Levison. *Deutschlands Geschichtsquellen im Mittelalter. Vorzeit und Karolinger*, H. 1 (Weimar 1951)

Weibull, Curt. *Die Auswanderung der Goten aus Schweden* (Göteborg 1958)

Weidemann, Margerete. *Kulturgeschichte der Merowingerzeit nach der Werken Gregors von Tours*, 2 vols., Römisch-germanisches Zentralmuseum, Forschungsinstitut für Vor- und Frühgeschichte, Monographien 3 (Mainz 1982)

Wenskus, Reinhard. *Stammesbildung und Verfassung. Das Werden der frühmittelalterlichen gentes* (Cologne 1961)

Wes, Marinus. *Das Ende des Kaisertums im Westen des Römischen Reiches* (The Hague 1967)

Weston, Arthur A. *Latin Satirical Writing Subsequent to Juvenal* (Lancaster, Pa. 1915)

White, Hayden. "The Fictions of Factual Representation," in Angus Fletcher, ed., *The Literature of Fact* (New York 1976), pp. 21-44

———. "The Historical Text as Literary Artifact," in Robert H. Canary and Henry Kozicki, eds., *The Writing of History: Literary Form and Historical Understanding* (Madison, Wis. 1978), pp. 41-62

———. "Historicism, History, and the Figurative Imagination," in *Essays on Historicism, History and Theory* Beiheft 14 (1975) 48-67

———. *Metahistory: The Historical Imagination in Nineteenth-Century Europe* (Baltimore-London 1973)

———. "The Value of Narrativity in the Representation of Reality," *Critical Inquiry* 7 (1980-81) 5-27

Whitelock, Dorothy. "Bede and His Teachers and Friends," in *Famulus Christi*, pp. 19-39

Williams, Schafer. "Visio aetatis aureae ecclesiae Pseudo-Isidoriana," thesis, University of California, Berkeley 1951

Wiseman, T. P. "Practice and Theory in Roman Historiography," *History* 66 (1981) 375-93

Wolfram, Herwig. "Einige Überlegungen zur gotischen *Origo gentis*," in *Studia linguistica Alexandro Vasilii filio Issatschenko oblata*, ed. Henrik Birnbaum *et al.* (Lisse [Lund] 1978), pp. 487-99

———. *Geschichte der Goten. Von den Anfängen bis zur Mitte des sechsten Jahrhunderts. Entwurf einer historischen Ethnographie*, 2d ed. (Munich 1980)

———. "Gothic History and Historical Ethnography," *Journal of Medieval History* 7 (1981) 309-19

———. "Methodische Frage zur Kritik am 'sakralen' Königtum germanische Stämme," in *Festschrift für Otto Höfler zum 65. Geburtstag*, ed. H. Birkan and O. Gschwantler, 2 vols. (Vienna 1968) II, 479-82

———. "Theogonie, Ethnogenese und ein kompromittierter Grossvater im Stammbaum Theoderichs des Grossen," in *Festschrift für Helmut Beumann*, ed. K.-U. Jäschke and R. Wenskus (Sigmaringen 1977), pp. 80-97

Wood, Ian N. "Gregory of Tours and Clovis," *Revue belge de philologie et d'histoire* 63 (1985) 249-72

Wood, Susan. "Bede's Northumbrian Dates Again," *English Historical Review* 98 (1983) 280-96

Wormald, Patrick. "Bede and Benedict Biscop," in *Famulus Christi*, pp. 141-69

———. "Bede, *Beowulf*, and the Conversion of the Anglo-Saxon Aristocracy," in R. T. Farrell, ed., *Bede and Anglo-Saxon England*, British Archaeological Reports, British Series 46 (Oxford 1978), pp. 32-95

———. "Bede, the *Bretwaldas*, and the Origins of the *Gens Anglorum*," in *Studies Presented to J. M. Wallace-Hadrill*, pp. 99-129

———. Review of Musca, *Venerabile Beda*, in *Durham University Journal* 67, N.S. 36 (1974-75) 231-33

Wozniak, Frank E. "Byzantine Diplomacy and the Lombard-Gepidic Wars," *Balkan Studies* 20 (1979) 138-58

Wright, C. E. *The Cultivation of Saga in Anglo-Saxon England* (Edinburgh-London 1934)

Wyckham, Chris. *Early Medieval Italy* (London 1981)

Zachariae, Theodor. "Ihr sagt er, nicht ich," *Zeitschrift für Volkskunde* 25 (1915) 402-408

Zelzer, Klaus. "Zur Frage des Autors der Miracula B. Andreae apostoli und zur Sprache des Gregor von Tours," *Grazer Beiträge. Zeitschrift für die klassischen Altertumswissenschaften* 6 (1977) 217-41

Zöllner, Erich. *Geschichte der Franken bis zur Mitte des sechsten Jahrhunderts* (Munich 1970)

Zurli, Loriano. "Le 'proprietà' del motivo dello 'scambio de persona' nella narrativa classica e nel 'racconto storico' di Paolo Diacono," Università di Perugia, Istituto di filologia Latina, *Materiali et contributi per la storia della narrativa Greco-Latina* 2 (1978) 71-104

Index of Passages Cited

BEDE

Chron.
244, 245, 248, 274, 284, 303, 387

Anon. *Cuthbert*
entire, 11, 249, 269; preface, 273, 283; 1., 268; 1.3, 270, 283; 1.4, 283; 1.5, 283; 1.6, 304; 1.7, 276, 283; 2., 268; 2.1, 276, 283; 2.2, 268, 283; 2.3, 283, 322; 2.4, 283; 2.5-6, 292; 3.1, 268, 276, 283; 3.2, 268, 276; 3.3, 268, 283; 3.4-5, 268; 3.6, 268, 270; 3.7, 268; 4.1, 268, 269, 283; 4.2, 283; 4.3, 268, 283, 284; 4.4, 268; 4.5, 268, 292; 4.6, 268, 284; 4.7, 268, 284; 4.8, 270; 4.10, 284; 4.11-13, 268; 4.14, 259, 263; 4.15, 268, 270, 283, 291; 4.16-17, 268

Historia abbatum
entire, 274; 1, 294; 2, 294, 323; 3-5, 294; 6, 294, 314; 7, 278, 294; 8, 294; 9, 294; 11, 292, 294, 315; 12, 292, 294; 13, 292, 294; 14, 292, 294; 15, 294; 16, 278; 20, 278; 22, 294

Historia Ecclesiastica gentis Anglorum
entire, 14, 359, 370, 388; *Epist. ad. Albinum*, 297; praef., 155, 251, 252, 284, 297, 298; 1.1, 88, 252, 299, 300, 310, 348, 378; 1.2, 300, 348; 1.2-14, 252, 299, 300; 1.3, 300, 348; 1.4, 300; 1.5, 300, 302; 1.6-11, 300; 1.12, 300-2; 1.13, 300; 1.14, 300; 1.15, 252, 299, 300; 1.16, 300, 302; 1.16-22, 299, 300, 302; 1.17-21, 300, 302; 1.22, 244, 254, 300, 302, 322; 1.23-26, 252, 303; 1.25, 214, 252, 303, 305; 1.26, 252, 255, 303; 1.27, 250, 252, 255; 1.27-32, 252, 303; 1.29, 251; 1.33, 252, 303; 1.34, 240, 252, 303; 2.1, 250, 251, 265, 266, 303, 371, 372; 2.2-8, 252; 2.4, 254; 2.5, 251; 2.9, 218, 251, 252, 304, 305; 2.10-14, 218, 252, 304; 2.12, 265, 305; 2.13, 252, 306; 2.15, 251, 252; 2.16, 251, 252, 309; 2.17, 252; 2.18, 250, 252; 2.19, 252, 310; 2.20, 252, 254, 262, 267, 305, 309, 368; 2.22, 254; 3., 363; 3.1, 218, 252, 363, 373; 3.2, 218, 250, 252, 260, 261, 426; 3.3, 218, 252, 306; 3.4, 252, 310, 324, 327; 3.5, 252, 255, 306; 3.6, 218, 252, 260, 263; 3.7, 251, 252, 254, 312; 3.8, 251, 252; 3.9, 218, 250, 252, 254, 260, 426; 3.10, 250, 252, 260, 426; 3.11, 250, 252, 260, 261, 426; 3.12, 218, 250, 252, 260, 426; 3.13, 250, 252, 261, 317, 327, 426; 3.14, 218, 252; 3.15, 252, 276, 426; 3.16, 252, 254, 306, 426; 3.17, 254, 257, 306, 310, 426; 3.18, 251, 252, 254; 3.19, 250-52; 3.20, 251, 252; 3.21, 251, 252, 254; 3.22, 251, 252; 3.23, 252, 254, 255, 316; 3.24, 218, 252, 262, 305, 316; 3.25, 252, 257, 309, 311-13; 3.26, 252, 310; 3.27, 252, 310; 3.28, 252, 311, 315, 316; 3.29, 251, 253; 3.30, 251, 252; 4.1, 251, 252; 4.2, 251, 252, 257, 258, 309, 314-16; 4.3, 250-52, 255, 310, 315, 316; 4.4, 218; 4.5, 218, 315, 323; 4.6, 250-52; 4.7-11, 250-52, 426; 4.12, 218, 251, 252, 255, 269, 315, 317; 4.13, 252, 318, 319, 321; 4.14, 251, 252, 261, 321; 4.15, 218, 251, 252, 319, 321, 373; 4.16, 218, 251, 252, 319-21, 373; 4.17, 251, 252; 4.18, 252, 314; 4.19, 250, 252, 260, 261, 322; 4.20, 249, 252, 259, 323; 4.21, 252, 261, 321; 4.22, 252, 321; 4.23, 250, 252, 262, 290, 322; 4.24, 252, 322; 4.25, 252, 322; 4.26, 252, 270, 310, 321; 4.27, 252, 255, 262, 269, 310, 313, 322, 426; 4.28, 252, 269, 313, 322, 426; 4.29, 252, 273, 276, 291, 322, 426; 4.30, 252, 260, 263, 278, 316, 322, 426; 4.31, 252, 316, 322, 426; 4.32, 252, 316, 322, 426; 5.1, 252, 322, 426; 5.2, 252, 262, 322, 426; 5.3, 252, 273, 322, 426; 5.4, 252, 322, 426; 5.5, 252, 273, 322, 426; 5.6, 252, 273, 290, 316, 322, 426; 5.7, 218, 251, 252, 320, 323, 416, 417; 5.8, 251, 252, 260, 316; 5.9, 251, 252, 310, 318, 322; 5.10, 251, 252, 310, 318; 5.11, 252, 318; 5.12, 252, 255, 273, 321; 5.13, 252; 5.14, 252; 5.15, 252, 322; 5.16, 250, 252; 5.17, 250, 252; 5.18, 254, 375; 5.19, 250, 252, 269, 271, 307, 315, 317, 321, 324; 5.20, 251, 252, 262, 273, 287, 324; 5.21, 252, 311; 5.22, 251, 252, 254,

PAUL THE DEACON

OTHER AUTHORS

General Index

472